35TH ANNUAL EDITION

2O12

SONGWRITER'S

MARKET

REFERENCE BOOK

Not to be taken from the
Library

Adria Haley, Editor

WD

WRITER'S DIGEST
BOOKS

WritersDigest.com
Cincinnati, Ohio

D1502240

Writer's Market website: www.writersmarket.com
Writer's Digest website: www.writersdigest.com
Writer's Digest Bookstore: www.writersdigestshop.com

Distributed in Canada by Fraser Direct
100 Armstrong Avenue
Georgetown, Ontario, Canada L7G 5S4
Tel: (905) 877-4411

Distributed in the UK and Europe by F&W Media International
Brunel House, Newton Abbot, Devon, TQ12 4PU, England
Tel: (+44) 1626-323200, Fax: (+44) 1626-323319
E-mail: postmaster@davidandcharles.co.uk

Distributed in Australia by Capricorn Link
P.O. Box 704, Windsor, NSW 2756 Australia
Tel: (02) 4577-3555

ISBN 13: 978-1-59963-232-2 (pbk:alk.paper)

Attention Booksellers: This is an annual directory of F+W Media, Inc.
Return deadline for this edition is December 31, 2012.

Edited by: Adria Haley
Editorial assistance by: Marielle Murphy
Cover designed by: Jessica Boonstra
Interior designed by: Claudean Wheeler
Page layout by: Terri Woesner
Production coordinated by: Greg Nock
Cover illustration by: Emily Keafer

CONTENTS

FROM THE EDITOR...1

GETTING STARTED

HOW TO USE *SONGWRITER'S MARKET*..2

WHERE SHOULD I SEND MY SONGS?...5

DEMO RECORDINGS..9

HOW DO I SUBMIT MY DEMO?...12

HOW DO I AVOID THE RIP-OFFS?...17

SUBMISSION STRATEGIES..21

MUSIC BIZ BASICS

ROYALTIES..25

COPYRIGHT...30

CAREER SONGWRITING..33

CONTRACTS..35

ARTICLES & INTERVIEWS

HILLARY SCOTT: *SESAC Songwriter of the Year*
   by Annie Downs 39

ONE OUT OF TENN: *Andy Davis & the Evolving Artist*
   by Lyndsay Rush..44

MUSIC LICENSING: *Rethinking How to Grow Your Audience Base*
   by Sarah Gavigan 51

ANDY HUNT: *Sound Advice From a Producer*
   by Adria Haley 58

LEARNING TO SAY *NO*: *How Being Selective Can Improve Your Lyrics*
   by Pat Pattison...64

SOCIAL MEDIA: *How Social Networking Can Impact Your Career*
   by Jamie Wilson Young 75

AMANDA PALMER: *On the Art of Songwriting, Staying Busy, & Being Honest*
   by Vanessa Wieland 82

DIY MUSICIANS: *Gavin Castleton & Matt Fazzi on Going Label-Free*
by *Vanessa Wieland* 87

BANDBOX: *Buying and Selling in a Digital World*
by *Lyndsay Rush* 93

MANAGING YOUR WORK

SONGWRITING CALENDAR 99

MARKETS

MUSIC PUBLISHERS *117*

RECORD COMPANIES *155*

RECORD PRODUCERS *185*

MANAGERS & BOOKING AGENTS *200*

MUSIC FIRMS *216*

PLAY PRODUCERS & PUBLISHERS *223*

CLASSICAL PERFORMING ARTS *228*

CONTESTS & AWARDS *245*

RESOURCES

ORGANIZATIONS *256*

WORKSHOPS & CONFERENCES *275*

RETREATS & COLONIES *283*

VENUES *287*

STATE & PROVINCIAL GRANTS *305*

PUBLICATIONS OF INTEREST *311*

WEBSITES OF INTEREST *319*

GLOSSARY *327*

INDEXES

GENERAL INDEX *337*

NAMES INDEX *349*

FROM THE EDITOR

It's no big surprise that the last decade or so has been a pivotal time in the music industry. Through social media tools like Facebook and MySpace, you can now access fans from every corner of the globe. That's why staying tuned in to the latest market trends and improving your business savvy have never been more important.

Regardless of what kind of lyrics you write, you need the best information possible on how to successfully present your music to producers, publishers, record companies, and other industry professionals. For thirty-five years now, *Songwriter's Market* is here to help. This edition of *SM* has an incredible lineup of articles filled with updates on today's music business landscape. Learn how to network, find licensing placements for your music, locate venues to begin booking your own tours, and hear some seasoned advice from successful songwriters currently making it in the industry.

I hope that 2012 brings you much success in your songwriting. But, most importantly, keep honing your craft, learning the business, and enjoying the journey!

Adria Haley
Managing Editor, Writer's Digest Books
http://www.writersmarket.com
adriahaley@fwmedia.com

Follow me on Twitter @adria_haley (http://twitter.com/adria_haley)

HOW TO USE *SONGWRITER'S MARKET*

//

Before you dive into the *Songwriter's Market* listings and start submitting songs willy-nilly, it's a good idea to take the time to read the following information. By educating yourself on how to best use this book, you'll be better prepared when you actually do send off your tape or CD.

Let's take a look at what is actually inside *Songwriter's Market*, why these articles were put into the book in the first place, and why they can actually help you in your career.

THE LISTINGS

Beyond the articles, there are eleven sections in this book, from Music Publishers and Record Companies to Contests & Awards. Each section begins with an introduction detailing how the different types of companies function—what part of the music industry the work in, how they make money, and what you need to think about when approaching them with your music.

These listings are the heart of *Songwriter's Market*. They are the names, addresses and contact information of music biz companies looking for songs and artists, as well as descriptions of the types of music they are looking for.

So how do I use *Songwriter's Market*?

The quick answer is that you should use the indexes to find companies who are interested in your type of music; then read the listings for details on how they want the music submitted. For support and help of all sorts, join a songwriting or other music industry association (see the Organizations section of this book). Read everything you can about songwriting (see the Publications of Interest section at the back of this book). Talk to other songwriters. That's a good start!

How does *Songwriter's Market* work?

The listings in *Songwriter's Market* are packed with a lot of information. It can be intimidating at first, but they are put together in a structured way to make them easy to work with. Take a few minutes to get used to how the listings are organized, and you'll have it down in no time. For more detailed information about how the listings are put together, skip ahead to the Where Should I Send My Songs? section.

The following are general guidelines about to how to use the listings:

1. **READ THE ENTIRE LISTING** to decide whether to submit your music. Please do not use this book as a mass mailing list. If you blindly mail out demos by the hundreds, you'll waste a lot of money on postage, annoy a lot of people, and your demos will wind up in the trash anyway.

2. **PAY CLOSE ATTENTION TO THE "MUSIC" SECTION IN EACH LISTING.** This will tell you what kind of music the company is looking for. If they want rockabilly only and you write heavy metal, don't submit to that company. That's just common sense.

3. **PAY CLOSE ATTENTION TO SUBMISSION INSTRUCTIONS** shown under How to Contact and follow them to the letter. A lot of listings are very particular about how they want submissions packaged. Pay close attention. If you do not follow their instructions, they will probably throw your submission in the garbage. If you are confused about their directions, contact the company for clarification.

4. **IF IN DOUBT, CONTACT THE COMPANY FOR PERMISSION TO SUBMIT.** This is a good general rule. Many companies don't mind if you send an unsolicited submission, but some will want you to get special prior permission from them. Contacting a company first is also a good way to find out their latest music needs. This is also a chance to briefly make contact on a personal level.

5. **BE COURTEOUS, BE EFFICIENT AND ALWAYS HAVE A PURPOSE** to your personal contact. Do not waste their time. If you call, always have a reason for making contact—permission to submit, checking on guidelines, following up on a demo, etc. These are solid reasons to make personal contact, but once you have their attention, do not wear out your welcome. Always be polite.

6. **CHECK FOR A PREFERRED CONTACT.** A lot of listings have a designated contact person shown after a bolded Contact in the heading. This is the person you should contact with questions or to whom you should address your submission.

7. **READ THE "TIPS" SECTION.** This part of the listing provides extra information on how to submit or what it might be like to work with the company. This is just the beginning. For more detailed information about the listings, see the next section—Where Should I Send My Songs?—and check out the sidebar with the sample listing called A Sample Listing Decoded.

FREQUENTLY ASKED QUESTIONS

How do these companies get listed in the book anyway?

No company pays to be included—all listings are free. The listings come from a combination of research the editor does on the music industry and questionnaires requested by companies who want to be listed (many of them contact us to be included). All questionnaires are screened for known sharks and to make sure they meet our requirements.

Why aren't other companies I know about listed in the book?

We may have sent them a questionnaire, but they did not return it, were removed for complaints, went out of business, specifically asked not to be listed, could not be contacted for an update, etc.

What's the deal with companies that don't take unsolicited submissions?

In the interest of completeness, the editor will sometimes include listings of crucial music companies and major labels she thinks you should be aware of. We want you to at least have some idea of what their policies are.

A company said in their listing that they take unsolicited submissions. But my demo came back unopened. What happened?

Some companies needs' change rapidly and may have changed since we contacted them for this edition of the book. This is another reason why it's often a good idea to contact a company before submitting.

So that's it. You now have the power at your fingertips to go out and become the professional songwriter you've always wanted to be. Let us know how you're doing. Drop us a line at marketbooks@fwmedia.com and tell us about any successes you have had because you used the materials found in this book.

Don't forget your webinar!

To access the webinar that is included with your book, go to writersmarket.com/2012sm and learn how to find new placements for your music.

WHERE SHOULD I SEND MY SONGS?

It depends a lot on whether you write mainly for yourself as a performer, or if you only write and want someone else to pick up your song for his or her recording (often the case in country music, for example). Are you mainly a performing songwriter or a nonperforming songwriter? This is important for figuring out what kind of companies to contact, as well as how you contact them. (For more detail, skip to the Submission Strategies section.)

What if I'm a nonperforming songwriter?

Many well-known songwriters are not performers in their own right. Some are not skilled instrumentalists or singers, but they understand melody, lyrics and harmony and how they go together. They can write great songs, but they need someone else to bring their music to life through skilled musicianship. A nonperforming songwriter will usually approach music publishers first for access to artists looking for songs, as well as artists' managers, their producers, and their record companies. On the flip side, many incredibly talented musicians can't write to save their lives and need someone else to provide them with good songs to perform. (For more details on the different types of companies and the roles they play for nonperforming and performing songwriters, see the section introductions for Music Publishers, Record Companies, Record Producers, and Managers & Booking Agents.)

What if I am a performing songwriter?

Many famous songwriters are also famous performers. They are skilled interpreters of their own material, and they also know how to write to suit their own particular talents as musicians. In this case, their intention is also usually to sell themselves as a performer in hopes of recording and releasing an album, or they have an album and want to find gigs and people who can help guide

TYPES OF MUSIC COMPANIES

- **MUSIC PUBLISHERS**—evaluate songs for commercial potential, find artists to record them, finds other uses for the songs such as film or TV, collects income from songs, protects copyrights from infringement

- **RECORD COMPANIES**—sign artists to their labels, finance recordings, promotion and touring, releases songs/albums to radio and TV

- **RECORD PRODUCERS**—works in the studio and records songs (independently or for a record company), may be affiliated with a particular artist, sometimes develop artists for record labels, locates or co-writes songs if an artist does not write their own

- **MANAGERS & BOOKING AGENTS**—works with artists to manage their careers, finds gigs, locates songs to record if the artist does not write their own

their careers. They will usually approach record companies or record producers first, on the basis of recording an album. For gigs and career guidance, they talk to booking agents and managers.

A smaller number also approach publishers in hopes of getting others to perform their songs, much like nonperforming songwriters. Some music publishers in recent years have also taken on the role of developing artists as both songwriters and performers, or are connected to a major record label, so performing songwriters might go to them for these reasons.

How do I use *Songwriter's Market* to narrow my search?

Once you've identified whether you are primarily interested in getting others to perform your songs (nonperforming songwriter) or you perform your own songs and want a record deal, etc., there are several steps you can take:

1. **IDENTIFY WHAT KIND OF MUSIC COMPANY YOU WISH TO APPROACH.** Based on whether you're a performing or nonperforming songwriter, do you want to approach a music publisher for a publishing deal? Do you want to approach a record producer because you need someone to help you record an album in the studio? Maybe you want to approach a producer in hopes that an act he's performing needs songs to complete his album.

2. **CHECK FOR COMPANIES BASED ON LOCATION.** Maybe you need a manager located close by. Maybe you need to find as many Nashville-based companies as you can because you write country music and most country publishers are in Nashville. In this case, start with the Geographic Index. You can also tell Canadian and foreign listings by the icons in the listing (see "A Sample Listing Decoded" on the next page).

3. **LOOK FOR COMPANIES BASED ON THE TYPE OF MUSIC THEY WANT.** Some companies want country. Some record labels want only punk. Read the listings carefully to make

sure you're maximizing your time and sending your work to the appropriate markets.

4. **LOOK FOR COMPANIES BASED ON HOW OPEN THEY ARE TO BEGINNERS.** Some companies are more open than others to beginning artists and songwriters. Maybe you are a beginner and it would help to approach these companies first. Some music publishers are hoping to find that wild card hit song and don't care if it comes from an unknown writer. Maybe you are just starting out looking for gigs or record deals, and you need a manager willing to help build your band's career from the ground up.

A SAMPLE LISTING DECODED

What do the little symbols at the beginning of the listing mean?

Those are called "icons," and they give you quick information about a listing with once glance. Here is a list of the icons and what they mean:

Openness to Submissions

- ○ means the company is open to beginners' submissions, regardless of past success
- ◖ means the company is mostly interested in previously published songwriters/well-established acts*, but will consider beginners
- ● these companies do not want submissions from beginners, only from previously published songwriters/well-established acts
- ⊘ companies with this icon only accept material referred by a reputable industry source

ADDITIONAL RESOURCES

Songwriter's Market lists music publishers, record companies, producers and managers (as well as advertising firms, play producers and classical performing arts organizations) along with specifications on how to submit your material to each. If you can't find a certain person or company you're interested in, there are other sources of information you can try.

The Recording Industry Sourcebook, an annual directory published by Norris-Whitney Communications, lists record companies, music publishers, producers, and managers, as well as attorneys, publicity firms, media, manufacturers, distributors and recording studios around the U.S. Trade publications such as *Billboard* or *Variety*, available at most local libraries and bookstores, are great sources for up-to-date information. These periodicals list new companies as well as the artists, labels, producers and publishers for each song on the charts.

CD booklets can also be valuable sources of information, providing the name of the record company, publisher, producer and usually the manager of an artist or group. Use your imagination in your research, and be creative—any contacts you make in the industry can only help your career as a songwriter. See the Publications of Interest section.

TYPES OF MUSIC COMPANIES

- **MUSIC PUBLISHERS**—evaluate songs for commercial potential; find artists to record them; find other uses for the songs, such as film or TV; collect income from songs; protect copyrights from infringement
- **RECORD COMPANIES**—sign artists to their labels, finance recordings, manage promotion and touring, release songs/albums to radio and TV
- **RECORD PRODUCERS**—work in the studio and record songs (independently or for a record company)—may be affiliated with a particular artist, sometimes develop artists for record labels, locate or cowrite songs if an artist does not write his or her own
- **MANAGERS & BOOKING AGENTS**—work with artists to manage their careers, find gigs, locate songs to record if the artist does not write his or her own

Other icons

- means the listing is Canadian
- means the market is located outside of the U.S. and Canada
- means the market is new to this edition
- means the market places music in film/TV

EASY-TO-USE REFERENCE ICONS

E-MAIL AND WEBSITE INFORMTION

TERMS OF AGREEMENT

DETAILED SUBMISSION GUIDELINES

WHAT THEY'RE LOOKING FOR

INSIDER ADVICE

RUSTIC RECORDS

6337 Murray Lane, Brentwood, TN 37027. (615)371-8397. Fax: (615)370-0353. E-mail: rusticrecordsam@aol.com. Website: www.rusticrecordsinc.com. President: Jack Schneider. Executive VP & Operations Manager: Nell Schneider. VP Publishing and Catalog Manager: Amanda Mark. VP Marketing and Promotions: Ross Schneider. Videography, Photography, and Graphic Design: Wayne Hall. Image consultant: Jo Ann Rossi. Independent traditional country music label and music publisher (Iron Skillet Music/ ASCAP, Covered Bridge/ BMI, Old Town Square/ SESAC). Estab. 1979. Staff size: 6. Releases 2-3/year. Pays negotiable royalty to artists on contracts; statutory royalty to publisher per song on record.

DISTRIBUTED BY CD Baby.com and available on iTunes, MSN Music, Rhapsody, and more.

HOW TO CONTACT Submit professional demo package by mail. Unsolicited submissions are OK. CD only; no mp3s or e-mails. Include no more than 4 songs with corresponding lyric sheets and cover letter. Include appropriately sized SASE. Responds in 4 weeks.

MUSIC Good combination of traditional and modern country. 2008-09 releases: *Ready to Ride*—debut album from Nikki Britt, featuring "C-O-W-B-O-Y," "Do I Look Like Him," "Long Gone Mama," and "I'm So Lonesome I Could Cry."

TIPS "Professional demo preferred."

DEMO RECORDINGS

What is a "demo"?

The demo, shorthand for *demonstration recording*, is the most important part of your submission package. Demos are meant to give music industry professionals a way to hear all the elements of your song as clearly as possible so they can decide if it has commercial potential.

Should I send a cassette or a CD?

More and more music industry people want CDs, although the cassette may still be accepted. A few companies want demos sent on CD only. It's getting cheaper and easier all the time to burn recordings, so it is worth the investment to buy a burner or borrow one. Other formats, such as DAT (Digital Audio Tape) are rarely requested.

What should I send if I'm seeking management?

Some companies want a video of an act performing their songs. Check with the companies for specific requirements.

How many songs should I send, and in what order and length?

Most music industry people agree that three songs is enough. Most music professionals are short on time, and if you can't catch their attention in three songs, your songs probably don't have hit potential. Also, put three *complete songs* on your demo, not just snippets. Make sure to put your best, most commercial song first. An up-tempo number is usually best. If you send a cassette, *put all the songs on one side of the cassette and cue the tape to the beginning of the first song so no time is wasted fast-forwarding or rewinding.*

Should I sing my own songs on my demo?

If you can't sing well, you may want to find someone who can. There are many places to check for singers and musicians, including songwriter organizations, music stores, and songwriting magazines. Some aspiring professional singers will sing on demos in exchange for a copy they can use as a demo to showcase their singing.

Should I use a professional demo service?

Many songwriters find professional demo services convenient if they don't have time or the resources to put together musicians on their own. For a fee, a demo service will produce your songs in their studio using in-house singers and musicians (this is pretty common in Nashville). Many of these services advertise in music magazines, songwriting newsletters and bulletin boards at music stores. Make sure to hear samples of work they've done in the past. Some are mail-order businesses—you send a rough tape of your song or the sheet music, and they produce and record a demo within a month or two. Be sure you find a service that will let you have some control over how the demo is produced, and tell them exactly how you want your song to sound. As with studios, look around for a service that fits your needs and budget. (Some will charge as low as $300 for three songs, while others may go as high as $3,000 and boast a high-quality sound—*shop around and use your best judgment!*)

Should I buy equipment and record demos myself?

If you have the drive and focus to learn good recording techniques, yes. If not, it might be easier to have someone else do it. Digital multitrack recorders are now easily available and within reasonable financial reach of many people. For performing songwriters in search of record deals, the actual sound of their recordings can often be an important part of their artistic concept. Having the "means of production" within their grasp can be crucial to artists pursuing the independent route. But, if you don't know how to use the equipment, it may be better to go into a professional studio.

How elaborate and full should the demo production be if I'm a nonperforming songwriter?

Many companies listed in *Songwriter's Market* tell you what they prefer. If in doubt, contact them and ask. In general, country songs and pop ballads can often be demoed with just a vocal plus a guitar or piano, although, many songwriters in those genres still prefer to get a more complete recording with drums, guitars, and other backing instruments. Up-tempo pop, rock, and dance demos usually need a more full production.

What kind of production do I need if I'm a performing songwriter?

If you are a band or artist looking for a record deal, you will need a demo that is as fully produced as possible. Many singer/songwriters record their demos as if they were going to be released as an album. That way, if they don't get a deal, they can still release it on their own. Professionally pressed CDs are also now easily within reach of performing songwriters, and many companies offer graphic design services for a professional-looking product.

HOW DO I SUBMIT MY DEMO?

//

You have three basic options for submitting your songs: submitting by mail, submitting in person, and submitting over the Internet (the newest and least widely accepted option at this time).

SUBMITTING BY MAIL

Should I call, write, or e-mail first to ask for permission or submission requirements?

This is always a good idea, and many companies ask you to contact them first. If you call, be polite, brief, and specific. If you send a letter, make sure it is typed and to the point. Include a typed SASE they can use to reply. If you send an e-mail, again, be professional and to the point. Proofread your message before you send it, and then be patient. Give them some time to reply. Do not send out mass e-mails or otherwise spam their e-mail account.

What do I send with my demo?

Most companies have specific requirements, but here are some general pointers:

- Read the listing carefully and submit *exactly* what they ask for, in the exact way they describe. It's also a good idea to call first, just in case they've changed their submission policies.
- Listen to each demo to make sure they sound right and are in the right order (see the previous section—Demo Recordings).
- If you use cassettes, make sure they are cued up to the beginning of the first song.
- Enclose a *brief*, typed cover letter to introduce yourself. Tell them what songs you are sending and why you are sending them. If you are pitching your songs to a particular artist, say so in the letter. If you are an artist/songwriter looking for a record deal, you should say so. Be specific.

SUBMISSION MAILING POINTERS

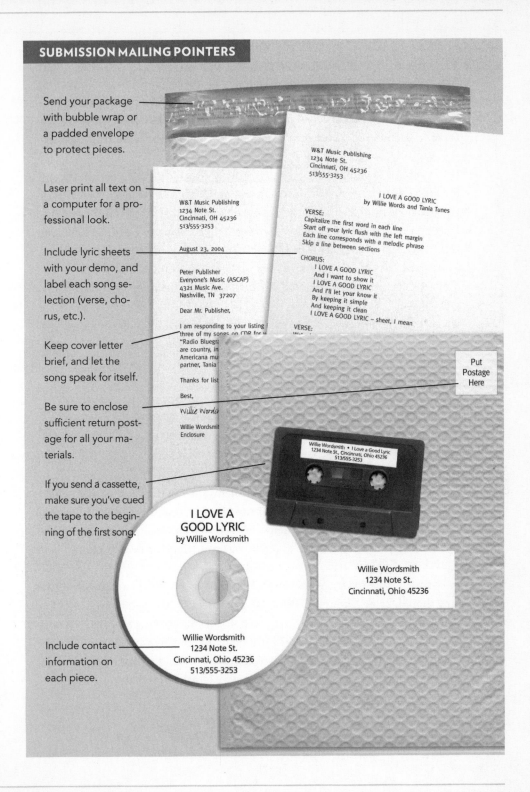

Send your package with bubble wrap or a padded envelope to protect pieces.

Laser print all text on a computer for a professional look.

Include lyric sheets with your demo, and label each song selection (verse, chorus, etc.).

Keep cover letter brief, and let the song speak for itself.

Be sure to enclose sufficient return postage for all your materials.

If you send a cassette, make sure you've cued the tape to the beginning of the first song.

Include contact information on each piece.

W&T Music Publishing
1234 Note St.
Cincinnati, OH 45236
513/555-3253

August 23, 2004

Peter Publisher
Everyone's Music (ASCAP)
4321 Music Ave.
Nashville, TN 37207

Dear Mr. Publisher,

I am responding to your listing
three of my songs on CDR for w
"Radio Bluegr
are country, in
Americana mu
partner, Tania

Thanks for list

Best,

Willie Wordsm

Willie Wordsmit
Enclosure

W&T Music Publishing
1234 Note St.
Cincinnati, OH 45236
513/555-3253

I LOVE A GOOD LYRIC
by Willie Words and Tania Tunes

VERSE:
Capitalize the first word in each line
Start off your lyric flush with the left margin
Each line corresponds with a melodic phrase
Skip a line between sections

CHORUS:
I LOVE A GOOD LYRIC
And I want to show it
I LOVE A GOOD LYRIC
And I'll let your know it
By keeping it simple
And keeping it clean
I LOVE A GOOD LYRIC – sheet, I mean

VERSE:

Put
Postage
Here

Willie Wordsmith • I Love a Good Lyric
1234 Note St., Cincinnati, Ohio 45236
513/555-3253

Willie Wordsmith
1234 Note St.
Cincinnati, Ohio 45236

I LOVE A
GOOD LYRIC
by Willie Wordsmith

Willie Wordsmith
1234 Note St.
Cincinnati, Ohio 45236
513/555-3253

- Include *typed* lyrics sheets or lead sheets, if requested. Make sure your name, address and phone number are on each sheet.
- Neatly label each tape or CD with your name, address, e-mail and phone number, along with the names of the songs in the order they appear on the recording.
- Include a SASE with sufficient postage and large enough to return all your materials. Warning: Many companies do not return materials, so read each listing carefully.
- If you submit to companies in other countries, include a self-addressed envelope (SAE) and International Reply Coupon (IRC), available at most post offices. Make sure the envelope is large enough to return all of your materials.
- Pack everything neatly. Neatly type or write the company's address and your return address so they are clearly visible. Your package is the first impression a company has of you and your songs, so neatness counts!
- Mail first class: Stamp or write "First Class Mail" on the package and the SASE you enclose.
- Do not use registered or certified mail unless requested. Most companies will not accept or open demos sent by registered or certified mail for fear of lawsuits.
- Keep records of the dates, songs, and companies you submit to.

Is it OK to send demos to more than one person or company at a time?

It is usually acceptable to make simultaneous submissions. One exception is when a publisher, artist, or other industry professional asks you to put your song "on hold."

What does it mean when a song is "on hold"?

This means they intend to record the song and don't want you to give the song to anyone else. This is not a guarantee, though. Your song may eventually be returned to you, even if it's been on hold for months. Or it may be recorded and included on the album. If either of these happens, you are free to pitch your song to other people again.

How can I protect myself from my song being put "on hold" indefinitely?

You can, and should, protect yourself. Establish a deadline for the person who asks for the hold, for example, "You can put my song on hold for [number of] months." Or you can modify the hold to specify that you will still pitch the song to others but won't sign another deal without allowing the person with the song on hold to make you an offer. Once you sign a contract with a publisher, they have exclusive rights to your song and you may not pitch it to other would-be publishers.

SUBMITTING IN PERSON

Is a visit to New York, Nashville, or Los Angeles to submit in person a good idea?

A trip to one of the major music hubs can be valuable if you are organized and prepared to make the most of it. You should have specific goals and set up appointments before you go. Some industry professionals are difficult to see and may not feel meeting out-of-town writers is a high priority. Others are more open and even encourage face-to-face meetings. By taking the time to travel, organize, and schedule meetings, you can appear more professional than songwriters who submit blindly through the mail.

What should I take?

Take several copies of your demo and typed lyric sheets of each of your songs. More than one company you visit may ask you to leave a copy for them to review. You can expect occasionally to find a person has canceled an appointment, but want you to leave a copy of your songs so they can listen and contact you later. (Never give someone the only or last copy of your demo if you absolutely want it returned, though.)

Where should I network while visiting?

Coordinate your trip with a music conference or make plans to visit ASCAP, BMI, or SESAC offices while you are there. For example, the South by Southwest Music Conference in Austin and NSAI Spring Symposium in Nashville often feature demo listening sessions, where industry professionals listen to demos submitted by songwriters attending the seminar. ASCAP, BMI, and SESAC also sometimes sponsor seminars or allow aspiring songwriters to make appointments with counselors who can give them solid advice.

How do I deal with rejection?

Many good songs have been rejected simply because they were not what the publisher or record company was looking for at that particular point. Do not take it personally. If few people like your songs, it does not mean they are not good. On the other hand, if you have a clear vision for what your particular songs are trying to convey, specific comments can also teach you a lot about whether your concept is coming across as you intended. If you hear the same criticisms of your songs over and over—for instance, the feel of the melody isn't right or the lyrics need work—give the advice serious thought. Listen carefully and use what the reviewers say constructively to improve your songs.

SUBMITTING OVER THE INTERNET

Is it OK to submit over the Internet?

It can be done, but it's not yet widely accepted. There can still be problems with audio file formats. Although e-mail is widely used now if you look through the listings in *Songwriter's Market*, not all music companies are necessarily equipped with computers or Internet access sufficient to make the process easy. But it shows a lot of promise for the future. Web-based companies like Tonos.com or TAXI, among many others, are making an effort to connect songwriters and industry professionals over the Internet. The Internet is proving important for networking. Garageband.com has extensive bulletin boards and allows members to post audio files of songs for critique. Stay tuned for future developments.

If I want to try submitting over the Internet, what should I do?

First, send an e-mail to confirm whether a music company is equipped to stream or download audio files properly (whether mp3 or real audio, etc). If they do accept demos online, one strategy becoming common is to build a website with audio files that can be streamed or downloaded. Then, when you have permission, send an e-mail with links to that website or to particular songs. All they have to do is click on the link and it launches their Web browser to the appropriate page. Do not try to send mp3s or other files as attachments. They are often too large for the free online e-mail accounts people commonly use, and they may be mistakenly erased as potential viruses.

HOW DO I AVOID THE RIP-OFFS?

The music industry has its share of dishonest, greedy people who will try to rip you off by appealing to your ambition, by stroking your ego, or by claiming special powers to make you successful—for a price, of course. Most of them use similar methods, and you can prevent a lot of heartbreak by learning to spot them and stay away.

What is a "song shark"?

"Song sharks," as they're called, prey on beginners—songwriters unfamiliar with how the music industry works and what the ethical standards are. Two general signs of a song shark are:

- song sharks will take *any* songs—quality doesn't count.
- they're not concerned with future royalties, since they get their money up front from songwriters who think they're getting a great deal.

What are some of the more blatant rip-offs?

A request for money up front is the most common element. Song sharks may ask for money in the form of submission fees, an outright offer to publish your song for a fee or an offer to rerecord your demo for a sometimes hefty price (with the implication that they will make your song wildly successful if you only pay to have it re-demoed in *their studio*). There are many variations on this theme.

Here is a list of rules that can help you avoid a lot of scams:

- **DO NOT SELL YOUR SONGS OUTRIGHT!** It's unethical for anyone to offer such a proposition. If your song becomes successful after you've sold it outright, you will never get royalties for it.

- **NEVER PAY ANY SORT OF "SUBMISSION FEES," "REVIEW FEES," "SERVICE FEES," "FILING FEES," ETC.** Reputable companies review material free of charge. If you encounter a company in this book who charges to submit, report them to the editor. If a company charges "only" $15 to submit your song, consider this: *if "only" 100 songwriters pay the $15, this company has made an extra $1,500 just for opening the mail!*

- **NEVER PAY TO HAVE YOUR SONGS PUBLISHED.** A reputable company interested in your songs assumes the responsibility and cost of promoting them, in hopes of realizing a profit once the songs are recorded and released. If they truly believe in your song, they will accept the costs involved.

- **DO NOT PAY A COMPANY TO PAIR YOU WITH A COLLABORATOR.** It's much better to contact a songwriting organization that offers collaboration services to their members.

- **NEVER PAY TO HAVE YOUR LYRICS OR POEMS SET TO MUSIC.** This is a classic rip-off. "Music mills"—for a price—may use the same melody for hundreds of lyrics and poems, whether it sounds good or not. Publishers recognize one of these melodies as soon as they hear it.

- **AVOID "PAY-TO-PLAY" CD COMPILATION DEALS.** It's totally unrealistic to expect this will open doors for you. These are mainly a moneymaker for the music company. CDs are cheap to manufacture, so a company that charges $100 to include your recording on a CD is making a killing. They claim they send these CDs to radio stations, producers, etc., but they usually wind up in the trash or as drink coasters. Music industry professionals have no incentive to listen to them. Everybody on the CD paid to be included, so it's not like they were carefully screened for quality.

- **AVOID "SONGPLUGGERS' WHO OFFER TO "SHOP" YOUR SONG FOR AN UP-FRONT FEE OR RETAINER.** This practice is not appropriate for *Songwriter's Market* readers, many of whom are beginners and live away from major music centers like Nashville. Professional, established songwriters in Nashville are sometimes known to work on a fee basis with songpluggers they have gotten to know over many years, *but the practice is controversial even for professionals.* Also, the songpluggers used by established professionals are very selective about their clients and have their own reputation to uphold. Companies who offer you these services but barely know you or your work are to be avoided. Also, contracting a songplugger long distance offers little or no accountability—you have no direct way of knowing what they're doing on your behalf.

- **AVOID PAYING A FEE UP FRONT TO HAVE A PUBLISHER MAKE A DEMO OF YOUR SONG.** Some publishers may take demo expenses out of your future royalties (a negotiable contract point usually meant to avoid endless demo sessions), but avoid paying up front for demo costs. Avoid situations where it is implied or expressed that a company will publish your song in return for you paying up front to use their demo services.

- **NO RECORD COMPANY SHOULD ASK YOU TO PAY THEM OR AN ASSOCIATED COMPANY TO MAKE A DEMO.** The job of a record company is to make records and decide which artists to sign *after* listening to demo submissions.
- **READ ALL CONTRACTS CAREFULLY BEFORE SIGNING.** And don't sign any contract you're unsure about or that you don't fully understand. It is well worth paying an attorney for the time it takes him to review a contract if you can avoid a bad situation that may cost you thousands of dollars.
- **BEFORE ENTERING A SONGWRITING CONTEST, READ THE RULES CAREFULLY.** Be sure what you're giving up in the way of entry fees, etc., is not more than what you stand to gain by winning the contest (see the Contests & Awards section).
- **VERIFY ANY SITUATION ABOUT AN INDIVIDUAL OR COMPANY IF YOU HAVE ANY DOUBTS AT ALL.** Contact the company's Performing Rights Society—ASCAP, BMI, SESAC, or SOCAN (in Canada). Check with the Better Business Bureau in the company's town, or contact the state attorney general's office. Contact professional organizations of which you're a member and inquire about the reputation of the company.
- **IF A RECORD COMPANY OR OTHER COMPANY ASKS YOU TO PAY EXPENSES UP FRONT, BE CAREFUL.** Record producers commonly charge up front to produce an artist's album. Small indie labels sometimes ask a band to help with recording costs (but seek less control than a major label might). It's up to you to decide whether or not it is a good idea. Talk to other artists who have signed similar contracts before you sign one yourself. Research companies to find out if they can deliver on their claims, and what kind of distribution they have. Visit their website, if they have one. Beware of any company that won't let you know what it has done in the past. If a company has had successes and good working relationships with artists, it should be happy to brag about them.

IF YOU WRITE LYRICS, BUT NOT MUSIC

- You must find a collaborator. The music business is looking for the complete package: music plus lyrics. If you don't write music, find a collaborator who does. The best way to find a collaborator is through songwriting organizations. Check the Organizations section for songwriting groups near you.
- Don't get ripped off. "Music mills" advertise in the back of magazines or solicit you through the mail. For a fee they will set your lyrics or poems to music. The rip-off is that they may use the same melody for hundreds of lyrics and poems, whether it sounds good or not. Publishers recognize one of these melodies as soon as they hear it.

HOW DO I FILE A COMPLAINT?

Write to the *Songwriter's Market* editor at: 4700 E. Galbraith Rd., Cincinnati, OH 45236. Include:

- a complete description of the situation, as best you can describe it
- copies of any materials a company may have sent you that we may keep on file

If you encounter situations similar to any of the "song shark" scenarios described previously, let us know about it.

I noticed record producers charge to produce albums. Is this bad?

Not automatically. Just remember what your goals are. If you write songs, but do not sing or perform, you are looking for publishing opportunities with the producer instead of someone who can help you record an album or CD. If you are a performing artist or band, then you might be in the market to hire a producer, in which case you will most likely pay them up front (and possibly give them a share in royalties or publishing, depending on the specific deal you negotiate). For more information see the Record Producers section introduction and the Royalties section.

Will it help me avoid rip-offs if I join a songwriting organization?

Yes. You will have access to a lot of good advice from a lot of experienced people. You will be able to research and compare notes, which will help you avoid a lot of pitfalls.

What should I know about contracts?

Negotiating a fair contract is important. You must protect yourself, and there are specific things you should look for in a contract. See the Contracts section for more information.

Are companies that offer demo services automatically bad?

No, but you are not obligated to make use of their services. Many music companies have their own or related recording studios, and with good recording equipment becoming so cheap and easy to use in recent years, a lot of them are struggling to stay afloat. This doesn't mean a company is necessarily trying to rip you off, but use your best judgment. In some cases, a company will submit a listing to *Songwriter's Market* for the wrong reasons—to pitch their demo services instead of finding songs to sign—in which case you should report them to the *Songwriter's Market* editor.

SUBMISSION STRATEGIES

//

NONPERFORMING SONGWRITERS

Here's a short list of avenues nonperforming songwriters can pursue when submitting songs:

1. **SUBMIT TO A MUSIC PUBLISHER.** This is the obvious one. Look at the information under Music in the listing to see examples of a publisher's songs and the artists they've found cuts with. Do you recognize the songs? Have you heard of the artists? Who are the writers? Do they have cuts with artists you would like to get a song to?

2. **SUBMIT TO A RECORD COMPANY.** Are the bands and artists on the record company's roster familiar? Do they tend to use outside songs on their albums? When pursuing this angle, it often helps to contact the record company first. Ask if they have a group or artist in development who needs material.

3. **SUBMIT TO A RECORD PRODUCER.** Do the producer's credits in the listings show songs written by songwriters other than the artist? Does he produce name artists known for using outside material? Be aware that producers themselves often write with the artists, so your song might also be competing against the producer's songwriting.

4. **SUBMIT TO AN ARTIST'S MANAGER.** If an artist needs songs, his or her manager is a prime gateway for your song. Contact the manager and ask if he has a act in need of material.

5. **JOIN A SONGWRITING ORGANIZATION.** Songwriting organizations are a good way to make contacts. You'll discover opportunities through the contacts you make that others might not hear about. Some organizations can put you in direct contact with publishers for song critique sessions. You can increase your chances of a hit by co-

writing with other songwriters. Your songs will get better because of the feedback from other members.

6. **APPROACH PERFORMING RIGHTS ORGANIZATIONS (PROS).** PROs like ASCAP and BMI have writer relation representatives who can sometimes (if they think you're ready) give you a reference to a music company. This is one of the favored routes to success in the Nashville music scene.

PERFORMING SONGWRITERS

This is a bit more complicated, because there are a lot of different avenues available.

Finding a record deal

This is often a performing songwriter's primary goal—to get a record deal and release an album. Here are some possible ways to approach it:

1. **APPROACH A RECORD COMPANY FOR A RECORD DEAL.** This is another obvious one. Independent labels will be a lot more approachable than major labels, who are usually deluged with demos. Independent labels give you more artistic freedom, while major labels will demand more compromise, especially if you do not have a previous track record. A compromise between the two is to approach one of the "fake indie" labels owned by a major. You'll get more of the benefits of an indie, but with more of the resources and connections of a major label.

2. **APPROACH A RECORD PRODUCER FOR A DEVELOPMENT DEAL.** Some producers sign artists, produce their albums and develop them like a record company, and then approach major labels for distribution deals. This has advantages and drawbacks. For example, the producer gives you guidance and connections, but it can also be harder to get paid because you are signed to the producer and not the label.

3. **GET A MANAGER WITH CONNECTIONS.** The right manager with the right connections can make all the difference in getting a record deal.

4. **ASK A MUSIC PUBLISHER.** Publishers are taking on more and more of a role of developing performing songwriters as artists. Many major publishers are sister companies to record labels and can shop you for a deal when they think you're ready. They do this in hopes of participating in the mechanical royalties from an album release, and these monies can be substantial when it's a major label release.

5. **APPROACH AN ENTERTAINMENT ATTORNEY.** Entertainment attorneys are a must when it comes to negotiating record contracts, and some moonlight by helping artists make connections for record deals (they will get their cut, of course).

6. **APPROACH PROS.** ASCAP and BMI can counsel you on your career and possibly make a referral. They also commonly put on performance showcases where A&R ("artist and repertoire') people from record labels attend to check out the new artists.

Finding a producer to help with your album

Independently minded performing songwriters often find they need help navigating the studio when it comes time to produce their own album. In this case, the producer often works for an up-front fee from the artist, for a percentage of the royalty when the album is released and sold (referred to as "points," as in "percentage points"), or a combination of both.

Things to keep in mind when submitting a demo to a producer on this basis:

1. **IS THE PRODUCER KNOWN FOR A PARTICULAR GENRE OR "SOUND"?** Many producers have a signature sound to their studio productions and are often connected to specific genres. Phil Spector had the "Wall of Sound." Bob Rock pioneered a glossy metal sound for Metallica and the Cult. Daniel Lanois and Brian Eno are famous for the atmospheres they created on albums by U2. Look at your favorite CDs to see who produced. Use these as touchstones when approaching producers to see if they are on your wavelength.

2. **WHAT ROLE DOES A PARTICULAR PRODUCER LIKE TO TAKE IN THE STUDIO?** The Tips information found at the end of many of the Record Producers listings often have notes from the producer about how they like to work with performing songwriters in the studio. Some work closely as a partner with the artist on developing arrangements and coaching performances. Some prefer final authority on creative decisions. Think carefully about what kind of working relationship you want.

Finding a manager

Many performing songwriters eventually find it necessary to find a manager to help with developing their careers and finding gigs. Some things to keep in mind when looking:

1. **DOES THE MANAGER WORK WITH ARTISTS IN MY GENRE OF MUSIC?** A manager who typically works with punk rock bands may not have as many connections useful to an aspiring country singer-songwriter. A manager who mainly works with gospel artists might not know what to do with a hedonistic rock band.

2. **HOW BIG IS THE MANAGER'S AGENCY?** If a manager is working with multiple acts, but has a small (or no) staff, you might not get the attention you want. Some of the listings have information in the heading about the agency's staff size.

3. **DOES THE MANAGER WORK WITH ACTS FROM MY REGION?** Many of the listings have information in their headings provided by the companies describing whether they work with regional acts only or artists from any region.

4. **DOES THE MANAGER WORK WITH NAME ACTS?** A manager with famous clients could work wonders for your career. Or you could get lost in the shuffle. Use your best judgment when sizing up a potential manager, and be clear with yourself about the

kind of relationship you would like to have and the level of attention you want for your career.

5. **IF I'M A BEGINNER, WILL THE MANAGER WORK FOR ME?** Check the listings for the Openness to Submissions icons ⊘◯◐● to find companies open to beginners. Some may suggest extensive changes to your music or image. On the other hand, you may have a strong vision of what you want to do and need a manager who will work with you to achieve that vision instead of changing you around. Decide for yourself how much you are willing to compromise in good faith.

REMEMBER THAT A RELATIONSHIP BETWEEN YOU AND A MANAGER IS A TWO-WAY STREET. You will have to earn each other's trust and be clear about your goals for mutual success.

ROYALTIES

NONPERFORMING SONGWRITERS

How do songwriters make money?

The quick answer is that songwriters make money through rights available to them through the copyright laws. For more details, keep reading and see the next section—Copyright.

What specific rights make money for songwriters?

There are two primary ways songwriters earn money on their songs: performance royalties and mechanical royalties.

What is a performance royalty?

When you hear a song on the radio, on television, in the elevator, in a restaurant, etc., the songwriter receives royalties, called performance royalties. Performing Rights Organizations (ASCAP, BMI and SESAC in the U.S.A.) collect payment from radio stations, television, etc., and distribute those payments to songwriters (see below).

What is a mechanical royalty?

When a record company puts a song onto a CD, cassette, etc., and distributes copies for sale, they owe a royalty payment to the songwriter for each copy they press of the album. It is called a mechanical royalty because of the mechanical process used to mass-produce a copy of a CD, cassette, or sheet music. The payment is small per song (see the "Royalty Provisions" subhead of the Basic Song Contract Pointers sidebar in the Contracts section), but the earnings can add up and reach massive proportions for songs appearing on success-

MUSIC PUBLISHING ROYALTIES

PERFORMANCE   **PRINT**   **SYNCHRONIZATION**   **MECHANICAL**

- Radio & TV Stations, Night Clubs, Concerts & Jukeboxes
- Sheet Music Orchestrations, Choral Arrangements & Folio Sales
- Films & TV Movies
- Record Stores & Record Clubs

- Performance Societies (ASCP, BMI, SESAC)
- Foreign Self-Publishing
- Record Company

- Music Publisher
- Harry Fox Agency or Other Collector

- Songwriter

ful label albums. Note: This royalty is totally different from the artist royalty on the retail price of the album.

Who collects the money for performance and mechanical royalties?

Performing Rights Organizations collect performance royalties. There are three organizations that collect performance royalties: ASCAP, BMI, and SESAC. These organizations arose many years ago when songwriters and music publishers gathered together to press for their rights and improve their ability to collect fees for the use of their songs. ASCAP, BMI, and SESAC collect fees for the use of songs and then pass along the money to their member songwriters and music publishers.

MECHANICAL RIGHTS ORGANIZATIONS COLLECT MECHANICAL ROYALTIES. There are three organizations that collect mechanical royalties: the Harry Fox Agency (HFA), the American Mechanical Rights Organization (AMRA) and the Songwriters Guild of America (SGA). These three organizations collect mechanical royalties from record companies of all sizes—major labels, midsize, and independents—and pass the royalties along to member music publishers and songwriters.

How do songwriters hook up with this system to earn royalties?

For performance royalties, individual songwriters affiliate with a Performing Rights Organization of their choice, and register their songs in the PRO database. Each PRO has a slightly different method of calculating payment, different ownership, and different membership structure, so choosing a PRO is an individual choice. Once a songwriter is affiliated and has registered his or her songs, the PROs then collect fees as described above and issue a check to the songwriter.

For mechanical royalties, three different things can happen:

1. The songwriter is signed to a publisher that is affiliated with the Harry Fox Agency. The Harry Fox Agency collects the mechanical royalties and passes them along to the publisher. The publisher then passes these along to the songwriter within thirty days. This case usually happens when a songwriter is signed to a major publisher and has a song on a major label album release.

2. The songwriter is not signed to a publisher and owns exclusive rights to his songs, and so works with AMRA or the Songwriters Guild of America, who cuts a check directly to the songwriter instead of passing him or her to the publisher first.

3. They are signed to a publisher, but the songs are being released on albums by independent labels. In this case, the songwriter often works with AMRA since they have a focus on the independent music publishing market.

PERFORMING SONGWRITERS / ARTISTS

How do performing songwriters make money?

Performing songwriters and artists (if they write their own songs) make money just like non-performing songwriters, as described previously, but they also make money through royalties made on the retail price of an album when it is sold online, in a store, etc.

What about all the stories of performing songwriters getting into bad deals?

The stories are generally true, but if they're smart, performing songwriters usually can hold on to the money they would be owed as songwriters (performing and mechanical royalties). But when it comes to retail sale royalties, all they will usually see is an "advance"—essentially a loan—which must then be paid off from record sales. You will not see a royalty check on retail sales until your advance is paid off. If you are given a $600,000 advance, for example, you will have to pay back the record company $600,000 out of your sales royalties before you see any more money.

Do performing songwriters and artists get to keep the advance?

Not really. If you have a manager who has gotten you a record deal, he or she will take a cut. You will probably be required in the contract to pay for the producer and studio time to make the album. Often the producer will take a percentage of subsequent royalties from album sales, which comes out of your pocket. Then there are also music video costs, promotion to radio stations, tour support, paying sidemen, etc. Just about anything you can think of is eventually paid for out of your advance or out of sales royalties. There are also deductions to royalties usually built into record company contracts that make it harder to earn out an advance.

What should a performing songwriter wanting to sign with a major label do?

Songwriters' best option is to negotiate a fair contract, get as big of an advance as possible, and then manage that advance money the best they can. A good contract will keep the songwriting royalties described above completely separate from the flow of sales royalties, and will also cut down on the number of royalty deductions the record company builds into the contract. And because of the difficulty in earning out any size advance or auditing the record company, it makes sense to get as much cash up front as you can, then to manage that as best you can. You will need a good lawyer.

RECORD COMPANIES, PRODUCERS AND MANAGERS, & BOOKING AGENTS

How do music publishers make money?

A publisher works as a songwriter's agent, looks for profitable commercial uses for the songs he or she represents, and then takes a percentage of the profits. This is typically 50 percent of all earning from a particular song—often referred to as the *publisher's share*. A successful publisher stays in contact with several A&R reps, finding out what upcoming projects are in need of new material, and whether any songs he or she represents will be appropriate.

How do record companies make money?

Record companies primarily make their money from profits made selling CDs, cassettes, DVDs, etc. Record companies keep most of the profit after subtracting manufacturing costs, royalties to recording artists, distribution fees and the costs of promoting songs to radio (which for major labels can reach up to $300,000 per song). Record companies also usually have music publishing divisions that make money performing all the functions of publishers.

How do record producers make money?

Producers mostly make their money by charging a flat fee up front to helm a recording project, by sharing in the royalties from album sales, or both. A small independent producer might charge $10,000 (or sometimes less) up front to produce a small indie band, while a "name" producer such as Bob Rock, who regularly works with major label bands, might charge $300,000. Either of these might also take a share in sales royalties, referred to as "points"—as in "percentage points." A producer might say, "I'll produce you for $10,000 and 2 points." If an artist is getting a 15 percent royalty on album sales, then two of those percentage points will go to the producer instead. Producers also make money by cowriting with the artists to get publishing royalties, or they may ask for part of the publishing from songs written by outside songwriters.

How do managers make money?

Most managers make money by taking a percentage commission of their clients' income, usually 10–25 percent. If a touring band finishes a show and makes a $2,000 profit, a manager on 15 percent commission would get $300. If an artist gets a $40,000 advance from a midsize label, the manager would get $6,000. Whether an artist's songwriting income is included in the manager's commission comes down to negotiation. The commission should give the manager incentive to make things happen for your career, so avoid paying flat fees up front.

COPYRIGHT

How am I protected by the copyright laws?

Copyright protection applies to your songs the instant you put them down in fixed form—a recording, sheet music, lead sheet, etc. This protection lasts for your lifetime plus 70 years (or the lifetime of the last surviving writer, if you cowrote the song with somebody else). When you prepare demos, place notification of copyright on all copies of your song—the lyric sheets, lead sheets, and labels for cassettes, CDs, etc. The notice is simply the word "copyright" or the symbol © followed by the year the song was created (or published) and your name (Example: © 2005 by John Q. Songwriter).

What parts of a song are protected by copyright?

Traditionally, only the melody line and the lyrics are eligible for copyright. Period. Chords and rhythm are virtually never protected. An incredibly original arrangement can sometimes qualify. Sound recordings can also be copyrighted, but this applies strictly to the actual sounds on the recording, not the song itself (this copyright is usually owned by record companies).

What songs are not protected?

Song titles or mere ideas for music and lyrics cannot be copyrighted. Very old songs in the "public domain" are not protected. You could quote a melody from a Bach piece, but you could not then stop someone else from quoting the same melody in his song.

When would I lose or have to share the copyright?

If you collaborate with other writers, they are assumed to have equal interests unless you state some other arrangement, in writing. If you write under a work-for-hire arrangement, the company or person who hired you to write the song then owns the copyright. Sometimes your spouse may automatically be granted an interest in your copyright as part of his or her spousal rights, which might then become important if you get divorced.

Should I register my copyright?

Registering your copyright with the Library of Congress gives the best possible protection. Registration establishes a public record of your copyright—even though a song is legally protected whether or not it is registered—and could prove useful in any future court cases involving the song. Registration also entitles you to a potentially greater settlement in a copyright infringement lawsuit.

How do I register my song?

To register your song, request government form PA from the Copyright Office. Call the 24-hour hotline at (202)707-9100 and leave your name and address on the messaging system. Once you receive the PA form, you must return it, along with a registration fee and a CD (or tape) and lead sheet of your song. Send these to the Register of Copyrights, Copyright Office, Library of Congress, Washington DC 20559. It may take several months to receive your certificate of registration from the Copyright Office, but your songs are protected from the date of creation (the date of registration will reflect the date you applied). For more information, call the Copyright Office's Public Information Office at (202)707-3000 or visit their website at www.copyright.gov.

How likely is it that someone will try to steal my song?

Copyright infringement is very rare. But if you ever feel that one of your songs has been stolen—that someone has unlawfully infringed on your copyright—you must prove that you created the work and that the person you are suing had access to your song. Copyright registration is the best proof of a date of creation. You must have your copyright registered in order to file a lawsuit. Also, it's helpful if you keep your rough drafts and revisions of songs, either on page or on tape.

Why did song sharks begin soliciting me after I registered my song?

This is one potential, unintended consequence of registering your song with the Library of Congress. The copyright indexes are a public record of your songwriting, and song sharks often search the copyright indexes and mail solicitations to songwriters who live out away from major music centers such as Nashville. They figure these songwriters don't know any better and are easy prey. *Do not allow this possibility to stop you from registering your songs!* Just be aware, educate yourself, and then throw the song sharks' mailings in the trash.

What if I mail a tape to myself to get a postmark date on a sealed envelope?

The "poor man's copyright" has not stood up in court, and is not an acceptable substitute for registering your song. If you feel it's important to shore up your copyright, register it with the Library of Congress.

CAREER SONGWRITING

//

What career options are open to songwriters who do not perform?

The possibilities range from a beginning songwriter living away from a music center like Nashville who lands an occasional single-song publishing deal, to a staff songwriter signed to a major publishing company. And there are songwriters like Desmond Child who operate independently, have developed a lot of connections, work with numerous artists, and have set up their own independent publishing operations.

What is "single-song" songwriting about?

In this case, a songwriter submits songs to many different companies. One or two songs gain interest from different publishers, and the songwriter signs separate contracts for each song with each publisher. The songwriter can then pitch other songs to other publishers. In Nashville, for instance, a single-song contract is usually the first taste of success for an aspiring songwriter on his or her way up the ladder. Success of this sort can induce a songwriter to move to a music center like Nashville (if he or she hasn't already), and is a big boost for a struggling songwriter already living there. A series of single-song contracts often signals a songwriter's maturing skill and marketability.

What is a "staff songwriter"?

A staff songwriter usually works for a major publisher and receives a monthly stipend as an advance against the royalties he or she is likely to earn for the publisher. The music publisher has exclusive rights to everything the songwriter writes while signed to the company. The publisher also works actively on the writer's behalf to hook him or her up with cowriters and other opportunities. A staff songwriting position is highly treasured by many because it offers a steady income, and in Nashville is a sign the songwriter "has arrived."

What comes after the staff songwriting position?

Songwriters who go to the next level have a significant reputation for their ability to write hit songs. Famous artists seek them out, and they often write actively in several markets at once. They often write on assignment for film and television, and commonly keep their own publishing companies to maximize their income.

As my career grows, what should I do about keeping track of expenses, etc.?

You should keep a ledger or notebook with records on all financial transactions related to your songwriting—royalty checks, demo costs, office supplies, postage, travel expenses, dues to organizations, class and workshop fees, plus any publications you purchase pertaining to songwriting. You may also want a separate checking account devoted to your songwriting activities. This will make record keeping easier and help to establish your identity as a business for tax purposes.

What should I know about taxes related to songwriting income?

Any royalties you receive will not reflect taxes or any other mandatory deductions. It is your responsibility to keep track of income and file the correct tax forms. For specific information, contact the IRS or talk to an accountant who serves music industry clients.

CONTRACTS

//

COWRITING

What kind of agreements do I need with cowriters?

You may need to sign a legal agreement between you and a cowriter to establish percentages you will each receive of the writer's royalties. You will also have to iron out what you will do if another person, such as an artist, wants to change your song and receive credit as a cowriter. For example, in the event a major artist wants to cut your song for his or her album—but also wants to rewrite some lyrics and take a share of the publishing—you and your cowriter need to agree whether it is better to get a song on an album that might sell millions (and make a lot of money) or pass on it because you don't want to give up credit. The situation could be uncomfortable if you are not in sync on the issue.

When do I need a lawyer to look over agreements?

When it comes to doing business with a publisher, producer, or record company, you should always have the contract reviewed by a knowledgeable entertainment attorney. As long as the issues at stake are simple, the cowriters respect each other, and they discuss their business philosophies before writing a song together, they can probably write up an agreement without the aid of a lawyer.

SINGLE-SONG CONTRACTS

What is a single-song contract?

A music publisher offers a single-song contract when he or she wants to sign one or more of your songs, but doesn't want to hire you as a staff songwriter. You assign your rights to a particular song to the publisher for an agreed-upon number of years, so that he or she may represent the song and find uses profitable for both of you. This is a common contract and quite possibly will be the first you encounter in your songwriting career.

What basic elements should every single-song contract contain?

Every contract should have the publisher's name, the writer's name, the song's title, the date, and the purpose of the agreement. The songwriter also declares the song is an original work and he is creator of the work. The contract *must* specify the royalties the songwriter will earn from various uses of the song, including performance, mechanical, print, and synchronization royalties.

How should the royalties usually be divided in the contract?

The songwriter should receive no less than 50 percent of the income his or her song generates. That means the songwriter and publisher split the total royalties 50/50. The songwriter's half is called the "writer's share" and the publisher's half is called the "publisher's share." If there is more than one songwriter, the songwriters split the writer's share. Sometimes, successful songwriters will bargain for a percentage of the publisher's share, negotiating what is basically a copublishing agreement. For a visual explanation of how royalties are collected and flow to the songwriter, see the chart called Music Publishing Royalties in the Royalties section.

What should the contract say about a "reversion clause"?

Songwriters should always negotiate for a "reversion clause," which returns all rights back to the songwriter if some provision of the contract is not met. Most reversion clauses give a publisher a set amount of time (usually one or two years) to work the song and make money with it. If the publisher can't get the song recorded and released during the agreed-upon time period, the songwriter can then take his song to another publisher. The danger of not getting some sort of reversion clause is that you could wind up with a publisher sitting on your song for the entire life-plus-70-years term of the copyright—which may as well be forever.

Is a reversion clause difficult to get?

Some publishers agree to it, and figure if they can't get any action with the song in the first year or two, they're not likely to ever have much luck with it. Other publishers may be reluctant to agree to a reversion clause. They may invest a lot of time and money in demoing and pitching a song to artists and want to keep working at it for a longer period of time. Or, for example, a producer might put a song on hold for a while and then go into a lengthy recording project. A year can easily go by before the artist or producer decides which songs to release as singles. This means you may have to agree to a longer time period, be flexible, and trust that the publisher has your best mutual interests in mind. Use your judgment.

The following list, taken from a Songwriters Guild of America publication, enumerates the basic features of an acceptable songwriting contract:

1) **WORK FOR HIRE.** When you receive a contract covering just one composition, you should make sure the phrases "employment for hire" and "exclusive writer agreement" are not included. Also, there should be no options for future songs.

2) **PERFORMING RIGHTS AFFILIATION.** If you previously signed publishing contracts, you should be affiliated with ASCAP, BMI, or SESAC. All performance royalties must be received directly by you from your performing rights organization, and this should be written into your contract.

3) **REVERSION CLAUSE.** The contract should include a provision that if the publisher does not secure a release of a commercial sound recording within a specified time (one year, two years, etc.), the contract can be terminated by you.

4) **CHANGES IN THE COMPOSITION.** If the contract includes a provision that the publisher can change the title, lyrics, or music, this should be amended so that only with your consent can such charges be made.

5) **ROYALTY PROVISIONS.** You should receive 50 percent of all publisher's income on all licenses issued. If the publisher prints and sells his own sheet music, your royalty should be 10 percent of the wholesale selling price. The royalty should not be stated in the contract as a flat rate ($.05, $.07, etc.).

6) **NEGOTIABLE DEDUCTIONS.** Ideally, demos and all other expenses of publication should be paid 100 percent by the publisher. The only allowable fee is for the Harry Fox Agency collection fee, whereby the writer pays one-half of the amount charged to the publisher for mechanical rights. The current mechanical royalty collected by the Harry Fox Agency is 9.1 cents per cut for songs under 5 minutes; and 1.75 cents per minute for songs over 5 minutes.

7) **ROYALTY STATEMENTS AND AUDIT PROVISION.** Once the song is recorded, you are entitled to receive royalty statements at least once every six months. In addition, an audit provision with no time restriction should be included in every contract.

8) **WRITER'S CREDIT.** The publisher should make sure that you receive proper credit on all uses of the composition.

9) **ARBITRATION.** In order to avoid large legal fees in case of a dispute with your publisher, the contract should include an arbitration clause.

10) **FUTURE USES.** Any use not specifically covered by the contract should be retained by the writer to be negotiated as it comes up.

What other basic issues should be covered by a single-song contract?

The contract should also address these issues:

- Will an advance be paid, and if so, how much will the advance be?
- When will royalties be paid (annually or semiannually)?
- Who will pay for demos—the publisher, songwriter or both?
- How will lawsuits against copyright infringement be handled, including the cost of lawsuits?
- Will the publisher have the right to sell its interest in the song to another publisher without the songwriter's consent?
- Does the publisher have the right to make changes in a song, or approve changes by someone else, without the songwriter's consent?
- The songwriter should have the right to audit the publisher's books if he feels it is necessary and gives the publisher reasonable notice.

WHEN DOES 50% EQUAL 100%?

NOTE: The publisher's and songwriter's share of the income are sometimes referred to as each being 100%—for 200% total! You might hear someone say, "I'll take 100% of the publisher's share." Do not be needlessly confused! If the numbers confuse you, ask for the terms to be clarified.

Where else can I go for advice on contracts?

The Songwriters Guild of America has drawn up a Popular Songwriter's Contract, which it believes to be the best minimum songwriter contract available (see the Basic Song Contract Pointers sidebar). The Guild will send a copy of the contract at no charge to any interested songwriter upon request (see the Songwriters Guild of America listing in the Organizations section). SGA will also review—free of charge—any contract offered to its members, and will check it for fairness and completeness. Also check out these two books published by Writer's Digest Books: *The Craft and Business of Songwriting*, 3rd edition, by John Braheny; and *The New Songwriter's Guide to Music Publishing*, 3rd edition, by Randy Poe.

HILLARY SCOTT

SESAC Songwriter of the Year

....

by Annie Downs

Hillary Scott is best known as "the lady" from Lady Antebellum, country music's hottest trio. With four number one hits ("Run to You", "Need You Now", "American Honey", "Our Kind of Love"), six Grammy Awards, and numerous CMA, AMA, and ACM Awards, Lady Antebellum has sealed their spot in music history. They have toured with many of country's greatest stars, including Martina McBride, Kenny Chesney, Tim McGraw, and Keith Urban. They are now headlining tours themselves. Crowds are pouring into venues around the country to hear the songs that the audience knows by heart.

What is lesser known about Hillary is her many accomplishments as a songwriter. At just twenty-four years old, Hillary has already garnered much praise for her writing ability, including being crowned SESAC Writer of the Year in 2008 and 2010. Hillary cowrites with her bandmates, Charles Kelley and Dave Haywood, but she also has penned songs with Tom Douglas, Dallas Davidson, Miranda Lambert, Dave Barnes, and Luke Laird, just to name a few.

A young, fresh voice in this historic genre, Hillary's songwriting continues to grow and evolve as her career and relationships do the same. She is redefining the world of female songwriters, and we are benefiting from it. Greatly.

Do you enjoy cowriting or do you write better songs alone?

I love cowriting. I like that it is collaborative. I like that it is not just your voice and your life experiences. You can pull from someone else's. For me, because I don't play an instrument well, it's better for me to write with someone who can.

When you started writing songs, how did you do that? Since you don't play...

I would write some by myself—I play a little guitar and piano—but I would also write with high school friends. I remember the first song I wrote-—I was six or seven. I wrote it with one of my friends.

My story is a little different. I started working with Victoria Shaw when I was sixteen, and started writing when I was seventeen. I had someone mentor me, take me under her wing, and teach me. So a lot of my first writing sessions were like going to school. I had never professionally written before, and I would be in a room with two amazingly talented songwriters. I would always give input, like, "I would say it like this" or "I wouldn't say that." You have to be honest when you write—you can't sing something or say something that you don't feel. But I had a mentor who taught me how to do that well.

What makes a good cowriter?

A lot of it has to do with being compatible with the person. Being able to carry on a good conversation brings connection. Other times, there are people that aren't easy to connect with—you can't talk for hours and hours about life—but you start to play music and putting words to that music, the connection comes and it is really special.

For me, a good cowriter is someone who listens—I'm always going to come in and talk about what is going on and what is inspiring me. And I like to hear what is going on with them as well—so an open-hearted person. Someone who will bear it all at times, lyrically, because I just appreciate honesty. Dave Haywood [member of Lady Antebellum] is one of my favorite cowriters. He is a very melodic guitar player and a very melodic piano player. And for me, since I don't play an instrument well, to have someone like him who does play well and has a really special way of playing those instruments, it opens up a lot of different vocal melodies or directions that you could go with the instrumentation.

It's talent, but it is also chemistry.

So can you teach someone to write a great song?

I think you can teach someone to get better at writing songs. Anyone can read a book and learn, but I truly believe that it is a gift. But it is a gift that you can improve, that you can hone and make better.

It's like a muscle—if you don't write for two months, you are out of shape—you get rusty.

How often is personal experience involved in your songwriting?

Probably 90 percent of the time. I don't feel comfortable writing songs about things I do not know about or haven't experienced firsthand. That's the other thing about cowriting. We can start to talk about someone else's life experiences, so you can see from someone else's point of view.

The best example is that I don't know how to write a song about how to change the world because I am just trying to love people and treat them well. I've been in love, I've been out of love, but I'm not going to write a huge political statement about how we should change the world. I'm only twenty-four years old. There are many people who are smarter and know more about that than I do.

I would rather write about what love has been for me. And what brokenness, heart-brokenness, has been for me. The songs I look back at from over the years, the ones I gravitate toward and love, are the ones that expressed how I felt in a moment or a situation better than I ever could.

So when you write a song, are you thinking about yourself performing it?

Not really. I get into the story more when writing the song. I get lost in it. If it is about something I personally have been through, I will go back there. I will go back to that place.

It takes a willingness to re-feel emotions. You have to allow yourself to go there again even if you are in a different place now. I am in love today, but tomorrow, we might write a song about being heartbroken, and I have to let myself go back to that place to pull from those emotions.

It's the same for performing. "Need You Now" is the furthest thing from my personal life, but every night I have to find those old emotions to feel what I'm singing.

Which do you prefer, then? The songwriting or the performing?

Songwriting, for sure. There is nothing better than being there and helping create a song from the infantile stages. Performing is a very rewarding feeling, especially when people know the words and sing along. But the actual songwriting, the song creation process, is what I love the most.

Do you know a great song when you write it? For example, did you know "Need You Now" would be a huge hit?

No, honestly.

We liked "Need You Now". I remember that—I remember liking it. But it wasn't until we got into the studio and got into preproduction, where we work out the arrangements, when it really took on a life of its own. That song is special. It is a combination of a relatable lyric, a singable melody, and the instrumentation exudes so much emotion. We have our producer and the musicians to thank for that.

The three of you [in Lady Antebellum] write songs all the time. So how do you decide what is a good song and what is a great song?

Because we write, record, and perform these songs—you know pretty quickly when you put an arrangement behind a song and put our voices on it. It makes itself evident what works and what does not work. Everyone says, "The last thing you write is your favorite" because it is what is fresh, but that isn't always the case when you get into a studio environment. Sometimes a song is better acoustic; sometimes it needs a full band to take it to the next level.

There are times you just know—when the song is something you love and believe in and the power is undeniable. There are other times, like "Need You Now", that it wasn't until we recorded it that we knew. And that was literally the last song we played for the label when we were making the record—and it ended up being the single and changed our career!

Are there advantages to being a female songwriter?

Yes. I think we have more freedom and can take more liberties with our emotions—to not be ashamed or afraid to say that we are feeling emotions. We can also be strong. Women can be strong in songs. We can in our everyday lives, but there is something so empowering about singing a song.

For example, I wrote "Long Gone", a song from our first album, before Lady Antebellum ever formed. Every night I sing that song from stage, it is the most empowering moment— I am able to say these things in a song that I never had the guts to say to the dude's face. Like, "I'm long gone. You missed the boat. Our ship has sailed." I would never have the guts to look at a boy and say, "OUR SHIP HAS SAILED" and slam the door in his face. So you have the opportunity to be really honest and really strong and gutsy.

What is your biggest moment as a songwriter thus far?

When "Need You Now" won the 2011 Grammy for the Song of the Year, because that award honors the writer of the song. But, you know, the other thing that is right up there was at the CMT Artist of the Year Awards in 2010. Adele and Darius Rucker sang "Need You Now". We got to sit in the audience and listen. It was really cool to have your song performed to you. I am so used to performing it myself that when that happened, that was a really cool moment. As a songwriter, hearing it and it not being our voices but someone else's inflection and delivery, that was amazing.

Will you write songs after your performance career slows down (if it ever does)?

For sure. That has always been my plan.

Thinking into your future as a songwriter, what are some goals you have?

I would love to write with other artists for their projects. I would love to write music for a movie or a soundtrack. We [Lady Antebellum] had the opportunity to write songs for a movie one time, and it was so neat to be given thirty pages of the script and a synopsis of the film and have to write about it. It mixes up the everyday routine of just sitting down and writing a song. It was fun, like a puzzle. You are given tools, information, and hints to make the songs specifically about the film.

What would you say to new songwriters who are looking to make it in the industry?

Come to Nashville and make friends. Write with people. This is such a friendly place—it's like one big neighborhood. That's one of the coolest things about Nashville—the songwriting community. There isn't anywhere like this. Nashville is in a league of its own as far as cowriting goes; there are so many collaborations. The songwriting community in Nashville unites together and supports each other. So I would say, move to Nashville and make friends and write and continue to write on your own, but get out and write with your friends.

What about the people who don't want to write country music? Is Nashville still the town for them?

Hands down, yes. For sure. It's Music City. Not Country Music City. There are tons of rock writers—lots of rock bands are coming out of here; there's a huge Christian market, a huge alternative/indie/singer-songwriter scene. There is everything. I definitely think it is the place to be.

ANNIE DOWNS is a freelance writer in Nashville, Tennessee. With several Bible studies and many articles under her literary belt, Annie also writes books for teen girls and women braving college and the years after. Her first book, *From Head to Foot,* released in 2010. She is a huge fan of the Internet, singer/songwriters, waffles with peanut butter, and sports of all kinds, especially four square. Read more at annieblogs.com.

PHOTO: Jeremy Cowart

ONE OUT OF TENN

Andy Davis & the Evolving Artist

....

by Lyndsay Rush

Today, in a sea of millions of songwriters, it can be difficult—if not impossible—to stand out from the crowd. Bringing new life to the old phrase, "little fish in a big pond," artists everywhere struggle to get their songs out, get their name out; get their story out. But for many singer/songwriters, like Andy Davis of Baton Rouge, LA, the problem is less about standing out in a crowd and more about getting the crowd to allow you to stay standing.

Or rather, to stand wherever you want.

As an independent artist some seven years into his career, Davis has felt the growing pains of changing direction, exploring new sounds, redefining himself. And a lot of times, what your fans want is not always what you want to give them.

Undeniably, at the end of the day every songwriter is a brand and, according to Davis, being marketable is about "selling yourself and your stories and your uniqueness."

So what happens when those things change? How do you stay true to yourself and still appease your fans? How do you walk the fine line between art and business, creativity and work? How, pray tell, do you evolve as an artist and maintain brand loyalty throughout multiple albums?

According to Andy Davis, the answer may be simpler than you think.

ANDY DAVIS HISTORY

When Andy Davis first arrived at Belmont University in Nashville, TN, to study music, he likened his surroundings to "the Olympic Village of songwriting." At Belmont to study recording, producing, and engineering, Davis recalls being cautious of putting himself out there before he was ready. "I kinda laid low for a couple of years," he says. "I was still writing but spent more time watching other people than really playing out."

As his education continued, he found himself "recording and performing songs here and there, or for school assignments," most of which, at the time, were love songs. "I was really into Frank Sinatra and Billy Joel and so I was writing these sort of crooner-ish, love songs," recalls Davis.

> "I think some songs are meant to be headphone experiences and some are meant to be live experiences."

Then, in 2003, friends Dave Barnes and Matt Wertz (both established performers at the time) heard Andy play and invited him to open for them on tour. Thus began the first branding of Andy Davis as an artist. Knowing that this was his opportunity to establish a fan base and get his music into the hands of potential listeners, Andy took to his laptop and burned about sixty CDs for the first show, handwriting all of the track titles on the CD jacket and numbering and initialing each one. That night he sold every single CD.

"I walked away from this concert where I had just played music, sold a bunch of CDs, made a bunch of money (for me at that point as a college kid), and it was like, wow, this is totally what I want to keep doing," remembers Davis. As the tour went on, Andy continued hand-making his CDs—all the way up to "around 900," adding a couple of new songs to the album including, "Brown Eyes," and "Please Turn Red." This "test marketing" CD ended up becoming Davis's first album, *Thinks of Her*, as well as the doorway to establishing a connection with a dedicated fan base.

"[That first tour] served as a great launching pad for me to start a career where I was being introduced to a lot of fans that were really excited about music," says Andy. "Those same cities where I opened for Wertz and Barnes, I went back and performed on my own afterward to the same fans."

Fast-forward past a second EP, *Fine China*, and Andy found himself in LA, recording a full-length album with a producer whom Andy had always admired, Mitchel Froom. The final product, 2007's *Let the Woman*, earned Davis a distribution deal through Barnes and Noble and sold over ten thousand copies. Andy went on to put out another EP in 2009 and joined up with a community of independent Nashville artists called Ten Out Of Tenn—joining them for a tour, the filming of a documentary, and several compilation albums. Andy is set to release a new, full-length album in April of 2010.

TEN OUT OF TENN • 10OUTOFTENN.COM // @TENOUTOFTENN

Ten Out Of Tenn is a collection of Nashville-based artists, a talented collection of individual singer-songwriters, who have all released their own albums and have their own fan base— but come together to tour and showcase the eclectic musicality Nashville has to offer.

The first Ten Out Of Tenn tour and compilation *(Ten Out Of Tenn Volume I)* was put together by Kristen Dabbs and her husband and songwriter Trent Dabbs in 2005:

TRENT DABBS - trentdabbs.com // @trentdabbs

KATE YORK - myspace.com/kateyork // @kateyorkmusic

GRIFFIN HOUSE - griffinhousemusic.com // @griffinhouse

DISAPPOINTED BY CANDY - myspace.com/disappointedbycandy

THE LONELY HEARTS - thelonelyhearts.net // @thelonelyhearts

PAPER ROUTE - paperrouteonline.com // @paperroute

SHORTWAVERADIO - myspace.com/shortwaveradio

BETSY ROO - @BetsyRoo

TYLER JAMES - tylerjames.com // @tylerjames

THE GOLDEN SOUNDS - thegoldensounds.com

2008's Ten Out Of Tenn tour *(Ten Out Of Tenn Volume II)* included the following lineup:

GRIFFIN HOUSE - griffinhousemusic.com // @griffinhouse

BUTTERFULY BOUCHER - butterflyboucher.com

ANDY DAVIS - andydavisonline.com // @andydavis

TYLER JAMES - tylerjames.com // @tylerjames

ERIN MCCARLEY - myspace.com/erinmccarley

JEREMY LISTER - jeremylister.com // @JeremyBlister

TRENT DABBS - trentdabbs.com // @trentdabbs

KATIE HERZIG - katieherzig.com // @KatieHerzig

KS RHOADS - ksrhoads.com // @ksrhoads

MATTHEW PERRYMAN JONES - mpjmusic.com // @mpjmusic

The recently announced third tour *(Ten Out Of Tenn Volume III)* features these talents:

AMY STROUP - amystroup.com // @amystroup

GABE DIXON - gabedixon.com // @gabedixonmusic

KATIE HERZIG - katieherzig.com // @KatieHerzig

KS RHOADS - ksrhoads.com // @ksrhoads

TYLER JAMES - tylerjames.com // @tylerjames

MATTHEW PERRYMAN JONES - mpjmusic.com // @mpjmusic

TRENT DABBS - trentdabbs.com // @trentdabbs
BUTTERFLY BOUCHER - butterflyboucher.com
JEREMY LISTER - jeremylister.com // @JeremyBlister
ANDREW BELLE - andrewbelle.com // @andrewbelle

A SECOND FIRST IMPRESSION (OR A NEW HISTORY)

From guitar to piano, from acoustic love songs to jazz-infused rock hits, Andy's sound has deeply evolved throughout his career.

"You sort of discover what you love and what you just tolerate," says Andy of exploring different instruments and musical expressions. But above all, says Andy, the best rule to follow as a writer is to "do what sounds cool to you. If it doesn't sound cool to you, don't do it."

The trouble, it seems, comes when it's time to move past what used to sound cool to you—and what your fans associate with you—and on to what sounds cool to you now. So how does one stay true to oneself while also being sensitive to the tastes and expectations of his or her established fan base?

WRITING FOR YOUR FANS

"Every time I finish a song, I feel like it is the best song I've ever written," confesses Andy when asked about how he knows when he's written a hit, "but then I have to get away from it, forget about it, and find it again. And then if I really love it, I put it into a set list to test it off the crowd." And, Davis admits, not every song gets the response he's expecting from fans.

"I think some songs are meant to be headphone experiences and some are meant to be live experiences," he says. "There are songs that I love that I've tried live that didn't really work. The song was right; it just wasn't meant to be played live." Both of Andy's most popular songs—"Black Keys" and "Brown Eyes"—were written in only about one to two hours each, but, according to Davis, were "honest snapshots of right where I was at the time." A quality in a song that he says really resonates with people.

....

"I learned not to brand until you know what you want to be long-term; before you make a career out of whatever that image is."

....

But several years have passed since Andy wrote those songs. And, admittedly, he is looking to move forward, to progress and evolve as an artist.

"It is really encouraging to have a song in the set every night that the crowd expects you to play," comments Davis. "But I've changed a lot since I wrote those songs so the issue now is writing new songs that will take the place of the old songs as people's favorites."

EDITING YOURSELF

When it comes to songwriting, there is a fine line that exists between honest self-expression and compelling storytelling. This can be a difficult dance—trying to be emotionally honest, while also crafting a song into a story that people want to hear. There's a well-known saying by author Anne Lamott that favors brutal honesty in writing. "Write as though your parents are dead," she says. This implies that your words—whether in song or in print—are to be honest reflections of what you are feeling regardless of the reception. Marketability be damned.

"I think that's what it means to grow in your craft—becoming a better editor to let your inner child play around, but you know what is the good stuff and what is the bad stuff."

But for an artist looking to make a living off of music, it is important to sometimes look past the therapeutic expression of songwriting and understand what is right for a song, for a listener. For Davis, songwriting can mostly be placed into two categories: therapeutic or entertaining. With room for crossover, of course.

"You make a choice when you become a performing artist or a professional writer," he says. "Is the purpose of your writing therapeutic or is it entertainment? The truth is, sometimes there can be things that you want to get out for therapeutic reasons that may not be the best choices to release professionally, or on an album." A practice, he admits, that isn't always easy.

"It's a very grey area and one where I've gotten close to and crossed the line," he says. "And I think it's good in the privacy of your home or in your journal to write out everything," he continues. "Sometimes really sensitive issues have a lot of heat that need to be explored." Above all else, says Davis, "You have to learn to filter what you're releasing and why you are releasing it."

Songwriting, it seems, is just as much about honesty as it is about learning to filter your feelings into a story worth telling.

REDEFINING SUCCESS

Art and success often don't have a smooth working relationship. More often than not, the notion of success in the independent music world can be a vague and mysterious thing. Especially for an independent artist often on, as Andy calls it, a "DIY budget."

Does success lie simply in the number of records sold? Or in the personal growth or accomplishment felt by the artist? Both?

When asked what his biggest personal success has been thus far, Andy suggests that often his criteria for success is less about sales and more about personal growth.

"I feel inspired now the same way I did when I was fifteen," he says, "but I've learned to edit my ideas better now. I think that's what it means to grow in your craft—becoming a better editor to let your inner child play around, but you know what is the good stuff and what's the bad stuff. As you grow, you learn to distinguish the keeper stuff and the other stuff."

BEING INDEPENDENT

The choice to make music independently wasn't hard for Andy Davis. Indeed, he can't imagine where he would be had he not taken the independent road some seven years ago.

"I've learned a lot throughout the years," comments Andy. " I learned how important it is to put out a ton of music before being married to an image. I learned not to brand until you know what you want to be long-term, before you make a career out of whatever that image is." Additionally, being an independent artist taught Davis to wear multiple hats.

"The writer and craftsman in me wants to be able to write everything that comes to my head and follow whatever the song wants," Andy observes. "But the businessman in me had to grow up a lot as an independent artist and ask myself, 'What does this need to look like?'"

Still, the potential to reach the masses and gain radio play undeniably favors artists who are picked up by a label. Something Andy admittedly considers as a way to explore new projects and new listeners. At the end of the day, though, for Davis it's about being excellent at your craft. And if that includes notoriety and fame, great, but it's about more than that he says.

"For me, I'm not going out there wanting to be the next Elton John, Billy Joel, or Paul McCartney," Andy explains. "But I would love to sit at a table with the three of them and feel like all three of them go, 'You know what you're doing and we're impressed.' Or 'you can hold your own.'" That, Davis admits, is real success.

CLOSING REMARKS

It would be an easier world to live in if everything had a formula. If unfailingly a + b equaled songwriting success, there would be no reason to explore ideas like artistic expression, branding, marketing, evolving identities.

But, alas, this is not the case. And for Davis, as is certainly the truth for other independent songwriters, writers must dedicate themselves to their craft, be good at listening to their fans as well as listening to themselves, and above all else, truly be in love with what they do.

"First ask yourself what you want out of it [music] and what you want to do and how willing you are to invest in it," he advises. "Are you willing to spend the next ten to fifteen years? Do you love it enough?" And that truly is what true art comes down to. Do you love what you do enough to do what it takes to do it for the rest of your life?

Ask yourself the good questions, the hard questions, suggests Davis. The more you figure out now, the better you'll be down the road.

LYNDSAY RUSH is a freelance writer from Nashville, TN. As she tells it, all of the things she spent time doing as a kid are what make her perfectly suited for her job: storytelling, playing make-believe, and trying to make people laugh. Whether in advertising, publishing, or journalism, Lyndsay combines insight and ingenuity to turn words into stories. Her passions include puns, slogans, and wordplay, and her dream job is working for *The Onion* or creating OPI nail polish names. When she's not hard at work, you can find her hardly working, drinking too much coffee, and walking around barefoot. Usually all at the same time. For more from Lyndsay check out her blog, www.lyndsights.com.

MUSIC LICENSING

Rethinking How to Grow Your Audience Base

···

by Sarah Gavigan

A highly visible music placement in a film, television show, or commercial has been hailed "the golden ticket" for any recording artist, singer, performer, or band who is lucky enough to land one. Just a few years ago these highly sought-after slots were seemingly reserved for the big players, the major labels, and even the major indies, but today you can hear veritably unknown and unsigned artists on a major Ford television commercial.

Shortly after that Ford commercial has aired, you may hear that same unsigned band on Top 40 radio, swiftly followed by a major label signing and record release.

For anyone who has been around the music business for a few years knows that this scenario plays like a film rolling backward. Industry standard has always been, STEP ONE: get signed; STEP TWO: release a record; STEP THREE: get radio play; STEP FOUR: land a juicy license.

Leading a band's career with a music placement is a new phenomenon that has reshaped the way bands release music and are introduced to the public.

It is a new world in today's music business. YouTube is turning the corner to become the number one search engine in the world, Twitter can help you build a fan base, and music licensing is quickly becoming the number one source of revenue.

So how does music licensing happen for a band, and is it just about luck? Not today it isn't. To get your music licensed, you need to have a strategy.

Synchronization music licensing has seen a decade of growth that has changed the way people think about lending their music to films, television shows, ads, and video games. The days of being seen as a "sell out" for licensing your music to a television commercial are long gone as band after band places their music, which plays an incredible role in their success.

Rising steadily by 30 percent a year for the past four years, sync music licensing is drawing in reported revenues of over two billion a year. Television shows and films are being made at breakneck speeds to fill the airtime of fledgling and expanding networks, while advertisers have begun to utilize the freedom of the Internet with web films and longer commercials that are only made for Internet. This "middle market" of music licensing has opened up an entirely new sector of the business that independent and unsigned artists can take great advantage of, as the major labels and publishers rarely clear tracks at lower license fees. Ten thousand dollars to an unsigned artist is a nice check. You would have to sell roughly 12,000 songs on iTunes to equal that payout.

Musicians, managers, record labels, and publishers have begun to see sync licensing for what it is—a quickly growing market that is a vital part of a marketing and distribution strategy for an artist.

> Music licensing is a serious distribution channel that rivals traditional radio both in its reach, influence, and most important, its ability to drive sales.

A few lucky artists and bands can say music placements in films, television shows, and ads have molded or even made their careers. Starting in 1999, Moby's release *Play* was the first album to license every song on the record to a film, television show, soundtrack, or ad once (or more).

Jumping ahead a decade to 2010, the Black Keys released their fifth studio album, titled *Brothers*, which within the course of a year became the most licensed record of that year for Warner Brothers Records. This is a band that has built a fan base over time through touring and writing great record after great record. For them, licensing was not as much a strategy as it was a testament to how much the sound and the music itself resonated with people. Warner Brothers estimates that tracks off the record *Brothers* were licensed over 100 times in the year 2010.

"For us licensing is like radio exposure," said the Black Keys manager Ryan Harrington at QPrime in Nashville, TN.

The long-term impact of a song placement packs a serious punch for artists, not simply in the money made from the licensing fees, but that it has the power to create new fans for a band literally overnight. Sync licensing is the equivalent of being paid to have your music distributed for you. Major labels pay millions of dollars to market and distribute their artists' music. For an example of this distribution, take a television commercial that is in heavy rotation; let's say it is an AT&T wireless commercial. That commercial will easily run over 20,000 times in one week, and hundreds of thousands of people will see that television commercial each time it airs. Potentially over a million "spins" a week. *American Idol* boasts 3.8 million viewers each week!

Concurrently, a television show or feature film will run repeatedly on cable channels and On-Demand. Music licensing is a serious distribution channel that rivals traditional radio both in its reach, influence, and most important, its ability to drive sales. It takes more effort and money than ever to promote a song to radio, and many still believe it is the best way to break a band, but there are more opportunities for a music placement than there are in Top 40 radio. Some have even said that television IS the *new radio* for the music industry.

Radio's power is in it ability to repeat a song to the same listener. That repetition is a powerful motivator, and drives consumers to engage with a band, become a fan and eventually buy their music. How many times have you found yourself humming a jingle you heard on television? Are you humming it because you like it, or because you have heard it so many times? That is what advertisers are banking on, and as licensed songs have begun to take the place of jingles in television commercials, we find ourselves humming the last song we heard in an Apple (computers) commercial.

This repetition and residual stickiness of the song from a placement is what an artist should look for to take his or her career to the next level. Music licensing is a strategy that is replacing mainstream radio for many artists, and the best news is that it can work for a band no matter where they may be in their careers. Licensing has become the main source of income for a growing number of artists in every genre imaginable. I spoke with a few.

Adam Foley, manager at Red Light Management, manages two artists—UNKLE and Ki:Theory. Both lean strongly on music licensing as both an income stream and as a strategy for drawing new fans and keeping loyal fans engaged.

Ki:Theory is an electronic and alternative rock artist whose music has been featured on the television show CSI; on the National Geographic Channel; in commercials for Audi, Converse, and Billabong; and in numerous films and video games.

James Lavelle, under the artist name UNKLE, has scored music for movies like *Sexy Beast*, *X-Files*, and major brands like BMW, Johnnie Walker, and Lexus. UNKLE's music has been licensed to numerous movies (*3:10 to Yuma*, *21*), television shows (*CSI*, *Friday Night Lights*), and video games (*Grand Theft Auto*, *Assassins Creed*). The founder of legendary record label Mo' Wax released DJ Shadow's groundbreaking album *Entroducing*. Clearly a very accomplished musician and artist, Lavelle attributes over 90 percent of his income to music licensing. Was that a part of the overall strategy of his career? His manager, Foley, responds:

"Both of my guys release their records independently. They do a lot of placements, both licensing and original music." To put a rough percentage on it, I asked Adam how much the licensing business means to their overall business strategy. "Their entire business model is built around their film scoring, licensing business."

Another artist who goes by the name RJD2, also in the electronic genre, has heard his music placed in ESPN, Saturn, Blackberry and Radio Shack ads, and in several movies. But most widely heard is his track "A Beautiful Mine," which was chosen as the theme to the wildly successful series *Mad Men* on AMC.

"Touring still outweighs licensing for me as far as overall income goes, but I see licensing as luxury income that allows me to be independent and to write whatever I choose when it comes to my records," RJ said. "Licensing allows me to stay independent. When I did my first license in 2003, [licensing] was a hotly debated topic, and frankly speaking, at the time it seemed like a bad idea, like you couldn't take it back. What I didn't expect was the [positive] response to my music through licensing it to an advertisement. I honestly was not expecting that."

Some artists even choose to focus their careers on writing and releasing music through the licensing world and foregoing touring altogether.

Musician Tim Myers started his career by joining a band and getting signed by a major label. At eighteen he joined the band One Republic, and left a few years later to pursue his solo career. In less than five years Myers has seen his music licensed in more than six national television commercials, including Target, Google, Macy's, Lens Crafters, Saturn, ABC TV, and JC Penney. The day I spoke with him he had a song running in ten simultaneous Chase Bank spots.

"Music Licensing is where it's at as a songwriter, especially in wanting to be a creative and independent songwriter. I have been involved in the major pop world, but for me the real heart and soul of a song is in the melody and the chord progressions and the best way to create a writing career is to write for the industry. I love to collaborate, and this business allows me to do that successfully."

The national retailer Target, known for using catchy upbeat music in their ads, chose his song "A Beautiful World"—featuring singer-songwriter Lindsey Ray—for a six-spot campaign, practically making it the Target anthem for almost a year.

"I write a ton of songs. I try to write a song every day. A lot are bad and a lot are good. It's about creating a body of work; it's about doing your craft."

When you listen to Myers's music, it's clear he has learned to capture emotion in a hook, and that talent has made his music very licensable.

"When I sit down to write, I have to feel it first emotionally, *always*. If you are going to write a feel-good song, you better feel that way when you sit down to write that song. The same goes for a cinematic or dramatic song for a television show drama. It all stems from emotion, and if you can make them feel something, you have got it."

On top of his incredible success with licensing in advertising, Myers has been just as successful in film and television, with placements in *The Waterhorse*, *Grey's Anatomy*, *One Tree Hill*, and many more.

When I asked Myers if he felt like he was writing to the trends in music licensing or staying just ahead of them, he answered:

"I think having the influences of the Beatles and Bob Dylan helped me be a great writer for music licensing, at the root of 1960s rock. From a licensing standpoint I think it benefits me as well. I love following trends, but it's my roots that I think favor me the most."

The idea of licensing his music was foreign to Myers until one night when he was performing and his (now) rep from Zync Music approached him after the show. Soon after that chance meeting took place, his reps were able to place one of his song in the season finale of *Grey's Anatomy*. He added that immediately after the finale the placement resulted in over 40,000 downloads of the song from iTunes. "I can't say how much the license fee was, of course, but it was more than my advance when I was signed to a major label.

"It was an eye-awakening moment, because it made me look at my career as One Republic . . . then consider how happy I would be to focus my career on being in the studio and writing songs. That sounded like heaven to me, and music licensing has allowed me to do that. Being in the studio is my absolute favorite thing. Touring and performing is not as appealing to me as writing."

Myers stays current by continuing to get out and see music as much as he can, and by continually collaborating with other artists he feels inspire him to stay really fresh and keep his work honest.

Some artists even choose to focus their careers on writing and releasing music through the licensing world and foregoing touring altogether.

So how do you create a strategy to license your music? Start by taking a few simple steps; you will learn more about the business at large, and begin to see where your music fits in best.

First, you need to identify what markets your music is best suited to. Watch the television shows, advertisements, and films specifically to take note of what kind of music they are using, and you will begin to see the attributes and trends that make a song "licensable."

Next, hone in on the television shows that license the style and feel of music similar to yours. MTV is well known in industry circles for licensing music from independent artists. The demographic is younger, and they tend to use all styles of music. You may also wonder where you can see commercials other than constantly watching television. YouTube. Most major brands have created YouTube channels and end up posting their commercials online.

Licensing trends are similar to consumer trends in many ways, especially in film and television. In the advertising world, songs are judged by a different set of attributes that qualify it as licensable in the non-narrative category. A commercial is essentially a film made in thirty seconds to promote a brand. Like all shows and films, it has a build, a break, and a payoff. Unlike shows and films, it happens in thirty seconds. So more often than not, music chosen for ads will be upbeat and quirky, then have a build, a break around twenty seconds, and a payoff.

The next step is to do your research and find the people who work on those specific projects. Music supervisors receive hundreds of unsolicited e-mails and packages a week; so don't blend in by sending a mass e-mail. Do your homework, know whom you are talking to, and reach out to people on a personal level. You will be surprised at the response.

So you get a placement, you negotiate a great deal, and the check is in the mail. What next? Can you use this opportunity to market and introduce your band to thousands of new people? You bet you can.

What should be the beginning of a new relationship between a fan and an artist is, sadly, many times the end. As technology continues to move at breakneck speeds, connecting us at every cyber turn, the music industry at large has continued to miss out on incredible opportunities for greater engagement. As you move forward with your licensing business, make sure that you build in some strategy to maximize the license placement itself. Use your existing fans to help bring you new fans. Connect the dots for consumers by making it easy for them to find your name and your music after they have heard your music in a television show, film, or advertisement. YouTube can be a very powerful tool in these circumstances.

Many bands and shows these days now have YouTube channels to house their content and promote and distribute it beyond the television. Think like a stealth marketing ninja and you will begin to see the incredible opportunity that lies here. I'll give you a big hint: if your song is used in an ad, then your band should be credited in the TAGS of the video when it is uploaded to the brand's site. When people go to YouTube to find the commercial, they will also find you!

No matter what strategy or technology you end up using, music licensing can help you, or your band, collect on the kind of financial security and fan base that will sustain your music career for years to come.

(1) http://www.wired.com/wired/archive/10.05/moby.html

SARAH GAVIGAN has been an entrepreneur in the music licensing space for close to ten years. After owning and running her own talent agency for seven years, Gavigan was drawn to the burgeoning world of music licensing by a conversation started in a van in Iceland in 1999. The conversation with Eric Hilton of Theivery Corporation led Sarah to understand that Indies were interested in finding a way to get their music to brands and agencies. In 2000 Ten Music was born to provide exactly that service to the growing Indie music community.

"It wast not a matter of if, but when. It was obvious that music licensing was to become the next major source of revenue for the music industry, and I wanted to find a way to enable the Indies to be at the front of the game."

Ten Music pioneered a business model that enabled representation for Indies, allowing their music access to the brightest and best in the vast national advertising network. The company placed well over 1,000 artists and bands to commercials in the last nine years.

"Licensing was not very popular with either artists or bands when we began in 2000," Gavigan laughs. "Agency creatives and producers either felt it was somehow too risky, or that Indie music was somehow lesser than major label music. I used to get questions like, "Why would I want to use music that no one knows?"

It didn't take long before Gavigan's new company was the de facto for music licensing in advertising. In the ten years since the company was formed, Gavigan and her team placed music for brands such as Nissan, Ford, Target, Payless, Microsoft, Samsung, Adidas, Nike, and many more.

In 2005 Gavigan stepped forward again into unchartered territory by creating HANK™, an online music supervisor.

Today Gavigan is consulting for agencies and brands on music licensing, music supervising on commercials, teaching at Belmont University, and writing about her experiences in music licensing and the music industry.

Check out her online education series, GET YOUR MUSIC LICENSED, which you can learn more about on her website: www.sarahgavigan.com.

ANDY HUNT

Sound Advice From a Producer

....

by Adria Haley

It was Christmastime of 1999 in Mississippi, when Andy Hunt's mom, sister, and grandmother bought him a 4-track tape recorder with the hopes of one day hearing some of his music. Little did they know he would fall in love with the recording process from that one simple gift. "I recorded myself and friends like crazy. I just loved creating good music and the challenge of making it sound great." However, Hunt quickly outgrew the 4-track. While working as a bartender, he saved up enough cash for a 24-track home studio.

By late 2000, two of Hunt's songs were on college radio in medium to heavy rotation. Both songs he wrote, produced, recorded, and mixed himself, playing all the instruments except for drums. A year later, Hunt officially started his own recording studio, Wide Studios. He began producing bands from country to rock, and solo projects from gospel to pop. Though he was still honing his craft, Hunt craved more. "I was having a blast working with artists, but I really wanted to speed up my learning curve. The only way for me to do that was to work alongside a well-established producer and learn from him."

In early 2002, Hunt began to work with Grammy-award-winning producer Dennis Herring (Buddy Guy, Jars of Clay, Counting Crows, Modest Mouse, Elvis Costello). Herring, also a Mississippi native, has a studio in Oxford, Mississippi, where national acts would come to record. "The studio is Dennis's private setup, so there wasn't any staff, just us. I was able to spend so much one-on-one time with him. He taught me a ton: production technique, songwriting; not to mention his gear was incredible. I got to cut my teeth on some really great equipment."

While working with Herring, Hunt met Nashville-based Grammy-award-winning producer/engineer/mixer Jacquire King (Tom Waits, Third Eye Blind, Buddy Guy, Modest Mouse, Smash Mouth). "[Jacquire] is great. Such an amazing person. He is truly gifted. He repeatedly took the time to talk me through his thought process when making decisions, whether it was regarding song arrangement, mic choice and placement, or moments spent just listening to music and talking about the mix."

Hunt and King worked on projects in Mississippi with Herring for nearly two years. But then, Hunt was off again. "Jacquire brought me to Nashville to work with him. He and I are still close. I consider him a mentor, for sure. Nashville is an amazing town and community full of talented musicians and people, in general. It's a perfect atmosphere to grow musically and hone your craft."

Tell me about the origin, or thought process, behind the naming of your studio, Wide Studios? How did that name come to be?

It had to do with a couple of things: I like a wide variety of music, and I like my mixes to sound *wide*. In other words, the sound pushes the boundaries of the sonic landscape.

Give me a rundown of the equipment you're working with? What equipment do you prefer to work with and why?

I work in a hybrid world of digital and analog. I use Pro Tools as my DAW (digital audio workstation) but enjoy the benefits of analog gear as well. Pro Tools is the most commonly used DAW. Vintage microphones and outboard gear really do sound the best—so I like to use them whenever I can.

What would you say is the basic equipment needed—the bare necessities—for a producer just getting started?

Production is really less about equipment than it is about the ability to see a record through to the end. However, having the right gear to make music (i.e., produce music) is important. Having a DAW like Pro Tools is essential if you want to share sessions with other musicians and so that you can edit your work.

Do you keep up with technology? If so, what resources do you keep a pulse on to try to stay in the know?

I try my best. There is always new gear popping up, and I get my info from various vendors, sites, and friends. Gearslutz.com is a great online forum to learn about trends and all things music.

What goes into making a decision on whether or not you want to work with an artist?

The artist and I should share a similar vision for the project. Everyone has his or her own style, but it's the producer's job to find the uniqueness that makes the artist who he or she is and bring that out of him or her.

How do you go about establishing a working relationship with an artist/band that you're working with for the very first time?

I'm all about "the Hang." I just try and get to know them. It's a courting process for sure—learning little things about them and building a friendship with them. We'll talk about what music they like, or who, or what inspires them. It's also important to ask them about *their* songs and why they wrote them.

Tell me about some of the people you've worked with. And possibly what you've learned with each artist/experience. What is particularly memorable about a few of those recordings?

I've been blessed to work with many artists over the last ten years. While working with Smash Mouth, they asked to hear a few songs of mine. After playing a few, they invited me to open up for them at Riverfest in Columbus, Georgia. That was an awesome experience. Those guys are so great.

I also traveled to Atlanta, Georgia, to work the talented group Third Day. I worked for a month with them alongside a great and talented friend and producer, Paul Moak. Third Day was actually a piece of cake to work with—so hospitable and welcoming.

A lot of the records I do in Nashville are with solo artists and need musicians to play on their records. A majority of the players are close friends of mine—and super talented. Add that to a talented artist and that always makes the process enjoyable.

How did you go about finding the sound you wanted for Drew Holcomb and the Neighbors' album?

For Drew Holcomb and the Neighbors' album, *Chasing Someday*, Drew and I talked about his vision for the project. We wanted modern sounds with a unique spin on them. We experimented with various mikes and techniques and printed effects to tape, committing to the sound. Drew's such a great storyteller, so his voice is key. We just needed to find the right stuff to support it. Fortunately, his band is incredibly talented, and we had legendary producer Brown Bannister lending his genius as well.

What genres of music do you enjoy working on the most?

Again, I like working with a wide range of music. But working with a singer/songwriter is particularly fun because I enjoy the space and it's organic nature. I also enjoy pop/rock music and its aggressive nature and creating melodic hooks around every corner.

It's really all about the song. That's where it all starts. If the song is good, the productions falls into place.

Should producers also be musicians?

I think new-school producers should be musicians. More and more labels or artists are looking for someone who can work with a band or artist and help take them to the next level for as little financial expense as possible. This usually lends itself to a producer that can do multiple things and do them well, so as to cut down on the expense of outside talent. It's also good for a producer to be a musician for communication purposes with the musicians he's working with—to understand their language.

In what ways are you still growing as a producer?

I'm still growing in all the ways possible. The day I stop growing is a sad day. I'm always trying to find new ways to create music. I like experimenting with new gear and challenging myself to support the vocal in new ways.

What's the best advice you have to up-and-coming songwriters and/or performers trying to locate a good producer to work with?

Read the back of your favorite CDs and find the guy that made those records. Look for a producer that you click with and who understands your vision. It's a relationship.

How is it different—from the position of a producer—having to work with an indie artist/band versus an artist/band signed to a label? Are their managers involved? And if so, what are the logistics of that?

There is always someone paying for the project. With indies, usually there are less cooks in the kitchen.

What are the pros and cons of having a home studio to work out of versus working at a major label's studio?

I wouldn't say "major label" studio. I'd say "large production" studio. I've done several major label projects out of my home studio, and the term "home studio" can make it sound like a less-than-ideal situation. When the reality is, I've got equal—if not better—gear in my home studio than some large production studios. Recording in your own studio, whether at home or elsewhere, is a plus because you save money on renting a space.

A con would be that on occasion larger facilities have access to more gear and a wider variety of gear, and sometimes they have a larger space to record in.

Does the musician in you ever conflict with the producer?

Nah. They get along pretty well. The producer in me is always challenging the musician in me to be better and vice versa.

How crucial is post-production? And what exactly are you listening for in this process?

Post-production—to me—is more of a video term. But if I were to equate that to music, I would say that's the mixing and mastering portion of the record-making process. If that's the case, I would say it's *very* important. A good mix engineer can make a great production even better. During this process, I'm listening for emotion and making sure the story of the song is conveyed through the balance of the music and vocals.

If you had to predict the future, where would you like to see your career five years from now? What, or who, would you still like to produce?

I'd like to still be making records that people enjoy. I'd like to make a couple of records across the country and overseas. Destination records are always fun.

What producers do you admire/respect?

There are a handful: Jacquire King, Eric Valentine, Mutt Lang, T-Bone Burnett, Brian Eno, Brendan O'Brien, George Martin, and Timbaland.

ANDY INTERVIEWS HIS MENTOR, JACQUIRE KING

HOW DID YOU GET STARTED AS A PRODUCER?

I have always had an opinion to offer when asked, and work to put my influence into something I'm working on while keeping the artist vision in mind. Even starting out as an engineer, I felt I was a capable producer. I would engage opportunities to do both from the start of my career. There wasn't any official point of "now you're a producer"—it has just come into being the main thing I do.

IN YOUR LONG LIST OF VARIED AND ACCOMPLISHED CREDITS AS A PRODUCER, WHAT PROJECT ARE YOU MOST PROUD OF AND WHY?

I view my body of work as a whole and have found that to be the greatest feeling of accomplishment—to have contributed to so many different things and feel like I made some difference for the artist is what I'm proud of. I'm not just proud of the ones that sold the most copies; the one artist I was an incredible fan of before being involved with and almost every person I've worked with since has commented on is Tom Waits. I'm very grateful to have worked on three albums ith him.

HOW DO YOU DECIDE IF YOU WANT TO WORK WITH A PARTICULAR ARTIST/BAND ON A PROJECT?

In all honesty, it can be complicated. But I really do make the choice based on my connection and reaction to their music or songs. It has to move me in some way that I feel like gives it meaning to me.

DO YOU JUGGLE MULTIPLE PROJECTS AT ONE TIME OR PREFER TO STAY FO-CUSED ON ONE THING AT A TIME?

I definitely prefer to be focused on one project, but do get in situations where they overlap. I try to avoid at all costs having to be in two or more places at the same time.

WHAT PROJECT OR ARTIST ARE YOU WORKING WITH NOW?

I'm on a break from producing Trixie Whitley while she has some touring commitments. I've just completed mixing Rayland Baxter's album. Currently, I'm mixing some songs for The Hives—and just before that, producing an EP for Amber Rubarth.

WHAT IS YOUR BEST PIECE OF ADVICE TO INDIE ARTISTS WHO ARE LOOKING FOR A PRODUCER TO WORK WITH?

Do you like the work that they have done before? And I don't mean the artist, but that there is the feeling that the producer helped the artist be at their best and showed them in a good light. Talk to them and make sure communication styles and methods of recording line up with your desires.

LEARNING TO SAY *NO*

How Being Selective Can Improve Your Lyrics

by Pat Pattison

Writing a lyric is like getting a gig: If you're grateful for any idea that comes along, you're probably not getting the best stuff. But if you have lots of legitimate choices, you won't end up playing six hours in Bangor, Maine, for twenty bucks. Look at it this way: The more often you can say no, the better your gigs get. That's why I suggest that you learn to build a worksheet—a specialized tool for brainstorming that produces bathtubs full of ideas and, at the same time, tailors the ideas specifically for a lyric.

Simply, a worksheet contains two things: a list of key ideas and a list of rhymes for each one. There are three stages to building a worksheet.

I. FOCUS YOUR LYRIC IDEA AS CLEARLY AS YOU CAN

Let's say you want to write about homelessness. Sometimes, you'll start the lyric from an emotion: "That old homeless woman with everything she owns in a shopping cart really touches me. I want to write a song about her." Sometimes you'll write from a cold, calculated idea: "I'm tired of writing love songs. I want to do one on a serious subject, maybe homelessness." Or, you may write from a title you like, maybe "Risky Business." Then the trick is to find an interesting angle on it, perhaps: "What do you do for a living?" "I survive on the streets." "That's pretty risky business."

In each case, it's up to you to find the angle, brainstorm the idea, and create the world the idea will live in. Since you always bring your unique perspective to each experience, you will have something interesting to offer. But you'll have to look at enough ideas to find the best perspective.

Object writing is the key to developing choices. You must dive into your vaults of sense material—those unique and secret places—to find out what images you've stored away, in the present example, around the idea of homelessness.

EXERCISE ///

Stop reading, get out a pen, and dive into homelessness for ten minutes. Stay sense-bound and very specific. How do you connect to the idea? Did you ever get lost in the woods as a child? Run away from home? Sleep in a car in New York?

Now, did you find an expressive image, like a broken wheel on a homeless woman's shopping cart, that can serve as a metaphor—a vehicle to carry your feelings? Did you see some situation, like your parents fighting, that seems to connect you with her situation? These expressive objects or situations are what T.S. Eliot calls "objective correlatives"— objects anyone can touch, smell, and see that correlate with the emotion you want to express. Broken wheels or parents fighting work nicely as objective correlatives.

Even if you find ideas that work well, keep looking a while longer. When you find a good idea, there is usually a bunch more behind it. (The gig opening for Aerosmith could be the next offer.) Jot down your good ideas on a separate sheet of paper.

---

2. MAKE A LIST OF WORDS THAT EXPRESS YOUR IDEA

You'll need to look further than the hot ideas from your object writing. Get out a thesaurus, one set up according to Roget's original plan according to the flow of ideas—a setup perfect for brainstorming. Dictionary-style versions (set up alphabetically) are useful only for finding synonyms and antonyms. They make brainstorming a cumbersome exercise in cross-referencing.

Your thesaurus is better than a good booking agent. It can churn up images and ideas you wouldn't ever get to by yourself, stimulating your diver to greater and greater depths until a wealth of choices litter the beaches.

Let's adopt the working title "Risky Business" and continue brainstorming the idea of homelessness. In the index (the last half of your thesaurus), locate a word that expresses the general idea, for example, *risk*. From the list below it, select the word most related to the lyric idea. My thesaurus lists these options for *risk*: *gambling 618n*; *possibility 469n*; *danger 661n*; *speculate 791vb*. The first notation should be read as follows: "You will find the word *risk* in the noun group of section 618 under the key word gambling."

Key words are always in italics. They set a general meaning for the section, like a key signature sets the tone center in a piece of music.

Probably the closest meaning for our purposes with "Risky Business" is *danger 661n*. Look in the text (front half) of the thesaurus for section 661 (or whatever number your thesaurus lists; numbers will appear at the tops of the pages). If you peruse the general area around danger for a minute, you will find several pages of related material. Here are the surrounding section headings in my thesaurus:

Ill health, disease	Insalubrity	Deterioration
Relapse	Bane	Danger
Pitfall	Danger signal	Escape
Salubrity (well-being)	Improvement	Restoration
Remedy	Safety	Refuge. Safeguard
Warning	Preservation	Deliverance

This related material runs for sixteen pages in double-column entries. Risk is totally surrounded by its relatives, so if you look around the neighborhood, you'll find a plethora of possibilities. Start building your list.

Look at these first few entries under danger: *N. danger, peril; . . . shadow of death, jaws of d., dragon's mouth, dangerous situation, unhealthy s., desperate s., forlorn hope 700n. predicament; emergency 137n. crisis; insecurity, jeopardy, risk, hazard, ticklishness . . .*

Look actively. If you take each entry for a quick drive through your sense memories, you should have a host of new ideas within minutes. (Frequent object writing pays big dividends here. The more familiar you are with the process, the quicker these quick dives get. If you are slow at first, don't give up—you'll get faster. Just vow to do more object writing.) Jot down the best words on your list and keep at it until you're into serious overload.

Now the fun begins. Start saying no to words in your list until you've trimmed it to about ten or twelve words with different vowel sounds in their stressed syllables. Put these survivors in the middle of a blank sheet of paper, number them, and enclose them in a box for easy reference later on. Keep these guidelines in mind:

1. If you are working with a title, be sure to put its key vowel sounds in the list.
2. Most of your words should end in a stressed syllable, since they work best in rhyming position.
3. Put any interesting words that duplicate a vowel sound in parentheses.

Your goal is to create a list of words to look up in your rhyming dictionary. Here's what I got banging around in the thesaurus, looking through the lens of homelessness:

1. risk
2. business
3. left out
4. freeze (wheel, shield)
5. storm
6. dull (numb)

7. night (child)
8. change
9. defense
10. home (hope, broken, coat)

This is not a final list. Don't be afraid to switch, add, or take out words as the process continues.

3. LOOK UP EACH WORD IN YOUR RHYMING DICTIONARY

Be sure to extend your search to imperfect rhyme types, and to select only words that connect with your ideas. Above all, don't bother with cliché rhymes or other typical rhymes. First, a quick survey of rhyme types.

Perfect Rhyme

Don't let yourself be seduced by the word "perfect." It doesn't mean "better," it only means:

1. The syllables' vowel sounds are the same.
2. The consonant sounds after the vowels (if any) are the same.
3. The sounds before the vowels are different.

Remember, lyrics are sung, not read or spoken. When you sing, you exaggerate vowels. And since rhyme is a vowel connection, lyricists can make sonic connections in ways other than perfect rhyme.

Family Rhyme

1. The syllables' vowel sounds are the same.
2. The consonant sounds after the vowels belong to the same phonetic families.
3. The sounds before the vowels are different.

Here's a chart of the three important consonant families:

		PLOSIVES	FRICATIVES	NASALS	
VOICED	t	b d g	v TH z zh j	m n ng	← companions
UNVOICED	n	p t k	f th s sh ch	← companions	

Each of the three boxes—plosives, fricatives, and nasals—form a phonetic family. When a word ends in a consonant on one of the boxes, you can use the other members of the family to find perfect rhyme substitutions.

Rub/up/thud/putt/bug/stuck are members of the same family—plosives—so they are family rhymes.

Love/buzz/judge/fluff/fuss/hush/touch are members of the fricative family, so they also are family rhymes.

Strum/run/sung rhyme as members of the nasal family.

Say you want to rhyme this line:

> *I'm stuck in a rut*

First, look up perfect rhymes for *rut: cut, glut, gut, hut, shut.*

The trick to saying something you mean is to expand your alternatives. Look at the table of family rhymes below and introduce yourself to t's relatives:

ud	uk	ub	up	ug
blood	buck	club	hard up	bug
flood	duck	hub	makeup	jug
mud	luck	pub	cup	unplug
stud	muck	scrub		plug
thud	stuck	tub		shrug
	truck			snug
				tug

That's much better. Now we find that we have a lot of interesting stuff to say no to.

What if you want to rhyme this:

> *There's nowhere I can feel safe*

First, look up perfect rhymes for *safe* in your rhyming dictionary. All we get is *waif.* Not much.

Now look for family rhymes under f's family, the fricatives. We add these possibilities:

as	av	az	aj
case	behave	blaze	age
ace	brave	craze	cage
breathing-space	cave	daze	page
chase	grave	haze	rage
face	shave	phrase	stage
disgrace	slave	paraphrase	
embrace	wave	praise	
grace			
lace			

resting-place	**ath**	**aTH**
space	faith	bathe

Finally, nasals. The word "nasals" means what you think it means: All the sound comes out of your nose. Rhyme this line:

> *My head is pounding like a drum*

Look up perfect rhymes for *drum*: *hum, pendulum, numb, slum, strum.*

Go to the table of family rhymes and look at m's relatives:

un	**ung**
fun	hung
gun	flung
overrun	wrung
won	sung
jettison	
skeleton	

Finding family rhyme isn't difficult, so there's no reason to tie yourself in knots using only perfect rhyme. Family rhyme sounds so close that when sung, the ear won't know the difference.

Additive Rhyme

1. The syllables' vowel sounds are the same.
2. One of the syllables add extra consonants after the vowel.
3. The sounds before the vowels are different.

When the syllable you want to rhyme ends in a vowel (e.g., play, free, fly), the only way to generate alternatives is to add consonants after the vowel. The guideline is simple: The less sound you add, the closer you stay to perfect rhyme.

Look again at the table of family rhymes. Voiced plosives—b, d, g—put out the least sound. Use them first, rhyming, for example, *ricochet* with *paid*; then the unvoiced plosives, rhyming *free* with *treat*. Next, voiced fricatives, rhyming *fly* and *alive*. Then on to unvoiced fricatives, followed by the most noticeable consonants (aside from l and r), the nasals. You'd end up with a list moving from closest to perfect rhyme to furthest away from perfect rhyme. For example, for *free*, we find: *speed, cheap, sweet, grieve, belief, dream, clean, deal.*

You can also add consonants even if there are already consonants after the vowel, for example: street/sweets, alive/drives, dream/screamed, trick/risk.

You can even combine this technique with family rhymes, such as dream/cleaned, club/floods/shove/stuffed. This gives you even more options, making it easier to say what you mean.

Subtractive Rhyme

1. The syllables' vowel sounds are the same.
2. One of the syllables adds an extra consonant after the vowel.
3. The sounds before the vowels are different.

Subtractive rhyme is basically the same as additive rhyme. The difference is practical. If you start with *fast*, *class* is subtractive. If you start with *class*, *fast* is additive.

> Help me please, I'm sinking fast
> Girl, you're in a different class

For *fast*, you could also try: *glass*, *flat*, *mashed* (family), *laughed* (family), *crash* (fam. subt.).

> *The possibilities grow.*

Assonance Rhyme

1. The syllables' vowel sounds are the same.
2. The consonant sounds after the vowels are unrelated.
3. The sounds before the vowels are different.

Assonance rhyme is the furthest you can get from perfect rhyme without changing vowel sounds. Consonants after the vowels have nothing in common. Try rhyming:

> *I hope you're satisfied*

For *satisfied*, we come up with: *life, trial, crime, sign, rise, survive, surprise.*

Use these rhyming techniques: You'll have much more leeway saying what you mean, and your rhymes will be fresh and useful. Again, look actively at each word. Use them to dive through your senses, as though you were object writing.

You'll find more on these rhyme types, including helpful exercises, in my book *Songwriting: Essential Guide to Rhyming.*

Rhymes and Chords

You can think about rhyme in the same way you think about chords. Go to the piano and play three chords: an F chord with an F as the bass note in the left hand, then G7 with G as the bass note, then, finally, C. Play the C chord with the notes C, E, and G in the right hand, and a C as a bass note in the left hand. Sing a C, too. It really feels like you've arrived home, doesn't it?

Next, do the same thing again with your right hand, singing a C when you get to the C chord, but this time, put a G in the left hand. It still feels like you're home, though not quite as solidly as when you played C in the bass. Still, it's difficult to notice the difference.

Do it all again, this time playing the third in the bass, an E. It still feels like a version of home, but less stable. It seems to have some discomfort at home—a very expressive chord.

Do it again, keeping the E in the bass, but this time take the C out of the chord in your right hand. Sing the C. This feels even less comfortable.

Last time, add a B to the right hand, still leaving the C out. Now, you're actually playing an E minor chord, the three minor in the key of C, still singing the C. Now we have only a suggestion of home, rather than sitting down to the supper table.

All of these voicings are useful, and all of these voicings are tonic (home) functions. Some land solidly and bring motion to a complete halt. Others express a desire to keep moving somewhere else—a kind of wanderlust. Each has its own identity and emotion.

Rhymes work the same way. Some are stronger than others and express a desire to stay put; they are stable. Others may have a foot at home, but their minds are looking for the next place to go. They feel less stable.

Here are the rhyme types, listed like the chords you played, in a scale from most stable to least stable:

RHYME TYPES: SCALE OF RESOLUTION STRENGTHS

Most Resolved | Least Resolved

Family Rhyme | Assonance Rhyme

Perfect Rhyme | Additive/Subtractive Rhyme | Consonance Rhyme

Look at the simple example below—a stable, four-stress couplet. With perfect rhyme, it feels very solid and resolved.

> A lovely day to have some fun
> Hit the beach, get some sun

As we move through the rhyme types, things feel less and less stable, even though the structure remains the same:

Family rhyme:

> A lovely day to have some fun
> Hit the beach, bring the rum (a lot like C with G in the bass)

Additive rhyme:

> A lovely day to have some fun
> Hit the beach, get some lunch (a lot like C with E in the bass)

Subractive rhyme:

> Hit the beach and get some lunch
> A lovely day, have some fun (a lot like C with E in the bass)

Assonance rhyme:

> A lovely day to have some fun
> Hit the beach, bring it on (a lot like the E minor in the key of C)

Consonance rhyme:

> A lovely day to have some fun
> Hit the beach, bring it on (a lot like the E minor in the key of C)

Expanding your rhyming possibilities accomplishes three things:

1. It multiplies the possibility of saying what you mean (and still rhyming) exponentially.
2. It guarantees the rhymes will not be predictable or cliché.
3. Most important, it allows you to control, like chords do, how stable or unstable the rhyme feels, allowing you to support or even create emotion with your rhymes.

Together, these offer a pretty good argument against the proponents of "perfect rhyme only."

> Baby baby take my hand
> Let me know you_____

Ah yes, understand. Telegraphed and locked down. Mostly, I find it disappointing when I know what's coming. When it's already telegraphed and waltzing in your brain, why say it? If you instead said something different, you'd have both messages at the same time:

> Baby baby take my hand
> Let me know you'll take a stand (*understand*, the expected cliché, is still present)

I like the perfect rhyme here. The full resolution seems to support the idea. Now, how about:

> Baby baby take my hand
> Let me know you'd like to dance

I love the surprise here. It also uses the telegraphing of *understand* as a second message. It's not a cliché rhyme. Pretty close, though, with n in common but d against c. That little bit of difference introduces something that perfect rhyme can't: a tinge of longing created by the difference at the end. The lack of perfect rhyme creates the same kind of instability as, say, the C major triad with a G in the bass. Almost, but not fully resolved. Just as a chord can create an emotional response, so can a less-perfect rhyme:

> Baby baby take my hand
> Let me know you're making plans

The same tinge of instability.

> Baby baby take my hand
> Let me know you want to laugh

What do you think the chances of hooking up are now? They seem about as remote as the assonance rhyme. Yup, the rhyme type really can affect and color the idea.

It's still a "tonic" function, but now it seems more like a C major triad with an E in the bass. Finally:

> Baby baby take my hand
> Let me know I'm on your mind

Now there's curiosity and uncertainty, expressed completely and only by the consonance rhyme. Pretty neat, huh?

WORKSHEET: RISKY BUSINESS

1. risk	2. business	3. left out	4. freeze	5. storm
cliff	collisions	proud	grieve	reform
fist	visions	bound	leave	(re)born
kissed	frigid	count	peace	court
stiff	forgiveness	vowed	appeased	cord
itch	submissive	aloud	street	scorn
pitch	delicious	renowned	debris	divorce
drift	riches	aroused	diseased	reward
switch	suspicious	crowned	guarantee(s)	warm
shift	kisses		wheel	torn
pinched	finish		shield	ignored
chips	wind			

6. dull	7. night	8. change	9. defense	10. home
sulk	flight	cage	expense	disowned
annulled	spite	slave	bench	blown
cult	bride	grave	trench	bone

pale	strike	safe	drenched	unknown
brawl	prize	faith	friend	stoned
numb	despised	castaway	revenge	dethroned
opium	deprived	ricochet	content	zone
martyrdom	child	haste	condemned	hope
crumbs	fault		contempt	coat
gun	crawl			throat
young				remote
				ghost
				Job
				load
				broken

Brainstorming

Brainstorming with a rhyming dictionary prepares you to write a lyric. At the same time you are brainstorming your ideas, you are also finding sounds you can use later. With solid rhyming techniques that include family rhymes, additive and subtractive rhymes, assonance and even consonance rhymes (especially for l and r), using a rhyming dictionary can be as relaxed and easy as brainstorming with a friend, except it's more efficient than a friend, and it won't whine for a piece of the song if you get a hit.

A worksheet externalized the inward process of lyric writing. It slows your writing process down so you can get to know it better, like slowing down when you play a scale to help get it under your fingers. The more you do it, the faster and more efficient you'll get.

The sample worksheet on the previous pages includes both perfect and imperfect rhymes. Reading this worksheet should be stimulating. But doing your own worksheet will set you on fire. Decide now that you will do a complete worksheet for each of your next ten lyrics, then stick to it. The first one will be slow and painful, but full of new and interesting options. By the third one, ideas will be coming fast and furious. You will have too much to say, too many choices, and too many rhymes. Though getting to this point takes work, it will be well worth the effort. Think of all the times you'll get to say no. No more clichés. No more forced rhymes. No more helpless gratitude that some idea, any idea at all, came along. No more six-hour gigs in Bangor for twenty bucks. Trust me.

Excerpted from *Writing Better Lyrics* © 2009 by **PAT PATTISON**. Used with the kind permission of Writer's Digest Books, an imprint of F+W Media Inc. Visit writersdigestshop.com or call (800)448-0915 to obtain a copy.

SOCIAL MEDIA

How Social Networking Can Impact Your Career

....

by Jamie Wilson Young

Most Americans take advantage of social networking in their personal lives, but have you wondered how you can improve your online connections professionally? Social networking is pervasive in our culture, and as a songwriter and/or performer, you don't want to miss out on golden opportunities to connect with new friends or potential fans and collaborators. We're approaching the time where all creatives must be engaged in social networking to further their craft, and as a writer, you should consider your online presence an extension of yourself and your brand. Justin Bieber was discovered thanks to online efforts—you could be too.

Below, two music business professionals weigh in on social media and how you can use it to to your advantage. If you're not familiar with Facebook and Twitter yet, those websites are highly recommended. Sign up today and begin building your brand. Sharing new songs, connecting with other writers, and creating a fan base has never been easier thanks to technology.

Southern Illinois native **JOHN CLORE** has actively been a part of the music industry since his 2003 graduation from Belmont University's Music Business program in Nashville. In that time, he has handled publicity and online marketing efforts for a variety of musicians, ranging from country music legend Ray Price to Grammy Award winners Jars of Clay to Poison front man Bret Michaels. Clore's first book, *The Music Industry Doesn't Have to Kill You*, releases in August 2011.

Proudly raised in New Jersey . . . far from the Jersey Shore, **PHIL COBUCCI** spent much of his childhood obsessing about brands and business, and from a young age, his parents knew that he was destined for a life of marketing and communications. Some of his highlighted achievements as a child were making friends with Wendy the Snapple Lady, collecting thousands upon thousands of Pepsi Points, and creating popular music mix tapes for his child-hood friends.

Somehow or other, he ended up at Liberty University, and the result was a degree in communications and a job with Warner Bros. Records. Despite his affinity for terrible early '90s music, Phil worked in the music industry for five years before realizing that it was going in an unfortunate downward spiral. He reinvented his life and moved to Nashville, Tennessee, in 2010, where he founded BAM! Solutions, a boutique social media firm for independent business owners.

While in the midst of launching his own social media marketing firm, Phil has played an integral role in the launch of direct-to-consumer eyewear company Tortoise & Blonde. As chief communications officer, Phil has played a strong role in the overall marketing strategy and implementation of the brand throughout the country. Certainly this is no small task, but you better believe it's a highly rewarding one. You can learn more about this venture at tortoiseandblonde.com.

What social networks should every artist sign up for, in order of relevance/importance?

CLORE: Facebook, Twitter. Beyond that, you will be talking to very small groups of people, which is not a bad thing, but good luck finding the network that's appropriate for your brand.

COBUCCI:

1) Facebook
2) Twitter
3) YouTube
4) Tumblr and/or Wordpress
5) MySpace (if it still exists by the time of publication)

How often should an artist engage with fans?

CLORE: Frequency is very much a case-by-case call, but I don't think you can ever go longer than one week without saying anything. You don't want to wear people out with your thoughts/comments/etc., but don't be the guy that tweets once every three or four months. Every day is totally fine, even multiple times a day; just be very careful to remain true to your brand and keep in mind the long-term impact of everything you say.

COBUCCI: At minimum, artists should engage and interact with fans on a daily basis. Your copy needs to be engaging so that your fans come back for more—but at the same time you don't want to sound like you are always trying to sell something. Engaging with fans versus always pushing your music are two different things. Your goal should be to keep your fans interested in your art, who you are as a person (without being too personal) and what you are listening to/reading/performing in.

How can an artist improve his or her numbers?

CLORE: First, I will say to not worry about numbers, but I realize most of us are only human and need approval from others to maintain forward momentum. Considering that, just do the best you can to not worry about your numbers. Focus on the quality of what you say: give people something to think about; point them to a worthwhile URL; give them something to respond to that keeps the conversation going. Yes, run promotions every now and then to give your numbers a little boost, but don't get caught up on this side of things—it's not worth it.

COBUCCI: First off—engaging your fans. Secondly, ensuring that your social sites and website are very easy to navigate. Lastly, making your fans feel like they are important. Respond to your fans' comments and questions publicly, respond to fan mail, and let your fans know that you want to develop a relationship with them. However, be sure that you don't give your fans too much personal information—because that can come back to haunt you. Your fans are obviously your greatest asset—they are going to be the ones that will talk about you. While they are going to talk about you, make sure that it is easy for them to share information—utilize the Facebook Developer features to promote your music. Remember you are not going to increase your numbers by solely "pushing" to sell—so it is key to make sure it is also easy for your fans to buy your music whether it is by iTunes, another DSP, or the actual CD

How can an artist improve the connection wtih his or her fans?

CLORE: Don't just talk to them, but listen and respond to what they have to say—consistently. Most artists really miss some great opportunities because they don't really stop and read/respond to what fans have asked on Facebook, etc. Also, reward them. That can mean lots of things, but determine what that is for your brand and determine what your fans are looking for. What are you looking for from the artists you love? Go and do that for your fans.

COBUCCI: As stated above, engaging your fans is key. Make sure your fans can interact with you and get to know your personality, while also ensuring that your personal life stays private.

Should an artist censor him- or herself when posting online? How personal should the artist get?

CLORE: [An artist] absolutely should. You have got to be careful when you are sharing information that could be seen potentially be anyone. Have fun with it, but put some thought into what you share. And personal information should absolutely be kept to a minimum—for your own safety, and more so, the safety of your family. Just because you can say something, that absolutely does not mean you should.

COBUCCI: Censor yourself to the point where your fans don't know where you live, your personal contact information, or your political beliefs. I have seen instances where politics can destroy friendships, lose fans, and turn a once positive, engaged fan to a negative, disinterested fan. If you are an artist that sings religious music, it is okay to share your religious beliefs—but other than that, I would encourage artists to keep that aligned with your private, personal life as well.

How should an artist handle damage control of an offensive posting?

CLORE: This is potentially one of those situations where you simply don't respond. Hopefully the person will stop. If not, I would maybe say one thing to them. If that doesn't work, just ignore it. I would also recommend dealing with a truly volatile situation in a manner where it is not visible to the general public, and keep records of the conversation, just in case. All in all, be very careful.

COBUCCI: It really depends on the post from a fan. If the post is offensive to your art— e.g., your music sucks—I would delete it and block the person from posting again in your open forum. However, if it is an instance where a fan is confused by a lyric or annoyed by something you said in a public forum (like from the stage)—this gives the artist the opportunity to either fully explain him- or herself, clear up the misunderstanding, or in some cases, agree to disagree. If the conversation takes a nasty or extremely negative turn, I would say that it would be necessary to delete it from public view.

What has been the most innovative use of social media by an artist?

CLORE: As I think about this question, all I can really think of is the end result of the social media campaign, i.e., that which was being promoted by social media, not the social media itself. Honestly, I feel like that's the whole point anyway, so I'm going to share what I feel was a huge point in the combined history of social media and music, and that was Arcade Fire's "The Wilderness Downtown" HTML5 video. I will never forget the tweets and articles I initially saw about that. I couldn't wait to check it out myself, and it did not disappoint. What an amazing combination of technology, great music, video, and social media.

COBUCCI: There are quite a few wonderful third-party applications that can be used on Facebook for an artist to deliver information that is engaging to his/her fanbase. Damn-TheRadio via Fan Bridge is certainly one of the most innovative that I have seen—and they do offer a freemium version if you are an artist just starting out. The beauty of the application is that in order for the potential fan to listen to new music from that specific artist, the fan has to "like" the Facebook page, and in order for them to download a free song, for example, the fan must submit their e-mail address. The most valuable piece of "real estate" in the online world these days is the fan's email address. Once you garner that valuable piece of information, you are now able to push more information directly to your fan's in-box. Other applications that I have used in the past that are fantastic for artists are RootMusic and TopSpin. If you haven't already set up accounts with ArtistData / SonicBids—stop what you are doing and do that now. It is the most valuable key for your business as an artist. The wealth of applications and services that are available are via Artist Data will make your life as an artist so incredibly easy its worth the time to spend on it now.

What has been a social media campaign that you've seen gone awry? What is the most innovative social network?

CLORE: It is really hard to top Facebook, and I think it is going to remain that way for a good, long while. There is something different about the overall flow of information from MySpace to Facebook, and in actuality, those two are not even close to being in the same league anymore. Facebook certainly has room for improvement, relative to what it offers artists, but I think that's part of the reason for its success, because the focus of Facebook has been on the regular, non-famous individual. Now that almost literally everyone is on seemingly multiple times per week, artists can really begin to take advantage of the avenues on Facebook to put their work in front of fans and potential fans.

COBUCCI: The artist that does not use social media at all—is the biggest mistake. With over 500 million people on Facebook alone, the opportunities to reach new fans are endless. The combination of reaching new fans by writing engaging copy and making your social media sites interactive will start creating deeper relationships with your fans. Facebook is the most innovative social network. The functionality that is allowed is clean, it's easy to understand, and most important—it has the most fans.

What technology is going to change the game dramatically?

CLORE: I'm still holding out on check-in technology. It has made blips on the radar over the past couple of years, but as the general public becomes more accustomed to having their smart phones with them all of the time, the technology they offer, and wanting to share even more unnecessary information about themselves with others who don't really care, I think people are going to become more and more interested in telling people where they are, or where they just were. In that will continue to be great opportunities for artists to "find" their fans, to literally physically engage with them, or set up promos to get the attention of consumers.

COBUCCI: Personally, the iPad is poised to revolutionize the world in terms of computing. The changes that we saw just between the iPad and the iPad 2 have turned other PC manufacturers on their head. This will change the way that musicians work, businesses run, and consumers purchase goods.

What trends are you seeing in social media? Kickstarter seems pretty revolutionary. Do you think kickstarter is here to stay?

CLORE: Unfortunately it probably is, at least in some form or another. Personally, I am not a fan. I understand and fully appreciate the concept, but I do not believe the "talent" should have to be funded by the general public just to get their work off the ground. Maybe that's old-school of me, but I really don't think it is. Side note, just because something is "old school," that does not make it wrong. Frankly, I think people that believe they have a creative endeavor worth sharing with the world should be able to figure out how to get the initial step funded, then hopefully sell enough to create or make more; then it hopefully continues to sell. Or maybe they should adjust what they think they need to get started. Why risk putting all of your worth in the hands of the public, even your "biggest" fans, right off the bat? Seriously, people have got to learn to keep some things close to the vest. For example, I'm currently writing my first book. I am busting it to get this project done. It is not easy. It is extremely time-consuming. It is not free. In the end it may not cost me as much as if I were recording my first EP, but it is far from free. I can genuinely tell you that I have never even considered using the Kickstarter model to raise funds for my book. If this thing flops, I'd rather deal with the financials of that on a personal level. Even if my first round of funding were to go through and things were off to a good start, I'd rather the general public have no idea how much it cost me to get started. I just hope they buy the finished product, and we all walk away with a clear conscience.

COBUCCI: The connectivity between your website and the socials is the biggest trend. It seems like Facebook is rolling out a new change or update nearly every month—and the opportunities that are given to developers to integrate Facebook into a website are amazing. Additionally, the sharing platform that is available to push information out via other social media sites like Tumblr, Twitter, and Wordpress are changing the way that we communicate. We are also going to see great changes in the way that we interact—Mobile is growing and it is certainly not going away. And do I think Kickstarter is here to stay? Without a doubt.

How can artists guarantee their projects get funded via kickstarter?

CLORE: Despite my aforementioned personal thoughts, I have seen some extremely successful Kickstarter campaigns, and my hat's off to those people. Namely, my friend Zach Prichard, who with his friend Jonathan Frazier, pretty much single-handedly saved the *Blue Like Jazz* movie. They simply worked their tails off to make certain that the word got out and that appropriate exchanges were in place for donors. They did a tremendous job on that project. All in all, it starts with a great concept/project; then you have to be strong and effective with your communication, and give your fans unique access that will make them want to join in the effort.

COBUCCI: It really comes back to your fans . . . are you engaging your fans with new and interesting happenings? That's the question you need to ask yourself.

Do you have any other thoughts on social networking?

CLORE: Put some thought into what you are doing, saying, posting. Again, just because we have access to communication channels, that does not mean we should use and abuse them. Take a couple of extra minutes and really consider what you are about to say—is that really going to help your brand? Are people going to be annoyed or turned off by it? Just be careful. There is a ridiculous amount of information flying past all of us. Do your part to truly stand out, gain people's respect and trust, then continue to show them why they gave it to you in the first place. Social media can be extremely fun and effectivee, but without at least a little bit of strategy, I would say you are wasting your time.

COBUCCI: If you are not on it now . . . do it before it's too late. There are a wealth of knowledge bases on the web that can and will help you succeed—don't pay for services that promise to get you 10,000 fans. The best way to grow your fan base is to engage them and make them feel appreciated, wanted, loved, and needed. Without that, you are just saying things that have no meaning to their lives. The best way to put it would be, would you rather eat a chicken that ate all natural foods and grew to its normal size or would you rather eat a chicken that has been plugged up with all sorts of steroids and unnatural growth hormones? The best growth for your business is organic growth—don't rely on false methods to grow your fan base. You want fans that are here to stay.

The moral of the story? Dive in and explore the possibilities of technology to make it work for you. Empower yourself to know the ins and outs of social media and to stay on top of the trends and developments. As you become more aware of social media, your brand awareness will inevitably increase.

JAMIE WILSON YOUNG launched her music business career in 2004 at the Nashville Songwriters Association International. Her experience at NSAI combined with her outside efforts of promoting independent artists allowed her to move into a content management position with HearItFirst.com, a leading Christian music website. Since her arrival at HearItFirst, the website has grown immensely and she is now the director of content, overseeing all content and promotions.

PHOTO: Breezy Baldwin

AMANDA PALMER

On the Art of Songwriting, Staying Busy, & Being Honest

....

by Vanessa Wieland

Few people have as much energy as Amanda Palmer. Seemingly constantly cooking up new ideas and performing twice as many shows as other artists (Amanda regularly hosts "ninja" gigs in the cities she tours), she also maintains a witty, vibrant online presence through her blog and Twitter accounts, which feel far more like conversations in a roomful of friends than performer-fan interactions. And that doesn't even include her music! Having built a loyal following as one-half of the Dresden Dolls with Brian Viglione, Amanda has also collaborated with fellow musicians such as Jason Webley, the Young Punx, and Tristan Allen, and worked with other visual artists and writer Neil Gaiman (the two have since married).

You can find Amanda's most recent work as of press time, *Amanda Palmer Goes Down Under*, along with her other albums at music.AmandaPalmer.net, as well as Dresden Dolls and Evelyn Evelyn.

Recently, she took some time out of her insane schedule to give us some insight into her touring and writing process, as well as her take on the present and future of the music industry. Her answers show the same honesty and sense of humor that has made her music so compelling.

Between your solo work, the Dresden Dolls reunion tour, Evelyn Evelyn, your comic with Dark Horse, curating and emceeing *Cabaret*, helping fund promising new artists, and your fan interactions on Twitter and through your blog, you seem to be everywhere at once. Where do you find the time?

I don't know. I think it's my stark and humorless New England work ethic that keeps me going. If I ever sit down to rest, an imaginary horseman who looks like a cross between the Grim Reaper and Paul Revere starts galloping behind me, shouting "WORK, YOU LAZY ARTIST, WORK!"

Seriously? I always wonder when people have the time to understand current events and watch movies and television. So maybe the secret is to never watch television, movies, or pick up a newspaper. Seems to work for me.

You fought to be released from your label. Would you ever be willing to sign with a label again? What advantages or enticements would a future label have to offer?

Labels are just groups of people. I need groups of people to get things done, since I can't do everything myself. So I have absolutely nothing against labels, or being signed to a label, if it would happen that the group of people are the right group and would do the right work. But I think the term "label" might have to die. I'm assuming that the labels of the future will more resemble marketing, management, and promotions offices than distribution. The distribution is the easy part, nowadays. Upload it, BAM, you're done.

For a songwriter/performer starting [his/her] professional career, is it better to go it alone or try to get on a label? Could you have accomplished the same level of recognition and put out records without label funding?

There's absolutely no way the Dresden Dolls would have gone as far as fast had we not signed. Was it worth it? I'll never know. At the time we signed, I just knew I absolutely couldn't keep up with the workload of running our own label and I couldn't find any responsible help. So a label was the only option if we wanted to continue to tour; otherwise we were going to have to start canceling dates so I could man the computer and the mail room.

If you look at the long term . . . yes, had we not signed, we would have just grown more slowly. We were well on our way to recognition before getting signed. But would we be known in places like New Zealand, Japan, Belgium? Without the office-might of the label to do our press and radio there, no way, not to the degree it happened.

It seems like there are a lot of people in the industry who are, if not outright scamming, at least not keeping the songwriter's interests at heart. How do you recognize a good deal or one that is too good to be true?

The moment you meet people, they'll usually tell you what their interests are. If people are interested in pure profit, you can smell it a mile away and start running. People who are interested in a more careful merging of art and business are hard to come by, but they're out there if you look, and their sincerity is usually easy to detect.

I'm no expert, though. I still get burned all the time. But that's the game. You don't play without taking risks.

What is the biggest change you've seen in the music business since you started your career?

The biggest change? Well, maybe it's obvious, but MySpace and YouTube. They've changed the protocol completely for how acts connect with each other, their fans, and their prospective fans and bookers/agents. It happened fast. It only took a year or so to transition from a life where hopeful CDS arrived in the mail on a daily basis to links being e-mailed.

In the past, you've talked about how the current model of payment for musicians needs to be adapted. You've had performers with you pass around a tip jar and recently you've used Kickstarter to help fund recording for your protégé, Tristan Allen. What tools or methods are proving to be most effective?

I can only speak for myself, but I'm a huge fan of the pay-what-you-will model of music downloading. I think a faith-based system is key. Nobody in the industry will like it, but they're dying a slow death anyway. This is the way I think the world of content and art online might move forward and actually make an artist a living.

On your website, you allow your fans to set the price to download some of your CDs. Have people generally been willing to pay a reasonable amount when it has been their choice?

Yes, they have. Part of the trick, I'll admit, is to have a minuscule minimum. Once people have to pay a few cents, they'll often opt to add a few dollars, because what's a few dollars? But that's the money that will pave the future of many artists.

One of the points of contention you had with your previous label was your image, which sparked your female fans to come to your defense with the ReBelly-on campaign. Is it more difficult to be taken seriously both as a songwriter and a performer as a female? How do you get past that?

I don't think much about it. I think if I think too much about it, I might get trapped in there. Being female in the industry has massive pros and cons just like being a female in the "Real World." You have a mysterious power over people, because you're this slightly odd beast in a zoo of men. But you also have to be the kind of person who can make poop jokes on a tour bus with your all-male crew for months on end. Otherwise, forget it; you'll go bonkers trying to relate to them on a feminine level.

Your relationship with your fans feels far more reciprocal than many fan-performer relationships. Where do you draw the line between public and private? Is there even a line to be drawn?

Oh yes, there's a line. There's a lot of information that I keep to myself. A lot of my love life, friendships, and family life are strictly off-limits. But I don't make any pretensions with my fan base that I'm telling All. Telling All would be incredibly tedious, don't you think?

But I do like sharing life and truth and stories with my fans, and I count myself incredibly lucky that I came of age as a rock star in the era of the forum, the blog, and the Twitter account. But that in itself has caused some hard problems; namely, where does the songwriting time go when you spend too much energy chatting to and relating to your fans? (Answer: out the window. And perhaps this is a more honest answer to the first question.)

Your music, whether it be the raw honesty of family illness and personal traumas or dressing up as conjoined twins with Jason Webley for *Evelyn Evelyn*, has brought its share of controversy. How do you defend yourself, your music, and keep writing honestly?

I think the key is to NOT defend yourself too much. Haters gonna hate, especially in the age of the Internet, where everyone can hide behind their walls and masks while spewing venom, truisms, and righteousness. The moment you start constantly having to defend your art, you're wasting your energy.

How does an Amanda Palmer song come into existence? Where does the inspiration come from, and do you start with lyrics or melody first?

I write simply as I write, when I have time, inspiration and energy, and often those never align. I've barely written in the past year. My songwriter has probably spent about 24 hours total truly at work. I try not to feel guilty about that. The time will come, or it won't, and that's fine. I try not to overthink. I try not to write for the audience, any audience. When I do that, I get thrown off track.

I hear songs in my head, and they usually start with lyrics. Those little lines and melodies bounce around in there, looking for a place to land, and if I'm around an instrument and not feeling too lazy, I'll sit down and record the idea. If a miracle occurs, I'll take that idea and flesh it out into a real song. But the distance from idea-birth to song-birth has to be a short one—after more than a few days, the idea gets stale. I've found that I have to write 80 percent of a song in one sitting or it won't be a great one. If I can write it 100 percent in one sitting, I'll often have a winner.

When writing, do you prefer collaboration or solo?

I like both, but I haven't collaborated very much. The album I wrote with Jason (Evelyn Evelyn) was a surprise . . . I thought it would be harder than it was. But we were both so careful of each other and trying so hard to make the other laugh that it worked like a charm. I'd be curious to see what happened if I tried it with someone else. But I like writing alone. It's a process that's hard to share, sort of like showering, or bedding down with someone. You have to really, really like the person to share a space that intimate.

What advice would you give to songwriters who are trying to build a career?

Write good music. You'll know if it's good, because people will tell you. If you aren't writing good music, try being more honest. If that doesn't work, quit.

But seriously, I suggest not over-pimping yourself until your shit is good enough. And you'll know; your inner voice will tell you if you're good enough to go out there and start peddling your wares. Once you start peddling, have no Plan B. Plan B will kill you. People won't believe you're committed to your career as an artist if you've got a whole backup plan. I certainly won't.

And lastly, I always tell everyone to leave no contact un-followed-up on. Anytime you meet anybody who takes an interest in your work, get an e-mail address from them, and keep them informed. It is these people, not a savior from the magical music business, who will build your career and your success. So don't take them for granted. And did I mention you have to get their e-mail address? You have to get their e-mail address and use it.

Also, don't take touring on the road as an excuse not to floss. [Bleeping] FLOSS!

VANESSA WIELAND is an associate editor with North Light and IMPACT Books and former assistant editor for *Songwriter's Market.* Her previous gigs include interviews in *Artist's and Graphic Designer's Market,* a column in *Writer's Digest* magazine, fiction in *Pindeldyboz* and poetry in *Crash.* She's still waiting for *Rolling Stone* and *Spin* to call.

DIY MUSICIANS

Gavin Castleton & Matt Fazzi
on Going Label-Free

by Vanessa Wieland

GAVIN CASTLETON's debut album, which he streamed online through his website, chronicled the disintegration of a relationship through the lens of a zombie attack, with dark, atmospheric music that left the listener both haunted and entertained. The epitome of a self-starter, Gavin's experience with funding and distributing music on his own gives him a profound and valuable insight into the music business for someone who has never been on a label.

MATT FAZZI started working on Happy Body, Slow Brain even when he was still performing in other bands. As a member of Facing New York and later Taking Back Sunday, Matt has experienced both ends of the spectrum. The two musicians have formed a close friendship performing Gavin's music together when Castleton opened for Taking Back Sunday.

Though neither is currently on a label, their varying experiences and outlooks highlight the variety of paths songwriters may find themselves traveling, and their friendship is testament to one of the great advantages of finding other musicians to tour with. Read on to get their take on the state of the music industry, setting up a tour, and gaining an audience.

So let's talk about not being on a label. What are the advantages and disadvantages? Are you seeking label representation, or do you prefer going the DIY route?

FAZZI: One of the biggest advantages/rewards of not being bound by a label is that you retain the full rights and control and the freedom to do whatever you want with your own music. Oftentimes, when a label is investing in you, they want a say in the "product" you are making, which can cause a band to have to alter their artistic vision to suit that of the label. The flipside sometimes is a label often has lots of money up front to put into the marketing of your band, recording, or pressing of your album, as well as connections in the industry that many up-and-coming bands might not have. However, if you DO have the means and the know-how to be able to record yourself well, market yourself, press your own albums, a band can easily become its own label. It's already easy enough for the independent musician to secure their own online distribution via iTunes, Amazon, CDBaby, etc., and the industry is changing more and more in favor of the DIY musician. I've personally always found that the more self-sufficient you can be, the better. Labels tend to be more attracted to a band making things happen themselves. The trends seem to suggest that labels won't be necessary in the not-so-distant future, so we're trying the DIY route for now.

CASTLETON: I'd say the main advantage of working alone is unencumbered publishing of content and 100 percent of the profits. The disadvantages would depend on what the label was bringing to the table, the list of which is no longer standardized. For me it was primarily a recording and promotion budget that I have to now work without. As far as if I would like to work with a label right now, I'd say it would be ideal to have a competent team of people working on my behalf, but I am not willing to do the political work that seems necessary in order to garner that kind of interest. The DIY route is my default, not necessarily my preference.

How are you building your audiences? What steps have seemed to work best, and are there any steps that haven't worked out for you?

CASTLETON: Touring, social networking, constant content provision, encouraging my listeners to share my music—these are all daily tasks that I have to do instead of making art. As the industry is (and has been for years now) in a total state of flux, our strategies have to evolve constantly. I've recently given up touring, as doing so for five years (excluding the nine years I toured in a band before my solo career began) has proven financially disastrous, even with a beat-up '94 minivan and a solid trio of pro musicians maintaining a very low overhead. I think touring does wonders for some bands, but I'd suggest that those bands have effective booking agents and the type of live music that doesn't require as much context as mine does.

As far as any other effective methods, I keep my eye on lots of new startups offering services to artists, but I find that the majority of them are designed to help you annoy your listeners and re-centralize your traffic onto their servers; few offer you new impressions. And most don't stick around very long, maybe due to the fact that they're marketing to artists, the poorest demographic in the country.

The only axiom I don't think I'll ever contradict is: improving your music increases your impact.

FAZZI: We are trying to build our audience through efficient touring and through a lot of social networking on sites like Twitter and Facebook, among others. We also try and keep the content as real and personal as we can and keep it updated somewhat regularly. With social networking sites breaking down the barriers between musician and fan more and more, I find that you are selling not only music but your personality as well so the more YOU that you can put into it, the more people will be attracted to take an interest and support what you do. Otherwise, I have found that making friends with other bands and cross promoting that way really always has and always will be one of the best ways to grow your band organically.

What lessons have you learned about the business side that, as an artist, you wish you'd known beforehand?

FAZZI: I've learned that there's so much REAL business you need to know if you really want to be a legit independent musician. From how to handle your taxes, to keeping track of band/business expenses and receipts, to exploring publishing options, licensing your music, dealing with a label, etc. There's tons of information out there; you just have to make it your priority to understand it as an independent musician because it will most certainly benefit you in the future on your journey.

CASTLETON: Too many to list here. But I've written several essays detailing them at http://gavincastleton.blogspot.com/search/label/Essay.

Does the Internet make it easier or harder for you to reach your audience?

CASTLETON: Easier.

FAZZI: The Internet definitely makes the world much smaller and more accessible to a band, but it also makes it much easier for the average person to record their starter band, put it online, and clog up the system a bit. I find there's a lot more fluff you have to sift through now to get to the great bands because it takes zero effort to have a page online.

Audience does not necessarily translate into sales, though. Or does it? Does streaming your songs, even whole albums online, help or hinder your ability to make a living creating music?

CASTLETON: I've recently opted to cancel my involvement with all paid and unpaid streaming sites (aside from my website, gavincastleton.com, where I stream both my recent two albums for free). I'm of the opinion that since people can now stream my music for free direct from their mobile devices, it would be ridiculous to expect those same people to pay for it. And the dividends I receive from paid streams is literally pennies.

FAZZI: I think for a band like Happy Body Slow Brain, starting new and streaming our entire album gives people a more complete picture of where our music is at. It's that try-it-before-you-buy-it–type thing that the music industry has adopted over the last several years. Having a record nowadays is more like a business card to get people in the door and interested in you. The hope is if they dig you and your music enough that they'll come out to a show and buy a shirt and support the artist that way.

Gavin, you recently used Kickstarter to finance your album *Won over Frequency*. How did that work? Would you call that a success, and is that something you would do again? What would you change?

CASTLETON: It worked better than I expected, and I would call it a success in that I reached and surpassed my initial funding goal. Unfortunately, I greatly underestimated my mixing costs, and am now still a few thousand dollars away from breaking even. I don't think I would work with Kickstarter again, as their fees are unreasonable and their limitations—though few—were frustrating. If I were to do it again, I would build the site myself instead of paying a percentage for an automated UI.

Who sets up your live shows and tours? Do you go through a management or booking agency for that? Or do it yourself? What do you look at when approaching a venue to play?

CASTLETON: I book them all myself. I've been unable to acquire either management or booking. When approaching a venue, I look at their sound system, current listings, location, and eventually, their money dealings.

FAZZI: I handle the Happy Body Slow Brain booking, and most times I work together with the bands we are playing with to set the shows up. I also send a lot of cold e-mails out to venues that seem like good places to play that work with the tour routing. Mainly, we are looking for a place that will take care of the bands, pay a decent guarantee, do some promo work, and is easy to find location-wise. As an up-and-coming band, we can't be too picky about where we play yet until we start building a stronger fan base. More than anything, getting the band in front of new people is always one of the top priorities.

For someone setting up their first tour out of town, what advice would you give them?

CASTLETON: Keep spreadsheets of everything. Have promo copies of things to give away. Rehearse much more than you think you should. Read my "The Keys to Failure: Tour Edition" essay (http://gavincastleton.blogspot.com/2009/11/keys-to-failure-tour-edition.html).

FAZZI: I suggest for a band doing their first tour, to do some research and reach out to other bands from the areas you intend to visit to set up and exchange shows. They'll know better what venues are best for their local scene and what promoters do a good job and which bands or spots to steer clear from. Make sure your transportation is in order, and try to crunch expense numbers to know what your costs will be (gas, van rental, merchandise, oil change, etc.) and what amount you'll need to make up to at least break even. Top priority is always making sure the band is as tight and exciting live as it can be, so make sure to rehearse!!!

Any favorite places to play? Cities, venues, etc.? What makes them so special?

CASTLETON: I like Boston, Providence, LA, San Jose, Reno, and Murfreesboro. I like those towns because they like me, and their enthusiasm gets me pumped.

FAZZI: I love playing Bottom of the Hill in San Francisco. It's a great venue, good size, and I've always played awesome shows there. I have a nostalgic connection to it for sure.

Matt, do you do all the songwriting for Happy Body, Slow Brain, or is that done in collaboration with Isaac and Eduardo?

FAZZI: I do the majority of the songwriting in Happy Body Slow Brain, with Isaac contributing some music as well. It's sort of been my baby since about 2007 when I was still in one of my previous bands, Facing New York. It's my first band where I'm the main contributor and writer, and it's been the most rewarding musical experience for me yet.

What's your writing process like?

FAZZI: My songwriting process starts in many ways. It could be a tiny melodic idea, a guitar riff, a smooth bass line, or a really interesting drum pattern that sparks the rest of the song. I'll try and come up with a music arrangement skeleton to start with, then work on a chorus melody and lyric theme. From there, I then try to rework the music/lyric ideas to support that main chorus idea and vibe a bit better. Sometimes, though, the immediate inspiration isn't there to complete a song, so I'll put the song away for a while and come back with fresh ears and ideas to make it better later on.

Matt, you've played with Gavin before. Have the two of you thought about further collaboration together, maybe some songwriting?

CASTLETON: Yes, we've been talking about that lately. I know it will happen; it's just a matter of when we'll be in the same place, at the same time, in matching sweat pants.

FAZZI: I've always wanted to do some sort of split with HBSB and Gavin; whether that means collaboration on all the songs or just contributing new, unused tracks, we'd be honored and stoked to do it. Collectively, HBSB owes a lot of influence and inspiration to Gavin and his music, so any chance we have at playing shows with Gav, playing on his records, or potentially doing a split, we'll jump at.

What advice and encouragement would you give to songwriters just starting out?

CASTLETON: Don't write a word until you have something to say. Don't get in the way of the song. Never lose respect for yourself or your abilities.

FAZZI: Soak up everything you can about your favorite music, and try to really get inside of it and understand what you love about it so much. Pay attention to the way the singer delivers their notes and words, the way the drummer and bassist fill the rhythm section pocket, the way the guitarist crafts his leads, or the way the band arranges their songs. You can always learn something new. Listen to lots of styles, and always, constantly be trying to grow your playing skills and style repertoire. Learn to play more than one instrument proficiently. You make yourself much more valuable as a musician in doing so.

You can listen to and buy Gavin's music at his website: http://www.gavincastleton.com/ as well as reading more about his inspiration and experiences creating and distributing music.

Happy Body, Slow Brain can be found at: http://happybodyslowbrain.bandcamp.com.

BANDBOX

Buying and Selling in a Digital World

....

by Lyndsay Rush

Sell your music, make 100 percent.

This is a claim that, as a songwriter with songs to sell, certainly catches the eye. And when prefaced with the expression "giving artists what they deserve," what else could you ask for?

That's exactly the question, though, that musicians all over the world are asking themselves as buying and selling music has gone digital, "What do I need?" In an online world, every artist must decide for themselves what program makes the most sense for them; who to use, who to trust. As any singer-songwriter would say, music is about artistry, creation, craft, story. But it's also undeniably about turning that art into a dollar. Or a million.

So when it comes time to sell your music, where do you go? What do you do? How do you even begin such a daunting task? Enter: Bandbox—a program boasting ease, simplicity, usability, and most important—100 percent of the profits.

Not too shabby.

THE SALES DEBATE

Bandbox has helped artists like Taylor Swift, Keith Urban, Jewel, Reba McEntire, and thousands of independents successfully sell their music directly to their fans. But what makes Bandbox better than Bandcamp or iTunes, Amazon.com, Snocap, Topspin, or a host of others? More important, what factors should you consider when deciding who to sell your music through? What is the key element that makes all of the difference?

For Los Angeles–based folk band Wing and Hollow, the most important factor is simply getting your music out there. "We feel that the big boys—iTunes and Amazon, are the best choice, simply because everyone knows of them and they sell the most music," says lead singer Jill Lamoureux. "When you're at the beginning of your career, just trying to 'get noticed,' the few cents more you might get out of each sale by choosing a smaller online vendor isn't worth sacrificing usability, management etc."

For other artists, like singer-songwriter John Goolsby of Nashville, TN, the most important factor in choosing a place online to sell your music is knowing the goal of selling your music to begin with. Which, undoubtedly brings many questions to the surface: "Do you want to get the word out and just want more people to know about you and your music?" John quips, "Do you want people to have access in a familiar setting that can bring you some notoriety? Are you looking for a place that maximizes the amount of money you make per track/album?"

Regardless of what your personal goals are with your music, it helps to be informed on a variety of services and programs that exist to help you, the artist, make the most of your music. Let's take a look at a few of the reasons why Bandbox may be a good fit for you.

Bandbox Basics

Right now, according to Bandbox, you could write a song, record it on your computer, and start selling it within ten minutes. That is nothing to sneeze at.

Bandbox offers the option to sell your digital music and CDs virtually anywhere online —your blog, your website, Facebook, MySpace—wherever your fans are. It's a "take your music to your fans" versus a "make your fans come to you" reasoning.

Bandbox is the perfect option for the artist looking to maintain control over how and where their music is sold. Offering the ability to set your own pricing on your music, several features and options exist to tailor a pricing plan that suits your personal needs.

Features at Your Fingertips

So what exactly are these tools that help you sell your music directly to your fans?

"Bandbox Basic" ($9.95/month) and "Bandbox Pro" ($14.95/month) offer the option to choose among the following features:

- 100 percent of net proceeds on all sales
- Unlimited digital albums
- Unlimited tracks
- Set your own pricing
- Free download capability
- Sell physical albums
- Detailed sales reporting
- Non-exclusivity
- Sell both in the U.S. and outside of the U.S.
- Payments issued monthly

Where to Begin?

Bandbox—a self-proclaimed "DIY" program—boasts a free thirty-day trial and a step-by-step setup for your personal digital music distribution. It's like the microwave of digital music, without the radiation.

According to the Bandbox website, getting started is as easy as 1, 2, 3. Quite literally:

Step 1: Sign up for a free account

Step 2: Upload your MP3s and set the price

Step 3: Copy the embed code and paste it into your MySpace, Facebook, website, blog, etc. —just like you would with a YouTube video

Making Money

The real question any artist wants to know when choosing a place to sell their songs is, "How do I get paid?" And rightly so. Especially for independent artists, the profit margin is without a doubt an important factor in the digital sales game.

Joel Rakes, Nashville folk singer, insists that where you decide to sell your music should be based on "where you have the best odds of connecting and converting a fan into a buyer." Says Rakes, "Who doesn't want to be more profitable?"

As far as Bandbox is concerned, 100 percent of the profits go in your pocket. Every time. They offer the following example as proof, "If you sell a $1 download, roughly 10 cents goes to the wonderful credit card companies and 90 cents goes back into your pocket. You literally keep 100 percent of the profit, Bandbox doesn't take a penny. If you sell a $10 CD, $9.45 comes back to you. Sound fair? Sound crazy? You're right on both accounts."

With detailed sales reports at your disposal, it's easy to track the analytics and metrics of your song success: see where you're at, how you're doing and who's buying. And when it comes to getting the actual money into your actual pocket, Bandbox directly deposits your profits into your bank account or PayPal account every thirty days. Quick, easy, and secure—what better way is there to get paid?

THE OTHER GUYS

No research is complete without a look at the competition.From top dog, iTunes, to fellow-widget makers Bandcamp, the song-selling world is full of services and products that are tailored to fit whatever needs you and your music have.

A brief glimpse at a few of the other places to sell your music will give you a better idea of what's out there and what will work best for you.

Bandcamp

Pop singer David Marshall chose Bandcamp due to its accessibility and audience awareness. "The potential consumer needs to be aware of the service to know where to spend their money," says Marshall. "I guess in essence the chosen program used needs to have a bigger consumer name/presence than the artist themselves."

....

Bandbox offers the option to sell your digital music and CDs virtually anywhere online—your blog, your website, Facebook, MySpace—wherever your fans are.

....

Bandcamp—which offers the ability to sell music and merchandise—offers a variety of features in a fan-friendly site built on social media values of discussion and sharing. From a plethora of file formats to name-your-price downloads, to viral distribution and discount codes, Bandcamp provides a site that can become the hub for your music and your fans.

Bandcamp wants to become your new artist site—one that is unique to your brand, offers a variety of download file formats, keeps your music streaming and downloading seamlessly, handles technical issues, keeps your site top-ranked in Google, makes it easy for your fans to share your music and gives you intelligent analytics to understand how your music is spreading. In a nutshell, Bandcamp is the website you never knew you always needed.

iTunes

If there is a household name for buying music online, it's iTunes. "Nothing seems to touch iTunes when it comes to the established music community and its buyers," insists singer-singwriter John Goolsby. "There's a sense of professionalism associated with getting your music on there, and it legitimizes your work in a way that other sites and programs cannot." And while that may certainly be the case, independent artists often need third-party vendors—such as CDBaby or TuneCore—to gain access to its services.

Additionally, with iTunes you miss out on the luxury of uploading music as soon as you've recorded it. According to independent artist Joel Rakes, "sometimes you may have to wait a few weeks before the music goes lives (on iTunes.) This can be frustrating if you're trying to get a release out fast or last minute."

There is no denying the powerhouse that is iTunes, but where it once seemed to be the only legitimate place to sell your music online, today there exist countless alternatives.

Amazon

Taking its place alongside iTunes as a well-known brand name and behemoth operation, Amazon offers some attractive features and options to sell your music. Using Artist Central, in just a few steps you can upload mp3s for free streaming. You can also customize your information with a personal page banner, official photos and videos, Twitter feed, and more. After you're finished, Amazon publishes your content to the site and you're set. If your first priority is to have your music heard, then Amazon is the place to go. Tens of millions of people use Amazon each day, which means millions of people could be listening to your music each day. How's that for exposure?

Topspin

Like most other digital media platforms, Topspin lets you manage your music, videos, images, and more, but Topspin's core M.O. is making your life easier in a variety of ways. For example, Topspin enables you to book your own shows, sell your own tickets, and even check people in at the door using your iPhone. You've needed a reason to buy that iPhone, right? So, there it is.

Topspin strongly encourages a close relationship with your fans. By using a state-of-the-art SAAS platform to build fan connections, Topspin allows you to gather your supporters' information (e-mail address, geographic information, mobile numbers, etc.) and then communicate with them via e-mail, Facebook, and Twitter. You can also create exclusive VIP memberships and fan clubs. "Merely a vessel through which your genius flows," Topspin is a simple and ideal way for artists to connect with their supporters.

NoiseTrade

Similar to Topspin, NoiseTrade pushes artists to form a meaningful bond with fans. Using NoiseTrade, artists upload their music and create their own artist page that comes with a customized widget. This widget can be embedded anywhere—Facebook, Twitter, e-mail, or any other social networking website. Fans can choose any amount up to $100 to download your music, using the "tip jar."

But what if people choose to download your music for free? That's the beauty of NoiseTrade: fans are able to grab the widget and add it to their own website or blog, and so begins the fresh circle of sharing and promoting music. NoiseTrade believes that you need to establish a fan base, and if you stay true to your fans, the money will come. According to NoiseTrade's website, "it's time to stop applying the old rules to a new model. If artists and music fans can work together, they'll find that they can all get what they want."

Decisions Made Easy

When all is said and done, buying and selling your music online can be like anything else digital these days: vast, overwhelming, but undeniably powerful. The most critical decision for you to make will lie not in choosing a service, but more so in understanding and prioritizing what factors matter the most to you.

In looking at several different options for selling your music, you have already begun to discern what priorities you have right now, where you're at with your music and in your career. Is it ease? Cost? Upkeep? Return on Investment?

The very best way to begin anything is to discover what you value. This way you're able to explore the different options according to their strong suits. At the end of the day, only you know best what matters most to you, to your music, and to your fans. The rest, as they say, will fall in place. It's the best part about living in a world of a million choices: once you know what is important to you, the right choice becomes easy.

SONGWRITING CALENDAR

The best way for songwriters to achieve success is by setting goals. Goals are usually met by songwriters who give themselves or are given deadlines. Something about having an actual date to hit helps create a sense of urgency for most writers. This songwriting calendar is a great place to keep your important deadlines.

Also, this calendar is a good tool for recording upcoming events you'd like to attend or contests you'd like to enter. Or use this calendar to block out time for yourself—to just create.

Of course, you can use this calendar to record other special events, especially if you have a habit of remembering to write but of forgetting birthdays or anniversaries. After all, this calendar is now yours. Do with it what you will.

AUGUST 2011

SUN	MON	TUE	WED	THURS	FRI	SAT
	1	2	3	4	5	6
7	8	9	10	11	12	13
14	15	16	17	18	19	20
21	22	23	24	25	26	27
28	29	30	31			

Start a blog and make at least one post per week.

SEPTEMBER 2011

SUN	MON	TUE	WED	THU	FRI	SAT
				1	2	3
4	5	6	7	8	9	10
11	12	13	14	15	16	17
18	19	20	21	22	23	24
25	26	27	28	29	30	

Try sending out one targeted demo per day.

OCTOBER 2011

SUN	MON	TUE	WED	THU	FRI	SAT
						1
2	3	4	5	6	7	8
9	10	11	12	13	14	15
16	17	18	19	20	21	22
23	24	25	26	27	28	29
30	31					

Are you on Twitter? Try leaving a meaningful tweet daily.

NOVEMBER 2011

SUN	MON	TUE	WED	THU	FRI	SAT
		1	2	3	4	5
6	7	8	9	10	11	12
13	14	15	16	17	18	19
20	21	22	23	24	25	26
27	28	29	30			

Find a songwriting workshop to attend.

_____

_____

_____

_____

_____

DECEMBER 2011

SUN	MON	TUE	WED	THU	FRI	SAT
				1	2	3
4	5	6	7	8	9	10
11	12	13	14	15	16	17
18	19	20	21	22	23	24
25	26	27	28	29	30	31

Evaluate your 2011 accomplishments and make 2012 goals.

_____

_____

_____

_____

_____

JANUARY 2012

SUN	MON	TUE	WED	THU	FRI	SAT
1	2	3	4	5	6	7
8	9	10	11	12	13	14
15	16	17	18	19	20	21
22	23	24	25	26	27	28
29	30	31				

Make 2012 your best year songwriting yet!

FEBRUARY 2012

SUN	MON	TUE	WED	THU	FRI	SAT
			1	2	3	4
5	6	7	8	9	10	11
12	13	14	15	16	17	18
19	20	21	22	23	24	25
26	27	28	29			

Use the extra day in February to submit a song.

MARCH 2012

SUN	MON	TUE	WED	THU	FRI	SAT
				1	2	3
4	5	6	7	8	9	10
11	12	13	14	15	16	17
18	19	20	21	22	23	24
25	26	27	28	29	30	31

Don't wait until April to file your 2011 taxes.

_____

_____

_____

_____

_____

APRIL 2012

SUN	MON	TUE	WED	THU	FRI	SAT
1	2	3	4	5	6	7
8	9	10	11	12	13	14
15	16	17	18	19	20	21
22	23	24	25	26	27	28
29	30					

Create a MySpace music page (or other social network platform) for people to hear your songs.

MAY 2012

SUN	MON	TUE	WED	THU	FRI	SAT
		1	2	3	4	5
6	7	8	9	10	11	12
13	14	15	16	17	18	19
20	21	22	23	24	25	26
27	28	29	30	31		

Try to find a new cowriter to work with.

_____

_____

_____

_____

_____

JUNE 2012

SUN	MON	TUE	WED	THU	FRI	SAT
					1	2
3	4	5	6	7	8	9
10	11	12	13	14	15	16
17	18	19	20	21	22	23
24	25	26	27	28	29	30

Develop one song idea each week.

JULY 2012

SUN	MON	TUE	WED	THU	FRI	SAT
1	2	3	4	5	6	7
8	9	10	11	12	13	14
15	16	17	18	19	20	21
22	23	24	25	26	27	28
29	30	31				

Organize your records for next tax season.

AUGUST 2012

SUN	MON	TUE	WED	THU	FRI	SAT
			1	2	3	4
5	6	7	8	9	10	11
12	13	14	15	16	17	18
19	20	21	22	23	24	25
26	27	28	29	30	31	

Find a show or concert to attend for inspiration.

SEPTEMBER 2012

SUN	MON	TUE	WED	THU	FRI	SAT
						1
2	3	4	5	6	7	8
9	10	11	12	13	14	15
16	17	18	19	20	21	22
23	24	25	26	27	28	29
30						

Try an unfamiliar writing style to help you grow as a writer.

OCTOBER 2012

SUN	MON	TUE	WED	THU	FRI	SAT
	1	2	3	4	5	6
7	8	9	10	11	12	13
14	15	16	17	18	19	20
21	22	23	24	25	26	27
28	29	30	31			

Remember to hit the Save button when you're writing.

NOVEMBER 2012

SUN	MON	TUE	WED	THU	FRI	SAT
				1	2	3
4	5	6	7	8	9	10
11	12	13	14	15	16	17
18	19	20	21	22	23	24
25	26	27	28	29	30	

Look for a songwriting organization to join, if you haven't already.

DECEMBER 2012

SUN	MON	TUE	WED	THU	FRI	SAT
						1
2	3	4	5	6	7	8
9	10	11	12	13	14	15
16	17	18	19	20	21	22
23	24	25	26	27	28	29
30	31					

If you don't have it yet, find a copy of *2013 Songwriter's Market*.

MUSIC PUBLISHERS

Music publishers find songs and then get them recorded. In return for a share of the money made from your songs, they work as an agent for you by plugging your songs to recording artists, taking care of paperwork and accounting, setting you up with cowriters (recording artists or other songwriters), and so on.

HOW DO MUSIC PUBLISHERS MAKE MONEY FROM SONGS?

Music publishers make money by getting songs recorded onto albums, film and TV soundtracks, commercials, etc., and other areas. While this is their primary function, music publishers also handle administrative tasks such as copyrighting songs; collecting royalties for the songwriter; negotiating and issuing synchronization licenses for use of music in films, television programs, and commercials; arranging and administering foreign rights; auditing record companies and other music users; suing infringers; and producing new demos of new songs. In a small, independent publishing company, one or two people may handle all these jobs. Larger publishing companies are more likely to be divided into the following departments: creative (or professional), copyright, licensing, legal affairs, business affairs, royalty, accounting, and foreign.

HOW DO MUSIC PUBLISHERS FIND SONGS?

The creative department is responsible for finding talented writers and signing them to the company. Once a writer is signed, it is up to the creative department to develop and nurture the writer so he will write songs that create income for the company. Staff members often put writers together to form collaborative teams. And, perhaps most important, the creative department is responsible for securing commercial recordings of songs and pitching them for use in film and other media. The head of the creative department—usually called the "professional manager"—is charged with locating talented writers for the company.

HOW DO MUSIC PUBLISHERS GET SONGS RECORDED?

Once a writer is signed, the professional manager arranges for a demo to be made of the writer's songs. Even though a writer may already have recorded his own demo, the publisher will often re-demo the songs using established studio musicians in an effort to produce the highest-quality demo possible.

Once a demo is produced, the professional manager begins shopping the song to various outlets. He may try to get the song recorded by a top artist on his or her next album or get the song used in an upcoming film. The professional manager uses all the contacts and leads he has to get the writer's songs recorded by as many artists as possible. Therefore, he must be able to deal efficiently and effectively with people in other segments of the music industry, including A&R personnel, recording artists, producers, distributors, managers and lawyers. Through these contacts, he can find out what artists are looking for new material, and who may be interested in recording one of the writer's songs.

HOW IS A PUBLISHING COMPANY ORGANIZED?

After a writer's songs are recorded, the other departments at the publishing company come into play.

- The *licensing and copyright departments* are responsible for issuing any licenses for use of the writer's songs in film or TV and for filing various forms with the copyright office.
- The *legal affairs department and business affairs department* works with the professional department in negotiating contracts with its writers.
- The *royalty and accounting departments* are responsible for making sure that users of music are paying correct royalties to the publisher and ensuring the writer is receiving the proper royalty rate as specified in the contract and that statements are mailed to the writer promptly.
- Finally, the *foreign department*'s role is to oversee any publishing activities outside of the United States, to notify sub-publishers of the proper writer and ownership information of songs in the catalog and update all activity and new releases, and to make sure a writer is being paid for any uses of his material in foreign countries.

LOCATING A MUSIC PUBLISHER

How do you go about finding a music publisher that will work well for you? First, you must find a publisher suited to the type of music you write. If a particular publisher works mostly with alternative music and you're a country songwriter, the contacts he has within the industry will hardly be beneficial to you.

Each listing in this section details, in order of importance, the type of music that publisher is most interested in; the music types appear in boldface to make them easier to locate. It's also very important to submit only to companies interested in your level of experience (see A Sample Listing Decoded). Publishers placing music in film or TV will be proceded by a ⊛.

Do your research!

It's important to study the market and do research to identify which companies to submit to.

- Many record producers have publishing companies or have joint ventures with major publishers who fund the signing of songwriters and who provide administration services. Since producers have an influence over what is recorded in a session, targeting the producer/publisher can be a useful avenue.
- Since most publishers don't open unsolicited material, try to meet the publishing representative in person (at conferences, speaking engagements, etc.) or try to have an intermediary intercede on your behalf (for example, an entertainment attorney, a manager, an agent, etc.).
- As to demos, submit no more than 3 songs.
- As to publishing deals, copublishing deals (where a writer owns part of the publishing share through his or her own company) are relatively common if the writer has a well-established track record.
- Are you targeting a specific artist to sing your songs? If so, find out if that artist even considers outside material. Get a copy of the artist's latest album, and see who wrote most of the songs. If they were all written by the artist, he's probably not interested in hearing material from outside writers. If the songs were written by a variety of different writers, however, he may be open to hearing new songs.
- Check the album liner notes, which will list the names of the publishers of each writer. These publishers obviously have had luck pitching songs to the artist, and they may be able to get your songs to that artist as well.
- If the artist you're interested in has a recent hit on the *Billboard* charts, the publisher of that song will be listed in the "Hot 100 A-Z" index. Carefully choosing which publishers will work best for the material you write may take time, but it will only increase your chances of getting your songs heard. "Shotgunning" your demo packages (sending out many packages without regard for music preference or submission policy) is a waste of time and money and will hurt, rather than help, your songwriting career.

Once you've found some companies that may be interested in your work, learn what songs have been successfully handled by those publishers. Most publishers are happy to provide you with this information in order to attract high-quality material. As you're researching music publishers, keep in mind how you get along with them personally. If you can't work with a publisher on a personal level, chances are your material won't be represented as you would like it to be. A publisher can become your most valuable connection to all other segments of the music industry, so it's important to find someone you can trust and feel comfortable with.

Independent or major company?

Also consider the size of the publishing company. The publishing affiliates of the major music conglomerates are huge, handling catalogs of thousands of songs by hundreds of songwriters. Unless you are an established songwriter, your songs probably won't receive enough attention from such large companies. Smaller, independent publishers offer several advantages. First, independent music publishers are located all over the country, making it easier for you to work face-to-face rather than by mail or phone. Smaller companies usually aren't affiliated with a particular record company and are therefore able to pitch your songs to many different labels and acts. Independent music publishers are usually interested in a smaller range of music, allowing you to target your submissions more accurately. The most obvious advantage to working with a smaller publisher is the personal attention they can bring to you and your songs. With a smaller roster of artists to work with, the independent music publisher is able to concentrate more time and effort on each particular project.

SUBMITTING MATERIAL TO PUBLISHERS

When submitting material to a publisher, always keep in mind that a professional, courteous manner goes a long way in making a good impression. When you submit a demo through the mail, make sure your package is neat and meets the particular needs of the publisher. Review each publisher's submission policy carefully, and follow it to the letter. Disregarding this information will only make you look like an amateur in the eyes of the company you're submitting to.

Listings of companies in Canada are preceded by a ☺, and international markets are designated with a ☺. You will find an alphabetical list of these companies at the back of the book, along with an index of publishers by state in the Geographic Index.

PUBLISHING CONTRACTS

Once you've located a publisher you like and he's interested in shopping your work, it's time to consider the publishing contract—an agreement in which a songwriter grants certain rights to a publisher for one or more songs. The contract specifies any advances offered to the writer, the rights that will be transferred to the publisher, the royalties a songwriter is to receive, and the length of time the contract is valid.

- When a contract is signed, a publisher will ask for a 50-50 split with the writer. *This is standard industry practice*; the publisher is taking that 50 percent to cover the overhead costs of running his business and for the work he's doing to get your songs recorded.
- It is always a good idea to have a publishing contract (or any music business contract) reviewed by a competent entertainment lawyer.
- There is no "standard" publishing contract, and each company offers different provisions for their writers.

Make sure you ask questions about anything you don't understand, especially if you're new in the business. Songwriter organizations such as the Songwriters Guild of America (SGA) provide contract review services, and can help you learn about music business language and what constitutes a fair music publishing contract. Be sure to read the Contracts section for more information on contracts. See the Organizations section for more information on the SGA and other songwriting groups.

When signing a contract, it's important to be aware of the music industry's unethical practitioners. The "song shark," as he's called, makes his living by asking a songwriter to pay to have a song published. The shark will ask for money to demo a song and promote it to radio stations; he may also ask for more than the standard 50 percent publisher's share or ask you to give up all rights to a song in order to have it published. Although none of these practices is illegal, it's certainly not ethical, and no successful publisher uses these methods. *Songwriter's Market* works to list only honest companies interested in hearing new material. (For more on "song sharks," see the How Do I Avoid the Rip-Offs? section.)

Icons

For more instructional information on the listings in this book, including explanations of the icons, read the article How to Use *Songwriter's Market*.

ⓓ ABEAR PUBLISHING (BMI)/ SONGTOWN PUBLISHING (ASCAP)

Nashville TN. E-mail: ronhebert@gmail.com. **Contact:** Ron Hebert, publisher. Estab. 2000. Pays standard royalty.

HOW TO CONTACT Submit mp3 by e-mail. Unsolicited submissions are OK. Prefers 3 songs with lyric sheets. Responds in 1 week if interested.

MUSIC Mostly **country**, **country/pop**, **pop**, **dance**, and **Christian**.

ⓓ◑ ALL ROCK MUSIC

P.O. Box 1200, 3260 AE Oud Beijerland The Netherlands. (31) 186-604266. E-mail: info@collectorrecords.nl. Website: www.collectorrecords.nl. **Contact:** Cees Klop, president. Music publisher, record company (Collector Records), and record producer. Estab. 1967. Publishes 40 songs/year; publishes several new songwriters/year. Staff size: 3. Pays standard royalty.

> ◐ Also see the listings for Collector Records in the Record Companies and Record Producers sections of this book.

AFFILIATES All Rock Music (United Kingdom).

HOW TO CONTACT Submit demo package by mail. Unsolicited submissions are OK. Prefers cassette. SAE, and IRC. Responds in 2 months.

MUSIC Mostly '50s rock, **rockabilly,** and **country rock**; also **piano boogie woogie**. Published *Rock Crazy Baby* (album), written and recorded by Art Adams (1950s rockabilly), released 2004; *Marvin Jackson* (album), by Marvin Jackson (1950s rockers), released 2005; *Western Australian Snake Pit R&R* (album), recorded by various (1950s rockers), released 2005, all on Collector Records.

TIPS "Send only the kind of material we issue/produce as listed."

ⓓ✹ ALPHA MUSIC INC.

Dept. SM, One International Blvd Suite 212, Mahwah NJ 07495. (201)335-0005. Fax: (201)335-0004. E-mail: info@trfmusic.com. Website: www.trfmusic.com. **Contact:** Michael Nurko. Music publisher. Estab. 1931. Pays standard royalty. Affiliate(s) Dorian Music Publishers, Inc. (ASCAP) and TRF Music Inc.

> ◐ Also see listing for TRF Production Music Libraries in the Advertising, Audiovisual, and Commercial Music Firms section of this book.

HOW TO CONTACT "We accept submissions of new compositions. Submissions are not returnable."

MUSIC All categories, mainly **instrumental** and **acoustic** suitable for use as **production music**, including **theme and background music for television and film**. "Have published over 50,000 titles since 1931."

ⓓ A NEW RAP JAM PUBLISHING

(BMI) P.O. Box 683, Lima OH 45802. E-mail: jamesmilliganjr@yahoo.com. Professional Managers: William Roach (rap, clean); James Milligan (country, 70s music, pop). **Contact:** A&R Dept. Music publisher and record company (New Experience/Faze 4 Records, Pump It Up Records, and Rough Edge Records). Publishes 50-100 songs/year; Grind Blocc Rec Touch Tone Digital International Records publishes 5-10 new songwriters/year. Hires staff songwriters. Staff size: 6. Pays standard royalty.

AFFILIATES Songwriters Party House Publishing (BMI), Creative Star Management, and Rough Edge Records. Distribution through NER/The Orchard/Interscope Digital, and The State51 Conspiracy LTD Distribution United Kingdom, a distribution service.

HOW TO CONTACT *Write first to arrange personal interview or submit demo CD by mail.* Unsolicited submissions are OK. Prefers CD with 3-5 songs and lyric or lead sheet. Include SASE. Responds in 6-8 weeks. "Visit myspace.com/newexperiencerecords2 for more information."

MUSIC Mostly **R&B**, **pop**, **blues,** and **rock/rap** (clean); also **contemporary**, **gospel**, **country,** and **soul**. Published "Lets Go Dancing" (single by Dion Mikel), recorded and released 2006 on Faze 4 Records/New Experience Records; "The Broken Hearted" (single) from *The Final Chapter* (album), recorded by T.M.C. the milligan connection (R&B/gospel); James Jr.; Girl Like You feat. Terry Zapp Troutman, additional appearances by Kurtis Blow, King MC, Sugarfoot Lead Singer (Ohio Players) Lavel Jackson 2009/10 on New Experience/Pump It Up Records. Other artists include singer-songwriter James, Jr. on Faze 4 Records/Rough Edge Records Grind Blocc Records.

TIPS "We are seeking hit artists from the '70s, '80s, and '90s who would like to be signed, as well as new talent and female solo artists. Send any available information supporting the group or act. We are a label that does not promote violence, drugs, or anything that we feel is a bad example for our youth. Establish music industry contacts, write and keep writing, and most of all, believe in yourself. Use a good recording studio, but be very professional. Just take your time and produce the best music possible. Sometimes you only get one chance. Make sure you place your best song on your demo first. This will increase your chances greatly. If you're the owner of your own small label and have a finished product, please send it. And if there is interest, we will contact you. Also be on the lookout for new artists on Rough Edge Records and Touch Tone Digital International Records. Now reviewing blues and soul music. If you have a developing record label and would like distribution, send us your artist listing record label information to be considered, and thank you for considering us for your next project."

⭘ ANTELOPE PUBLISHING INC.

(BMI) P.O. Box 55, Rowayton CT 06853. **Contact:** Tony LaVorgna, owner/president. Music publisher. Estab. 1982. Publishes 5-10 new songs/year; publishes 3-5 new songwriters/year. Pays standard royalty.

HOW TO CONTACT Submit demo by mail. Unsolicited submissions are OK. Prefers cassette with lead sheet. Does not return material. Responds in 1 month "only if interested."

MUSIC Only **bebop** and **1940s swing**. Does not want anything electronic. Published "Somewhere Near" (single by Tony LaVorgna) from *Just for My Friends* (album), recorded by Jeri Brown (easy listening); "Cookie Monster" and "The Lady from Mars" (singles by Tony LaVorgna) from *Just for My Friends* (album), recorded by Tony LaVorgna (jazz/easy listening), released 2007 on Antelope.

TIPS "Put your best song first with a short intro."

⦿ BAITSTRING MUSIC

(ASCAP) 2622 Kirtland Rd., Brewton AL 36426. (251)867-2228. **Contact:** Roy Edwards, president. Music publisher and record company (Bolivia Records). Estab. 1972. Publishes 20 songs/year; publishes 10 new songwriters/year. Hires staff songwriters. Pays standard royalty.

⭘ Also the listings for Cheavroia Music in this section, Bolivia Records in the Record Companies section, and Known Artist Productions in the Record Producers section of this book.

AFFILIATES Cheavoria Music Co. (BMI).

HOW TO CONTACT Submit demo by mail. Unsolicited submissions are OK. Prefers CD with 3 songs and lyric sheet. Does not return material. Responds in 1 month.

MUSIC Mostly **R&B**, **pop,** and **easy listening**; also **country** and **gospel**. Published "Forever and Always," written and recorded by Jim Portwood (pop); and "Make Me Forget" (by Horace Linsley) and "Never Let Me Go" (by Cheavoria Edwards), both recorded by Bobbie Roberson (country), all on Bolivia Records.

TIPS "We need some good gospel."

⭘ BARKIN' FOE THE MASTER'S BONE

405 Broadway St. Suite 900, Cincinnati OH 45202-3329. (513)546-2537 (cell). E-mail: autoredcurtis@aol.com. Company owner (rock, R&B): Kevin Curtis. Professional managers: Shonda Barr (country, jazz, pop, rap, gospel, soul, soft rock). Music publisher. Estab. 1989. Publishes 4 songs/year; publishes 1 new songwriter/year. Staff size: 4. Pays standard royalty.

AFFILIATES Beat Box Music (ASCAP) and Feltstar (BMI).

HOW TO CONTACT Submit demo by mail. Unsolicited submissions are OK. Prefers CD (or VHS videocassette) with 3 songs. Include SASE. Responds in 2 weeks.

MUSIC Mostly **top 40** and **pop**; also **soul**, **gospel,** **rap,** and **jazz**. Does not want classical. Published "Lover, Lover" (single by J Tea/Jay B./Skylar) from *The Time Has Come* (album), recorded by J-Trey (rap), released 2003 on East Side Records; "Been A Long Time" (single by J Tea/Jay B./Skylar), from *The Time Has Come* (album), recorded by J-Trey (rap), released 2003 on East Side Records; "No Worries" (single by Mejestic/7-Starr/D-Smooy/Hardhead), from *Home Grown* (album), recorded by Low Down Boyz (rap), released 2002 on Untamed Records.

⦾ BEARSONGS

(PRS)Box 944, Edgbaston, Birmingham B16 8UT United Kingdom. 44-121-454-7020. E-mail: agency@bigbearmusic.com. Website: www.bigbearmusic.com. Managing director: Jim Simpson. Professional manager: Russell Fletcher. Music publisher and record company (Big Bear Records). Member PRS, MCPS. Publishes 25 songs/year; publishes 15-20 new songwriters/year. Pays standard royalty.

○ Also see the listings for Big Bear Records in the Record Companies section and Big Bear in the Record Producers section of this book.

HOW TO CONTACT Submit demo by mail. Unsolicited submissions are OK. Prefers CD. Does not return material. Responds in 3 months.

MUSIC Mostly **blues**, **swing**, and **jazz**. Published *Blowing with Bruce* and *Cool Heights* (by Alan Barnes), recorded by Bruce Adams/Alan Barnes Quintet; and *Blues for My Baby* (by Charles Brown), recorded by King Pleasure & The Biscuit Boys, all on Big Bear Records.

TIPS "Have a real interest in jazz, blues, swing."

BIG FISH MUSIC PUBLISHING GROUP

12720 Burbank Blvd., Suite 124, Valley Village, CA, 91607. (818) 508-9777. Email: clisag21@yahoo.com. Estab. 1971. President, CEO and music publisher: Chuck Tennin. Producer: Gary Black (country, pop, adult contemporary, rock, crossover songs, other styles). Professional music manager: Lora Sprague (jazz, New Age, instrumental, pop rock, R&B). Professional music manager: B.J. (pop, TV, film, and special projects). Professional music and vocal consultant: Zell Black (country, pop, gospel, rock, blues). Producer, Independent Artists: Darryl Harrelson—Major Label Entertainment (country, pop and other genres). Nashville music associate: Ron Hebert (Abear/Songtown Publishing). Songwriter/consultant: Jerry Zanandrea (Z Best Muzic). Staff songwriters: BillyO'Hara, Joe Rull, Lisa Faye. Music publisher, record company (California Sun Records) and production company. Publishes 10-20 songs/year; publishes 5-10 new songwriters/year. Staff size: 10. Pays standard royalty. "We also license songs and music copyrights to users of music, especially TV and film, commercials, and recording projects." Member: BMI, ASCAP, CMA and ACM.

AFFILIATES Big Fish Music (BMI) and California Sun Music (ASCAP).

HOW TO CONTACT *Write first and obtain permission to submit.* Include SASE for reply. "**Please do not call** or e-mail submissions. After permission to submit is confirmed, we will assign and forward to you a submission code number allowing you to submit up to 4 songs maximum, preferably on CD. Include a properly addressed cover letter, signed and dated, with your source of referral (*Songwriter's Market*)

with your assigned submission code number and an SASE for reply and/or return of material. Include lyrics. *Unsolicited material will not be accepted.* This is our submission policy to review outside and new material." Responds in 2 weeks.

FILM & TV Places 6 songs on TV/year. Recently published "Even the Angels Knew" (by Cathy Carlson/Craig Lackey/Marty Axelrod); "Stop before We Start" (by J.D. Grieco); "Oh Santa" (by Christine Bridges/John Deaver), all recorded by the Black River Girls in *Passions* (NBC); licensed "A Christmas Wish" (by Ed Fry/Eddie Max), used in *Passions* (NBC); "Girls Will Be Girls" (by Cathy Carlson/John LeGrande), recorded by the Black River Girls, used in *All My Children* (ABC); "The Way You're Drivin' Me" and "Ain't No Love 'Round Here" (by Jerry Zanandrea), both recorded by the Black River Girls, used in *Passions* (NBC); "Since You Stole My Heart" (by Rick Colmbra/Jamey Whiting), used in *Passions* (NBC); "Good Time to Fly," "All I Need Is a Highway," and "Eyes of the Children" (by Wendy Martin), used in *Passions* (NBC); "It's an Almost Perfect Christmas" (by Michael Martin), used in *Passions* (NBC).

MUSIC Country, including **country pop, country A/C,** and **country crossover** with "a cutting edge"; also **pop, rock, pop ballads, adult contemporary, uplifting, praise, worship, spiritual**, and **inspirational adult contemporary gospel** "with a powerful message," **instrumental background and theme music** for TV, film, and commercials, **New Age/instrumental jazz** and **novelty, orchestral classical, R&B,** and **children's music,** for all kinds of commercial use. Published "If Wishes Were Horses" (single by Billy O'Hara); "Purple Bunny Honey" (single by Robert Lloyd/Jim Love); "Leavin' You for Me" (single by J.D. Grieco).

TIPS "Demo should be professional, high quality, clean, simple, dynamic, and must get the song across on the first listen. Good, clear vocals, a nice melody, a good musical feel, good musical arrangement, strong lyrics and chorus—a unique, catchy, clever song that sticks with you. Looking for unique country and pop songs with a different edge that can cross over to the mainstream market for ongoing Nashville music projects and songs for hot female country acts that can cross over to adult contemporary and pop with great lush harmonies. Also, catchy, up-tempo songs with an attitude and a groove, preferably rock, that can be marketed to today's youth."

⊘⊛ BIXIO MUSIC GROUP & ASSOCIATES/IDM MUSIC

(ASCAP) 111 E. 14th St., Suite 140, New York NY 10003. (212)695-3911. E-mail: info@bixio.com. Website: www.bixio.com and www.idmmusic.com. Administrator: Miriam Westercappel (all styles). A&R director, office manager: Courtney Stack-Slutsky. Administrative assistant: Karlene Evans (soundtracks). Creative director: Robert Draghi (all styles). Senior creative director/Producer: Tomo. A&R: Claudene Neysmith (world/New Age). Music publisher, record company, and rights clearances. Estab. 1985. Publishes a few hundred songs/year; publishes 2 new songwriters/year. Staff size: 6. Pays standard royalty.
HOW TO CONTACT *Does not accept unsolicited material.*
MUSIC Mostly **soundtracks**. Published "La Strada Nel Bosco," included in the TV show *Ed* (NBC); "La Beguine Du Mac," included in the TV show *The Chris Isaac Show* (Showtime); and "Alfonsina Delle Camelie," included in the TV show *UC: Undercover* (NBC).

ⓞ BOUQUET-ORCHID PUBLISHING

Bouquet-Orchid Enterprises, P.O. Box 1335, Norcross GA 30091. Phone/fax: (770)339-9088. **Contact:** Bill Bohannon, president. Music publisher, record company, record producer (Bouquet-Orchid Enterprises) and artist management. Member: CMA, AFM. Publishes 10-12 songs/year; publishes 3 new songwriters/year. Pays standard royalty.
HOW TO CONTACT Submit demo by mail. Unsolicited submissions are OK. Prefers cassette or CD with 3-5 songs and lyric sheet. "Send biographical information if possible—even a photo helps." Include SASE. Responds in 1 month.
MUSIC Mostly **religious** ("Amy Grant, etc., contemporary gospel"); **country** ("Garth Brooks, Trisha Yearwood–type material"); and **top 100/pop** ("Bryan Adams, Whitney Houston–type material"). Published "Blue as Your Eyes" (single), written and recorded by Adam Day; "Spare My Feelings" (single by Clayton Russ), recorded by Terri Palmer; and "Trying to Get By" (single by Tom Sparks), recorded by Bandoleers, all on Bouquet Records.

⊘ BOURNE CO. MUSIC PUBLISHERS

5 W. 37th St., New York NY 10018. (212)391-4300. Fax: (212)391-4306. E-mail: bourne@bournemusic.com. Website: www.bournemusic.com. **Contact:** Professional Manager. Music publisher. Estab. 1919. Publishes educational material and popular music.
AFFILIATES ABC Music, Ben Bloom, Better Half, Bogat, Burke & Van Heusen, Goldmine, Harborn, Lady Mac and Murbo Music.
HOW TO CONTACT *Does not accept unsolicited submissions.*
MUSIC Piano/vocal, band pieces, and **choral pieces**. Published "Amen" and "Mary's Little Boy Child" (singles by Hairston); "When You Wish upon a Star" (single by Washington/Harline); and "San Antonio Rose" (single by Bob Willis, arranged John Cacavas).

⊙ BRANDON HILLS MUSIC, LLC (BMI)

N. 3425 Searle County Line Rd., Brandon WI 53919. (920)398-3279 or (920)570-1076. E-mail: martab@centurytel.net. www.brandonhillsmusic.com. **Contact:** Marsha Brown, president. Music publishers. Estab. 2005. Publishes 4 new songwriters/year. Staff size: 2. Pays standard royalty of 50%.
HOW TO CONTACT Submit demo package by mail. Unsolicited submissions are OK. Prefers CD with 1-4 songs and cover letter. Does not return submissions. Responds only if interested.
MUSIC Mostly **country (traditional, modern, country rock)**, **contemporary Christian, blues**; also **children's** and **bluegrass** and **rap**. Published "Let It Rain," recorded by Steff Nevers, written by Larry Migliore and Kevin Gallarello (Universal Records, Norway); "Do You Like My Body," recorded by Ginger-Ly, written by Nisa McCall (SEI Corp and Big Daddy G Music, CA); "Did I Ever Thank You Lord," recorded by Jacob Garcia, written by Eletta Sias (TRW Records); "Honky Tonk in Heaven," recorded by Buddy Lewis, written by Mike Heath and Bob Alexander (Ozark Records).
TIPS "We prefer studio-produced CDs. The lyrics and the CD must match. Cover letter, lyrics, and CD should have a professional look. Demos should have vocals up front, and every word should be distinguishable. Please make sure your lyrics match your song. Submit only your best. The better the demo, the better the chance of getting your music published and recorded."

⊘ BUG MUSIC, INC.

7750 Sunset Blvd., Los Angeles CA 90046. (323)969-0988. Fax: (323)969-0968. E-mail: buginfo@bugmusic.com. Website: www.bugmusic.com. Senior vice president of creative: Eddie Gomez. Creative manager: Mara Schwartz. Creative coordinator: Laura Scott. **Nashville:** 33 Music Square W Suite 104B, Nashville TN 37203. (615)313-7676. Fax: (615)313-7670. Director of creative services: Ed Williams; creative manager: Tyler Pickens. **New York:** 347 W. 36th St., Suite 1203, New York NY 10018. (212)643-0925. Fax: (212)643-0897. Senior vice president: Garry Valletri. Music publisher. Estab. 1975. "We handle administration."

AFFILIATES Bughouse (ASCAP).

HOW TO CONTACT *Does not accept unsolicited submissions.*

MUSIC All genres. Published "You Were Mine" (by E. Erwin/M. Seidel), recorded by Dixie Chicks on Monument.

○ CALIFORNIA COUNTRY MUSIC

(BMI)112 Widmar Pl., Clayton CA 94517. (925)833-4680. **Contact:** Edgar J. Brincat, owner. Music publisher and record company (Roll On Records). Estab. 1985. Staff size: 1. Pays standard royalty. Affiliate(s) Sweet Inspirations Music (ASCAP).

🔾 Also see the listing for Roll On Records in the Record Companies section of this book.

HOW TO CONTACT Submit demo by mail. Unsolicited submissions are OK. "Do not call or write. Any calls will be returned collect to caller." Send CD with 3 songs and lyric sheet. Include SASE. Responds in 6 weeks.

MUSIC Mostly **MOR**, **contemporary country,** and **pop**. Does not want rap, metal, or rock. Published *For Realities Sake* (album by F.L. Pittman/R. Barretta) and *Maddy* (album by F.L. Pittman/M. Weeks), both recorded by Ron Banks & L.J. Reynolds on Life & Bellmark Records; and *Quarter Past Love* (album by Irwin Rubinsky/Janet Fisher), recorded by Darcy Dawson on NNP Records.

○⊕ CHRISTMAS & HOLIDAY MUSIC

26642 Via Noveno, Mission Viejo CA 92691. (949)859-1615. E-mail: justinwilde@christmassongs.com. Website: www.christmassongs.com. **Contact:** Justin Wilde, president. Music publisher. Estab. 1980. Publishes 8-12 songs/year; publishes 8-12 new songwriters/year. Staff size: 1. "All submissions must be complete songs (i.e., music and lyrics)." Pays standard royalty.

AFFILIATES Songcastle Music (ASCAP).

HOW TO CONTACT Submit demo CD by mail. Unsolicited submissions are OK. *Do not call. Do not send unsolicited mp3s or links to websites.* See website for submission guidelines. "First Class Mail only. Registered or certified mail not accepted." Prefers CD with no more than 3 songs with lyric sheets. Do not send lead sheets or promotional material, bios, etc." Include SASE but does not return material out of the US. Responds only if interested.

FILM & TV Places 10-15 songs in TV/year. Published Barbara Streisand's "It Must Have Been the Mistletoe."

MUSIC Strictly **Christmas**, **Halloween**, **Hanukkah**, **Mother's Day**, **Thanksgiving**, **Father's Day,** and **New Year's Eve music** in every style imaginable: easy listening, rock, pop, blues, jazz, country, reggae, rap, children's secular, or religious. *Please do not send anything that isn't a holiday song.* Published "It Must Have Been the Mistletoe" (single by Justin Wilde/Doug Konecky) from *Christmas Memories* (album), recorded by Barbra Streisand (pop Christmas), by Columbia; "What Made the Baby Cry?" (single by Toby Keith) and "Mr. Santa Claus" (single by James Golseth) from *Casper's Haunted Christmas* soundtrack (album), recorded by Scotty Blevins (Christmas) on Koch International.

TIPS "We only sign one out of every 200 submissions. Please be selective. If a stranger can hum your melody back to you after hearing it twice, it has 'standard' potential. Couple that with a lyric filled with unique, inventive imagery, that stands on its own, even without music. Combine the two elements, and workshop the finished result thoroughly to identify weak points. Submit to us only when the song is polished to perfection. Submit positive lyrics only. Avoid negative themes like 'Blue Christmas.'"

⊘ CHRYSALIS MUSIC GROUP

(ASCAP, BMI) 8447 Wilshire Boulevard, Suite 400, Beverly Hills CA 90211. (323)658-9125. Fax: (323)658-8019. Website: http://chrysalismusicusa.com. **Contact:** David Stamm, vice president of A&R. Music publisher. Estab. 1968.

HOW TO CONTACT *Chrysalis Music does not accept any unsolicited submissions.*

MUSIC Published "Sum 41" (single), written and recorded by OutKast; "Light Ladder" (single), written and recorded by David Gray. Administer, David Lee Roth, Andrea Boccelli, Velvet Revolver, and Johnta Austin.

◐ COME ALIVE COMMUNICATIONS, INC. (ASCAP)

348 Valley Rd., Suite A, P.O. Box 436, West Grove PA 19390-0436. (610)869-3660. Fax: (610)869-3660. E-mail: info@comealivemusic.com. Website: www.comealiveusa.com. Professional managers: Joseph L. Hooker (pop, rock, jazz); Bridget G. Hylak (spiritual, country, classical). Music publisher, record producer, and record company. Estab. 1985. Publishes 4 singles/year. Staff: 7. Pays standard royalty of 50%.

○ Come Alive Communications received a IHS Ministries Award in 1996, John Lennon Songwriting Contest winner, 2003.

HOW TO CONTACT *Call first to obtain permission to submit a demo.* For song publishing submissions, prefers CD with 3 songs, lyric sheet, and cover letter. Does not return submissions. Responds only if interested.

MUSIC Mostly **pop**, **easy listening**, **contemporary Christian**, and **patriotic**; also **country** and **spiritual**. Does not want obscene, suggestive, violent, or morally offensive lyrics. Produced "In Search of America" (single) from *Long Road to Freedom* (album), written and recorded by J. Hooker (patriotic), released 2003 on ComeAliveMusic.com; "Our Priests/Nuestros Sacerdotes," named CMN's official theme song for the Vatican Designated Year of the Priest (2009-10). See www.ourpriests.com.

⊘ COPPERFIELD MUSIC GROUP/PENNY ANNIE MUSIC (BMI)/TOP BRASS MUSIC (ASCAP)/BIDDY BABY MUSIC (SESAC)

1400 South St., Nashville TN 37212. (615)726-3100. E-mail: ken@copperfieldmusic.com. Website: www.copperfieldmusic.com **Contact**: Ken Biddy, president/CEO.

HOW TO CONTACT Contact first and obtain permission to submit a demo by e-mail only. Does not return submissions or accept phone calls. Responds only if interested.

MUSIC Mostly **country**; also **modern bluegrass**. Does not want rap or heavy/metal/rock. Recently published "Daddy Won't Sell the Farm" from *Tat-

toos and Scars (album), recorded by Montgomery Gentry (country).

○ CORELLI MUSIC GROUP

(BMI/ASCAP) P.O. Box 2314, Tacoma WA 98401-2314. (253)273-6205. E-mail: JerryCorelli@yahoo.com. Website: www.CorelliMusicGroup.com. **Contact:** Jerry Corelli, owner. Music publisher, record company (Omega III Records), record producer (Jerry Corelli/Angels Dance Recording Studio), and booking agency (Tone Deaf Booking). Estab. 1996. Publishes 12 songs/year; publishes 6 new songwriters/year. Staff size: 3. Pays standard royalty.

AFFILIATES My Angel's Songs (ASCAP); Corelli's Music Box (BMI).

HOW TO CONTACT Submit demo by mail. Unsolicited submissions are OK. "No phone calls, e-mails, or letters asking to submit." CD only with no more than 3 songs, lyric sheet and cover letter. *"We DO NOT accept mp3s vie e-mail.* We want love songs with a message and overtly Christian songs. Make sure all material is copyrighted. *You MUST include SASE or we DO NOT respond!"* Responds in 2 months

MUSIC Mostly **contemporary Christian**, **Christian soft rock,** and **Christmas**; also **love songs**, **ballads,** and **new country**. Does not want songs without lyrics or lyrics without music. Published "I'm Not Dead Yet" (by Jerry Corelli), "Fried Bologna" (by Jerry Corelli), and "His Name Is Jesus" (by Jerry Corelli), all from *I'm Not Dead Yet* (album), released 2010 on Omega III Records.

TIPS "Success is obtained when opportunity meets preparation! If a SASE is not sent with demo, we don't even listen to the demo. Be willing to do a rewrite. Don't send material expecting us to place it with a Top Ten artist. Be practical. Do your songs say what's always been said, except differently? Don't take rejection personally. Always send a #10 self-adhesive envelope for your SASE."

◐ THE CORNELIUS COMPANIES/ GATEWAY ENTERTAINMENT, INC.

(BMI, ASCAP, SESAC) Dept. SM, 9 Music Square South, Suite 92, Nashville TN 37203. (615)321-5333. E-mail: corneliuscompanies@bellsouth.net. Website: www.corneliuscompanies.com. **Contact:** Ron Cornelius, owner/president. Music publisher and record producer (Ron Cornelius). Estab. 1986. Publishes 60-80 songs/year; publishes 2-3 new songwriters/year. Occasionally hires staff writers. Pays standard royalty.

AFFILIATES RobinSparrow Music (BMI), Strummin' Bird Music (ASCAP) and Bridgeway Music (SESAC).

HOW TO CONTACT *Contact by e-mail or call for permission to submit material.* Submit demo package by mail. Unsolicited submissions are OK. "Send demo on CD format only with 2-3 songs." Include SASE. Responds in 2 months.

MUSIC Mostly **country** and **pop**; also **positive country**, **gospel,** and **alternative**. Published songs by Confederate Railroad, Faith Hill, David Allen Coe, Alabama, and over 50 radio singles in the positive Christian/country format.

TIPS "Looking for material suitable for film."

◕ CRINGE MUSIC (PRS, MCPS)

The Cedars, Elvington Lane, Hawkinge, Kent CT18 7AD United Kingdom. (01)(303)893-472. Fax: (01)(303)893-833. E-mail: info@cringemusic.co.uk. Website: www.cringemusic.co.uk. **Contact:** Christopher Ashman. Music publisher and record company (Red Admiral Records). Estab. 1979. Staff size: 2.

HOW TO CONTACT Submit demo package by mail. Unsolicited submissions are OK. CD only with unlimited number of songs and lyric sheet, lead sheet. Submission materials are not returned. Responds if interested.

MUSIC All styles.

◑ THE CROSSWIND CORPORATION

PO Box 120816, Nashville TN 37212. (615)467-3860. Fax: (615)467-3859. E-mail: tdchoate@aol.com. Website: http://crosswindcorporation.com. **Contact:** Terry Choate.

⊘ CURB MUSIC

(ASCAP, BMI, SESAC) 48 Music Square East, Nashville TN 37203. Website: www.curb.com.

> ◗ *Curb Music only accepts submissions through reputable industry sources and does not accept unsolicited demos.*

AFFILIATES Mike Curb Music (BMI); Curb Songs (ASCAP); and Curb Congregation Songs (SESAC).

● JOF DAVE MUSIC

1055 Kimball Ave., Kansas City KS 66104. (913)593-3180. **Contact:** David Johnson, CEO. Music publisher, record company (Cymbal Records). Estab. 1984. Pub-

lishes 30 songs/year; publishes 12 new songwriters/year. Pays standard royalty.

HOW TO CONTACT *Contact first and obtain permission to submit.* Prefers CD. Include SASE. Responds in 1 month.

MUSIC Mostly **gospel** and **R&B**. Published "The Woman I Love" (single) from *Sugar Bowl* (album), written and recorded by King Alex, released 2001 on Cymbal Records; and "Booty Clap" (single by Johnny Jones) from *Gotta Move On* (album), recorded by Jacuzé, released 2005 on Cymbal Records.

DEFINE SOMETHING IN NOTHING MUSIC

(ASCAP) 11213 W. Baden Street, Avondale AZ 85323. (360)421-9225. E-mail: definesinm@gmail.com. **Contact**: Jaime Reynolds, president. Estab. 2008. Music agency. Staff Size: 5. Pays 75% of gross revenue.

HOW TO CONTACT Prefers MP3s sent to e-mail only. "Please do not contact for permission, just send your music." Does not return submissions. Responds in 2 weeks if interested.

MUSIC Interested in all styles. "We welcome everything all over the world."

TIPS "Please e-mail a zip file via yousendit.com. No phone calls or mail, no CDs or cassettes."

⊘ DELEV MUSIC COMPANY

(ASCAP, BMI)7231 Mansfield Ave., Philadelphia PA 19138-1620. (215)276-8861. Fax: (215)276-4509. E-mail: delevmusic@msn.com. President/CEO: William L. Lucas. A&R: Darryl Lucas. Music publisher. Publishes 6-10 songs/year; publishes 6-10 new songwriters/year. Pays standard royalty.

AFFILIATES Sign of the Ram Music (ASCAP) and Delev Music (BMI).

HOW TO CONTACT *Does not accept unsolicited material. Write or call first to obtain permission to submit.* Prefers CD format only—no cassettes—with 1-4 songs and lyric sheet. "We will not accept certified mail or SASE." Does not return material. Responds in 1-2 months.

MUSIC Mostly **R&B ballads** and **dance oriented**; also **pop ballads**, **Christian/gospel**, **crossover** and **country/western**. We do not accept rap song material. Published "Angel Love" (single by Barbara Heston/Geraldine Fernandez) from *The Silky Sounds of Debbie G* (album), recorded by Debbie G (light R&B/easy listening), released 2000 on Blizzard Records; *Variety* (album), produced by Barbara Heston, released on Luvya Records; and "Ever Again" by Bernie Williams, released 2003 on Sun-Dazed Records.

TIPS "Persevere regardless if it is sent to our company or any other company. Most of all, no matter what happens, believe in yourself."

◑⊛ THE EDWARD DE MILES MUSIC COMPANY

(BMI)10573 W. Pico Blvd., #352, Los Angeles CA 90064-2348. Phone: (310)948-9652. E-mail: info@edmsahara.com. Website: www.edmsahara.com. **Contact:** Professional Manager. Music publisher, record company (Sahara Records), record producer, management, bookings and promotions. Estab. 1984. Publishes 50-75 songs/year; publishes 5 new songwriters/year. Hires staff songwriters. Pays standard royalty.

> ◯ Also see the listings for Edward De Miles in the Record Producers and Managers & Booking Agents sections, and Sahara Records and Filmworks Entertainment in the Record Companies section of this book.

HOW TO CONTACT *Write first and obtain permission to submit.* Prefers CD with 1-3 songs and lyric sheet. Does not return material. Reponds in 1 month.

MUSIC Mostly **top 40 pop/rock, R&B/dance,** and **country**; also **musical scores for TV, radio, films,** and **jingles**. Published "Dance wit Me" and "Moments" (singles), written and recorded by Steve Lynn; "Games" (single), written and recorded by D'von Edwards (jazz), all on Sahara Records. Other artists include Multiple Choice.

TIPS "Copyright all materials before submitting. Equipment and showmanship a must."

⊘ DISNEY MUSIC PUBLISHING

(ASCAP, BMI)500 S. Buena Vista St., Burbank CA 91521-6182. (818)569-3241. Fax: (818)845-9705. Website: home.disney.go.com/music/. Affiliate(s) Seven Peaks Music and Seven Summits Music.

> ◯ part of the Buena Vista Music Group.

HOW TO CONTACT *"We cannot accept any unsolicited material."*

● DUANE MUSIC, INC.

382 Clarence Ave., Sunnyvale CA 94086. (408)739-6133. **Contact:** Garrie Thompson, President. Music

publisher and record producer. Publishes 10-20 songs/year; publishes 1 new songwriter/year. Pays standard royalty.

AFFILIATES Morhits Publishing (BMI).

HOW TO CONTACT Submit demo by mail. Unsolicited submissions are OK. Prefers CD with 1-2 songs. Include SASE. Responds in 2 months.

MUSIC Mostly **blues**, **country**, **disco**, and **easy listening**; also **rock**, **soul** and **top 40/pop**. Published "Little Girl" (single), recorded by the Syndicate of Sound & Ban (rock); "Warm Tender Love" (single), recorded by Percy Sledge (soul); and "My Adorable One" (single), recorded by Joe Simon (blues).

DUNSDON MUSIC PUBLISHING

Estab. 2006. E-mail: info@dunsdonmusic.com. Website: www.dunsdonmusic.com. **Contact:** Ian Dunsdon. Estab. 2006. Published 3 songs in the last year; published 2 new songwriters in the last year. Staff size: 2. Hires staff writers. Pays standard royalty of 50%.

AFFILIATES Newave Music Publishing (BMI).

HOW TO CONTACT Contact first and obtain permission to submit a demo. Include CD or e-mail a download link, lyric sheet, and cover letter. Does not return submissions. Responds only if interested.

FILM & TV Placed 3 songs in film/year. Recently published "Pennyless," "Already Know by Now," and "Coming Down" by Mark Mullane, recorded by the Misery Loves, in *Jumping Up and Down* (film) (Pragma Records).

MUSIC Mostly **rock/pop, hip hop**, and **dance**; also **country** and **alternative**.

◑ EARTHSCREAM MUSIC PUBLISHING CO.

(BMI) 8375 Westview Dr., Houston TX 77055. (713)464-GOLD. E-mail: jeffwells@soundartsrecording.com. Website: www.soundartsrecording.com. **Contact:** Jeff Wells; Brian Baker, Nick Cooper. Music publisher, record company, and record producer. Estab. 1975. Publishes 12 songs/year; publishes 4 new songwriters/year. Pays standard royalty.

> ◯ Also see the listing for Sound Arts Recording Studio in the Record Producers section of this book.

AFFILIATES Reach for the Sky Music Publishing (ASCAP).

HOW TO CONTACT Submit demo by mail. Unsolicited submissions are OK. Prefers CD or videocassette with 2-5 songs and lyric sheet. Does not return material. Responds in 6 weeks.

MUSIC Mostly **new rock**, **country**, **blues**. Published "Baby Never Cries" (single by Carlos DeLeon), recorded by Jinkies on Surface Records (pop); "Telephone Road" (single), written and recorded by Mark May(blues) on Icehouse Records; "Do You Remember" (single by Barbara Pennington), recorded by Perfect Strangers on Earth Records (rock), and "Sheryl Crow" (single), recorded by Dr. Jeff and the Painkillers (pop); "Going Backwards" (single), written and recorded by Tony Vega (Gulf Swamp Blues), released on Red Onion Records.

◐ ELECTRIC MULE PUBLISHING COMPANY (BMI)/NEON MULE MUSIC (ASCAP)

1019 17th Ave. S, Nashville TN 37212. (615)321-4455. E-mail: emuleme@aol.com. **Contact:** Jeff Moseley, President.

MUSIC Country, pop.

◐ EMF PRODUCTIONS

(ASCAP) 1000 E. Prien Lake Rd., Suite D, Lake Charles LA 70601. Website: www.emfproductions. com. President: Ed Fruge. Music publisher and record producer. Estab. 1984. Pays standard royalty.

HOW TO CONTACT Submit demo package by mail. Unsolicited submissions are OK. Prefers CD or DVDs with 3 of your best songs and lyric sheets. Does not return material. Responds in 6 weeks.

MUSIC Mostly **R&B**, **pop** and **rock**; also **country** and **gospel**.

⊘ EMI CHRISTIAN MUSIC PUBLISHING

(ASCAP, BMI, SESAC) P.O. Box 5084, Brentwood TN 37024. (615)371-4300. Website: www.EMICMGPublishing.com. Music publisher. Publishes more than 100 songs/year. Represents more than 35,000 songs and over 300 writers. Hires staff songwriters. Pays standard royalty.

AFFILIATES Birdwing Music (ASCAP), Sparrow Song (BMI), His Eye Music (SESAC), Ariose Music (ASCAP), Straightway Music (ASCAP), Shepherd's Fold Music (BMI), Songs of Promise (SESAC), Dawn Treader Music (SESAC), Meadowgreen Music Company (ASCAP), River Oaks Music Company (BMI), Stonebrook Music Company (SESAC), Bud John Songs, Inc. (ASCAP), Bud John Music, Inc. (BMI), Bud John Tunes, Inc. (SESAC), WorshipTogether Songs, ThankYou Music, Thirst Moon River.

HOW TO CONTACT *"We do not accept unsolicited submissions."*

MUSIC Published Chris Tomlin, Toby Mac, David Crowder, Jeremy Camp, Stephen Curtis Chapman, Delirious, Tim Hughes, Matt Redman, Demon Hunter, Underoath, Switchfoot, Third Day, Casting Crowns, and many others.

TIPS "Do what you do with passion and excellence and success will follow; just be open to new and potentially more satisfying definitions of what 'success' means."

⊘ EMI MUSIC PUBLISHING

75 Ninth Ave., 4th Floor, New York NY 10011. (212)492-1200. Fax: (212)492-1865. Also 2700 Colorado Ave., Suite 450, Santa Monica CA 90404; (310)586-2700. Fax: (310)586-2758. Also 404 Washington Ave., Miami Beach FL 33139. (305)695-6400. Fax: (305)695-6440. Also 35 Music Square E, Nashville TN 37203. (615)457-6900. Website: www.emimusicpub.com. Music publisher.

HOW TO CONTACT *EMI does not accept unsolicited material.*

MUSIC Published "All Night Long" (by F. Evans/R. Lawrence/S. Combs), recorded by Faith Evans featuring Puff Daddy on Bad Boy; "You" (by C. Roland/ J. Powell), recorded by Jesse Powell on Silas; and "I Was" (by C. Black/P. Vassar), recorded by Neal McCoy on Atlantic.

TIPS "Don't bury your songs. Less is more—we will ask for more if we need it. Put your strongest song first."

◐ EMSTONE MUSIC PUBLISHING

(BMI)Box 398, Hallandale FL 33008. E-mail: webmaster@emstonemusicpublishing.com. Website: www. emstonemusicpublishing.com. **Contact:** Mitchell Stone. Vice President: Madeline Stone. Music publisher. Estab. 1997. Pays standard royalty.

HOW TO CONTACT Submit demo CD by mail with any number of songs. Unsolicited submissions are OK. Does not return material. Responds only if interested. "Also check our sister company at SongwritersBestSong.com."

MUSIC All types. Published *Greetings from Texas* (2009) (album), by Greetings from Texas; "Gonna Recall My Heart" (written by Dan Jury) from *No Tears* (album), recorded by Cole Seaver and Tammie

Darlene, released on CountryStock Records; and "I Love What I've Got" (single by Heather and Paul Turner) from *The Best of Talented Kids* (compilation album) recorded by Gypsy; "My Christmas Card to You" (words and music by Madeline and Mitchell Stone); and "Your Turn to Shine" (words and music by Mitchell Stone).

TIPS "Keep the materials inside your demo package as simple as possible. Just include a brief cover letter (with your contact information) and lyric sheets. Avoid written explanations of the songs; if your music is great, it'll speak for itself. We only offer publishing contracts to writers whose songs exhibit a spark of genius. Anything less can't compete in the music industry."

FATT CHANTZ MUSIC

(BMI) 2535 Winthrope Way, Lawrenceville GA 30044. Estab. 2009. (770)982-7055. Website: www.jeromepromotions.com. Contact: Bill Jerome, president and CEO. Music Publisher. Estab. 2009. Staff size: 3. Pays standard royalty of 50%.

HOW TO CONTACT Contact first and obtain permission to submit a demo. Include CD or mp3 and cover letter. Does not return submissions. Responds in 1 week.

MUSIC Top 40, alt country. Also **alternative**, crossover **R&B,** and **hip-hop**. Does not want rap, gospel, country. Published "She's My Girl," written by Lefkowith/Rogers, recorded by Hifi on Red/Generic (2009).

●◐⊛ FIRST TIME MUSIC (PUBLISHING) U.K.

Sovereign House, 12 Trewartha Rd., Praa Sands, Penzance, Cornwall TR20 9ST United Kingdom. +44(01736)762826. Fax: +44(01736)763328. E-mail: panamus@aol.com. Website: www.panamamusic.co/uk. **Contact:** Roderick G. Jones, CEO. Music publisher, record company (Digimix Records Ltd www.digimaxrecords.com, Rainy Day Records, Mohock Records, Pure Gold Records). Estab. 1986. Publishes 500-750 songs/year; 20-50 new songwriters/year. Staff size: 6. Hires staff writers. Pays standard royalty; "50-60% to established and up-and-coming writers with the right attitude."

AFFILIATES Scamp Music Publishing, Panama Music Library, Musik Image Library, Caribbean Music Library, PSI Music Library, ADN Creation Music Library, Promo Sonor International, Eventide Music, Melody First Music Library, Piano Bar Music Library, Corelia Music Library, Panama Music Ltd, Panama Music Productions, Digimix Worldwide Digital Distribution Services.

HOW TO CONTACT Submit demo package by mail. Unsolicited submissions are OK. Submit on CD only, "of professional quality" with unlimited number of songs/instrumentals and lyric or lead sheets. Responds in 1 month. SAE and IRC required for reply.

FILM & TV Places 200 songs in film and TV/year. "Copyrights and phonographic rights of Panama Music Limited and its associated catalogue idents have been used and subsist in many productions broadcasts and adverts produced by major and independent production companies, television, film/video companies, radio broadcasters (not just in the UK, but in various countries worldwide) and by commercial record companies for general release and sale. In the UK & Republic of Ireland they include the BBC networks of national/regional television and radio, ITV network programs and promotions (Channel 4, Border TV, Granada TV, Tyne Tees TV, Scottish TV, Yorkshire TV, HTV, Central TV, Channel TV, LWT, Meridian TV, Grampian TV, GMTV, Ulster TV, Westcountry TV, Channel TV, Carlton TV, Anglia TV, TV3, RTE (Ireland), Planet TV, Rapido TV, VT4 TV, BBC Worldwide, etc.), independent radio stations, satellite Sky Television (BskyB), Discovery Channel, Learning Channel, National Geographic, Living Channel, Sony, Trouble TV, UK Style Channel, Hon Cyf, CSI, etc., and cable companies, GWR Creative, Premier, Spectrum FM, Local Radio Partnership, Fox, Manx, Swansea Sound, Mercury, 2CRFM, Broadland, BBC Radio Collection, etc. Some credits include copyrights in programs, films/videos, broadcasts, trailers and promotions such as *Desmond's, One Foot in the Grave, EastEnders, Hale and Pace, Holidays from Hell, A Touch of Frost, 999 International,* and *Get Away.*"

MUSIC All styles. Published "I Get Stoned" (hardcore dance), recorded by AudioJunkie & Stylus, released by EMI records (2009) on *Hardcore Nation 2009*; "Long Way to Go" (country/MOR) on *Under Blue Skies*, recorded by Charlie Landsborough, released on Rosette Records (2008); "Mr Wilson" (folk) from *Only the Willows Are Weeping*, released on Digimix Records (2009); "Blitz" (progressive rock/goth rock), recorded by Bram Stoker on *Rock*

Paranoia, released by Digimix Records, and many more.

TIPS "Have a professional approach—present well-produced demos. First impressions are important and may be the only chance you get. Writers are advised to join the Guild of International Songwriters and Composers in the United Kingdom (www. songwriters-guild.co.uk and www.myspace.com/ guildofsongwriters)."

◑ FRICON MUSIC COMPANY

11 Music Square E, Nashville TN 37203. (615)826-2288. Fax: (615)826-0500. E-mail: fricon@comcast. net. President: Terri Fricon. **Contact:** Madge Benson, professional manager. Music publisher. Estab. 1981. Publishes 25 songs/year; publishes 1-2 new songwriters/year. Staff size: 6. Pays standard royalty.

AFFILIATES Fricout Music Company (ASCAP) and Now and Forever Songs (SESAC).

HOW TO CONTACT *Contact first and obtain permission to submit.* Prefers CD with 3-4 songs and lyric or lead sheet. "Prior permission must be obtained or packages will be returned." Include SASE. Responds in 2 months.

MUSIC Mostly **country**.

◯ GLAD MUSIC CO.

14340 Torrey Chase, Suite 380, Houston TX 77014. (281)397-7300. Fax: (281)397-6206. E-mail: hwesdaily@gladmusicco.com. Website: www.gladmusicco. com. **Contact:** Wes Daily, A&R Director (country). Music publisher, record company, and record producer. Estab. 1958. Publishes 3 songs/year; publishes 2 new songwriters/year. Staff size: 2. Pays standard royalty.

AFFILIATES Bud-Don (ASCAP), Rayde (SESAC), and Glad Music (BMI).

HOW TO CONTACT Submit via CD or mp3 with 3 songs maximum, lyric sheet, and cover letter. Lyric sheet should be folded around CD and submitted in a rigid case and secured with rubber band. Does not return material. Responds in 6 weeks. SASE or e-mail address for reply.

MUSIC Mostly **country**. Does not want weak songs. Published *Love Bug* (album by C. Wayne/W. Kemp), recorded by George Strait, released 1995 on MCA; *Walk through This World with Me* (album), recorded by George Jones; and *Race Is On* (album by D. Rol-

lins), recorded by George Jones, both released 1999 on Asylum.

◑ G MAJOR PUBLISHING

P.O. Box 3331, Fort Smith AR 72913. E-mail: Alex@ Gmajor.org. Website: www.GMajorPublishing.com. Professional managers: Alex Hoover. Music publisher. Estab. 1992. Publishes 10 songs/year; publishes 2 new songwriters/year. Staff size: 2. Pays standard royalty.

HOW TO CONTACT *No unsolicited submissions.* Submit inquiry by mail with SASE. Prefers CD or mp3. Submit up to 3 songs with lyrics. Include SASE. Responds in 4-6 weeks.

MUSIC Mostly **country** and **contemporary Christian**. Published *Set The Captives Free* (album by Chad Little/Jeff Pitzer/Ben Storie), recorded by Sweeter Rain (contemporary Christian), for Cornerstone Television; "Hopes and Dreams" (single by Jerry Glidewell), recorded by Carrie Underwood (country), released on Star Rise; and "Be Still" (single by Chad Little/Dave Romero/Bryan Morse/Jerry Glidewell), recorded CO3 (contemporary Christian), released on Flagship Records.

TIPS "We are looking for 'smash hits' to pitch to the Country and Christian markets."

◑⊛ GOODNIGHT KISS MUSIC

(BMI, ASCAP) 10153½ Riverside Dr. #239, Toluca Lake CA 91602. (831)479-9993. Website: www.goodnightkiss.com. **Contact:** Janet Fisher, managing director. Music publisher, record company and record producer. Estab. 1986. Publishes 6-8 songs/year; publishes 4-5 new songwriters/year. Pays standard royalty.

◯ Goodnight Kiss Music specializes in placing music in movies and TV.

AFFILIATES Scene Stealer Music (ASCAP).

HOW TO CONTACT "Check our website or subscribe to newsletter (www.goodnightkiss.com) to see what we are looking for and to obtain codes. Packages must have proper submission codes, or they are discarded." Only accepts material that is requested on the website. Does not return material. Responds in 6 months.

FILM & TV Places 3-5 songs in film/year. Published "I Do, I Do, Love You" (by Joe David Curtis), recorded by Ricky Kershaw in Road Ends; "Bee Charmer's Charmer" (by Marc Tilson) for the MTV movie *Love*

Song; "Right When I Left" (by B. Turner/J. Fisher) in the movie *Knight Club*.

MUSIC **All modern styles.** Published and produced Addiction: *Highs & Lows* (CD), written and recorded by various artists (all styles), released 2004; *Tall Tales of Osama Bin Laden* (CD), written and recorded by various artists (all styles parody), released 2004; and *Rhythm of Honor* (CD), written and recorded by various artists (all styles), slated release 2005, all on Goodnight Kiss Records.

TIPS "The absolute best way to keep apprised of the company's needs is to subscribe to the online newsletter. Only specifically requested material is accepted, as listed in the newsletter (what the industry calls us for is what we request from writers). We basically use an SGA contract, and there are never fees to be considered for specific projects or albums. However, we are a real music company, and the competition is just as fierce as with the majors."

○ L.J. GOOD PUBLISHING

(ASCAP) 33 Appleway Rd., Okanogan WA 98840. (509)422-1400. E-mail: ljgood@wingsforchrist.com. Website: www.wingsforchrist.com. **Contact:** Lonnie Good, president. Music publisher. Estab. 2006. Publishes 5 songs/year. Publishes 1 new songwriters/year. Staff size: 1. Pays standard royalty of 50%.

AFFILIATES L.J. Good Publishing (ASCAP).

HOW TO CONTACT Prefers CD or mp3 with 3 songs and lyric sheet, cover letter. Does not e-mailed mp3s. Does not return submissions.

MUSIC Mostly **country**, **blues**, **soft rock**, contemporary **Christian/Praise and Worship**.

○ R L HAMMEL ASSOCIATES, INC.

"Consultants to the Music, Recording & Entertainment Industries," P.O. Box 531, Alexandria IN 46001. E-mail: rlh@rlhammel.com. Website: www.rlhammel.com. **Contact:** A&R Department. President: Randal L. Hammel. Music publisher, record producer, and consultant. Estab. 1974. Staff size: 3-5. Pays standard royalty.

AFFILIATES LADNAR Music (ASCAP) and LEMMAH Music (BMI).

HOW TO CONTACT Submit demo package and brief bio by mail. Unsolicited submissions are OK. Prefers CD, DAT, or VHS/8mm videocassette with a maximum of 3 songs and typed lyric sheets. "Please notate three (3) best songs—no time to listen to a full project." Does not return material. Responds ASAP. "No fixed timeline."

MUSIC Mostly **pop**, **R&B** and **Christian**; also MOR, **light rock**, **pop country,** and **feature film title cuts**. Produced/arranged *The Wedding Collection Series* for Word Records. Published *Lessons For Life* (album by Kelly Hubbell/Jim Boedicker) and *I Just Want Jesus* (album by Mark Condon), both recorded by Kelly Connor, released on iMPACT Records.

● ◐ ⊛ HEUPFERD MUSIKVERLAG GMBH

Ringwaldstr. 18, Dreieich 63303. Germany. E-mail: heupferd@t-online.de. Website: www.heupferd-musik.de. **Contact:** Christian Winkelmann, general manager. Music publisher and record company (Viva La Difference). GEMA. Publishes 30 songs/year. Staff size: 3. Pays "royalties after GEMA distribution plan."

AFFILIATES Song Buücherei (book series). "Vive la Difference!" (label).

HOW TO CONTACT *Does not accept unsolicited submissions.*

FILM & TV Places 1 song in film/year. Published "El Grito y el Silencio" (by Thomas Hickstein), recorded by Tierra in *Frauen sind was Wunderbares*.

MUSIC Mostly **folk**, **jazz,** and **fusion**; also **New Age**, **rock,** and **ethnic music**. Published "Mi Mundo" (single by Denise M'Baye/Matthias Furstenberg) from *Havana—Vamos A Ver* (album), recorded by Havana (Latin), released 2003 on Vive La Difference. Printed *Andy Irvine: Aiming For the Heart—Irish Song Affairs*, released in 2007.

○ ⊘ HICKORY LANE PUBLISHING AND RECORDING

(ASCAP, SOCAN) 2713 Oakridge Crescent, Prince George BC V2K 3Y2 Canada. (250)962-5135. E-mail: kobzar@telus.net. Website: http://chrisurbanski.weebly.com. **Contact:** Chris Urbanski, president. Music publisher, record company, and record producer. Estab. 1988. Hires staff writers. Publishes 30 songs/year; publishes 5 new songwriters/year. Pays standard royalty.

HOW TO CONTACT *Does not accept unsolicited submissions.*

MUSIC Mostly **country** and **country rock**. Published "Just Living for Today" (single by Chris Urbanski), recorded by Chris Michaels (country), released 2005 on Hickory Lane Records; "This Is My Sons" (single by Tyson Avery/Chris Urbanski/Alex

Bradshaw), recorded by Chris Michaels (country), released 2005 on Hickory Lane Records; "Stubborn Love" (single by Owen Davies/Chris Urbanski/John Middleton), recorded by Chris Michaels (country), released 2005 on Hickory Lane Records.

TIPS "Send us a professional quality demo with the vocals up front. We are looking for hits, and so are the major record labels we deal with. Be original in your approach, don't send us a cover tune."

⭕ HITSBURGH MUSIC CO.

P.O. Box 1431, 233 N. Electra, Gallatin TN 37066. (615)452-0324. Contact: Harold Gilbert, president/general manager. Music publisher. Estab. 1964. Publishes 12 songs/year. Staff size: 4. Pays standard royalty.

AFFILIATES 7th Day Music (BMI).

HOW TO CONTACT Submit demo by mail. Unsolicited submissions are OK. Prefers cassette or quality videocassette with 2-4 songs and lead sheet. Prefers studio produced demos. Include SASE. Responds in 6 weeks.

MUSIC Mostly **country gospel** and **MOR**. Published "That Kind'a Love" (single by Kimolin Crutchet and Dan Serafini), from *Here's Cissy* (album), recorded by Cissy Crutcher (MOR), released 2005 on Vivaton; "Disorder at the Border" (single), written and recorded by Donald Layne, released 2001 on Southern City; and "Blue Tears" (single by Harold Gilbert/Elaine Harmon), recorded by Hal, released 2006 (reissue) on Southern City.

⭕ HOME TOWN HERO'S PUBLISHING (BMI)

112 West Houston, Leonard TX 75452. E-mail: hometownheroes1@verizon.net. Website: www.myspace.com/hometownheroespublishing1. **Contact:** Tammy Wood, owner. Music publisher. Estab. 2003. Staff size: 2. Pays standard royalty.

HOW TO CONTACT Submit demo by mail. Unsolicited submissions are OK. Prefers CD with 3-6 songs, lyric sheet, and cover letter. Does not return submissions. Responds only if interested.

MUSIC Mostly **country (all styles)**, **pop**, **Southern rock**; also **ballads**, **gospel**, and **blues**. Does not want heavy metal and rap.

TIPS "Most of all, believe in yourself. The best songs come from the heart. Don't get discouraged, be tough, keep writing, and always think positive. Songwriters,

no calls please. I will contact you if interested. Send me your best."

IAMA (INTERNATIONAL ACOUSTIC MUSIC AWARDS)

2881 E. Oakland Park Blvd., Ft. Lauderdale FL 33306.(954)537-3127. E-mail: info@inacoustic.com. Website: www.inacoustic.com.

IDOL PUBLISHING

P.O. Box 720043, Dallas TX 75372.Estab. 1992. (214)321-8890. E-mail: info@idolrecords.com. Website: www.IdolRecords.com. **Contact:** Erv Karwelis, president. Record publisher. Estab. 1992. Releases 30 singles, 80 LPs, 20 EPs, and 10-15 CDs/year. Pays negotiable royalty to artists on contract; negotiable rate to publisher per song on record.

HOW TO CONTACT See website at www.IdolRecords.com for submission policy. No phone calls or e-mail follow-ups.

MUSIC Mostly **rock, pop**, and **alternative**. Released *The Boys Names Sue—The Hits Vol. Sue!* (album), The O's—*We are the Os* (album), Little Black Dress —*Snow in June (album), The Man* recorded by Sponge (alternative); *Movements* (album), recorded by Black Tie Dynasty (alternative); *In Between Days* (album), recorded by Glen Reynolds (rock), all released 2006/2006 on Idol Records. Other artists include Flickerstick, DARYL, Centro-matic, the Deathray Davies, GBH, PPT, The Crash That Took Me, Shibboleth, Trey Johnson.

➕ 💬 ⭕ INSIDE RECORDS/OK SONGS

St.-Jacobsmarkt 76 (B1), Antwerp 2000 Belgium. 32+(0)3+226-77-19. Fax: 32+(0)3+226-78-05. **Contact:** Jean Meeusen, MD. Music publisher and record company. Estab. 1989. Publishes 50 songs/year; publishes 30-40 new songwriters/year. Hires staff writers. Royalty varies "depending on teamwork."

HOW TO CONTACT Submit demo by mail. Unsolicited submissions are OK. Prefers cassette with complete name, address, telephone, and fax number. SAE and IRC. Responds in 2 months.

MUSIC Mostly **dance, pop,** and **MOR contemporary**; also **country, reggae,** and **Latin**. Published *Fiesta de Bautiza* (album by Andres Manzana); *I'm Freaky* (album by Maes-Predu'homme-Robinson); and *Heaven* (album by KC One-King Naomi), all on Inside Records.

🎬🎵✪ INTOXYGENE SARL

283 rue du Fbg St. Antoine, 75011 Paris France. 011(33)1 43485151. Fax: 011(33)1 43485753. Website: www.intoxygene.com or www.intoxygene.net. E-mail: infos@intoxygene.com. **Contact:** Patrick Jammes, managing director. Music publisher and record company. Estab. 1990. Staff size: 1. Publishes 30 songs/year. Pays 50% royalty.

HOW TO CONTACT *Does not accept unsolicited submissions.*

FILM & TV Places 3/5 songs in film and in TV/year.

MUSIC Mostly **new industrial** and **metal**, **lounge**, **electronic**, and **ambient**. Publisher for Peepingtom (trip-hop), Djaimin (house), Missa Furiosa by Thierry Zaboitzeff (progressive), The Young Gods (alternative), Alex Carter, Love Motel, Steve Tallis, and lo'n, among others.

🎵◐ ISLAND CULTURE MUSIC PUBLISHERS

(BMI) 7005 Bordeaux, St. John 00830-9510. U.S. Virgin Islands. E-mail: islandking@islandkingrecords. com. Website: www.IslandKingRecords.com. **Contact:** Liston Monsanto Jr., president. Music publisher and record company (Island King Records). Estab. 1996. Publishes 10 songs/year; publishes 3 new songwriters/year. Hires staff songwriters. Staff size: 3. Pays standard royalty.

HOW TO CONTACT Submit demo package by mail. Unsolicited submissions are OK. Prefers CD with 8 songs and lyric sheet. Send bio and 8×10 glossy. Does not return material. Responds in 1 month.

MUSIC Mostly **reggae**, **calypso**, and **zouk**; also **house**. Published *De Paris a Bohicon* (album), recorded by Rasbawa (reggae), released 2006 on Island King Records; "Jah Give Me Life" (single by Chubby) from *Best of Island King* (album), recorded by Chubby (reggae), released 2003 on Island King Records; "When People Mix Up" (single by Lady Lex/L. Monsanto/Chubby) and "I Am Real" (single by L. Monsanto) from *Best of Island King* (album), recorded by Lady Lex (reggae), released 2003 on Island King Records.

◐ IVORY PEN ENTERTAINMENT

(ASCAP) P.O. Box 1097, Laurel MD 20725. Fax: (240)786-6744. E-mail: ivorypen@comcast.net. Professional managers: Steven Lewis (R&B, pop/rock, inspirational); Sonya Lewis (AC, dance) Wandaliz Co-

lon (Latin, Ethnic); Cornelius Roundtree (gospel/inspirational). Music publisher. Estab. 2003. Publishes 10 songs/year. Staff size: 4. Pays standard royalty.

HOW TO CONTACT E-mail electronic press kit or mp3 no less than 128k. Unsolicited submissions are OK. Prefers CD with 3-5 songs and cover letter. Does not return material. Responds in 4 months. "Don't forget contact info with e-mail address for faster response! Always be professional when you submit your work to any company. Quality counts."

MUSIC Mostly **R&B**, **dance**, **pop/rock**, **Latin**, **adult contemporary**, and **inspirational**. Published Ryan Vetter (single), writer recorded by Alan Johnson (pop/rock), released on Ivory Pen Entertainment; and "Mirror" (single), by Angel Demone, on Vox Angel Inc./Ivory Pen Entertainment.

TIPS "Learn your craft. Always deliver high quality demos. 'Remember, if you don't invest in yourself, don't expect others to invest in you. Ivory Pen Entertainment is a music publishing company that caters to the new songwriter, producer, and aspiring artist. We also place music tracks (no vocals) with artists for release."

◑ JANA JAE MUSIC

P.O. Box 35726, Tulsa OK 74153. (918)786-8896. E-mail: janajae@janajae.com. Website: www.janajae. com. **Contact:** Kathleen Pixley, secretary. Music publisher, record company (Lark Record Productions, Inc.), and record producer (Lark Talent and Advertising). Estab. 1980. Publishes 5-10 songs/year; publishes 1-2 new songwriters/year. Staff size: 8. Pays standard royalty.

HOW TO CONTACT Submit demo by mail. Unsolicited submissions are OK. Prefers CD or DVD with 3-4 songs and typed lyric and lead sheet if possible. Does not return material. Responds only if accepted for use.

MUSIC Mostly **country**, **bluegrass**, **jazz**, and **instrumentals** (**classical** or **country**). Published *Mayonnaise* (album by Steve Upfold), recorded by Jana Jae; and *Let the Bible Be Your Roadmap* (album by Irene Elliot), recorded by Jana Jae, both on Lark Records.

🎵◐ JA/NEIN MUSIKVERLAG GMBH

(GEMA) Oberstr. 14 A, D - 20144, Hamburg Germany. Fax: (49)(40)448 850. E-mail: janeinmv@aol. com. General manager: Mary Dostal. Music publisher, record company, and record producer. Member of GEMA. Publishes 50 songs/year; publishes 5 new songwriters/year. Staff size: 3. Pays 50-66% royalty.

AFFILIATES Pinorrekk Mv., Star-Club Mv. (GEMA).

HOW TO CONTACT Submit audio (visual) carrier by mail. Unsolicited submissions are OK. "We do not download unsolicited material, but visit known websites." Prefers CD or DVD. Enclose e-mail address. Responds in maximum 2 months.

MUSIC Mostly **jazz**, **world** (**klezmer**), **pop**, **rap**, and **rock**.

TIPS "We do not return submitted material. Send your best A-Side works only, please. Indicate all rights owners, like possible co-composer/lyricist, publisher, sample owner. Write what you expect from collaboration. If artist, enclose photo. Enclose lyrics. Be extraordinary! Be fantastic!"

○ JERJOY MUSIC

(BMI)P.O. Box 1264, Peoria IL 61654-1264. (309)673-5755. Fax: (309)673-7636. Website: www.unitedcyber.com and www.myspace.com/jerryhanlon. **Contact:** Jerry Hanlon, professional manager. Music publisher and record company (UAR Records). Estab. 1978. Publishes 10+ songs/year; publishes numerous new songwriters/year. Staff size: 3. Pays standard royalty.

○ Also see the listing for Kaysarah Music in this section and UAR Records in the Record Companies section of this book.

AFFILIATES Kaysarah Music (ASCAP); Abilite Music (BMI).

HOW TO CONTACT *Write first and obtain permission to submit. "WE DO NOT RESPOND TO TELEPHONE CALLS.* Unsolicited submissions are OK, but be sure to send SASE and/or postage or mailing materials if you want a reply and/or a return of all your material. *WE DO NOT OFFER CRITIQUES OF YOUR WORK UNLESS SPECIFICALLY ASKED.* Simple demos—vocal plus guitar or keyboard—are acceptable. We DO NOT require a major demo production to interpret the value of a song." Prefers CD with 4-8 songs and lyric sheet. Responds in 2 weeks.

MUSIC Mostly **American country, Irish Country,** and **religious**. Published "Philomena from Ireland," "I Wanted You for Mine," and "Lisa, Dance with Me" written by the Heggarty Twins of Northern Ireland (recorded by the Heggarty Twins and Jerry Hanlon, country), and "Things My Daddy Used to Do" written by Mark Walton (recorded by Jerry Hanlon,

country); "That Little Irish Church" written and recorded by Jerry Hanlon, country gospel Irish). "I'd Better Stand Up" written by Gene Gillen and Will Herring (recorded by the Heggarty Twins and Jerry Hanlon, country); "Rainbow" written by Dwight Howell (recorded by the Heggarty Twins and Jerry Hanlon, Irish country). "All Your Little Secrets" and "The Girl from Central High" written by Ron Czikall (recorded by Tracy Wells, country); all released on UAR Records.

TIPS "Don't submit any song that you don't honestly feel is well constructed and strong in commercial value. Be critical of your writing efforts. Be sure you use each and every one of your lyrics to its best advantage. 'Think Big!' Make your songs tell a story and don't be repetitious in using the same or similar ideas or words in each of your verses. Would your musical creation stand up against the major hits that are making the charts today? Think of great hooks you can work into your song ideas."

⊘ QUINCY JONES MUSIC

(ASCAP) 6671 Sunset Blvd., #1574A, Los Angeles CA 90028. (323)957-6601. Fax: (323)962-5231. E-mail: info@quincyjonesmusic.com. Website: www.quincyjonesmusic.com. Music publisher.

HOW TO CONTACT *Quincy Jones Music does not accept unsolicited submissions.*

MUSIC The Quincy Jones Music Publishing catalog is home to more than 1,600 titles spanning five decades of music covering numerous musical genres including jazz, R&B, pop, rock-n-roll, Brazilian, alternative, and hip-hop. Over the years, such legendary performers as Frank Sinatra, Count Basie, Sarah Vaughan, Louis Jordan, Lesley Gore, Barbra Streisand, Billy Eckstine, and Tony Bennett have recorded our songs. We remain a presence in today's market by way of such artists as Michael Jackson, 98°, Tevin Campbell, K-Ci & Jo Jo, George Benson, Ivan Lins, S.W.V., Vanessa Williams, Patti Austin, The Manhattan Transfer, James Ingram, Barry White, and Ray Charles. Our current roster of talent includes lyricists, composers, musicians, performers, and producers.

○ KAUPPS & ROBERT PUBLISHING CO.

(BMI)P.O. Box 5474, Stockton CA 95205. (209)948-8186. Fax: (209)942-2163. **Contact:** Melissa Glenn, A&R coordinator (all styles). Production manager (country, pop, rock): Rick Webb. Professional manager (country, pop, rock): Bruce Bolin. President: Nancy L. Merrihew. Music publisher, record company (Kaupp Records), manager, and booking agent (Merri-Webb Productions and Most Wanted Bookings). Estab. 1990. Publishes 15-20 songs/year; publishes 5 new songwriters/year. Pays standard royalty.

HOW TO CONTACT *Write first and obtain permission to submit.* Prefers cassette or VHS videocassette (if available) with 3 songs maximum and lyric sheet. "If artist, send PR package." Include SASE. Responds in 6 months.

MUSIC Mostly **country**, **R&B,** and **A/C rock**; also **pop**, **rock,** and **gospel**. Published "Rushin' In" (singles by N. Merrihew/B. Bolin), recorded by Valerie; "Goin Postal" (singles by N. Merrihew/B. Bolin), recorded by Bruce Bolin (country/rock/pop); and "I Gotta Know" (single by N. Merrihew/B. Bolin), recorded by Cheryl (country/rock/pop), all released on Kaupp Records.

TIPS "Know what you want, set a goal, focus in on your goals, be open to constructive criticism, polish tunes and keep polishing."

◯ KAYSARAH MUSIC

(ASCAP, BMI) P.O. Box 1264, 6020 W. Pottstown Rd., Peoria IL 61654-1264. (309)673-5755. Fax: (309)673-7636. E-mail: jerryhanlon33@yahoo.com. Website: www.unitedcyber.com and www.myspace.com/jerryhanlon. **Contact:** Jerry Hanlon, owner/producer. Music publisher, record company (UAR Records), and record producer. Estab. 2000. Publishes 2 new songwriters/year. Staff size: 3. Pays standard royalty.

○ Also see the listing for Jerjoy Music in this section and UAR Records in the Record Companies section of this book.

AFFILIATES Jerjoy Music (BMI); Abilite Music (BMI).

HOW TO CONTACT *Write first and obtain permission to submit.* "WE DO NOT RESPOND TO TELEPHONE CALLS. Unsolicited submissions are OK, but be sure to send SASE and/or postage or mailing materials if you want a reply and/or a return of all your material. WE DO NOT OFFER CRITIQUES OF YOUR WORK UNLESS SPECIFICALLY ASKED." Prefers CD with 4 songs and lyric sheet and cover letter. Include SASE. Responds in 2 weeks.

MUSIC Mostly **traditional country** and **country gospel**; also **Irish country**, **Irish ballads,** and **Irish folk/traditional**.

TIPS "Be honest and self-critical of your work. Make every word in a song count. Attempt to create work that is not over 2:50 minutes in length. Compare your work to the songs that seem to be what you hear on radio. A good A&R person or professional recording artist with a creative mind can determine the potential value of a song simply by hearing a melody line (guitar or keyboard) and the lyrics. DON'T convince yourself that your work is outstanding if you feel that it will not be able to compete with the tough competition of today 's market."

◑ LAKE TRANSFER PRODUCTIONS & MUSIC

11300 Hartland St., North Hollywood CA 91605. (818)508-7158. **Contact:** Jim Holvay, professional manager (pop, R&B, soul); Tina Antoine (hip-hop, rap); Steve Barri Cohen (alternative rock, R&B). Music publisher and record producer (Steve Barri Cohen). Estab. 1989. Publishes 11 songs/year; publishes 3 new songwriters/year. Staff size: 6. Pay "depends on agreement, usually 50% split."

AFFILIATES Lake Transfer Music (ASCAP) and Transfer Lake Music (BMI).

HOW TO CONTACT Accepting unsolicited submissions through mid-2008.

MUSIC Mostly **alternative pop**, **R&B/hip-hop** and **dance**. Does not want country & western, classical, New Age, jazz, or swing. Published "Tu Sabes Que Te Amo (Will You Still Be There)" (single by Steve Barri Cohen/Rico) from *Rico: The Movement II* (album), recorded by Rico (rap/hip-hop), released 2004 on Lost Empire/Epic-Sony; "When Water Flows" (single by Steve Barri Cohen/Sheree Brown/Terry Dennis) from *Sheree Brown "83"* (album), recorded by Sheree Brown (urban pop), released 2004 on BBEG Records (a division of Saravels, LLC); and "Fair Game" (single by LaTocha Scott/Steve Barri Cohen) *Soundtrack from the Movie Fair Game* (album), recorded by LaTocha Scott (R&B/hip-hop), released 2004 on Raw Deal Records, College Park, Georgia. "All our staff are songwriters/producers. Jim Holvay has written hits like 'Kind of a Drag' and 'Hey Baby They're Playin our Song' for the Buckinghams. Steve Barri Cohen has worked with every one from Evelyn 'Champagne' King (RCA), Phantom Planets (Epic),

Meredith Brooks (Capitol) and Dre (Aftermath/Interscope)."

TIPS "Trends change, but it's still about the song. Make sure your music and lyrics have a strong (POV) point of view."

○ LITA MUSIC

(ASCAP)P.O. Box 40251, Nashville TN 37204. (615)269-8682. Fax: (615)269-8929. E-mail: justin-peters@songsfortheplanet.com; songsfortheplanet@songsfortheplanet.com. Website: www.songsfortheplanet.com. **Contact:** Justin Peters, president. Music publisher. Estab. 1980.

AFFILIATES Justin Peters Music, Platinum Planet Music and Tourmaline (BMI).

HOW TO CONTACT Submit demo package by mail. Unsolicited submissions are OK. Prefers CD with 5 songs and lyric sheet. Does not return material. "Place code '2011' on each envelope submission."

MUSIC Mostly **country, classic rock, Southern rock, inspirational AC Pop, Southern gospel/ Christian,** and **worship songs.** Published "The Bottom Line" recorded by Charley Pride on Music City Records (written by Art Craig, Drew Bourke, and Justin Peters); "No Less Than Faithful" (single by Don Pardoe/Joel Lyndsey), recorded by Ann Downing on Daywind Records, Jim Bullard on Genesis Records and Melody Beizer (#1 song) on Covenant Records; "No Other Like You" (single by Mark Comden/Paula Carpenter), recorded by Twila Paris and Tony Melendez (#5 song) on Starsong Records; "Making a New Start" and "Invincible Faith" (singles by Gayle Cox), recorded by Kingdom Heirs on Sonlite Records; "I Don't Want to Go Back" (single by Gayle Cox), recorded by Greater Vision on Benson Records; and "He Had Mercy On Me" (by Constance and Justin Peters) recorded by Shining Grace.

○ M & T WALDOCH PUBLISHING, INC.

(BMI)4803 S. Seventh St., Milwaukee WI 53221. (414)482-2194. VP, Creative management (rockabilly, pop, country): Timothy J. Waldoch. Professional manager (country, top 40): Mark T. Waldoch. Music publisher. Estab. 1990. Publishes 2-3 songs/year; publishes 2-3 new songwriters/year. Staff size: 2. Pays standard royalty.

HOW TO CONTACT Submit demo package by mail. Unsolicited submissions are OK. Prefers CD with 3-6 songs and lyric or lead sheet. "We will also accept a studio produced demo tape." Include SASE. Responds in 3 months.

MUSIC Mostly **country/pop, rock, top 40 pop**; also **melodic metal, dance**, R&B. Does not want rap. Published "It's Only Me" and "Let Peace Rule the World" (by Kenny LePrix), recorded by Brigade on SBD Records (rock).

TIPS "Study the classic pop songs from the 1950s through the present time. There is a reason why good songs stand the test of time. Today's hits will be tomorrow's classics. Send your best well-crafted, polished song material."

◐ MAKERS MARK GOLD

Publishing (ASCAP) 534 W. Queen Lane, Philadelphia PA 19144. E-mail: MakersMark@verizon.net. **Contact:** Paul Hopkins, producer/publisher. Music publisher and record producer. Estab. 1991. Pays standard royalty.

HOW TO CONTACT Submit demo CD or tape by mail. Unsolicited submissions are OK. Prefers 2-4 songs. Does not return material. Responds in 6 weeks if interested.

MUSIC "Our publishing and productions has changed to total **Christian/Inspirational. gospel/ Christian** only. All genres **contemporary, traditional, pop, dance, hip-hop gospel**." Historically mostly **R&B, hip-hop, gospel, pop,** and **house.** Published "Silent Love," "Why You Want My Love" and "Something for Nothing," (singles), written and recorded by Elaine Monk, released on Black Sands Records/Metropolitan Records; "Get Funky" (single), written and recorded by Larry Larr, released on Columbia Records; and "He Made a Way" (single by Kenyatta Arrington), "We Give All Praises unto God" (single by Jacqueline D. Pate), "I Believe He Will" (single by Pastor Alyn E. Waller), and "Psalms 146" (single by Rodney Roberson), all songs recorded by the Enon Tabernacle Mass Choir from *Pastor Alyn E. Waller Presents: The Enon Tabernacle Mass Choir*, released on ECDC Records (www.enontab.org). Also produces and publishes music for Bunim/Murray productions network television, MTV's *Real World, Road Rules, Rebel Billionaire, Simple Life,* and movie soundtracks worldwide. Also produced deep soul remixes for Brian McKnight, Musiq Soulchild, Jagged Edge, John Legend, and Elaine Monk.

⊙ ◐ MANY LIVES MUSIC PUBLISHERS (SOCAN)

RR #1, Kensington PE COB 1MO Canada. (902)836-4571 (studio). E-mail: musicpublisher@amajorsound.com. Website: www.amajorsound.com/manylivespublishers.html. **Contact:** Paul C. Milner, publisher. Music publisher. Estab. 1997. "Owners of Shell Lane Studio www.shelllanestudio.com complete in-house production facility. Many Lives Music Publishers was also involved in the production and recording of all projects listed below." Pays standard royalty.

HOW TO CONTACT Submit demo by mail, MySpace, or SonicBids. Unsolicited submissions are OK. Prefers CD and lyric sheet (lead sheet if available). Does not return material. Responds in 3 months if interested.

MUSIC All styles. *Six Pack EP* and *Colour* (album), written and recorded by Chucky Danger (Pop/Rock), released 2005 on Landwash Entertainment. Chucky Danger's *Colour* album was named Winner Best Pop Recording at the East Coast Music Awards 2006, "Sweet Symphony" was nominated for Single of the Year, and Chucky Danger was nominated for Best New Group. Released *Temptation* (album by various writers), arrangement by Paul Milner, Patrizia, Dan Cutrona (rock/opera), released 2003 on United One Records; *The Edge of Emotion* (album by various writers), arrangement by Paul Milner, Patrizia, Dan Cutrona (rock/opera), released 2006 on Nuff entertainment/United One Records. The Single "Temptation" won a SOCAN #1 award. *Saddle River Stringband* (album) written and recorded by the Saddle River Stringband (Bluegrass) released on Panda Digital/Save as Music 2007. Winners of best Bluegrass recording East Coast Music Awards 2007. *Pat Deighan and the Orb Weavers* (album) "In a Fever in a Dream" (Alternative Rock) written by Pat Deighan, released on Sandbar Music April 2008.

◐ JOHN WELLER MARVIN PUBLISHING

(ASCAP) P.O. Box 513, Akron OH 44309. (330)733-8585. Fax: (330)733-8595. E-mail: stephanie.arble@jwmpublishing.net. Website: www.jwmpublishing.net. **Contact:** Stephanie Arble, president. Music Publisher. Estab. 1996. Pays standard royalty.

HOW TO CONTACT Submit demo by mail. Unsolicited submissions are OK. Prefers cassette, CD or VHS and lyric or lead sheet. Responds in 6 weeks.

MUSIC All genres, mostly **pop**, **R&B**, **rap**; also **rock**, and **country**. Published "Downloading Files" (single by S. Arble/R. Scott), recorded by Ameritech Celebration Choir (corporate promotional). "We work with a promoter, booking major label artists, and we're also involved in television and corporate promotional recordings."

MATERIAL WORTH PUBLISHING

(ASCAP) 46 First St., Walden, NY, 12586. (845)778-7768. E-mail: materialworthpub@aol.com. Website: www.materialworth.com. **Contact:** Frank Sardella, owner. Music publisher. Estab. 2003. Staff size: 3. Pays standard royalty of 50%.

HOW TO CONTACT *E-mail or visit website for how to obtain permission to submit. Must have permission before sending.* Do not call first. Prefers mp3 or online player. CD, lyric sheet, and cover letter are also accepted; "no cassette tapes, please." Does not return submissions. Responds in 6-8 weeks.

MUSIC Mostly **female pop** or **pop/country crossover**, **singer-songwriter**, **male pop alternative rock**.

◐ MAUI ARTS & MUSIC ASSOCIATION/ SURVIVOR RECORDS/TEN OF DIAMONDS MUSIC

(BMI) PMB 208, P.O. Box 79-1540, Paia Maui HI 96779. (808)874-5900. E-mail: mamamaui@dreammaui.com. Website: www.dreammaui.com. Music publisher and record producer. Estab. 1974. Publishes 1-2 artists/year. Staff size: 2. Pays standard royalty.

HOW TO CONTACT *Prefers that submitters send a sound file submission via e-mail, maximum of 5 minutes in length.*

MUSIC Mostly **pop**, **country**, **R&B**, and **New Age**. Does not want rock. Published "In the Morning Light" (by Jack Warren), recorded by Jason (pop ballad); "Before the Rain" (by Giles Feldscher), recorded by Jason (pop ballad), both on Survivor; and "Then I Do" (single), written and recorded by Lono, released on Ono Music.

TIPS "Looking for a great single only!"

◐ MCCLURE & TROWBRIDGE PUBLISHING, LTD (ASCAP, BMI)

P.O. Box 148548, Nashville TN 37214. (615)902-0509. Website: http://trowbridgeplanetearth.com. Music publisher, and record label (JIP Records) and production company (George McClure, producer). Estab. 1983. Publishes 35 songs/year. Publishes 5 new songwriters/year. Staff size: 8. Pays standard royalty of 50%.

HOW TO CONTACT *Follow directions ONLINE ONLY—obtain Control Number to submit a demo via US Mail.* Requires CD with 1-5 songs, lyric sheet, and cover letter. Does not return submissions. Responds in 3 weeks if interested.

MUSIC Pop, **country**, **gospel**, **Latin,** and **swing**. Publisher of Band of Writers (BOW) series. Published "Experience (Should Have Taught Me)" album 2010 on JIP Records; "The Lights of Christmas" album; "PlayboySwing," released 2008 on JIP Records; "Miles Away" (single) on DiscoveryChannel's "The Deadliest Catch"; and "I'm a Wild One" (single), recorded by Veronica Leigh, released 2006 on Artist Choice CD.

○ JIM MCCOY MUSIC

(BMI) 25 Troubadour Lane, Berkeley Springs WV 25411. (304)258-9381 or (304)258-8314. E-mail: mccoytroubadour@aol.com. Website: www.troubadourlounge.com. **Contact:** Bertha and Jim McCoy, owners. Music publisher, record company (Winchester Records) and record producer (Jim McCoy Productions). Estab. 1973. Publishes 20 songs/year; publishes 3-5 new songwriters/year. Pays standard royalty.

AFFILIATES New Edition Music (BMI).

HOW TO CONTACT Submit demo by mail with lyric sheet. Unsolicited submissions are OK. Prefers cassette or CD with 6 songs. Include SASE. Responds in 1 month.

MUSIC Mostly **country**, **country/rock** and **rock**; also **bluegrass** and **gospel**. Published *Jim McCoy and Friends Remember Ernest Tubb*; "She's the Best" recorded by Matt Hahn on Troubadour Records (written by Jim McCoy); "Shadows on My Mind" recorded by Sandy Utley (written by Jim McCoy), "Rock and Roll Hillbilly Redneck Girl" recorded by Elaine Arthur (written by Jim McCoy), released in 2007.

⊘⊕ MCJAMES MUSIC INC.

(ASCAP) 1724 Stanford St., Suite B, Santa Monica CA 90404. (310)712-1916. Fax: (419)781-6644. E-mail: tim@mcjamesmusic.com; steven@mcjamesmusic.com. Website: www.mcjamesmusic.com. Professional managers: Tim James (country/pop); Steven

McClintock (pop/country). Music publisher, record company (37 Songs) and record producer (Steven McClintock). Estab. 1977. Writers include: Pamela Phillips Oland, Stephen Petree, Jeremy Dawson, Chad Petree, Brian Stoner, Tom Templeman, Cathy-Anne McClintock, Tim James, Steven McClintock, Ryan Lawhon. Publishes 50 songs/year. Staff size: 4. Pays standard royalty. Does administration and collection for all foreign markets for publishers and writers.

AFFILIATES 37 Songs (ASCAP) and McJames Music, Inc. (BMI).

HOW TO CONTACT *Only accepts material referred by a reputable industry source.* Prefers CD with 2 songs and cover letter. Does not return material. Responds in 6 months.

FILM & TV Places 2 songs in film and 3 songs in TV/year. Music supervisor: Tim James/Steven McClintock. *Blood & Chocolate, 3-Day Weekend, Dirty Sexy Money, Brothers & Sisters, Dancing with the Stars, Dexter, Always Sunny in Philadelphia, America's Top Model.* Commercials include Honda Australia, Scion California, Motorola Razr 2 worldwide.

MUSIC Mostly **modern rock, country, pop, jazz,** and **euro dance**; also **bluegrass** and **alternative**. Will accept some mainstream rap but no classical. Published "Le Disko"; "You are the One"; "Rainy Monday" (singles from Shiny Toy Guns on Universal), "Be Sure"; "What It Is" (singles from Cris Barber), "Keeps Bringing Me Back" (from Victoria Shaw on Taffita), "Christmas Needs Love to Be Christmas" (single by Andy Williams on Delta), recent cover by ATC on BMG/Universal with "If Love Is Blind"; single by new Warner Bros. act Sixwire called "Look at Me Now."

TIPS "Write a song we don't have in our catalog or write an undeniable hit. We will know it when we hear it."

⊘⊕ MIDI TRACK PUBLISHING (BMI)

P.O. Box 1545, Smithtown NY 11787. (718)767-8995. E-mail: info@allrsmusic.com. Website: www.allrsmusic.com. **Contact:** Renee Silvestri-Bushey, president. F.John Silvestri, founder; Leslie Migliorelli, director of operations. Music publisher, record company (MIDI Track Records), music consultant, artist management, record producer. Voting member of NARAS/National Academy of Recording Arts and Sciences (the Grammy Awards), voting member of the Country Music Association (CMA Awards); SGMA/Southern Gospel Music Association, SGA/Songwriters Guild of America (Diamond Member). Estab. 1994. Staff size: 6. Publishes 3 songs/year; publishes 2 new songwriters/year. Pays standard royalty. Affiliate(s) ALLRS Music Publishing Co. (ASCAP).

HOW TO CONTACT "Write or e-mail first to obtain permission to submit. We do not accept unsolicited submissions." Prefers CD with 3 songs, lyric sheet, and cover letter. Does not return material. Responds in 6 months only if interested.

FILM & TV Places 1 song in film/year. Published "Why Can't You Hear My Prayer" (single by F. John Silvestri/Leslie Silvestri), recorded by Iliana Medina in a documentary by Silvermine Films.

MUSIC Mostly **country**, **gospel**, **top 40**, **R&B**, **MOR** ,and **pop**. Does not want show tunes, jazz, classical or rap. Published "Why Can't You Hear My Prayer" (single by F. John Silvestri/Leslie Silvestri), recorded by eight-time Grammy nominee Huey Dunbar of the group DLG (Dark Latin Groove), released on MIDI Track Records (including other multiple releases); "Chasing Rainbows" (single by F. John Silvestri/Leslie Silvestri/Darin Kelly), recorded by Tommy Cash (country), released on MMT Records (including other multiple releases); "Because of You" (single by F. John Silvestri/Leslie Silvestri), recorded by Iliana Medina, released 2002 on MIDI Track Records (including other multiple releases also recorded by Grammy nominee Terri Williams, of Always, Patsy Cline, Grand Ole Opry member Ernie Ashworth), released on KMA Records and including other multiple releases; "My Coney Island" (single by F. John Silvestri/Leslie Silvestri), recorded by eight-time Grammy nominee Huey Dunbar, released 2005-2009 on MIDI Track Records.

TIPS "Attend workshops, seminars, and visit our blog on our website for advice, tips, and info on the music industry."

THE MUSIC ROOM PUBLISHING GROUP

(ASCAP)/MRP MUSIC (BMI) 525 S. Francisca Ave., Redondo Beach CA 90277. (310)316-4551. E-mail: mrp@aol.com. Website: http://musicroomonline.com; www.musicroom.us. **Contact:** John Reed, president/owner. Music publisher and record producer. Estab. 1982. Pays standard royalty.

AFFILIATES MRP Music (BMI).

HOW TO CONTACT *Not accepting unsolicited material.*

MUSIC Mostly **pop/rock/R&B** and **crossover**. Published "That Little Tattoo," "Mona Lisa" and "Sleepin' with an Angel" (singles by John E. Reed) from *Rock with an Attitude* (album), recorded by Rawk Dawg (rock), released 2002; "Over the Rainbow" and "Are You Still My Lover" (singles) from *We Only Came to Rock* (album), recorded by Rawk Dawg, released 2004 on Music Room Productions.

MUST HAVE MUSIC

(ASCAP, BMI) P.O. Box 361326, Los Angeles CA 90036-1326. (323)932-9524. E-mail: info@musthavemusic.com. Website: www.musthavemusic.com. **Contact:** Kenneth R. Klar, managing director. Music publisher and music library. Estab. 1990. Pays standard royalty.

AFFILIATES Must Have More Music (ASCAP); Must Have Music (BMI).

HOW TO CONTACT Submit demo by mail with a personal e-mail address included for directors response. Unsolicited submissions are OK. Prefers CD with lyric sheet and cover letter. Does not return submissions. Responds in 2 months.

FILM & TV Music supervisor: Ken Klar, managing director.

MUSIC Mostly **pop/ R& B**, **pop/country,** and **rock**; also **AAA**, **adult contemporary**, and **contemporary Christian/gospel**. Does not want instrumental music. "We only work with completed songs with lyric and vocal."

TIPS "Write what you know and what you believe. Then rewrite it!"

NERVOUS PUBLISHING

5 Sussex Crescent, Northolt, Middlesex UB5 4DL United Kingdom. +44(020) 8423 7373. Fax: +44(020) 8423 7773. E-mail: info@nervous.co.uk. Website: www.nervous.co.uk. **Contact:** Roy Williams, owner. Music publisher, record company (Nervous Records), and record producer. MCPS, PRS and Phonographic Performance Ltd. Estab. 1979. Publishes 100 songs/year; publishes 25 new songwriters/year. Pays standard royalty; royalties paid directly to US songwriters.

Nervous Publishing's record label, Nervous Records, is listed in the Record Companies section.

HOW TO CONTACT Submit demo by mail. Unsolicited submissions are OK. Prefers CD with 3-10 songs and lyric sheet. "Include letter giving your age and mentioning any previously published material." SAE and IRC. Responds in 3 weeks.

MUSIC Mostly **psychobilly, rockabilly,** and **rock** (impossibly fast music—e.g.: Stray Cats but twice as fast); also **blues, country, R&B,** and **rock** ('50s style). Published *Trouble* (album), recorded by Dido Bonneville (rockabilly); *Rockabilly Comp* (album), recorded by various artists; and *Nervous Singles Collection* (album), recorded by various artists, all on Nervous Records.

TIPS "Submit *no* rap, soul, funk—we want *rockabilly*."

ⓘ NEWBRAUGH BROTHERS MUSIC

(ASCAP, BMI) 228 Morgan Lane, Berkeley Springs WV 25411-3475. (304)261-0228. E-mail: Nbtoys@verizon.net. **Contact:** John S. Newbraugh, owner. Music publisher, record company (NBT Records, BMI/ASCAP). Estab. 1967. Publishes 124 songs/year. Publishes 14 new songwriters/year. Staff size: 1. Pays standard royalty.

AFFILIATES NBT Music (ASCAP) and Newbraugh Brothers Music (BMI).

HOW TO CONTACT Submit demo by mail. Unsolicited submissions are OK. Prefers cassette or CD with any amount of songs, a lyric sheet, and a cover letter. Include SASE. Responds in 6 weeks. "Please don't call for permission to submit. Your materials are welcomed."

MUSIC Mostly **rockabilly, hillbilly, folk,** and **bluegrass;** also **rock, country,** and **gospel**. "We will accept all genres of music except songs with vulgar language." Published "*Ride the Train Series Vol. 25; Layin' It on the Line* by Night Drive (2009); "Love Notes" The Sisters Two; "The Country Cowboy" by Jack Long; "Original Praise Songs" by Russ and Donna Miller.

TIPS "Find out if a publisher/record company has any special interest. NBT, for instance, is always hunting 'original' train songs. Our 'registered' trademark is a train and from time to time we release a compilation album of all train songs. We welcome all genres of music for this project."

ⓞ NEWCREATURE MUSIC

P.O. Box 1444, Hendersonville TN 37077-1444. (615)585-9301. E-mail: ba@landmarkcommunicationsgroup.com. Website: www.landmarkcommunicationsgroup.com. **Contact:** Bill Anderson, Jr., president. Professional manager: G.L. Score. Music publisher, record company, record producer (Landmark Communications Group), and radio and TV syndicator. Publishes 25 songs/year; publishes 2 new songwriters/year. Pays standard royalty.

AFFILIATES Mary Megan Music (ASCAP).

HOW TO CONTACT *Contact first and obtain permission to submit.* Prefers CD or videocassette with 4-10 songs and lyric sheet. Include SASE. Responds in 6 weeks.

MUSIC Mostly **country, gospel, jazz, R&B, rock** and **top 40/pop**. Published *Let This Be the Day* by C.J. Hall; *When a Good Love Comes Along* by Gail Score; *The Wonder of Christmas* by Jack Mosley.

ⓞ⊛ OLD SLOWPOKE MUSIC

(BMI) P.O. Box 52626 Utica Square Station, Tulsa OK 74152. (918)742-8087. Fax: (888)878-0817. E-mail: ryoung@oldslowpokemusic.com. Website: http://oldslowpokemusic.com. **Contact:** Steve Hickerson, professional manager. President: Rodney Young. Music publisher and record producer. Estab. 1977. Publishes 10-20 songs/year; publishes 2 new songwriters/year. Staff size: 2. Pays standard royalty.

HOW TO CONTACT CDs only, no cassettes.

FILM & TV 1 song in film/year. Recently published "Samantha," written and recorded by George W. Carroll in Samantha. Placed two songs for Tim Drummond in movies: "Hound Dog Man" in *Loving Lu Lu* and "Fur Slippers" in a CBS movie *Shake, Rattle & Roll*.

MUSIC Mostly **rock, country,** and **R&B;** also **jazz**. Published *Promise Land* (album), written and recorded by Richard Neville on Cherry Street Records (rock).

TIPS "Write great songs. We sign only artists who play an instrument, sing and write songs."

ⓞ PEERMUSIC

2397 Shattuck Ave., Suite 202, Berkeley CA 94704. (510)848-7337. Fax: (510)848-7355. E-mail: sfcorp@peermusic.com. Website: www.peermusic.com. Music publisher and artist development promotional label. Estab. 1928. Hires staff songwriters. "All deals negotiable."Affiliate(s) Songs of Peer Ltd. (ASCAP) and Peermusic III Ltd. (BMI).

HOW TO CONTACT "We do NOT accept unsolicited submissions. We only accept material through agents, attorneys and managers." Prefers CD and lyric sheet. Does not return material.

MUSIC Mostly **pop, rock** and **R&B**. Published music by David Foster (writer/producer, pop); Andrew Williams (writer/producer, pop); Christopher "Tricky" Stewart (R&B, writer/producer).

➕🌐⚫ PEGASUS MUSIC

Otago, New Zealand. Website: www.myspace.com/pegasusmusicpublishing. Professional managers: Errol Peters (country, rock); Ginny Peters (gospel, pop). Music publisher and record company. Estab. 1981. Publishes 20-30 songs/year; publishes 5 new songwriters/year. Pays standard royalty.

HOW TO CONTACT Submit demo package by mail. Unsolicited submissions are OK. Prefers CD with 3-5 songs and lyric sheet. SAE and IRC. Responds in 1 month.

MUSIC Mostly **country**; also **bluegrass**, **easy listening,** and **top 40/pop**. Published "Beyond the Reason," written and recorded by Ginny Peters (Pegasus Records); "I Only See You," written by Ginny Peters, recorded by Dennis Marsh (Rajon Records, New Zealand); "The Mystery of God," written and recorded by Ginny Peters (NCM Records, England).

TIPS "Get to the meat of the subject without too many words. Less is better."

⊘ PERLA MUSIC

(ASCAP) 134 Parker Ave., Easton PA 18042. (212)957-9509. Fax: (917)338-7596. E-mail: PM@PMRecords. Org. Website: www.PMRecords.org. **Contact:** Gene Perla (jazz). Music publisher, record company (PM-Records.org), record producer (Perla.org), studio production (TheSystemMSP.com) and Internet Design (CCINYC.com). Estab. 1971. Publishes 5 songs/year. Staff size: 5. Pays 75%/25% royalty.

HOW TO CONTACT *E-mail first and obtain permission to submit.*

MUSIC Mostly **jazz** and **rock**.

⭕ JUSTIN PETERS MUSIC

(BMI)P.O. Box 40251, Nashville TN 37204. (615)269-8682. Fax: (615)269-8929. E-mail: justinpeters@songsfortheplanet.com; songsfortheplanet@songsfortheplanet.com. Website: http://songsfortheplanet.com. **Contact:** Justin Peters, president. Music publisher. Estab. 1981.

AFFILIATES Platinum Planet Music (BMI), Tourmaline (BMI), and LITA Music (ASCAP).

HOW TO CONTACT Submit demo package by mail. Unsolicited submissions are OK. Prefers CD with

5 songs and lyric sheet. Does not return material. "Place code '2010' on each envelope submission."

MUSIC Mostly **pop**, **reggae**, **country**, and **comedy**. Published "Saved by Love" (single), recorded by Amy Grant on A&M Records; "From the Center of My Heart," by Shey Baby on JAM Records; "A Gift That She Don't Want" (single), recorded by Bill Engvall on Warner Brother Records; "The Bottom Line," recorded by Charley Pride on Music City Records, cowritten by Justin Peters; "Heaven's Got to Help Me Shake These Blues" (single), written by Vickie Shaub and Justin Peters, recorded by B.J. Thomas; "Virginia Dreams" and "Closer to You" (Jimmy Fortune/Justin Peters), recorded by Jimmy Fortune.

⊘ PHOEBOB MUSIC

(BMI) 5181 Regent Dr., Nashville TN 37220. (615)832-4199. **Contact:** Phoebe Binkley.

HOW TO CONTACT "We do not want unsolicited submissions."

MUSIC Mostly **country**, **Christian**, and **theatre**.

ⓓ PIANO PRESS

(ASCAP)P.O. Box 85, Del Mar CA 92014-0085. (619)884-1401. Fax: (858)755-1104. E-mail: pianopress@pianopress.com. Website: www.pianopress.com. **Contact:** Elizabeth C. Axford, M.A., owner. Music publisher and distributor. Publishes songbooks & CDs for music students and teachers. Estab. 1998. Licenses 32-100 songs/year; publishes 1-24 new songwriters/year. Staff size: 5. Pays standard print music and/or mechanical royalty; songwriter retains rights to songs.

HOW TO CONTACT *E-mail first to obtain permission to submit.* Prefers CD with 1-3 songs, lyric and lead sheet, cover letter, and sheet music/piano arrangements. "Looking for children's songs for young piano students and arrangements of public domain folk songs of any nationality." Currently accepting submissions for various projects. Include SASE. Responds in 2-3 months.

MUSIC Mostly **children's songs**, **folk songs,** and **holiday songs**; also **teaching pieces**, **piano arrangements**, **lead sheets with melody, chords, and lyrics** and **songbooks**. Published *My Halloween Fun Songbook* and CD and *My Christmas Fun Songbook* series, *The Holiday Fun* series, *The Pieces for Piano* series, *The Piano Composers* series, and *The Kidtunes* series.

TIPS "Songs should be simple, melodic, and memorable. Lyrics should be for a juvenile audience and well-crafted."

○ PLATINUM PLANET MUSIC, INC.

(BMI) P.O. Box 40251, Nashville TN 37204. (615)269-8682. Fax: (615)269-8929. E-mail: justinpeters@songsfortheplanet.com. Website: http://songsfortheplanet.com. **Contact:** Justin Peters, president. Music publisher. Estab. 1997.

AFFILIATES Justin Peters Music (BMI), Tourmaline (BMI) and LITA Music (ASCAP).

HOW TO CONTACT Submit demo package by mail. Unsolicited submissions are OK. Prefers CD with 5 songs and lyric sheet. Does not return material. "Place code '2011' on each envelope submission."

MUSIC Mostly **R&B, reggae, sports themes, dance,** and **country**; also represents many **Christian** artists/writers. Published "Happy Face" (single by Dez Dickerson/Jordan Dickerson), recorded by Squirt on Absolute Records; "Buena Vida" (Daron Glenn and Justin Peters), recorded by Daron Glenn on PPMI; "Love's Not a Game" (single), written by Art Craig and J. Peters and recorded by Kashief Lindo on Heavybeat Records; "Place Called Heaven" written by Armond Morales and Kevin Wicker and released by the Imperials, "Love Won't Let Me Leave" (Art Craig and Justin Peters), recorded by Jason Rogers on Independent; and "Loud" (single), written and recorded by These Five Down on Absolute Records.

⊘ PORTAGE MUSIC (BMI)

16634 Gannon Ave. W., Rosemount MN 55068. (952)432-5737. E-mail: olrivers@earthlink.net. President: Larry LaPole. Music publisher. Publishes 0-5 songs/year. Pays standard royalty.

HOW TO CONTACT *Call or e-mail first for permission to submit.*

MUSIC Mostly **country** and **country rock**. Published "Lost Angel," "Think It Over" and "Congratulations to Me" (by L. Lapole), all recorded by Trashmen on Sundazed.

TIPS "Keep songs short, simple, and upbeat with positive theme."

○ ⊛ QUARK, INC.

P.O. Box 452, Newtown, CT 06470. (917)687-9988. E-mail: quarkent@aol.com. **Contact:** Curtis Urbina, manager. Music publisher, record company (Quark Records), and record producer (Curtis Urbina). Estab. 1984. Publishes 12 songs/year; 2 new songwriters/year. Staff size: 4. Pays standard royalty.

AFFILIATES Quarkette Music (BMI), Freedurb Music (ASCAP), and Quark Records.

HOW TO CONTACT Prefers CD only with 2 songs. No cassettes. Include SASE. Responds in 2 months.

FILM & TV Places 10 songs in film/year. Music Supervisor: Curtis Urbina.

MUSIC Pop. Does not want anything short of a hit.

⊘ ⊛ RAINBOW MUSIC CORP.

45 E. 66 St., New York NY 10021. (212)988-4619. E-mail: fscam45@aol.com. **Contact:** Fred Stuart, vice president. Music publisher. Estab. 1990. Publishes 25 songs/year. Staff size: 2. Pays standard royalty.

AFFILIATES Tri-Circle (ASCAP).

HOW TO CONTACT *Only accepts material referred by a reputable industry source.* Prefers CD with 2 songs and lyric sheet. Include SASE. Responds in 1 week.

FILM & TV Published "You Wouldn't Lie to an Angel, Would Ya?" (single by Diane Lampert/Paul Overstreet) from *Lady of the Evening* (album), recorded by Ben te Boe (country), released 2003 on Mega International Records; "Gonna Give Lovin' a Try" (single by Cannonball Adderley/Diane Lampert/Nat Adderley) from *The Axelrod Chronicles* (album), recorded by Randy Crawford (jazz), released 2003 on Fantasy Records; "Breaking Bread" (single by Diane Lampert/Paul Overstreet) from *Unearthed* (album), recorded by Johnny Cash (country), released 2003 on Lost Highway Records; "Gonna Give Lovin' a Try" (single by Cannonball Adderley/Diane Lampert/Nat Adderley) from *Day Dreamin'* (album), recorded by Laverne Butler (jazz), released 2002 on Chesky Records; "Nothin' Shakin' (But the Leaves on the Trees)" (single by Diane Lampert; John Gluck, Jr./Eddie Fontaine/Cirino Colcrai) recorded by the Beatles, from *Live at the BBC* (album).

MUSIC Mostly **pop, R&B,** and **country**; also **jazz**. Published "Break It to Me Gently" (single by Diane Lampert/Joe Seneca) from *TIME/LIFE* compilations *Queens of Country* (2004), *Classic Country* (2003), and *Glory Days of Rock 'N Roll* (2002), recorded by Brenda Lee.

☼○❀ RANCO MUSIC PUBLISHING

(formerly Lilly Music Publishing) 61 Euphrasia Dr., Toronto ON M6B 3V8 Canada. (416)782-5768. Fax: (416)782-7170. E-mail: panfilo@sympatico.ca; obbie-music@sympatico.ca. Website: www.myspace.com/rancorecords; www.obbiemusic.com **Contact:** Panfilo Di Matteo, president. Music publisher and record company (P. & N. Records). Estab. 1992. Publishes 20 songs/year; publishes 8 new songwriters/year. Staff size: 3. Pays standard royalty.

AFFILIATES San Martino Music Publishing and Paglieta Music Publishing (CMRRA).

HOW TO CONTACT Submit demo by mail. Unsolicited submissions are OK. Prefers CD (or videocassette if available) with 3 songs and lyric and lead sheets. "We will contact you only if we are interested in the material." Responds in 1 month.

FILM & TV Places 12 songs in film/year.

MUSIC Mostly **dance**, **ballads,** and **rock**; also **country**. Published "I'd Give It All" (single by Glenna J. Sparkes), recorded by Suzanne Michelle (country crossover), released 2005 on Lilly Records.

RAZOR & TIE ENTERTAINMENT

214 Sullivan St., Suite 4A, New York NY 10012. (212)473-9173. E-mail: bprimont@razorandtie.com. Website: www.razorandtiemusicpublishing.com. Music publisher.

HOW TO CONTACT *Does not accept unsolicited material.*

MUSIC Songwriters represented include Natalie Grant, Phillip LaRue, Matisyahu, Drive-By Truckers, Dave Barnes, Melinda Watts, and many more.

○ RED SUNDOWN RECORDS

(BMI) 1920 Errel Dowlen Rd., Pleasant View TN 37146. (615)746-0844. E-mail: rsdr@bellsouth.net. **Contact:** Ruby Perry.

HOW TO CONTACT *Does not accept unsolicited submissions.* Submit CD and cover letter. Does not return submissions.

MUSIC Country, rock, and **pop**. Does not want rap or hip-hop. Published "Take a Heart" (single by Kyle Pierce) from *Take Me with You* (album), recorded by Tammy Lee (country) released in 1998 on Red Sundown Records.

⊘ RONDOR MUSIC INTERNATIONAL/ALMO/IRVING MUSIC, A UNIVERSAL MUSIC GROUP COMPANY

(ASCAP, BMI) 2440 Sepulveda Blvd., Suite 119, Los Angeles CA 90064. (310)235-4800. Fax: (310)235-4801. E-mail: rondorla@umusic.com. Website: www.universalmusicpublishing.com. **Contact:** Creative Staff Assistant.

AFFILIATES Almo Music Corp. (ASCAP) and Irving Music, Inc. (BMI).

HOW TO CONTACT *Does not accept unsolicited submissions.*

◗○ R.T.L. MUSIC

Perthy Farm, The Perthy, Shropshire SY12 9HR United Kingdom. (01691)623173. **Contact:** Tanya Woof, international A&R manager. Professional managers: Ron Dickson (rock/rock 'n' roll); Katrine LeMatt (MOR/dance); Xavier Lee (heavy metal); Tanya Lee (classical/other types). Music publisher, record company (Le Matt Music) and record producer. Estab. 1971. Publishes approximately 30 songs/year. Pays standard royalty.

AFFILIATES Lee Music (publishing), Swoop Records, Grenouille Records, Check Records, Zarg Records, Pogo Records, R.T.F.M. (all independent companies).

HOW TO CONTACT Submit demo by mail. Unsolicited submissions are OK. Prefers CD, cassette, MDisc, or DVD (also VHS 625/PAL system videocassette) with 1-3 songs and lyric and lead sheets; include still photos and bios. "Make sure name and address are on CD or cassette." Send IRC. Responds in 6 weeks.

MUSIC All types. Published "The Old Days" (single by Ron Dickson) from *Groucho* (album), recorded by Groucho (pop); "Orphan in the Storm" (single by M.J. Lawson) from *Emmit Till* (album), recorded by Emmit Till (blues); "Donna" (single by Mike Sheriden) from *Donna* (album), recorded by Mike Sheriden (pop), all released 2006 on Swoop.

○ RUSTIC RECORDS, INC. PUBLISHING

(ASCAP, BMI, SESAC) 6337 Murray Lane, Brentwood TN 37027. (615)371-0646. E-mail: rusticrecordsam@aol.com. Website: www.rusticrecordsinc.com. **Contact:** Jack Schneider, president. Vice president: Claude Southall. Office manager: Nell Tolson. Music publisher, record company (Rustic Records Inc.), and record producer. Estab. 1984. Publishes 20 songs/year. Pays standard royalty.

AFFILIATES Covered Bridge Music (BMI), Town Square Music (SESAC), Iron Skillet Music (ASCAP).

HOW TO CONTACT Submit demo by mail. Unsolicited submissions are OK. Prefers CD with 3-4 songs and lyric sheet. Include SASE. Responds in 3 months.

MUSIC Mostly **country**. Published "In Their Eyes" (single by Jamie Champa); "Take Me as I Am" (single by Bambi Barrett/Paul Huffman); and "Yesterday's Memories" (single by Jack Schneider), recorded by Colte Bradley (country), released 2003.

TIPS "Send three or four traditional country songs, novelty songs 'foot-tapping, hand-clapping' gospel songs with strong hook for male or female artist of duet. Enclose SASE (manila envelope)."

○ RUSTRON MUSIC PUBLISHERS/WHIMSONG MUSIC

1156 Park Lane, West Palm Beach FL 33417-5957. (561)686-1354. E-mail: rmp_wmp@bellsouth.net. **Contact:** Sheelah Adams, office administrator (for current submission guidelines). Professional managers: Rusty Gordon (adult contemporary, acoustic-electric, New Age instrumentals, folk fusions, children's, blues, cabaret, soft vocal & instrumental jazz fusions, soft rock, women's music, world music); Ron Caruso (all styles); Davilyn Whims (folk fusions, country, R&B). Music publisher, record company, management firm, and record producer (Rustron Music Productions). Estab. 1972. Publishes 100-150 songs/year; publishes 10-20 new songwriters/year. Staff size: 9. Pays standard royalty.

AFFILIATES Whimsong Publishing (ASCAP).

HOW TO CONTACT Submit demo by mail. Cover letter should explain reason for submitting and what songwriter needs from Rustron-Whimsong. Unsolicited submissions are OK. Current submission guidelines will be sent by e-mail upon request. If requesting by snail mail, include SASE. All songs submitted must be copyrighted by the songwriter(s) on Form PA with the U.S. Library of Congress prior to submitting. For freelance songwriters we prefer CD with up to 10 songs or cassette with 1-3 songs and typed lyric sheets (1 sheet for each song). For performing songwriters we prefer CD with up to 15 songs. A typed lyric sheet for each song submitted is required. "Clearly label your tape container or jewel box. We don't review songs on websites." SASE or International Reply Coupon (IRC) required for all correspondence. No exceptions. Responds in 4 months.

MUSIC Mostly **pop** (ballads, blues, theatrical, cabaret), **progressive country,** and **folk/rock**; also **R&B, New Age** (instrumental fusions with classical, jazz or pop themes), **women's music**, **children's music** and **world music**. Does not publish Youth Music—rap, hip-hop, new wave, hard rock, heavy metal, or punk. Published "White House Worries" (single) from *Whitehouse Worries* (album), written and recorded by the Ramifications (progressive country-folk/socio-political-topical), released 2007 on Rustron Records; "Sanibel-Captiva and the Gulf of Mexico" (single—historical song) from *Song of Longboat Key* (album), recorded by Florida Rank & File (Florida folk); "Take the High Road" (single) from *Voting for Democracy* (album), recorded by the Panama City Pioneers (progressive-political-folk), released 2007 on Whimsong Records.

TIPS "Accepting performing and freelance songwriter's CD for full 'Body of Work' product review of all songs on CD. Write strong hooks. For single-song marketing, songs should have definitive verse melody. Keep song length 3-3¹/₂ minutes or less. Avoid predictability—create original and unique lyric themes. Tell a story. Develop a strong chorus with well-planned phrasing that can build into song titles and/or tags. Tune in to the trends and fusions indicative of commercially viable new music for the new millennium. All songs reviewed for single-song marketing must be very carefully crafted. Album cuts can be eclectic."

○ SABTECA MUSIC CO. (ASCAP)

P.O. Box 10286, Oakland CA 94610. (510)520-3527. Fax: (510)832-0464. E-mail: sabtecarecords@aol.com. Website: http://sabtecamusiccompany.com. **Contact:** Duane Herring, owner; Romare Herring, representative. Music publisher and record company (Sabteca Record Co., Andre Romare). Estab. 1980. Publishes 8-10 songs/year; 1-2 new songwriters/year. Pays standard royalty.

AFFILIATES Toyiabe Publishing (BMI).

HOW TO CONTACT *Write first and obtain permission to submit.* Prefers cassette with 2 songs and lyric sheet. Include SASE. Responds in 1 month.

MUSIC Mostly **R&B**, **pop,** and **country**. Published "Walking My Baby Home" (single by Reggie Walker) from *Reggie Walker* (album), recorded by Reggie Walker (pop), 2002 on Andre Romare Records/Sabteca; "Treat Me Like a Dog" (single by Duane Herring/Thomas Roller), recorded by John Butterworth (pop), released 2004 Sabteca Music Co; "Sleeping Beauty," recorded by C Haynace, released 2008, Sabteca Music Co.

TIPS "Listen to music daily, if possible. Keep improving writing skills."

SALT WORKS MUSIC

80 Highland Dr., Jackson OH 45640-2074. (740)286-1514 or (740)286-6561. Professional managers: Jeff Elliott (country/gospel); Mike Morgan (country). Music publisher and record producer (Mike Morgan). Staff size: 2. Pays standard royalty.

AFFILIATES Salt Creek Music (ASCAP) and Sojourner Music (BMI).

HOW TO CONTACT Submit demo package by mail. Unsolicited submissions are OK. Prefers cassette or CD. Include SASE. Responds in 2 weeks.

MUSIC Mostly **country**, **gospel**, and **pop**. Does not want rock, jazz, or classical. Published "The Tracks You Left on Me" (single by Ed Bruce/Jeff Elliott/MikeMorgan) and "Truth Is I'm a Liar" (single by Jeff Elliott/Mike Morgan) from *This Old Hat* (album), recorded by Ed Bruce (country), released 2002 on Sony/Music Row Talent.

SANDALPHON MUSIC PUBLISHING

(BMI) P.O. Box 542407, Grand Prairie TX 75054. (972)333-0876. E-mail: jackrabbit01@comcast.net. **Contact:** Ruth Otey, president. Music publisher, record company (Sandalphon Records), and management agency (Sandalphon Management). Estab. 2005. Staff size: 2. Pays standard royalty of 50%.

HOW TO CONTACT Submit demo by mail. Unsolicited submissions are fine. Prefers CD with 1-5 songs, lyric sheet, and cover letter. Include SASE or SAE and IRC for outside United States. Responds in 6-8 weeks.

MUSIC Mostly **rock**, **country**, and **alternative**; also **pop**, **blues**, and **gospel**.

SHAWNEE PRESS, INC.

1221 17th Ave. S, Nashville TN 37212. (615)320-5300. Fax: (615)320-7306. E-mail: info@shawneepress.com. Website: www.ShawneePress.com. **Contact:** Director of Church Music Publications (sacred choral music): Joseph M. Martin. Director of School Music Publica-

tions (secular choral music): Greg Gilpin. Music publisher. Estab. 1939. Publishes 150 songs/year. Staff size: 12. Pays negotiable royalty.

AFFILIATES GlorySound, Harold Flammer Music, Mark Foster Music, Wide World Music, Concert Works.

HOW TO CONTACT Submit manuscript. Unsolicited submissions are OK. See website for guidelines. Prefers manuscript; recording required for instrumental submissions. Include SASE. Responds in 4 months. "No unsolicited musicals or cantatas."

MUSIC Mostly **church/liturgical**, **educational choral**, and **instrumental**.

TIPS "Submission guidelines appear on our website."

SILICON MUSIC PUBLISHING CO.

222 Tulane St., Garland TX 75043-2239. Website: http://siliconmusic.us. President: Gene Summers. Vice president: Deanna L. Summers. Public relations: Steve Summers. Music publisher and record company (Front Row Records). Estab. 1965. Publishes 10-20 songs/year; publishes 2-3 new songwriters/year. Pays standard royalty.

◖ Also see the listing for Front Row Records in the Record Companies section of this book.

HOW TO CONTACT Submit demo package by mail. Unsolicited submissions are OK. Prefers cassette with 1-2 songs. Does not return material. Responds ASAP.

MUSIC Mostly **rockabilly** and **'50s material**; also **old-time blues/country**, and **MOR**. Published "Rockaboogie Shake" (single by James McClung) from *Rebels and More* (album), recorded by Lennerockers (rockabilly), released 2002 on Lenne (Germany); "Be-Bop City" (single by Dan Edwards), "So" (single by Dea Summers/Gene Summers), and "Little Lu Ann" (single by James McClung) from *Do Right Daddy* (album), recorded by Gene Summers (rockabilly/'50s rock and roll), released 2004 on Enviken (Sweden).

TIPS "We are very interested in '50s rock and rockabilly original masters for release through overseas affiliates. If you are the owner of any '50s masters, contact us first! We have releases in Holland, Switzerland, United Kingdom, Belgium, France, Sweden, Norway and Australia. We have the market if you have the tapes! Our staff writers include James McClung, Gary Mears (original Casuals), Robert Clark, Dea Summers,

Shawn Summers, Joe Hardin Brown, Bill Becker and Dan Edwards."

⊘⊛ SILVER BLUE MUSIC/OCEANS BLUE MUSIC

(ASCAP, BMI) 3940 Laurel Canyon Blvd., Suite 441, Studio City CA 91604. (818)980-9588. E-mail: jdiamond20@aol.com. **Contact:** Joel Diamond, president. Music publisher and record producer (Joel Diamond Entertainment). Estab. 1971. Publishes 50 songs/year. Pays standard royalty.

HOW TO CONTACT *Does not accept unsolicited material.* "No tapes returned."

FILM & TV Places 4 songs in film and 6 songs in TV/year.

MUSIC Mostly **pop** and **R&B**; also **rap** and **classical**. Produced and managed The 5 Browns-3 #1 CDs on Sony. Published "After the Lovin" (by Bernstein/Adams), recorded by Engelbert Humperdinck; "This Moment in Time" (by Alan Bernstein/Ritchie Adams), recorded by Engelbert Humperdinck. Other artists include David Hasselhoff, Kaci (Curb Records), Ike Turner, Andrew Dice Clay, Gloria Gaynor, Tony Orlando, Katie Cassidy, and Vaneza.

⊛◑ SINUS MUSIK PRODUKTION, ULLI WEIGEL

Geitnerweg 30a, D-12209, Berlin Germany. +49-30-7159050. Fax: +49-30-71590522. E-mail: ulli.weigel@arcor.de. Website: www.ulli-weigel.de. **Contact:** Ulli Weigel, owner. Music publisher, record producer, and screenwriter. Wrote German lyrics for more than 500 records. Member: GEMA, GVL. Estab. 1976. Publishes 20 songs/year; publishes 6 new songwriters/year. Staff size: 3. Pays standard royalty.

AFFILIATES Sinus Musikverlag H.U. Weigel GmbH.

HOW TO CONTACT Submit demo package by mail. Prefers CD or cassette with up to 10 songs and lyric sheets. If you want to send mp3 attachments, you should contact me before. Attachments from unknown senders will not be opened. Responds in 2 months by e-mail. "If material should be returned, please send 2 International Reply Coupons (IRC) for cassettes and 3 for a CD. No stamps."

MUSIC Mostly **rock**, **pop**, and **New Age**; also **background music for movies and audiobooks**. Published "Simple Story" (single), recorded by MAANAM on RCA (Polish rock); *Die Musik Maschine*

(album by Klaus Lage), recorded by CWN Productions on Hansa Records (pop/German), "Villa Woodstock" (film music/comedy) Gebrueder Blattschuss, Juergen Von Der Lippe, Hans Werner Olm (2005).

TIPS "Take more time working on the melody than on the instrumentation. I am also looking for master-quality recordings for non-exclusive release on my label (and to use them as soundtracks for multimedia projects, TV and movie scripts I am working on)."

◑ SIZEMORE MUSIC

P.O. Box 210314, Nashville TN 37221. (615)356-3453. E-mail: americanabooks@comcast.net. Website: www.sizemoremusic.com. Contact: Gail Rhine. Music publisher, record company (Willowind) and record producer (G.L. Rhine). Estab. 1960. Publishes 5 songs/year; 1 new songwriter/year. Pays standard royalty.

HOW TO CONTACT Submit demo by mail. Unsolicited submissions are OK. Prefers CD with 2 songs and lyric sheets. Does not return material. Responds in 3 months.

MUSIC Mostly **hip-hop**, **soul**, **blues**, and **country**. Published "Liquor and Wine" and "The Wind," written and recorded by K. Shackleford (country), released on Heart Records.

◐⊘⊛ S.M.C.L. PRODUCTIONS, INC.

P.O. Box 84, Boucherville QC J4B 5E6 Canada. (450)641-2266. **Contact:** Christian Lefort, president. Music publisher and record company. SOCAN. Estab. 1968. Publishes 25 songs/year. Pays standard royalty.

AFFILIATES A.Q.E.M. Ltee, Bag Music, C.F. Music, Big Bazaar Music, Sunrise Music, Stage One Music, L.M.S. Music, ITT Music, Machine Music, Dynamite Music, Cimafilm, Coincidence Music, Music and Music, Cinemusic Inc., Cinafilm, Editions La Fete Inc., Groupe Concept Musique, Editions Dorimen, C.C.H. Music (PRO/SDE) and Lavagot Music.

HOW TO CONTACT *Write first and obtain permission to submit.* Prefers CD with 4-12 songs and lead sheet. SAE and IRC. Responds in 3 months.

FILM & TV Places songs in film and TV. Recently published songs in French-Canadian TV series and films, including *Young Ivanhoe, Twist of Terror, More Tales of the City, Art of War, Lance & Comte (Nouvelle Generation), Turtle Island* (TV series), *Being Dorothy,*

The Hidden Fortress, Lance et Compte: La Revanche (TV series), and *A Vos Marques, Party* (film).

MUSIC Mostly **dance, easy listening,** and **MOR**; also **top 40/pop** and **TV and movie soundtracks**. Published *Always and Forever* (album by Maurice Jarre/Nathalie Carien), recorded by N. Carsen on BMG Records (ballad); *Au Nom De La Passion* (album), written and recorded by Alex Stanke on Select Records.

SME PUBLISHING GROUP

(ASCAP, BMI) P.O. Box 1150, Tuttle OK 73089. (405)381-3754. E-mail: smemusic@juno.com. Website: www.smepublishinggroup.com. Professional managers: Cliff Shelder (Southern gospel); Sharon Kinard (country gospel). Music publisher. Estab. 1994. Publishes 6 songs/year; publishes 2 new songwriters/year. Staff size: 2. Pays standard royalty.

AFFILIATES Touch of Heaven Music (ASCAP) and SME Music (BMI).

HOW TO CONTACT Submit demo package by mail. Unsolicited submissions are OK. Prefers CD with 3 songs and lyric sheet. Make sure tapes and CDs are labeled and include song title, writer's name, e-mail address, and phone number. Do not send SASE. Does not return or critique material. Responds only if interested.

MUSIC Mostly **Southern gospel, country gospel,** and **Christian country**. Does not want Christian rap, rock and roll, and hard-core country. Released "I Love You Son" (single), by Jeff Hinton and Quint Randle, from *My Oasis* (album), recorded by the Crist Family (Southern gospel) on Crossroads Records; "Look Who's in the Ship" (single by Mike Spanhanks) from *How I Picture Me* (album), recorded by the Skyline Boys (Southern Gospel) on Journey Records; "My Oasis" from *My Oasis* (album), recorded by the Crist Family (Southern gospel) on Crossroads Records.

TIPS "Always submit good quality demos. Never give up."

SONY/ATV MUSIC PUBLISHING

(ASCAP, BMI, SESAC) 8 Music Square W, Nashville TN 37203. (615)726-8300. Fax: (615)726-8329. E-mail: info@sonyatv.com. Website: www.sonyatv.com. **Santa Monica**: 10635 Santa Monica Blvd., Suite 300, Los Angeles CA 90025. (310)441-1300. **New York**:

550 Madison Ave., 5th Floor, New York NY 10022. (212)833-7730.

HOW TO CONTACT *Sony/ATV Music does not accept unsolicited submissions.*

SOUND CELLAR MUSIC

(BMI) 703 N. Brinton Ave., Dixon IL 61021. (815)297-2800. E-mail: revelators@cellarrecords.com. Website: www.cellarrecords.com. **Contact:** Todd Joos (country, pop, Christian), president. Professional managers: James Miller (folk, adult contemporary); Mike Thompson (metal, hard rock, alternative). Music publisher, record company (Sound Cellar Records), record producer, and recording studio. Estab. 1987. Publishes 15-25 songs/year. Publishes 5 or 6 new songwriters/year. Staff size: 7. Pays standard royalty.

HOW TO CONTACT Submit demo by mail. Unsolicited submissions are OK. Prefers CD with 3 or 4 songs and lyric sheet. Does not return material. "We contact by phone in 3-4 weeks only if we want to work with the artist."

MUSIC Mostly **metal, country,** and **rock**; also **pop** and **blues**. Published "Problem of Pain" (single by Shane Sowers) from *Before the Machine* (album), recorded by Junker Jorg (alternative metal/rock), released 2000; "Vaya Baby" (single by Joel Ramirez) from *It's about Time* (album), recorded by Joel Ramirez and the All-Stars (Latin/R&B), released 2000; and "X" (single by Jon Pomplin) from *Project 814* (album), recorded by Project 814 (progressive rock), released 2001, all on Cellar Records. "Vist our website for up-to-date releases."

STILL WORKING MUSIC GROUP

(ASCAP, BMI, SESAC) 1625 Broadway, Suite 200, Nashville TN 37203. (615)242-0567. Website: www.myspace.com/stillworkingmusic. **Owner:** Barbara Orbison. Music publisher and record company (Orby Records, Inc.). Estab. 1994.

AFFILIATES Still Working for the Woman Music (ASCAP), Still Working for the Man Music (BMI) and Still Working for All Music (SESAC).

HOW TO CONTACT *Does not accept unsolicited submissions.*

FILM & TV Published "First Noel," recorded by the Kelions in *Felicity*.

MUSIC Mostly **rock, country,** and **pop**; also **dance** and **R&B**. Published "If You See Him/If You See Her" (by Tommy Lee James), recorded by Reba Mc-

Intire/Brooks & Dunn; "Round about Way" (by Wil Nance), recorded by George Strait on MCA; and "Wrong Again" (by Tommy Lee James), recorded by Martina McBride on RCA (country).

TIPS "If you want to be a country songwriter, you need to be in Nashville where the business is. Write what is in your heart."

🎵○✿ SUCCES

Pijnderslaan 84, Dendermonde 9200 Belgium. (052)218 987. Fax: (052) 225 260. E-mail: deschuyteneer@hotmail.com. **Contact:** Deschuyteneer Hendrik, director. Music publisher, record company, and record producer. Estab. 1978. Publishes 400 songs/year. Hires staff songwriters. Staff size: 4. Pays standard royalty.

HOW TO CONTACT Submit demo by mail. Unsolicited submissions are OK. Prefers cassette or VHS videocassette with 3 songs. SAE and IRC. Responds in 2 months.

FILM & TV Places songs in TV. Recently released "Werkloos" (by Deschuyteneer), recorded by Jacques Vermeire in *Jacques Vermeire Show.*

MUSIC Mostly **pop**, **dance,** and **variety**; also **instrumental** and **rock**. Published "Hoe Moet Dat Nou" (single by Henry Spider), recorded by Monja (ballad), released 2001 on MN; "Liefde" (single by H. Spider), recorded by Rudy Silvester (rock), released 2001 on Scorpion; and "Bel Me Gauw" (single by H. Spider), recorded by Guy Dumon (ballad), released 2001 on BM Records.

❶ SUPREME ENTERPRISES INT'L CORP.

(ASCAP, BMI) Music publisher, record company, and record producer. Publishes 20-30 songs/year; publishes 2-6 new songwriters/year. Pays standard royalty. E-mail: seicorp@earthlink.net. Website: www.seicorp.ne.

AFFILIATES Fuerte Suerte Music (BMI), Big Daddy G. Music (ASCAP).

HOW TO CONTACT *No phone calls.* Submit demo by mail. Unsolicited submissions are OK. Prefers CD. Does not return material and you must include an e-mail address for a response. **Mail Demos To:** P.O. Box 1373, Agoura Hills CA 91376. "Please copyright material before submitting and include e-mail." Responds in 12-16 weeks if interested.

MUSIC Mostly **reggae**, **rap**, and **dance**. Published "Paso La Vida Pensando," recorded by Jose Feliciano on Universal Records; "Cucu Bam Bam" (single by David Choy), recorded by Kathy on Polydor Records (reggae/pop); "Volvere Alguna Vez" recorded by Matt Monro on EMI Records and "Meneaito" (single), recorded by Gaby on SEI Records.

TIPS "A good melody is a hit in any language."

❶ T.C. PRODUCTIONS/ETUDE PUBLISHING CO.

(BMI)121 Meadowbrook Dr., Hillsborough NJ 08844. (908)359-5110. Fax: (908)359-1962. E-mail: tony@tc-productions2005.com. Website: www.tonycamillo.com. President: Tony Camillo. Music publisher and record producer. Estab. 1992. Publishes 25-50 songs/year; publishes 3-6 new songwriters/year. Pays negotiable royalty.

AFFILIATES We Iz It Music Publishing (ASCAP), Etude Publishing (BMI), and We B Records (BMI).

HOW TO CONTACT *Write or call first and obtain permission to submit.* Prefers CD or cassette with 3-4 songs and lyric sheet. Include SASE. Responds in 1 month.

MUSIC Mostly **R&B** and **dance**; also **country** and **outstanding pop ballads**. Published "I Just Want to Be Your Everything" (single) from *A Breath of Fresh Air* (album), recorded by Michelle Parto (spiritual), released 2006 on Chancellor Records; and *New Jersey Jazz* (album).

TIPS "Michelle Parto will soon be appearing in the film musical *Sing Out*, directed by Nick Castle and written by Kent Berhard."

○✿ THISTLE HILL (BMI)

P.O. Box 707, Hermitage TN 37076. (615)889-7105. E-mail: billyherzig@hotmail.com. **Contact:** Arden Miller.

HOW TO CONTACT Submit demo by mail. Unsolicited submissions OK. Prefers CD with 3-10 songs. *No* lyric sheets. Responds only if interested.

MUSIC **Country**, **pop**, and **rock**; also **songs for film/TV**. Published "Angry Heart " (single) from *See What You Wanna See* (album), recorded by Radney Foster (Americana); and "I Wanna be Free" (single) from *I Wanna be Free* (album), recorded by Jordon MyCoskie (Americana), released 2003 on Ah! Records; "Que Vamos Hacer" (single) from *Rachel Rodriguez* (album), recorded by Rachel Rodriguez.

⊙ TIKI STUDIOS-O'NEAL PRODUCTIONS (ASCAP, BMI)

195 S. 26th St., San Jose CA 95116. (408)286-9840. E-mail: onealprod@gmail.com. Website: www.oneal-prod.com. **Contact**: Gradie O'Neal, president. Professional manager: Jeannine O'Neil. Music publisher, record company (Rowena Records) and record producer (Jeannine O'Neal and Gradie O'Neal). Estab. 1967. Publishes 40 songs/year; publishes 12 new songwriters/year. Staff size: 3. Pays standard royalty.

AFFILIATES Tooter Scooter Music (BMI), Janell Music (BMI), and O'Neal & Friend (ASCAP).

HOW TO CONTACT Submit demo by mail. Unsolicited submissions are OK. Prefers CD with 3 songs and lyric or lead sheets. Include SASE. Responds in 2 weeks.

MUSIC Mostly **country**, **Mexican**, **rock/pop**, **gospel**, **R&B**, and **New Age**. Does not want atonal music. Published "You're Looking Good to Me" (single) from *A Rock 'n' Roll Love Story* (album), written and recorded by Warren R. Spalding (rock 'n' roll), released 2003-2004; "I Am Healed" (single) from *Faith on the Front Lines* (album), written and recorded by Jeannine O'Neal (praise music), released 2003-2004; and "It Amazes Me" (single by David Davis/Jeannine O'Neal) from *The Forgiven Project* (album), recorded by David Davis and Amber Littlefield, released 2003, all on Rowena Records.

TIPS "For up-to-date published titles, review our website. Keep writing and sending songs in. Never give up—the next hit may be just around the bend."

⊙ TOURMALINE MUSIC, INC.

(BMI)2831 Dogwood Place, Nashville TN 37204. (615)269-8682. Fax: (615)269-8929. E-mail: justinpeters@songsfortheplanet.com. Website: www.songsfortheplanet.com. **Contact**: Justin Peters, president. Music publisher. Estab. 1980.

AFFILIATES Justin Peters Music (BMI), LITA Music (ASCAP) and Platinum Planet Music (BMI).

HOW TO CONTACT Submit demo package by mail. Unsolicited submissions are OK. Prefers CD with 5 songs and lyric sheet. Does not return material. "Place code '2012' on each envelope submissions."

MUSIC Mostly **rock and roll**, **classy alternative**, **adult contemporary**, **classic rock**, **country**, **Spanish gospel**, and some **Christmas music**. Published "Making War in the Heavenlies," written by George Searcy, recorded by Ron Kenoly (Integrity); "The Hurt Is Worth the Chance," by Justin Peters/Billy Simon, recorded by Gary Chapman on RCA/BMG Records, and "The Bottom Line," by Art Craig, Drew Bourke, and Justin Peters, recorded by Charley Pride (Music City Records).

⊙⊛ TOWER MUSIC GROUP

(ASCAP, BMI) 19 Music Square W, Suite U-V-W, Nashville TN 37203. (615)401-7111. Fax: (615)401-7119. E-mail: towermanagementgroup@castlerecords.com. Website: www.castlerecords.com. **Contact**: Dave Sullivan, A&R Director. Professional Managers: Ed Russell; Eddie Bishop. Music publisher, record company (Castle Records), and record producer. Estab. 1969. Publishes 50 songs/year; publishes 10 new songwriters/year. Staff size: 15. Pays standard royalty.

AFFILIATES Cat's Alley Music (ASCAP) and Alley Roads Music (BMI).

HOW TO CONTACT See submission policy on website. Prefers CD with 3 songs and lyric sheet. Does not return material. "You may follow up via e-mail." Responds in 3 months only if interested.

FILM & TV Places 2 songs in film and 26 songs on TV/year. Published "Run Little Girl" (by J.R. Jones/Eddie Ray), recorded by J.R. Jones in *Roadside Prey*.

MUSIC Mostly **country** and **R&B**; also **blues**, **pop** and **gospel**. Published "If You Broke My Heart" (single by Condrone) from *If You Broke My Heart* (album), recorded by Kimberly Simon (country); "I Wonder Who's Holding My Angel Tonight" (single) from *Up Above* (album), recorded by Carl Butler (country); and "Psychedelic Fantasy" (single by Paul Sullivan/Priege) from *The Hip Hoods* (album), recorded by the Hip Hoods (power/metal/y2k), all released 2001 on Castle Records. "Visit our website for an up-to-date listing of published songs."

TIPS "Please follow our Submission Policy at our website www.CastleRecords.com."

⊙⊙⊛ TRANSAMERIKA MUSIKVERLAG KG

Wilhelmstrasse 10, Bad Schwartau 23611 Germany. (00) (49) 4512 1530. E-mail: transamerika@online.de. Website: www.TRANSAMERIKAmusik.de. General Manager: Pia Kaminsky. License Dept: Cubus Medienverlag GMGH. **Hamburg**: Knauerstr 1, 20249 Hamburg, Germany.Phone: 0049-40-46 06 3394. License Manager: Kirsten Jung. Member: GEMA, KODA, NCB. Music publisher and administrator. Estab. 1978.

Staff size: 3. Pays 50% royalty if releasing a record; 85% if only administrating.

AFFILIATES Administrative agreements with: German Fried Music, Rock and Roll Stew Music, Cas Music Edition, MCI Music Publishing (UK), Native Tongue Music Pty. (Australia and New Zealand), Sinless Music (USA), Sinpays Publishing (USA), Pacific Electric Music Publishing (USA), Evolution Music Partners (USA), Justin Faye (composer), and Don Crouse (composer) (USA).

HOW TO CONTACT "We accept only released materials—no demos!" Submit CD or MP3. Does not return material. Responds only if interested.

FILM & TV administration.

MUSIC Mostly **pop**; also **rock, country, reggae,** and especially **film music.**

TIPS "We are specializing in administering (filing, registering, licensing and finding unclaimed royalties, and dealing with counter-claims) publishers worldwide."

○ TRANSITION MUSIC CORPORATION

E-mail: submissions@transitionmusic.com. Website: www.transitionmusic.com. Publishes 250 songs/year; publishes 50 new songwriters/year. Variable royalty based on song placement and writer.

AFFILIATES Pushy Publishing (ASCAP), Creative Entertainment Music (BMI) and One Stop Shop Music (SESAC).

HOW TO CONTACT Submit one song (make it your best) online only to submissions@transitionmusic. com. We accept all genres and unsolicited music. **Responses will not be given due to the high volume of submissions daily. Please do not call/e-mail to inquire about us receiving your submission. TMC will only contact whom they intend on signing.**

FILM & TV "TMC provides music for all forms of visual media. Mainly television." Music—all styles.

MUSIC TMC is a music library and publishing company generating over 95,000 performances in film, TV, commercials, games, Internet, and webisodes over the past year. In the last few months, TMC launched its newest division, Ultimate Exposure, exposing new independent artists to the world of visual media.

TIPS "Supply master quality material with great songs."

⊘ TRIO PRODUCTIONS, INC/ SONGSCAPE MUSIC, LLC

1026 15th Ave. S, Nashville TN 37212. (615)726-5810. E-mail: info@trioproductions.com; robyn@trioproductions.com. Website: www.trioproductions.com. **Contact:** Robyn Taylor-Drake.

AFFILIATES ASCAP, BMI, SESAC, Harry Fox Agency, CMA, WMBA, IPA

HOW TO CONTACT Contact first by e-mail to obtain permission to submit demo. *Unsolicited material will not be listened to or returned.* Submit CD with 3-4 songs and lyric sheet. Submit via mp3 once permission to send has been received. Include a lyric sheet.

MUSIC Country, pop, and **Americana**.

⊘ UNIVERSAL MUSIC PUBLISHING

(ASCAP, BMI, SESAC) 2100 Colorado Ave., Santa Monica CA 90404. (310)235-4700. Fax: (310)235-4900. Website: www.umusicpub.com.

HOW TO CONTACT *Does not accept unsolicited submissions.*

⊕ ◑ UNKNOWN SOURCE MUSIC (ASCAP)

120-4d Carver Loop, Bronx NY 10475. **Contact:** James Johnson, A&R. Music publisher, record company (Smokin Ya Productions) and record producer. Estab. 1993. Publishes 5-10 songs/year; publishes 5-10 new songwriters/year. Hires staff songwriters. Staff size: 10. Pays standard royalty.

AFFILIATES Sundance Records (ASCAP), Critique Records, WMI Records, and Cornell Entertainment.

HOW TO CONTACT *Send e-mail first, then mail.* Unsolicited submissions are OK. Prefers mp3s. Responds within 6 weeks.

MUSIC Mostly **rap/hip-hop, R&B**, and **alternative**. Published "LAH" recorded by Force Dog; "Changed My World" recorded by Crysto.

TIPS "Keep working with us, be patient, be willing to work hard. Send your very best work."

◑ VAAM MUSIC GROUP

(BMI) P.O. Box 29550, Hollywood CA 90029. E-mail: request@vaammusic.com. Website: www.VaamMusic.com. **Contact:** Pete Martin, president. Music publisher and record producer (Pete Martin/Vaam Productions). Estab. 1967. Publishes 9-24 new songs/year. Pays standard royalty.

AFFILIATES Pete Martin Music (ASCAP).

HOW TO CONTACT Send CD with 2 songs and lyric sheet. Include SASE. Responds in 1 month. "Small packages only."

MUSIC Mostly **top 40/pop**, **country**. "Submitted material must have potential of reaching top 5 on charts."

TIPS "Study the top 10 charts in the style you write. Stay current and up-to-date with today's market."

VINE CREEK MUSIC

(ASCAP) P.O. Box 171143, Nashville TN 37217. E-mail: vinecreek1@aol.com. Website: www.myspace.com/vinecreekmusic or www.darleneaustin.com **Contact:** Darlene Austin, Brenda Madden. Administration: Jayne Negri. Creative director: Brenda Madden.

HOW TO CONTACT *Vine Creek Music does not accept unsolicited submissions.* "Only send material of good competitive quality. We do not return tapes/CDs unless SASE is enclosed."

WALKERBOUT MUSIC GROUP

(ASCAP, BMI, SESAC), P.O. Box 24454, Nashville TN 37202. (615)269-7071. Fax: (888)894-4934. E-mail: matt@walkerboutmusic.com. Website: www.walkerboutmusic.com. **Contact:** Matt Watkins, director of operations. Estab. 1988. Publishes 50 songs/year; 5-10 new songwriters/year. Pays standard royalty.

AFFILIATES Goodland Publishing Company (ASCAP), Marc Isle Music (BMI), Gulf Bay Publishing (SESAC), Con Brio Music (BMI), Wiljex Publishing (ASCAP), Concorde Publishing (SESAC).

HOW TO CONTACT "Please see website for submission information."

MUSIC Mostly **country/Christian** and **adult contemporary**.

WARNER/CHAPPELL MUSIC, INC.

10585 Santa Monica Blvd., Los Angeles CA 90025. (310)441-8600. Fax: (310)441-8780. Website: www.warnerchappell.com. Music publisher.

HOW TO CONTACT *Warner/Chappell does not accept unsolicited material.*

WEAVER OF WORDS MUSIC

(BMI) (administered by Bug Music), P.O. Box 803, Tazewell VA 24651. (276)988-6267. E-mail: cooksong@verizon.net. Website: www.weaverofwordsmusic.com. **Contact:** H.R. Cook, president. Music publisher and record company (Fireball Records). Estab. 1978. Publishes 12 songs/year. Pays standard royalty.

AFFILIATES Weaver of Melodies Music (ASCAP).

HOW TO CONTACT Submit demo by mail. Unsolicited submissions are OK. Prefers CD with 3 songs and lyric or lead sheets. "We prefer CD submissions but will accept mp3s—limit 2." Include SASE. Responds in 3 weeks.

MUSIC Mostly **country, pop, bluegrass, R&B, film and television,** and **rock**. Published "Zero to Love" (single by H. Cook/Brian James Deskins/Rick Tiger) from *It's Just the Night* (album), recorded by Del McCoury Band (bluegrass), released 2003 on McCoury Music; "Muddy Water" (Alan Johnston) from *The Midnight Call* (album), recorded by Don Rigsby (bluegrass), released 2003 on Sugar Hill; "Ol Brown Suitcase" (H.R. Cook) from *Lonesome Highway* (album), recorded by Josh Williams (bluegrass), released 2004 on Pinecastle; and "Mansions of Kings" from *Cherry Holmes II* (album), recorded by IBMA 2005 Entertainer of the Year Cherry Holmes (bluegrass), released 2007 on Skaggs Family Records.

BERTHOLD WENGERT (MUSIKVERLAG)

Hauptstrasse 36, Pfinztal-Söllingen, D-76327 Germany. **Contact:** Berthold Wengert. Music publisher. Pays standard GEMA royalty.

HOW TO CONTACT Prefers cassette and complete score for piano. SAE and IRC. Responds in 1 month. "No cassette returns!"

MUSIC Mostly **light music** and **pop**.

WILCOM PUBLISHING

(ASCAP) B248 Deano Rd, Branson MO 65616. (4170)559-5256. Fax: (870)847-1721. E-mail: william@wilcompublishing.com. **Contact:** William Clark, owner. Music publisher. Estab. 1989. Publishes 10-15 songs/year; publishes 1-2 new songwriters/year. Staff size: 2. Pays standard royalty.

HOW TO CONTACT *Write or call first and obtain permission to submit.* Prefers CD with 1-2 songs and lyric sheet. Include SASE. Responds in 3 weeks.

MUSIC Mostly **R&B, pop,** and **rock**; also **country**. Does not want rap. Published "Girl Can't Help It" (single by W. Clark/D. Walsh/P. Oland), recorded by Stage 1 on Rockit Records (top 40). Also produced a cover of "D'yer M'aker" by Mylo Bigsby on MGL Records.

❶ ZOMBA MUSIC PUBLISHING

(ASCAP, BMI) 245 Fifth Avenue., 8th Floor, New York NY 10001. (212)727-0016. Website: www.zomba.com. **Contact:** Jennifer Blakeman (pop/rock), Peter Visvardis (pop/rock), or Tanya Brown (urban). **Beverly Hills:** 8750 Wilshire Blvd., Beverly Hills CA 90211. (310)358-4200. **Contact:** Andrea Torchia (pop/rock). Music publisher. Publishes 5,000 songs/year.

AFFILIATES Zomba Enterprises, Inc. (ASCAP); Zomba Songs, Inc. (BMI).

HOW TO CONTACT *Zomba Music Publishing does not accept unsolicited material.* "Contact us through management or an attorney."

MUSIC Mostly **R&B**, **pop**, and **rap**; also **rock** and **alternative**. Published "Baby One More Time" (single by M. Martin), recorded by Britney Spears on Jive; "Home Alone" (single by R. Kelly/K. Price/K. Murray), recorded by R. Kelly featuring Keith Murray on Jive; and "Taking Everything" (single by G. Levert/ D. Allamby/L. Browder/A. Roberson), recorded by Gerald Levert on EastWest.

RECORD COMPANIES

Record companies release and distribute records, cassettes, and CDs—the tangible products of the music industry. They sign artists to recording contracts, decide what songs those artists will record, and determine which songs to release. They are also responsible for providing recording facilities, securing producers and musicians, and overseeing the manufacture, distribution, and promotion of new releases.

MAJOR LABELS & INDEPENDENT LABELS

Major labels and independent labels—what's the difference between the two?

The majors

As of this writing, there are four major record labels, commonly referred to as the "Big 4":

- **THE EMI GROUP** (Capitol Music Group, Angel Music Group, Astralwerks, Chrysalis Records, etc.)
- **SONY BMG** (Columbia Records, Epic Records, RCA Records, Arista Records, J Records, Provident Label Group, etc.)
- **UNIVERSAL MUSIC GROUP** (Universal Records, Interscope/Geffen/A&M, Island/Def Jam, Dreamworks Records, MCA Nashville Records, Verve Music Group, etc.)
- **WARNER MUSIC GROUP** (Atlantic Records, Bad Boy, Asylum Records, Warner Bros. Records, Maverick Records, Sub Pop, etc.)

Each of the "Big 4" is a large, publicly traded corporation beholden to shareholders and quarterly profit expectations. This means the major labels have greater financial resources and promotional muscle than a smaller "indie" label, but it's also harder to get signed to a major. A big major label may also expect more contractual control over an artist or band's sound and image.

As shown in the above list, they also each act as umbrella organizations for numerous other well-known labels—former major labels in their own right, well-respected former independent/boutique labels, as well as subsidiary "vanity" labels fronted by successful major label recording artists. Each major label also has its own related worldwide product distribution system, and many independent labels will contract with the majors for distribution into stores.

If a label is distributed by one of these major companies, you can be assured any release coming out on that label has a large distribution network behind it. It will most likely be sent to most major retail stores in the United States.

The independents

Independent labels go through smaller distribution companies to distribute their product. They usually don't have the ability to deliver records in massive quantities as the major distributors do. However, that doesn't mean independent labels aren't able to have hit records just like their major counterparts. A record label's distributors are found in the listings after the "Distributed By" heading.

Which do I submit to?

Many of the companies listed in this section are independent labels. They are usually the most receptive to receiving material from new artists. Major labels spend more money than most other segments of the music industry; the music publisher, for instance, pays only for items such as salaries and the costs of making demos. Record companies, at great financial risk, pay for many more services, including production, manufacturing, and promotion. Therefore, they must be very selective when signing new talent. Also, the continuing fear of copyright infringement suits has closed avenues to getting new material heard by the majors. Most don't listen to unsolicited submissions, period. Only songs recommended by attorneys, managers, and producers whom record company employees trust and respect are being heard by A&R people at major labels (companies with a referral policy have a ● preceding their listing). But that doesn't mean all major labels are closed to new artists. With a combination of a strong local following, success on an independent label (or strong sales of an independently produced and released album) and the right connections, you could conceivably get an attentive audience at a major label.

But the competition is fierce at the majors, so you shouldn't overlook independent labels. Since they're located all over the country, indie labels are easier to contact and can be important in building a local base of support for your music. Independent labels usually concentrate on a specific type of music, which will help you target those companies your submissions should be sent to. And since the staff at an indie label is smaller, there are fewer channels to go through to get your music heard by the decision makers in the company.

HOW RECORD COMPANIES WORK

Independent record labels can run on a small staff, with only a handful of people running the day-to-day business. Major record labels are more likely to be divided into the following departments: A&R, sales, marketing, promotion, product management, artist development, production, finance, business/legal and international.

- The *A&R department* is staffed with A&R representatives who search out new talent. They go out and see new bands, listen to demo tapes, and decide which artists to sign. They also look for new material for already signed acts, match producers with artists, and oversee recording projects. Once an artist is signed by an A&R rep and a record is recorded, the rest of the departments at the company come into play.
- The *sales department* is responsible for getting a record into stores. They make sure record stores and other outlets receive enough copies of a record to meet consumer demand.
- The *marketing department* is in charge of publicity, advertising in magazines and other media, promotional videos, album cover artwork, in-store displays, and any other means of getting the name and image of an artist to the public.
- The *promotion department*'s main objective is to get songs from a new album played on the radio. They work with radio programmers to make sure a product gets airplay.
- The *product management department* is the ringmaster of the sales, marketing, and promotion departments, assuring that they're all going in the same direction when promoting a new release.
- The *artist development department* is responsible for taking care of things while an artist is on tour, such as setting up promotional opportunities in cities where an act is performing.
- The *production department* handles the actual manufacturing and pressing of the record and makes sure it gets shipped to distributors in a timely manner.
- People in the *finance department* compute and distribute royalties, as well as keep track of expenses and income at the company.
- The *business/legal department* takes care of contracts, not only between the record company and artists but with foreign distributors, record clubs, etc.
- And finally, the *international department* is responsible for working with international companies for the release of records in other countries.

LOCATING A RECORD LABEL

With the abundance of record labels out there, how do you go about finding one that's right for the music you create? First, it helps to know exactly what kind of music a record label releases. Become familiar with the records a company has released, and see if they fit in with what you're doing. Each listing in this section details the type of music a particular record company is interested in releasing. You should only approach companies open to your level of experience (see A Sample Listing Decoded). Visiting a company's website can also provide valuable information about a company's philosophy, the artists on the label, and the music they work with.

Networking

Recommendations by key music industry people are an important part of making contacts with record companies. Songwriters must remember that talent alone does not guarantee success in the music business. You must be recognized through contacts, and the only way to make contacts is through networking. Networking is the process of building an interconnecting web of acquaintances within the music business. The more industry people you meet, the larger your contact base becomes, and the better are your chances of meeting someone with the clout to get your demo into the hands of the right people. If you want to get your music heard by key A&R representatives, networking is imperative.

Networking opportunities can be found anywhere industry people gather. A good place to meet key industry people is at regional and national music conferences and workshops. There are many held all over the country for all types of music (see the Workshops & Conferences section for more information). You should try to attend at least one or two of these events each year; it's a great way to increase the number and quality of your music industry contacts.

Creating a buzz

Another good way to attract A&R people is to make a name for yourself as an artist. By starting your career on a local level and building it from there, you can start to cultivate a following and prove to labels that you can be a success. A&R people figure if an act can be successful locally, there's a good chance they could be successful nationally. Start getting booked at local clubs, and start a mailing list of fans and local media. Once you gain some success on a local level, branch out. All this attention you're slowly gathering, this "buzz" you're generating, will not only get to your fans but to influential people in the music industry as well.

SUBMITTING TO RECORD COMPANIES

When submitting to a record company, major or independent, a professional attitude is imperative. Be specific about what you are submitting and what your goals are. If you are strictly a songwriter and the label carries a band you believe would properly present your song, state that in your cover letter. If you are an artist looking for a contract, showcase your strong points as a performer. Whatever your goals are, follow submission guidelines closely, be as neat as possible, and include a top-notch demo. If you need more information concerning a company's requirements, write or call for more details. (For more information on submitting your material, see the sections Where Should I Send My Songs? and Demo Recordings.)

RECORD COMPANY CONTRACTS

Once you've found a record company that is interested in your work, the next step is signing a contract. Independent label contracts are usually not as long and complicated as major label ones, but they are still binding, legal contracts. Make sure the terms are in the best interest of both you and the label. Avoid anything in your contract that you feel is too restrictive. It's important to have your contract reviewed by a competent entertainment lawyer. A basic recording contract can run from 40 to 100 pages, and you need a lawyer to help you understand it. A lawyer will also be essential in helping you negotiate a deal that is in your best interest.

Recording contracts cover many areas, and just a few of the things you will be asked to consider will be: What royalty rate is the record label willing to pay you? What kind of advance are they offering? How many records will the company commit to? Will they offer tour support? Will they provide a budget for video? What sort of a recording budget are they offering? Are they asking you to give up any publishing rights? Are they offering you a publishing advance? These are only a few of the complex issues raised by a recording contract, so it's vital to have an entertainment lawyer at your side as you negotiate.

ADDITIONAL RECORD COMPANIES

The Case for Independents

If you're interested in getting a major label deal, it makes sense to look to independent record labels to get your start. Independent labels are seen by many as a stepping-stone to a major recording contract. Very few artists are signed to a major label at the start of their careers; usually, they've had a few independent releases that helped build their reputation in the industry. Major labels watch independent labels closely to locate up-and-coming bands and new trends. In the current economic atmosphere at major labels—with extremely high overhead costs for developing new bands and the fact that only 10 percent of acts on major labels actually make any profit—they're not willing to risk everything on an unknown act. Most major labels won't even consider signing a new act that hasn't had some indie success.

But independents aren't just farming grounds for future major label acts; many bands have long-term relationships with indies, and prefer it that way. While they may not be able to provide the extensive distribution and promotion that a major label can (though there are exceptions), indie labels can help an artist become a regional success, and may even help the performer to see a profit as well. With the lower overhead and smaller production costs an independent label operates on, it's much easier to "succeed" on an indie label than on a major.

Icons

For more instructional information on the listings in this book, including explanations of the icons, read the article How to Use *Songwriter's Market*.

4AD

Beggar's Group, 17-19 Alma Rd., London, SW18 1AA, United Kingdom. (020)8870-9912. E-mail: 4AD@4AD.com. Website: www.4ad.com.

HOW TO CONTACT Submit demo (CD or vinyl only) by mail, attention A&R, 4AD. "Sadly, there just aren't enough hours in the day to respond to everything that comes in. We'll only get in touch if we really like something."

MUSIC Mostly rock, indie/alternative. Current artists include Blonde Redhead, Bon Iver, Camera Obscura, the Breeders, the National, TV On The Radio, and more.

ALTERNATIVE TENTACLES

Attn: New Materials, P.O. Box 419092, San Francisco, CA 94141.(510)596-8981. Fax: (510)596-8982. E-mail: jb@alternativetentacles.com. Website: www.alternativetentacles.com. **Contact:** Jello Biafra. Estab. 1979. Staff size: 4. Releases 15-20 albums/year.

DISTRIBUTED BY Lumberjack/Mordam Records.

HOW TO CONTACT Unsolicited submissions OK. Prefers CD or cassette. Does not return material. Responds only if interested. *"We accept demos by postal mail ONLY! We do not accept mp3s sent to us.* We will not go out and listen to your mp3s on Web sites. If you are interested in having ATR hear your music, you need to send us a CD, tape or vinyl. We cannot return your demos either, so please don't send us your originals or ask us to send them back. Sometimes Jello replies to people submitting demos; sometimes he doesn't. There is no way for us to check on your 'status,' so please don't ask us."

MUSIC Mostly **punk rock**, **spoken word**, **Brazilian hardcore**, **bent pop**, **faux-country**, and **assorted rock & roll**. Released *It's Not the Eat, It's the Humidity* (album), recorded by the Eat (punk); *Fuck World Trade* (album), recorded by Leftover Crack (punk); *Live from the Armed Madhouse* (album), recorded by Greg Palast (spoken word); *Dash Rip Rock* (album), recorded by Hee Haw Hell (Southern country punk); *Homem Inimigo Do Homem* (album), recorded by Ratos De Parao (Brazilian hardcore). Other artists include Jello Biafra, the (International) Noise Conspiracy, Subhumans, Butthole Surfers, Dead Kennedys, DOA, Pansy Division, and Melvins.

AMERICAN RECORDINGS

8920 Sunset Blvd., 2nd Floor, W. Hollywood, CA 90069. (310)288-5300. Website: www.americanrecordings.com. A&R: Dino Paredes, George Drakoulias, Antony Bland. Labels include Too Pure, Infinite Zero, UBL, Venture and Onion. Record company. American Recordings is a subsidiary of Sony BMG, one of the "Big 4" major labels.

DISTRIBUTED BY Sony.

HOW TO CONTACT Submit demo by mail. Unsolicited submissions are OK. Prefers CD, cassette or videocassette with lyric and lead sheet.

MUSIC Released *Unchained*, recorded by Johnny Cash, released on American Recordings. Other artists include Slayer, System of a Down, the Jayhawks, Rahat Feteh Ali Khan, Paloalto, Noise Ratchet, and the (International) Noise Conspiracy.

ANGEL RECORDS

150 Fifth Ave., 6th Floor, New York NY 10011. (212)786-8600. E-mail: EMIClassicsUS@gmail.com. Website: www.angelrecords.com. Record company. Labels include EMI Classics, Manhattan Records, and Virgin Classics.

Angel Records is a subsidiary of the EMI Group, one of the "Big 4" major labels. EMI is a British-based company.

DISTRIBUTED BY EMI Music Distribution.

HOW TO CONTACT *Angel/EMI Records does not accept unsolicited submissions.*

MUSIC Artists include Sarah Brightman, Sir Paul McCartney, and Bernadette Peters.

ARIANA RECORDS

1312 S. Avenida Polar, Tucson, AZ 85710. Website: www.arianarecords.net. Labels include Smart Monkey Records, the MoleHole Studio, Chumway Studios. Record company, music publisher (Myko Music/BMI) and record producer. Estab. 1980. Releases 5 CDs a year and 1 compilation/year. Pays negotiable rates.

DISTRIBUTED BY LoneBoy Records London, the Yellow Record Company in Germany, and Groovetune Music distributors in Alberta, Canada.

HOW TO CONTACT "Send finished masters only. No demos! Unsolicited material okay."

MUSIC Mostly rock, funk, jazz, anything weird, strange, or lo-fi (must be mastered to CD). Released *Rustling Silk* (electronic) by BuddyLoveBand; *Porn-Muzik 2* (ambient); *T.G.I.F4* (electronica); *Under-*

Cover Band; 2010 (pop rock and funk); *Catch the Ghost* (hard rock).

TIPS "Keep on trying."

● ARKADIA ENTERTAINMENT CORP.

11 Reservoir Rd., Saugerties, NY 12477. (845)246-9955. Fax:(845)246-9966. E-mail: info@view.com. Website: www.arkadiarecords.com. **Contact:** A&R Song Submissions, acquisitions@view.com. Labels include Arkadia Jazz and Arkadia Chansons. Record company, music publisher (Arkadia Music), record producer (Arkadia Productions), and Arkadia Video. Estab. 1995.

HOW TO CONTACT *Write or call first and obtain permission to submit.*

MUSIC Mostly **jazz**, **classical**, and **pop/R&B**; also **world**.

● ASTRALWERKS

ATTN: A&R Dept. 150 5th Ave, New York, NY 10011. E-mail: A&R@astralwerks.net. Website: www.astralwerks.com. **Contact:** A&R. Record company. Estab. 1979. Releases 10-12 12" singles and 100 CDs/year. Pays varying royalty to artists on contract; statutory rate to publisher per song.

   ○ Astralwerks is a subsidiary of the EMI Group, one of the "Big 4" major labels. EMI is a British-based company.

HOW TO CONTACT Send submissions to: "A&R Dept." to address above. No unsolicited phone calls please. Prefers CD. "Please include any pertinent information, including your group name, track titles, names of members, bio background, successes, and any contact info. Do not send e-mail attachments."

MUSIC Mostly **alternative/indie/electronic**. Artists include VHS or BETA, Badly Drawn boy, the Beta Band, Chemical Brothers, Turin Breaks, and Fatboy Slim.

TIPS "We are open to artists of unique quality and enjoy developing artists from the ground up. We listen to all types of 'alternative' music regardless of genre. It's about the aesthetic and artistic quality first. We send out rejection letters so do not call to find out what's happening with your demo."

○ ATLAN-DEC/GROOVELINE RECORDS

Record company, music publisher, and record producer. Staff size: 2. Releases 3-4 singles, 3-4 LPs and 3-4 CDs/year. Pays 10-25% royalty to artists on contract; statutory rate to publisher per song on record.

DISTRIBUTED BY C.E.D. Entertainment Dist.

HOW TO CONTACT Submit demo package by mail. Unsolicited submissions are OK. Prefers CD with lyric sheet. Does not return material. Responds in 3 months.

MUSIC Mostly R&B/urban, hip-hop/rap, and contemporary jazz; also soft rock, gospel, dance, and new country. Released "Temptation" by Shawree, released 2004 on Atlan-Dec/Grooveline Records; *Enemy of the State* (album), recorded by Lowlife (rap/hip-hop); *I'm The Definition* (album), recorded by L.S. (rap/hip-hop), released 2007; "AHHW" (single), recorded by LeTebony Simmons (R&B), released 2007. Other artists include Furious D (rap/hip-hop), Mark Cocker (new country), and Looka, "From the Top" (rap/hip-hop) recorded in 2008.

◐◑ ATLANTIC RECORDS

1290 Avenue of the Americas, New York, NY 10104. (212)707-2000. Fax: (212)581-6414. Website: www.atlanticrecords.com. **Los Angeles:** 3400 W. Olive Ave., 3rd Floor, Burbank, CA 91505. (818)238-6800. Labels include Big Beat Records, LAVA, Nonesuch Records, Atlantic Classics, and Rhino Records. Record company. Pays negotiable royalty to artists on contract; negotiable rate to publisher per song on record.

   ○ Atlantic Records is a subsidiary of Warner Music Group, one of the "Big 4" major labels.

DISTRIBUTED BY WEA.

HOW TO CONTACT *Does not accept unsolicited material.* "No phone calls, please."

MUSIC Artists include Missy Elliott, Simple Plan, Lupe Fiasco, Phil Collins, B.O.B., Jason Mraz, and Death Cab for Cutie.

◑ AVITA RECORDS

P.O. Box 764, Hendersonville, TN 37077-0764. (615)824-9313. Fax: (615)824-0797. E-mail: tachoir@bellsouth.net. Website: www.tachoir.com. **Contact:** Robert Kayne, manager. Record company, music publisher (Riohcat Music, BMI), and record producer (Jerry Tachoir). Estab. 1976. Staff size: 8. Releases 2 LPs and 2 CDs/year. Pays negotiable royalty to artists on contract; statutory rate to publisher per song on record.

   ○ Also see the listing for Riohcat Music in the "Managers & Booking Agents" section of this book.

HOW TO CONTACT *Contact first and obtain permission to submit.* "We only accept material referred to us by a reputable industry source." Prefers CD, cassette, or DAT. Does not return materials. Responds only if interested.

MUSIC Mostly **jazz**. Released *Improvised Thoughts* (album by Marlene Tachoir/Jerry Tachoir/Van Manakas), recorded by Jerry Tachoir and Van Manakas (jazz), released 2001 on Avita Records. Other artists include Van Manakas.

● ◑ AWAL UK LIMITED

Sheffield Technology Park, Arundel St., Sheffield S1 2NS, United Kingdom. E-mail: info@awal.com. Website: www.awal.com. **Contact:** A&R Department. President: Denzyl Feigelson. Record company. Estab. 1996.

DISTRIBUTED BY Primarily distributes via digital downloads but physical distribution available.

HOW TO CONTACT Submit demo by mail. Unsolicited submissions are OK. Prefers CD with 5 songs, lyric sheet, cover letter, and press clippings. Does not return materials.

MUSIC Mostly **pop**, **world**, and **jazz**; also **techno**, **teen**, and **children's**. Released *Go Cat Go* (album by various), recorded by Carl Perkins on ArtistOne. com; *Bliss* (album), written and recorded by Donna Delory (pop); and *Shake a Little* (album), written and recorded by Michael Ruff, both on Awal Records.

⊘ AWARE RECORDS

1316 Sherman Ave., #215, Evanston, IL 60201. (847)424-2000. E-mail: awareinfo@awaremusic.com. Website: www.awaremusic.com. A&R: Steve Smith. President: Gregg Latterman. Record company. Estab. 1993. Staff size: 6. Releases 5 LPs, 1 EP and 3 CDs/year. Pays negotiable royalty to artists on contract; statutory rate to publisher per song on record.

HOW TO CONTACT *Does not accept unsolicited submissions.*

MUSIC Mostly **rock/pop**. Artists include Mat Kearney and Guster.

● BIG BEAR RECORDS

P.O. Box 944, Edgbaston, Birmingham B16 8UT, United Kingdom. 44-121-454-7020. Fax: 44-121-454-9996. E-mail: jim@bigbearmusic.com. Website: www.bigbearmusic.com. A&R Director: Jim Simpson. Labels include Truckers Delight and Grandstand Records. Record company, record producer, and music publisher

(Bearsongs). Releases 6 LPs/year. Pays 8-10% royalty to artists on contract; $8\frac{1}{4}$% to publishers for each record sold. Royalties paid directly to songwriters and artists or through US publishing or recording affiliate.

> ◯ Big Bear's publishing affiliate, Bearsongs, is listed in the "Music Publishers" section, and Big Bear is listed in the "Record Producers" section of this book.

HOW TO CONTACT Submit demo by mail. Unsolicited submissions are OK. Prefers CD. Does not return material. Responds in 3 weeks.

MUSIC **Blues** and **jazz**. Released *I've Finished with the Blues* and *Blues for Pleasure* (by Skirving/Nicholls), both recorded by King Pleasure and the Biscuit Boys (jazz); and *Side-Steppin'* (by Barnes), recorded by Alan Barnes/Bruce Adams Quintet (jazz), all on Big Bear Records. Other artists include Lady Sings the Blues, Drummin' Man, Kenny Baker's Dozen, Tipitina, and Dr. Teeth Big Band.

◑ BLACKHEART RECORDS

636 Broadway, New York, NY 10012. (212)353-9600. Fax: (212)353-8300. E-mail: blackheart@blackheart. com. Website: www.blackheart.com. **Contact:** Zander Wolff, A&R. Record label. Estab. 1982.

HOW TO CONTACT Unsolicited submissions are OK. Prefers CD with 1-3 songs and lyric sheets. Include SASE. Responds only if interested.

MUSIC Mostly **rock**. Artists include Joan Jett & the Blackhearts, the Dollyrots, the Vacancies, Girl in a Coma, and the Eyeliners.

● CAMBRIA RECORDS & PUBLISHING

P.O. Box 374, Lomita, CA 90717. (310)831-1322. Fax: (310)833-7442. E-mail: cambriamus@aol.com. Website: cambriamus.com. **Contact:** Lance Bowling, director of recording operations. Record company and music publisher. Estab. 1979. Staff size: 3. Pays 5-8% royalty to artists on contract; statutory rate to publisher for each record sold.

DISTRIBUTED BY Albany Distribution.

HOW TO CONTACT *Write first and obtain permission to submit.* Prefers cassette. Include SASE. Responds in 1 month.

MUSIC Mostly *classical*. Released *Songs of Elinor Remick Warren* (album) on Cambria Records. Other artists include Marie Gibson (soprano), Leonard Pennario (piano), Thomas Hampson (voice), Mischa Leftkowitz (violin), Leigh Kaplan (piano), North Wind Quintet, and Sierra Wind Quintet.

● CANTILENA RECORDS

740 Fox Dale Ln. Knoxville, TN. 37934. E-mail: llzz@ aol.com. Website: www.cantilenarecords.com. A&R: Laurel Zucker, owner. A&R: B. Houseman. Record company. Estab. 1993. Releases 3 CDs/year. Pays Harry Fox standard royalty to artists on contract; statutory rate to publishers per song on record.

HOW TO CONTACT *Write first and obtain permission to submit or to arrange personal interview.* Prefers CD. Does not return material.

MUSIC Classical, jazz. Released "Caliente!" (single by Christopher Caliendo) from *Caliente! World Music for Flute & Guitar* (album), recorded by Laurel Zucker and Christopher Caliendo! (world crossover); *Suites No. 1 & 2 For Flute & Jazz Piano Trio* (album by Claude Bolling), recorded by Laurel Zucker, Joe Gilman, David Rokeach, Jeff Neighbor (jazz); and *HOPE! Music for Flute, Soprano, Guitar* (album by Daniel Akiva, Astor Piazzolla, Haim Permont, Villa-Lobos) (classical/world), recorded by Laurel Zucker, Ronit Widmann-Levy, Daniel Akiva, all released in 2004 by Cantilena Records. Other artists include Tim Gorman, Prairie Prince, Dave Margen, Israel Philharmonic, Erkel Chamber Orchestra, Samuel Magill, Renee Siebert, Robin Sutherland, and Gerald Ranch.

⊘ CAPITOL RECORDS

1750 N. Vine St., Hollywood, CA 90028. (323)462-6252. Fax: (323)469-4542. Website: www.hollywood-andvine.com. **Nashville:** 3322 West End Ave., 11th Floor, Nashville, TN 37203. (615)269-2000. Labels include Blue Note Records, Grand Royal Records, Pangaea Records, The Right Stuff Records, and Capitol Nashville Records. Record company.

    ◯ Capitol Records is a subsidiary of the EMI Group, one of the "Big 4" major labels.

DISTRIBUTED BY EMD.

HOW TO CONTACT *Capitol Records does not accept unsolicited submissions.*

MUSIC Artists include Coldplay, the Decemberists, Beastie Boys, Katy Perry, Interpol, Lily Allen, and Depeche Mode.

◐❀ CAPP RECORDS

P.O. Box 150871, San Rafael, CA 94915-0871. Phone/fax: (415)457-8617. E-mail: manus@capprecords.com.

Website: www.capprecords.com. CEO/International Manager: Dominique Toulon (pop, dance, New Age); Creative Manager/A&R: Manus Buchart (dance, techno). President: Rudolf Stember. Vice president/Publisher: Radi Tamimi (tamimi@capprecords.com); Public Relations/A&R: Michael Oliva (oliva@capprecords.com). Music publisher (Cappster music/ASCAP and CIDC Music/BMI) and record company. Member: NARAS, NCSA, Songwriter's Guild of America. Estab. 1993. Publishes 100 songs/year; publishes 25 new songwriters/year. Pays standard royalty.

HOW TO CONTACT Submit demo package by mail. Unsolicited submissions are OK. Prefers CD or NTSC videocassette with 3 songs and cover letter. "E-mail us in advance for submissions, if possible." Include SASE. Only responds if interested.

FILM & TV Places 20 songs in film and 7 songs on TV/year. Music supervisors: Dominique Toulon (pop, dance, New Age). "Currently doing music placement for television—*MTV*, *VH1*, *Oprah*, *A&E Network*, and *Discovery Channel*."

MUSIC Mostly **pop**, **dance**, and **techno**; also **New Age**. Does not want country. Released "It's Not a Dream" (single by Cary August/Andre Pessis), recorded by Cary August on CAPP Records (dance). "Visit our website for new releases."

◑ CHERRY STREET RECORDS

P.O. Box 52626, Tulsa OK 74152. (918)925-9736. Fax: (888)878-0817. E-mail: ryound@cherrystreetrecords. com. Website: www.cherrystreetrecords.com. President: Rodney Young. Record company and music publisher. Estab. 1990. Staff size: 1. Releases 1 CD/year. Pays 50% royalty to artists on contract; statutory rate to publisher per song on record.

DISTRIBUTED BY Internet.

HOW TO CONTACT *Write first and obtain permission to submit.* Prefers CD with 4 songs and lyric sheet. Include SASE. Responds in 4 months.

MUSIC Rock, **country**, and **R&B**; also **jazz**. Released *Promised Land* (album), written and recorded by Richard Neville on Cherry Street (rock). Other artists include George W. Carroll and Chris Blevins.

TIPS "We sign only artists who play an instrument, sing, and write songs. Send only your best 4 songs."

◗◯ COLLECTOR RECORDS

P.O. Box 1200, 3260 AE Oud Beijerland, The Netherlands. (31)186 604266. Fax: (31)186 604366. E-mail:

info@collectorrecords.nl. Website: www.collector-records.nl. **Contact:** Cees Klop, president. Manager: John Moore. Labels include All Rock, Downsouth, Unknown, Pro Forma, and White Label Records. Record company, music publisher (All Rock Music Publishing) and record producer (Cees Klop). Estab. 1967. Staff size: 4. Release 25 LPs/year. Pays 10% royalty to artist on contract.

HOW TO CONTACT Submit demo package by mail. Unsolicited submissions are OK. Prefers cassette. SAE and IRC. Responds in 2 months.

MUSIC Mostly **'50s rock, rockabilly, hillbilly boogie,** and **country/rock**; also **piano boogie woogie**. Released *Rock Crazy Baby* (album), by Art Adams (1950s rockabilly), released 2005; *Marvin Jackson* (album), by Marvin Jackson (1950s rockers), released 2005; *Western Australian Snake Pit R&R* (album), recorded by various (1950s rockers), released 2005, all on Collector Records. Other artists include Henk Pepping, Rob Hoeke, Eric-Jan Overbeek, and more. "See our website."

⊘ COLUMBIA RECORDS

555 Madison Ave., 10th Floor, New York NY 10022. (212)833-4000. Fax: (212)833-4389. E-mail: sonymusiconline@sonymusic.com. Website: www.columbiarecords.com. **Santa Monica:** 2100 Colorado Ave., Santa Monica CA 90404. (310)449-2100. Fax: (310)449-2743. **Nashville:** 34 Music Square E., Nashville TN 37203. (615)742-4321. Fax: (615)244-2549. Record company.

◐ Columbia Records is a subsidiary of Sony BMG, one of the "Big 4" major labels.

DISTRIBUTED BY Sony.

HOW TO CONTACT *Columbia Records does not accept unsolicited submissions.*

MUSIC Artists include Aerosmith, Marc Anthony, Beyonce, Bob Dylan, and Patti Smith.

⊘ COSMOTONE RECORDS

2951 Marina Bay Dr., Suite 130, PMB 501, League City, TX 77573-2733. E-mail: marianland@earthlink.net. Website: www.cosmotonerecords.com. Record company, music publisher (Cosmotone Music, ASCAP) and record producer (Rafael Brom). Estab. 1984.

DISTRIBUTED BY marianland.com

HOW TO CONTACT "Sorry, we do not accept material at this time." Does not return materials.

MUSIC Mostly **Christian pop/rock**. Released *Rafael Brom I, Padre Pio Lord Hamilton, Dance for Padre Pio, Peace of Heart, Music for Peace of Mind, The Sounds of Heaven, The Christmas Songs, Angelophany, The True Measure of Love, All My Love to You Jesus* (albums), and *Rafael Brom Unplugged* (live concert DVD), *Life Is Good, Enjoy It While You Can, Change,* by Rafael Brom, *Refugee from Socialism* by Rafael Brom, and *Move Your Ass,* by Rafael Brom.

⊖ CREATIVE IMPROVISED MUSIC PROJECTS (CIMP) RECORDS

CIMP LTD, Cadence Building, Redwood, NY 13679. (315)287-2852. Fax: (315)287-2860. E-mail: cimp@cadencebuilding.com Website: www.cimprecords.com. **Contact:** Bob Rusch, producer. Labels include Cadence Jazz Records. Record company and record producer (Robert D. Rusch). Estab. 1980. Releases 25-30 CDs/year. Pays negotiable royalty to artists on contract; pays statutory rate to publisher per song on record. Distributed by North Country Distributors.

◐ CIMP specializes in jazz and creative improvised music.

HOW TO CONTACT Submit demo by mail. Unsolicited submissions are OK. Prefers cassette or CD. "We are not looking for songwriters but recording artists." Include SASE. Responds in 1 week.

MUSIC Mostly **jazz** and **creative improvised music**. Released *The Redwood Session* (album), recorded by Evan Parker, Barry Guy, Paul Lytton, and Joe McPhee; *Sarah's Theme* (album), recorded by the Ernie Krivda Trio, Bob Fraser, and Jeff Halsey; and *Human Flowers* (album), recorded by the Bobby Zankel Trio, Marily Crispell, and Newman Baker, all released on CIMP (improvised jazz). Other artists include Arthur Blythe, Joe McPhee, David Prentice, Anthony Braxton, Roswell Rudd, Paul Smoker, Khan Jamal, Odean Pope, etc.

TIPS "CIMP Records are produced to provide music to reward repeated and in-depth listenings. They are recorded live to two-track which captures the full dynamic range one would experience in a live concert. There is no compression, homogenization, eq-ing, post-recording splicing, mixing, or electronic fiddling with the performance. Digital recording allows for a vanishingly low noise floor and tremendous dynamic range. This compression of the dynamic range is what limits the 'air' and life of many recordings. Our recordings capture the dynamic intended by the musicians. In this regard these recordings are demanding. Treat the recording as your private concert. Give it your undivided attention and it will reward you. CIMP Records are not intended to be background music. This method is demanding not only on the listener but on the performer as well. Musicians must be able to play together in real time. They must understand the dynamics of their instrument and how it relates to the others around them. There is no fix-it-in-the-mix safety; either it works or it doesn't. What you hear is exactly what was played. Our main concern is music not marketing."

⊘ CURB RECORDS

49 Music Square E., Nashville TN 37203. (615)321-5080. Fax: (615)327-1964. Website: www.curb.com. **Contact:** John Ozier, A&R coordinator. Record company.

HOW TO CONTACT *Curb Records does not accept unsolicited submissions; accepts previously published material only. Do not submit without permission.*

MUSIC Released *Everywhere* (album), recorded by Tim McGraw; *Sittin' on Top of the World* (album), recorded by LeAnn Rimes; and *I'm Alright* (album), recorded by Jo Dee Messina, all on Curb Records. Other artists include Mary Black, Merle Haggard, David Kersh, Lyle Lovett, Tim McGraw, Wynonna, and Sawyer Brown.

◐ DEEP SOUTH ENTERTAINMENT

P.O. Box 17737, Raleigh, NC 27619. (919)844-1515. Fax: (919)847-5922. E-mail: info@deepsouthentertainment.com. Website: www.deepsouthentertainment.com. Manager: Amy Cox. Record company and management company. Estab. 1996. Staff size: 10. Pays negotiable royalty to artists on contract; statutory rate to publisher per song on record.

DISTRIBUTED BY Redeye Distribution, Valley, Select-O-Hits, City Hall, AEC/Bassin, Northeast One Stop, Pollstar, and Koch International.

HOW TO CONTACT Submit demo by mail. Unsolicited submissions are OK. Prefers cassette or CD with 3 songs, cover letter, and press clippings. Does not return material. Responds only if interested.

MUSIC Mostly **pop**, **modern rock**, and **alternative**; also **swing**, **rockabilly**, and **heavy rock**. Does not want rap or R&B. Artists include Bruce Hornsby, Little Feat, Mike Daly, SR-71, Stretch Princess, Darden Smith, and Vienna Teng.

◐ DENTAL RECORDS

P.O. Box 20058, New York NY 10017. E-mail: info@dentalrecords.com. Website: www.dentalrecords.com. **Contact:** Rick Sanford, owner. Record company. Estab. 1981. Staff size: 1. Releases occasional material, primarily digitally. Pays negotiable royalty to artists on contract; statutory rate to publisher per song on record.

HOW TO CONTACT "Check website to see if your material is appropriate." *Not currently accepting unsolicited submissions.*

MUSIC **Pop-derived structures**, **jazz-derived harmonies**, and **neo-classic-wannabee-pretenses**. Claims no expertise, nor interest, in urban, heavy metal, or hard core. Released *Perspectivism* (album), written and recorded by Rick Sanford (instrumental), released 2003 on Dental Records. Other artists include Les Izmor.

◑ DRUMBEAT INDIAN ARTS, INC.

4143 N. 16th St., Phoenix, AZ 85016. (602)266-4823. Fax: (602)265-2402. E-mail: info@drumbeatindianarts.com. Website: www.DrumbeatIndianArts.com. **Contact:** Bob Nuss, president. Record company and distributor of American Indian recordings. Estab. 1984. Staff size: 8. Releases 100 CDs/year. Royalty varies with project.

🎧 Note that Drumbeat Indian Arts is a very specialized label, and only wants to receive submissions by Native American artists.

HOW TO CONTACT *Call first and obtain permission to submit.* Include SASE. Responds in 2 months.

MUSIC Music by American Indians—any style (must be enrolled tribal members). Does not want New Age "Indian-style" material. Released Pearl Moon (album), written and recorded by Xavier (native Amerindian). Other artists include Black Lodge Singers, R. Carlos Nakai, Lite Foot, and Joanne Shenandoah.

TIPS "We deal only with American Indian performers. We do not accept material from others. Please include tribal affiliation."

EARACHE RECORDS

4402 11th St., #507A Long Island City, NY 11101. (718)786-1707. Fax: (718)786-1756. E-mail: usaproduction@earache.com. Website: www.earache.com. Estab. 1993 (US).

MUSIC Rock, industrial, heavy metal techno, death metal, grindcore. Artists include Municipal Waste, Dillinger Escape Plan, Bring Me the Horizon, Deicide, Oceano, and more.

⊘ ELEKTRA RECORDS

75 Rockefeller Plaza, 17th Floor, New York, NY 10019. Website: www.elektra.com. Record company.

○ Elektra Records is a subsidiary of Warner Music Group, one of the "Big 4" major labels.

DISTRIBUTED BY WEA.

HOW TO CONTACT *Elektra does not accept unsolicited submissions.*

Music Mostly alternative/modern rock. Artists include Bruno Mars, Cee Lo, Justice, Little Boots, and True Blood.

⊘ EPIC RECORDS

550 Madison Ave., 22nd Floor, New York NY 10022. (212)833-8870. Fax: (212)833-4054. Website: www. epicrecords.com. **A&R:** Rose Noone. **Santa Monica:** 2100 Colorado Ave., Santa Monica, CA 90404. (310)449-2100 Fax: (310)449-2848. A&R: Mike Flynn. Labels include Beluga Heights, Daylight Records, and E1 Music. Record company.

○ Epic Records is a subsidiary of Sony BMG, one of the "Big 4" major labels.

DISTRIBUTED BY Sony Music Distribution.

HOW TO CONTACT *Write or call first and obtain permission to submit* (New York office only). Does not return material. Responds only if interested. *Santa Monica and Nashville offices do not accept unsolicited submissions.*

MUSIC Artists include Sade, Shakira, Modest Mouse, the Fray, Natasha Bedingfield, Sean Kingston, Incubus, the Script.

TIPS "Do an internship if you don't have experience or work as someone's assistant. Learn the business and work hard while you figure out what your talents are and where you fit in. Once you figure out which area of the record company you're suited for, focus on that, work hard at it and it shall be yours."

⊘ EPITAPH RECORDS

2798 Sunset Blvd., Los Angeles CA, 90026. (213)355-5000. Website: www.epitaph.com. Contact: Brett Gurewitz, founder. Record company. Contains imprints Hellcat Records and Anti. "Epitaph Records was founded by Bad Religion guitarist Brett Gurewitz

with the aim of starting an artist-friendly label from a musician's point of view. Perhaps most well known for being the little indie from L.A. that spawned the 90s punk explosion."

HOW TO CONTACT "Post your demos on-line at one of the many free music portals, then simply fill out the Demo Submission-form" on website.

MUSIC Artists include Social Distortion, Alkaline Trio, Rancid, the Weakerthans, Weezer, Bad Religion, Every Time I Die.

EYEBALL RECORDS

P.O. Box 400, Ridgewood, NJ 07451. E-mail: info@ eyeballrecords.com. Website: www.eyeballrecords. com. **Contact:** A&R.

HOW TO CONTACT "Familiarize yourself with the bands we work with." Submit demo by mail. "You don't have to call or e-mail us to follow up."

MUSIC New London Fire, Pompeii, the Blackout Pact, United Nations, Wolftron, and more.

FAT WRECK CHORDS

P.O. Box 193690, San Francisco CA 94119. E-mail: mailbag@fatwreck.com. Website: www.fatwreck. com. Contact: Mike.

HOW TO CONTACT Accepts demos by mail at: Asian Man Records, ATTN: Mike, P.O. Box 35585, Monte Soreno, CA 95030. Responds via e-mail or through the post "in time."

MUSIC Punk, rock, alternative. Artists include NOFX, Rise Against, the Lawrence Arms, Anti-Flag, Me First and the Gimme Gimmes, Propagandhi, Dillinger Four, Against Me! and more.

FEARLESS RECORDS

13772 Goldenwest St., #545, Westminster, CA 92683. (562)592-3438. E-mail: shervon@fearlessrecords.com. Website: www.fearlessrecords.com.

HOW TO CONTACT Send all demos to mailing address. "Do not e-mail us about demos or with links to mp3s."

MUSIC Alternative, pop, indie, rock, metal. Artists include Plain White T's, At the Drive-in, the Maine, Mayday Parade, Sugarcult, Every Avenue, Alesana, Blessthefall, Breathe Carolina, Artist vs Poet, and more.

◐ FIREANT

2009 Ashland Ave., Charlotte, NC 28205. E-mail: LewH@fireantmusic.com. Website: www.fireantmusic.com. **Contact:** Lew Herman, owner. Record company, music publisher (Fireant Music) and record producer (Lew Herman). Estab. 1990. Releases several CDs/year. Pays negotiable royalty to artists on contract; statutory royalty to publisher per song on record.

DISTRIBUTED BY eMusic.com.

HOW TO CONTACT Submit demo by mail. Unsolicited submissions are OK. Prefers cassette, DAT, or videocassette. Does not return material.

MUSIC Mostly **progressive**, **traditional**, and **musical hybrids**. "Anything except New Age and MOR." Released *Loving the Alien: Athens Georgia Salutes David Bowie* (album), recorded by various artists (rock/alternative/electronic), released 2000 on Fireant; and *Good Enough* (album), recorded by Zen Frisbee. Other artists include Mr. Peters' Belizean Boom and Chime Band.

O FLYING HEART RECORDS

4015 NE 12th Ave., Portland, OR 97212. E-mail: flyheart@teleport.com. Website: http://home.teleport.com/~flyheart. **Contact:** Jan Celt, owner. Record company and record producer (Jan Celt). Estab. 1982. Releases 2 CDs/year. Pays variable royalty to artists on contract; negotiable rate to publisher per song on record.

DISTRIBUTED BY Burnside Distribution Co.

HOW TO CONTACT Submit demo by mail. Unsolicited submissions are OK. Prefers cassette with 1-10 songs and lyric sheets. Does not return material. "SASE required for *any* response." Responds in 3 months.

MUSIC Mostly **R&B**, **blues**, and **jazz**; also **rock**. Released *Vexatious Progr.* (album), written and recorded by Eddie Harris (jazz); *Juke Music* (album), written and recorded by Thara Memory (jazz); and *Lookie Tookie* (album), written and recorded by Jan Celt (blues), all on Flying Heart Records. Other artists include Janice Scroggins, Tom McFarland, Thara Memory, and Snow Bud & the Flower People.

FUELED BY RAMEN

1290 Avenue of the Americas, New York, NY 10104. Website: www.fueledbyramen.com. Contact: Johnny Minardi.

HOW TO CONTACT Send demos by mail to address above.

MUSIC Alternative, Rock, Indie. Artists include The Academy Is . . . , Cobra Starship, Gym Class Heroes, Panic! at the Disco, Paramore, Sublime with Rome, This Providence, and more.

O GOTHAM RECORDS

Attn: A&R, P.O. Box 7185, Santa Monica, CA 90406. E-mail: ar@gothamrecords.com. Website: www.gothamrecords.com. Record company. Estab. 1994. Staff size: 3. Releases 8 LPs and 8 CDs/year. Pays negotiable royalty to artists on contract; statutory rate to publisher per song on record. "Gotham Music Placement is Gotham Records' main focus. Gotham Music Placement places recorded material with motion picture, TV, advertising, and video game companies. GMP supervises full feature films and releases full soundtracks, and represents artists from all over the world and all types of genres."

DISTRIBUTED BY Sony RED.

HOW TO CONTACT Submit demo by mail "in a padded mailer or similar package." Unsolicited submissions are OK. Prefers CD and bios, pictures, and touring information. Does not return material.

MUSIC All genres. Artists include SLANT, Red Horizon, The Day After . . . , and the Vicious Martinis.

TIPS "Send all submissions in regular packaging. Spend your money on production and basics, not on fancy packaging and gift wrap."

O HACIENDA RECORDS & RECORDING STUDIO

1236 S. Staple St., Corpus Christi TX 78404. (361)882-7066. E-mail: info@haciendarecords.com. Website: www.haciendarecords.com. **Contact:** Rick Garcia, executive vice president. Founder/CEO: Roland Garcia. Record company, music publisher, and record producer. Estab. 1979. Staff size: 10. Releases 12 singles and 15 CDs/year. Pays negotiable royalty to artists on contract; negotiable rate to publisher per song on record.

HOW TO CONTACT Submit demo package by mail. Unsolicited submissions are OK. Prefers CD with cover letter. Does not return material. Responds in 6 weeks.

MUSIC Mostly **tejano**, **regional Mexican**, **country** (Spanish or English), and **pop**. Released "Chica Bonita" (single), recorded by Albert Zamora and D.J. Cubanito, released 2001 on Hacienda Records; "Si Quieres Verme Llorar" (single) from *Lisa Lopez* con *Mariachi* (album), recorded by Lisa Lopez (mariachi), released 2002 on Hacienda; "Tartamudo" (single) from *Una Vez Mas* (album), recorded by Peligro (norteno); and "Miento" (single) from *Si Tu Te Vas* (album), recorded by Traizion (tejano), both released 2001 on Hacienda. Other artists include, Gary Hobbs, Steve Jordan, Grammy Award nominees Mingo Saldivar and David Lee Garza, Michelle, Victoria y Sus Chikos, La Traizion.

● HEADS UP INT., LTD.

23309 Commerce Park Rd., Cleveland OH 44122. (216)765-7381. Fax: (216)464-6037. E-mail: dave@headsup.com. Website: www.headsup.com. **Contact:** Dave Love, president. Record company, music publisher (Heads Up Int., Buntz Music, Musica de Amor), and record producer (Dave Love). Estab. 1980. Staff size: 57. Releases 13 LPs/year. Pays negotiable royalty to artists on contract.

DISTRIBUTED BY Universal Fontana (domestically).

HOW TO CONTACT Submit demo by mail. Unsolicited submissions are OK. Prefers CD. Does not return material. Responds to all submissions.

MUSIC Mostly **jazz, R&B, pop,** and **world**. Does not want anything else. Released *Long Walk to Freedom* (album), recorded by Ladysmith Black Mambazo (world); *Pilgrimage* (album), recorded by Michael Brecker (contemporary jazz); *Rizing Sun* (album), recorded by Najee (contemporary jazz). Other artists include Diane Schuur, Mateo Parker, Victor Wooten, Esperanza Spalding, Incognito, George Doke, Take 6, Fourplay.

⊘ HEART MUSIC, INC.

P.O. Box 160326, Austin, TX 78716-0326. (512)795-2375. E-mail: info@heartmusic.com. Website: www.heartmusic.com. **Contact:** Tab Bartling, president. Record company and music publisher (Coolhot Music). "Studio available for artists." Estab. 1989. Staff size: 2. Releases 1-2 CDs/year. Pays statutory rate to publisher per song on record.

HOW TO CONTACT *Not interested in new material at this time.* Does not return material. Responds only if interested.

MUSIC Mostly **folk-rock, pop**, and **jazz**; also **blues** and **contemporary folk**. Libby Kirkpatrick's Heroine in early 2011; released *The Fisherman* (album), recorded by Darin Layne/Jason McKensie; re-

leased The Fisherman by Darin Layne; Joe LoCascio Woody Witt Seasons Ago In the City of Lost Things (jazz), recorded by Joe LoCascio, both released in 2007; *Collaborations* (album), recorded by Will Taylor and Strings Attached, featuring Eliza Gilkyson, Shawn Colvin, Patrice Pike, Ian Moore, Guy Forsyth, Ruthie Foster, Libby Kirkpatrick, Jimmy LaFave, Slaid Cleaves, and Barbara K., released 2006; *Goodnight Venus* (album), recorded by Libby Kirkpatrick, released in 2003, and *Be Cool Be Kind* (album), recorded by Carla Helmbrecht (jazz), released January 2001.

HOLOGRAPHIC RECORDING COMPANY

700 West Pete Rose Way, Suite 390, Cincinnati, OH 45203. (513)442-3886. Fax: (513)834-9390. E-mail: info@holographicrecords.com. Website: http://holographicrecords.com. **Contact**: James Sfarnas, president. Label. Estab. 1983. Releases recordings from artists and groups from anywhere; current roster includes 7 acts.

HOW TO CONTACT Call first and obtain permission to submit.

MUSIC **Jazz, progressive**. Current acts include Acumen (progressive jam rock), John Novello (fusion), Alex Skolnick Trio (progressive jazz), Jeff Berlin (jazz), Poogie Bell Band (urban jazz), Dave LaRue (fusion), Mads Eriksen (fusion).

○ HOTTRAX RECORDS

1957 Kilburn Dr., Atlanta, GA 30324. (770)662-6661. E-mail: hotwax@hottrax.com. Website: www.hottrax.com. **Contact:** George Burdell, vice president, A&R. Labels include Dance-A-Thon and Hardkor. Record company and music publisher (Starfox Publishing). Staff size: 6. Releases 8 singles and 3-4 CDs/year. Pays 5-15% royalty to artists on contract. Estab. 1975.

◖ Also see the listing for Alexander Janoulis Productions/Big Al Jano Productions in the "Record Producers" section of this book.

DISTRIBUTED BY Get Hip Inc., DWM Music and Super D.

HOW TO CONTACT *E-mail first to obtain permission to submit.* Prefers an e-link to songs and lyrics in the e-mail. Does not return CDs or printed material. Responds in 6 months. "When submissions get extremely heavy, we do not have the time to respond/return material we pass on. We do notify those sending the most promising work we review, however. Current economic conditions may also affect song acceptance and response."

MUSIC Mostly **blues/blues rock**, some **top 40/pop, rock**, and **country**; also **hardcore punk** and **jazz-fusion**. Released *Power Pop Deluxe* (album), by Secret Lover featuring Delanna Protas, *Some of My Best Friends Have the Blues* (album), by Big Al Jano, *Hot to Trot* (album), written and recorded by Starfoxx (rock); *Lady That Digs the Blues* (album), recorded by Big Al Jano's Blues Mafia Show (blues rock); and *Vol. III, Psychedelic Era. 1967-1969* (album), released 2002 on Hottrax. Other artists include Big Al Jano, Sammy Blue, and Sheffield & Webb. Released in 2010: *So Much Love* (album), by Michael Rozakis & Yorgos; Beyond the Shadows—Then and Now, by Little Phil. Scheduled: *Rare Pidgeon* (CD) by Rick Ware.

◑ IDOL RECORDS

DISTRIBUTED BY Super D (SDID).

HOW TO CONTACT See website at www.IdolRecords.com for submission policy. No phone calls or e-mail follow-ups.

MUSIC Mostly **rock**, **pop**, and **alternative**; also some **hip-hop**. *The O's—Between the Two* (album), *Here Holy Spain—Division* (album), *Calhoun—Heavy Sugar* (album), *Little Black Dress—Snow in June* (album), all released 2009-12 on Idol Records. Other artists include Flickerstick, DARYL, Centromatic, the Deathray Davies, GBH, PPT, the Crash That Took Me, Shibboleth, Trey Johnson, Black Tie Dynasty, Old 97's.

◑ ⦸ INTERSCOPE/GEFFEN/A&M RECORDS

2220 Colorado Ave., Santa Monica, CA 90404. (310)865-1000. Fax: (310)865-7908. Website: www.interscoperecords.com. Labels include Blackground Records, Cherrytree Records, will.i.am music group, and Aftermath Records. Record company.

◖ Interscope/Geffen/A&M is a subsidiary of Universal Music Group, one of the "Big 4" major labels.

HOW TO CONTACT *Does not accept unsolicited submissions.*

MUSIC Released *Worlds Apart*, recorded by . . . And You Will Know Us by the Trail of Dead; and *Guero*, recorded by Beck. Other artists include U2, M.I.A, Keane, and Lady Gaga.

⦸ ISLAND/DEF JAM MUSIC GROUP

825 Eighth Ave., New York, NY 10019. (212)333-8000. Fax: (212)603-7654. Website: www.islanddefjam.com. Executive A&R: Paul Pontius. Labels include Island Records, Def Jam Recordings, and Mercury Records. Record company.

◖ Island/Def Jam is a subsidiary of Universal Music Group, one of the "Big 4" major labels.

HOW TO CONTACT *Island/Def Jam Music Group does not accept unsolicited submissions. Do not send material unless requested.*

MUSIC Artists include Bon Jovi, Fall Out Boy, Kanye West, Rihanna, The Killers, Jay-Z, and Ludacris.

JEROME PRODUCTIONS

2535 Winthrope Way, Lawrenceville GA 30044. (770)982-7055. Fax: (770)982-1882. E-mail: hitcd@bellsouth.net. Website: www.jeromepromotions.com. **Contact**: Bill Jerome, president and CEO. Estab: 2009. Record company. Staff size: 3. Royalties are negotiable.

HOW TO CONTACT Contact first and obtain permission to submit a demo. Include CD with 5 songs and cover letter. Does not return submissions. Responds in 1 week.

MUSIC Mostly interested in **top 40**, **adult contemporary, hot AC**; also **R&B, alternative** and **hip-hop crossover**. Does not want rap, country, gospel, hard rock.

⦸ J RECORDS

745 Fifth Ave., 6th Floor, New York NY 10151. (212)833-8000. Website: www.jrecords.com. Part of Arista Records.

HOW TO CONTACT *J Records does not accept unsolicited submissions.*

MUSIC Artists include Alicia Keys, Rod Stewart, and Pitbull.

◑ KILL ROCK STARS

1526 NE Alberta St. #231, Portland, OR 97211. E-mail: krs@killrockstars.com. Website: www.killrockstars.com. Estab. 1991. Releases 4 singles, 10 LPs, 4-6 EPs and 35 CDs/year. Pays 50% of net profit to artists on contract; negotiated rate to publisher per song on record.

DISTRIBUTED BY Redeye Distribution.

HOW TO CONTACT *Does not accept or listen to demos sent by mail.* Will listen to links online only if in a touring band coming through Portland. "If you are not touring through Portland, don't send us anything." Prefers link to Web page or EPK. Does not return material.

MUSIC Mostly **punk rock**, **neo-folk** or **anti-folk** and **spoken word**. Artists include Deerhoof, Xiu Xiu, Mary Timony, the Gossip, Erase Errata, and Two Ton Boa.

TIPS "We will only work with touring acts, so let us know if you are playing Olympia, Seattle or Portland. Particularly interested in young artists with indie-rock background."

⦿ LANDMARK COMMUNICATIONS GROUP

P.O. Box 1444, Hendersonville TN 37077. E-mail: ba@landmarkcommunicationsgroup.com. Website: www.landmarkcommunicationsgroup.com. **Contact:** Bill Anderson, Jr., president (all styles). Professional manager (western): Dylan Horse. Labels include Jana and Landmark Records. Record company, record producer, music publisher (Newcreature Music/BMI and Mary Megan Music/ASCAP) and management firm (Landmark Entertainment). Releases 6 singles, 8 CDs/year. Pays 5-7% royalty to artists on contract; statutory rate to publisher for each record sold.

HOW TO CONTACT Submit demo tape by mail. Unsolicited submissions are OK. Prefers mp3 or CD with 2-4 songs and lyric sheet. Responds in 1 month.

MUSIC Mostly **country/crossover**, **Christian**. Recent projects: *Smoky Mountain Campmeeting* by Various Artists; *The Pilgrim & the Road* by Tiffany Turner; *Fallow Ground* by C.J. Hall; *Prince Charming Is Dead* by Kecia Burcham.

TIPS "Be professional in presenting yourself."

⦿ LARK RECORD PRODUCTIONS, INC.

P.O. Box 35726, Tulsa OK 74153. (918)786-8896. Fax: (918)786-8897. E-mail: janajae@janajae.com. Website: www.janajae.com. **Contact:** Kathleen Pixley, vice president. Record company, music publisher (Jana Jae Music/BMI), management firm (Jana Jae Enterprises), and record producer (Lark Talent and Advertising). Estab. 1980. Staff size: 8. Pays negotiable royalty to artists on contract; statutory rate to publisher per song on record.

HOW TO CONTACT Submit demo by mail. Unsolicited submissions are OK. Prefers CD or DVD with 3 songs and lead sheets. Does not return material. Responds only if interested.

MUSIC Mostly **country**, **bluegrass**, and **classical**; also **instrumentals**. Released "Fiddlestix" (single by Jana Jae); "Mayonnaise" (single by Steve Upfold); and "Flyin' South" (single by Cindy Walker), all recorded by Jana Jae on Lark Records (country). Other artists include Sydni, Hotwire, and Matt Greif.

⦿ MAGNA CARTA RECORDS

A-1 Country Club Rd., East Rochester, NY 14445. (585)381-5224. Fax: (585)381-0658. E-mail: info@magnacarta.net. Website: www.magnacarta.net. **Contact:** Pete Morticelli. Record label.

HOW TO CONTACT Contact first and obtain permission to submit. *No unsolicited material.*

MUSIC Mostly **progressive metal**, **progressive rock**, and **progressive jazz**.

⦿ MARTY GARRETT ENTERTAINMENT

320 West Utica Place, Broken Arrow, OK 74011. (888)HE4-GAVE. E-mail: musicbusiness@telepath.com. Website: www.martygarrettentertainment.com and http://breakintothemusicbiz.com. Marty R. Garrett, president. Labels include MGE Records and Lonesome Wind Records. Record company, record producer, music publisher, and entertainment consultant. Estab. 1988. Releases 1-2 EPs and 1 CD/year. Pays negotiable royalty to artists on contract; statutory rate to publisher per song on record.

HOW TO CONTACT *Call or check Internet site first and obtain permission to submit.* Prefers CD with 4-5 songs and lyric or lead sheet with chord progressions listed. Does not return material. No press packs or bios, unless specifically requested. Responds in 4-6 weeks.

MUSIC Mostly **honky tonk**, **progressive/traditional country**, or **scripture-based gospel**. Released *Drinking the New Wine* (album) by Marty Garrett on MGE Records. Released singles include "He Brought Me Back Again," "My Father Made the Jailhouse Rock," "Drinking the New Wine," "Get Myself off My Mind," "What Would God Say Then"; all singles released on MGE Records.

TIPS "We help artists secure funding to record and release major label quality CD products to the public for sale through 1-800 television and radio advertising and on the Internet. Although we do submit finished products to major record companies for review, our main focus is to establish and surround the artist with their own long-term production, promotion and distribution organization. Professional studio demos are not required, but make sure vocals are distinct, up-front and up-to-date. I personally listen and respond to each submission received, so check website to see if we are reviewing for an upcoming project."

MATADOR RECORDS

Beggar's Group, 304 Hudson St., New York, NY 10013. (212)995-5882. Fax: (212)995-5883. E-mail: webmaster@matadorrecords.com. Website: www.matadorrecords.com. **UK address:** 17-19 Alma Rd., London, SW18 1AA, United Kingdom.
HOW TO CONTACT "We are sorry to say that we *no longer accept unsolicited demo submissions.*"
MUSIC Alternative rock. Artists include Lou Reed, Pavement, Belle and Sebastian, Cat Power, Jay Reatard, Sonic Youth, Yo La Tengo, Mogwai, the New Pornographers, and more.

MCA NASHVILLE

(formerly MCA Records), 1904 Adelicia St., Nashville TN 37212. (615)244-8944. Fax: (615)880-7447. Website: www.umgnashville.com Record company and music publisher (MCA Music).

> MCA Nashville is a subsidiary of Universal Music Group, one of the "Big 4" major labels.

HOW TO CONTACT *MCA Nashville cannot accept unsolicited submissions.*
MUSIC Artists include Tracy Byrd, George Strait, Vince Gill, Sugarland, the Mavericks, and Shania Twain.

MEGAFORCE RECORDS

P.O. Box 1955, New York, NY 10113. E-mail: gregaforce@aol.com. Website: www.megaforcerecords.com. **Contact:** Robert John, president. General manager: Missi Callazzo. Record company. Estab. 1983. Staff size: 5. Releases 6 CDs/year. Pays various royalties to artists on contract; 3/4 statutory rate to publisher per song on record.
DISTRIBUTED BY Red/Sony Distribution.
HOW TO CONTACT *Contact first and obtain permission to submit.* Submissions go to the Philadelphia office.
MUSIC Mostly **rock**. Artists include Truth and Salvage, the Meat Puppets, and the Disco Biscuits.

METAL BLADE RECORDS

5737 Kanan Rd., #143, Agoura Hills, CA 91301. (805)522-9111. Fax: (805)522-9380. E-mail: metalblade@metalblade.com. Website: www.metalblade.com. **Contact:** A&R. Record company. Estab. 1982. Releases 20 LPs, 2 EPs and 20 CDs/year. Pays negotiable royalty to artists on contract.
HOW TO CONTACT Submit demo through website form. Does not accept physical copies of demos. Unsolicited submissions are OK. Response time varies, but "be patient."
MUSIC Mostly **heavy metal** and **industrial**; also **hardcore, gothic,** and **noise.** Released "Gallery of Suicide," recorded by Cannibal Corpse; "Voo Doo," recorded by King Diamond; and "A Pleasant Shade of Gray," recorded by Fates Warning, all on Metal Blade Records. Other artists include As I Lay Dying, The Red Chord, the Black Dahlia Murder, and Unearth.
TIPS "Metal Blade is known throughout the underground for quality metal-oriented acts."

MODAL MUSIC, INC.

P.O. Box 6473, Evanston, IL 60204-6473. Phone/Fax: (847)864-1022. E-mail: info@modalmusic.com. Website: www.modalmusic.com. President: Terran Doehrer. Assistant: J. Distler. Record company and agent. Estab. 1988. Staff size: 2. Releases 1-2 LPs/year. Pays negotiable royalty to artists on contract; negotiable rate to publisher per song on record.
HOW TO CONTACT Submit demo package by mail. Unsolicited submissions are OK. Prefers CD with bio, PR, brochures, any info about artist and music. Does not return material. Responds in 4 months.
MUSIC Mostly **ethnic** and **world**. Released "St. James Vet Clinic" (single by T. Doehrer/Z. Doehrer) from *Wolfpak Den Recordings* (album), recorded by Wolfpak, released 2005; "Dance the Night Away" (single by T. Doehrer) from *Dance the Night Away* (album), recorded by Balkan Rhythm Band™; "Sid Beckerman's Rumanian" (single by D. Jacobs) from *Meet Your Neighbor's Folk Music* (album), recorded by Jutta & the Hi-Dukes; and *Hold Whatcha Got* (album), recorded by Razzemetazz, all on Modal Music Records. Other artists include Ensemble M'chaiya, Nordland Band and Terran's Greek Band.
TIPS "Please note our focus is primarily traditional and traditionally-based ethnic which is a very limited, non-mainstream market niche. You waste your time

and money by sending us any other type of music. If you are unsure of your music fitting our focus, please call us before sending anything. Put your name and contact info on every item you send!"

⦿◯ NERVOUS RECORDS

Record company (Nervous Records), record producer and music publisher (Nervous Publishing and Zorch Music). Member: MCPS, PRS, PPL, ASCAP, NCB. Releases 2 albums/year. Pays 8-12% royalty to artists on contract; statutory rate to publisher per song on records. Royalties paid directly to US songwriters and artists or through US publishing or recording affiliate.

> ◯ Nervous Records' publishing company, Nervous Publishing, is listed in the "Music Publishers" section.

HOW TO CONTACT Unsolicited submissions are OK. Prefers CD with 4-15 songs and lyric sheet. SAE and IRC. Responds in 3 weeks.

MUSIC Mostly **psychobilly** and **rockabilly**. "No heavy rock, AOR, stadium rock, disco, soul, pop—only wild rockabilly and psychobilly." Released *Extra Chrome*, written and recorded by Johnny Black; *It's Still Rock 'n' Roll to Me*, written and recorded by The Jime. Other artists include Restless Wild and Taggy Tones.

◑ NEURODISC RECORDS, INC.

3801 N. University Dr., Suite 403, Ft. Lauderdale FL 33351. (954)572-0289. Fax: (954)572-2874. E-mail: info@neurodisc.com. Website: www.neurodisc.com or www.myspace.com/neurodiscrecords. President: Tom O'Keefe. New media manager: Pasha Love. Record company and music publisher. Estab. 1992. Releases 6 singles and 10 CDs/year. Pays negotiable royalty to artists on contract.

DISTRIBUTED BY Fontana Distribution.

HOW TO CONTACT Submit demo package by mail. Unsolicited submissions are OK. Prefers CD, mp3 or DVD. Include SASE and contact information. Responds only if interested.

MUSIC Mostly **electronic**, **chillout in lounge**, **down tempo**, **New Age**, and **electro-bass**. Released albums from The Egg, Sleepthief, Blue Stone, Peplab, Etro Anime, Deviations Project, Ryan Farish & Amethystium, as well as Bass Lo-Ryders and Bass Crunk. Other artists include DaKsha, Eric Hansen, Bella Sonus and NuSound.

◯ NORTH STAR MUSIC

338 Compass Circle A1, North Kingstown, RI 02852. (401)886-8888 or (800)346-2706. Fax: (401)294-3687. E-mail: info@northstarmusic.com. Website: www. northstarmusic.com. **Contact:** Richard Waterman, president. Record company. Estab. 1985. Staff size: 15. Releases 12-16 LPs/year. Pays 9% royalty to artists on contract; ³/₄ statutory rate to publisher per song on record.

DISTRIBUTED BY Goldenrod and in-house distribution.

HOW TO CONTACT Submit demo CD by mail. Unsolicited submissions are OK. Prefers finished CD. Does not return material. Responds in 2 months.

MUSIC Mostly **instrumental**, **traditional** and **contemporary jazz**, **New Age**, **traditional world** (**Cuban, Brazilian, singer/songwriter, Hawaiian, and Flamenco**) and **classical**. Released *Sacred* (album), written and recorded by David Tolk (inspirational), released 2003; *An Evening in Tuscany* (album), written and recorded by Bruce Foulke/Howard Kleinfeld (contemporary instrumental), released 2004; *Always & Forever* (album), written and recorded by David Osborne (piano), released 2003, all on North Star Music. Other artists include Judith Lynn Stillman, David Osborne, Emilio Kauderer, Gerry Beaudoin, Cheryl Wheeler, and Nathaniel Rosen.

● OGLIO RECORDS

P.O. Box 404, Redondo Beach, CA 90277. (310)791-8600. Fax: (310)791-8670. E-mail: getinfo4@oglio.com. Website: www.oglio.com. Record company. Estab. 1992. Releases 20 LPs and 20 CDs/year. Pays negotiable royalty to artist on contract; statutory rate to publisher per song on record.

HOW TO CONTACT *No unsolicited demos.*

MUSIC Mostly **alternative rock** and **comedy**. Released *Shine* (album), recorded by Cyndi Lauper (pop); *Live at the Roxy* (album), recorded by Brian Wilson (rock); *Team Leader* (album), recorded by George Lopez (comedy).

◑ OUTSTANDING RECORDS

P.O. Box 2111, Huntington Beach, CA 92647. (714)377-7447. E-mail: beecher@outstandingmusic.com Website: www.outstandingmusic.com. **Contact:** Earl Beecher, owner. Labels include Outstanding, Morrhythm (mainstream/commercial), School Band (educational/charity), Church Choir (religious charity), and Empowerment (educational CDs and DVDs). Record company, music publisher (Earl Beecher Publishing/BMI and Beecher Music Publishing/ASCAP), and record producer (Earl Beecher). Estab. 1968. Staff size: 1. Releases 100 CDs/year. Pays $2/CD royalty to artists on contract; statutory rate to publisher per song on record.

DISTRIBUTED BY All full CDs listed on the website can be ordered directly through the website. Most of them are now available via download through iTunes, Napster, Rhapsody, Amazon/mp3, Emusic, or Yahoo. Whenever wholesale distributors contact me for specific orders, I am happy to work with them, especially distributors overseas.

HOW TO CONTACT Submit demo by mail. Unsolicited submissions are OK. Prefers CD (full albums), lyric sheet, photo, and cover letter. Include SASE. Responds in 3 weeks.

MUSIC Mostly **jazz**, **rock,** and **country**; also **everything else, especially Latin**. Does not want music with negative, antisocial or immoral messages. "View our website for a listing of all current releases."

TIPS "We prefer to receive full CDs, rather than just three numbers. A lot of submitters suggest we release their song in the form of singles, but we just can't bother with singles at the present time. Especially looking for performers who want to release their material on my labels. Some songwriters are pairing up with performers and putting out CDs with a 'Writer Presents the Performer' concept. No dirty language. Do not encourage listeners to use drugs, alcohol or engage in immoral behavior. I'm especially looking for upbeat, happy, danceable music."

●❶ THE PANAMA MUSIC GROUP OF COMPANIES

(formerly Audio-Visual Media Productions), Sovereign House, 12 Trewartha Rd., Praa Sands, Penzance, Cornwall TR20 9ST, England. +44 (0)1736 762826. Fax: +44 (0)1736 763328. E-mail: panamus@aol.com. Website: www.songwriters-guild.co.uk and www.panamamusic.co.uk. **Contact:** Roderick G. Jones, CEO, A&R. Labels include Pure Gold Records, Panama Music Library, Rainy Day Records, Panama Records, Mohock Records, Digimix Records (www.digimixrecords.com and www.myspace.com/digimixrecords). Registered members of Phonographic Performance Ltd. (PPL). Record company, music publisher, production and development company (Panama Music Library, Melody First Music Library, Eventide Music Library, Musik Image Music Library, Promo Sonor International Music Library, Caribbean Music Library, ADN Creation Music Library, Piano Bar Music Library, Corelia Music Library, PSI Music Library, Scamp Music, First Time Music Publishing U.K.), registered members of the Mechanical Copyright Protection Society (MCPS) and the Performing Right Society (PRS) (London, England UK), management firm, and record producer (First Time Management & Production Co.). Estab. 1986. Staff size: 6. Pays variable royalty to artists on contract; statutory rate to publisher per song on record subject to deal.

DISTRIBUTED BY Media U.K. Distributors and Digimix Worldwide Digital Distribution.

HOW TO CONTACT Submit demo package by mail. Unsolicited submissions are OK. CD only with unlimited number of songs/instrumentals and lyric or lead sheets where necessary. "We do not return material so there is no need to send return postage. We will, due to volume of material received only respond to you if we have any interest. Please note: no MP3 submissions, attachments, downloads, or referrals to Web sites in the first instance via e-mail. Do not send anything by recorded delivery or courier as it will not be signed for. If we are interested, we will follow up for further requests and offers as necessary."

MUSIC **All styles**. Published by Scamp Music: "F*ck Me I'm Famous" written by Paul Clarke & Matthew Dick (film/DVD & single & album track), released worldwide in *Get Him to the Greek*, starring Russell Brand, recorded by Dougal & Gammer, released as an album track by Gut Records Ltd. and as a single by Essential Platinum Records in 2010. Also published "The River" (soul/R&B), recorded by Leonie Parker, released by Diximax Records, Ltd.; "Wait a Second" (hard dance), recorded by DJ Matt Lee, released by TidyTrax Records; "Break It" (hardcore), recorded by Dougal & Gammer, released by Universal Records/All around the World; Published by Panama Music Library: "I Get Stoned" (hardcore dance) recorded by AudioJunkie & Stylus, released by EMI records on *Hardcore Nation 2009,* and more.

PAPER + PLASTICK

Website: paperandplastick.com. **Contact:** through form on website. Paper+Plastick handles both visual artwork and music.

MUSIC **Rock, punk**, and more. Artists include: Do-pamines, Andrew Dost, Coffee Project, Foundation, Gatorface, Blacklist Royals, Landmines, We Are the Union, and more.

○ PARLIAMENT RECORDS

357 S. Fairfax Ave., #430, Los Angeles, CA 90036. (323)653-0693. Fax: (323)653-7670. E-mail: parlirec@aol.com. Website: www.parliamentrecords.com. **Contact:** Ben Weisman, owner. Record company, record producer (Weisman Production Group) and music publisher (Audio Music Publishers, Queen Esther Music Publishing). Estab. 1965. Produces 30 singles/year. Fee derived from sales royalty when song or artist is recorded.

○ Also see the listings for Audio Music Publishers and Queen Esther Music Publishing in the "Music Publishers" section and Weisman Production Group in the "Record Producer" section.

HOW TO CONTACT Submit demo package by mail. Unsolicited submissions are OK. Prefers CD with 3-10 songs and lyric sheet. Include SASE. "Mention *Songwriter's Market*. Please make return envelope the same size as the envelopes you send material in, otherwise we cannot send everything back." Responds in 6 weeks.

MUSIC Mostly **R&B**, **soul**, **dance**, and **top 40/pop**; also **gospel** and **blues**. Arists include Rapture 7 (male gospel group), Wisdom Gospel Singers (male gospel group), Chosen Gospel Recovery (female gospel group), Jewel with Love (female gospel group), Apostle J. Dancy (gospel), TooMiraqulas (rap), the Mighty Voices of Joy (male gospel group) L'Nee (hip-hop/soul).

TIPS "Parliament Records will also listen to 'tracks' only. If you send tracks, please include a letter stating what equipment you record on—ADAT, Protools or Roland VS recorders."

○ RADICAL RECORDS

77 Bleecker St., Suite C2-21, New York, NY 10012. (212)475-1111. Fax: (212)475-3676. E-mail: Bryan@radicalrecords.com. Website: www.radicalrecords.com. **Contact:** Bryan Mechutan. Record company. Estab. 1986. Staff size: 4. Releases 1 single and 6 CDs/year. Pays 14% royalty to artists on contract; statutory rate to publisher per song on record.

DISTRIBUTED BY City Hall, Revelation, Select-O-Hits, Choke, Southern, Carrot Top, and other indie distributors.

HOW TO CONTACT *E-mail first for permission to submit demo.* Prefers CD. Does not return material. Responds in 1 month.

MUSIC Mostly **punk**, **hardcore**, **glam,** and **rock**. Released *New York City Rock N Roll* (compilation album featuring 22 NYC bands); *Too Legit for the Pit-Hardcore Takes the Rap* (compilation album), recorded by various; *Punk's Not Dead—A Tribute to the Exploited* (compilation album), recorded by various; *East Coast of Oi!* (compilation album), recorded by various; *Ramones Forever* (compilation album), recorded by various; *Sex Pistols Tribute—Never Mind the Sex Pistols, Here's the Tribute* (compilation album), recorded by various; and 3 volumes of OI!/Skampilation (compilation albums, recorded by various shi and oi! punk bands). Artists include Sex Slaves, 5¢ Deposit, Blanks '77, Speedealer, the Agents, Inspector 7, and I.C.U.

TIPS "Create the best possible demos you can and show a past of excellent self-promotion."

○ RAVE RECORDS, INC.

Attn: Production Dept., 13400 W. Seven Mile Rd., Detroit, MI 48235. E-mail: info@raverecords.com. Website: www.raverecords.com. **Contact:** Carolyn and Derrick, production managers. Record company and music publisher (Magic Brain Music/ASCAP). Estab. 1992. Staff size: 2. Releases 2-4 singles and 2 CDs/year. Pays various royalty to artists on contract; statutory rate to publisher per song on record.

DISTRIBUTED BY Action Music Sales.

HOW TO CONTACT *"We do not accept unsolicited submissions."* Submit demo package by mail. Prefers CD with 3 songs, lyric sheet. "Include any bios, fact sheets, and press you may have. We will contact you if we need any further information." Does not return materials.

MUSIC Mostly **alternative rock** and **dance**. Artists include Cyber Cryst, Dorothy, Nicole, and Bukimi 3.

○○ RCA RECORDS

550 Madison Ave, New York, NY 10022. (212)833-6200. Website: www.rcarecords.com. A&R: Ashley Newtown. Labels include RCA Records Nashville and RCA Victor. Record company.

○ RCA Records is a subsidiary of Sony BMG, one of the "Big 4" major labels.

DISTRIBUTED BY BMG.

HOW TO CONTACT *RCA Records does not accept unsolicited submissions.*

MUSIC Artists include the Strokes, Dave Matthews Band, Christina Aguilera, and Foo Fighters.

RED ADMIRAL RECORDS LLP

The Cedars, Elvington Lane, Folkestone, Kent CT18 7AD, United Kingdom. (01)(303)893-472. Fax: (01)(303)893-833. E-mail: info@redadmiralrecords.com. Website: www.redadmiralrecords.com. **Contact:** Chris Ashman. Estab. 1979. Registered members of MCPS, PRS, and PPL. Record company and music publisher (Cringe Music (MCPS/PRS)). Estab. 1979.

HOW TO CONTACT Submit demo package by mail. Unsolicited submissions are OK. Submit CD only with unlimited number of songs. Submission materials are not returned. Responds if interested.

MUSIC All styles. Artists include Crispian St. Peters, Rik Waller, Wim Hautekiet, Mirkwood, David Hay, The Silent Kingdom, Peter Dinsley, Carmen Wiltshire, Hardly Mozart, The Sharpee's.

RED ONION RECORDS

8377 Westview, Houston TX 77055. (713)464-4653. Fax: (713)464-2622. E-mail: jeffwells@soundartsrecording.com. Website: www.redonionrecords.com; www.soundartsrecording.com. **Contact:** Jeff Wells, president. A&R: Peter Verkerk. Record company, music publisher (Reach for the Sky Music Publishing/ASCAP; Earthscream Music Publishing Co./BMI) and record producer (Jeff Wells). Estab. 2007. Releases 4 CDs/year. Pays negotiable royalty to artists on contract; statutory rate to publisher per song on record.

DISTRIBUTED BY Earth Records.

HOW TO CONTACT Submit demo by mail. Unsolicited submissions are OK. Prefers CD with 4 songs and lyric sheet. Does not return material. Responds in 6 weeks.

MUSIC Mostly **country, blues,** and **pop/rock.** Released *Glory Baby* (album), recorded by Tony Vega Band (blues); *Two for Tuesday* (album), recorded by Dr. Jeff and the Painkilllers (blues), all released 2007 on Red Onion Records.

REPRISE RECORDS

3300 Warner Blvd., 4th Floor, Burbank, CA 91505. (818)846-9090. Fax: (818)840-2389. Website: www.repriserecords.com. Record company.

Reprise Records is a subsidiary of Warner Music Group, one of the "Big 4" major labels.

DISTRIBUTED BY WEA.

HOW TO CONTACT *Reprise Records does not accept unsolicited submissions.*

MUSIC Artists include Eric Clapton, My Chemical Romance, Michael Bublé, the Used, Green Day, Alanis Morissette, Fleetwood Mac, and Neil Young.

RISE RECORDS

421 SW 6th Ave., Suite 1400, Portland, OR 97204. E-mail: Matthew@RiseRecords.com. Website: www.riserecords.com.

HOW TO CONTACT E-mail a link to music, either on Purevolume or MySpace. "Please save your money and don't mail a press kit."

MUSIC Rock, metal, alternative. Artists include Dance Gavin Dance, Emarose, The Devil Wears Prada, Of Mice & Men, and more.

ROADRUNNER RECORDS

902 Broadway, 8th Floor, New York, NY 10010. (212)274-7500. Fax: (212)505-7469. E-mail: roadrunner@roadrunnerrecords.com. Website: www.roadrunnerrecords.com.

HOW TO CONTACT Submit demo by e-mail at signmeto@roadrunnerrecords.com. Submissions are currently open.

MUSIC Rock, metal, alternative. Artists include Korn, Killswitch Engage, Opeth, Nickelback, Lenny Kravitz, Lynyrd Skynyrd, Megadeth, Slipknot, and more.

ROBBINS ENTERTAINMENT LLC

35 Worth St., 4th Floor, New York, NY 10013. (212)675-4321. Fax: (212)675-4441. E-mail: info@robbinsent.com. Website: www.robbinsent.com. **Contact:** Matt D'Arduini, director of A&R. Record company and music publisher (Rocks, No Salt). Estab. 1996. Staff size: 10. Releases 25 singles and 12-14 CDs/year. Pays negotiable royalty to artists on contract; statutory rate to publisher per song on record.

DISTRIBUTED BY Sony/BMG.

HOW TO CONTACT Accepts unsolicited radio edit demos as long as it's dance music. Prefers CD with 2 songs or less. "Make sure everything is labeled with the song title information and your contact information. This is important in case the CD and the jewel case get separated. Do not call us and ask if you can send your package. The answer is yes."

MUSIC Commercial **dance** only. Released top 10 pop smashes, "Heaven" (single), recorded by DJ Sammy; "Everytime We Touch" (single), recorded by Cascada; "Listen to Your Heart" (single), recorded by DHT; as well as Hot 100 records from Rockell, Lasgo, Reina, and K5. Other artists includel, September, Andain, Judy Torres, Jenna Drey, Marly, Dee Dee, Milky, Kreo, and many others.

TIPS "Do not send your package 'Supreme-Overnight-Before-You-Wake-Up' delivery. Save yourself some money. Do not send material if you are going to state in your letter that, 'If I had more (fill in the blank) it would sound better.' We are interested in hearing your best and only your best. Do not call us and ask if you can send your package. The answer is yes. We are looking for dance music with crossover potential."

ROLL ON RECORDS

112 Widmar Place, Clayton, CA 94517. (925)833-4680. E-mail: rollonrecords@aol.com. **Contact:** Edgar J. Brincat, owner. Record company and music publisher (California Country Music). Estab. 1985. Pays 10% royalty to artists on contract; statutory rate to publisher per song on record. Member of Harry Fox Agency.

DISTRIBUTED BY Tower.

HOW TO CONTACT Submit demo package by mail. Unsolicited submissions are OK. "Do not call or write for permission to submit, if you do you will be rejected." Prefers CD with 3 songs and lyric sheet. Include SASE and phone number. Responds in 6 weeks.

MUSIC Mostly **contemporary/country** and **modern gospel**. Released "Broken Record" (single by Horace Linsley/Dianne Baumgartner), recorded by Edee Gordon on Roll On Records; *Maddy* and *For Realities Sake* (albums both by F.L. Pittman/Madonna Weeks), recorded by Ron Banks/L.J. Reynolds on Life Records/Bellmark Records.

TIPS "Be patient and prepare to be in it for the long haul. A successful songwriter does not happen overnight. It's rare to write a song today and have a hit tomorrow. If you give us your song and want it back, then don't give it to us to begin with."

ROTTEN RECORDS

Attn: A&R Dept., P.O. Box 56, Upland, CA 91785. (909)920-4567. E-mail: rotten@rottenrecords.com. Website: www.rottenrecords.com. President: Ron Peterson. Promotions/Radio/Video: Andi Jones. Record company. Estab. 1988. Releases 3 LPs, 3 EPs, and 3 CDs/year.

DISTRIBUTED BY RIOT (Australia), Sonic Rendezvous (NL), RED (US) and PHD (Canada).

HOW TO CONTACT Submit demo package by mail. Unsolicited submissions are OK. Prefers CD or MySpace link. Does not return material.

MUSIC Mostly **rock**, **alternative,** and **commercial**; also **punk** and **heavy metal**. Released *Paegan Terrorism* (album), written and recorded by Acid Bath; *Kiss the Clown* (album by K. Donivon), recorded by Kiss the Clown; and *Full Speed Ahead* (album by Cassidy/Brecht), recorded by D.R.T., all on Rotten Records.

TIPS "Be patient."

ROUGH TRADE RECORDS

Beggar's Group, 66 Golborne Rd., London W10 5PS. +44 020 8960 9888. Fax: (+44)(020)-8968-6715. Website: www.roughtraderecords.com.

HOW TO CONTACT Demos should be marked for attention of Paul Jones.

MUSIC Alternative. Artists include Super Furry Animals, Jarvis Cocker, the Hold Steady, Emiliana Torrini, British Sea Power, the Libertines, My Morning Jacket, Jenny Lewis, the Strokes, the Mystery Jets, the Decemberists, and more.

RUSTIC RECORDS

6337 Murray Lane, Brentwood, TN 37027. (615)371-0646. Fax: (615)370-0353. E-mail: rusticrecordsinc@aol.com. Website: www.rusticrecordsinc.com. President: Jack Schneider. Executive VP & operations manager: Nell Schneider. Independent traditional country music label and music publisher (Iron Skillet Music/ASCAP, Covered Bridge/ BMI, Old Towne Square/SESAC). Estab. 1979. Staff size: 6. Releases 2-3/year. Pays negotiable royalty to artists on contracts; statutory royalty to publisher per song on record.

DISTRIBUTED BY CDBaby.com and available on iTunes, MSN Music, Rhapsody, and more.

HOW TO CONTACT Submit professional demo package by mail. Unsolicited submissions are OK. CD only; no mp3s or e-mails. Include no more than 4 songs with corresponding lyric sheets and cover letter. Include appropriately sized SASE. Responds in 4 weeks.

MUSIC Good combination of traditional and modern **country**. 2008-09 releases: *Ready to Ride*—debut album from Nikki Britt, featuring "C-O-W-B-O-Y," "Do I Look Like Him," "Star in My Car," and "You Happened"; *Hank Stuff* from DeAnna Cox—featuring "I'm a Long Gone Mama," and "I'm So Lonesome I Could Cry."

TIPS "Professional demo preferred."

SAHARA RECORDS AND FILMWORKS ENTERTAINMENT

10573 W. Pico Blvd., #352, Los Angeles, CA 90064-2348. Phone: (310)948-9652. Fax: (310)474-7705. E-mail: info@edmsahara.com. Website: www.edmsahara.com. **Contact:** Edward De Miles, president. Record company, music publisher (EDM Music/BMI, Edward De Miles Music Company) and record producer (Edward De Miles). Estab. 1981. Releases 15-20 CD singles and 5-10 CDs/year. Pays $9^{1}/_{2}$-11% royalty to artists on contract; statutory rate to publishers per song on record.

HOW TO CONTACT *Does not accept unsolicited submissions.*

MUSIC Mostly **R&B/dance**, **top 40 pop/rock,** and **contemporary jazz**; also **TV-film themes, musical scores and jingles**. Released "Hooked on U," "Dance wit Me" and "Moments" (singles), written and recorded by Steve Lynn (R&B) on Sahara Records. Other artists include Lost in Wonder, Devon Edwards, and Multiple Choice.

TIPS "We're looking for strong mainstream material. Lyrics and melodies with good hooks that grab people's attention."

○ SANDALPHON RECORDS

P.O. Box 542407, Grand Prairie TX 75054. (972)333-0876. E-mail: jackrabbit01@comcast.net. **Contact:** Ruth Otey, president. Record company, music publisher (Sandalphon Music/BMI), and management agency (Sandalphon Management). Estab. 2005. Staff size: 2. Pays negotiable royalty to artists on contract; statutory royalty to publisher per song on record.

DISTRIBUTED BY "We are currently negotiating for distribution."

HOW TO CONTACT Submit demo package by mail. Unsolicited submissions are fine. Prefers CD with 1-5 songs with lyric sheet and cover letter. Returns submissions if accompanied by a SASE or SAE and IRC for outside the United States. Responds in 6-8 weeks.

MUSIC Mostly **rock**, **country**, and **alternative**; also **pop**, **gospel**, and **blues**.

SILVER WAVE RECORDS

P.O. Box 7943, Boulder, CO 80306. (303)443-5617. Fax: (303)443-0877. E-mail: info@silverwave.com. Website: www.silverwave.com. **Contact:** James Marienthal. Record company. Estab. 1986. Releases 3-4 CDs/year. Pays varying royalty to artists on contract and to publisher per song on record.

HOW TO CONTACT *Call first and obtain permission to submit.* Prefers CD. Include SASE. Responds only if interested.

MUSIC Mostly **Native American** and **world**.

SIMPLY GRAND MUSIC INC

P.O. Box 770208, Memphis, TN 38177-0208.Estab. 1965. (901)763-4787. Fax: (901)763-4883. E-mail: wahani@aol.com. Website: www.simplygrandmusic.com. **Contact:** Linda Lucchesi, president. Record company (Memphis Town Music) and music publisher (Beckie Publishing Company). Estab. 1965. Staff size: 2. Released 9 CDs last year. Royalties are negotiable.

DISTRIBUTED BY Ace Records and various others.

HOW TO CONTACT Contact first and obtain permission to submit a demo. Include CD with 1-3 songs and lyric sheet. Returns submissions if accompanied by an SASE with ample postage. Responds in 3 months.

MUSIC Mostly interested in **country**, **soul/R&B**, **pop**; also interested in **top 40**, **soft rock**. Recently published "Can't Find Happiness" written by Charlie Chalmers and Paul Selph Jr., recorded by Barbara & the Browns (soul) for *Can't Find Happiness* (album) on Ace Records; "Hooked on a Feeling" written by Mark James, recorded by the Ovations feat. Louis Williams (soul) for *One in a Million* (album) on Ace Records; "Love Made a Fool of Me" written by Gary McEwen and Louis Paul Jr., recorded by Bettye LaVette (soul/R&B) for *Take Another Little Piece of My Heart* (album) on Varese Sarabande Records.

SKELETON CREW

NJ. E-mail: info@skeletoncrewonline.com. Website: www.skeletoncrewonline.com.

HOW TO CONTACT E-mail or send message through MySpace page for directions on sending material.

MUSIC Punk, indie, rock, alternative. Artists include David Costa, the Architects, New Tomorrow, the Mean Reds, and more.

◑ SMALL STONE RECORDS

P.O. Box 02007, Detroit, MI 48202. (248)219-2613. Fax: (248) 541-6536 E-mail: sstone@smallstone.com. Website: www.smallstone.com. Owner: Scott Hamilton. Record company. Estab. 1995. Staff size: 1. Releases 2 singles, 2 EPs, and 10 CDs/year. Pays negotiable royalty to artists on contract; statutory rate to publisher per song on record.

DISTRIBUTED BY A EC, Allegro/Nail, Carrot Top.

HOW TO CONTACT Submit CD/CD Rom by mail. Unsolicited submissions are OK. Does not return material. Responds in 2 months.

MUSIC Mostly **alternative**, **rock,** and **blues**; also **funk (not R&B)**. Released *Fat Black Pussy Cat*, written and recorded by Five Horse Johnson (rock/blues); *Wrecked & Remixed*, written and recorded by Morsel (indie rock, electronica); and *Only One Division*, written and recorded by Soul Clique (electronica), all on Small Stone Records. Other artists include Acid King, Perplexa, and Novadriver.

TIPS "Looking for esoteric music along the lines of Bill Laswell to Touch & Go/Thrill Jockey records material. Only send along material if it makes sense with what we do. Perhaps owning some of our records would help."

SMOG VEIL RECORDS

1658 N. Milwaukee Ave., #284, Chicago IL 60647. (773)706-0450. Fax: (312)276-8519. E-mail: franklisa@aol.com. Website: www.smogveil.com. **Contact**: Frank Mauceri. "Smog Veil Records focuses primarily on underground, challenging, unknown, and/or bombastic rock'n'roll."

HOW TO CONTACT Submit CD or CD-R to Frank Mauceri by mail. Does not accept submissions by e-mail or links to website. Submissions must include a contact, press kit, and plans for touring. Response time is slow. "Note that if your band is playing the Chicago area, we cannot help with booking, but may be interested in seeing you perform live. Therefore, please email gig details. Demo submissions cannot be returned to the submitter."

MUSIC Artists include Batusis, David Thomas, Thor, This Moment in Black History, Butcher Boys, and Prisoners.

◐◯ SONIC UNYON RECORDS CANADA

P.O. Box 57347, Jackson Station, Hamilton, ON L8P 4X2, Canada. (905)777-1223. Fax: (905)777-1161. E-mail: jerks@sonicunyon.com. Website: www.sonicunyon.com. Co-owners: Tim Potocic; Mark Milne. Record company. Estab. 1992. Releases 2 singles, 2 EPs and 6-10 CDs/year. Pays negotiable royalty to artists on contract; statutory rate to publisher per song on record.

DISTRIBUTED BY Caroline Distribution.

HOW TO CONTACT *Call first and obtain permission to submit.* Prefers CD or cassette. "Research our company before you send your demo. We are small; don't waste my time and your money." Does not return material. Responds in 4 months.

MUSIC Mostly **rock**, **heavy rock,** and **pop rock**. Released *Doberman* (album), written and recorded by Kittens (heavy rock); *What a Life* (album), written and recorded by Smoother; and *New Grand* (album), written and recorded by New Grand on sonic unyon records (pop/rock). Other artists include Ad Astra Per Aspera, Wooden Stars, The Ghost Is Dancing, the Nein, Simply Saucer, Raising the Fawn, and Aereogramme.

TIPS "Know what we are about. Research us. Know we are a small company. Know signing to us doesn't mean that everything will fall into your lap. We are only the beginning of an artist's career."

⊘ SONY BMG

550 Madison Ave., New York, NY 10022. Website: www.sonymusic.com.

◯ Sony BMG is one of the primary "Big 4" major labels.

HOW TO CONTACT For specific contact information see the listings in this section for Sony subsidiaries Columbia Records, Epic Records, Sony Nashville, RCA Records, J Records, Arista, and American Recordings.

⊘ SONY MUSIC NASHVILLE

8 Music Square W., Nashville TN 37203-3204. (615)301-4300. Website: www.sonymusic.com. Labels include Columbia Nashville, Arista Nashville, RCA, BNA, and Provident Music Group.

◯ Sony Music Nashville is a subsidiary of Sony BMG, one of the "Big 4" major labels.

HOW TO CONTACT *Sony Music Nashville does not accept unsolicited submissions.*

⊘ SUGAR HILL RECORDS

E-mail: info@sugarhillrecords.com. Website: www.
sugarhillrecords.com. Record company. Estab. 1978.

   ○ Welk Music Group acquired Sugar Hill Records in 1998.

HOW TO CONTACT *No unsolicited submissions.*
"If you are interested in having your music heard by
Sugar Hill Records or the Welk Music Group, we
suggest you establish a relationship with a manager,
publisher, or attorney that has an ongoing relationship with our company. We do not have a list of such
entities."

MUSIC Mostly **Americana**, **bluegrass**, and **country**.
Artists include Nitty Gritty Dirt Band, Sarah Jarosz, Donna the Buffalo, The Infamous Stringdusters,
Joey + Rory, and Sam Bush.

① TEXAS MUSIC CAFE

P.O. Box 50273, Austin, TX 78763. E-mail: info@texasmusiccafe.com. Website: www.texasmusiccafe.com.
Contact: Aubin Hagelstein, booking. Television show.
Estab. 1997. Staff size: 10. Releases 26 TV programs/
year. Pays opportunity to perform on national television. Original music only.

DISTRIBUTED BY PBS in high definition and surround sound.

HOW TO CONTACT Submit demo by mail or email a link. Unsolicited submissions are OK. Prefers
CD, videocassette (VHS/DVD) with sample songs.
Does not return material. Responds only if interested.

TIPS "Must be willing to travel to Texas at your expense to be taped. Let us know if you are traveling
near central Texas."

① TEXAS ROSE RECORDS

2002 Platinum St., Garland, TX 75042. (972)272-3131.
Fax: (972)272-3155. E-mail: txrr1@aol.com. Website:
www.texasroserecords.com. **Contact:** Nancy Baxendale, president. Record company, music publisher
(Yellow Rose of Texas Publishing) and record producer (Nancy Baxendale). Estab. 1994. Staff size: 3.
Releases 3 CDs/year. Pays negotiable royalty to artists on contract; statutory rate to publisher per song
on record.

DISTRIBUTED BY Self distribution.

HOW TO CONTACT *E-mail first for permission
to submit.* Submit maximum of 2 songs on CD and

lyrics. Does not return material. Responds only if
interested.

MUSIC Mostly **country**, **soft rock,** and **blues**; also
pop. Does not want hip-hop, rap, heavy metal. Released *Flyin' High over Texas* (album), recorded by
Dusty Martin (country); *High on the Hog* (album),
recorded by Steve Harr (country); *Time for Time to
Pay* (album), recorded by Jeff Elliot (country); *Double XXposure* (album), recorded by Jeff Elliott and
Kim Neeley (country), Pendulum Dream (album)
recorded by Maureen Kelly (Americana) and "Cowboy Super Hero" (single) written and recorded by
Robert Mauldin.

TIPS "We are interested in songs written for today's
market with a strong musical hook. No home recordings, please."

⊘ TOMMY BOY ENTERTAINMENT LLC

120 Fifth Ave., 7th Floor, New York, NY 10011.
(212)388-8300. Fax: (212)388-8431. E-mail: info@
tommyboy.com. Website: www.tommyboy.com. Record company.

DISTRIBUTED BY WEA, Subway Records.

HOW TO CONTACT E-mail to obtain current
demo submission policy.

MUSIC Artists include Chavela Vargas, Afrika
Bambaataa, Biz Markie, Kool Keith, and INXS.

○ TON RECORDS

E-mail: tonmusic@earthlink.net. Website: www.ton-records.com or www.myspace.com/tonrecords. Vice
president: Jay Vasquez. Labels include 7" collectors
series and Ton Special Projects. Record company and
record producer (RJ Vasquez). Estab. 1992. Releases
6-9 LPs, 1-2 EPs and 10-11 CDs/year. Pays negotiable
royalty to artists on contract; statutory rate to publisher per song on record.

HOW TO CONTACT Not signing at present time.

MUSIC Mostly **new music**; also **hard new music**.
Released *Intoxicated Birthday Lies* (album), recorded by shoegazer (punk rock); *The Good Times R Killing Me* (album), recorded by Top Jimmy, all on Ton
Records. Other artists include Why? Things Burn,
Sarge Inc., and the Ramblers.

TIPS "Work as hard as we do."

① TOPCAT RECORDS

P.O. Box 670234, Dallas, TX 75367. (972)484-4141. Fax:
(972)620-8333. E-mail: info@topcatrecords.com. Web-

site: www.topcatrecords.com or www.myspace.com/top-catrecords. President: Richard Chalk. Record company and record producer. Estab. 1991. Staff size: 3. Releases 4-6 CDs/year. Pays 10-15% royalty to artists on contract; statutory rate to publisher per song on record.

DISTRIBUTED BY City Hall.

HOW TO CONTACT *Call first and obtain permission to submit.* Prefers CD. Does not return material. Responds in 1 month.

MUSIC Mostly **blues**, **swing**, **rockabilly**, **Americana**, **Texana** and **R&B**. Released *If You Need Me* (album), written and recorded by Robert Ealey (blues); *Texas Blueswomen* (album by 3 Female Singers), recorded by various (blues/R&B); and *Jungle Jane* (album), written and recorded by Holland K. Smith (blues/swing), all on Topcat. Released CDs: *Jim Suhler & Alan Haynes—Live*; Bob Kirkpatrick *Drive across Texas*; *Rock My Blues to Sleep* by Johnny Nicholas; *Walking Heart Attack*, by Holland K. Smith; *Dirt Road* (album), recorded by Jim Suhler; *Josh Alan Band* (album), recorded by Josh Alan; *Bust Out* (album), recorded by Robin Sylar. Other artists include Grant Cook, Muddy Waters, Big Mama Thornton, Big Joe Turner, Geo. "Harmonica" Smith, J.B. Hutto and Bee Houston. "View our website for an up-to-date listing of releases."

TIPS "Send me blues (fast, slow, happy, sad, etc.) or good blues oriented R&B. No pop, hip-hop, or rap."

TOUCH AND GO/QUARTERSTICK RECORDS

P.O. Box 25520, Chicago, IL 60625. Phone: (773)388-3888. Fax: (773)388-8888. E-mail: info@tgrec.com. Website: www.touchandgorecords.com. Quarterstick Records: P.O. Box 25342, Chicago, IL 60625.

HOW TO CONTACT Mail to one or the other (staffed by same people; no need to send to both labels). "Demos are listened to by any and all staffers who want to or have time to listen to them. Do not call or e-mail us about your demo." Do not e-mail mp3s or web URLs.

MUSIC All Styles. Artists include Therapy?, TV on the Radio, Pinback, Naked Raygun, Blonde Redhead, Henry Rollins, Yeah Yeah Yeahs, Girls against Boys, and more.

TRANSDREAMER RECORDS

P.O. Box 1955, New York, NY 10113. (212)741-8861. Website: www.transdreamer.com. **Contact:** Greg Caputo, marketing savant. President: Robert John. Record company. Estab. 2002. Staff size: 5. Released 4 CDs/year. Pays negotiable rate to artists on contract; 3/4 statutory rate to publisher per song on record.

Also see the listing for Megaforce in this section of the book.

DISTRIBUTED BY Red/Sony.

HOW TO CONTACT *Contact first and obtain permission to submit.*

MUSIC Mostly **alternative/rock**. Artists include the Delgados, Arab Strap, Dressy Bessy, the Dig, and Holly Golightly.

UAR RECORDS

P.O. Box 1264, 6020 W. Pottstown Rd., Peoria, IL 61654-1264. (309)673-5755. Fax: (309)673-7636. E-mail: uarltd@a5.com. Website: www.unitedcyber.com/uarltd. Contact: Jerry Hanlon, A&R director. Record company and music publisher (Jerjoy Music/BMI and Katysarah Music/ASCAP). Estab. 1978. Staff size: 2. Releases 3 or more CDs/year.

Also see the listings for Kaysarah Music (ASCAP) and Jerjoy Music (BMI) in the "Music Publishers" section of this book.

HOW TO CONTACT "If you are an artist seeking a record deal, please send a sample of your vocal and/or songwriting work—guitar and vocal is fine, no more than 4 songs. Fully produced demos are NOT necessary. Also send brief information on your background in the business, your goals, etc. If you are NOT a songwriter, please send 4 songs maximum of cover tunes that we can use to evaluate your vocal ability. If you wish a reply, please send a SASE, otherwise, you will not receive an answer. If you want a critique of your vocal abilities, please so state as we do not routinely offer critiques. Unsolicited submissions are OK. If you wish all of your material returned to you, be sure to include mailing materials and postage. WE DO NOT RETURN PHONE CALLS."

MUSIC Mostly **American** and **Irish country**. Released "When Jackie Sang the Walking Talking Dolly," "Far Side Banks of Jordan," "There's You," all recorded by Jerry Hanlon. "Lisa Dance with Me," "Philomena from Ireland," "Rainbow," "I'd Better Stand Up," all recorded by the Heggarty Twins from Northern Ireland and Jerry Hanlon. "An Ordinary Woman," "All Your Little Secrets," recorded by Anne More.

TIPS "We are a small independent company, but our belief is that every good voice deserves a chance to be heard and our door is always open to new and aspiring artists."

⊘ UNIVERSAL MOTOWN RECORDS

1755 Broadway, #6, New York, NY 10019. (212)841-8600. Website: www.universalmotown.com. Vice presidents A&R: Bruce Carbone. Labels include Cash Money Records, SRC Records, Derrty Entertainment, and Rowdy Records. Record company.

○ Universal Motown Records is a subsidiary of Universal Music Group, one of the "Big 4" major labels.

HOW TO CONTACT *Does not accept unsolicited submissions.*

MUSIC Artists include Lil' Wayne, Erykah Badu, Days Difference, Kem, Paper Route, and Kelly Rowland.

VAGRANT RECORDS

2118 Wilshire Blvd. #361, Santa Monica, CA 90403. E-mail: info@vagrant.com. Website: www.vagrant.com. United Kingdom: 3rd Floor, 1a Adpar St., London W2 1DE. E-mail: vagrantuk@vagrant.com.

HOW TO CONTACT Send demos to demosubmissions@vagrant.com.

MUSIC Rock, alternative. Artists include Black Rebel Motorcycle Club, Electric Owls, J Roddy Walston and the Business, Murder by Death, Protest the Hero, School of Seven Bells, Senses Fail, Stars, the Hold Steady, Thrice, and more.

🎧⊘ THE VERVE MUSIC GROUP

1755 Broadway, 3rd Floor, New York, NY 10019. (212)331-2000. Fax: (212)331-2064. E-mail: contact@vervemusicgroup.com. Website: www.vervemusicgroup.com. A&R Director: Dahlia Ambach. Los Angeles: 100 N. First St., Burbank CA 91502. Vice president A&R: Bud Harner. Record company. Labels include Verve, GRP, and Impulse! Records.

○ Verve Music Group is a subsidiary of Universal Music Group, one of the "Big 4" major labels.

HOW TO CONTACT *The Verve Music Group does not accept unsolicited submissions.*

MUSIC Artists include Boney James, Diana Krall, Ledisi, Herbie Hancock, Queen Latifah, and Bruce Hornsby & the Noisemakers.

VICTORY RECORDS

346 N. Justine St., 5th Floor, Chicago, IL 60607. (312)666-8661. Fax: (312)666-8665. Website: www.victoryrecords.com.

HOW TO CONTACT Send press kit by mail.

MUSIC Alternative, metal, rock. Artists include the Audition, Bayside, Catch 22, Funeral for A Friend, Otep, Hawthorne Heights, Ringworm, Secret Lives of the Freemasons, Silverstein, the Tossers, Voodoo Glow Skulls, William Control, Streetlight Manifesto, and more.

⊘ VIRGIN MUSIC GROUP

5750 Wilshire Blvd., Los Angeles CA 90036. (323)462-6252. Website: www.virginrecords.com. New York office: 150 5th Ave., 3rd Floor, New York, NY 10016. (212)786-8200. Fax:(212)786-8343. Labels include Virgin Records, Pointblank Records, Astralwerks Records, and Relentless Records. Record company.

○ Virgin Records is a subsidiary of the EMI Group, one of the "Big 4" major labels.

DISTRIBUTED BY EMD.

HOW TO CONTACT *Virgin Music Group does not accept recorded material or lyrics unless submitted by a reputable industry source.* "If your act has received positive press or airplay on prior independent releases, we welcome your written query. Send a letter of introduction accompanied by all pertinent artist information. Do not send a tape until requested. All unsolicited materials will be returned unopened."

MUSIC Mostly **rock** and **pop**. Artists include Lenny Kravitz, Placebo, Joss Stone, Ben Harper, Iggy Pop, and Gorillaz.

◐ WAREHOUSE CREEK RECORDING CORP.

P.O. Box 102, Franktown, VA 23354. (757)442-6883. E-mail: warehousecreek@verizon.net. Website: www.warehousecreek.com. President: Billy Sturgis. Record company, music publisher (Bayford Dock Music) and record producer (Billy Sturgis). Estab. 1993. Staff size: 1. Releases 11 singles and 1 CD/year. Pays negotiable royalty to artists on contract; statutory rate to publisher per song on record.

DISTRIBUTED BY City Hall Records.

HOW TO CONTACT Submit demo by mail. Unsolicited submissions are OK. Prefers cassette, CD, or VHS videocassette with lyric sheet. Does not return material.

MUSIC Mostly **R&B**, **blues** and **gospel**. Released *Nothin' Nice* (album), recorded by Guitar Slim Jr. (blues); *Frank Town Blues* (album), recorded by the Crudup Brothers (blues); *Hi-Fi Baby* (album), recorded by Greg "Fingers" Taylor (blues), all released on Warehouse Creek Records.

WARNER BROS. RECORDS

3300 Warner Blvd., 3rd Floor, Burbank CA 91505. (818)846-9090. Fax: (818)953-3423. Website: www.wbr.com. **New York:** 75 Rockefeller Plaza, New York, NY 10019. (212)275-4500 Fax:(212)275-4596. A&R: James Dowdall, Karl Rybacki. **Nashville:** 20 Music Square E., Nashville, TN 37203. (615)748-8000 Fax:(615)214-1567. Labels include American Recordings, Eternal Records, Imago Records, Mute Records, Giant Records, Malpaso Records, and Maverick Records. Record company.
DISTRIBUTED BY WEA.
HOW TO CONTACT *Warner Bros. Records does not accept unsolicited material.* "All unsolicited material will be returned unopened. Those interested in having their tapes heard should establish a relationship with a manager, publisher or attorney that has an ongoing relationship with Warner Bros. Records."
MUSIC Released *Van Halen 3* (album), recorded by Van Halen; *Evita* (soundtrack); and *Dizzy Up the Girl* (album), recorded by Goo Goo Dolls, both on Warner Bros. Records. Other artists include Faith Hill, Tom Petty & the Heartbreakers, Jeff Foxworthy, Porno for Pyros, Travis Tritt, Yellowjackets, Bela Fleck and the Flecktones, Al Jarreau, Joshua Redmond, Little Texas, and Curtis Mayfield.

⊕ WATERDOG MUSIC

A.K.A Waterdog Records. Labels include Whitehouse Records. Record company. Estab. 1991. Staff size: 2. Releases 2 CDs/year. Pays negotiable royalty to artists on contract; statutory rate to publisher per song on record.
HOW TO CONTACT "Not accepting unsolicited materials, demos at this time. If submission policy changes, it will be posted on our website."
MUSIC Mostly **rock** and **pop**. *Smash Record*, by the Bad Examples, released 2011. Other artists have included Middle 8, Al Rose & the Transcendos, Kat Parsons, Torben Floor (Carey Ott), MysteryDriver, Joel Frankel, Dean Goldstein & Coin, and Matt Tiegler.

TIPS "Ralph Covert's children's music (Ralph's World) is released on Disney Sound and Bar/None Records. We are not looking for any other children's music performers or composers."

⊙ WINCHESTER RECORDS

25 Troubadour Lane, Berkeley Springs WV 25411. (304)258-9381. E-mail: mccoytroubadour@aol.com. Website: www.troubadourlounge.com. **Contact:** Jim or Bertha McCoy, owners. Labels include Master Records and Real McCoy Records. Record company, music publisher (Jim McCoy Music, Alear Music, New Edition Music/BMI), record producer (Jim McCoy Productions) and recording studio. Releases 20 singles and 10 LPs/year. Pays standard royalty to artists; statutory rate to publisher for each record sold.
HOW TO CONTACT *Write first and obtain permission to submit.* Prefers CD with 5-10 songs and lead sheet. Include SASE. Responds in 1 month.
MUSIC Mostly **bluegrass**, **church/religious**, **country**, **folk**, **gospel**, **progressive,** and **rock**. Released "Runaway Girl" (single by Earl Howard/Jim McCoy) from *Earl Howard Sings His Heart Out* (album), recorded by Earl Howard (country), released 2002 on Winchester; *Jim McCoy and Friends Remember Ernest Tubb* (album), recorded by Jim McCoy (country), released January 2003 on Winchester; *The Best of Winchester Records* (album), recorded by RileeGray/J.B. Miller/Jim McCoy/Carroll County (country), released 2002 on Winchester.

⊘ WIND-UP ENTERTAINMENT

72 Madison Ave., 7th Floor, New York NY 10016. (212)895-3100. Website: www.winduprecords.com. **Contact:** A&R. Record company. Estab. 1997. Releases 6-7 CDs/year. Pays negotiable royalty to artists on contract; statutory rate to publisher per song on record.
DISTRIBUTED BY BMG.
HOW TO CONTACT *Write first and obtain permission to submit.* Prefers CD or DVD. Does not return material or respond to submissions.
MUSIC Mostly **rock**, **folk,** and **hard rock**. Artists include Seether, Evanescence, Finger Eleven, Creed, and People In Planes.
TIPS "We rarely look for songwriters as opposed to bands, so writing a big hit single would be the rule of the day."

○ WORLD BEATNIK RECORDS

121 Walnut Lane, Rockwallm TX 75032. Phone/Fax: (972)771-3797. E-mail: tropikalproductions@gmail.com. Website: www.tropikalproductions.com/label.html. Producers: J. Towry (world beat, reggae, ethnic, jazz); Jimbe (reggae, world beat, ethnic); Arik Towry (ska, pop, ragga, rock). Labels include World Beatnik Records. Record company and record producer (Jimi Towry). Estab. 1983. Staff size: 4. Releases 6 singles, 6 LPs, 6 EPs, and 6 CDs/year. Pays negotiable royalty to artists on contract; statutory rate to publisher per song on record.

DISTRIBUTED BY Midwest Records, Southwest Wholesale, Reggae OneLove, Ejaness Records, Ernie B's, CD Wareouse, and Borders.

HOW TO CONTACT Submit demo tape by mail. Unsolicited submissions are OK. Prefers cassette, DAT, mini disk, or VHS videocassette with lyric sheet. Include SASE. Responds in 2 weeks.

MUSIC Mostly **world beat, reggae,** and **ethnic**; also **jazz, hip-hop/dance,** and **pop**. Released *I and I* (album by Abby I/Jimbe), recorded by Abby I (African pop); *Rastafrika* (album by Jimbe/Richard Ono), recorded by Rastafrika (African roots reggae); and *Vibes* (album by Jimbe/Bongo Cartheni), recorded by Wave (worldbeat/jazz), all released 2001/2002 on World Beatnik. Other artists include Ras Richi (Cameroon), Wisdom Ogbor (Nigeria), Joe Lateh (Ghana), Dee Dee Cooper, Ras Lyrix (St. Croix), Ras Kumba (St. Kitts), Gary Mon, Darbo (Gambia), Ricki Malik (Jamaica), Arik Miles, Narte's (Hawaii), Gavin Audagnotti (South Africa) and Bongo (Trinidad).

○ XEMU RECORDS

2 E. Broadway, Suite 901, New York, NY 10038. (212)807-0290. E-mail: XemuRecord@aol.com. Website: www.xemu.com. Record company. Estab. 1992. Releases 4 CDs/year. Pays negotiable royalty to artists on contract; statutory rate to publisher per song on record.

DISTRIBUTED BY Redeye Distribution.

HOW TO CONTACT *Write first and obtain permission to submit.* Prefers CD with 3 songs. Does not return material. Responds in 2 months.

MUSIC Mostly **alternative**. Released *Happy Suicide, Jim!* (album) by The Love Kills Theory (alternative rock); *Howls from the Hills* (album) by Dead Meadow; *The Fall* (album), recorded by Mikki James (alternative rock); *A Is for Alpha* (album), recorded by Alpha Bitch (alternative rock); *Hold the Mayo* (album), recorded by Death Sandwich (alternative rock); *Stockholm Syndrome* (album), recorded by Trigger Happy (alternative rock) all released on Xemu Records. Other artists include Morning After Girls, Spindrift, and Rumpleville.

○ XL RECORDINGS

Beggar's Group, One Codrington Mews, London W11 2EH, United Kingdom. Website: www.xlrecordings.com. **US**: 304 Hudson St., 7th Floor, New York, NY 10013.

MUSIC Alternative rock. Artists include Adele, Basement Jaxx, Radiohead, Beck, M.I.A, Peaches, Radiohead, Sigur Ros, the Horrors, the Raconteurs, the White Stripes, Thom Yorke, Vampire Weekend, and more.

RECORD PRODUCERS

The independent producer can best be described as a creative coordinator. He's often the one with the most creative control over a recording project and is ultimately responsible for the finished product. Some record companies have in-house producers who work with the acts on that label (although, in more recent years, such producer-label relationships are often non-exclusive). Today, most record companies contract out-of-house, independent record producers on a project-by-project basis.

WHAT RECORD PRODUCERS DO

Producers play a large role in deciding what songs will be recorded for a particular project and are always on the lookout for new songs for their clients. They can be valuable contacts for songwriters because they work so closely with the artists whose records they produce. They usually have a lot more freedom than others in executive positions and are known for having a good ear for potential hit songs. Many producers are songwriters and musicians themselves. Since they wield a great deal of influence, a good song in the hands of the right producer at the right time stands a good chance of being cut. And even if a producer is not working on a specific project, he is well acquainted with record company executives and artists and can often get material through doors not open to you.

SUBMITTING MATERIAL TO PRODUCERS

It can be difficult to get your tapes to the right producer at the right time. Many producers write their own songs, and even if they don't write, they may be involved in their own publishing companies so they have instant access to all the songs in their catalogs. Also, some genres are more dependent on finding outside songs than others. A producer working with a rock group or a singer-songwriter will rarely take outside songs.

It's important to understand the intricacies of the producer/publisher situation. If you pitch your song directly to a producer first, before another publishing company publishes the song, the producer may ask you for the publishing rights (or a percentage thereof) to your song. You must decide whether the producer is really an active publisher who will try to get the song recorded again and again or whether he merely wants the publishing because it means extra income for him from the current recording project. You may be able to work out a copublishing deal, where you and the producer split the publishing of the song. That means he will still receive his percentage of the publishing income, even if you secure a cover recording of the song by other artists in the future. Even though you would be giving up a little bit initially, you may benefit in the future.

Some producers will offer to sign artists and songwriters to "development deals." These can range from a situation where a producer auditions singers and musicians with the intention of building a group from the ground up, to development deals where a producer signs a band or singer-songwriter to his production company with the intention of developing the act and producing an album to shop to labels (sometimes referred to as a "baby record deal").

You must carefully consider whether such a deal is right for you. In some cases, such a deal can open doors and propel an act to the next level. In other worst-case scenarios, such a deal can result in loss of artistic and career control, with some acts held in contractual bondage for years at a time. Before you consider any such deal, be clear about your goals, the producer's reputation, and the sort of compromises you are willing to make to reach those goals. If you have any reservations whatsoever, don't do it.

The listings that follow outline which aspects of the music industry each producer is involved in, what type of music he or she is looking for, and what records and artists he or she has recently produced. Study the listings carefully, noting the artists each producer works with, and consider if any of your songs might fit a particular artist's or producer's style. Then determine whether they are open to your level of experience (see the A Sample Listing Decoded).

ADDITIONAL RECORD PRODUCERS

Icons

For more instructional information on the listings in this book, including explanations of the icons, read the article How to Use *Songwriter's Market*.

WILLIAM ACKERMAN

P.O. Box 419, Bar Mills ME 04004. (207)929-5777. E-mail: will@williamackerman.com. Website: www. williamackerman.com.

MUSIC Has worked with George Winston, Michael Hedges, Heidi Anne Breyer, Fiona Joy Hawkins, Devon Rice, Erin Aas. Music: acoustic, alternative, instrumental.

⊘ ADR STUDIOS

(formerly Stuart J. Allyn), 250 Taxter Rd., Irvington, NY 10533. (914)591-5616. Fax: (914)591-5617. E-mail: ardstudios@adrinc.org. Website: www.adrinc.org. Associate: Jack Walker. **Contact:** Jack Walker, general manager. President: Stuart J. Allyn. Record producer. Estab. 1972. Produces 6 singles and 3-6 CDs/year. Fee derived from sales royalty and outright fee from recording artist and record company.

HOW TO CONTACT *Does not accept unsolicited submissions.*

MUSIC Mostly **pop**, **rock**, **jazz**, and **theatrical**; also **R&B** and **country**. Produced *Thad Jones Legacy* (album), recorded by Vanquard Jazz Orchestra (jazz), released 2000 on New World Records. Other artists include Billy Joel, Aerosmith, Carole Demas, Michael Garin, the Magic Garden, Bob Stewart, the Dixie Peppers, Nora York, Buddy Barnes, and various video and film scores.

🎧 🌓 AL DELORY AND MUSIC MAKERS

E-mail: aldelory@mn.rr.com. Website: www.aldelory. com. **Contact:** Al DeLory, president. Record producer and career consultant (MUSIC MAKERS/ASCAP). Estab. 1987. Fee derived from outright fee from recording artist.

> ○ Al DeLory has won two Grammy Awards and has been nominated five times.

HOW TO CONTACT *E-mail first and obtain permission to submit.* Prefers CD. Include SASE. Responds in 2-3 months only if interested.

MUSIC Mostly **pop** and **Latin**. Produced "Gentle on My Mind" (single), "By the Time I Get to Phoenix" (single) and "Wichita Lineman" (single), all recorded by Glen Campbell. Other artists include Lettermen, Wayne Newton, Bobbie Gentry, and Anne Murray.

TIPS "Seek advice and council only with professionals with a track record and get the money up front."

ALLRS MUSIC PUBLISHING CO. (ASCAP)

P.O. Box 1545, Smithtown, NY 11787. (718)767-8995. E-mail: info@allrsmusic.com. Website: www.allrs music.com. **Contact:** Renee Silvestri-Bushey, president. F.John Silvestri, founder. Leslie Migliorelli, director of operations. Henry Carotenuto, adviser. Bob McDonald, assistant. Music publisher, record company (MIDI Track Records), music consultant, artist management, record producer. Voting member of NARAS (the Grammy Awards), voting member of the Country Music Association (the CMA Awards), SGMA, Songwriters Guild of America (Diamond Member). Estab. 1994. Staff size: 5. Publishes 3 songs/year; publishes 2 new songwriters/year. Pays standard royalty. Affiliate(s) Midi-Track Publishing Co. (BMI).

HOW TO CONTACT "Write/e-mail to obtain permission to submit. *We do not accept unsolicited submissions.*" Prefers CD with 3 songs, lyric sheet, and cover letter. Responds via e-mail in 6 months only if interested.

MUSIC Mostly **country**, **gospel**, **top 40**, **R&B**, **MOR**, and **pop**. Does not want show tunes, jazz, classical, or rap. Published "Why Can't You Hear My Prayer" (single by F. John Silvestri/Leslie Silvestri), recorded by 10-time Grammy nominee Huey Dunbar of the group DLG (Dark Latin Groove) released on Midi Track Records including other multiple releases); "Chasing Rainbows" (single by F. John Silvestri/Leslie Silvestri), recorded by Tommy Cash (country), released on MMT Records (including other multiple releases); "Because of You" (single by F. John Silvestri/Leslie Silvestri), recorded by Iliana Medina, released 2002 on MIDI Track Records, also recorded by Grammy nominee Terri Williams of Always... Patsy Cline, released on MIDI Track Records; also recorded by Grand Ole Opry member Ernie Ashworth, and other multiple releases.

TIPS "Attend workshops, seminars, and visit our blog on our website for advice and info on the music industry."

🌓 🌓 A MAJOR SOUND CORPORATION

RR #1, Kensington, PE C0B 1M0, Canada. (902)836-4571. E-mail: info@amajorsound.com. Website: www. amajorsound.com. **Contact:** Paul C. Milner, producer. Record producer and music publisher. Estab. 1989. Produces 8 CDs/year. Fee derived in part from sales royalty when song or artist is recorded, and/or outright fee from recording artist or record company, or investors.

HOW TO CONTACT Submit demo package by mail. Unsolicited submissions are OK. Prefers CD with 5 songs and lyric sheet (lead sheet if available). Does not return material. Responds only if interested in 3 months.

MUSIC Mostly **rock**, **A/C**, **alternative** and **pop**; also **Christian** and **R&B**. Produced *COLOUR* (album written by J. MacPhee/R. MacPhee/C. Buchanan/D. MacDonald), recorded by the Chucky Danger Band (pop/rock), released 2006; Winner of ECMA award; *Something In Between* (album, written by Matt Andersen), recorded by Matt Andersen and Friends (Blues), released 2008 on Weatherbox/Andersen; *In a Fever in a Dream* (album, written by Pat Deighan), recorded by Pat Deighan and the Orb Weavers (Rock), released in 2008 on Sandbar Music; *Saddle River String Band* (album, written by Saddle River Stringband), recorded by Saddle River Stringband (Blue Grass) released 2007 on Save As Music; Winner of ECMA award.

TIM ANDERSEN

(651)271-0515. E-mail: tandersen2005@yahoo.com. Website: www.timandersenrecordengineer.com. "Can offer all those techniques to make your project rise above "the usual" to something extraordinary, the way real records are made."

MUSIC Has worked with House of Pain, Shaq, Judgement Night, SDTRK, De Jef, Patti LaBelle, Temptations, Hiroshima, Krazy Bone, Snoop Dogg. Music: Rock, R&B, Hip-hop, rap, acoustic.

AUDIO 911

(formerly Steve Wytas Productions), P.O. Box 212, Haddam, CT 06438. (860)916-9947. E-mail: request@audio911.com. Website: www.audio911.com. **Contact:** Steven J. Wytas. Record producer. Estab. 1984. Produces 4-8 singles, 3 LPs, 3 EPs, and 4 CDs/year. Fee derived from outright fee from recording artist or record company.

HOW TO CONTACT Submit demo by mail. Unsolicited submissions are OK. Prefers CD or VHS videocassette with several songs and lyric or lead sheet. "Include live material if possible." Does not return material. Responds in 3 months.

MUSIC Mostly **rock**, **pop**, **top 40**, and **country/acoustic**. Produced *Already Home* (album, record-ed by Hannah Cranna on Big Deal Records (rock); *Under the Rose* (album), recorded by Under the Rose on Utter Records (rock); and *Sickness & Health* (album), recorded by Legs Akimbo on Joyful Noise Records (rock). Other artists include King Hop!, the Shells, the Gravel Pit, G'nu Fuz, Tuesday Welders, and Toxic Field Mice.

WILLIE BASSE

(519)759-3003. E-mail: williebasse@gmail.com. Website: www.williebasse.com. Contact: James Wright.

MUSIC Has worked with: Canned Heat, Finis Tasby, Frank Goldwasser, Paul Shortino, Jeff Nothrup, Black Sheep. Music: rock, blues, heavy metal.

EVAN BEIGEL

5618 Vineland Ave., N. Hollywood CA 91601. (818)321-5472. E-mail: mail@evanjbeigel.com. Website: www.evanjbeigel.com.

MUSIC Has worked with Ray Kurzweil, Badi Assad, Ted Nugent, EightStopSeven, Test Your Reflex, Ford, Budweiser. Music: rock, indie, alternative.

BIG BEAR

P.O. Box 944, Edgbaston, Birmingham B16 8UT, United Kingdom. (0)(121)454-7020. E-mail: agency@bigbearmusic.com. Website: www.bigbearmusic.com. Managing director: Jim Simpson. Record producer, music publisher (Bearsongs) and record company (Big Bear Records). Produces 10 LPs/year. Fee derived from sales royalty.

Also see the listings for Bearsongs in the "Music Publishers" section of this book and Big Bear Records in the "Record Companies" section of this book.

HOW TO CONTACT *Write first about your interest; then submit demo tape and lyric sheet.* Does not return material. Responds in 2 weeks.

MUSIC **Blues**, **swing**, and **jazz**.

BLUES ALLEY RECORDS

Rt. 1, Box 288, Clarksburg, WV 26301. (304)598-2583. E-mail: info@bluesalleymusic.com. Website: www.bluesalleymusic.com. **Contact:** Joshua Swiger, producer. Record producer, record company and music publisher (Blues Alley Publishing/BMI). Produces 4-6 LPs and 2 EPs/year. Fee derived from sales royalty when song or artist is recorded.

HOW TO CONTACT Submit demo package by mail. Unsolicited submissions are OK. Will only accept

CDs with lead sheets and typed lyrics. Does not return material. Responds in 6 weeks.

MUSIC Mostly **country, pop, Christian**, and **rock**. Produced *Monongalia*, recorded by The New Relics (country), 2009; *Chasing Venus*, recorded by The New Relics (acoustic rock), 2006; *Sons of Sirens*, recorded by Amity (rock), 2004; and *It's No Secret*, recorded by Samantha Caley (pop country), 2004.

CLIFF BRODSKY

E-mail: cliff@brodskyentertainment.com. Website: www.cliffbrodsky.com.

MUSIC Has worked with Rose Rossi, Jason Kirk, Warner Brothers, Universal, Sony, MCA, Virgin, Interscope. Music: indie, pop, rock.

⊘ CABIN-ON-THE-LAKE MUSIC

4120 Dale Rd., Suite J-8, #180, Modesto, CA 95356. (608)239-4121. Fax: (209)409-8343. E-mail: cotlmusic@aim.com. Website: www.cabin-on-the-lake.com. **Contact:** James Miksche, producer. Estab. 2002. Produces 12-20 singles; 2 albums per year. Fees derived from sales royalty when song or artist is recorded.

HOW TO CONTACT Submit demo by mail. Unsolicited submissions are OK. Send CD with 3 songs, lyric sheet, and cover letter. Does not return submissions. Responds only if interested.

MUSIC Mostly interested in singer/songwriters, folk; also country/crossover, blues rock. Does not want rap, hard rock, hip-hop, or jazz. Produced "The Legend of Coby Gill" (single by Chris Lawrence) from *The Legend of Coby Gill* (album), recorded by Coby Gill (folk/country), 2010; "Give Me a Call" (single by Chris Lawrence), from *The Legend of Coby Gill* (album), recorded by Coby Gill (folk/country), 2010; "I Could Swear" written and recorded by Tom Davis, 2009.

○ COACHOUSE MUSIC

P.O. Box 1308, Barrington, IL 60011. (847)382-7631. Fax: (847)382-7651. E-mail: coachouse1@aol.com or michael@coachousemusic.com. Website: coachousemusic.com. **Contact:** Michael Freeman, president. Record producer. Estab. 1984. Produces 6-8 CDs/year. Fee derived from flat fee and/or sales royalty when song or artist is recorded.

HOW TO CONTACT *Write or e-mail first and obtain permission to submit.* Prefers CD with 3-5 songs and lyric sheet. Include SASE. Responds in 6 weeks.

MUSIC Mostly **rock, pop,** and **blues**; also **alternative rock** and **country/Americana/roots**. Produced *Casque Nu* (album), written and recorded by Charlelie Couture on Chrysalis EMI France (contemporary pop); *Time Will Tell* (album), recorded by Studebaker John on Blind Pig Records (blues); *Where Blue Begins* (album by various/ D. Coleman), recorded by Deborah Coleman on Blind Pig Records (contemporary blues); *A Man Amongst Men* (album), recorded by Bo Diddley (blues); and *Voodoo Menz* (album), recorded by Corey Harris and Henry Butler. Two WC Handy nominations; produced *Pinetop Perkins & Friends* on Telarc, recorded by Pinetop Perkins—Grammy nominated. Other artists include Paul Chastain, Candi Station, Eleventh Dream Day, Magic Slim, the Tantrums, the Pranks, the Bad Examples, Mississippi Heat, and Sherri Williams.

TIPS "Be honest, be committed, strive for excellence."

ERIC CORNE

(310)500-8831. E-mail: eeric@ericcornemusic.com; ericcorne@gmail.com. Website: www.ericcornemusic.com. Contact: Eric Corne, producer. Contact via e-mail or e-mail submission form on website.

MUSIC Has worked with Glen Campbell, Michelle Shocked, DeVotchKa, Instant Karma. Music: rock, indie, Americana, country, blues, jazz, folk.

◑ CREATIVE SOUL

Nashville, TN 37179. (615)400-3910. E-mail: firstcontact@creativesoulrecords.com. Website: www.creativesoulonline.com. **Contact:** Eric Copeland, producer/writer. Record producer. Produces 5-10 singles and 8-15 albums/year. Fee derived from outright fee from recording artist or company. Other services include consulting/critique/review services.

HOW TO CONTACT *Contact first by e-mail to obtain permission to submit demo.* Prefers CD with 2-3 songs and lyric sheet and cover sheet. Does not return submissions. Responds only if interested.

MUSIC contemporary, **Christian, jazz,** and **instrumental**; also **R&B** and **pop/rock**. "If you are a Christian jazz or instrumentalist, then all the better!" Produced *Cedars Gray*, recorded by Cedars Gray (contemporary Christian); *It Is of You*, recorded by Matt Pitzl (contemporary Christian); *Fairytale Life*, recorded by Stephanie Newton (contemporary Christian); all released on Creative Soul Records. Other artists include Brett Rush, Frances Drost, Kristyn Leigh, Tom Dolan, and Canopy Red

TIPS "Contact us first by e-mail; we are here in Nashville for you. We offer monthly information and special consults in Nashville for artists and writers. We want to meet you and talk with you about your dreams. E-mail us and let's start talking about your music and ministry!"

⊘⊛ THE EDWARD DE MILES MUSIC COMPANY

10573 W. Pico Blvd., #352, Los Angeles CA 90064-2348. Phone: (310)948-9652. Fax: (310)474-7705. E-mail: info@edmsahara.com. Website: www.edmsahara.com. **Contact:** Edward De Miles, president. Record producer, music publisher (Edward De Miles Music Co./BMI) and record company (Sahara Records and Filmworks Entertainment). Estab. 1981. Produces 5-10 CDs/year. Fee derived from sales royalty when song or artist is recorded.

> ◯ Also see the listing for Edward De Miles in the "Music Publishers" and "Managers & Booking Agents" sections, as well as Sahara Records and Filmworks Entertainment in the "Record Companies" section of this book.

HOW TO CONTACT Does not accept unsolicited submissions.

MUSIC Mostly **R&B/dance**, **top 40 pop/rock,** and **contemporary jazz**; also **country**, **TV, and film themes—songs and jingles**. Produced "Moments" and "Dance Wit Me" (singles) (dance), both written and recorded by Steve Lynn; and "Games" (single), written and recorded by D'von Edwards (jazz), all on Sahara Records. Other artists include Multiple Choice.

TIPS "Copyright all material before submitting. Equipment and showmanship a must."

MARC DESISTO

(818)522-0214. E-mail: mdaudiomix@roadrunner.com; marcdmix@gmail.com; imixit2010@gmail.com. Website: www.marcdesisto.com.

MUSIC Has worked with Stevie Nicks, Michelle Branch, Unwritten Law, Melissa Ethridge, Rick Knowles, Don Henley, Patti Smith, Mark Opitz, Tom Petty, U2. Music: rock, alternative, pop, indie.

JEANNIE DEVA

P.O. Box 4636, Sunland CA 91041. (818)446-0932. E-mail: JeannieDeva@gmail.com. Website: www.jeanniedeva.com.

MUSIC Has worked with Rounder Records, Charisse Arrington, MCA, Dar Williams, Razor and Tie Records, Alldaron West. Music: all contemporary styles.

⊘ JOEL DIAMOND ENTERTAINMENT

3940 Laurel Canyon Blvd., Suite 441, Studio City, CA 91604. (818)980-9588. Fax: (818)980-9422. E-mail: jdiamond20@aol.com. Website: www.joeldiamond.com. **Contact:** Joel Diamond. Record producer, music publisher and manager. Fee derived from sales royalty when song is recorded or outright fee from recording artist or record company.

> ◯ Also see the listing for Silver Blue Music/ Oceans Blue Music in the "Music Publishers" section of this book.

HOW TO CONTACT Does not return material. Responds only if interested.

MUSIC Mostly **dance**, **R&B**, **soul,** and **top 40/pop**. The 5 Browns—3 number 1 CDs for Sony/BMG, David Hasselhoff; produced "One Night in Bangkok" (single by Robey); "I Think I Love You," recorded by Katie Cassidy (daughter of David Cassidy) on Artemis Records; "After the Loving" (single), recorded by E. Humperdinck; "Forever Friends," recorded by Vaneza (featured on Nickelodeon's *The Brothers Garcia*); and "Paradise" (single), recorded by Kaci.

LES DUDEK

P.O. Box 726, Auburndale FL 33823. (863)967-0977. Website: www.lesdudek.com.

HOW TO CONTACT E-mail using submission form found on website.

MUSIC Has worked with Stevie Nicks, Steve Miller Band, Cher, Dave Mason, the Allman Brothers, Mike Finnigan, Bobby Whitlock. Music: Southern rock.

● FINAL MIX INC.

(formerly Final Mix Music), 2219 W. Olive Ave., Suite 102, Burbank, CA 91506. E-mail: rob@finalmix.com. Website: www.finalmix.com. **Contact:** Theresa Frank, A&R. Record producer/remixer/mix engineer, independent label (3.6 Music, Inc.) and music publisher (Ximlanif Music Publishing). Estab. 1989. Releases 12 singles and 3-5 LPs and CDs/year. Fee derived from sales royalty when song or artist is recorded.

HOW TO CONTACT *Does not accept unsolicited submissions.*

MUSIC Primarily **pop**, **rock**, **dance**, **R&B**, and **rap**. Produced and/or mixer/remixer for Mary Mary, New Boyz, Kirk Franklin, Charlie Wilson, LeAnn Rimes, Charice, Train, Aaliyah, Hilary Duff, Jesse McCartney, Christina Aguilera, *American Idol*, Ray Charles, Quincy Jones, Michael Bolton, K-Ci and Jo Jo, Will Smith, and/or mixer/remixer for Janet Jackson, Ice Cube, Queen Latifah, Jennifer Paige, and the Corrs.

RICHARD FINK IV

P.O. Box 127, Bergen NY 14416. (646)233-3393. E-mail: voice@richardiv.com. Website: www.richardiv.com.

MUSIC Has worked with Carmireli, Meredith Haight, Scattered Ink, Johnny Cummings, Krista Marie. Music: pop, rock, alternative, hard rock, metal, R&B.

MAURICE GAINEN

4470 Sunset Blvd. Suite 177, Hollywood CA 90027. (323)662-3642. E-mail: info@mauricegainen.com. Website: www.mauricegainen.com. "We provide complete start-to-finish CD production, including help in choosing songs and musicians through CD Mastering. We also pride ourselves on setting a budget and keeping to it."

MUSIC Has worked with Stacy Golden, Yuka Takara, Donna Loren, James Webber, Andy McKee, Rafael Moreira, Alex Skolnick Trio, Metro, Mel Elias, Shelly Rudolph, Kenny Tex, Rachael Owens. Music: R&B, jazz, alternative, rock, pop.

BRIAN GARCIA

(626)487-0410. E-mail: info@briangarcia.net; record@wt.net. Website: www.briangarcia.net.

MUSIC "Producer-Mixer-Engineer Brian Garcia specializes in the genres of rock & pop. He has been part of 22 million records sold, debuts at number 1 in 30 countries, a Grammy winning album and a number 1 single on iTunes as a co-writer/producer/mixer. Brian has taken artists from development to securing record deals & producing the albums for EMI and Sony/BMG." Has worked with Our Lady Peace, Earshot, Until June, Galactic Cowboys, Avril Lavigne, Kelly Clarkson, Michelle Branch, Dizmas, Chantal Kreviazuk, King's X, Diana Degarmo, the Library, Pushmonkey, the Daylights, Precious Death, Joy Drop. Music: rock, pop, indie.

MCKAY GARNER

c/o Bounce Inventive Audio, 1873 Eighth Ave. Suite A, San Francisco CA 94122. (323)912-9119. E-mail: info@mckaygarner.com. Website: www.mckaygarner.com.

MUSIC Has worked with Red Hot Chili Peppers, Styles of Beyond, Flogging Molly, Valencia, Mike Shinoda, Michael Buble, Sara Melson, Elyzium.

CARMEN GRILLO

Big Surprise Music, 1616 Ventura Blvd. Suite 522, Encino CA 91436. (818)905-7676. E-mail: info@carmengrillo.com. Website: www.carmengrillo.com.

MUSIC Has worked with Manhattan, Transfer, Chicago, Bill Champlin, Mike Finnigan, Tower of Power. Music: R&B, pop, rock, jazz, blues.

◐ HAILING FREQUENCY MUSIC PRODUCTIONS

7438 Shoshone Ave., Van Nuys, CA 91406. (818)881-9888. Fax: (818)881-0555. E-mail: blowinsmokeband@ktb.net. Website: www.blowinsmokeband.com. President: Lawrence Weisberg. Vice president: Larry Knight. Record producer, record company (Blowin' Smoke Records), management firm (Blowin' Smoke Productions) and music publisher (Hailing Frequency Publishing). Estab. 1992. Produces 3 LPs and 3 CDs/year. Fee derived from sales royalty when song or artist is recorded or outright fee from artist.

⊙ Also see the listing for Blowin' Smoke Productions/Records in the Managers & Booking Agents section of this book.

HOW TO CONTACT *Write or call first and obtain permission to submit.* Prefers CD or DVD. "Write or print legibly with complete contact instructions." Include SASE. Responds in 1 month.

MUSIC Mostly **contemporary R&B**, **blues**, and **blues-rock**; also **songs for film**, **jingles for commercials**, and **gospel (contemporary)**. Produced Sky King's "Tales from the Left Coast" (2010). Other artists include the Fabulous Smokettes. New division creates songs and music tracks for both the mainstream and adult film industries.

◐ HEART CONSORT MUSIC

410 First St. SW., Mt. Vernon, IA 52314. E-mail: mail@heartconsortmusic.com. Website: www.heartconsortmusic.com. **Contact:** Catherine Lawson, manager. Record producer, record company, and music publisher.

Estab. 1980. Produces 2-3 CDs/year. Fee derived from sales royalty when song or artist is recorded.

HOW TO CONTACT Submit demo package by mail. Unsolicited submissions are OK. Prefers CD or cassette with 3 songs and 3 lyric sheets. Include SASE. Responds in 3 months.

MUSIC Mostly **jazz**, **New Age,** and **contemporary**. Produced *New Faces* (album), written and recorded by James Kennedy on Heart Consort Music (world/jazz).

TIPS "We are interested in jazz/New Age artists with quality demos and original ideas. We aim for an international audience."

HEATHER HOLLEY

E-mail: info@heatherholley.com. Website: http://heatherholley.com. "Heather Holley is a New York–based multi-platinum songwriter/arranger/producer whose credits have yielded combined sales of over 29 million, and climbing."

MUSIC Has worked with Christina Aguilera, Katie Costello, Holly Brook, Caitlin Moe. Music: pop, dance, indie, R&B.

JIMMY HUNTER

(323)655-0615. E-mail: jimmy@jimmyhunter.com. Website: www.jimmyhunter.com. "When you work with Jimmy Hunter, you find a fellow artist who will help you to achieve and refine your vision. He has the experience and tools to get the ultimate sound for your music and bring out the very best in you."

MUSIC Has worked with Cher, Savannah Phillips, Smoove, Jared Justice, Lisa Rine, Lynn Tracy, Mark R. Kent, Della Reese, Lisa Gold, Jamie Palumbo, the Ramblers. Music: rock, pop, R&B.

SIMON ILLA

E-mail: info@simonilla.com. Website: www.simonilla.com.

MUSIC Has worked with Onyx, Vivian Green, Floetry, Roscoe P. Coldchain, the Answer. Music: hip-hop, R&B, pop, folk, rock, gospel, emo.

◑ INTEGRATED ENTERTAINMENT

1815 JFK Blvd., #1612, Philadelphia, PA 19103. (267)408-0659. E-mail: lawrence@gelboni.com. Website: www.gelboni.com. **Contact:** Gelboni, president. Record producer. Estab. 1991. Produces up to 6 projects/year. Compensation is derived from outright fee from recording artist or record company and sales royalties.

HOW TO CONTACT Submit demo package by mail. Solicited submissions only. CD only with 3 songs. "Draw a guitar on the outside of envelope so we'll know it's from a songwriter." Will respond if interested.

MUSIC Mostly **rock** and **pop**. Produced *Gold Record* (album), written and recorded by Dash Rip Rock (rock) on Ichiban Records and many others.

◑ JAN CELT MUSICAL SERVICES

4015 NE 12th Ave., Portland OR 97212. E-mail: flyheart@teleport.com. Website: http://home.teleport.com/~flyheart. **Contact:** Jan Celt, owner. Record producer, music producer and publisher (Wiosna Nasza Music/BMI) and record company (Flying Heart Records). Estab. 1982. Produces 3-5 CDs/year.

◐ Also see the listing for Flying Heart Records in the Record Companies section of this book.

HOW TO CONTACT Submit demo tape by mail. Unsolicited submissions are OK. Prefers high-quality cassette with 1-10 songs and lyric sheet. "SASE required for any response." Does not return materials. Responds in 4 months.

MUSIC Mostly **R&B**, **rock,** and **blues**; also **jazz**. Produced "Vexatious Progressions" (single), written and recorded by Eddie Harris (jazz); "Bong Hit" (single by Chris Newman), recorded by Snow Bud & the Flower People (rock); and "She Moved Away" (single by Chris Newman), recorded by Napalm Beach, all on Flying Heart Records. Other artists include the Esquires and Janice Scroggins.

MICHAEL JOST

1305 Ocean Front Walk, Suite 301, Venice CA 90291. (310)450-9276. E-mail: michaeljost@jostmusic.com; cosrev1@jostmusic.com. Website: www.jostmusic.com.

HOW TO CONTACT Has worked with Aino Laos, George Clinton, Titus. Music: electronica, acoustic, rock, world, funk.

CHRIS JULIAN

4872 Topanga Canyon Blvd. Suite 406, Woodland Hills CA 91364. (310)924-7849. E-mail: chris@ChrisJulian.com. Website: www.ChrisJulian.com. "Owned and operated solely by engineer/producer Chris Julian, the studio is oriented towards personal service."

MUSIC Has worked with David Bowie, Vanessa Williams, Jimmy Webb, De La Soul, Queen Latifah, Biz Markie, A Tribe Called Quest, Fat Joe, Peter Moffitt,

Danielle Livingston, Bobbi Humphrey, Mint, Just James, Brenda K. Star, Naughty By Nature. Music: R&B, pop, rock, soul, hip-hop, jazz.

KAREN KANE PRODUCER/ENGINEER

(910)681-0220. E-mail: karenkane@mixmama.com. Website: www.mixmama.com. **Contact:** Karen Kane, producer/ recording and live sound engineer/audio instructor. Record producer and recording engineer. Estab. 1978. Produces 3-5 CDs/year. Fee derived from sales royalty when song or artist is recorded or outright fee from recording artist or record company.

HOW TO CONTACT *E-mail first and obtain permission to submit. Unsolicited submissions are not OK.* "Please note: I am not a song publisher. My expertise is in album production." Does not return material. Responds in 1 week.

MUSIC Mostly **acoustic music of any kind**, **rock**, **blues**, **pop**, **alternative**, **R&B/reggae**, **country**, and **bluegrass**. Produced *Good to Me* (album), recorded by Nina Repeta; *Topless* (Juno-nominated album), recorded by Big Daddy G, released on Reggie's Records; *Mixed Wise and Otherwise* (Juno-nominated album), recorded by Harry Manx (blues). Other artists include Tracy Chapman (her first demo), Katarina Bourdeaux, Crys Matthews, Laura Bird, L Shape Lot, the Hip Hop Co-op, Barenaked Ladies (live recording for a TV special), and the Coolidge Band.

TIPS "Get proper funding to be able to make a competitive, marketable product."

TIM DAVID KELLY

10061 Riverside Dr. Suite 343, Toluca Lake CA 91602. (818)601-7047. E-mail: info@timdavidkelly.com. Website: www.timdavidkelly.com.

MUSIC Has worked with Kicking Harold, Shiny Toy Guns, Dokken. Music: alternative, metal, Americana, rock, acoustic pop.

L.A. ENTERTAINMENT, INC.

7095 Hollywood Blvd., #826, Hollywood, CA 90028. (800)579-9157. Fax: (323)924-1095. E-mail: info@warriorrecords.com. Website: www.WarriorRecords.com. **Contact:** Jim Ervin, A&R. Record producer, record company (Warrior Records) and music publisher (New Entity Music/ASCAP, New Copyright Music/BMI, New Euphonic Music/SESAC). Estab. 1988. Fee derived from sales royalty when song or artist is recorded.

HOW TO CONTACT Submit demo package by mail. Unsolicited submissions are OK. Prefers CD and/or videocassette with original songs, lyric, and lead sheet if available. "We do not review Internet sites. Do not send MP3s, unless requested. All written submitted materials (e.g., lyric sheets, letter, etc.) should be typed." Does not return material unless SASE is included. Responds in 2 months only via e-mail or SASE.

MUSIC All styles. "All genres are utilized with our music supervision company for Film & TV, but our original focus is on **alternative rock** and **urban genres** (e.g., **R&B**, **rap**, **gospel**).

LANDMARK COMMUNICATIONS GROUP

P.O. Box 1444, Hendersonville, TN 37077. E-mail: ba@landmarkcommunicationsgroup.com. **Contact:** Bill Anderson Jr., producer. Record producer, record company, music publisher (Newcreature Music/BMI) and TV/radio syndication. Produces 6 singles and 6 LPs/year. Fee derived from sales royalty.

○ Also see the listings for Landmark Communications Group in the "Record Companies" section of this book.

HOW TO CONTACT *Write first and obtain permission to submit.* Prefers CD, mp3 with 4-10 songs and lyric sheet. Include SASE.

MUSIC Country crossover. Recent projects: *Smoky Mountain Campmeeting* by Various Artists; *The Pilgrim & the Road* by Tiffany Turner; *Fallow Ground* by C.J. Hall; *Prince Charming is Dead* by Kecia Burcham.

LARK TALENT & ADVERTISING

P.O. Box 35726, Tulsa, OK 74153. (918)786-8896. Fax: (918)786-8897. E-mail: janajae@janajae.com. Website: www.janajae.com. **Contact:** Kathleen Pixley, vice president. Owner: Jana Jae. Record producer, music publisher (Jana Jae Music/BMI) and record company (Lark Record Productions, Inc.). Estab. 1980. Fee derived from sales royalty when song or artist is recorded.

○ Also see the listings for Jana Jae Music in the "Music Publishers" section, Lark Record Productions in the "Record Companies" section, and Jana Jae Enterprises in the "Managers & Booking Agents" section of this book.

HOW TO CONTACT Submit demo by mail. Unsolicited submissions are OK. Prefers CD or DVD with 3 songs and lead sheet. Does not return material. Responds in 1 month only if interested.

MUSIC Mostly **country**, **bluegrass**, and **classical**; also **instrumentals**. Produced "Bussin' Ditty" (single by Steve Upfold); "Mayonnaise" (single by Steve Upfold); and "Flyin' South" (single by Cindy Walker), all recorded by Jana Jae on Lark Records (country). Other artists include Sydni, Hotwire, and Matt Greif.

BOB LUNA

(310)202-8043 or (310)508-1356. E-mail: bobluna@earthlink.net. Website: www.boblunamusic.com. Contact: Bob Luna, arranger/composer/producer.
MUSIC Music: live and midi orchestration.

O MAC-ATTACK PRODUCTIONS

868 NE 81 St., Miami FL 33138. (305)757-4750. E-mail: GoMacster@aol.com. **Contact:** Michael McNamee, engineer/producer. Record producer and music publisher (Mac-Attack Publishing/ASCAP). Estab. 1986. Fee derived from outright fee from recording artist or record company.

HOW TO CONTACT Submit demo by mail. Unsolicited submissions are OK. Prefers CD or DVD with 3-5 songs, lyric sheet, and bio. Does not return material. Responds in up to 3 months.

MUSIC Mostly **pop**, **alternative rock,** and **dance**. Recorded artists include: Caution Automatic, Bruce Jordan, Acidosis, Kaseeno, Blowfly, Tally Tal, Fire Bush, Nina Llopis, the Lead, Girl Talk, Tyranny of Shaw, Jacobs Ladder, South Beach Chamber Ensemble, Cari Shurman, Nostalgic Ensemble of Miami, and 40 Days.

PETER MALICK

(886)884-9919 ext. 2. E-mail: peter@petermalick.com. Website: www.petermalick.com.
MUSIC Has worked with Fast Heart Mart, Henry Gummer, Chelsea Williams, Hope Waits, Norah Jones, Kirsten Proffit, Whitey Conwell, Free Dominguez, Suzanne Santos. Music: indie, rock, roots, Americana.

GUY MARSHALL

c/o Tutt & Babe Music, 6506 Penfield Ave., Woodland Hills CA 91367. (818)621-3181. Fax: (323)585-0011. E-mail: guymarshallmusic@hotmail.com.

MUSIC Has worked with Pat Benatar, the Tuesdays, Baywatch, Lionheart, Cobra, Venus & Mars. Music: rock, alternative.

O MEGA TRUTH RECORDS

P.O. Box 4988, Culver City, CA 90231. E-mail: jonbare@aol.com. Website: www.jonbare.net. **Contact:** Jon Bare, CEO. Record producer and record company. Estab. 1994. Produces 2 CDs/year. Fee negotiable.

HOW TO CONTACT Submit demo package by mail. Unsolicited submissions are OK. Prefers CD. "We specialize in recording world-class virtuoso musicians and bands with top players." Does not return material. Responds in 2 weeks only if interested.

MUSIC Mostly **rock**, **blues**, and **country rock**; also **swing**, **dance** and **instrumental**. Produced Party Platter recorded by Hula Monsters (swing); and Killer Whales, Shredzilla and Orcastra (by Jon Bare and the Killer Whales) (rock), all on Mega Truth Records. Other artists include the Rich Harper Blues Band, Aeon Dream & the Dream Machine and Techno Dudes.

TIPS "Create a unique sound that blends great vocals and virtuoso musicianship with a beat that makes us want to get up and dance."

BILL METOYER

16209 Victory Blvd. #132, Lake Balboa CA 91406. (818)780-5394. E-mail: bill@skullseven.com. Website: www.billmetoyer.com.
MUSIC Has worked with Salyer, W.A.S.P., Fates Warning, Six Feet Under, Armored Saint, Tourniquet, Skrew, Rigor Mortis, Sacred Steel, Cement. Music: hard rock, metal.

BILLY MITCHELL

P.O. Box 284, S. Pasadena CA91031. (626)574-5040. Fax: (626)446-2584. E-mail: billymitchell2k@aol.com. Website: www.billy-mitchell.com.
MUSIC Has worked with Chartmaker Records, Vista Records, PRC Records, USA Music Group. Music: contemporary jazz, pop.

ADAM MOSELEY

(323)316-4932. E-mail: adammoseley@mac.com. Website: www.adammoseley.com.
MUSIC Has worked with Claudio Valenzuela, Lisbeth Scott, Wolfmother, Nikka Costa, Abandoned Pools, John Cale, AJ Croce, Lucybell, the Cure, KISS, Rush, Roxette, Maxi Priest. Music: rock, alternative, electronica, acoustic.

O MUSICJONES RECORDS

(formerly Sound Works Entertainment Productions Inc.) P.O. Box 6984, Charlottesville, VA 22906. (434)632-7860. E-mail: info@musicjones.com. Website: www.musicjones.com. **Contact:** Michael E. Jones, president. Record producer, record company (MusicJones Records) and music publisher (MusicJones Music). Estab. 1989. Produces 16 singles, 2 LPs, and 20 CDs/year. Fee derived from sales royalty when song or artist is recorded or outright fee from recording artist or record company.

HOW TO CONTACT Submit demo package by mail. Unsolicited submissions are OK. Prefers cassette with 3-6 songs and lyric sheet. "Please include short bio and statement of goals and objectives." Does not return material. Responds in 6 weeks.

MUSIC Mostly **country**, **folk**, and **pop**; also **rock**. Recent album releases: *The Highway* featuring Mike Jones and "Oops My Bad" featuring Ginger Granger. Also produced "Lonelyville," and "Alabama Slammer" (singles), both written and recorded by Wake Eastman; and "Good Looking Loser" (single), written and recorded by Renee Rubach, all on Sound Works Records (country). Other artists include Matt Dorman, Steve Gilmore, the Tackroom Boys, the Las Vegas Philharmonic, and J.C. Clark.

TIPS "Put your ego on hold. Don't take criticism personally. Advice is meant to help you grow and improve your skills as an artist/songwriter. Be professional and businesslike in all your dealings."

XAVIER NATHAN

524 Raymond Ave. #4, Santa Monica CA 90405. (818)339-3238. E-mail: zave2004@yahoo.com. Website: http://xavierjnathan.com.

HOW TO CONTACT E-mail or use e-mail submission form found on website.

MUSIC Has worked with Headsandwich, Sahaloop, The Joy House, Dan Bern, Indya, Edouardo Torres. Music: rock, blues, R&B, funk, acoustic, hard rock.

O NEU ELECTRO PRODUCTIONS

P.O. Box 1582, Bridgeview, IL 60455. (630)257-6289. E-mail: neuelectro@email.com. Website: www.neu electro.com. **Contact:** Bob Neumann, owner. Record producer and record company. Estab. 1984. Produces 16 singles, 16 12" singles, 20 LPs, and 4 CDs/year. Fee derived from outright fee from record company or recording artist.

HOW TO CONTACT Submit demo package by mail. Unsolicited submissions are OK. Prefers CD with 3 songs and lyric sheet or lead sheet. "Provide accurate contact phone numbers and addresses, promo packages and photos." Include SASE for reply. Responds in 2 weeks. "A production fee estimate will be returned to artist."

MUSIC Mostly **dance**, **house**, **techno**, **rap,** and **rock**; also **experimental**, **New Age,** and **top 40**. Produced "Juicy" (single), written and recorded by Juicy Black on Dark Planet International Records (house); "Make Me Smile" (single), written and recorded by Roz Baker (house); *Reactovate-6* (album by Bob Neumann), recorded by Beatbox-D on N.E.P. Records (dance); and *Sands of Time* (album), recorded by Bob Neumann (New Age). Other artists include Skid Marx and the Deviants.

CARLA OLSON

11684 Ventura Blvd. Suite 583, Studio City CA 91604. (818)761-2621. E-mail: contactcarla2@aol.com.

MUSIC Has worked with Paul Jones, Jake Andrews, Davis Gaines, Joe Louis Walker, Astrella Celeste, Youngblood Hart, Billy Joe Royal, Kim Wilson.

① PETE MARTIN/VAAM MUSIC PRODUCTIONS

P.O. Box 29550, Hollywood CA 90029-0550. (323)664-7765. E-mail: request@vaammusic.com. Website: www.VaamMusic.com. **Contact:** Pete Martin, president. Record producer, music publisher (Vaam Music/BMI and Pete Martin Music/ASCAP) and record company (Blue Gem Records). Estab. 1982.

> ○ Also see the listings for Vaam Music Group in the "Music Publishers" section of this book and Blue Gem Records in the "Record Companies" section of this book.

HOW TO CONTACT Send CD or cassette with 2 songs and a lyric sheet. Send small packages only. Include SASE. Responds in 1 month.

MUSIC Mostly **top 40/pop, country,** and **R&B**.

TIPS "Study the market in the style that you write. Songs must be capable of reaching top 5 on charts."

PLATINUM STUDIOS

(818)994-5368. E-mail: paulhilton123@scglobal.net. Website: www.paulhiltonmusic.com. "Platinum sound at affordable rates."

MUSIC Has worked with Janet Klein, Matt Zane & Society 1, Bon Jovi, Spencer Davis, Big Joe Turner, Billy Vera, Metallica, Ratt, Motley Crue, Morgana King, Jack Mack & the Heart Attack, Rodney O & Joe Cooley, WASP, Carlos Rico, Mera, Sam Glaser. Music: Latin, rock, blues.

WILL RAY

P.O. Box 9222, Asheville NC 28815. (828)296-0107. E-mail: will@willray.biz. Website: www.willray.biz.
MUSIC Has worked with the Hellecasters, Solomon Burke, Wylie & the Wild West Show, Candye Kane, Jeffrey Steele, Clay DuBose, the Buzzards, Carrie James. Music: country, folk, blues.

◯ RN'D DISTRIBUTION, LLC

(formerly RN'D Productions), P.O. Box 540102, Houston, TX 77254-0102. (713)521-2616, ext. 10. Fax: (713)529-4914. E-mail: Music@RNDDistribution. com. Website: www.rnddistribution.com **Contact:** Byron Gates, A&R director. National sales director: Ramon Smith. Record producer, record company (Albatross Records), distributor (labels distributed include Albatross Records, TDA Music, and Ball In' Records) and music publisher (Ryedale Publishing). Estab. 1986. Produces 25 singles, 20 LPs, 4 EPs, and 21 CDs/year.
HOW TO CONTACT Submit demo package by mail. Unsolicited submissions are OK. Prefers CD with 4 songs and lyric sheet. Does not return material. Responds in 1 month.
MUSIC All types.

TODD ROSENBERG

(310)926-5059. E-mail: todd@toddrosenberg.net. Website: www.toddrosenberg.net.
MUSIC Has worked with Pressure 45, Devil Driver, Mad Caddies, Motograter, Honda, Mitsubishi, Panasonic, Grooveworks. Music: indie, rock, Americana, country, ska, punk.

MARK SAUNDERS

Beat 360 Studios, 630 Ninth Ave. Suite 710, New York NY 10036. (212)262-4932. E-mail: info@marksaun ders.com; ollie@rocketmusic.com. Website: www. marksaunders.com. Contact: Ollie Hammett.
MUSIC Has worked with the Cure, Tricky, Depeche Mode, Marilyn Manson, David Byrne, Shiny Toy Guns, Yaz, the Sugarcubes, Gravity Kills, Neneh Cherry. Music: electronic, rock.

☊◯ SCOTT MATHEWS, D/B/A HIT OR MYTH PRODUCTIONS INC.

246 Almonte Blvd., Mill Valley CA 94941. E-mail: scott@scottmathews.com. Website: www.Scott Mathews.com. Contact: Mary Ezzell, A&R Director. President: Scott Mathews. Assistant: Tom Luekens. Record producer, song doctor, studio owner and music publisher (Hang on to Your Publishing/BMI). Estab. 1990. Produces 6-9 CDs/year. Fee derived from recording artist or record company (with royalty points).

◯ Scott Mathews has several gold and platinum awards for sales of more than 15 million records. He has worked with more than 60 Rock & Roll Hall of Fame inductees and on several Grammy and Oscar-winning releases. He is currently working primarily with emerging artists while still making music with his legendary established artists.

HOW TO CONTACT "No phone calls or publishing submissions, please." Submit demo CD by mail or an mp3 by email. "Unsolicited submissions are often the best ones and readily accepted. Include SASE if e-mail is not an option. Also include your e-mail address on your demo CD." Responds in 2 months.
MUSIC Mostly rock/pop, alternative, and singer/songwriters of all styles. In 2009 and 2010 Mathews made music with Jimmy Buffett, Bonnie Raitt, Brian Wilson, Zac Brown, Chris Isaak, and a long list of emerging artists. Produced 4 tracks on *Anthology* (best of), recorded by John Hiatt (rock/pop), released 2001 on Hip-O. Has produced Elvis Costello, Roy Orbison, Rosanne Cash, Jerry Garcia, Huey Lewis, and many more. Has recorded classics with everyone from Barbra Streisand to John Lee Hooker, including Keith Richards, George Harrison, Mick Jagger, Van Morrison, Bonnie Raitt, and Eric Clapton to name but a few.
TIPS "These days if you are not independent, you are dependent. The new artists that are coming up and achieving success in the music industry are the ones that prove they have a vision and can make incredible records without the huge financial commitment of a major label. When an emerging artist makes great product for the genre they are in, they are in the driver's seat to be able to make a fair and equitable deal for distribution, be it with a major or independent label. My philosophy is to go where

you are loved. The truth is, a smaller label that is completely dedicated to you and shares your vision may help your career far more than a huge label that will not keep you around if you don't sell millions of units. Perhaps no label is needed at all, if you are up for the challenge of wearing a lot of hats. I feel too much pressure is put on the emerging artist when they have to pay huge sums back to the label in order to see their first royalty check. We all know those records can be made for a fraction of that cost without compromising quality or commercial appeal. I still believe in potential and our company is in business to back up that belief. It is up to us as record makers/visionaries to take that potential into the studio and come out with music that can compete with anything else on the market. Discovering, developing and producing artists that can sustain long careers is our main focus at Hit or Myth Productions. We are proud to be associated with so many legendary and timeless artists and our track record speaks for itself. If you love making music, don't let anyone dim that light. We look forward to hearing from you. (Please check out www.ScottMathews.com for more info, and also www.allmusic.com—keyword: Scott Mathews.) Accept no substitutes!"

① SOUND ARTS RECORDING STUDIO

8377 Westview Dr., Houston, TX 77055. (713)464-GOLD. E-mail: jeffwells@soundartsrecording.com. Website: www.soundartsrecording.com. **Contact:** Jeff Wells, president. Record producer and music publisher (Earthscream Music). Estab. 1974. Produces 12 singles and 3 CDs/year. Fee derived from sales royalty when song or artist is recorded.

   Also see the listing for Earthscream Music Publishing in the "Music Publishers" section of this book.

HOW TO CONTACT Submit demo by mail. Unsolicited submissions are OK. Prefers CD with 2-5 songs and lyric sheet. Does not return material. Responds in 6 weeks.

MUSIC Mostly **pop/rock**, **country,** and **blues**. Produced Texas Johnny Brown (album), written and recorded by Texas Johnny Brown on Quality (blues); and "Sheryl Crow" (single), recorded by Dr. Jeff and the Painkillers. Other artists include Tim Nichols, Perfect Strangers, B.B. Watson, Jinkies, Joe "King" Carasco (on Surface Records), Mark May (on Icehouse Records), the Barbara Pennington Band (on

Earth Records), Tempest, Atticus Finch, Tony Vega Band (on Red Onion Records), Saliva (Island Records), Earl Gillian, Blue October (Universal Records), and the Wiggles.

CHRIS STAMEY

(919)929-5008. E-mail: info@chrisstamey.com. Website: www.chrisstamey.com. "The central philosophy behind my production and mixing these days is that the best records combine the recording of transcendent musical moments with the structuring of the carefully considered arrangement details that frame those moments. And the point of recording is to add new entries to that select list of best records."

HOW TO CONTACT See website for rates.

MUSIC Has worked with Alejandro Escovedo, Ryan Adams, Amy Ray, Squirrel Nut Zippers, Patrick Park, Jeremy Larson, Chatham Country Line. Music: rock, indie, alternative.

○ STEVE SATKOWSKI RECORDINGS

P.O. Box 3403, Stuart, FL 34995. (772)225-3128. Website: www.clearsoulproductions.com/SteveSatkowski. html. Engineer/producer: Steven Satkowski. Record producer, recording engineer, management firm and record company. Estab. 1980. Produces 20 CDs/year. Fee derived from outright fee from recording artist or record company.

HOW TO CONTACT Submit demo by mail. Unsolicited submissions are OK. Prefers CD or cassette. Does not return material. Responds in 2 weeks.

MUSIC Mostly **classical**, **jazz,** and **big band**. Produced recordings for National Public Radio and affiliates. Engineered recordings for Steve Howe, Patrick Moraz, Kenny G, and Michael Bolton.

○ STUDIO SEVEN

417 N. Virginia, Oklahoma City OK 73106. (405)236-0643. Fax: (405)236-0686. **Contact:** Dave Copenhaver, Producer. Record producer, record label (Lunacy Records) and music publisher (Lunasong Music). Estab. 1990. Produces 10-12 CDs/year. Fee is derived from sales royalty when song or artist is recorded or outright fee from recording artist or record company. "All projects are on a customized basis."

HOW TO CONTACT *Contact first and obtain permission to submit.* Prefers CD or cassette with lyric sheet. Include SASE. Responds in 6 weeks.

MUSIC Mostly **rock**, **jazz-blues**, **country**, and **Native American**. Releases in 2009: Morris McCraven;

Ben Treffer (*What Would You Do?*), Scott King (*Let's Get Something Straight Between Us*) Bailey Wilton (*Bailey*), Lorraine Worth (*The Greatest Hero*); Curt Shoemaker; the Boys of the Fort; Jack Hughes; Les Gilliam; Frosty; Jeff Fenholt; Joe Merrick; Ronnie and Imods; Leroy Jones.

RANDALL MICHAEL TOBIN

2219 W. Olive Ave. Suite 226, Burbank CA 91506. (818)955-5888. E-mail: rmt@rmtobin.com. Website: www.rmtobin.com.

MUSIC Has worked with Mel Carter, Bettie Ross, Isla St. Clair, Margaret MacDonald, Katheryne Levin. Music: pop, rock, R&B, jazz, alternative, country.

DAVE TOUGH

5801 Tee Pee Dr., Nashville TN 37013. (615)554-6693. E-mail: dave@davetough.com. Website: www.davet ough.com.

HOW TO CONTACT See website for rates.

MUSIC Has worked with Come & Go, Cindy Alter, Matt Heinecke, Craig Winquist. Music: country, pop.

BIL VORNDICK

6090 Fire Tower Rd., Nashville TN 37221. (615)352-1227. E-mail: bilinstudio@comcast.net. Website: www.bilvorndick.com. "Helping artists realize their dreams."

MUSIC Has worked with Alison Krauss, Rhonda Vincent, Jerry Douglas, Bela Fleck, Jim Lauderdale, Ralph Stanley, Lynn Anderson, Bob Dylan, John Oates.

DICK WAGNER

17032 E. Parlin Dr., Fountain Hills AZ 85268. (989)295-9247. E-mail: wagnerrocks@gmail.com. Website: www.wagnermusic.com.

MUSIC Has worked with Wensday, Robert Wagner, Chris de Marco, Bleedstreet, Janis Leigh, DWB, Matt Besey, Darin Scott, Skinner Rat, Gwen Goodman, Adam Smith. Music: rock, pop, modern country, spiritual.

DAVE WATERBURY

Laurel Canyon and Magnolia, Valley Village CA 91607. (818)505-8080. E-mail: DaveWaterbury91607@ yahoo.com. Website: www.davewaterbury.net.

MUSIC Has worked with the XOTX, Robbie Krieger, Pink, Mark Krendal, David Eagle, Irv Kramer. Music: rock, dance, electronica, pop.

ⓘ WESTWIRES RECORDING USA

(formerly Westwires Digital USA) 1042 Club Ave., Allentown, PA 18109. (610)435-1924. E-mail: info@west wires.com. Website: www.westwires.com. **Contact:** Wayne Becker, owner/producer. Record producer and production company. Fee derived from outright fee from record company or artist retainer.

HOW TO CONTACT *Contact via e-mail for permission to submit.* "No phone calls, please." Submit demo by mail or mp3 by e-mail. Unsolicited submissions are OK. Prefers mp3 with lyrics in MS Word or Adobe PDF file format, or CD, DVD, or VHS videocassette with 3 songs and lyric sheet. Does not return material. Responds in 1 month.

MUSIC Mostly **rock**, **R&B**, **dance**, **alternative**, **folk**, and **eclectic**. Produced Ye Ren (Dimala Records), Weston (Universal/Mojo), Zakk Wylde (Spitfire Records). Other artists include Ryan Asher, Paul Rogers, Anne Le Baron, and Gary Hassay

TIPS "We are interested in singer/songwriters and alternative artists living in the mid-Atlantic area. Must have steady gig schedule and established fan base."

ⓘ WLM MUSIC/RECORDING

2808 Cammie St., Durham NC 27705-2020. (919)471-3086. Fax: (919)471-4326. E-mail: wlm-musicrecord ing@nc.rr.com or wlm-band@nc.rr.com. **Contact:** Watts Lee Mangum, owner. Record producer. Estab. 1980. Fee derived from outright fee from recording artist. "In some cases, an advance payment requested for demo production."

HOW TO CONTACT Submit demo by mail. Unsolicited submissions are OK. Prefers CD with 2-4 songs and lyric or lead sheet (if possible). Include SASE. Responds in 6 months.

MUSIC Mostly **country**, **country/rock,** and **blues/rock**; also **pop**, **rock**, **blues**, **gospel,** and **bluegrass**. Produced "911," and "Petals of an Orchid" (singles), both written and recorded by Johnny Scoggins (country); and "Renew the Love" (single by Judy Evans), recorded by Bernie Evans (country), all on Independent. Other artists include Southern Breeze Band and Heart Breakers Band.

MICHAEL WOODRUM

(818)848-3393. E-mail: michael@woodrumproduc tions.com . Website: www.woodrumproductions.com. "Michael Woodrum is a Producer who's also an accomplished engineer. He gets sounds faster than you can think them up. You won't sit around waiting for something to sound right."

MUSIC Has worked with 3LW, Juvenile, Tupac, Linkin Park, MC Lyte, Mary J. Blige, Eric Clapton, Joss Stone, Snoop Dogg, Bobby Rydell, B2K, Rocio Banquells, Queen Latifah, JoJo, Dr. Dre, John Guess, Tiffany Evans, Samantha Jade. Music: rock, pop, R&B, rap, hip-hop, alternative, acoustic, indie, Americana, country, soul.

◑ WORLD RECORDS

5798 Deertrail Dr., Traverse City, MI 49684. E-mail: jack@worldrec.org. Website: www.worldrec.org. **Contact:** Jack Conners, producer. Record producer, engineer/technician and record company (World Records). Estab. 1984. Produces 1 CD/year. Fee derived from outright fee from recording artist.

HOW TO CONTACT *Write first and obtain permission to submit.* Prefers CD with 1 or 2 songs. Include SASE. Responds in 6 weeks.

MUSIC Mostly **classical**, **folk**, and **jazz**. Produced *Mahler, Orff, Collins* (album), recorded by Traverse Symphony Orchestra (classical), released 2006; *Reflections on Schubert* (album) recorded by Michael Coonrod (classical), released 2007. Other artists include Jeff Haas and the Camerata Singers.

◑ ZIG PRODUCTIONS

P.O. Box 120931, Arlington, TX 76012. (214)354-8401. E-mail: billyherzig@hotmail.com. Website: www.zigproductions.com. **Contact:** Billy Herzig or Wendy Mazur. Record producer. Music publisher (Thistle Hill/BMI). Estab. 1998. "Occasionally I produce a single that is recorded separate from a full CD project." Produces 6-10 albums. Fee derived from sales royalty when song or artist is recorded and/or outright fee from recording artist. "Sometimes there are investors."

HOW TO CONTACT Submit a demo by mail. Unsolicited submissions are OK. "We do not return submissions." Responds only if interested.

MUSIC Mostly **country**, **Americana**, and **rock**; also **pop**, **r&b**, and **alternative**. Produced "Ask Me to Stay" (single by King Cone/Josh McDaniel) from *Gallery*, recorded by King Cone (Texas country/Americana). released 2007 on King Cone; "A Cure for Awkward Silence" (single), recorded by Tyler Stock (acoustic rock), released 2007 on Payday Records; "Take Me Back" (single) from *Peace, Love & Crabs*, written and recorded by Deanna Dove (folk-rock), released 2007 on Island Girl. Also produced Robbins & Jones (country), Jordan Mycoskie (country), Carla Rhodes (comedy), Four Higher (alternative), Charis Thorsell (country), Shane Mallory (country), Rachel Rodriguez (blues-rock), Jessy Daumen (country), Frankie Moreno (rock/r&b), Shawna Russell (country), and many others.

SAUL ZONANA

606 Stone Mill Circle, Murfreesboro TN 37130. (914)610-5342. E-mail: zonana@comcast.net. Website: http://saulzonana.com.

MUSIC Has worked with Crash Test Dummies, Adrian Belew, Blue Oyster Cult, Nicole McKenna, Ace Frehley. Music: rock, electronica.

MANAGERS & BOOKING AGENTS

Before submitting to a manager or booking agent, be sure you know exactly what you need. If you're looking for someone to help you with performance opportunities, the booking agency is the one to contact. They can help you book shows either in your local area or throughout the country. If you're looking for someone to help guide your career, you need to contact a management firm. Some management firms may also handle booking; however, it may be in your best interest to look for a separate booking agency. A manager should be your manager—not your agent, publisher, lawyer, or accountant.

MANAGERS

Of all the music industry players surrounding successful artists, managers are usually the people closest to the artists themselves. The artist manager can be a valuable contact, both for the songwriter trying to get songs to a particular artist and for the songwriter/performer. A manager and his connections can be invaluable in securing the right publishing deal or recording contract if the writer is also an artist. Getting songs to an artist's manager is yet another way to get your songs recorded, since the manager may play a large part in deciding what material his client uses. For the performer seeking management, a successful manager should be thought of as the foundation for a successful career.

The relationship between a manager and his client relies on mutual trust. A manager works as the liaison between you and the rest of the music industry, and he must know exactly what you want out of your career in order to help you achieve your goals. His handling of publicity, promotion, and finances, as well as the contacts he has within the industry, can make or break your career. You should never be afraid to ask questions about any aspect of the relationship between you and a prospective manager.

Always remember that a manager works *for the artist*. A good manager is able to communicate his opinions to you without reservation, and should be willing to explain any confusing terminology or discuss plans with you before taking action. A manager needs to be able to communicate successfully with all segments of the music industry in order to get his client the best deals possible. He needs to be able to work with booking agents, publishers, lawyers, and record companies.

Keep in mind that you are both working together toward a common goal: success for you and your songs. Talent, originality, professionalism, and a drive to succeed are qualities that will attract a manager to an artist—and a songwriter.

BOOKING AGENTS

The function of the booking agent is to find performance venues for his clients. Agents usually represent many more acts than a manager does, and have less contact with their acts. A booking agent charges a commission for his services, as does a manager. Managers usually ask for a 15–20% commission on an act's earnings; booking agents usually charge around 10%. In the area of managers and booking agents, more successful acts can negotiate lower percentage deals than the ones set forth above.

SUBMITTING MATERIAL TO MANAGERS & BOOKING AGENTS

The firms listed in this section have provided information about the types of music they work with and the types of acts they represent. Read each listing carefully to determine whether a firm is open to your level of experience (see A Sample Listing Decoded). Each listing also contains submission requirements and information about what items to include in a press kit and will also specify whether the company is a management firm or a booking agency. Remember that your submission represents you as an artist, and should be as organized and professional as possible.

Icons

For more information on the listings in this book, including explanations of symbols (or icons), read the section How To Use *Songwriter's Market*.

◑ AIR TIGHT MANAGEMENT

115 West Rd., P.O. Box 113, Winchester Center, CT 06094. (860)738-9139. Fax: (860)738-9135. E-mail: mainoffice@airtightmanagement.com. Website: www.airtightmanagement.com. **Contact:** Jack Forchette, president. Management firm. Estab. 1969. Represents individual artists, groups or songwriters from anywhere; currently handles 8 acts. Receives 15-20% commission. Reviews material for acts.

HOW TO CONTACT *Write e-mail first and obtain permission to submit.* Prefers CD or VHS videocassette. If seeking management, press kit should include photos, bio, and recorded material. "Follow up with a fax or e-mail, not a phone call." Does not return material. Responds in 1 month.

MUSIC Mostly **rock**, **country**, and **jazz**. Current acts include P.J. Loughran (singer/songwriter), Johnny Colla (songwriter/producer, and guitarist/songwriter for Huey Lewis and the News), Jason Scheff (lead singer/songwriter for the group Chicago), Gary Burr (Nashville songwriter/producer), Nathan East (singer/songwriter/bassist—Eric Clapton, Michael Jackson, Madonna, 4-Play and others), Rocco Prestia (legendary R&B musician, Tower of Power bassist), Steve Oliver (contemporary jazz/pop songwriter/guitarist/vocalist, recording artist), Kal David (blues), Warren Hill (saxophonist/recording artist), and Harvey Mason (percussionist/composer).

☺◑ ALERT MUSIC INC.

51 Hillsview Ave., Toronto ON M6P 1J4 Canada. (416)364-4200. Fax: (416)364-8632. E-mail: contact@alertmusic.com. Website: www.alertmusic.com. **Contact:** W. Tom Berry, president. Management firm, record company, and recording artist. Represents local and regional individual artists and groups; currently handles 5 acts. Reviews material for acts.

HOW TO CONTACT *Write first and obtain permission to submit.* Prefers CD. If seeking management, press kit should include finished CD, photo, press clippings and bio. Include SASE.

MUSIC All types. Works primarily with bands and singer/songwriters. Current acts include Holly Cole (jazz vocalist), Kim Mitchell (rock singer/songwriter), Michael Kaeshammer (pianist/singer), and Roxanne Potvin (blues, singer/songwriter).

◑ MICHAEL ALLEN ENTERTAINMENT DEVELOPMENT

P.O. Box 111510, Nashville, TN 37222. (615)754-0059. E-mail: gmichaelallen@comcast.net. Website: www.gmichaelallen.com. **Contact:** Michael Allen. Management firm and public relations. Represents individual artists, groups, and songwriters; currently handles 2 acts. Receives 15-25% commission. Reviews material for acts.

HOW TO CONTACT Submit demo package by mail. Unsolicited submissions are OK. Prefers CD/DVD with 3 songs and lyric or lead sheets. If seeking management, press kit should include photo, bio, press clippings, letter, and CD/DVD. Include SASE. Responds in 3 months.

MUSIC Mostly **country** and **pop**; also **rock** and **gospel**. Works primarily with vocalists and bands. Currently doing public relations for Brenda Lee, the Imperials, Ricky Lynn Gregg, Kyle Rainer, and Lee Greenwood.

○ AMERICAN BANDS MANAGEMENT

3300 S. Gessner, Suite 207, Houston TX 77063. (713)785-3700. Fax: (713)785-4641. E-mail: johnblomstrom@aol.com. President: John Blomstrom. Senior Vice President: Cheryl Byrd. Management firm. Estab. 1973. Represents groups from anywhere; currently handles 3 acts. Receives 15-25% commission. Reviews material for acts.

HOW TO CONTACT Submit demo package by mail prior to making phone contact. Unsolicited submissions are OK. Prefers live videos. If seeking management, press kit should include cover letter, bio, photo, demo tape/CD, press clippings, video, résumé and professional references with names and numbers. Does not return material. Responds in 1 month.

MUSIC Mostly **rock (all forms)** and **modern country**. Works primarily with bands. Current acts include The Scars Heal In Time, Trey Gadler & Dead Man's Hand, Zak Perry Band, the Standells, Love It To Death (Alice Cooper tribute), Unchain The Night (Dokken tribute), and Pearl (Janis Joplin tribute).

◑ BILL ANGELINI ENTERPRISES/ BOOKYOUREVENT.COM

(formerly Management Plus), P.O. Box 132, Seguin TX 78155. (830)401-0061. Fax: (830)401-0069. E-mail: bill@bookyourevent.com. Website: www.bookyourevent.com. **Contact:** Bill Angelini, owner. Management firm and booking agency. Estab. 1980. Represents individual artists and groups from anywhere; currently handles 6 acts. Receives 10-15% commission. Reviews material for acts.

HOW TO CONTACT Submit demo package by mail or EPK. Unsolicited submissions are OK. Press kit should include pictures, bio, and discography. Does not return material. Responds in 1 month.

MUSIC Mostly **Latin American**, **Tejano**, and **International**; also **Norteno** and **country**. Current acts include Jay Perez (Tejano), Ram Herrera (Tejano), Michael Salgado (Tejano), Flaco Jimenez (Tex-Mex), Electric Cowboys (Tex-Mex), Los Palominos (Tejano), Grupo Vida (Tejano), and Texmaniacs (Tex-Mex).

APODACA PROMOTIONS INC.

717 E. Tidwell Rd., Houston TX 77022. (713)691-6677. Fax: (713)692-9298. E-mail: houston@apodacapromotions.com. Website: www.apodacapromotions.com. Manager: Domingo A. Barrera. Management firm, booking agency, music publisher (Huina Publishing, Co. Inc.). Estab. 1991. Represents songwriters and groups from anywhere; currently handles 40 acts. Reviews material for acts.

HOW TO CONTACT Submit demo package by mail. Unsolicited submissions are OK. Prefers CD and lyric and lead sheet. Include SASE. Responds in 2 months.

MUSIC Mostly **international** and **Hispanic**; also **rock**. Works primarily with bands and songwriters. Current acts include Boby Pulldo, Los Super Reyes, Fanny Lu, Elephant, Dinora, Apollo Sunshine, and Ninel Conde.

ARTIST REPRESENTATION AND MANAGEMENT

1257 Arcade St., St. Paul, MN 55106. (651)483-8754. Fax: (651)776-6338. E-mail: ra@armentertainment.com. Website: www.armentertainment.com. Contact: Roger Anderson, agent/manager. Management firm and booking agency. Estab. 1983. Represents artists from USA/Canada; currently handles 15 acts. Receives 15% commission. Reviews material for acts.

HOW TO CONTACT Submit CD and DVD (preferable) by mail. Unsolicited submissions are OK. Please include minimum 3 songs. If seeking management, current schedule, bio, photo, press clippings should also be included. "Priority is placed on original artists with product who are currently touring." Does not return material. Responds only if interested within 30 days.

MUSIC Mostly **melodic rock**. Current acts include Warrant, Firehouse, Winger, Skid Row, Head East, Frank Hannon of Tesla, LA Guns featuring Phil Lewis, Dokken, Adler's Appetite, and Bret Michaels of Poison.

BACKSTREET BOOKING

Longworth Hall Office Complex, 700 W. Pete Rose Way, Lobby B, 3rd Floor, Suite 390, Box 18, Cincinnati OH 45203. (513)442-4405. Fax: (513)834-9390. E-mail: info@backstreetbooking.com. Website: www.backstreetbooking.com. **Contact:** James Sfarnas, president. Booking agency. Estab. 1992. Represents individual artists and groups from anywhere; currently handles 30 acts. Receives 10-15% commission. Reviews material for acts.

HOW TO CONTACT *Call first and obtain permission to submit.* Accepts only signed acts with product available nationally and/or internationally.

MUSIC Mostly **niche-oriented music**. Current acts include Acumen (progressive jam rock), Niacin (fusion), John Novello (Fusion), Novello B3 Soul (Urban Jazz), Alex Skolnick Trio (progressive jazz), Jeff Berlin (Jazz), Greg Howe (Fusion), American English (Beatles Tribute), the Van Dells (50s-60s Review).

TIPS "Build a base on your own."

B.C. FIEDLER MANAGEMENT

53 Seton Park Rd., Toronto, ON M3C 3Z8, Canada. (416)421-4421. Fax: (416)421-0442. E-mail: info@bcfiedler.com. **Contact:** B.C. Fiedler. Management firm, music publisher (B.C. Fiedler Publishing) and record company (Sleeping Giant Music Inc.). Estab. 1964. Represents individual artists, groups and songwriters from anywhere; currently handles 4 acts. Receives 20-25% or consultant fees. Reviews material for acts.

HOW TO CONTACT *Call first and obtain permission to submit.* Prefers CD or VHS videocassette with 3 songs and lyric sheet. If seeking management, press kit should include bio, list of concerts performed in past 2 years including name of venue, repertoire, reviews and photos. Does not return material. Responds in 2 months.

MUSIC Mostly **classical/crossover**, **voice**, and **pop**. Works primarily with classical/crossover ensembles, instrumental soloists, operatic voice, and pop singer/songwriters. Current acts include Gordon Lightfoot, Dan Hill, Quartetto Gelato, and Patricia O'Callaghan.

TIPS "Invest in demo production using best quality voice and instrumentalists. If you write songs, hire the vocal talent to best represent your work. Submit CD and lyrics. Artists should follow up 6-8 weeks after submission."

◑ BLANK & BLANK

One Belmont Ave., Suite 602, Bala Cynwyd PA 19004. (610)667-9900. Fax: (610)667-9901. E-mail: erblank1950@aol.com. **Contact:** E. Robert Blank, manager. Management firm. Represents individual artists and groups. Reviews material for acts.

HOW TO CONTACT *Contact first and obtain permission to submit.* Prefers CD, DVD, or videocassette. If seeking management, press kit should include cover letter, demo tape/CD, and video. Does not return material.

◐ BLOWIN' SMOKE PRODUCTIONS/RECORDS

7438 Shoshone Ave., Van Nuys CA 91406-2340. (818)881-9888. Fax: (818)881-0555. E-mail: blowin smokeband@ktb.net. Website: www.blowinsmoke band.com. **Contact:** Larry Knight, president. Management firm and record producer. Estab. 1990. Represents local and West Coast individual artists and groups; currently handles 6 acts. Receives 15-20% commission. Reviews material for acts.

> ◌ Also see the listing for Hailing Frequency Music Productions in the "Record Producers" section of this book.

HOW TO CONTACT *Write or call first and obtain permission to submit.* Prefers cassette or CD. If seeking management, press kit should include cover letter, demo tape/CD, lyric sheets, press clippings, video if available, photo, bios, contact telephone numbers and any info on legal commitments already in place. Include SASE. Responds in 1 month.

MUSIC Mostly **R&B**, **blues**, and **blues-rock**. Works primarily with single and group vocalists and a few R&B/blues bands. Current acts include Larry "Fuzzy" Knight (blues singer/songwriter), King Floyd (R&B artist), the Blowin' Smoke Rhythm & Blues Band, The Fabulous Smokettes, Joyce Lawson, Sky King (rock/blues), and Guardians of the Clouds (alternative rock).

● THE BLUE CAT AGENCY

E-mail: bluecat_agency@yahoo.com. **Contact:** Karen Kindig, owner/agent. Management firm and booking agency. Estab. 1989. Represents established individual artists and/or groups from anywhere; currently handles 5 acts. Receives 10-15% commission. Reviews material for acts.

HOW TO CONTACT *E-mail only for permission to submit.* Prefers cassette or CD. If seeking management, press kit should include CD or tape, bio, press clippings, and photo. SASE. Responds in 2 months.

MUSIC Mostly **rock/pop "en espanol"** and **jazz/Latin jazz**. Works primarily with bands (established performers only). Current acts include Ylonda Nickell, Kai Eckhardt, Alejandro Santos, Ania Paz, Gabriel Rosati.

◌ BREAD & BUTTER PRODUCTIONS

P.O. Box 1539, Wimberley TX 78676. (512)301-7117. E-mail: sgladson@gmail.com. **Contact:** Steve Gladson, managing partner. Management firm and booking agency. Estab. 1969. Represents individual artists, songwriters, and groups from anywhere; currently handles 6 acts. Receives 10-20% commission. Reviews material for acts.

HOW TO CONTACT Submit demo package by e-mail or mail. Unsolicited submissions OK. Prefers e-mail. If seeking management, press kit should include cover letter, demo tape/CD, lyric sheets, press clippings, video, résumé, picture, and bio or a list of your social networking sites. Does not return material. Responds in 1 month.

MUSIC Mostly **alternative rock**, **country,** and **R&B**; also **classic rock**, **folk,** and **Americana**. Works primarily with singer/songwriters and original bands. Current acts include Lou Cabaza (songwriter/producer/manager), Duck Soup (band), and Gaylan Ladd (songwriter/singer/producer).

TIPS "Remember why you are in this biz. The art comes first."

◐ BROTHERS MANAGEMENT ASSOCIATES

141 Dunbar Ave., Fords, NJ 08863. (732)738-0880. Fax: (732)738-0970. E-mail: bmaent@yahoo.com. Website: www.bmaent.com. **Contact:** Allen A. Faucera, president. Management firm and booking agency. Estab. 1972. Represents artists, groups, and song-

writers; currently handles 25 acts. Receives 15-20% commission. Reviews material for acts.

HOW TO CONTACT *Write first and obtain permission to submit.* Prefers CD or DVD with 3-6 songs and lyric sheets. Include photographs and résumé. If seeking management, include photo, bio, tape, and return envelope in press kit. Include SASE. Responds in 2 months.

MUSIC Mostly **pop, rock, MOR,** and **R&B.** Works primarily with vocalists and established groups. Current acts include Nils Lofgren of the E Street Band, Cover Girls, Harold Melvin's Blue Notes, and Gloria Gaynor.

TIPS "Submit very commercial material—make demo of high quality."

CHERYL K. WARNER PRODUCTIONS

P.O. Box 179, Hermitage TN 37076. Phone: (615)429-7849. E-mail: cherylkwarner@tds.net (primary); cherylkwarner@comcast.net (secondary). Website: www.cherylkwarner.com. **Contact:** Cheryl K. Warner. Recording and stage production, music consulting, music publisher, record label, A&R. Currently works with 2 acts with expansion in the works. Reviews material for acts.

HOW TO CONTACT Submit demo package by mail or e-mail. Unsolicited submissions are OK. Prefers CD or DVD, but will accept CD with 3 best songs, lyric or lead sheet, bio, and picture. Press kit should include CD, DVD with up-to-date bio, cover letter, lyric sheets, press clippings, and picture. Does not return material. Responds in 6 weeks if interested.

MUSIC Mostly **country/traditional and contemporary, Christian/gospel,** and **A/C/pop/rock.** Works primarily with singer/songwriters and bands with original and versatile style. Current acts include Cheryl K. Warner (recording artist/entertainer) and Cheryl K. Warner Band (support/studio).

CLASS ACT PRODUCTIONS/ MANAGEMENT/PETER KIMMEL'S MUSIC CATALOG

P.O. Box 55252, Sherman Oaks CA 91413. (818)980-1039. E-mail: peter.kimmel@sbcglobal.net. **Contact:** Peter Kimmel, president. Management firm; independent song plugger; composer rep. Estab. 1985. Currently represents music artists for licensing to media; must have broadcast-quality, mastered recordings. Receives 50/50 split of licensing income from place-ments onto soundtracks of motion pictures, TV shows, commercials, etc.

HOW TO CONTACT "Music artists: Submit broadcast-quality, mastered recordings via mail or high quality MP3s derived from your mastered recordings, via e-mail. Unsolicited submissions are OK. For mail, include CD, cover letter (mentioning *Songwriter's Market*), lyric sheets (mandatory) or submit electronic press kit by e-mail. Responds in 1 month.

MUSIC **All styles.** Represents select first-rate music material to music supervisors of films, television, commercials, etc.

TIPS "We cannot use just-printed lyrics. Songwriting must be professional quality, music must be highly accomplished, andrecordings must be professional, broadcast-quality and mastered."

CLOUSHER PRODUCTIONS

P.O. Box 1191, Mechanicsburg, PA 17055. (717)766-7644. Fax: (717)766-1490. E-mail: cpinfo@msn.com. Website: www.clousher.com. **Contact:** Fred Clousher, owner. Booking agency and production company. Estab. 1972. Represents groups from anywhere; currently handles over 100 acts.

HOW TO CONTACT Submit demo package by mail. Please, no electronic press kits. Unsolicited submissions are OK. Prefers CDs or DVD. Press kit should include bio, credits, pictures, song list, references, and your contact information. Does not return material. "Performer should check back with us!"

MUSIC Mostly **country, oldies rock & roll,** and **ethnic** (German, Hawaiian, etc.); also **dance bands** (regional), **Dixieland,** and **classical musicians.** "We work mostly with country, old-time R&R, regional variety dance bands, tribute acts, and all types of variety acts." Current acts include Jasmine Morgan (country/pop vocalist), Robin Right (country vocalist and Tammy Wynette tribute artist) and Stanky & the Coalminers (polka band).

TIPS "The songwriters we work with are entertainers themselves, which is the aspect we deal with. They usually have bands or do some sort of show, either with tracks or live music. We engage them for stage shows, concerts, etc. We DO NOT review songs you've written. We do not publish music, or submit performers to recording companies for contracts. We strictly set up live performances for them."

CONCEPT 2000 INC.

P.O. Box 2950, Columbus, OH 43216-2950. (614)276-2000. Fax: (614)275-0163. E-mail: info2k@concept2k.com. Website: www.concept2k.com. **Florida office:** P.O. Box 2070, Largo, FL 33779-2070. (727)585-2922. Fax: (727)585-3835. **Contact:** Brian Wallace, president. Management firm and booking agency. Estab. 1981. Represents international individual artists, groups and songwriters; currently handles 4 acts. Receives 20% commission. Reviews material for acts.

HOW TO CONTACT Submit demo by mail. Unsolicited submissions are OK. Prefers CD with 4 songs. If seeking management, include demo tape, press clips, photo, and bio. Does not return material. Responds in 2 weeks.

MUSIC Mostly **rock, country, pop,** and **contemporary gospel.** Current acts include Satellites Down (rock); Gene Walker (jazz); Endless Summer (show group); Thomas Wynn and the Believers (country).

TIPS "Send quality songs with lyric sheets. Production quality is not necessary."

DAS COMMUNICATIONS, LTD.

83 Riverside Dr., New York, NY 10024. (212)877-0400. Fax: (212)595-0176. Management firm. Estab. 1975. Represents individual artists, groups, and producers from anywhere; currently handles 25 acts. Receives 20% commission.

HOW TO CONTACT *Does not accept unsolicited submissions.*

MUSIC Mostly **rock**, **pop**, **R&B**, **alternative,** and **hip-hop**. Current acts include Joan Osborne (rock), Wyclef Jean (hip-hop), Black Eyed Peas (hip-hop), John Legend (R&B), Spin Doctors (rock), the Bacon Brothers (rock).

DCA PRODUCTIONS

676A 9th Ave., #252, New York, NY 10036. (800)659-2063. Fax: (609)259-8260. Website: www.dcaproductions.com. **Contact:** Suzanne Perrotta, office manager. President: Daniel Abrahamsen. Vice president: Geraldine Abrahamsen. Management firm. Estab. 1975. Represents individual artists, groups and songwriters from anywhere.

HOW TO CONTACT If seeking management, press kit should include cover letter, bio, photo, demo tape/CD, and video. Prefers cassette or DVD with 2 songs. "All materials are reviewed and kept on file for future consideration. Does not return material. We respond only if interested."

MUSIC Mostly **acoustic**, **rock** and **mainstream**; also **cabaret** and **theme**. Works primarily with acoustic singer/songwriters, top 40 or rock bands. Current acts include And Jam Band (soulful R&B), Lorna Bracewell (singer/songwriter), Lisa Bouchelle (singer/songwriter), and Jimmy and the Parrots (Jimmy Buffett cover band). "Visit our website for a current roster of acts."

TIPS "Please do not call for a review of material."

DEBORAH PEACOCK PRODUCTIONS

P.O. BOX 300127, Austin, TX78703. (512) 970-9024. E-mail: photo@deborahpeacock.com. Website: www.deborahpeacock.com; www.art-n-music.com. Graphic design, public relations, promotions, photography, and consultancy. Deborah Peacock Photography & Public Relations caters to businesses, products, actors and musicians, performing and visual artists; product photography, special events, videography and graphic/web design.

HOW TO CONTACT Visit website.

MUSIC Visit website.

THE EDWARD DE MILES MUSIC COMPANY

10573 W. Pico Blvd., #352, Los Angeles, CA 90064-2348. Phone: (310)948-9652. Fax: (310)474-7705. E-mail: info@edmsahara.com. Website: www.edmsahara.com. **Contact:** Edward de Miles, president. Management firm, booking agency, entertainment/sports promoter, and TV/radio broadcast producer. Estab. 1984. Represents film, television, radio and musical artists; currently handles 15 acts. Receives 10-20% commission. Reviews material for acts. Regional operations in Chicago, Dallas, Houston, and Nashville through marketing representatives. Licensed A.F. of M. booking agent.

Also see listings for Edward De Miles in the "Music Publishers" and "Record Producers" sections, and Sahara Records and Filmworks Entertainment in the "Record Companies" section of this book.

HOW TO CONTACT *Does not accept unsolicited materials.* Prefers CD with 3-5 songs, 8×10 b&w photo, bio, and lyric sheet. "Copyright all material before submitting." If seeking management, include cover letter, bio, demo CD with 3-5 songs, 8×10 b&w

photo, lyric sheet, press clippings, and video if available in press kit. Include SASE. Does not return material. Responds in 1 month.

MUSIC Mostly **country**, **dance**, **R&B/soul**, **rock**, **top 40/pop**, and **urban contemporary**; also looking for material for **television, radio, and film** productions. Works primarily with dance bands and vocalists. Current acts include Steve Lynn (R&B/dance), Multiple Choice (rap) and Devon Edwards (jazz).

TIPS "Performers need to be well prepared with their presentations (equipment, showmanship a must)."

☯◑ DIVINE INDUSTRIES

(formerly Gangland Artists), Unit 191, #101-1001 W. Broadway, Vancouver, BC V6H 4E4, Canada. Fax: (604)737-3602. E-mail: divine@divineindustries.com. Website: www.divineindustries.com. **Contact:** Allen Moy. Management firm, production house and music publisher. Estab. 1985. Represents artists and songwriters; currently handles 5 acts. Reviews material for acts.

HOW TO CONTACT *Write first and obtain permission to submit.* Prefers audio links. "Videos are not entirely necessary for our company. It is certainly a nice touch. If you feel your audio cassette is strong—send the video upon later request." Does not return material. Responds in 2 months.

MUSIC **Rock**, **pop**, and **roots**. Works primarily with rock/left-of-center folk show bands. Current acts include 54-40 (rock/pop), Blackie & the Rodeo Kings (folk rock), Ridley Bent, Barney Bentall, John Mann (of Spirit of the West).

◑ JOHN ECKERT ENTERTAINMENT CONSULTANTS

(formerly Pro Talent Consultants), 7723 Cora Dr., Lucerne, CA 95458. (707)349-1809, (323)325-6662 (Los Angeles, CA). E-mail: talentconsultants@gmail.com. **Contact:** John Eckert, coordinator or Rich Clark. MarVista/Santa Monica management firm and booking agency. Estab. 1979. Represents individual artists and groups; currently handles 12 acts. Receives 15% commission. Reviews material for acts.

HOW TO CONTACT Submit demo package by mail. Unsolicited submissions are OK. "We prefer CD (4 songs). Submit videocassette with live performance only." If seeking management, press kit should include an 8×10 photo, a cassette or CD of at least 4-6 songs, a bio on group/artist, references, cover letter, press clippings, video, and business card, or a phone number with address. Does not return material. Responds in 5 weeks.

MUSIC Mostly **country**, **country/pop,** and **rock**. Works primarily with vocalists, show bands, dance bands, and bar bands. Current acts include the Rose Garden (pop/rock/country band); the Royal Guardsmen (pop/rock/top 40); the Hullaballoos (top 40/pop band); and Don Grady, (singer/songwriter, actor).

☯◑◐ S.L. FELDMAN & ASSOCIATES & MACKLAM FELDMAN MANAGEMENT

1505 W. Second Ave. #200, Vancouver, BC V6H 3Y4, Canada. (604)734-5945. Fax: (604)732-0922. E-mail: feldman@slfa.com. Website: www.slfa.com. Booking agency and artist management firm. Estab. 1970. Agency represents mostly established Canadian recording artists and groups; currently handles over 200 acts.

HOW TO CONTACT *Write or call first to obtain permission to submit a demo.* Prefers CD, photo, and bio. If seeking management, contact Watchdog for consideration and include video in press kit. SAE and IRC. Responds in 2 months.

MUSIC Current acts include the Chieftains, Joni Mitchell, Diana Krall, FeFe Dobson, Pink Martini, Plain White Ts, Sarah McLachlan, Michael Buble, and Melody Gardot.

◒◑◐ FIRST TIME MANAGEMENT

Sovereign House, 12 Trewartha Rd., Praa Sands-Penzance, Cornwall TR20 9ST, England (01736)762826. Fax: (01736)763328. E-mail: panamus@aol.com. Website: www.songwriters-guild.co.uk and www.myspace.com/guildofsongwriters. **Contact:** Roderick G. Jones, managing director. Management firm, record company (Digimix Records Ltd www.digimixrecords.com, Rainy Day Records, Mohock Records, Pure Gold Records), and music publisher (Panama Music Library, Melody First Music Library, Eventide Music Library, Musik' Image Music Library, Promo Sonor International Music Library, Caribbean Music Library, ADN Creation Music Library, Piano Bar Music Library, Corelia Music Library, PSI Music Library, Scamp Music Publishing, First Time Music [Publishing] U.K. [www.panamamusic.co.uk and www.myspace.com/scampmusicpublishing] —registered members of the Mechanical Copyright Protection Society [MCPS] and the Performing Right Society [PRS]). Estab. 1986. Represents local, regional, and international individual artists, groups, composers, DJs, and songwriters. Receives 15-25% commission. Reviews material for acts.

○ Also see the listings for First Time Music (Publishing) in the "Music Publishers" section of this book.

HOW TO CONTACT Submit demo package by mail. Unsolicited submissions are OK. Prefers CD with 3 songs, lyric sheets, and also complete album projects where writer/performer has finished masters. If seeking management, press kit should include cover letter, bio, photo, demo tape/CD, press clippings, and anything relevant to make an impression. Does not return material. Responds in 1 month only if interested.

MUSIC All styles. Works primarily with songwriters, composers, DJs, rappers, vocalists, bands, groups, and choirs. Current acts include Willow (pop), Bram Stoker (prog rock/gothic rock group), Kevin Kendle (New Age, holistic) Peter Arnold (folk/roots), David Jones (urban/R&B), Shanelle (R&B/dance), AudioJunkie & Stylus (dance/hardcore/funky house/electro house) Ray Guntrip (jazz); DJ Gammer (hardcore/hardhouse/dance).

TIPS "Become a member of the Guild of International Songwriters and Composers (www.songwriters-guild.co.uk). Keep everything as professional as possible. Be patient and dedicated to your aims and objectives."

○ GARY SMELTZER PRODUCTIONS

P.O. Box 201112, Austin, TX 78720. (512)478-6020. Fax:(512)478-8979. E-mail: info@garysmeltzerproductions.com. Website: www.garysmeltzerproductions.com. Estab. 1967. Management firm and booking agency. Represents individual artists and groups from anywhere. Currently handles 20 acts. "We book about 100 different bands each year—none are exclusive." Receives 20% commission. Reviews material for acts.

HOW TO CONTACT Submit demo package by mail. Unsolicited submissions are OK. Prefers CD or DVD. If seeking management, press kit should include cover letter, résumé, CD/DVD, bio, picture, lyric sheets, press clippings, and video. Does not return material. Responds in 1 month.

MUSIC Mostly **alternative**, **R&B**, and **country**. Current acts include Rotel & the Hot Tomatoes (nostalgic '60s show band).

TIPS "We prefer performing songwriters who can gig their music as a solo or group."

○ HARDISON INTERNATIONAL ENTERTAINMENT CORPORATION

P.O. Box 1732, Knoxville, TN 37901-1732 (prefers e-mail contact). (865)688-8680. E-mail: dennishardin

son@bellsouth.net. Website: www.dynamoreckless.com. **Contact:** Dennis K. Hardison, CEO/founder. Dennis K. Hardison II, president; Travis J. Hardison, president, Denlatrin Record, a division of Hardison International Entertainment Corp. Contact: Management firm, booking agency, music publisher (Denlatrin Music) BMI, record label (Denlatrin Records) and record producer. Estab. 1984. Represents individual artists from anywhere; currently handles 3 acts. Receives 20% commission. Reviews material for acts. "We are seeking level-minded and patient individuals. Our primary interests are established recording acts with prior major deals."

○ This company has promoted many acts in show business for over 30 years.

HOW TO CONTACT Submit demo package by mail. Unsolicited submissions are OK. Prefers CD with 3 songs only. If seeking management, press kit should include bio, promo picture, and CD. Does not return materials. Responds in 6 weeks to the best material. Critiques available through MySpace, so enclose your MySpace address.

MUSIC Mostly **R&B**, **hip-hop**, and **rap**. Current acts include Dynamo (hip-hop), the Nafro Queens of Lagos, Nigeria, Triniti (record producer, Universal Music, Public Enemy, Dynamo, among others; current engineer for Chuck D), and RapStation artists.

TIPS "We respond to the hottest material, so make it hot!"

∅ INTERNATIONAL ENTERTAINMENT BUREAU

3612 N. Washington Blvd., Indianapolis IN 46205-3592. (317)926-7566. E-mail: ieb@prodigy.net. Booking agency. Estab. 1972. Represents individual artists and groups from anywhere; currently handles 145 acts. Receives 20% commission.

HOW TO CONTACT *No unsolicited submissions.*

MUSIC Mostly **rock**, **country**, and **A/C**; also **jazz**, **nostalgia**, and **ethnic**. Works primarily with bands, comedians, and speakers. Current acts include Five Easy Pieces (A/C), Scott Greeson (country), and Cool City Swing Band (variety).

① JANA JAE ENTERPRISES

P.O. Box 35726, Tulsa OK 74153. (918)786-8896. Fax: (918)786-8897. E-mail: janajae@janajae.com. Website: www.janajae.com. **Contact:** Kathleen Pixley, agent.

Booking agency, music publisher (Jana Jae Publishing/BMI) and record company (Lark Record Productions, Inc.). Estab. 1979. Represents individual artists and songwriters; currently handles 12 acts. Receives 15% commission. Reviews material for acts.

🎧 Also see the listings for Jana Jae Music in the "Music Publishers" section, Lark Record Productions in the "Record Companies" section and Lark Talent & Advertising in the "Record Producers" section of this book.

HOW TO CONTACT Submit demo by mail. Unsolicited submissions are OK. Prefers CD or DVD of performance. If seeking management, press kit should include cover letter, bio, photo, demo tape/CD, lyric sheets, and press clippings. Does not return material.

MUSIC Mostly **country, classical,** and **jazz instrumentals**; also **pop**. Works with vocalists, show and concert bands, solo instrumentalists. Represents Jana Jae (country singer/fiddle player), Matt Greif (classical guitarist), Sydni (solo singer) and Hotwire (country show band).

○ KUPER PERSONAL MANAGEMENT/ RECOVERY RECORDINGS

515 Bomar St., Houston, TX 77006. (713)520-5791. Fax: (713)527-0202. E-mail: info@recoveryrecord ings.com. Website: www.recoveryrecordings.com. **Contact:** Koop Kuper, owner. Management firm, music publisher (Kuper-Lam Music/BMI, Uvula Music/BMI, and Meauxtown Music/ASCAP) and record label (Recovery Recordings). Estab. 1979/2002. Represents individual artists, groups, and songwriters from Texas. Receives 20% commission. Reviews material for acts.

HOW TO CONTACT Submit demo package by mail. Unsolicited submissions are OK. Prefers CD. If seeking management, press kit should include cover letter, press clippings, photo, bio (1 page) tearsheets (reviews, etc.), and demo CD. Does not return material. Responds in 2 months.

MUSIC Mostly **singer/songwriters, AAA, roots rock,** and **Americana**. Works primarily with self-contained and self-produced artists. Current acts include Philip Rodriguez (singer/songwriter), David Rodriguez (singer/songwriter), Def Squad Texas (hip-hop). U.S. representative for the following Dutch groups: the Watchman (Dutch singer/songwriter), and the Very Girls (Dutch vocal duo).

TIPS "Create a market value for yourself, produce your own master tapes, and create a cost-effective situation."

○ LOGGINS PROMOTION

5018 Franklin Pike, Nashville TN 37220. (310)325-2800. Fax: (615)323-2200. E-mail: staff@Loggin sPromotion.com. Website: www.logginspromotion. com. **Contact:** Paul Loggins, CEO. Management firm and radio promotion. Represents individual artists, groups, and songwriters from anywhere; currently handles 6 acts. Receives 20% commission. Reviews material for acts.

HOW TO CONTACT If seeking management, press kit should include picture, short bio, cover letter, press clippings, and CD (preferred). "Mark on CD which cut you, as the artist, feel is the strongest." Does not return material. Responds in 2 weeks.

MUSIC Mostly **adult, top 40,** and **AAA**; also **urban, rap, alternative, college, smooth jazz,** and **Americana**. Works primarily with bands and solo artists.

● MANAGEMENT BY JAFFE

68 Ridgewood Ave., Glen Ridge, NJ 07028. (973)743-1075. Fax: (973)743-1075. E-mail: jerjaf@aol.com. President: Jerry Jaffe. Management firm. Estab. 1987. Represents individual artists and groups from anywhere; currently handles 2 acts. Receives 20% commission. Reviews material for acts "rarely." Reviews for representation "sometimes."

HOW TO CONTACT *Write or call first to arrange personal interview.* Prefers CD or DVD with 3-4 songs and lyric sheet. Does not return material. Responds in 2 months.

MUSIC Mostly **rock/alternative, pop,** and **Hot AC**. Works primarily with groups and singers/songwriters.

TIPS "If you are influenced by Jesus & Mary Chain, please e-mail. Create some kind of 'buzz' first."

○ RICK MARTIN PRODUCTIONS

E-mail: rick@easywaysystems.com. Website: www. rickmartinproductions.com and www.myspace.com/ rickmartinproductions. **Contact:** Rick Martin, president. Personal manager and independent producer. Held the office of secretary of the National Conference of Personal Managers for 22 years. Represents vocalists; currently produces pop and country crossover music artists in private project studio and looking for a female vocalist in the general area of Greenwich, CT, for production project. Receives 15% commission as a personal manager and/or customary production and publishing distributions.

HOW TO CONTACT "Please e-mail for initial contact with your web link. Do not submit unless permission received to do so."

MUSIC Any genre but hip-hop or rap.

TIPS "Your demo does not have to be professionally produced to submit to producers, publishers, or managers. In other words, save your money. It's really not important what you've done. It's what you can do now that counts."

MIDCOAST, INC.

1002 Jones Rd., Hendersonville TN 37075. (615)400-4664. E-mail: mid-co@ix.netcom.com. Managing director: Bruce Andrew Bossert. Management firm and music publisher (MidCoast, Inc./BMI). Estab. 1984. Represents individual artists, groups, and songwriters; currently handles 2 acts. Reviews material for acts.

HOW TO CONTACT Submit demo package by mail. Unsolicited submissions are OK. Prefers CD, cassette, VHS videocassette, or DAT with 2-4 songs and lyric sheet. If seeking management, press kit should include cover letter, "short" bio, tape, video, photo, press clippings, and announcements of any performances in Nashville area. Does not return material. Responds in 6 weeks if interested.

MUSIC Mostly **rock, pop,** and **country**. Works primarily with original rock and country bands and artists. Current acts include Room 101 (alternative rock).

NOTEWORTHY PRODUCTIONS

124¹/₂ Archwood Ave., Annapolis, MD 21401. (410)268-8232. Fax: (410)268-2167. E-mail: mcshane@mcnote.com. Website: www.mcnote.com. **Contact:** McShane Glover, president. Management firm and booking agency. Estab. 1985. Represents individual artists, groups, and songwriters from everywhere; currently handles 6 acts. Receives 15-20% commission. Reviews material for acts.

HOW TO CONTACT *Write first and obtain permission to submit.* Prefers CD/CDR with lyric sheet. If seeking management, press kit should include CD, photo, bio, venues played, and press clippings (preferably reviews). "Follow up with a phone call 3-5

weeks after submission." Does not return material. Responds in 2 months.

MUSIC Mostly **Americana, folk,** and **Celtic**. Works primarily with performing singer/songwriters. Current acts include Toby Walker (blues) and Pat Wictor (roots).

PARADIGM TALENT AGENCY

360 N. Crescent Dr., North Bldg., Beverly Hills, CA 90210. (310)288-8000. Fax: (310)288-2000. Website: www.paradigmagency.com. **Nashville:** 124 12th Ave. S., Suite 410, Nashville TN 37203. (615)251-4400. Fax: (615)251-4401. **New York:** 260 Park Ave. S., 16th Floor, New York, NY 10010. (212)897-6400. Fax: (212)764-8941. **Monterey:** 404 W. Franklin St., Monterey, CA 93940. (831)375-4889. Fax: (831)375-2623. Website: www.paradigmagency.com. Booking agency. Represents individual artists, groups from anywhere. Receives 10% commission. Reviews material for acts.

HOW TO CONTACT *Write or call first to arrange personal interview.*

MUSIC Current acts include Ricky Skaggs, Junior Brown, Toby Keith, Grand Funk Railroad, Kasey Chambers, Uncle Kracker, Black Eyed Peas, Kirk Franklin, Lily Allen, My Chemical Romance, and Lauryn Hill.

PRIME TIME ENTERTAINMENT

2430 Research Dr., Livermore, CA 94550. (925)449-1724. Fax: (925)605-0379. E-mail: info@primetimeentertainment.com. Website: www.primetimeentertainment.com. Owner: Jim Douglas. Management firm and booking agency. Estab. 1988. Represents individual artists, groups, and songwriters from anywhere. Receives 10-20% commission. Reviews material for acts.

HOW TO CONTACT Submit demo package by mail. Unsolicited submissions are OK. Prefers CD with 3-5 songs. If seeking management, press kit should include 8×10 photo, reviews, and CDs/tapes. Include SASE. Responds in 1 month.

MUSIC Mostly **jazz, country,** and **alternative**; also **ethnic**. Artists include Grant Geissman (fusion/jazz), Jody Watley (R&B), Ray Parker Jr. (jazz/R&B), and Craig Chaquico (jazz).

TIPS "It's all about the song."

RAINBOW TALENT AGENCY LLC

146 Round Pond Lane, Rochester, NY 14626. (585)723-3334. Fax: (585)720-6172. E-mail: carl@rainbowtalent

agency.com. Website: www.rainbowtalentagency.com. **Contact:** Carl Labate, president. Management firm and booking agency. Represents artists and groups; currently handles 4 acts. Receives 15-25% commission.

HOW TO CONTACT Submit demo package by mail. Unsolicited submissions are OK. Prefers CD with minimum 3 songs. May send DVD if available; "a still photo and bio of the act; if you are a performer, it would be advantageous to show yourself or the group performing live. Theme videos are not helpful." If seeking management, include photos, bio, markets established, CD/DVD. Does not return material. Responds in 1 month.

MUSIC Mostly **blues**, **rock**, and **R&B**. Works primarily with touring bands and recording artists. Current acts include Kristen Maxfield (R&B), Russell Thompkins Jr. & the New Stylistics (R&B), Nevergreen (pop) and Spanky Haschmann Swing Orchestra (high energy swing).

TIPS "My main interest is with groups or performers that are currently touring and have some product. And are at least 50% original. Strictly songwriters should apply elsewhere."

O RASPBERRY JAM MUSIC

(formerly Endangered Species Artist Management) 4 Berachah Ave., South Nyack NY 10960-4202. (845)353-4001. Fax: (845)353-4332. E-mail: muzik@ verizon.net. Website: www.musicandamerica.com or www.anyamusic.com. President: Fred Porter. Vice president: Suzanne Buckley. Management firm. Estab. 1979. Represents individual artists, groups and songwriters from anywhere; currently handles 3 acts. Receives 20% commission. Reviews material for acts.

HOW TO CONTACT *Call first and obtain permission to submit.* Prefers CD with 3 or more songs and lyric sheet. "Please include a demo of your music, a clear, recent photograph as well as any current press, if any. A cover letter indicating at what stage in your career you are and expectations for your future. Please label the cassette and/or CD with your name and address as well as the song titles." If seeking management, press kit should include cover letter, bio, photo, demo/CD, lyric sheet, and press clippings. Include SASE. Responds in 6 weeks.

MUSIC Mostly **pop**, **rock**, and **world**; also **Latin/heavy metal**, **R&B**, **jazz** and **instrumental**. Current acts include Jason Wilson & Tabarruk (pop/reggae, nominated for Juno award 2001), and Anya (pop singer).

TIPS "Listen to everything, classical to country, old to contemporary, to develop an understanding of many writing styles. Write with many other partners to keep the creativity fresh. Don't feel your style will be ruined by taking a class or a writing seminar. We all process moods and images differently. This leads to uniqueness in the music."

O REIGN MUSIC AND MEDIA, LLC

(formerly Bassline Entertainment, Inc.) P.O. Box 2394, New York, NY 10185. E-mail: online@reignmm.com. Website: www.reignmm.com. **Contact:** Talent Relations Dept. Multimedia/Artist Development firm. Estab. 1993 as Bassline Entertainment. Promotes/develops primarily local and regional vocalists, producers, and songwriters. Receives 20-25% commission. Reviews material for artists.

HOW TO CONTACT Submit demo package by mail or e-mail. Unsolicited submissions are OK. Prefers CD, mp3, or video. Standard hard copy press kit or EPK should include cover letter, press clippings and/or reviews, bio, demo (in appropriate format), picture, and accurate contact telephone number. Include SASE. Usually responds in 3 weeks.

MUSIC Mostly **pop**, **R&B**, **club/dance**, and **hip-hop/rap**; some **Latin**. Works primarily with singer/songwriters, producers, rappers, and bands. Current acts include Sincere (hip hop/R&B); R. Notes (pop/R&B), and Iceman (hip hop).

● RICK LEVY MANAGEMENT

4250 A1AS, D-11, St. Augustine FL 32080. (904)806-0817. Fax: (904)460-1226. E-mail: rick@ricklevy.com. Website: www.ricklevy.com. **Contact:** Rick Levy, president. Management firm, music publisher (Flying Governor Music/BMI) and record company (Luxury Records). Estab. 1985. Represents local, regional, or international individual artists and groups; currently handles 5 acts. Receives 15-20% commission. Reviews material for acts.

HOW TO CONTACT *Write or call first and obtain permission to submit.* Prefers CD or DVD with 3 songs and lyric sheet. If seeking management, press kit should include cover letter, bio, demo tape/CD, DVD demo, photo, and press clippings. Include SASE. Responds in 2 weeks.

MUSIC Mostly **R&B** (no rap), **pop**, **country**, and **oldies**; also **children's** and **educational videos** for schools. Current acts include Jay & the Techniques

('60s hit group), the Original Box Tops ('60s), the Limits (pop), Freddy Cannon ('60s), the Fallin Bones (Blues/rock), Tommy Roe ('60s), the Bushwhackers (country).

TIPS "If you don't have 200% passion and commitment, don't bother. Be sure to contact only companies that deal with your type of music."

◑ RIOHCAT MUSIC

P.O. Box 764, Hendersonville, TN 37077-0764. (615)824-9313. Fax: (615)824-0797. E-mail: tachoir@bellsouth.net. Website: www.tachoir.com. **Contact:** Robert Kayne, manager. Management firm, booking agency, record company (Avita Records), and music publisher. Estab. 1975. Represents individual artists and groups; currently handles 4 acts. Receives 15-20% commission.

○ Also see the listing for Avita Records in the "Record Companies" section of this book.

HOW TO CONTACT *Contact first and obtain permission to submit.* Prefers CD, and lead sheet. If seeking management, press kit should include cover letter, bio, photo, demo tape/CD and press clippings. Does not return material. Responds in 6 weeks.

MUSIC Mostly **contemporary jazz** and **fusion**. Works primarily with jazz ensembles. Current acts include Group Tachoir (jazz), Tachoir/Manakas Duo (jazz) and Jerry Tachoir (jazz vibraphone artist).

◐○ ROBERTSON ENTERTAINMENT

106 Harding Rd., Kendenup 6323, Western Australia. (618)9851-4311. Fax: (618)9851-4225. E-mail: info@robertsonentertainment.com. Website: www.robertsonentertainment.com. **Contact:** Eddie Robertson. Booking agency. Estab. 1991. Represents individual artists and/or groups; currently handles 50 acts. Receives 20% commission. Reviews material for acts.

HOW TO CONTACT *Write first and obtain permission to submit.* Unsolicited submissions are OK. Prefers cassette or videocassette with photo, information on style and bio. If seeking management, press kit should include photos, bio, cover letter, press clippings, video, demo, lyric sheets, and any other useful information. Does not return material. Responds in 1 month.

MUSIC Mostly **top 40/pop, jazz** and **'60s-'90s**; also **reggae** and **blues**. Works primarily with show bands and solo performers. Current acts include Faces

(dance band), Heart & Soul (easy listening), and Ruby Tuesday (contemporary pop/rock/classics).

TIPS "Send as much information as possible. If you do not receive a call after four to five weeks, follow up with letter or phone call."

◑ SA'MALL MANAGEMENT

P.O. Box 261488, Encino CA 91426. (818)506-8533. Fax: (818)506-8534. E-mail: samusa@aol.com. Website: www.pplentertainmentgroup.com; www.pplzmi.com. **Vice president of talent:** Ted Steele. Management firm, music publisher (Pollybyrd Publications), and record company (PPL Entertainment Group). Estab. 1990. Represents individual artists, groups and songwriters worldwide; currently handles 10 acts. Receives 10-25% commission. Reviews material for acts.

○ Also see the listings for Pollybyrd Publications Limited and Zettitalia Music International in the "Music Publishers" section and PPL Entertainment Group in the "Record Companies" section of this book.

HOW TO CONTACT *E-mail first and obtain permission to submit.* "Only professional full-time artists who tour and have a fan base need apply. No weekend warriors, please." Prefers CD or cassette. If seeking management, press kit should include picture, bio and tape. Include SASE. Responds in 2 months.

MUSIC **All types.** Current acts include Riki Hendrix (rock), Buddy Wright (blues), Fhyne, Suzette Cuseo, The Band AKA, LeJenz, B.D. Fuoco, MoBeatz, and Kenyatta Jarrett (Prince Ken).

○ SANDALPHON MANAGEMENT

P.O. Box 542407, Grand Prairie TX 75054. (972)333-0876. E-mail: jackrabbit01@comcast.net. **Contact:** Ruth Otey, president. Management firm, music publisher (Sandalphon Music Publishing/BMI), and record company (Sandalphon Records). Estab. 2005. Represents individual artists, groups, songwriters; works with individual artists and groups from anywhere. Currently handles 0 acts. Receives negotiable commission. Reviews material for acts.

HOW TO CONTACT Submit demo by mail. Unsolicited submissions are fine. Prefers CD with 1-5 songs and lyric sheet, cover letter. "Include name, address, and contact information." Include SASE or SAE and IRC for outside the United States. Responds in 6-8 weeks.

MUSIC Mostly **rock**, **country**, and **alternative**; also **pop**, **gospel**, and **blues**. "We are looking for singers, bands, and singer/songwriters who are original but would be current in today's music markets. We help singers, bands, and singer-songwriters achieve their personal career goals."

TIPS "Submit material you feel best represents you, your voice, your songs, or your band. Fresh and original songs and style are a plus. We are a West Coast management company looking for singers, bands, and singer-songwriters who are ready for the next level. We are looking for those with talent who are capable of being national and international contenders."

○ SCOTT EVANS PRODUCTIONS

P.O. Box 814028, Hollywood FL 33081-4028. (954)963-4449. E-mail: evansprod@hotmail.com. Website: www.theentertainmentmall.com. **Contact:** Ted Jones, new artists, or Jeanne K., Internet marketing and sales. Management firm and booking agency. Estab. 1979. Represents local, regional, or international individual artists, groups, songwriters, comedians, novelty acts, and dancers; currently handles over 200 acts. Receives 10-50% commission. Reviews material for acts.

HOW TO CONTACT New artists can make submissions through the "Auditions" link located on the website. Unsolicited submissions are OK. "Please be sure that all submissions are copyrighted and not your original copy as we do not return material."

MUSIC Mostly **pop**, **R&B**, and **Broadway**. Deals with "all types of entertainers; no limitations." Current acts include Scott Evans and Company (variety song and dance), Dorit Zinger (female vocalist), Jeff Geist, Actors Repertory Theatre, Entertainment Express, Joy Deco (dance act), Flashback (musical song and dance revue), and Around the World (international song and dance revue).

TIPS "Submit a neat, well put together, organized press kit."

●⊛ SERGE ENTERTAINMENT GROUP

P.O. Box 2760, Acworth, GA 30102. (678)445-0006. Fax: (678)494-9289. E-mail: sergeent@aol.com. Website: www.sergeentertainmentgroup.com. **Contact:** Sandy Serge, president. Management and PR firm and song publishers. Estab. 1987. Represents individual artists, groups, songwriters from anywhere; currently handles 20 acts. Receives 20% commission for management. Monthly fee required for PR acts.

HOW TO CONTACT E-mail first for permission to submit. Submit demo package by mail. Unsolicited submissions are OK. Prefers CD with 4 songs and lyric sheet. If seeking management, press kit should include 8×10 photo, bio, cover letter, lyric sheets, max of 4 press clips, DVD, performance schedule, and CD. "All information submitted must include name, address and phone number on each item." Does not return material. Responds in 6 weeks if interested.

MUSIC Mostly **rock**, **pop**, and **country**; also **New Age**. Works primarily with singer/songwriters and bands. Current acts include Kevin Carlson (folk), ASIA featuring John Payne (classic rock), Erik Norlander (prog rock), and Sonics (punk/garage rock).

◐● SIEGEL ENTERTAINMENT LTD.

1736 W. 2nd Ave., Vancouver, BC V6J 1H6 Canada. (604)736-3896. Fax: (604)736-3464. E-mail: siegelent@telus.net. Website: www.siegelent.com. **Contact:** Robert Siegel, president. Management firm and booking agency. Estab. 1975. Represents individual artists, groups, and songwriters from anywhere; currently handles more than 100 acts (for bookings). Receives 15-20% commission. Reviews material for acts.

HOW TO CONTACT Does not accept unsolicited submissions. E-mail or write for permission to submit. Does not return material. Responds in 1 month.

MUSIC Mostly **rock**, **pop**, and **country**; also **specialty** and **children's**. Current acts include Johnny Ferreira & the Swing Machine, Lee Aaron, Kenny Blues Boss Wayne (boogie), and Tim Brecht (pop/children's).

◑ T. SKORMAN PRODUCTIONS, INC.

5156 S. Orange Ave., Orlando FL 32809. (407)895-3000. Fax: (407)895-1422. E-mail: ted@tskorman.com. Website: www.tskorman.com. **Contact:** Ted Skorman, president. Management firm and booking agency. Estab. 1983. Represents groups; currently handles 40 acts. Receives 10-25% commission. Reviews material for acts.

HOW TO CONTACT E-mail first for permission to submit. Prefers CD with 2 songs, or videocassette of no more than 6 minutes. "Live performance—no trick shots or editing tricks. We want to be able to view act as if we were there for a live show." If seeking management, press kit should include cover letter, bio, photo, and demo CD or video. Does not return material. Responds only if interested.

MUSIC Mostly **top 40**, **dance, pop**, and **country**. Works primarily with high-energy dance acts, recording acts, and top 40 bands. Current acts include Steph Carse (pop).

SOUTHEASTERN ATTRACTIONS

1025 23rd St. S., Suite 302, Birmingham AL 35205. (205)307-6790. Fax: (205)307-6798. E-mail: info@ seattractions.com. Website: www.seattractions.com. **Contact:** Agent. Booking agency. Estab. 1967. Represents groups from anywhere; currently handles 200 acts. Receives 20% commission.
HOW TO CONTACT Submit demo package by mail. Unsolicited submissions are OK. Prefers CD or DVD. Does not return material. Responds in 2 months.
MUSIC Mostly **rock**, **alternative**, **oldies**, **country**, and **dance**. Works primarily with bands. Current acts include Leaderdog (rock), Undergrounders (variety to contemporary), Style Band (Motown/dance), The Connection (Motown/dance), Rollin' in the Hay (bluegrass).

STARKRAVIN' MANAGEMENT

11135 Weddington St., Suite 424, North Hollywood, CA 91601. (818)587-6801. Fax: (818)587-6802. E-mail: bcmclane@aol.com. Website: www.benmclane. com. **Contact:** B.C. McLane, Esq. Management and law firm. Estab. 1994. Represents individual artists, groups and songwriters. Receives 20% commission (management); $300/hour as attorney.
HOW TO CONTACT Submit demo package by mail. Unsolicited submissions are OK. Prefers cassette. Does not return material. Responds in 1 month if interested.
MUSIC Mostly **rock**, **pop,** and **R&B**. Works primarily with bands.

ST. JOHN ARTISTS

P.O. Box 619, Neenah WI 54957-0619. (920)722-2222. Fax: (920)725-2405. E-mail: jon@stjohn-artists.com. Website: www.stjohn-artists.com/. **Contact:** Jon St. John and Gary Coquoz, agents. Booking agency. Estab. 1968. Represents local and regional individual artists and groups; currently handles 20 acts. Receives 15-20% commission. Reviews material for acts.
HOW TO CONTACT *Call first and obtain permission to submit.* Prefers CD or DVD. If seeking management, press kit should include cover letter, bio, photo, demo tape/CD, video, and résumé. Include SASE.

MUSIC Mostly **rock** and **MOR**. Current acts include Boogie & the Yo-Yo's ('60s to 2000s), Vic Ferrari (Top 40 '80s-2000s), Little Vito & the Torpedoes (variety '50s-2000s), and Da Yoopers (musical comedy/novelty).

TAS MUSIC CO./DAVE TASSE ENTERTAINMENT

N2467 Knollwood Dr., Lake Geneva, WI 53147. (262)245-1335. E-mail: info@baybreezerecords.com. Website: www.baybreezerecords.com. **Contact:** David Tasse. Booking agency, record company and music publisher. Represents artists, groups and songwriters; currently handles 21 acts. Receives 10-20% commission. Reviews material for acts.
HOW TO CONTACT Submit demo tape by mail. Unsolicited submissions are OK. Prefers cassette with 2-4 songs and lyric sheet. Include performance videocassette if available. If seeking management, press kit should include tape, bio, and photo. Does not return material. Responds in 3 weeks.
MUSIC Mostly **pop** and **jazz**; also **dance, MOR, rock, soul,** and **top 40**. Works primarily with show and dance bands. Current acts include Maxx Kelly (pop/rock) and Walter Thomas (smooth R&B).

THE MANAGEMENT TRUST, LTD.

411 Queen St. W, 3rd Floor, Toronto ON M5V 2A5 Canada. (416)979-7070. Fax: (416)979-0505. E-mail: mail@mgmtrust.ca. Website: www.mgmtrust.ca. Manager: Jake Gold. Manager: R.J. Guha. General Manager: Shelley Stertz. Management firm. Estab. 1986. Represents individual artists and/or groups; currently handles 8 acts.
HOW TO CONTACT Submit demo package by mail (Attn: A&R Dept.). Unsolicited submissions are OK. If seeking management, press kit should include CD, bio, cover letter, photo and press clippings. Does not return material. Responds in 2 months.
MUSIC All types.

T.L.C. BOOKING AGENCY

37311 N. Valley Rd., Chattaroy, WA 99003. (509)292-2201. Fax: (509)292-2205. E-mail: tlcagent@ix.netcom. com. Website: www.tlcagency.com. **Contact:** Tom or Carrie Lapsansky, agent/owners. Booking agency. Estab. 1970. Represents individual artists and groups from anywhere; currently handles 17 acts. Receives 10-15% commission. Reviews material for acts.

HOW TO CONTACT *Call first and obtain permission to submit.* Prefers CD with 3-4 songs. Does not return material. Responds in 3 weeks.

MUSIC Mostly **rock**, **country**, and **variety**; also **comedians** and **magicians**. Works primarily with bands, singles, and duos. Current acts include Nobody Famous (variety/classic rock), Mr. Happy (rock), and Jimmy Buffett Review.

○ UNIVERSAL MUSIC MARKETING

P.O. Box 2297, Universal City TX 78148. (210)653-3989. Website: www.bsw-records.com. **Contact:** Frank Willson, president. Management firm, record company (BSW Records), booking agency, music publisher and record producer (Frank Wilson). Estab. 1987. Represents individual artists and groups from anywhere; currently handles 12 acts. Receives 15% commission. Reviews material for acts.

> ○ Also see the listings for BSW Records in the "Music Publishers" and "Record Companies" sections and Frank Wilson in the "Record Producers" section of this book.

HOW TO CONTACT Submit demo package by mail. Unsolicited submissions are OK. Prefers CD or DVD with 3 songs and lyric sheet. If seeking management, include tape/CD, bio, photo, and current activities. Include SASE. Responds in 6 weeks.

MUSIC Mostly **country** and **light rock**; also **blues** and **jazz**. Works primarily with vocalists, singer/songwriters, and bands. Current acts include Candee Land, Darlene Austin, Larry Butler, John Wayne, Sonny Marshall, Bobby Mountain, Crea Beal, and Butch Martin (country). "Visit our website for an up-to-date listing of current acts."

○ WORLDSOUND, LLC

17837 1st Ave. South Suite 3, Seattle WA, 98148. (206)444-0300. Fax: (206)244-0066. E-mail: music@worldsound.com. Website: www.worldsound.com. **Contact:** Warren Wyatt, A&R manager. Management firm. Estab. 1976. Represents individual artists, groups, and songwriters from anywhere; currently handles 8 acts. Receives 20% commission. Reviews material for acts.

HOW TO CONTACT "Online, send us an e-mail containing a link to your website where your songs can be heard and the lyrics are available—PLEASE DO NOT E-MAIL SONG FILES! By regular mail, unsolicited submissions are OK." Prefers CD with 2-10 songs and lyric sheet. "If seeking management, please send an e-mail with a link to your website—your site should contain song samples, band biography, photos, video (if available), press and demo reviews. By mail, please send the materials listed above and include SASE." Responds in 1 month.

MUSIC Mostly **rock**, **pop**, and **world**; also **heavy metal**, **hard rock**, and **top 40**. Works primarily with pop/rock/world artists. Current acts include Na Leo (contemporary/Hawaiian), and Keith Olsen (music producer).

TIPS "Always submit new songs/material, even if you have sent material that was previously rejected; the music biz is always changing."

● ZANE MANAGEMENT, INC.

1650 Market St., One Liberty Place, 56th Floor, Philadelphia PA 19103. (215)575-3803. Fax: (215)575-3801. E-mail: lzr@braverlaw.com. Website: www.zanemanagement.com. **Contact:** Lloyd Z. Remick, Esq., president. Entertainment/sports consultants and managers. Represents artists, songwriters, producers, and athletes; currently handles 7 acts. Receives 10-15% commission.

HOW TO CONTACT Submit demo tape by mail. Unsolicited submissions are OK. Prefers CD and lyric sheet. If seeking management, press kit should include cover letter, bio, photo, demo tape, and video. Does not return material. Responds in 3 weeks.

MUSIC Mostly **dance**, **easy listening**, **folk**, **jazz (fusion)**, **MOR**, **rock (hard and country)**, **soul**, and **top 40/pop**. Current acts include Bunny Sigler (disco/funk), Peter Nero and Philly Pops (conductor), Cast in Bronze (rock group), Pieces of a Dream (jazz/crossover), Don't Look Down (rock/pop), Christian Josi (pop-swing), Bishop David Evans (gospel), Kevin Roth (children's music), Rosie Carlino (standards/pop), and Tyrone Vaughan (country).

MUSIC FIRMS
Advertising, Audiovisual, & Commercial

It's happened a million times—you hear a jingle on the radio or television and can't get it out of your head. That's the work of a successful jingle writer, writing songs to catch your attention and make you aware of the product being advertised. But the field of commercial music consists of more than just memorable jingles. It also includes background music that many companies use in videos for corporate and educational presentations, as well as films and TV shows.

SUBMITTING MATERIAL

More than any other market listed in this book, the commercial music market expects composers to have made an investment in the recording of their material before submitting. A sparse, piano/vocal demo won't work here; when dealing with commercial music firms, especially audiovisual firms and music libraries, high-quality production is important. Your demo may be kept on file at one of these companies until a need for it arises, and it may be used or sold as you sent it. Therefore, your demo tape or reel must be as fully produced as possible.

The presentation package that goes along with your demo must be just as professional. A list of your credits should be a part of your submission, to give the company an idea of your experience in this field. If you have no experience, look to local television and radio stations to get your start. Don't expect to be paid for many of your first jobs in the commercial music field; it's more important to get the credits and exposure that can lead to higher-paying jobs.

Commercial music and jingle writing can be a lucrative field for the composer/songwriter with a gift for writing catchy melodies and the ability to write in many different music styles. It's a very competitive field, so it pays to have a professional presentation package that makes your work stand out.

Three different segments of the commercial music world are listed here: advertising agencies, audiovisual firms, and commercial music houses/music libraries. Each looks for a different type of music, so read these descriptions carefully to see where the music you write fits in.

ADVERTISING AGENCIES

Ad agencies work on assignment as their clients' needs arise. Through consultation and input from the creative staff, ad agencies seek jingles and music to stimulate the consumer to identify with a product or service.

When contacting ad agencies, keep in mind they are searching for music that can capture and then hold an audience's attention. Most jingles are short, with a strong, memorable hook. When an ad agency listens to a demo, it is not necessarily looking for a finished product so much as for an indication of creativity and diversity. Many composers put together a reel of excerpts of work from previous projects, or short pieces of music that show they can write in a variety of styles.

AUDIOVISUAL FIRMS

Audiovisual firms create a variety of products, from film and video shows for sales meetings, corporate gatherings and educational markets, to motion pictures and TV shows. With the increase of home video use, how-to videos are a big market for audiovisual firms, as are spoken word educational videos. All of these products need music to accompany them. For your quick reference, companies working to place music in movies and TV shows (excluding commercials) have a ⊕ preceding their listing.

Like ad agencies, audiovisual firms look for versatile, well-rounded songwriters. When submitting demos to these firms, you need to demonstrate your versatility in writing specialized background music and themes. Listings for companies will tell what facet(s) of the audiovisual field they are involved in and what types of clients they serve. Your demo tape should also be as professional and fully produced as possible; audiovisual firms often seek demo tapes that can be put on file for future use when the need arises.

COMMERCIAL MUSIC HOUSES & MUSIC LIBRARIES

Commercial music houses are companies contracted (either by an ad agency or the advertiser) to compose custom jingles. Since they are neither an ad agency nor an audiovisual firm, their main concern is music. They use a lot of it, too—some composed by in-house songwriters and some contributed by outside, freelance writers.

Music libraries are different in that their music is not custom composed for a specific client. Their job is to provide a collection of instrumental music in many different styles that, for an annual fee or on a per-use basis, the customer can use however he chooses.

In the following listings, commercial music houses and music libraries, which are usually the most open to works by new composers, are identified as such by **bold** type.

The commercial music market is similar to most other businesses in one aspect: experience is important. Until you develop a list of credits, pay for your work may not be high. Don't pass up opportunities if a job is non- or low-paying. These assignments will add to your list of credits, make you contacts in the field, and improve your marketability.

Money & Rights

Many of the companies listed in this section pay by the job, but there may be some situations where the company asks you to sign a contract that will specify royalty payments. If this happens, research the contract thoroughly, and know exactly what is expected of you and how much you'll be paid.

Depending on the particular job and the company, you may be asked to sell one-time rights or all rights. One-time rights involve using your material for one presentation only. All rights means the buyer can use your work any way he chooses, as many times as he likes. Be sure you know exactly what you're giving up, and how the company may use your music in the future.

In the commercial world, many of the big advertising agencies have their own publishing companies where writers assign their compositions. In these situations, writers sign contracts whereby they do receive performance and mechanical royalties when applicable.

ADDITIONAL LISTINGS

For additional names and addresses of ad agencies that may use jingles and/or commercial music, refer to the *Standard Directory of Advertising Agencies* (National Register Publishing). For a list of audiovisual firms, check out the latest edition of *AV Marketplace* (R.R. Bowker). Both these books may be found at your local library.

THE AD AGENCY

Advertising agency and jingle/commercial music production house. Clients include business, industry, and retail. Uses the services of music houses, independent songwriter/composers, and lyricists for scoring of commercials, background music for video production, and jingles for commercials. Commissions 20 composers and 15 lyricists/year. Pays by the job or by the hour. Buys all or one-time rights.

HOW TO CONTACT Submit demo tape of previous work. Prefers cassette with 5-8 songs and lyric sheet. Include SASE. Responds in 3 weeks. Uses variety of musical styles for commercials, promotion, TV, video presentations.

TIPS "Our clients and our needs change frequently."

ADVERTEL, INC.

P.O. Box 18053, Pittsburgh PA 15236-0053. (412)344-4700. Fax: (412)344-4712. E-mail: info@advertel.com. Website: www.advertel.com/home. **Contact:** Paul Beran, president/CEO. **Telephonic/Internet production company.** Clients include small and multinational companies. Estab. 1983. Uses the services of music houses and independent songwriters/composers for scoring of instrumentals (all varieties) and telephonic production. Commissions 3-4 composers/year. Pay varies. Buys all rights and phone exclusive rights.

HOW TO CONTACT Submit demo of previous work. Prefers CD. "Most compositions are 2 minutes strung together in 6, 12, 18 minute length productions." Does not return material; prefers to keep on file. Responds "right away if submission fills an immediate need."

MUSIC Uses all varieties, including unusual; mostly subdued music beds. Radio-type production used exclusively in telephone and Internet applications.

TIPS "Go for volume. We have continuous need for all varieties of music in 2 minute lengths. Advertel now produces a religious radio program called 'Prayer-in-the-Air.' Feel free to submit songs with lyrics taken from scripture. We also look for catchy, memorable melodies. For those pro bono submissions, no compensation is offered—only national recognition."

✪ ALLEGRO MUSIC

6516 Marquette St., Apt. E, Moorpark, CA 93021-3756. E-mail: dannymuse@roadrunner.com. Website: www.danielobrien.com. **Owner:** Daniel O'Brien. Scoring service, jingle/commercial music production

house. Clients include film-makers, advertisers, network promotions and aerobics. Estab. 1991. Uses the services of independent songwriters/composers and lyricists for scoring of films, TV, and broadcast commercials, jingles for ad agencies and promotions, and commercials for radio and TV. Commissions 3 composers and 1 lyricist/year. Pays 50% royalty. Buys one-time rights.

HOW TO CONTACT Does not accept unsolicited material. Query with résumé of credits or submit demo tape of previous work. Prefers CD, cassette and lyric sheet. Include SASE. Responds in 1 month (if interested).

MUSIC Varied: Contemporary to orchestral.

CEDAR CREST STUDIO

#17 CR 830, Henderson, AR 72544. Website: www.cedarcreststudio.com. **Contact:** Bob Ketchum, owner. **Audiovisual firm and jingle/commercial music production house.** Clients include corporate, industrial, sales, music publishing, training, educational, legal, medical, music, and Internet. Estab. 1973. Sometimes uses the services of independent songwriters/composers for background music for video productions, jingles for TV spots and commercials for radio and TV. Pays by the job or by royalties. Buys all rights or one-time rights.

HOW TO CONTACT Query with résumé of credits or submit demo tape of previous work. Prefers CD, cassette, or DVD. Does not return material. "We keep it on file for future reference." Responds in 2 months.

MUSIC Uses up-tempo pop (not too "rocky"), unobtrusive—no solos for commercials and background music for video presentations.

TIPS "Hang, hang, hang. Be open to suggestions. Improvise, adapt, overcome."

COMMUNICATIONS FOR LEARNING

395 Massachusetts Ave., Arlington, MA 02474. (781)641-2350. E-mail: comlearn@thecia.net. Website: www.communicationsforlearning.com. **Contact:** Jonathan L. Barkan, executive producer/director. Video, multimedia, exhibit and graphic design firm. Clients include multinationals, industry, government, institutions, local, national, and international nonprofits. Uses services of music houses and independent songwriters/composers as theme and background music for videos and multimedia. Com-

missions 1-2 composers/year. Pays $2,000-5,000/job and one-time use fees. Rights purchased vary.

HOW TO CONTACT Submit demo and work available for library use. Prefers CD to Web links. Does not return material; prefers to keep on file. "For each job we consider our entire collection." Responds in 3 months.

MUSIC Uses all styles of music for all sorts of assignments.

TIPS "Please don't call. Just send your best material available for library use on CD. We'll be in touch if a piece works and negotiate a price. Make certain your name and contact information are on the CD itself, not only on the cover letter."

DBF A MEDIA COMPANY

9683 Charles St., La Plata, MD 20646. (301)645-6110. E-mail: service@dbfmedia.com. Website: www.dbf-media.com. **Contact:** Randy Runyon, general manager. Video Production. Estab. 1981. Uses the services of music houses for background music for industrial, training, educational and promo videos, jingles, and commercials for radio and TV. Buys all rights. "All genre for MOH, industrial, training, video/photo montages and commercials."

HOW TO CONTACT Submit demo CD of previous work. Prefers CD or DVD with 5-8 songs and lead sheet. Include SASE, but prefers to keep material on file. Responds in 6 months.

○⊛ DISK PRODUCTIONS

1100 Perkins Rd., Baton Rouge, LA 70802. Fax: (225)343-5438. E-mail: disk_productions@yahoo.com. **Contact:** Joey Decker, director. **Jingle/production house.** Clients include advertising agencies and film companies. Estab. 1982. Uses the services of music houses, independent songwriters/composers and lyricists for scoring and background music for TV spots, films, and jingles for radio and TV. Commissions 7 songwriters/composers and 7 lyricists/year. Pays by the job. Buys all rights.

HOW TO CONTACT Submit demo of previous work. Prefers DVD, CD, cassette, or DAT. Does not return material. Responds in 2 weeks.

MUSIC Needs all types of music for jingles, music beds, or background music for TV and radio, etc.

TIPS "Advertising techniques change with time. Don't be locked in a certain style of writing. Give me music that I can't get from pay needle-drop."

⊛ FINE ART PRODUCTIONS/RICHIE SURACI PICTURES, MULTIMEDIA, INTERACTIVE

67 Maple St., Newburgh, NY 12550-4034. (914)527-9740. Fax: (845)561-5866. E-mail: rs7fap@bestweb.net. Website: www.idsi.net/~rs7fap/tentsales.htm. **Contact:** Richard Suraci, owner. Advertising agency, audiovisual firm, scoring service, **jingle/commercial music production house**, motion picture production company (Richie Suraci Pictures), and **music sound effect library**. Clients include corporate, industrial, motion picture, and broadcast firms. Estab. 1987. Uses services of independent songwriters/composers for scoring, background music and jingles for various projects and commercials for radio and TV. Commissions 1-2 songwriters or composers and 1-2 lyricists/year. Pays by the job, royalty, or by the hours. Buys all rights.

HOW TO CONTACT Submit demo tape of previous work or tape demonstrating composition skills, query with résumé of credits, or write or call first to arrange personal interview. Prefers CD, DVD, cassette (or $1/2$", $3/4$", or 1" videocassette) with as many songs as possible and lyric or lead sheets. Include SASE, but prefers to keep material on file. Responds in 1 year.

MUSIC Uses all types of music for all types of assignments.

HOME, INC.

165 Brookside Ave. Extension, Boston, MA 02135. E-mail: alanmichel@homeinc.org. Website: www.homeinc.org. **Director:** Alan Michel. Audiovisual firm and video production company. Clients include cable television, nonprofit organizations, pilot programs, entertainment companies, and industrial. Uses the services of music houses and independent songwriters/composers for scoring of music videos, background music, and commercials for TV. Commissions 2-5 songwriters/year. Pays up to $200-600/job. Buys all rights and one-time rights.

HOW TO CONTACT Submit demo tape of previous work. Prefers CD or website URL with 6 pieces. Does not return material; prefers to keep on file. Responds as projects require.

MUSIC Mostly synthesizer. Uses all styles of music for educational videos.

TIPS "Have a variety of products available and be willing to match your skills to the project and the budget."

K&R ALL MEDIA PRODUCTIONS LLC

(formerly K&R's Recording Studios) 28533 Greenfield, Southfield, MI 48076. (248)557-8276. E-mail: recordav@knr.net. Website: www.knr.net. **Contact:** Ken Glaza. Scoring service and **jingle/commercial music production house**. Clients include commercial and industrial firms. Services include sound for pictures (Foley, music, dialogue). Uses the services of independent songwriters/composers and lyricists for scoring of film and video, commercials and industrials, and jingles and commercials for radio and TV. Commissions 1 composer/month. Pays by the job. Buys all rights.

HOW TO CONTACT Submit demo tape of previous work. Prefers CD or VHS videocassette with 5-7 short pieces. "We rack your tape for client to judge." Does not return material.

TIPS "Keep samples short. Show me what you can do in five minutes. Go to knr.net 'free samples' and listen to the sensitivity expressed in emotional music."

KEN-DEL PRODUCTIONS INC.

First State Production Center, 1500 First State Blvd., Wilmington DE, 19804-3596. (302)999-1111. E-mail: info@ken-del.com. Website: www.ken-del.com. Estab. 1950. **Contact:** Edwin Kennedy, A&R manager. Clients include publishers, industrial firms and advertising agencies, how-to's and radio/TV. Uses services of songwriters for radio/TV commercials, jingles, and multimedia. Pays by the job. Buys all rights.

HOW TO CONTACT "Submit all inquiries and demos in any format to general manager." Does not return material. Will keep on file for 3 years. Generally responds in 1 month or less.

⬤✖ NOVUS COMMUNICATIONS

Cross media marketing and communications company. Clients include corporations and interactive media. Uses the services of music houses, independent songwriters/composers and lyricists for scoring, background music for documentaries, commercials, multimedia applications, website, film shorts, and commercials for radio and TV. Commissions 2 composers and 4 lyricists/year. Pay varies per job. Buys one-time rights.

HOW TO CONTACT *Request a submission of demo.* Query with résumé. Submit demo of work. Prefers CD with 2-3 songs. "We prefer to keep submitted

material on file, but will return material if SASE is enclosed. Responds in 6 weeks.

MUSIC Uses all styles for a variety of different assignments.

TIPS "Always present your best and don't add quantity to your demo. Novus is a creative marketing and communications company. We work with various public relations, artists managements, and legal advisors. We consult on multimedia events."

OMNI COMMUNICATIONS

Dept. SM, P.O. Box 302, Carmel, IN 46082-0302. (317)846-2345. E-mail: omni@omniproductions.com. Website: www.omniproductions.com. President: W. H. Long. Creative director: S.M. Long. Production manager: Jim Mullet. Television, digital media production, and audiovisual firm. Estab. 1978. Serves industrial, commercial, and educational clients. Uses the services of music houses and songwriters for scoring of films and television productions, DVDs, CD-ROMs, and Internet streams; background music for voice-overs; lyricists for original music and themes. Pays by the job. Buys all rights.

HOW TO CONTACT Submit demo tape of previous work. Prefers CD or DVD. Does not return material. Responds in 2 weeks.

MUSIC Varies with each and every project; from classical, contemporary to commercial industrial.

TIPS "Submit good demo tape with examples of your range to command the attention of our producers."

QUALLY & COMPANY INC.

1187 Wilmette Ave., Suite 160, Wilmette, IL 60091-2719. (312)280-1898. E-mail: ivamichael@hotmail.com. Website: www.quallycompany.com. **Contact:** Michael Iva, creative director. **Advertising agency.** Uses the services of music houses, independent songwriters/composers and lyricists for scoring, background music, and jingles for radio and TV commercials. Commissions 2-4 composers and 2-4 lyricists/year. Pays by the job. Buys various rights depending on deal.

HOW TO CONTACT Submit demo CD of previous work or query with résumé of credits. Include SASE, but prefers to keep material on file.

MUSIC Uses all kinds of music for commercials.

UTOPIAN EMPIRE CREATIVEWORKS

P.O. Box 9, Traverse City MI 49685-0009 or P.O. Box 458, Kapa'a (Kaua'i), HI 96746-0458. (231)943-5050 or (231)943-4000. E-mail: creativeservices@Utopi anEmpire.com. Website: www.UtopianEmpire.com. **Contact:** Ms. M'Lynn Hartwell, president. Web design, multimedia firm, and motion picture/video production company. Primarily serves commercial, industrial, and nonprofit clients. "We provide the following services: advertising, marketing, design/packaging, distribution and booking. Uses services of music houses, independent songwriters/composers for jingles and scoring of and background music for multi-image/multimedia, film and video." Negotiates pay. Buys all or one-time rights.

HOW TO CONTACT Submit CD of previous work, demonstrating composition skills or query with re-sume of credits. Prefers CD. Does not return material; prefers to keep on file. Responds only if interested.

MUSIC Uses mostly industrial/commercial themes.

⊗ VIDEO I-D, TELEPRODUCTIONS

Post production/teleproductions. Clients include law enforcement, industrial, and business. Uses the services of music houses and independent songwriters/composers for background music for video productions. Pays per job. Buys one-time rights.

HOW TO CONTACT Submit demo of previous work. Prefers CD with 5 songs and lyric sheet. Does not return material. Responds in 1 month.

PLAY PRODUCERS & PUBLISHERS

PLAY PRODUCERS

ARKANSAS REPERTORY THEATRE

601 Main, P.O. Box 110, Little Rock AR 72201. (501)378-0445. Website: www.therep.org. **Contact:** Robert Hupp, producing artistic director. Estab. 1976. Produces 6-10 plays and musicals/year. "We perform in a 354-seat house and also have a 99-seat 2nd stage." Pays 5-10% royalty or $75-150 per performance.

HOW TO CONTACT Query with synopsis, character breakdown, and set description. Include SASE. Responds in 6 months.

MUSICAL THEATER "Small casts are preferred, comedy or drama and prefer shows to run 1:45 to 2 hours maximum. Simple is better; small is better, but we do produce complex shows. We aren't interested in children's pieces, puppet shows or mime. We always like to receive a tape of the music with the book."

PRODUCTIONS *Disney's Beauty & the Beast*, by Woolverton/Ashman/Rice/Menken (musical retelling of the myth); *Crowns*, by Taylor/Cunningham/Marberry (on the significance of African-American women's hats); and *A Chorus Line*, by Kirkwood/Hamlisch/Kleban (auditions).

TIPS "Include a good cassette of your music, sung well, with the script."

WILLIAM CAREY UNIVERSITY DINNER THEATRE

William Carey University, Hattiesburg MS 39401. (601)318-6051. Website: www.wmcarey.edu. **Contact:** O.L. Quave, managing director. Play producer. Produces 2 musicals/year. "Our dinner theater operates only in summer and plays to family audiences." Payment negotiable.

HOW TO CONTACT Query with synopsis, character breakdown and set description. Does not return material. Responds in 1 month.

MUSICAL THEATER "Plays should be simply-staged, have small casts (8-10 maximum), and be suitable for family viewing; two hours maximum length. Score should require piano only, or piano, synthesizer."

PRODUCTIONS *Ring of Fire: The Johnny Cash Musical*; *Smoke on the Mountain*; *Spitfire Grill*; and *Pump Boys and Dinettes*.

CIRCA '21 DINNER PLAYHOUSE

1828 Third Ave., Rock Island IL 61201. (309)786-7733 ext 2. Website: www.circa21.com. Estab. 1977. Produces 1-2 plays and 4-5 musicals (1 new musical)/year. Plays produced for a general audience. Three children's works/year, concurrent with major productions. Payment is negotiable.

HOW TO CONTACT Query with synopsis, character breakdown, and set description or submit complete manuscript, score and tape of songs. Include SASE. Responds in 3 months.

MUSICAL THEATER "We produce both full length and one act children's musicals. Folk or fairy tale themes. Works that do not condescend to a young audience yet are appropriate for entire family. We're also seeking full-length, small cast musicals suitable for a broad audience." Would also consider original music for use in a play being developed.

PRODUCTIONS *A Closer Walk with Patsy Cline*, *Swingtime Canteen*, *Forever Plaid*, and *Lost Highway*.

TIPS "Small, upbeat, tourable musicals (like *Pump Boys*) and bright musically-sharp children's productions (like those produced by Prince Street Players) work best. Keep an open mind. Stretch to encompass a musical variety—different keys, rhythms, musical ideas and textures."

FOOLS COMPANY, INC.

423 W, 46th St., New York NY 10036. (212)307-6000. Collaborative new and experimental works producer. Estab. 1970. Produces 1 play and 1 musical (1 new musical) depending on available funding. "Audience is comprised of hip, younger New Yorkers. Plays are performed at various venues in NYC." Pay is negotiable.

MUSICAL THEATER "We seek new and unusual, contemporary and experimental material. We would like small, easy-to-tour productions. Nothing classical, folkloric or previously produced." Would also consider working with composers in collaboration or original music for use in plays being developed.

PRODUCTIONS Recent: *Rug Burn*; *Cathleen's Corsage* (alternative performance); and *Blunt Passage* (original drama).

TIPS "Come work in NYC!"

LA JOLLA PLAYHOUSE

P.O. Box 12039, La Jolla CA 92039. (858)550-1070. Fax: (858)550-1075. E-mail: information@ljp.org. Website: www.lajollaplayhouse.org. **Contact:** Shirley Fishman, director of play development; Christopher Ashley, artistic director. Estab. 1947. Produces 6-show season including 1-2 new musicals/year. Audience is University of California students to senior citizens. Performance spaces include a large proscenium theatre with 492 seats, a $^3/_4$ thrust (384 seats), and a black box with up to 400 seats.

HOW TO CONTACT Query with synopsis, character breakdown, 10-page dialogue sample, demo CD. Include SASE. Responds in 1-2 months.

MUSICAL THEATER "We prefer contemporary music but not necessarily a story set in contemporary times. Retellings of classic stories can enlighten us about the times we live in. For budgetary reasons, we'd prefer a smaller cast size."

PRODUCTIONS *Cry-Baby*, book and lyrics by Thomas Meehan and Mark O'Donnell, music by David Javerbaum and Adam Schlesinger; *Dracula, The Musical*, book and lyrics by Don Black and Christopher Hampton, music by Frank Wildhorn (adaptation of Bram Stoker's novel); *Thoroughly Modern Millie*, book by Richard Morris and Dick Scanlan, new music by Jeanine Tesori, new lyrics by Dick Scanlan (based on the 1967 movie); and *Jane Eyre*, book and additional lyrics by John Cairo, music and lyrics by Paul Gordon (adaptation of Charlotte Bronte's novel).

LOS ANGELES DESIGNERS' THEATRE

P.O. Box 1883, Studio City CA 91614. (323)650-9600. Fax: (323)654-3210. E-mail: ladesigners@juno.com. **Contact:** Richard Niederberg, artistic director. Play producer. Estab. 1970. Produces 20-25 plays and 8-10 new musicals/year. Audience includes Hollywood production executives in film, TV, records and multimedia. Plays are produced at several locations, primarily Studio City, California. Pay is negotiable.

HOW TO CONTACT Query first. Does not return material. Responds only if interested. *Send proposals only.*

MUSICAL THEATER "We seek out controversial material. Street language OK, nudity is fine, religious themes, social themes, political themes are encouraged. Our audience is very 'jaded' as it consists of TV, motion picture and music publishing executives who have 'seen it all'." Does not wish to see bland, 'safe' material. We like first productions. In the cover letter state in great detail the proposed involvement of the songwriter, other than as a writer (i.e., director, actor, singer, publicist, designer, etc.). Also, state if there are any liens on the material or if anything has been promised."

PRODUCTIONS *St. Tim*, by Fred Grab (historical '60s musical); *Slipper and the Rose* (gang musical); and *1593—The Devils Due* (historical musical).

TIPS "Make it very 'commercial' and inexpensive to produce. Allow for non-traditional casting. Be prepared with ideas as to how to transform your work to film or videotaped entertainment."

NORTH SHORE MUSIC THEATRE

62 Dunham Rd., Beverly MA 01915. (978)232-7200. Fax: (978)921-9999. E-mail: NorthShoreMusicTheatre@nsmt.org. Website: www.nsmt.org. **Contact:** Bill Hanney, owner/producer. Estab. 1955. Produces 1 Shakespearian play and 7 musicals (1 new musical)/year. General audiences. Performance space is an 1,500-seat arena theater, 120-seat workshop. Pays royalty (all done via individual commission agreements).

HOW TO CONTACT Submit synopsis and CD of songs. Include SASE. Responds within 6 months.

MUSICAL THEATER Prefers full-length adult pieces not necessarily arena-theater oriented. Cast sizes from 1 to 30; orchestras from 1 to 16.

PRODUCTIONS *Tom Jones*, by Paul Leigh, George Stiles; *I Sent A Letter to My Love*, by Melissa Manchester and Jeffrey Sweet; *Just So*, by Anthony Drewe & George Stiles (musical based on Rudyard Kipling's fables); *Letters from 'Nam*, by Paris Barclay (Vietnam War experience as told through letters from GIs); and *Friendship of the Sea*, by Michael Wartofsky & Kathleen Cahill (New England maritime adventure musical).

TIPS "Keep at it!"

THE OPEN EYE THEATER

P.O. Box 959, 960 Main St., Margaretville NY 12455. Phone/Fax: (845)586-1660. E-mail: openeye@catskill.net. Website: www.theopeneye.org. **Contact:** Amie Brockway, producing artistic director. Play producer. Estab. 1972. Produces approximately 3 full length or 3 new plays for multigenerational audiences. Pays on a fee basis.

HOW TO CONTACT Query first. "A manuscript will be accepted and read only if it is a play for all ages and is: 1) Submitted by a recognized literary agent; 2) Requested or recommended by a staff or company member; or 3) Recommended by a professional colleague with whose work we are familiar. Playwrights may submit a one-page letter of inquiry including a very brief plot synopsis. Please enclose a self-addressed (but not stamped) envelope. We will reply only if we want you to submit the script (within several months)."

MUSICAL THEATER "The Open Eye Theater is a not-for-profit professional company working in a community context. Through the development, production and performance of plays for all ages, artists and audiences are challenged and given the opportunity to grow in the arts. In residence, on tour, and in the classroom, The Open Eye Theater strives to stimulate, educate, entertain, inspire and serve as a creative resource."

PRODUCTIONS *The Tempest* and *As You Like It* by Shakespeare; John Dilworth Newman's *A Year Down Yonder* based on the novel for young readers by Richard Peck; Willy Russell's *Shirley Valentine*; Sandra Fenichel Asher's *The Princess and the Goblin* and *Keeping Mr. Lincoln*; Robert Harling's *Steel Magnolias*; Amie Brockway's *The Cricket on the Hearth*, based on the book by Charles Dickens.

PRIMARY STAGES

307 W. 38th St., Suite 1510, New York NY 10018. (212)840-9705. Fax: (212)840-9725. E-mail: info@primarystages.com. Website: www.primarystages.com. **Contact:** Michelle Bossy, associate artistic director. Play producer. Estab. 1984. Produces 4-5 plays/year. "New York theater-going audience representing a broad cross-section, in terms of age, ethnicity, and economic backgrounds. 199-seat, Off-Broadway theater."

HOW TO CONTACT *"No unsolicited scripts accepted. Submissions by agents only."* Include SASE. Responds in up to 8 months.

MUSICAL THEATER "We are looking for work of heightened theatricality, that challenges realism—musical plays that go beyond film and televisions standard fare. We are looking for small cast shows under 6 characters total, with limited sets. We are interested in original works, that have not been produced in New York."

PRODUCTIONS *I Sent a Letter to My Love*, by Melissa Manchester/Jeffrey Sweet; *Nightmare Alley*, by Jonathan Brielle; *Call the Children Home*, by Mildred Kayden and Thomas Babe; *Adrift in Macao*, by Christopher Durang and Peter Melnick.

PRINCE MUSIC THEATER

Play producer. Produces 4-5 musicals/year. "Our average audience member is in their mid-40s. We perform to ethnically diverse houses."

HOW TO CONTACT Submit two-page synopsis with tape or CD of 4 songs. Include SASE. "May include complete script, but be aware that response is at least 10 months."

TIPS "Innovative topics and use of media, music, technology a plus. Sees trends of arts in technology (interactive theater, virtual reality, sound design); works are shorter in length (1-1 & 1/2 hours with no intermissions or 2 hours with intermission)."

THE REPERTORY THEATRE OF ST. LOUIS

P.O. Box 191730, 130 Edgar Road, St. Louis MO 63119. (314)968-7340. E-mail: mail@repstl.org; swoolf@repstl.org. Website: www.repstl.org. **Contact:** Steven Woolf, artistic director. Play producer. Estab. 1966. Produces 9 plays and 1 or 2 musicals/year. "Conservative regional theater audience. We produce all our work at the Loretto Hilton Theatre." Pays by royalty.

HOW TO CONTACT Query with synopsis, character breakdown, and set description. Does not return material. Responds in 2 years.

MUSICAL THEATER "We want plays with a small cast and simple setting. No children's shows or foul language. After a letter of inquiry we would prefer script and demo tape."

PRODUCTIONS *Almost September* and *Esmeralda*, by David Schechter and Steve Lutvak; *Jack*, by Barbara Field and Hiram Titus; and *Young Rube*, by John Pielmeier and Nattie Selman, *Ace* by Robert Taylor and Richard Oberacker.

SHAKESPEARE SANTA CRUZ

Theater Arts Center, U.C.S.C., 1156 High Street, Santa Cruz CA 95064. (831)459-2121. Fax: (831)459-3316. E-mail: mbarrice@ucsc.edu. Website: www.shakespearesantacruz.org. **Contact:** Marco Barricelli, artistic director. Play producer. Estab. 1982. Produces 4 plays/year. Performance spaces are an outdoor redwood grove; and an indoor 540-seat thrust. Pay is negotiable.

HOW TO CONTACT Query first. Include SASE. Responds in 2 months.

MUSICAL THEATER "Shakespeare Santa Cruz produces musicals in its Winter Holiday Season (Oct-Dec). We are also interested in composers' original music for pre-existing plays—including songs, for example, for Shakespeare's plays."

PRODUCTIONS *Cinderella*, by Kate Hawley (book and lyrics) and Gregg Coffin (composer); and *Gretel and Hansel*, by Kate Hawley (book and lyrics) and composer Craig Bohmler; *The Princess and the Pea*, by Kate Hawley (book and lyrics) and composer

Adam Wernick; *Sleeping Beauty*, by Kate Hawley (book and lyrics) and composer Adam Wernick.

TIPS "Always contact us before sending material."

THUNDER BAY THEATRE

400 N. Second Ave., Alpena MI 49707. (989)354-2267. E-mail: TBT@ThunderBayTheatre.com; Artistic-Director@ThunderBayTheatre.com. Website: www.thunderbaytheatre.com. Artistic Director: J.R. Rodriguez. Play producer. Estab. 1967. Produces 12 productions/year including 5 musicals and 7 plays. Performance space is thrust stage. Pays variable royalty or per performance.

HOW TO CONTACT Submit complete manuscript, score and tape of songs. Include SASE.

MUSICAL THEATER Small cast. Not equipped for large sets. Considers original background music for use in a play being developed or for use in a pre-existing play.

PRODUCTIONS 2009 Musicals *Brigadoon, The Producers, The Rat Pack Lounge, White Christmas, Beauty and the Beast.*

WEST END ARTISTS

c/o St. Luke's Theatre, 308 W. 46th St., New York NY 10036. (212)947-3499. E-mail: stlukestheatre@gmail.com. Play producer. Estab. 1983. "We operate St. Luke's Theatre, Actors Temple Theatre, and Theatres at 45 Bleecker St. in New York City, and Whitmore-Lindley Theatre Center in Los Angeles." Produces 5 plays and 3 new musicals/year. Audience "covers a broad spectrum, from general public to heavy theater/film/TV industry crowds. Pays 6% royalty.

HOW TO CONTACT Submit complete manuscript, score and tape of songs. Include SASE. Responds in 3 months.

MUSICAL THEATER "Prefer small-cast musicals and revues. Full length preferred. Interested in children's shows also." Cast size: "Maximum 12; exceptional material with larger casts will be considered."

PRODUCTIONS Off-Broadway: *Picon Pie*-Lambs Theatre (2004-05); *Trolls*-Actors Playhouse, (2005); *The Big Voice: God or Merman?*-Actors Temple Theatre (2006-07); *Danny and Sylvia: The Danny Kaye Musical*-St. Luke's Theatre (2009-10); *Dietrich and Chevalier: The Musical*-St. Luke's Theatre (2010).

TIPS "If you feel every word or note you have written is sacred and chiseled in stone and are unwilling to work collaboratively with a professional director, don't bother to submit."

PLAY PUBLISHERS

BAKER'S PLAYS

45 W. 25th St., New York NY 10010. (323)876-0579. Fax: (323)876-5482. E-mail: publications@bakers plays.com. Website: www.bakersplays.com. Play publisher. Estab. 1845. Publishes 25-30 plays and 5-10 new musicals/year. Plays are used by children's theaters, junior and senior high schools, colleges, and community theaters. Pays negotiated book and production royalty.

◯ See the listing for Baker's Plays High School Playwriting Contest in the "Contests & Awards" section.

HOW TO CONTACT "Our submission policy has changed. As of November 1, 2010, Baker's Plays will accept only solicited and agent submitted manuscripts. Playwrights must send query letters regarding unsolicited submissions." See website for more details.

MUSICAL THEATER "Seeking musicals for teen production and children's theater production. We prefer large cast, contemporary musicals which are easy to stage and produce. Plot your shows strongly, keep your scenery and staging simple, your musical numbers and choreography easily explained and blocked out. Music must be camera-ready."

PRODUCTIONS *Stone Soup* by Anne Glasner & Betty Hollinger (children's musical); *A Walk in the Sky,* book and lyrics by Dale Wasserman, music by Allan Jay Friedman (family musical); *Beanstalk! The Musical!* book by Ross Mihalko and Donna Swift, music by Linda Berg, lyrics by Ross Mihalko (children's musical).

HEUER PUBLISHING CO.

P.O. Box 248, Cedar Rapids IA 52406. Main Office: 211 First Ave. SE, Cedar Rapids IA 52401. (319)368-8008. Fax: (319)368-8011. E-mail: editor@hitplays.com. Website: www.hitplays.com. Play publisher. Estab. 1928. Publishes plays, musicals, operas/operettas, and guides (choreography, costume, production/staging) for amateur and professional markets, including junior and senior high schools, college/university and community theaters. Focus includes comedy, drama, fantasy, mystery, and holiday. Pays by percentage royalty or outright purchase.

HOW TO CONTACT Query with musical CD/tape or submit complete manuscript and score. Include SASE. Responds in 2 months.

MUSICAL THEATER "We prefer one, two or three act comedies or mystery-comedies with a large number of characters."

PUBLICATIONS *Happily Ever After*, by Allen Koepke (musical fairy tale); *Brave Buckaroo*, by Renee J. Clark (musical melodrama); and *Pirate Island*, by Martin Follose (musical comedy).

TIPS "We are willing to review single-song submissions as cornerstone piece for commissioned works. Special interest focus in multicultural, historic, classic literature, teen issues, and biographies."

CLASSICAL PERFORMING ARTS

Finding an audience is critical to the composer of orchestral music. Fortunately, baby boomers are swelling the ranks of classical music audiences and bringing with them a taste for fresh, innovative music. So the climate is fair for composers seeking their first performance.

Finding a performance venue is particularly important because once a composer has his work performed for an audience and establishes himself as a talented newcomer, it can lead to more performances and commissions for new works.

BEFORE YOU SUBMIT

Be aware that most classical music organizations are nonprofit groups, and don't have a large budget for acquiring new works. It takes a lot of time and money to put together an orchestral performance of a new composition, therefore these groups are quite selective when choosing new works to perform. Don't be disappointed if the payment offered by these groups is small or even nonexistent. What you gain is the chance to have your music performed for an appreciative audience. Also realize that many classical groups are under-staffed, so it may take longer than expected to hear back on your submission. It pays to be patient, and employ diplomacy, tact, and timing in your follow-up.

In this section you will find listings for classical performing arts organizations throughout the U.S. But if you have no prior performances to your credit, it's a good idea to begin with a small chamber orchestra, for example. Smaller symphony and chamber orchestras are usually more inclined to experiment with new works. A local university or conservatory of music, where you may already have contacts, is a great place to start.

All of the groups listed in this section are interested in hearing new works from contemporary classical composers. Pay close attention to the music needs of each group, and when you find one you feel might be interested in your music, follow submission guidelines carefully.

ACADIANA SYMPHONY ORCHESTRA

412 Travis St., Lafayette LA 70503. (337)232-4277. Fax: (337)237-4712. E-mail: executivedirector@aca dianasymphony.org. Website: www.acadianasym phony.org. **Contact**: Jenny Krueger, executive director. Music director: Mariusz Smolij. Symphony orchestra. Estab. 1984. Members are amateurs and professionals. Performs 20 concerts/year, including 1 new work. Commissions 1 new work/year. Performs in 2,230-seat hall with "wonderful acoustics." Pays "according to the type of composition."

HOW TO CONTACT Call first. Does not return material. Responds in 2 months.

MUSIC Full orchestra: 10 minutes at most. Reduced orchestra, educational pieces: short, up to 5 minutes.

PERFORMANCES Quincy Hilliard's *Universal Covenant* (orchestral suite); James Hanna's *In Memoriam* (strings/elegy); and Gregory Danner's *A New Beginning* (full orchestra fanfare).

THE AMERICAN BOYCHOIR

19 Lambert Dr., Princeton NJ 08540. (609)924-5858. Fax: (609)924-5812. E-mail: admissions@american boychoir.org. Website: www.americanboychoir.org. General manager: Christie Starrett-Guillermo. Music director: Fernando Malvar-Ruiz. Professional boychoir. Estab. 1937. Members are musically talented boys in grades 4-8. Performs 150 concerts/year. Commissions 1 new work approximately every 3 years. Actively seeks high quality arrangements. Performs national and international tours, orchestral engagements, church services, workshops, school programs, local concerts, and at corporate and social functions.

HOW TO CONTACT Submit complete score. Include SASE. Responds in 1 year.

MUSIC Choral works in unison, SA, SSA, SSAA, or SATB division; unaccompanied and with piano or organ; occasional chamber orchestra or brass ensemble. Works are usually sung by 28 to 60 boys. Composers must know boychoir sonority.

PERFORMANCES *Four Seasons*, by Michael Torke (orchestral-choral); *Garden of Light*, by Aaron Kernis (orchestral-choral); *Reasons for Loving the Harmonica*, by Libby Larsen (piano); and *Songs Eternity*, by Steven Paulus (piano).

AMERICAN OPERA MUSICAL THEATRE CO.

400 W. 43rd St. #19D, New York NY 10036. (212)594-1839. Opera and musical theatre producing/presenting organization. Estab. 1995. Members are professionals with varying degrees of experience. Performs 2 operas, many concerts/year and 1 musical theater production each year. Audience is sophisticated and knowledgeable about music and theater. "We rent performance spaces in New York, and are either sponsored by a presenter, or are paid performance fees for opera and concerts."

HOW TO CONTACT "We are only accepting photos and resumes at this time—no CDs or DVDs."

MUSIC "Must be vocal (for opera or for music theater). Cast should not exceed 10. Orchestration should not exceed 30, smaller groups preferred. No rock 'n' roll, brassy pop."

PERFORMANCES Nationally and internationally: Puccini's *La Boheme*; Verdi's *Rigoletto*; *The Jewel Box*; *Iolanta*; *La Molinara,* and *The World Goes Round.*

ANDERSON SYMPHONY ORCHESTRA

1124 Meridian Plaza, Anderson IN 46016. (765)644-2111. E-mail: aso@andersonsymphony.org. Website: www.andersonsymphony.org. **Contact:** Dr. Richard Sowers, conductor. Symphony orchestra. Estab. 1967. Members are professionals. Performs 7 concerts/year. Performs for typical Midwestern audience in a 1,500-seat restored Paramount Theatre. Pay negotiable.

HOW TO CONTACT Query first. Include SASE. Responds in several months.

MUSIC "Shorter lengths better; concerti OK; difficulty level: mod high; limited by typically 3 full service rehearsals."

THE ATLANTA YOUNG SINGERS OF CALLANWOLDE

980 Briarcliff Rd. N.E., Atlanta GA 30306. (404)873-3365. Fax: (404)873-0756. E-mail: info@aysc.org. Website: www.aysc.org. **Contact:** Paige F. Mathis, music director. Children's chorus. Estab. 1975. Performs 3 major concerts/year as well as invitational performances and coproductions with other Atlanta arts organizations. Audience consists of community members, families, alumni, and supporters. Performs most often at churches. Pay is negotiable.

HOW TO CONTACT Submit complete score and tape of piece(s). Include SASE. Responds in accordance with request.

MUSIC "Subjects and styles appealing to 3rd-12th grade boys and girls. Contemporary concerns of the world of interest. Unusual sacred, folk, classic style. Internationally and ethnically bonding. Medium difficulty preferred, with or without keyboard accompaniment."

TIPS "Our mission is to promote service and growth through singing."

AUGSBURG CHOIR

Augsburg College, 2211 Riverside Ave. S, Minneapolis MN 55454. (612)330-1265. E-mail: brauer@augsburg.edu. Website: www.augsburg.edu. **Contact:** Tina Brauer, coordinator. **Director of Choral Activities**: Peter A. Hendrickson. Vocal ensemble (SATB choir). Members are amateurs. Performs 25 concerts/year, including 1-6 new works. Commissions 0-2 composers or new works/year. Audience is all ages, "sophisticated and unsophisticated." Concerts are performed in churches, concert halls, and schools. Pays for outright purchase.

HOW TO CONTACT Query first. Include SASE. Responds in 1 month.

MUSIC Seeking "sacred choral pieces, no more than 5-7 minutes long, to be sung a cappella or with obbligato instrument. Can contain vocal solos. We have 50-60 members in our choir."

PERFORMANCES Carol Barnett's *Spiritual Journey*; Steven Heitzeg's *Litanies for the Living* (choral/orchestral); and Morton Lanriclsen's *O Magnum Mysteries* (a cappella choral).

BILLINGS SYMPHONY

2721 Second Ave N., Suite 350, Billings MT 59101. (406)252-3610. Fax: (406)252-3353. E-mail: symphony@billingssymphony.org. Website: www.billingssymphony.org. **Contact:** Sandra Culhane, executive director. Symphony orchestra, orchestra, and chorale. Estab. 1950. Members are professionals and amateurs. Performs 12-15 concerts/year, including 6-7 new works. Traditional audience. Performs at Alberta Bair Theater (capacity 1,416). Pays by outright purchase (or rental).

HOW TO CONTACT Query first. Include SASE. Responds in 2 weeks.

MUSIC Any style. Traditional notation preferred.

PERFORMANCES 2010 Symphony in the Park includes: "Michael Jackson Spectacular"; "Glee" inspired versions of "Jump" by Van Halen and "Don't Stop Believing" by Journey. Highlights from our upcoming 60th Anniversary Season: Jenkins' "Palladio"; Mussorgsky's "Night on Bald Mountain"; A Tribute to the 50s Jukebox, and finale from Dvorak's "New World" Symphony.

TIPS "Write what you feel (be honest) and sharpen your compositional and craftsmanship skills."

BIRMINGHAM-BLOOMFIELD SYMPHONY ORCHESTRA

P.O. Box 1925, Birmingham MI 48012. (248)352-2276. E-mail: bbso@bbso.org. Website: www.bbso.org. **Contact:** Charles Greenwell, music director and conductor. Conductor laureate: Felix Resnick. Executive director: Maureen Kickham. Symphony orchestra. Estab. 1975. Members are professionals. Performs 5 concerts including 1 new work/year. Commissions 1 composer or new work/year "with grants." Performs for middle-to-upper class audience at Temple Beth El's Sanctuary. Pays per performance "depending upon grant received."

HOW TO CONTACT Query first. Does not return material. Responds in 6 months.

MUSIC "We are a symphony orchestra but also play pops. Usually 3 works on program (2 hrs.) Orchestra size 65-75. If pianist is involved, they must rent piano."

PERFORMANCES Brian Belanger's *Tuskegee Airmen Suite* (symphonic full orchestra); Larry Nazer & Friends' *Music from "Warm" CD* (jazz with full orchestra); and Mark Gottlieb's *Violin Concerto for Orchestra* (new world premiere, 2006).

THE BOSTON PHILHARMONIC

295 Huntington Ave., Suite 210, Boston MA 02115. (617)236-0999. E-mail: info@bostonphil.org. Website: www.bostonphil.org. **Music director:** Benjamin Zander. Symphony orchestra. Estab. 1979. Members are professionals, amateurs, and students. Performs 2 concerts/year. Audience is ages 30-70. Performs at New England Conservatory's Jordan Hall, Boston's Symphony Hall, and Sanders Theatre in Cambridge. Both Jordan Hall and Sanders Theatre are small (approximately 1,100 seats) and very intimate.

HOW TO CONTACT *Does not accept new music at this time.*

MUSIC Full orchestra only.

PERFORMANCES Dutilleux' *Tout un monde lointain* for cello and orchestra (symphonic); Bernstein's *Fancy Free* (symphonic/jazzy); Copland's *El Salon Mexico* (symphonic); Gershwin's *Rhapsody in Blue*; Shostakovitch's *Symphony No. 10*; Harbison's *Concerto for Oboe*; Holst's *The Planet Suite*; Schwantner's *New Morning for the World*; Berg's *Seven Early Songs*; and Ive's *The Unanswered Question*.

BRAVO! L.A.

(818)892-8737. Fax: (818)892-1227. E-mail: info@bravo-la.com. Website: www.bravo-la.com. **Contact:** Cellist Dr. Janice Foy, director. An umbrella organization of recording/touring musicians, formed in 1994. Includes the following musical ensembles: the New American Quartet (string quartet); the Ascending Wave (harp/cello duo); Celllissimo! L.A. (cello ensemble); Sierra Chamber Players (includes piano with strings or other combos); Trio Fantastico (piano, clarinet, and cello); the Happy Band and the World Peace Orchestra (jazz groups playing all styles). The latest combo is solo cello with flamenco dancer, Jani Quintero.

HOW TO CONTACT Submit scores/tape of pieces. Include SASE. Responds in a few months. "We also record DEMOS for those needing entry into various situations and we use a DEMO rate through the Musicians Union Local 47 as our contract for that. If you want to do a Limited Pressing recording, that also goes through the Union with an appropriate contract."

MUSIC "We do all styles from classical to jazz. You can hear examples of most of the above ensembles on the site. You may also read about the latest musical antics of these musicians at the site."

TIPS "Let Bravo! L.A. know about your latest or upcoming performances and if you have a tape/CD of it, please forward or send an audio clip! If you have trouble getting through the spam blocker, let me know! We do not provide funding but there are many different grants out there for different situations. Good luck!"

☻ CALGARY BOYS CHOIR

4825 Mt. Royal Gate SW, Calgary, AB, T3E 6K6 Canada. (403)440-6821. Fax: (403)440-6594. E-mail: lfcrawford@shaw.ca. Website: www.wix.com/levendis99/calgaryboyschoir. **Contact:** Paul Grindlay, artistic director. Boys choir. Estab. 1973. Members are amateurs age 5 and up. Performs 5-10 concerts/year including 1-2 new works. Pay negotiable.

HOW TO CONTACT Query first. Submit complete score and tape of piece(s). Include SASE. Responds in 6 weeks. Does not return material.

MUSIC "Style fitting for boys choir. Lengths depending on project. Orchestration preferable a cappella/for piano/sometimes orchestra."

PERFORMANCES Dr. William Jordan's *City of Peace* (world premiere Wednesday September 11, 2002); Lydia Adam's arrangement of *Mi'kmaq Honour Song* (May 26, 2002); *A Child's Evening Prayer*, Dr. Allan Bevan (May 10, 2008).

☻ CANADIAN OPERA COMPANY

227 Front St. E, Toronto ON M5A 1E8 Canada. (416)363-6671. Fax: (416)363-5584. E-mail: info@coc.ca; music@coc.ca. Website: www.coc.ca. **Contact:** Alexander Neef, general director. Opera company. Estab. 1950. Members are professionals. 68-72 performances, including a minimum of 1 new work/year. Pays by contract.

HOW TO CONTACT Submit complete CDs or DVDs of vocal and/or operatic works. "Vocal works, please." Include SASE. Responds in 5 weeks.

MUSIC Vocal works, operatic in nature. "Do not submit works which are not for voice. Ask for requirements for the Composers-In-Residence program."

PERFORMANCES Dean Burry's *Brothers Grimm* (children's opera, 50 minutes long); Dean Burry's *Isis and the Seven Scorpions* (45-minute opera for children); James Rolfe's *Swoon:* James Rolfe's *Donna* (work title for forthcoming work); *Nixon in China* by John Adams; *L'Amour Do Loin* by Saariaho.

TIPS "We have a Composers-In-Residence program which is open to Canadian composers or landed immigrants."

CANTATA ACADEMY

CHORALE P.O. Box 1958, Royal Oak MI 48084. (313)248-7282. E-mail: cantata@cantataacademy.org. Website: http://cantataacademy.org. **Contact:** Ashley M. Prescott, business manager; Susan Catanese, director. Vocal ensemble. Estab. 1961. Members are professionals. Performs 10-12 concerts/year including 1-3 new works. "We perform in churches and small auditoriums throughout the Metro Detroit area for audiences of about 500 people." Pays variable rate for outright purchase.

HOW TO CONTACT Submit complete score. Include SASE. Responds in 3 months.

MUSIC Four-part a cappella and keyboard accompanied works, two and three-part works for men's or women's voices. Some small instrumental ensemble accompaniments acceptable. Work must be suitable for forty-voice choir. No works requiring orchestra or large ensemble accompaniment. No pop.

PERFORMANCES Libby Larsen's *Missa Gaia:*

Mass for the Earth (SATB, string quartet, oboe, percussion, 4-hand piano); Dede Duson's *To Those Who See* (SATB, SSA); and Sarah Hopkins's *Past Life Melodies* (SATB with Harmonic Overtone Singing); Eric Whiteacre *Five Hebrew Love Songs*; Robert Convery's *Songs of the Children*.

TIPS "Be patient. Would prefer to look at several different samples of work at one time."

CARMEL SYMPHONY ORCHESTRA

P.O. Box 761, Carmel IN 46082. (317)844-9717. Fax: (317)844-9916. E-mail: info@carmelsymphony.org. Website: www.carmelsymphony.org. **Contact**: Allen Davis, president/CEO. Symphony orchestra. Estab. 1976. Members are paid and nonpaid professionals. Performs 15 concerts/year, including 1-2 new works. Performs in a 1,600-seat Palladium at the Center for the Performing Arts.

HOW TO CONTACT *Query first.* Include SASE. Responds in 3 months.

MUSIC "Full orchestra works, 5-60 minutes in length. Parents are encouraged to bring a child. 85-piece orchestra, medium difficult to difficult.

PERFORMANCES Brahms' *Concerto in D Major for Violin and Orchestra*, Op. 77; Debussy's "La Mer"; Ravel's Second Suite from "Daphnis and Chloe"; Dvorak's *Carnival Overture*, Op. 92; and Sibelius' *Symphony No. 5* in E-flat Major, Op. 82. Outstanding guest artists include Michael Feinstein, Sylvia McNair, Cameron Carpenter, Dale Clevenger, and Angela Brown.

CHATTANOOGA GIRLS CHOIR

1831 Hickory Valley Rd. Suite 400, Chattanooga TN 37421. (423)296-1006. E-mail: office@chattanoogagirlschoir.com. Website: chattanoogagirlschoir.com. **Contact**: Nicole Knauss, executive director. Vocal ensemble. Estab. 1986. Members are amateurs. Performs 2 concerts/year including at least 1 new work. Audience consists of cultural and civic organizations and national and international tours. Performance space includes concert halls and churches. Pays for outright purchase or per performance.

HOW TO CONTACT Query first. Include SASE. Responds in 6 weeks.

MUSIC Seeks renaissance, baroque, classical, romantic, twentieth century, folk and musical theatre for young voices of up to 8 minutes. Performers include 5 treble choices: 4th grade (2 pts.); 5th grade (2 pts.) (SA); grades 6-9 (3 pts.) (SSA); grades 10-12 (3-4 pts.) (SSAA); and a combined choir: grades 6-12 (3-4 pts.) (SSAA). Medium level of difficulty. "Avoid extremely high Tessitura Sop I and extremely low Tessitura Alto II."

PERFORMANCES Jan Swafford's *Iphigenia Book: Meagher* (choral drama); Penny Tullock's *How Can I Keep from Singing* (Shaker hymn).

CHEYENNE SYMPHONY ORCHESTRA

1904 Thomes Ave., Cheyenne WY 82001. (307)778-8561. E-mail: executivedirector@cheyennesymphony. org. Website: www.cheyennesymphony.org. **Contact:** Kim E. Lovett, executive director. Symphony orchestra. Estab. 1955. Members are professionals. Performs 5-6 concerts/year. "Orchestra performs for a conservative, mid-to-upper income audience of 1,200 season members."

HOW TO CONTACT Query first to music director William Intriligator. Does not return material.

CIMARRON CIRCUIT OPERA COMPANY

P.O. Box 1085, Norman OK 73070. (405)364-8962. Fax: (405)321-5842. E-mail: info@cimarronopera. org. Website: www.ccocopera.org. **Contact:** Kevin W. Smith, music director. Opera company. Estab. 1975. Members are semiprofessional. Performs 75 concerts/year including 1-2 new works. Commissions 1 or less new work/year. "CCOC performs for children across the state of Oklahoma and for a dedicated audience in central Oklahoma. As a touring company, we adapt to the performance space provided, ranging from a classroom to a full raised stage." Pay is negotiable.

HOW TO CONTACT Query first. Does not return material. Responds in 6 months.

MUSIC "We are seeking operas or operettas in English only. We would like to begin including new, American works in our repertoire. Children's operas should be no longer than 45 minutes and require no more than a synthesizer for accompaniment. Adult operas should be appropriate for families, and may require either full orchestration or synthesizer. CCOC is a professional company whose members have varying degrees of experience, so any difficulty level is appropriate. There should be a small to moderate number of principals. Children's work should have no more than four principals. Our slogan is 'Opera is a family thing to do.' If we cannot market a work to families, we do not want to see it."

PERFORMANCES Menotti's *Amahl & the Night Visitors*; and Barab's *La Pizza Con Funghi*.

TIPS "45-minute fairy tale-type children's operas with possibly a 'moral' work well for our market. Looking for works appealing to K-8 grade students. No more than four principles."

CONNECTICUT CHORAL ARTISTS/ CONCORA

90 Main St., New Britain CT 06051. (860)293-0567. Fax: (860)244-0073. E-mail: contact@concora.org; cbell@concora.org. Website: www.concora.org. **Contact:** Claudia Bell, executive director. Richard Coffey, artistic director. Professional concert choir, also an 18-voice ensemble dedicated to contemporary a cappella works. Estab. 1974. Members are professionals. Performs 15 concerts/year, including 3-5 new works. "Mixed audience in terms of age and background; performs in various halls and churches in the region." Payment "depends upon underwriting we can obtain for the project."

HOW TO CONTACT Query first. "No unsolicited submissions accepted." Include SASE. Responds in 1 year.

MUSIC Seeking "works for mixed chorus of 36 singers; unaccompanied or with keyboard and/or small instrumental ensemble; text sacred or secular/any language; prefers suites or cyclical works, total time not exceeding 15 minutes. Performance spaces and budgets prohibit large instrumental ensembles. Works suited for 750-seat halls are preferable. Substantial organ or piano parts acceptable. Scores should be very legible in every way."

PERFORMANCES Don McCullough's *Holocaust Contata* (choral with narration); Robert Cohen's *Sprig of Lilac: Peter Quince at the Clavier* (choral); Greg Bartholomew's *The 21st Century: A Girl Born in Afghanistan* (choral).

TIPS "Use conventional notation and be sure manuscript is legible in every way. Recognize and respect the vocal range of each vocal part. Work should have an identifiable rhythmic structure."

DUO CLASICO

1 Normal Ave., Montclair NJ 07043. (973)655-7212. Fax: (973)655-5279. E-mail: music@mail.montclair. edu. Website: www.montclair.edu/Arts/music/contact/index.html. **Contact:** David Witten, associate professor of music. Chamber music ensemble. Estab. 1986. Members are professionals. Performs 16 concerts/year including 4 new works. Commissions

1 composer or new work/year. Performs in small recital halls. Pays 10% royalty.

HOW TO CONTACT Query first. Include SASE. Responds in 6 weeks.

MUSIC "We welcome scores for flute solo, piano solo or duo. Particular interest in Latin American composers."

PERFORMANCES Diego Luzuriaga's *La Muchica* (modern, with extended techniques); Robert Starer's *Yizkor & Anima Aeterna* (rhythmic); and Piazzolla's *Etudes Tanguistiques* (solo flute).

TIPS "Extended techniques, or with tape, are fine!"

⬤ EUROPEAN UNION CHAMBER ORCHESTRA

Hollick, Yarnscombe EX31 3LQ United Kingdom. (44)1271 858249. Fax: (44)1271 858375. E-mail: eu corchl@aol.com. Website: www.etd.gb.com. **Contact:** Ambrose Miller, general director. Chamber orchestra. Members are professionals. Performs 70 concerts/ year, including 6 new works. Commissions 2 composers or new works/year. Performs regular tours of Europe, Americas, and Asia, including major venues. Pays per performance or for outright purchase, depending on work.

HOW TO CONTACT Query first. Does not return material. Responds in 6 weeks.

MUSIC Seeking compositions for strings, 2 oboes, and 2 horns with a duration of about 8 minutes.

PERFORMANCES Peeter Vahi "Prayer Wheel"; James MacMillan "Kiss on Wood," arr Karkof.

TIPS "Keep the work to less than 15 minutes in duration, it should be sufficiently 'modern' to be interesting but not too difficult as this could take up rehearsal time. It should be possible to perform without a conductor."

FONTANA CONCERT SOCIETY

359 S. Kalamazoo Mall, Suite 200, Kalamazoo MI 49007. (269)382-7774. Fax: (269)382-0812. E-mail: ab@fontanachamberarts.org. Website: www.fontana chamberarts.org. **Contact:** Mr. Ab Sengupta, artistic director/CEO. Chamber music ensemble presenter. Estab. 1980. Members are professionals. Fontana Chamber Arts presents over 45 events, including the 6-week Summer Festival of Music and Art, which runs from mid-July to the end of August. Regional and guest artists perform classical, contemporary, jazz, and nontraditional music. Commissions and performs new works each year. Fontana Chamber

Arts presents 7 classical and 2 jazz concerts during the Fall/Winter season. Audience consists of well-educated individuals who accept challenging new works, but like the traditional as well. Summer—180-seat hall; Fall/winter—various venues, from 400 to 1,500 seats.

HOW TO CONTACT Submit complete score, resume and tapes of piece(s). Include SASE. Responds in approximately 1 month. Music chamber music—any combination of strings, winds, piano. No "pop" music, New Age type. Special interest in composers attending premiere and speaking to the audience.

PERFORMANCES 2010—Juilliard String Quartet; Ben Allison and Man Size Safe; Esperanza Spalding; Cyro Baptista *Banquet of the Spirits*; Tord Gustavsen Trio; eighth blackbird; 2008—Imani Winds Josephine Baker: *A Life of Le Jazz Hot!*; Mitsuko Uchida & Friends; 2007—Billy Child's *The Path among the Trees* (Billy Child's Jazz Chamber Ensemble with Ying Quartet)

TIPS "Provide a résumé and clearly marked tape of a piece played by live performers."

FORT WORTH CHILDREN'S OPERA

1300 Gendy St., Fort Worth TX 76107. (817)731-0833, ext. 19. Fax: (817)731-0835. E-mail: clyde@fwopera. org. Website: www.fwopera.org. **Contact:** Clyde Berry. Opera company. Estab. 1946. Members are professionals. Performs over 180 in-school performances/ year." Audience consists of elementary school children; performs in major venues for district-wide groups and individual school auditoriums, cafeteriums and gymnasiums. Pays $40/performance.

HOW TO CONTACT Submit complete score and tape of piece(s). Include SASE. Responds in 6 months.

MUSIC "Familiar fairy tales or stories adapted to music of opera composers, or newly-composed music of suitable quality. Ideal length: 40-45 minutes. Piano or keyboard accompaniment. Should include moral, safety or school issues. Can be ethnic in subject matter and must speak to pre-K and grade 1-6 children. Prefer pieces with good, memorable melodies. Performed by young, trained professionals on 9-month contract. Requires work for four performers, doubled roles OK, SATB plus accompanist/narrator. Special interest in bilingual (Spanish/English) works."

GREATER GRAND FORKS SYMPHONY ORCHESTRA

3350 Campus Rd., Mail Stop 7084, Grand Forks ND 58202. (701)732-0579 or (701)777-3359. E-mail: symphony@ggfso.org. Website: www.ggfso.org. **Contact:** Alexander Platt, music director. Symphony orchestra. Estab. 1908. Members are professionals and/or amateurs. Performs 6 concerts/year. "New works are presented in 2-4 of our programs." Audience is "a mix of ages and musical experience. In 1997-98 we moved into a renovated, 420-seat theater." Pay is negotiable, depending on licensing agreements.

HOW TO CONTACT Submit complete score or complete score and tape of pieces. Include SASE. Responds in 6 months.

MUSIC "Style is open, instrumentation the limiting factor. Music can be scored for an ensemble up to but not exceeding: 3,2,3,2/4,3,3,1/3 perc./strings. Rehearsal time limited to 3 hours for new works."

PERFORMANCES Michael Harwood's *Amusement Park Suite* (orchestra); Randall Davidson's *Mexico Bolivar Tango* (chamber orchestra); and John Corigliano's *Voyage* (flute and orchestra); Linda Tutas Haugen's *Fable of Old Turtle* (saxophone concerto); Michael Wittgraf's *Landmarks*; Joan Tower's *Made in America*.

HEARTLAND MEN'S CHORUS

P.O. Box 32374, Kansas City MO 64171-5374. (816)931-3338. Fax: (816)531-1367. E-mail: hmc@hmckc.org. Website: www.hmckc.org. **Contact:** Joseph Nadeau, artistic director. Men's chorus. Estab. 1986. Members are professionals and amateurs. Performs 3 concerts/ year; 9-10 are new works. Commissions 1 composer or new works/year. Performs for a diverse audience at the Folly Theater (1,100 seats). Pay is negotiable.

HOW TO CONTACT Query first. Include SASE. Responds in 2 months.

MUSIC "Interested in works for male chorus (ttbb). Must be suitable for performance by a gay male chorus. We will consider any orchestration, or a cappella."

PERFORMANCES Mark Hayes's *Two Flutes Playing* (commissioned song cycle); Alan Shorter's *Country Angel Christmas* (commissioned children's musical); Kevin Robinson's *Life Is a Cabaret: The Music of Kander and Ebb* (commissioned musical).

TIPS "Find a text that relates to the contemporary gay experience, something that will touch peoples's lives."

HELENA SYMPHONY

P.O. Box 1073, Helena MT 59624. (406)442-1860. E-mail: llily@helenasymphony.org. Website: www.helenasymphony.org. **Contact:** Allan R. Scott, music director and conductor; Leatrice Lily, director of artistic planning. Symphony orchestra. Estab. 1955. Members are professionals and amateurs. Performs 7-10 concerts/year including new works. Performance space is an 1,800-seat concert hall. Payment varies.
HOW TO CONTACT Query first. Include SASE. Responds in 3 months.
MUSIC "Imaginative, collaborative, not too atonal. We want to appeal to an audience of all ages. We don't have a huge string complement. Medium to difficult okay—at frontiers of professional ability we cannot do."
PERFORMANCES Eric Funk's *A Christmas Overture* (orchestra); Donald O. Johnston's *A Christmas Processional* (orchestra/chorale); and Elizabeth Sellers's *Prairie* (orchestra/short ballet piece).
TIPS "Try to balance tension and repose in your works. New instrument combinations are appealing."

HENDERSONVILLE SYMPHONY ORCHESTRA

P.O. Box 1811, Hendersonville NC 28739. (828)697-5884. Fax: (828)697-5765. E-mail: hso1@bellsouth.net. Website: www.hendersonvillesymphony.org. **Contact:** Debra Anthony, general manager. Symphony orchestra. Estab. 1971. Members are professionals and amateurs. Performs 6 concerts/year. "We would welcome a new work per year." Audience is a cross-section of retirees, professionals, and some children. Performance space is a 857-seat high school audiorium.
HOW TO CONTACT Query first. Include SASE. Responds in 1 month.
MUSIC "We use a broad spectrum of music (classical concerts and pops)."
PERFORMANCES Nelson's *Jubilee* (personal expression in a traditional method); Britten's "The Courtly Dances" from Glorina (time-tested); and Chip Davis's arrangement for Mannheim Steamroller's *Deck the Halls* (modern adaptation of traditional melody).
TIPS "Submit your work even though we are a community orchestra. We like to be challenged. We have the most heavily patronized fine arts group in the county. Our emphasis is on education."

HERMANN SONS GERMAN BAND

P.O. Box 162, Medina TX 78055. (830)589-2268. E-mail: herbert@festmusik.com. Website: www.festmusik.com. **Contact:** Herbert Bilhartz, music director. Community band with German instrumentation. Estab. 1990. Members are both professionals and amateurs. Performs 4 concerts/year including 2 new works. Commissions no new composers or new works/year. Performs for "mostly older people who like German polkas, waltzes and marches. We normally play only published arrangements from Germany."
HOW TO CONTACT Query first; then submit full set of parts and score, condensed or full. Include SASE. Responds in 6 weeks.
MUSIC "We like European-style polkas or waltzes (Viennese or Missouri tempo), either original or arrangements of public domain tunes. Arrangements of traditional American folk tunes in this genre would be especially welcome. Also, polkas or waltzes featuring one or two solo instruments (from instrumentation below) would be great. OK for solo parts to be technically demanding. Although we have no funds to commission works, we will provide you with a cassette recording of our performance. Also, we would assist composers in submitting works to band music publishers in Germany for possible publication. Polkas and waltzes generally follow this format: Intro; 1st strain repeated; 2nd strain repeated; DS to 1 strain; Trio: Intro; 32 bar strain; 'break-up' strain; Trio DS. Much like military march form. Instrumentation: Fl/Picc, 3 clars in B flat, 2 Fluegelhorns in B flat; 3 Tpts in B flat, 2 or 4 Hns in F or E flat, 2 Baritones (melody/countermelody parts; 1 in B flat TC, 1 in BC), 2 Baritones in B flat TC (rhythm parts), 3 Trombones, 2 Tubas (in octaves, mostly), Drum set, Timpani optional. We don't use saxes, but a German publisher would want 4-5 sax parts. Parts should be medium to medium difficult. All brass parts should be considered one player to the part; woodwinds, two to the part. No concert type pieces; no modern popular or rock styles. However, a 'theme and variations' form with contrasting jazz, rock, country, modern variations would be clever, and our fans might go for such a piece (as might a German publisher)."
PERFORMANCES New music performed in 2005: Stefan Rundel's *Mein Glueckssktern (My Lucky Star)*.

TIPS "German town bands love to play American tunes. There are many thousands of these bands over there and competition among band music publishers in Germany is keen. Few Americans are aware of this potential market, so few American arrangers get published over there. Simple harmony is best for this style, but good counterpoint helps a lot. Make use of the dark quality of the Fluegelhorns and the bright, fanfare quality of the trumpets. Give the two baritones (one in TC and one in BC) plenty of exposed melodic material. Keep them in harmony with each other (3rds and 6ths), unlike American band arrangements, which have only one Baritone line. If you want to write a piece in this style, give me a call, and I will send you some sample scores to give you a better idea."

HERSHEY SYMPHONY ORCHESTRA

P.O. Box 93, Hershey PA 17033. (717)533-8449. E-mail: hsogm@itech.net. **Contact:** Dr. Sandra Dackow, music director. Symphony orchestra. Estab. 1969. Members are professionals and amateurs. Performs 8 concerts/year, including 1-3 new works. Commissions "possibly 1-2" composers or new works/year. Audience is family and friends of community theater. Performance space is a 1,900-seat grand old movie theater. Pays commission fee.

HOW TO CONTACT Submit complete score and tape of piece(s). Include SASE. Responds in 3 months.

MUSIC "Symphonic works of various lengths and types which can be performed by a non-professional orchestra. We are flexible but like to involve all our players."

PERFORMANCES Paul W. Whear's *Celtic Christmas Carol* (orchestra/bell choir) and Linda Robbins Coleman's *In Good King Charlie's Golden Days* (overture).

TIPS "Please lay out rehearsal numbers/letter and rests according to phrases and other logical musical divisions rather than in groups of ten measures, etc., which is very unmusical and wastes time and causes a surprising number of problems. Also, please do not send a score written in concert pitch; use the usual transpositions so that the conductor sees what the players see; rehearsal is much more effective this way. Cross cue all important solos; this helps in rehearsal where instruments may be missing."

HUDSON VALLEY PHILHARMONIC

35 Market St., Poughkeepsie NY 12601. (845)473-5288. Fax: (845)473-4259. Website: www.bardavon. org. **Contact:** Barbara Fehribach, director of development. Symphony orchestra. Estab. 1969. Members are professionals. Performs 20 concerts/year including 1 new work. "Classical subscription concerts for all ages; Pops concerts for all ages; New Wave concerts—crossover projects with a rock 'n' roll artist performing with an orchestra. HVP performs in three main theatres which are concert auditoriums with stages and professional lighting and sound." Pay is negotiable.

HOW TO CONTACT Query first. Include SASE. Responds only if interested.

MUSIC "HVP is open to serious classical music, pop music and rock 'n' roll crossover projects. Desired length of work between 10-20 minutes. Orchestrations can be varied by should always include strings. There is no limit to difficulty since our musicians are professional. The ideal number of musicians to write for would include up to a Brahms-size orchestra 2222, 4231, T, 2P, piano, harp, strings."

PERFORMANCES Joan Tower's *Island Rhythms* (serious classical work); Bill Vanaver's *P'nai El* (symphony work with dance); and Joseph Bertolozzi's *Serenade* (light classical, pop work).

TIPS "Don't get locked into doing very traditional orchestrations or styles. Our music director is interested in fresh, creative formats. He is an orchestrator as well and can offer good advice on what works well. Songwriters who are into crossover projects should definitely submit works. Over the past four years, HVP has done concerts featuring the works of Natalie Merchant, John Cale, Sterling Morrison, Richie Havens, and R. Carlos Naka (Native American flute player), all reorchestrated by our music director for small orchestra with the artist."

INDIANA UNIVERSITY NEW MUSIC ENSEMBLE

Indiana University Bloomington, School of Music, Bloomington IN 47405. E-mail: ddzubay@indiana. edu. Website: www.indiana.edu/~nme. **Contact**: David Dzubay, director. Performs solo, chamber and large ensemble works. Estab.1974. Members are students. Presents 4 concerts/year.

MUSIC Peter Lieberson's *Free and Easy Wanderer*; Sven-David Sandstrom's *Wind Pieces*; Atar

Arad's *Sonata*; and David Dzubay's *Dancesing in a Green Bay*.

KENTUCKY OPERA

323 West Broadway, Suite 601, Louisville KY 40202. (502)584-4500. Fax: (502)584-7484. E-mail: alise_oliver@kyopera.org. Website: www.kyopera.org. **Contact:** Alise Oliver, artistic administration. Opera. Estab. 1952. Members are professionals. Performs 3 main stage/year. Performs at Brown Theatre, 1,400. Pays by royalty, outright purchase or per performance.

HOW TO CONTACT *Write or call first before submitting. No unsolicited submissions.* Submit complete score. Include SASE. Responds in 6 months.

MUSIC Seeks opera—1 to 3 acts with orchestrations. No limitations.

PERFORMANCES *Cavalleria Rusticana, The Elixir of Love, Madame Butterfly*

LAMARCA AMERICAN VARIETY SINGERS

2655 W. 230th Place, Torrance CA 90505. (310)325-8708. **Contact:** Priscilla LaMarca-Kandell, director. Composer of children's songs for home and school use, educational, and entertaining. Also, vocal, ear training, and sight-singing exercises to help other songwriters improve their singing demo techniques.

HOW TO CONTACT Query first. Include SASE. Responds in 2 weeks.

MUSIC "Seeks 3-10 or 15 minute medleys; a variety of musical styles from Broadway—pop styles to humorous specialty songs. Top 40 dance music, light rock and patriotic themes. No rap or anything not suitable for family audiences."

PERFORMANCES *Disney Movie Music* (uplifting); *Children's Music* (educational/positive); and *Beatles Medley* (love songs).

LEXINGTON PHILHARMONIC SOCIETY

161 N. Mill St., Arts Place, Lexington KY 40507. (859)233-4226. E-mail: sterrell@lexphil.org. Website: www.lexphil.org. **Contact:** Scott Terrell, music director. Symphony orchestra. Estab. 1961. Members are professionals. Series includes "8 serious, classical subscription concerts (hall seats 1,500); 3 concerts called Pops the Series; 3 Family Concerts; 10 outdoor pops concerts (from 1,500 to 5,000 tickets sold); 5-10 runout concerts ($^1/_2$ serious/$^1/_2$ pops); and 10 children's concerts." Pays via ASCAP and BMI, rental purchase and private arrangements.

HOW TO CONTACT Submit complete score and tape of piece(s). Include SASE.

MUSIC Seeking "good current pops material and good serious classical works. No specific restrictions, but overly large orchestra requirements, unusual instruments and extra rentals help limit our interest."

PERFORMANCES "Visit our website for complete concert season listing."

TIPS "When working on large-format arrangement, use cross-cues so orchestra can be cut back if required. Submit good quality copy, scores and parts. Tape is helpful."

LIMA SYMPHONY ORCHESTRA

133 N. Elizabeth St., Lima OH 45801. (419)222-5701. Fax: (419)222-6587. Website: www.limasymphony.com. **Contact:** Crafton Beck, music conductor. Symphony orchestra. Estab. 1953. Members are professionals. Performs 17-18 concerts including at least 1 new work/year. Commissions at least 1 composer or new work/year. Middle to older audience; also Young People's Series. Mixture for stage and summer productions. Performs in Veterans' Memorial Civic & Convention Center, a beautiful hall seating 1,670; various temporary shells for summer outdoors events; churches; museums; and libraries. Pays $2,500 for outright purchase (Anniversary commission) or grants $1,500-5,000.

HOW TO CONTACT Submit complete score if not performed; otherwise submit complete score and tape of piece(s). Include SASE. Responds in 3 months.

MUSIC "Good balance of incisive rhythm, lyricism, dynamic contrast and pacing. Chamber orchestra to full (85-member) symphony orchestra." Does not wish to see "excessive odd meter changes."

PERFORMANCES Frank Proto's *American Overture* (some original music and fantasy); Werner Tharichen's *Concerto for Timpani and Orchestra*; and James Oliverio's *Pilgrimage—Concerto for Brass* (interesting, dynamic writing for brass and the orchestra).

TIPS "Know your instruments, be willing to experiment with unconventional textures, be available for in depth analysis with conductor, be at more than one rehearsal. Be sure that individual parts are correctly matching the score and done in good, neat calligraphy."

LYRIC OPERA OF CHICAGO

20 N. Wacker Dr., Chicago IL 60606. (312)332-2244 ext. 3500. Fax: (312)419-8345. Website: www.lyricopera.org. **Contact:** Thomas Young, music administrator. Opera company. Estab. 1953. Members are professionals. Performs 80 operas/year including 1 new work in some years. Commissions 1 new work every 4 or 5 years. "Performances are held in a 3,563 seat house for a sophisticated opera audience, predominantly 30+ years old." Payment varies.

HOW TO CONTACT Query first. Does not return material. Responds in 6 months.

MUSIC "Full-length opera suitable for a large house with full orchestra. No musical comedy or Broadway musical style. We rarely perform one-act operas. We are only interested in works by composers and librettists with extensive theatrical experience. We have few openings for new works, so candidates must be of the highest quality. Do not send score or other materials without a prior contact."

PERFORMANCES William Bolcom's *View from the Bridge*; John Corigliano's *Ghosts of Versailles*; and Leonard Bernstein's *Candide*.

TIPS "Have extensive credentials and an international reputation."

MILWAUKEE YOUTH SYMPHONY ORCHESTRA

325 W. Walnut St., Milwaukee WI 53212. (414)267-2950. Fax: (414)267-2960. E-mail: general@myso.org. Website: www.myso.org. **Contact:** Fran Richman, executive director. Multiple youth orchestras and other instrumental ensembles. Estab. 1956. Members are students. Performs 12-15 concerts/year including 1-2 new works. "Our groups perform in Uihlein Hall at the Marcus Center for the Performing Arts in Milwaukee plus area sites. The audiences usually consist of parents, music teachers and other interested community members, with periodic reviews in the Milwaukee *Journal Sentinel*." Payment varies.

HOW TO CONTACT Query first. Include SASE. Does not return material. Responds in 1 month.

PERFORMANCES James Woodward's *Tuba Concerto*.

TIPS "Be sure you realize you are working with *students* (albeit many of the best in southeastern Wisconsin) and not professional musicians. The music needs to be on a technical level students can handle. Our students are 8-18 years of age, in 2 full symphony orchestras, a wind ensemble and 2 string orchestras, plus two flute choirs, advanced chamber orchestra and 15-20 small chamber ensembles."

MOORES OPERA CENTER

University of Houston, 120 Moores School of Music Building, Houston TX 77204. (713)743-3009. Fax: (713)743-3166. E-mail: bross@uh.edu. Website: www.uh.edu/music/Mooresopera/. **Director of Opera:** Buck Ross. Opera/music theater program. Members are professionals, amateurs and students. Performs 12-14 concerts/year including 1 new work. Performs in a proscenium theater that seats 800. Pit seats approximately up to 75 players. Audience covers wide spectrum, from first time opera-goers to very sophisticated. Pays per performance.

HOW TO CONTACT Submit complete score and tapes of piece(s). Include SASE. Responds in 6 months.

MUSIC "We seek music that is feasible for high graduate level student singers. Chamber orchestras are very useful. No more than two and a half hours. No children's operas."

PERFORMANCES *The Grapes of Wrath*, *Florencia en el Amazonas*, *Elmer Gantry*, *A Wedding*.

OPERA MEMPHIS

6745 Wolf River Pkwy., Memphis TN 38120. (901)257-3100. Fax: (901)257-3109. E-mail: info@operamemphis.org. Website: www.operamemphis.org. Contact: Jonathan Ealy, artistic administrator. Opera company. Estab. 1955. Members are professionals. Performs 8-12 concerts/year including new works. Occasionally commissions composers. Audience consists of older, wealthier patrons, along with many students and young professionals. Pay is negotiable.

HOW TO CONTACT Query first. Include SASE. Responds in 1 year or less.

MUSIC Accessible practical pieces for educational or second stage programs. Educational pieces should not exceed 90 minutes or 4-6 performers. We encourage songwriters to contact us with proposals or work samples for theatrical works. We are very interested in crossover work.

PERFORMANCES Mike Reid's *Different Fields* (one act opera); David Olney's *Light in August* (folk opera); and Sid Selvidge's *Riversongs* (one-act blues opera).

TIPS "Spend many hours thinking about the synopsis (plot outline)."

ORCHESTRA SEATTLE/SEATTLE CHAMBER SINGERS

P.O. Box 15825, Seattle WA 98115. (206)682-5208. E-mail: osscs@osscs.org. Website: www.osscs.org. **Contact:** Laurie Medill, business manager. Symphony orchestra, chamber music ensemble and community chorus. Estab. 1969. Members are amateurs and professionals. Performs 8 concerts/year including 2-3 new works. Commissions 1-2 composers or new works/year. "Our audience is made up of both experienced and novice classical music patrons. The median age is 45 with an equal number of males and females in the upper income range. Most concerts now held in Benaroya Hall."

HOW TO CONTACT Query first. Include SASE. Responds in 1 year.

PERFORMANCES Beyer's *The Turns of a Girl*; Bernstein's Choruses from *The Lark*; Edstrom's Concerto for Jazz Piano and Orchestra.

PALMETTO MASTERSINGERS

(803)765-0777. E-mail: info@palmettomastersingers.org. Website: www.palmettomastersingers.org. **Contact:** Walter Cuttino, music director. 80-voice male chorus. Estab. 1981 by the late Dr. Arpad Darasz. Members are professionals and amateurs. Performs 8-10 concerts/year. Commissions 1 composer of new works every other year (on average). Audience is generally older adults, "but it's a wide mix." Performance space for the season series is the Koger Center (approximately 2,000 seats) in Columbia, SC. More intimate venues also available. Fee is negotiable for outright purchase.

HOW TO CONTACT Query first. Include SASE. Or e-mail to info@palmettomastersingers.org.

MUSIC Seeking music of 10-15 minutes in length, "not too far out tonally. Orchestration is negotiable, but chamber size (10-15 players) is normal. We rehearse once a week and probably will not have more than 8-10 rehearsals. These rehearsals (2 hours each) are spent learning a 1^1/$_2$-hour program. Only 1-2 rehearsals (max) are with the orchestra. Piano accompaniments need not be simplified, as our accompanist is exceptional."

PERFORMANCES Randal Alan Bass's *Te Deum* (12-minute, brass and percussion); Dick Goodwin's *Mark Twain Remarks* (40 minute, full symphony); and Randol Alan Bass's *A Simple Prayer* (a capella 6 minute).

TIPS "Contact us as early as possible, given that programs are planned by July. Although this is an amateur chorus, we have performed concert tours of Europe, performed at Carnegie Hall, The National Cathedral and the White House in Washington, DC. We are skilled amateurs."

PICCOLO OPERA COMPANY INC.

24 Del Rio Blvd., Boca Raton FL 33432-4734. (800)282-3161. Fax: (561)394-0520. E-mail: leejon51@msn.com. **Contact:** Marjorie Gordon, executive director. Traveling opera company. Estab. 1962. Members are professionals. Performs 1-50 concerts/year including 1-2 new works. Commissions 0-1 composer or new work/year. Operas are performed for a mixed audience of children and adults. Pays by performance or outright purchase. Operas in English.

HOW TO CONTACT Query first. Include SASE.

MUSIC "Productions for either children or adults. Musical theater pieces, lasting about one hour, for adults to perform for adults and/or youngsters. Performers are mature singers with experience. The cast should have few performers (up to 10), no chorus or ballet, accompanied by piano or local orchestra. Skeletal scenery. All in English."

PERFORMANCES Menotti's *The Telephone*; Mozart's *Cosi Fan Tutte*; and Puccini's *La Boheme* (repertoire of more than 22 productions).

PRINCETON SYMPHONY ORCHESTRA

P.O. Box 250, Princeton NJ 08542. (609)497-0020. Fax: (609)497-0904. E-mail: info@princetonsymphony.org. Website: www.princetonsymphony.org. **Contact:** Rossen Milanov, music director. Symphony orchestra. Estab. 1980. Members are professionals. Performs 6-10 concerts/year including some new works. Commissions 1 composer or new work/year. Performs in a "beautiful, intimate 800-seat hall with amazing sound." Pays by arrangement.

MUSIC "Orchestra usually numbers 40-60 individuals."

PRISM SAXOPHONE QUARTET

30 Seaman Av., #4M, New York NY 10034 or 257 Harvey St., Philadelphia PA 19144. (215)438-5282. E-mail: info@prismquartet.com. Website: www.prismquartet.com. President, New Sounds Music Inc. Prism Quartet: Matthew Levy. Chamber music ensemble. Estab. 1984. Members are professionals. Performs 80 concerts/year including 10-15 new works. Commissions

4 composers or new works/year. "Ours are primarily traditional chamber music audiences." Pays royalty per performance from BMI or ASCAP or commission range from $100 to $15,000.

HOW TO CONTACT Submit complete score (with parts) and tape of piece(s). Does not return material. Responds in 3 months.

MUSIC "Orchestration—sax quartet, SATB. Lengths—5-25 minutes. Styles—contemporary, classical, jazz, crossover, ethnic, gospel, avant-garde. No limitations on level of difficulty. No more than 4 performers (SATB sax quartet). No transcriptions. The Prism Quartet places special emphasis on crossover works which integrate a variety of musical styles."

PERFORMANCES David Liebman's *The Gray Convoy* (jazz); Bradford Ellis's *Tooka-Ood Zasch* (ethnic-world music); and William Albright's *Fantasy Etudes* (contemporary classical).

SACRAMENTO MASTER SINGERS

P.O. Box 417997, Sacramento CA 95841. (916)788-7464. E-mail: smsbusiness@surewest.net. Website: www.mastersingers.org. **Contact:** Ralph Hughes, conductor/artistic director. Vocal ensemble. Estab. 1984. Members are professionals and amateurs. Performs 9 concerts/year including 5-6 new works. Commissions 2 new works/year. Audience is made up of mainly college age and older patrons. Performs mostly in churches with 500-900 seating capacity. Pays $200 for outright purchase.

HOW TO CONTACT Submit complete score and tape of piece(s). Include SASE. Responds in 5 weeks.

MUSIC "A cappella works; works with small orchestras or few instruments; works based on classical styles with a 'modern' twist; multi-cultural music; shorter works probably preferable, but this is not a requirement. We usually have 38-45 singers capable of a high level of difficulty, but find that often simple works are very pleasing."

PERFORMANCES Joe Jennings's *An Old Black Woman, Homeless and Indistinct* (SATB, oboe, strings, dramatic).

TIPS "Keep in mind we are a chamber ensemble, not a 100-voice choir."

🎧 SAN FRANCISCO GIRLS CHORUS

44 Page St., Suite 200, San Francisco CA 94102. (415)863-1752. E-mail: info@sfgirlschorus.org. Website: www.sfgirlschorus.org. **Contact:** Susan McMane, artistic director. Choral ensemble. Estab. 1978. Advanced choral ensemble of young women's voices. Performs 8-10 concerts/year including 3-4 new works. Commissions 2 composers or new works/year. Concerts are performed for "choral/classical music lovers, plus family audiences and audiences interested in international repertoire. Season concerts are performed in an 800-seat church with excellent acoustics and in San Francisco's Davies Symphony Hall, a 2,800-seat state-of-the-art auditorium." Pay negotiable for outright purchase.

🎧 The San Francisco Girls Chorus has won three Grammy Awards as guest performers on the San Francisco Symphony's recordings.

HOW TO CONTACT Submit complete score and CD recording, if possible. Does not return material. Responds in 6 months.

MUSIC "Music for treble voices (SSAA); a cappella, piano accompaniment, or small orchestration; 3-10 minutes in length. Wide variety of styles; 45 singers; challenging music is encouraged."

PERFORMANCES See website under "Music/Commissions" for a listing of SFGC commissions. Examples: Jake Heggie's *Patterns* (piano, mezzo-soprano soloist, chorus); and Chen Yi's *Chinese Poems* (a cappella).

TIPS "Choose excellent texts and write challenging music. The San Francisco Girls Chorus has pioneered in establishing girls choral music as an art form in the United States. The Girls Chorus is praised for its 'stunning musical standard' (*San Francisco Chronicle*) in performances in the San Francisco Bay Area and on tour. SFGC's annual concert season showcases the organization's concert/touring ensemble, Chorissima, in performances of choral masterworks from around the world, commissioned works by contemporary composers, and 18th-century music from the Venetian Ospedali and Mexican Baroque which SFGC has brought out of the archives and onto the concert stage. Chorissima tours through California with partial support provided by the California Arts Council Touring Program and have represented the U.S. and the City of San Francisco nationally and abroad. The chorus provides ensemble and solo singers for performances and recordings with the San Francisco Symphony and San Francisco Opera, Women's Philharmonic, and many other music ensembles. The Chorus has produced six solo CD recordings including: *Voices of Hope and Peace*, a recording that includes

"Anne Frank: A Living Voice" by an American composer Linda Tutas Haugen; *Christmas*, featuring diverse holiday selections; *Crossroads*, a collection of world folk music; and *Music from the Venetian Ospedali*, a disc of Italian Baroque music of which the *New Yorker* described the Chorus as "tremendously accomplished." The Chorus can also be heard on several San Francisco Symphony recordings, including three GRAMMY Award winners."

SINGING BOYS OF PENNSYLVANIA

P.O. Box 206, Wind Gap PA 18091. (610)759-6002. Fax: (610)759-6042. Website: www.singingboysof pennsylvania.org. **Contact:** K. Bernard Schade, conductor. Vocal ensemble. Estab. 1970. Members are professional children. Performs 100 concerts/year including 3-5 new works. "We attract general audiences: family, senior citizens, churches, concert associations, university concert series and schools." Pays $300-3,000 for outright purchase.

HOW TO CONTACT *Query first.* Does not return material. Responds in 3 weeks.

MUSIC "We want music for commercials, voices in the SSA or SSAA ranges, sacred works or arrangements of American folk music with accompaniment. Our range of voices are from G below middle C to A (13th above middle C). Reading ability of choir is good but works which require a lot of work with little possibility of more than one performance are of little value. We sing very few popular songs except for special events. We perform music by composers who are well-known and works by living composers who are writing in traditional choral forms. Works which have a full orchestral score are of interest. The orchestration should be fairly light, so as not to cover the voices. Works for Christmas have more value than some other, since we perform with orchestras on an annual basis."

PERFORMANCES Don Locklair's *The Columbus Madrigals* (opera).

TIPS "It must be appropriate music and words for children. We do not deal in pop music. Folk music, classics and sacred are acceptable."

SOLI DEO GLORIA CANTORUM

3402 Woolworth Ave., Omaha NE 68105. (402)341-4111. Fax: (402)341-9381. E-mail: cantorum@ber key.com. Website: www.berkey.com. **Contact:** Almeda Berkey, music director. Professional choir. Estab. 1988. Members are professionals. Performs 5-7 concerts/year;

several are new works. Commissions 1-2 new works/year. Performance space: "cathedral, symphony hall, smaller intimate recital halls as well." Payment is "dependent upon composition and composer."

HOW TO CONTACT Submit complete score and tape of piece(s). Include SASE. Responds in 2 months.

MUSIC "Chamber music mixed with topical programming (e.g., all Celtic or all Hispanic programs, etc.). Generally a cappella compositions from very short to extended range (6-18 minutes) or multi-movements. Concerts are of a formal length (approx. 75 minutes) with 5 rehearsals. Difficulty must be balanced within program in order to adequately prepare in a limited rehearsal time. 28 singers. Not seeking orchestral pieces, due to limited budget."

PERFORMANCES Jackson Berkey's *Native Am Ambience* (eclectic/classical); John Rutter's *Hymn to the Creator of Light* (classical); and Arvo Part's *Te Deum* (multi-choir/chant-based classical).

ST. LOUIS CHAMBER CHORUS

P.O. Box 11558, Clayton MO 63105. (636)458-4343. E-mail: stlchamberchorus@gmail.com. Website: www.chamberchorus.org. **Contact:** Philip Barnes, artistic director. Vocal ensemble, chamber music ensemble. Estab. 1956. Members are professionals and amateurs. Performs 6 concerts/year including 5-10 new works. Commissions 3-4 new works/year. Audience is "diverse and interested in unaccompanied choral work and outstanding architectural/acoustic venues." Performances take place at various auditoria noted for their excellent acoustics—churches, synagogues, schools, and university halls. Pays by arrangement.

HOW TO CONTACT Query first. Does not return material. "Panel of 'readers' submit report to Artistic Director. Responds in 3 months. 'General Advice' leaflet available on request."Music "*Only a cappella writing!* No contemporary 'popular' works; historical editions welcomed. No improvisatory works. Our programs are tailored for specific acoustics—composers should indicate their preference."

PERFORMANCES Sir Richard Rodney Bennett's *A Contemplation upon Flowers* (a cappella madrigal); Ned Rorem's *Ode to Man* (a cappella chorus for mixed voices); and Sasha Johnson Manning's *Requiem* (a cappella oratorio).

TIPS "We only consider a cappella works which can be produced in five rehearsals. Therefore pieces of great complexity or duration are discouraged. Our seasons are planned 2-3 years ahead, so much lead time is required for programming a new work. We will accept hand-written manuscript, but we prefer typeset music."

SUSQUEHANNA SYMPHONY ORCHESTRA

P.O. Box 963, Abingdon, MD 21009. Fax: (410)306-6069. E-mail: sheldon.bair@ssorchestra.org. Website: www. ssorchestra.org. **Contact:** Sheldon Bair, founder/music director. Symphony orchestra. Estab. 1978. Members are amateurs. Performs 6 concerts/year including 1-2 new works. Composers paid depending on the circumstances. "We perform in 1 hall, 600 seats with fine acoustics. Our audience encompasses all ages."

HOW TO CONTACT Query first. Include SASE. Responds in 3 or more months.

MUSIC "We desire works for large orchestra, any length, in a 'conservative 20th and 21st century' style. Seek fine music for large orchestra. We are a community orchestra, so the music must be within our grasp. Violin I to 7th position by step only; Violin II—stay within 5th position; English horn and harp are OK. Full orchestra pieces preferred."

PERFORMANCES *Stabat Mater*, by Stanislaw Moryto; *Elegy*, Amanda Harberg; *I Choose the Mountain*, by Stacey Zyriek; *Little Gift*, by Benny Russell.

☼ TORONTO MENDELSSOHN CHOIR

60 Simcoe St., Toronto ON M5J 2H5 Canada. (416)598-0422. Fax: (416)598-2992. E-mail: manager@tmchoir. org. Website: www.tmchoir.org. **Contact:** Cynthia Hawkins, executive director. Vocal ensemble. Members are professionals and amateurs. Performs 25 concerts/year including 1-3 new works. "Most performances take place in Roy Thomson Hall. The audience is reasonably sophisticated, musically knowledgeable but with moderately conservative tastes." Pays by commission and ASCAP/SOCAN.

HOW TO CONTACT Query first or submit complete score and tapes of pieces. Include SASE. Responds in 6 months.

MUSIC All works must suit a large choir (180 voices) and standard orchestral forces or with some other not-too-exotic accompaniment. Length should be restricted to no longer than $\frac{1}{2}$ of a nocturnal concert. The choir sings at a very professional level and can sight-read almost anything. "Works should fit naturally with the repertoire of a large choir which performs the standard choral orchestral repertoire."

PERFORMANCES Holman's *Jezebel*; Orff's *Catulli Carmina*; and Lambert's *Rio Grande*.

☼ VANCOUVER CHAMBER CHOIR

1254 W. Seventh Ave., Vancouver BC V6H 1B6 Canada. E-mail: info@vancouverchamberchoir.com. Website: www.vancouverchamberchoir.com. **Contact:** Jon Washburn, artistic director. Vocal ensemble. Members are professionals. Performs 40 concerts/year including 5-8 new works. Commissions 2-4 composers or new works/year. Pays SOCAN royalty or negotiated fee for commissions.

HOW TO CONTACT Submit complete score and tape of piece(s). Does not return material. Responds in 6 months if possible.

MUSIC Seeks "choral works of all types for small chorus, with or without accompaniment and/or soloists. Concert music only. Choir made up of 20 singers. Large or unusual instrumental accompaniments are less likely to be appropriate. No pop music."

PERFORMANCES The VCC has commissioned and premiered over 200 new works by Canadian and international composers, including Alice Parker's *That Sturdy Vine* (cantata for chorus, soloists and orchestra); R. Murray Schafer's *Magic Songs* (SATB a cappella); and Jon Washburn's *A Stephen Foster Medley* (SSAATTBB/piano).

TIPS "We are looking for choral music that is performable yet innovative, and which has the potential to become 'standard repertoire.' Although we perform much new music, only a small portion of the many scores which are submitted can be utilized."

☼ VANCOUVER YOUTH SYMPHONY ORCHESTRA SOCIETY

3214 West 10th Ave., Vancouver BC V6K 2L2 Canada. (604)737-0714. Fax: (604)737-0739. E-mail: vyso@ telus.net. Website: www.vyso.com. **Music directors:** Roger Cole, artistic director and senior orchestra conductor; Jin Zhang, intermediate orchestra conductor; Margitta Krebs, debut and junior orchestra conductor. Youth orchestra. "Four divisions consisting of musicians ranging in age from 8-22 years old." Estab. 1930. Members are amateurs. Performs 10-15 concerts/year in various lower mainland venues. Concert admission by donation.

MUSIC "Extensive and varied orchestral repertoire is performed by all divisions. Please contact the VYSO for more information."

VIRGINIA OPERA

P.O. Box 2580, Norfolk VA 23501. (757)627-9545. E-mail: info@vaopera.com. Website: www.vaopera.org. Artistic administration director: Andrew Chugg. Opera company. Estab. 1974. Members are professionals. Performs more than 560 concerts/year. Commissions vary on number of composers or new works/year. Concerts are performed for schoolchildren throughout Virginia, grades K-5, 6-8, and 9-12 at the Harrison Opera House in Norfolk and at the Carpenter Theatre in Richmond. Pays on commission.

HOW TO CONTACT Query first. Include SASE. Response time varies.

MUSIC "Audience accessible style approximately 45 minutes in length. Limit cast list to three vocal artists of any combination. Accompanied by piano and/or keyboard. Works are performed before schoolchildren of all ages. Pieces must be age appropriate both aurally and dramatically. Musical styles are encouraged to be diverse, contemporary as well as traditional. Works are produced and presented with sets, costumes, etc." Limitations: "Three vocal performers (any combination). One keyboardist. Medium to difficult acceptable, but prefer easy to medium. Seeking only pieces which are suitable for presentation as part of an opera education program for Virginia Opera's education and outreach department. Subject matter must meet strict guidelines relative to Learning Objectives, etc. Musical idiom must be representative of current trends in opera, musical theater. Extreme dissonance, row systems not applicable to this environment."

PERFORMANCES Seymour Barab's *Cinderella*; John David Earnest's *The Legend of Sleepy Hollow*; and Seymour Barab's *The Pied Piper of Hamelin*.

TIPS "Theatricality is very important. New works should stimulate interest in musical theater as a legitimate art form for school children with no prior exposure to live theatrical entertainment. Composer should be willing to create a product which will find success within the educational system."

WHEATON SYMPHONY ORCHESTRA

344 Spring Ave., Glen Ellyn IL 60137. (630)790-1430. Fax: (630)790-9703. E-mail: info@wheatonsymphony. org. Website: www.wheatonsymphony.org. **Contact:** Don Mattison, manager. Symphony orchestra. Estab. 1959. Members are professionals and amateurs. Performs 6 concerts/year including a varying number of new works. "No pay for performance but can probably record your piece."

HOW TO CONTACT Query first. Include SASE. Responds in 1 month.

MUSIC "This is a good amateur orchestra that wants pieces to be performed in the mode of John Williams or Samuel Barber, Corliango, etc. Large scale works for orchestra only. No avant garde, 12-tone or atonal material. Pieces should be 20 minutes or less and must be prepared in 3 rehearsals. Instrumentation needed for woodwinds in 3s, full brass 4-3-3-1, 4 percussion and strings—full-instrumentation only. Selections for full orchestra only. No pay for reading your piece, but we will record it at our expense. We will rehearse and give a world premiere of your piece if it is in the stated orchestration, probably with keyboard added."

PERFORMANCES Richard Williams's *Symphony in G Minor* (4 movement symphony); Dennis Johnson's *Must Jesus Bear the Cross Alone, Azon* (traditional); and Michael Diemer's *Skating* (traditional style).

CONTESTS & AWARDS

Participating in contests is a great way to gain exposure for your music. Prizes vary from contest to contest, from cash to musical merchandise to studio time, and even publishing and recording deals. For musical theater and classical composers, the prize may be a performance of your work. Even if you don't win, valuable contacts can be made through contests. Many times, contests are judged by music publishers and other industry professionals, so your music may find its way into the hands of key industry people who can help further your career.

HOW TO SELECT A CONTEST

It's important to remember when entering any contest to do proper research before signing anything or sending any money. We have confidence in the contests listed in *Songwriter's Market*, but it pays to read the fine print. First, be sure you understand the contest rules and stipulations once you receive the entry forms and guidelines. Then you need to weigh what you will gain against what they're asking you to give up. If a publishing or recording contract is the only prize a contest is offering, you may want to think twice before entering. Basically, the company sponsoring the contest is asking you to pay a fee for them to listen to your song under the guise of a contest, something a legitimate publisher or record company would not do. For those contests offering studio time, musical equipment, or cash prizes, you need to decide if the entry fee you're paying is worth the chance to win such prizes.

Be wary of exorbitant entry fees, and if you have any doubts whatsoever as to the legitimacy of a contest, it's best to stay away. Songwriters need to approach a contest, award, or grant in the same manner as they would a record or publishing company. Make your submission as professional as possible; follow directions and submit material exactly as stated on the entry form.

Contests in this section encompass all types of music and levels of competition. Read each listing carefully and contact them if the contest interests you. Many contests now have websites that offer additional information and even entry forms you can print. Be sure to read the rules carefully and be sure you understand exactly what a contest is offering before entering.

AGO AWARD IN ORGAN COMPOSITION

American Guild of Organists, 475 Riverside Dr., Suite 1260, New York, NY 10115. (212)870-2310. Fax: (212)870-2163. E-mail: info@agohq.org. Website: www.agohq.org. **Contact:** Harold Calhoun, competitions administrator. For composers and performing artists. Biennial award.

REQUIREMENTS Organ solo, no longer than 8 minutes in duration. Specifics vary from year to year. Deadline: TBA, but usually early spring of odd-numbered year. Go to the website for application.

AWARDS $2,000; publication by Hinshaw Music Inc.; performance at the biennial National Convention of the American Guild of Organists.

AGO/ECS PUBLISHING AWARD IN CHORAL COMPOSITION

American Guild of Organists, 475 Riverside Dr., Suite 1260, New York NY 10115. (212)870-2310. Fax: (212)870-2163. E-mail: info@agohq.org. Website: www.agohq.org. **Contact:** Harold Calhoun, competitions administrator. Biannual award.

REQUIREMENTS Composers are invited to submit a work for SATB choir and organ in which the organ plays a significant and independent role. Work submitted must be unpublished and are usually 3.5 to 5 minutes in length. There is no age restriction. Deadline: TBA, "but usually late fall in even numbered years." Application information on the website.

AWARDS $2,000 cash prize, publication by ECS Publishing and premier performance at the AGO National Convention. Further details are published in *The American Organist.*

ALEA III INTERNATIONAL COMPOSITION PRIZE

855 Commonwealth Ave., Boston, MA 02215. (617)353-3340. E-mail: aleaiii@bu.edu. Website: www.aleaiii.com. For composers. Annual award.

PURPOSE To promote and encourage young composers in the composition of new music.

REQUIREMENTS Composers born after January 1, 1972 may participate; 1 composition per composer. Works may be for solo voice or instrument or for chamber ensemble up to 15 members lasting between 6 and 15 minutes. Available instruments are: one flute (doubling piccolo or alto), one oboe (doubling English horn), one clarinet (doubling bass clarinet), one bassoon, one saxophone, one horn, one trumpet, one trombone, one tuba, two percussion players, one harp, one keyboard player, one guitar, two violins, one viola, one cello, one bass, tape, and one voice. "One of the 15 performers could play an unusual, exotic or rare instrument, or be a specialized vocalist. For more info and guidelines, please refer to our website." All works must be unpublished and must not have been publicly performed or broadcast, in whole or in part or in any other version before the announcement of the prize in late September or early October of 2012. Works that have won other awards are not eligible. Deadline: March 15, 2012. Send for application. Submitted work required with application. "Real name should not appear on score; a nom de plume should be signed instead. Sealed envelope with entry form should be attached to each score."

AWARDS ALEA III International Composition Prize: $2,500. Awarded once annually. Between 6-8 finalists are chosen and their works are performed in a competition concert by the ALEA III contemporary music ensemble. At the end of the concert, one piece will be selected to receive the prize. One grand prize winner is selected by a panel of judges.

TIPS "Emphasis placed on works written in 20th and 21st century compositional idioms."

AMERICAN SONGWRITER LYRIC CONTEST

1303 16th Ave. S., 2nd Floor, Nashville, TN 37212. (615)321-6096. Fax: (615)321-6097. E-mail: info@americansongwriter.com. Website: www.americansongwriter.com. Estab. 1984. For songwriters and composers. Award for each bimonthly issue of *American Songwriter* magazine, plus grand prize winner at year-end.

PURPOSE To promote and encourage the craft of lyric writing.

REQUIREMENTS Contest is open to any amateur songwriter. AS defines an amateur as one who has not earned more than $5,000 from songwriting related to royalties, advances, or works for hire. Lyrics must be typed and a check for $12 (per entry) must be enclosed. Deadlines: January, March, May, July, September, November. See website for exact dates. Submit online through American Songspace or Sonicbids.com. Lyrics only. "If you enter two or more lyrics, you automatically receive a 1-year subscription to *American Songwriter* magazine (Canada: 3 or more; Other Countries: 4 or more)."

AWARDS A DX1 Martin Koa acoustic guitar valued at over $700 to bimonthly contest winner. The annual winner will be chosen from the six bimonthly contest winners. First place winners also receive one legendary Shure SM58 microphone and four sets of Elixir Strings, and one Elixir Guitar Cable. GRAND PRIZE: The annual winner, chosen from the six contest winners, will receive round-trip airfare to Nashville and a dream cowriting session. The May/June 2011 1st place winner was Laura Busey for "This Side of Sanity."

TIPS "You do not have to be a subscriber to enter or win. You may submit as many entries as you like. All genres of music accepted."

ANNUAL NSAI SONG CONTEST

1710 Roy Acuff Place, Nashville, TN 37203. (615)256-3354. E-mail: songcontest@nashvillesongwriters.com. Website: www.nsai.cmt.com. **Contact:** David Petrelli, NSAI event director.

PURPOSE "A chance for aspiring songwriters to be heard by music industry decision makers."

REQUIREMENTS Entry fee: $35 per song (NSAI member); $45 per song (non-member). Submissions accepted August 1-October 31. In order to be eligible contestants must not be receiving income from any work submitted—original material only. Mail-in submissions must be in CD form and include entry form, lyrics and melody. Online submissions available through nsai.cmt.com. Visit website for complete list of rules and regulations. Deadline is different each year; check website or send for application. Samples are required with application in the format of cassette or CD.

AWARDS Grand Prize winner receives a one-on-one mentoring session with music superstar Darius Rucker. CMT Listener's Choice award gives fans a chance to vote for their favorite song entry. Visit website for complete list of rules and prizes.

CRS NATIONAL COMPOSERS COMPETITION

724 Winchester Rd., Broomall, PA 19008. (610)544-5920. Fax:(610)544-5920. E-mail: crsnews@verizon.net. Website:www.crsnews.org. For songwriters, composers, and performing artists. College faculty and gifted artists. Each annual competition is limited to the first 300 applicants—ALL FEES BEYOND THIS LIMIT WILL BE RETURNED. Email: crsnews@verizon.net

REQUIREMENTS For composers, songwriters, performing artists, and ensembles. Each category requires a separate application fee. The work submitted must be unpublished (prior to acceptance) and not commercially recorded on any label. The work submitted must not exceed nine performers. Each composer/performer may submit one work for each application submitted. (Taped performances by composers are additionally encouraged.) Composition must not exceed sixteen minutes in length. CRS reserves the right not to accept a First Prize Winner. Write with SASE for application or visit website. Add $3.50 for postage and handling. Must send a detailed résumé with application form available on our Web page under "Events" category. Samples of work required with application. Send score and parts with optional CD or DAT. Application fee: $50.

AWARDS First prize will consist of a commercially distributed new compact disc recording grant featuring one composition along with other distinguished composers and performing artists. Second and Third Prizes will be awarded Honorable Mention toward future recordings with CRS and Honorary Life Membership to the Society. Applications are judged by a panel of judges determined each year.

EUROPEAN INTERNATIONAL COMPETITION FOR COMPOSERS/IBLA FOUNDATION

226 East 2nd St., Loft 1B, New York, NY 10009. (212)387-0111. E-mail: iblanewyork@gmail.com. Website: www.ibla.org. **Contact:** Michael Yasenak, executive director. Chairman: Dr. Salvatore Moltisanti. Estab. 1995. For songwriters and composers. Annual award.

PURPOSE "To promote the winners' career through exposure, publicity, recordings with Athena Records and nationwide distribution with the Empire Group."

REQUIREMENTS Deadline: April 30. Send for application. Music score and/or recording of one work are required with application. Application fee is refunded if not admitted into the program.

AWARDS Winners are presented in concerts in Europe-Japan, USA.

GRASSY HILL KERRVILLE NEW FOLK COMPETITION

(formerly New Folk Concerts For Emerging Songwriters) P.O. Box 291466, Kerrville, TX 78029. (830)257-3600. Fax:(830)257-8680. E-mail: info@kerrville music.com. Website:www.kerrvillefolkfestival.com. **Contact:** Dalis Allen, producer. For songwriters. Annual award.

⊙ Also see the listing for Kerrville Folk Festival in the "Workshops" section of this book.

PURPOSE "To provide an opportunity for emerging songwriters to be heard and rewarded for excellence."

REQUIREMENTS Songwriter enters 2 original songs burned to CD (cassettes no longer accepted), or uploaded to SonicBids, with entry fee; no more than one submission may be entered; 6-8 minutes total for 2 songs. Application online, no lyric sheets or press material needed. Submissions accepted between December 1 and March 15 or first 800 entries received prior to that date. Call or e-mail to request rules. Entry fee: $25.

AWARDS New Folk Award Winner. 32 finalists invited to sing the 2 songs entered during the Kerrville Folk Festival in May. Six writers are chosen as award winners. Each of the 6 receives a cash award of $450 or more and performs at a winner's concert during the Kerrville Folk Festival in June. Initial round of entries judged by the festival producer and a panel of online listeners from the music industry. 32 finalists judged by panel of 3 performer/songwriters.

TIPS "Do not allow instrumental accompaniment to drown out lyric content. Don't enter without complete copy of the rules. Former winners and finalists include Lyle Lovett, Nanci Griffith, Hal Ketchum, John Gorka, David Wilcox, Lucinda Williams and Robert Earl Keen, Tish Hinojosa, Carrie Newcomer, Jimmy Lafave, etc."

GREAT AMERICAN SONG CONTEST

PMB 135, 6327-C SW Capitol Hill Hwy., Portland, OR 97239-1937. E-mail: info@GreatAmericanSong.com. Website: www.GreatAmericanSong.com. **Contact:** Carla Starrett, event coordinator. Estab. 1998. For songwriters, composers and lyricists. Annual award.

⊙ Also see the listing for Songwriters Resource Network in the "Organizations" section of this book.

PURPOSE To help songwriters get their songs heard by music-industry professionals; to generate educational and networking opportunities for participating songwriters; to help songwriters open doors in the music business.

REQUIREMENTS Entry fee: $25. "Annual deadline. Check our website for details or send SASE along with your mailed request for information."

AWARDS Winners receive a mix of cash awards and prizes. The focus of the contest is on networking and educational opportunities. (All participants receive detailed evaluations of their songs by industry professionals.) Songs are judged by knowledgeable music-industry professionals, including prominent hit songwriters, producers and publishers.

TIPS "Focus should be on the song. The quality of the demo isn't important. Judges will be looking for good songwriting talent. They will base their evaluations on the song—not the quality of the recording or the voice performance."

HARVEY GAUL COMPOSITION CONTEST

The Pittsburgh New Music Ensemble, Inc., 527 Coyne Terrace, Pittsburgh, PA 15207. (412)889-7231. E-mail: contactpnme@gmail.com. Website: www.pnme.org. **Contact:** Jeffrey Nytch, DMA, managing director. For composers. Biennial.

PURPOSE Objective is to encourage composition of new music.

REQUIREMENTS "Must be citizen of the US. Please submit score and recording, if available (CDs only) of a representative instrumental score." Send SASE for application or download from www.pnme.org. Samples of work are required with application. Entry fee: $20. Deadline: January 1, 2013 (postmark).

AWARDS Harvey Gaul Composition Contest: $6,000. Winner will receive commission for new work to be premiered by the PNME.

IAMA (INTERNATIONAL ACOUSTIC MUSIC AWARDS)

2881 E. Oakland Park Blvd, Suite 414, Fort Lauderdale, FL 33306. (954)537-3127. **Contact:** Jessica Brandon, artist relations. Established 2004. E-mail: info@inacoustic.com. Website: www.inacoustic.com. For singer-songwriters, musicians, performing musicians in the acoustic genre.

PURPOSE "The purpose is to promote the excellence in Acoustic music performance and songwriting." Genres include: Folk, Alternative, Blue-grass, etc.

REQUIREMENTS Visit website for entry form and details. "All songs submitted must be original. There must be at least an acoustic instrument (voice) in any song. Electric and Electronic instruments, along with loops is allowed but acoustic instruments (or voice) must be clearly heard in all songs submitted. Contestants may enter as many songs in as many categories as desired but each entry requires a separate CD, entry form, lyric sheet and entry fee. CDs and lyrics will not be returned. Winners will be chosen by a Blue Ribbon Judging Committee comprised of music industry professionals including A&R managers from record labels, publishers and producers. Entries are judged equally on music performance, production, originality, lyrics, melody and composition. Songs may be in any language. Winners will be notified by e-mail and must sign and return an affidavit confirming that winner's song is original and he/she holds rights to the song." Entry fee: $35/entry.

AWARDS Prizes: Overall Grand Prize receives $11,000 worth of merchandise. First prizes in all categories win $900 worth of merchandise and services. Runner-up prizes in all categories receive $600 worth of merchandise and services. All first prizes and runner-up winners will receive a track on IAMA compilation CD which goes out to radio stations.

TIPS "Judging is based on music performance, music production, songwriting and originality/artistry."

KATE NEAL KINLEY MEMORIAL FELLOWSHIP

University of Illinois, College of Fine and Applied Arts, 608 E. Lorado Taft Dr., #100, Champaign, IL 61820. (217)333-1661. Website: www.faa.uiuc.edu. **Contact:** Chairperson. Estab. 1931. For students of architecture, art or music. Annual award.

PURPOSE The advancement of study in the fine arts.

REQUIREMENTS "The Fellowship will be awarded upon the basis of unusual promise in the fine arts. Open to college graduates whose principal or major studies have been in the fields of architecture, art or music." Deadline for 2012-2013 fellowship: December 1, 2011. Call or visit website for application. Samples of work are required with application.

AWARDS "One major fellowship which yield the sum of $20,000 each which is to be used by the recipients toward defraying the expenses of advanced study of the fine arts in America or abroad." Two or three smaller fellowships may also be awarded upon committee recommendations. Good for 1 year. Grant is nonrenewable.

L.A. DESIGNERS' THEATRE MUSIC AWARDS

P.O. Box 1883, Studio City, CA 91614-0883. (323)650-9600. Fax: (323)654-3210. E-mail: ladesigners@gmail.com. Artistic director: Richard Niederberg. For songwriters, composers, performing artists, musical playwrights and rights holders of music.

PURPOSE To produce new musicals, operettas, opera-boufes and plays with music, as well as new dance pieces with new music scores.

REQUIREMENTS Submit nonreturnable cassette, tape, CD, or any other medium by first, or fourth-class mail. "We prefer proposals to scripts." Acceptance: continuous. Submit nonreturnable materials with cover letter. No application form or fee is necessary.

AWARDS Music is commissioned for a particular project. Amounts are negotiable. Applications judged by our artistic staff.

TIPS "Make the material 'classic, yet commercial' and easy to record/re-record/edit. Make sure rights are totally free of all 'strings,' 'understandings,' 'promises,' etc. ASCAP/BMI/SESAC registration is OK, as long as 'grand' or 'performing rights' are available."

MAXIM MAZUMDAR NEW PLAY COMPETITION

1 Curtain Up Alley, Buffalo, NY 14202-1911. (716)852-2600. Fax: (716)852-2266. E-mail: newplays@alleyway.com. Website: www.alleyway.com. **Contact:** Literary Manager. For musical playwrights. Annual award.

PURPOSE Alleyway Theatre is dedicated to the development and production of new works. Winners of the competition will receive production and royalties.

REQUIREMENTS Unproduced full-length work not less than 90 minutes long with cast limit of 10 and unit or simple set, or unproduced one-act work less than 15 minutes long with cast limit of 6 and simple set; prefers work with unconventional setting that explores the boundaries of theatricality; limit of 1 submission in each category; guidelines available online, no entry form. $25 playwright entry fee. Script, resume, SASE optional. CD or cassette mandatory. Deadline: July 1.

AWARDS Production for full-length play or musical with royalty and production for one-act play or musical.

TIPS "Entries may be of any style, but preference will be given to those scripts which take place in unconventional settings and explore the boundaries of theatricality. No more than ten performers is a definite, unchangeable requirement."

MID-ATLANTIC SONG CONTEST

Songwriters' Association of Washington, PMB 106-137, 4200 Wisconsin Ave., NW, Washington DC 20016. E-mail: masc@saw.org. Website: www.saw.org. For songwriters and composers. Estab. 1982. Annual award.

○ Also see the listing for Songwriters Association of Washington in the "Organizations" section.

PURPOSE This is one of the longest-running contests in the nation; SAW has organized 27 contests since 1982. The competition is designed to afford rising songwriters in a wide variety of genres the opportunity to receive awards and exposure in an environment of peer competition.

REQUIREMENTS Amateur status is important. Applicants should request a brochure/application using the contact information above. Rules and procedures are clearly explained in the brochure and also online. CD and 3 copies of the lyrics are to be submitted with an application form and fee for each entry, or submit mp3 entries by applying online or through Sonicbids. Reduced entry fees are offered to members of Songwriters' Association of Washington; membership can be arranged simultaneously with entering. Multiple song discounts are also offered. Applications are mailed out and posted on their website around June 1; the submission deadline is September 15; awards are typically announced late in the fall.

AWARDS The two best songs in each of ten categories win prize packages donated by the contest's corporate sponsors: BMI, Oasis CD Manufacturing, Omega Recording Studios, Mary Cliff, and Sonic Bids. Winning songwriters are invited to perform in Washington, DC at the Awards Ceremony Gala, and the winning songs are included on a compilation CD.

The best song in each category is eligible for three grand cash prizes. Certificates are awarded to other entries meriting finalis and honorable mention.

TIPS "Enter the song in the most appropriate category. Make the sound recording the best it can be (even though judges are asked to focus on melody and lyric and not on production.) Avoid clichés, extended introductions, and long instrumental solos."

THELONIOUS MONK INTERNATIONAL JAZZ COMPOSERS COMPETITION

(Sponsored by BMI) Thelonious Monk Institute of Jazz, 5225 Wisconsin Ave., NW, #605, Washington DC 20015. (202)364-7272. Fax: (202)364-0176. E-mail: info@monkinstitute.org. Website: www.monkinstitute.org. **Contact:** Leonard Brown, program director. Estab. 1993. For songwriters and composers. Annual award.

PURPOSE The award is given to an aspiring jazz composer who best demonstrates originality, creativity and excellence in jazz composition.

REQUIREMENTS Deadline: See website. Send for application. Submission must include application form, resume of musical experience, CD or cassette, entry, four copies of the full score, and a photo. The composition features a different instrument each year. Entry fee: $35.

AWARDS $10,000. Applications are judged by panel of jazz musicians. "The Institute will provide piano, bass, guitar, drum set, tenor saxophone, and trumpet for the final performance. The winner will be responsible for the costs of any different instrumentation included in the composition."

NACUSA YOUNG COMPOSERS' COMPETITION

Contact: Daniel Kessner, president, NACUSA. Estab. 1978. For composers. Annual award.

○ Also see the National Association of Composers/USA (NACUSA) listing in the "Organizations" section.

PURPOSE Encourages the composition of new American concert hall music.

REQUIREMENTS Entry fee: $20 (membership fee). Deadline: October 30. Send for application. Samples are not required.

AWARDS 1st Prize: $400; 2nd Prize: $100; and possible Los Angeles performances. Applications are judged by a committee of experienced NACUSA composer members.

SAMMY NESTICO AWARD/USAF BAND AIRMEN OF NOTE

201 McChord St., Joint Base Anacostia-Bolling, Washington, DC 20032-0202. (202)767-1756. Fax: (202)767-0686. E-mail: USAFBand.af.mil. **Contact:** Alan Baylock, master sergeant. Estab. 1995. For composers. Annual award.

PURPOSE To carry on the tradition of excellence of Sammy Nestico's writing through jazz composition. The winner will have his/her composition performed by the USAF Airmen of Note, have it professionally recorded, and receive an opportunity for a $2,000 follow-up commission.

REQUIREMENTS Unpublished work for jazz ensemble instrumentation (5,4,4,4) style, form and length are unrestricted. Deadline: November 1, 2011. Send for application. Samples of work are required with full score and set of parts (or CD recording).

AWARDS Performance by the USAF Band Airmen of Note; expense paid travel to Washington DC for the performance; professionally produced recording of the winning composition; and an opportunity for a $2,000 follow up commission. Applications are judged by panel of musicians.

PULITZER PRIZE IN MUSIC

Columbia University, 709 Journalism Bldg., 2950 Broadway, New York, NY 10027. (212)854-3841. Fax: (212)854-3342. E-mail: pulitzer@www.pulitzer.org. Website: www.pulitzer.org. **Contact:** Music Secretary. For composers and musical playwrights. Annual award.

REQUIREMENTS "For distinguished musical composition by an American that has had its first performance or recording in the United States during the year." Entries should reflect current creative activity. Works that receive their American premiere between January 1, 2010 and December 31, 2011 are eligible. A public performance or the public release of a recording shall constitute a premiere. Deadline: December 31. Samples of work are required with application, biography and photograph of composer, date and place of performance, score or manuscript and recording of the work, entry form, and $50 entry fee.

AWARDS "One award: $10,000. Applications are judged first by a nominating jury, then by the Pulitzer Prize Board."

RICHARD RODGERS AWARDS

American Academy of Arts and Letters, 633 W. 155 St., New York, NY 10032. (212)368-5900. E-mail: academy@artsandletters.org. Website: www.artsandletters. org. **Contact:** Jane Bolster, coordinator. Estab. 1978. Deadline: November 1, 2011. "The Richard Rodgers Awards subsidize staged reading, studio productions, and full productions by nonprofit theaters in New York City of works by composers and writers who are not already established in the field of musical theater. The awards are only for musicals—songs by themselves are not eligible. The authors must be citizens or permanent residents of the United States." Guidelines for this award may be obtained by sending a SASE to above address or download from www. artsandletters.org.

ROCKY MOUNTAIN FOLKS FESTIVAL SONGWRITER SHOWCASE

Planet Bluegrass, ATTN: Songwriter Showcase, P.O. Box 769, Lyons, CO 80540. (800)624-2422 or (303)823-0848. Fax: (303)823-0849. E-mail: brian@bluegrass. com. Website: www.bluegrass.com. **Contact:** Steve Szymanski, director. Estab. 1993. For songwriters, composers, and performers. Annual award.

PURPOSE Award based on having the best song and performance.

REQUIREMENTS Deadline: June. Finalists notified by July. Rules available on website. Samples of work are required with application. Send CD with $10/song entry fee. Can now submit online at www. sonicbids.com. "Contestants cannot be signed to a major label or publishing deal. No backup musicians allowed. Awards: 1st Place is a 2012 Festival Main Stage set, custom Hayes Guitar, $100, and a free one song drumoverdubs (www.drumoverdubs.com) certificate (valued at $300); 2nd Place is $500 and a Baby Taylor Guitar; 3rd Place is $400 and a Baby Taylor Guitar; 4th Place is $300; 5th Place is $200; 6th to 10th Place is $100 each. Each finalist will also receive a complimentary 3-day Folks Festival pass that includes onsite camping, and a Songwriter In The Round slot during the Festival on our workshop stage."

ROME PRIZE COMPETITION FELLOWSHIP

American Academy in Rome, 7 E. 60 St., New York, NY 10022-1001. (212)751-7200. Fax: (212)751-7220. E-mail: info@aarome.org. Website: www.aarome.org.

Contact: Programs Department. For composers. Annual award.

PURPOSE "Through its annual Rome Prize Competition, the academy awards up to thirty fellowships in eleven disciplines, including musical composition. Winners of the Rome Prize pursue independent projects while residing at the Academy's eleven acre center in Rome."

REQUIREMENTS "Applicants for 11-month fellowships must be US citizens and hold a bachelor's degree in music, musical composition or its equivalent." Deadline: November 1. Entry fee: $30. Application guidelines are available through the Academy's website.

AWARDS "Up to two fellowships are awarded annually in musical composition. Fellowship consists of room, board, and a studio at the Academy facilities in Rome as well as a stipend of $26,000. In all cases, excellence is the primary criterion for selection, based on the quality of the materials submitted. Winners are announced in mid-April and fellowships generally begin in early September."

TELLURIDE TROUBADOUR CONTEST

Planet Bluegrass, ATTN: Troubadour Competition, P.O. Box 769, Lyons CO 80540. (303)823-0848 or (800)624-2422. Fax: (303)823-0849. E-mail: brian@bluegrass.com. Website: www.bluegrass.com. **Contact:** Steve Szymanski, director. Estab. 1991. For songwriters, composers, and performers. Annual award.

PURPOSE Award based on having best song and performance.

REQUIREMENTS Deadline: must be postmarked by April 15; notified May 6, if selected. Rules available on website. Send CD and $10/song entry fee (limit of 2 songs). Can now submit music online at www.sonicbids.com. Contestants cannot be signed to a major label or publishing deal. No backup musicians allowed.

AWARDS 1st: custom Shanti Guitar, $300 and Festival Main Stage Set; 2nd: $500; 3rd: $400; 4th: $300; 5th: $200. Applications judged by panel of judges.

THE ART OF MUSIC ANNUAL WRITING CONTEST

The Art of Music, Inc., P.O. Box 85, Del Mar CA 92014-0085. (619) 884-1401. Fax: (858) 755-1104. E-mail: info@theartofmusicinc.org. Website: www.theartofmusicinc.org. **Contact:** Elizabeth C. Axford. Offered annually. Categories are: essay, short story, poetry, song lyrics, and illustrations for cover art. The purpose of the contest is to promote the art of music through writing. Acquires one time rights. All entries must be accompanied by an entry form indicating category and age; parent signature is required of all writers under age 18. Poems may be of any length and in any style; essays and short stories should not exceed five double-spaced, typewritten pages. All entries shall be previously unpublished (except poems and song lyrics) and the original work of the author. Prize: Cash, medal, certificate, publication in the anthology titled *The Art of Music: A Collection of Writings*, and copies of the book. Judged by a panel of published poets, authors and songwriters. Entry fee: $20 fee. Inquiries accepted by e-mail, phone. **Deadline: June 30.** Short stories should be no longer than five pages typed and double spaced. Open to any writer. "Make sure all work is fresh and original. Music-related topics only." Results announced October 31. Winners notified by mail. For contest results, send SASE or visit website. Guidelines and entry form for SASE, on website, or by e-mail.

PURPOSE "The purpose of the contest is to promote the art of music through writing."

REQUIREMENTS "All writings must be music-related topics."

THE ASCAP DEEMS TAYLOR AWARDS

American Society of Composers, Authors & Publishers, One Lincoln Plaza, New York NY, 10023. (212)621-6323. E-mail: esansaurus@ascap.com. Website: www.ascap.com. **Contact:** Esther SanSaurus.

PURPOSE The ASCAP Deems Taylor Awards Competition offers $250-1,000 prize for books, articles, liner notes, broadcasts and websites on the subject of music.

REQUIREMENTS Deadline: See website. There is no fee or submission form required but must be submitted with a cover letter. Written works must be published in the United States in English, during the calendar year of 2011. The subject matter may be biographical or critical, reportorial or historical- almost any form of nonfiction prose about music and/or its creators. However, instructional textbooks, how-to-guides, or works of fiction will not be accepted.

AWARDS Prize: $250-1,000.

THE BLANK THEATRE COMPANY YOUNG PLAYWRIGHTS FESTIVAL

P.O. Box 38756, Hollywood, CA 90038. (323)871-8018. Fax: (323)661-3903. E-mail: submissions@youngplay wrights.com. Website: www.youngplaywrights.com. Estab. 1993. For both musical and nonmusical playwrights. Annual award.

PURPOSE "To give young playwrights an opportunity to learn more about playwriting and to give them a chance to have their work mentored, developed, and presented by professional artists."

REQUIREMENTS Playwrights must be 19 years old or younger on March 15, 2012. Send legible, original plays of any length and on any subject (cowritten plays are acceptable provided all cowriters meet eligibility requirements). Submissions must be postmarked by March 15 and must include a cover sheet with the playwright's name, date of birth, school (if any), home address, home phone number, e-mail address, and production history. Pages must be numbered and submitted unbound (unstapled). For musicals, a tape or CD of a selection from the score should be submitted with the script. Manuscripts will not be returned. Please do not send originals. Semifinalists and winners will be contacted in May.

AWARDS Winning playwrights receive a workshop presentation of their work.

THE JOHN LENNON SONGWRITING CONTEST

180 Brighton Rd., Suite 801, Clifton NJ 07012. (888)884-5572. E-mail: info@jlsc.com; tiana@jlsc. com. Website: www.jlsc.com. Contact: Tiana Lewis. Estab. 1996. For songwriters. Open year-round.

PURPOSE "The purpose of the John Lennon Songwriting Contest is to promote the art of songwriting by assisting in the discovery of new talent as well as providing more established songwriters with an opportunity to advance their careers."

REQUIREMENTS Each entry must consist of the following: completed and signed application; audiocassette, CD or mp3 containing 1 song only, 5 minutes or less in length; lyric sheet typed or printed legibly (English translation is required when applicable); $30 entry fee. Deadline: December 15, 2011. Applications can be found in various music-oriented magazines and on our website. Prospective entrants can send for an application or contact the contest via e-mail at info@jlsc.com.

AWARDS Entries are accepted in the following 12 categories: rock, country, jazz, pop, world, gospel/inspirational, R&B, hip-hop, Latin, electronic, folk, and children's music. Winners will receive EMI Publishing Contracts, Studio Equipment from Brian Moore Guitars, Roland, Edirol, and Audio Technica, 1,000 CDs in full color with premium 6-panel Digipaks courtesy of Discmakers, and gift certificates from Musiciansfriend.com. One entrant wil be chosen to TOUR and PERFORM for 1 week on Warped Tour 2012. One Lennon Award-winning song will be named "Song of the Year" and take home an additional $20,000 in cash.

U.S.A. SONGWRITING COMPETITION

2881 E. Oakland Park Blvd., Suite 414, Ft. Lauderdale FL 33306. (954)537-3127. Fax: (954)537-9690. E-mail: info@songwriting.net. Website: www.songwriting.net. **Contact:** Contest Manager. Estab. 1994. For songwriters, composers, performing artists, and lyricists. Annual award.

PURPOSE "To honor good songwriters/composers all over the world, especially the unknown ones."

REQUIREMENTS Open to professional and beginner songwriters. No limit on entries. Each entry must include an entry fee, a CD or audiocassette tape of song(s), and lyric sheet(s). Judged by music industry representatives. Past judges have included record label representatives and publishers from Arista Records, EMI, and Warner/Chappell. Deadline: To be announced. Entry fee: To be announced. Send SASE with request or e-mail for entry forms at any time. Samples of work are not required.

AWARDS Prizes include cash and merchandise in 15 different categories: pop, rock, country, Latin, R&B, gospel, folk, jazz, "lyrics only" category, instrumental, and many others.

TIPS "Judging is based on lyrics, originality, melody and overall composition. CD-quality production is great but not a consideration in judging."

U.S.-JAPAN CREATIVE ARTISTS EXCHANGE FELLOWSHIP PROGRAM

Japan-U.S. Friendship Commission, 1201 15th St. NW, Suite 330, Washington DC 20005. (202)653-9800. Fax: (202)653-9802. E-mail: jusfc@jusfc.gov. Website: www.jusfc.gov. **Contact:** Margaret Mihori, assistant executive director. Estab. 1980. For all creative artists. Annual award.

PURPOSE "For artists to go as seekers, as cultural visionaries, and as living liaisons to the traditional and contemporary life of Japan."

REQUIREMENTS "Artists' works must exemplify the best in U.S. arts." Deadline: Feb. 1, 2012. Send for application and guidelines. Applications available on website. Samples of work are required with application. Requires 2 pieces on CD or DVD.

AWARDS Five artists are awarded a 3-month residency anywhere in Japan. Awards monthly stipend for living expenses, housing, and professional support services; up to $6,000 for predeparture costs, including such items as language training and economy class round-trip airfare, plus 400,000 yen for monthly living expenses, housing allowance, and professional support services, as well as other arts professionals with expertise in Japanese culture.

TIPS "Applicants should anticipate a highly rigorous review of their artistry and should have compelling reasons for wanting to work in Japan."

Y.E.S. FESTIVAL OF NEW PLAYS

Northern Kentucky University, Dept. of Theatre, FA-205, Highland Heights, KY 41099-1007. (859)572-6303. Fax: (859)572-6057. E-mail: forman@nku.edu. **Contact:** Sandra Forman, project director. Estab. 1983. For musical playwrights. Biennial award (odd-numbered years).

PURPOSE "The festival seeks to encourage new playwrights and develop new plays and musicals. Three plays or musicals are given full productions."

REQUIREMENTS "No entry fee. Submit a script with a completed entry form. Musicals should be submitted with a piano/conductor's score and/or a vocal parts score. Scripts may be submitted May 1 through Sept. 30, 2012, for the New Play Festival occuring April 2013. Send SASE for application."

AWARDS Three awards of $500. "The winners are brought to NKU at our expense to view late rehearsals and opening night." Submissions are judged by a panel of readers.

TIPS "Plays/musicals which have heavy demands for mature actors are not as likely to be selected as an equally good script with roles for 18-30 year olds."

ORGANIZATIONS

One of the first places a beginning songwriter should look for guidance and support is a songwriting organization. Offering encouragement, instruction, contacts, and feedback, these groups of professional and amateur songwriters can help an aspiring songwriter hone the skills needed to compete in the ever-changing music industry.

The type of organization you choose to join depends on what you want to get out of it. Local groups can offer a friendly, supportive environment where you can work on your songs and have them critiqued in a constructive way by other songwriters. They're also great places to meet collaborators. Larger, national organizations can give you access to music business professionals and other songwriters across the country.

Most of the organizations listed in this book are nonprofit groups with membership open to specific groups of people—songwriters, musicians, classical composers, etc. They can be local groups with a membership of fewer than 100 people, or large national organizations with thousands of members from all over the country. In addition to regular meetings, most organizations occasionally sponsor events such as seminars and workshops to which music industry personnel are invited to talk about the business, and perhaps listen to and critique demo tapes.

Check the following listings, bulletin boards at local music stores, and your local newspapers for area organizations. If you are unable to locate an organization within an easy distance of your home, you may want to consider joining one of the national groups. These groups, based in New York, Los Angeles, and Nashville, keep their members involved and informed through newsletters, regional workshops, and large yearly conferences. They can help a writer who feels isolated in his hometown get his music heard by professionals in the major music centers.

In the following listings, organizations describe their purpose and activities, as well as how much it costs to join. Before joining any organization, consider what they have to offer and how becoming a member will benefit you.

ACADEMY OF COUNTRY MUSIC

5500 Balboa Blvd., Encino CA 91316. (818)788-8000. Fax: (818)788-0999. E-mail: info@acmcountry.com. Website: www.acmcountry.com. **Contact:** Bob Romeo, CEO. Estab. 1964. Serves country music industry professionals. Eligibility for professional members is limited to those individuals who derive some portion of their income directly from country music. Each member is classified by one of the following categories: artist/entertainer, club/venue operator, musician, on-air personality, manager, talent agent, composer, music publisher, public relations, publications, radio, TV/motion picture, record company, talent buyer, or affiliated (general). The purpose of ACM is to promote and enhance the image of country music. The Academy is involved year-round in activities important to the country music community. Some of these activities include charity fund-raisers, participation in country music seminars, talent contests, artist showcases, assistance to producers in placing country music on television and in motion pictures and backing legislation that benefits the interests of the country music community. The ACM is governed by directors and run by officers elected annually. Applications are accepted throughout the year. Membership is $75/year.

AMERICAN MUSIC CENTER, INC.

322 8th Ave., Suite 1401, New York NY 10001. (212)366-5260 x10. E-mail: allison@amc.net; deborah@amc.net. Website: www.amc.net. **Contact:** Membership Department. The American Music Center, founded by a consortium led by Aaron Copland in 1939, is the first-ever national service and information center for new classical music and jazz by American composers. The Center has a variety of innovative new programs and services, including a monthly Internet magazine (www.newmusicbox.org) for new American music, online databases of contemporary ensembles and ongoing opportunities for composers, an online catalog of new music for educators specifically targeted to young audiences, a series of professional development workshops, and an online listening library (www.newmusicjukebox.org). Each month, AMC provides its over 2,500 members with a listing of opportunities including calls for scores, competitions, and other new music performance information. Each year, AMC's Information Services Department fields thousands of requests concerning composers, performers,

data, funding, and support programs. The AMC Collection at the New York Public Library for the Performing Arts presently includes over 60,000 scores and recordings, many unavailable elsewhere. "AMC also continues to administer several grant programs: the Aaron Copland Fund for Music; the Henry Cowell Performance Incentive Fund; and its own programs Live Music for Dance and the Composer Assistance Program." Members also receive a link their websites on www.amc.net. The American Music Center is not-for-profit and has an annual membership fee.

AMERICAN SOCIETY OF COMPOSERS, AUTHORS AND PUBLISHERS (ASCAP)

One Lincoln Plaza, New York NY 10023. (212)621-6000 (administration); (212)621-6240 (membership). E-mail: info@ascap.com. Website: www.ascap.com. President and chairman of the board: Paul Williams. CEO: John LoFrumento. Executive vice president/Membership: Todd Brabec. **Contact:** Member Services at (800)95-ASCAP. **Regional offices—West Coast:** 7920 Sunset Blvd., Third Floor, Los Angeles CA 90046, (323)883-1000; **Nashville:** Two Music Square W., Nashville TN 37203, (615)742-5000; **Atlanta:** 950 Joseph E. Lowery Bldv. NW, Atlanta GA 30318, (404)685-8699; **Miami:** 420 Lincoln Rd., Suite 385, Miami Beach FL 33139, (305)673-3446; **United Kingdom:** 8 Cork St., London W1S 3LJ England, 011-44-207-439-0909; **Puerto Rico:** Ave. Martinez Nadal, c/ Hill Side 623, San Juan, Puerto Rico 00920, (787)707-0782. ASCAP is a membership association of over 240,000 composers, lyricists, songwriters, and music publishers, whose function is to protect the rights of its members by licensing and collecting royalties for the nondramatic public performance of their copyrighted works. ASCAP licensees include radio, television, cable, live concert promoters, bars, restaurants, symphony orchestras, new media, and other users of music. ASCAP is the leading performing rights society in the world. All revenues, less operating expenses, are distributed to members (about 86 cents of each dollar). ASCAP was the first US performing rights organization to distribute royalties from the Internet. Founded in 1914, ASCAP is the only society created and owned by writers and publishers. The ASCAP board of directors consists of 12 writers and 12 publishers, elected by the membership. ASCAP's Member Card provides exclusive benefits geared towards working music professionals.

Among the benefits are health, musical instrument and equipment, tour and studio liability, term life and long-term care insurance, discounts on musical instruments, equipment and supplies, access to a credit union, and much more. ASCAP hosts a wide array of showcases and workshops throughout the year, and offers grants, special awards, and networking opportunities in a variety of genres. Visit their website listed above for more information.

ARIZONA SONGWRITERS ASSOCIATION

428 E. Thunderbird Rd., #737, Phoenix AZ 85022. E-mail: azsongwriters@cox.net. Website: www.azsongwriters.com. **Contact:** Jon Iger, president. Estab. 1977. Members are all ages; all styles of music, novice to pro; many make money placing their songs in film and TV. Most members are residents of Arizona. Purpose is to educate about the craft and business of songwriting and to facilitate networking with business professionals and other songwriters, musicians, singers, and studios. Offers instruction, e-newsletter, workshops, performance, and song pitching opportunities. Applications accepted year-round. Membership fee: $25/year.

◎ ASSOCIATION DES PROFESSIONEL. LE.S DE LA CHANSON ET DE LA MUSIQUE

450 Rideau St., Suite 401, Ottawa ON K1N 5Z4 Canada. (613)745-5642. Fax: (613)745-9715. E-mail: communications@apcm.ca. Website: www.apcm.ca. **Contact:** Jean-Emmanuel Simiand, agent de communication. Director: Lucie Mailloux. Estab. 1989. Members are French Canadian singers and musicians. Members must be French singing and may have a CD to be distributed. Purpose is to gather French-speaking artists (outside of Quebec, mainly in Ontario) to distribute their material, other workshops, instructions, lectures, etc. Offers instruction, newsletter, lectures, workshops, and distribution. Applications accepted year-round. Membership fee: $60 (Canadian).

ASSOCIATION OF INDEPENDENT MUSIC PUBLISHERS

Los Angeles Chapter: P.O. Box 69473, Los Angeles CA 90069. (818)771-7301. New York line: (212)391-2532. E-mail: LAinfo@aimp.org or NYinfo@aimp.org. Website: www.aimp.org. Estab. 1977. Purpose is to educate members on new developments in the music publishing industry and to provide networking opportunities. Offers monthly panels and networking events.

Applications accepted year-round. Membership fee: NY: $75/year; LA: $76/year.

AUSTIN SONGWRITERS GROUP

P.O. Box 2578, Austin TX 78768. (512)698-4237. E-mail: info@austinsongwritersgroup.com. Website: www.austinsongwritersgroup.com. **Contact:** Lee Duffy, executive director. President: Rick Busby Estab. 1986. Serves all ages and all levels, from just beginning to advanced. "Prospective members should have an interest in the field of songwriting, whether it be for profit or hobby. The main purpose of this organization is to educate members in the craft and business of songwriting; to provide resources for growth and advancement in the area of songwriting; and to provide opportunities for performance and contact with the music industry." The primary benefit of membership to a songwriter is exposed to music industry professionals, which increases contacts and furthers the songwriter's education in both craft and business aspects. Offers competitions, instruction, lectures, library, newsletter, performance opportunities, evaluation services, workshops and contact with music industry professionals through special guest speakers at meetings, plus our yearly 'Austin Songwriters Symposium,' which includes instruction, song evaluations, and song pitching direct to those pros currently seeking material for their artists, publishing companies, etc." Applications accepted year-round. Membership fee: $100/year.

TIPS Our newsletter is top-quality-packed with helpful information on all aspects of songwriting-craft, business, recording and producing tips, and industry networking opportunities. Go to our website and sign up for emails to keep you informed about on going and up coming events!"

BALTIMORE SONGWRITERS ASSOCIATION

P.O. Box 22496, Baltimore MD 21203. (410)669-1075. E-mail: info@baltimoresongwriters.org. Website: www.baltimoresongwriters.org. **Contact:** Ken Gutberlet, president. Estab. 1997. "The BSA is an inclusive organization with all ages, skill levels and genres of music welcome." Offers instruction, newsletter, lectures, workshops, performance opportunities. Applications accepted year-round; membership not limited to location or musical status. Membership fee: $25.

TIPS "We are trying to build a musical community that is more supportive and less competitive. We are dedicated to helping songwriters grow and become better in their craft."

THE BLACK ROCK COALITION

P.O. Box 1054, Cooper Station, New York NY 10276. (212)713-5097. E-mail: ldavis@blackrockcoalition.org. Website: www.blackrockcoalition.org. **Contact**: LaRonda Davis, president. Estab. 1985. Serves musicians, songwriters—male and female ages 18-40 (average). Also engineers, entertainment attorneys and producers. Looking for members who are "mature and serious about music as an artist or activist willing to help fellow musicians. The BRC independently produces, promotes and distributes Black alternative music acts as a collective and supportive voice for such musicians within the music and record business. The main purpose of this organization is to produce, promote and distribute the full spectrum of black music along with educating the public on what black music is. The BRC is now soliciting recorded music by bands and individuals for Black Rock Coalition Records. Please send copyrighted and original material only." Offers instruction, newsletter, lectures, free seminars and workshops, monthly membership meeting, quarterly magazine, performing opportunities, evaluation services, business advice, full roster of all members. Applications accepted year-round. Bands must submit a tape, bio with picture and a self-addressed, stamped envelope before sending their membership fee. Membership fee: $25.

BROADCAST MUSIC, INC. (BMI)

7 World Trade Center, 250 Greenwich St., New York NY 10007. (212)220-3000. E-mail: newyork@bmi.com. Website: www.bmi.com. **Los Angeles:** 8730 Sunset Blvd., 3rd Floor West, Los Angeles CA 90069. (310)659-9109. E-mail: losangeles@bmi.com. **Nashville:** 10 Music Square East, Nashville TN 37203. (615)401-2000. E-mail: nashville@bmi.com. **Miami:** 1691 Michigan Av., Miami FL 33139. (305)673-5148. E-mail: miami@bmi.com. **Atlanta:** 3340 Peachtree Rd., NE, Suite 570, Atlanta GA 30326. (404)261-5151. E-mail: atlanta@bmi.com. **Puerto Rico:** 1250 Av. Ponce de Leon, San Jose Building Santurce PR 00907. (787)754-6490. **United Kingdom:** 84 Harley House, Marylebone Rd., London NW1 5HN United Kingdom. 011-44-207-486-2036. E-mail: london@bmi.com. President and CEO: Del R. Bryant. Senior vice presidents, New York: Phillip Graham, Writer/Publisher Relations; Alison Smith, Performing Rights. Vice presidents: New York: Charlie Feldman; Los Angeles: Barbara Cane and Doreen Ringer Ross; Nashville: Paul Corbin; Miami: Diane J. Almodovar; Atlanta: Catherine Brewton. Senior executive, London: Brandon Bakshi. BMI is a performing rights organization representing approximately 300,000 songwriters, composers, and music publishers in all genres of music, including pop, rock, country, R&B, rap, jazz, Latin, gospel, and contemporary classical. "Applicants must have written a musical composition, alone or in collaboration with other writers, which is commercially published, recorded or otherwise likely to be performed." Purpose: BMI acts on behalf of its songwriters, composers, and music publishers by insuring payment for performance of their works through the collection of licensing fees from radio stations, Internet outlets, broadcast and cable TV stations, hotels, nightclubs, aerobics centers and other users of music. This income is distributed to the writers and publishers in the form of royalty payments, based on how the music is used. BMI also undertakes intensive lobbying efforts in Washington DC on behalf of its affiliates, seeking to protect their performing rights through the enactment of new legislation and enforcement of current copyright law. In addition, BMI helps aspiring songwriters develop their skills through various workshops, seminars and competitions it sponsors throughout the country. Applications accepted year-round. There is no membership fee for songwriters; a onetime fee of $150 is required to affiliate an individually owned publishing company; $250 for partnerships, corporations and limited-liability companies. "Visit our website for specific contacts, e-mail addresses and additional membership information."

CALIFORNIA LAWYERS FOR THE ARTS

Fort Mason Center, Building C, Room 255, San Francisco CA 94123. (415)775-7200. Fax: (415)775-1143. E-mail: sanfrancisco@calawyersforthearts.org. Website: www.calawyersforthearts.org. **Southern California:** 1641 18th St., Santa Monica CA 90404. (310)998-5590. Fax: (310)998-5594. E-mail: losangeles@calawyersforthearts.org. **Sacramento Office:** 1418 20th St., Suite 201, Sacramento CA 95811. (916)442-6210. Fax: (916)441-1170. E-mail: sacramento@calawyersforthearts.org. **Contact:** Alma Robinson, executive director. Rob Woodworth, membership & outreach manager. Estab. 1974. "For artists of all disciplines, skill levels, and ages, supporting individuals and organizations, and arts organizations. Artists of all disciplines are welcome, whether professionals or amateurs. We also welcome groups and individuals who support the arts. We work most closely with the California arts community. Our mission is to establish a bridge between the legal and arts communities so that artists and art groups may handle their creative activities with greater business and legal competence; the legal profession will be more aware of issues affecting the arts community; and the law will become more responsive to the arts community." Offers newsletter, lectures, library, workshops, mediation service, attorney referral service, housing referrals, publications and advocacy. Membership fee: $20 for senior citizens and full-time students; $25 for working artists; $45 for general individual; $65 for panel attorney; $100 for patrons. Organizations: $50 for small organizations (budget under $100,000); $90 for large organizations (budget of $100,000 or more); $100 for corporate sponsors.

☯ CANADA COUNCIL FOR THE ARTS/ CONSEIL DES ARTS DU CANADA

350 Albert St., P.O. Box 1047, Ottawa ON K1P 5V8 Canada. (613)566-4414, ext. 4681. Website: www.can adacouncil.ca. **Contact:** Christian Mondor, information officer. Estab. 1957. An independent agency that fosters and promotes the arts in Canada by providing grants and services to professional artists including songwriters and musicians. "Individual artists must be Canadian citizens or permanent residents of Canada, and must have completed basic training and/or have the recognition as professionals within their fields. The Canada Council offers grants to professional musicians to pursue their individual artistic development and creation. There are specific deadline dates for the various programs of assistance. Visit our website at www.canadacouncil. ca/music for more details."

☯ CANADIAN ACADEMY OF RECORDING ARTS & SCIENCES (CARAS)

345 Adelaide Street West, 2nd Floor, Toronto, ON M5V 1R5. (416)485-3135. Fax: (416)485-4978. E-mail: info@carasonline.ca. Website: www.carasonline.ca. **Contact:** Meghan McCabe, manager, communications. President: Melanie Berry. Manager, Awards and Events: Brenna Knought. Membership is open to all employees (including support staff) in broadcasting and record companies, as well as producers, personal managers, recording artists, recording engineers, arrangers, composers, music publishers, album designers, promoters, talent and booking agents, record retailers, rack jobbers, distributors, recording studios, and other music industry-related professions (on approval). Applicants must be affiliated with the Canadian recording industry. Offers newsletter, nomination and voting privileges for Juno Awards and discount tickets to Juno Awards show. "CARAS strives to foster the development of the Canadian music and recording industries and to contribute toward higher artistic standards." Applications accepted year-round. Membership fee is $50/year (Canadian) + HST = $56.50. Applications accepted from individuals only, not from companies or organizations.

☯ CANADIAN COUNTRY MUSIC ASSOCIATION

120 Adelaide St. E, Suite 200, Toronto, ON M5C 1K9 Canada. (416)947-1331. Fax: (416)947-5924. E-mail: country@ccma.org. Website: www.ccma.org. **Contact:** Brandi Mills, manager of operations. Estab. 1976. Members are artists, songwriters, musicians, producers, radio station personnel, managers, booking agents, and others. Offers newsletter, workshops, performance opportunities, and the CCMA awards every September. "Through our newsletters and conventions we offer a means of meeting and associating with artists and others in the industry. The CCMA is a federally chartered, nonprofit organization, dedicated to the promotion and development of Canadian country music throughout Canada and the world and to providing a unity of purpose for the Canadian country music industry." See website for membership information and benefits.

☯ CANADIAN MUSICAL REPRODUCTION RIGHTS AGENCY LTD.

56 Wellesley St. W, #320, Toronto ON M5S 2S3 Canada. (416)926-1966. Fax: (416)926-7521. E-mail: inquiries@cmrra.ca. Website: www.cmrra.ca. **Contact:** Michael Mackie, membership services. Estab. 1975. Members are music copyright owners, music publishers, sub-publishers and administrators. Representation by CMRRA is open to any person, firm or corporation anywhere in the world, which owns and/or administers one or more copyrighted musical works. CMRRA is a music licensing agency—Canada's largest—which represents music copyright owners, publishers and administrators

for the purpose of mechanical and synchronization licensing in Canada. Offers mechanical and synchronization licensing. Applications accepted year-round.

CENTRAL CAROLINA SONGWRITERS ASSOCIATION (CCSA)

131 Henry Baker Rd., Zebulon NC 27597. (919) 269-6240. Website: www.ccsa-raleigh.com. **Contact:** Tony Dickens. Established in 1997, CCSA welcomes songwriters of all experience levels from beginner to professional within the local RDU/Triad/Eastern area of North Carolina to join our group. Our members' musical background varies, covering a wide array of musical genres. CCSA meets monthly in Raleigh, NC. We are unable to accept applications from incarcerated persons or those who do not reside in the local area, as our group's primary focus is on songwriters who are able to attend the monthly meetings to ensure members get the best value for their yearly dues. CCSA strives to provide each songwriter and musician a resourceful organization where members grow musically by networking and sharing with one another. Offers annual songwriters forum, periodic workshops, critiques at the monthly meetings, opportunities to perform and network with fellow members. Applications are accepted year-round. Dues are $24/year (pro-rated for new members at $2/month by date of application) with annual renewal each January.

CENTRAL OREGON SONGWRITERS ASSOCIATION

1900 NE Third St., Suite 106-132, Bend OR 97701. E-mail: dvdskelton@aol.com. Website: http://oregon songwriters.org. President: David Skelton. Estab. 1993. "Our members range in age from their 20s into their 80s. Membership includes aspiring beginners, accomplished singer/songwriter performing artists and all in between. Anyone with an interest in song-writing (any style) is invited to and welcome at COSA. COSA is a nonprofit organization to promote, educate and motivate members in the skills of writing, marketing and improving their craft." Offers competitions, instruction, newsletter, lectures, library, workshops, performance opportunities, songwriters round, awards, evaluation services and collaboration. Applications accepted year-round. Membership fee is $25.

THE COLLEGE MUSIC SOCIETY

312 E. Pine St., Missoula MT 59802. (406)721-9616. Fax: (406)721-9419. E-mail: cms@music.org. Website: www.music.org. Contact: Shannon Devlin, member services. Estab. 1959. Serves college, university and conservatory professors, as well as independent musicians. "The College Music Society promotes music teaching and learning, musical creativity and expression, research and dialogue, and diversity and inter-disciplinary interaction. A consortium of college, conservatory, university, and independent musicians and scholars interested in all disciplines of music, the Society provides leadership and serves as an agent of change by addressing concerns facing music in higher education." Offers journal, newsletter, lectures, workshops, performance opportunities, job listing service, databases of organizations and institutions, music faculty and mailing lists. Applications accepted year-round. Membership fee: $70 (regular dues), $35 (student dues), $35 (retiree dues).

CONNECTICUT SONGWRITERS ASSOCIATION

P.O. Box 511, Mystic CT 06355. E-mail: info@ctsongs.com. Website: www.ctsongs.com. **Contact:** Bill Pere, Executive Director. "We are an educational, nonprofit organization dedicated to improving the art and craft of original music. Founded in 1979, CSA has had almost 2,000 active members and has become one of the best known and respected songwriters' associations in the country. Membership in the CSA admits you to 12-18 seminars/workshops/song critique sessions per year throughout Connecticut and surrounding region. Out-of-state members may mail in songs for free critiques at our meetings. Noted professionals deal with all aspects of the craft and business of music including lyric writing, music theory, music technology, arrangement and production, legal and business aspects, performance techniques, song analysis and recording techniques. CSA offers song screening sessions for members and songs that pass become eligible for inclusion on the CSA sampler anthology through various retail and online outlets and are brought to national music conferences. CSA is well connected in both the independent music scene and the traditional music industry. CSA also offers showcases and concerts which are open to the public and designed to give artists a venue for performing their original material for an attentive, listening audience. CSA benefits help local soup kitchens, group homes, hospice, world hunger, libraries, nature centers, community centers, and more. CSA encompasses ballads to bluegrass and Bach to rock. Membership fee: $45/year.

DALLAS SONGWRITERS ASSOCIATION

Sammons Center for the Arts, 3630 Harry Hines Blvd., Box 20, Dallas TX 75219. (214)750-0916. E-mail: info@dallassongwriters.org. Website: www. dallassongwriters.org. **Contact:** Mary Guthrie, vice president of membership. President: Buck Morgan. Estab. 1986. Serves songwriters and lyricists of Dallas/Ft. Worth metroplex. Members are adults ages 18-75, Dallas/Ft. Worth area songwriters/lyricists who are or aspire to be professionals. Purpose is to provide songwriters an opportunity to meet other songwriters, share information, find cowriters and support each other through group discussions at monthly meetings; to provide songwriters an opportunity to have their songs heard and critiqued by peers and professionals by playing cassettes and providing an open mike at monthly meetings and open mics, showcases, and festival stages, and by offering contests judged by publishers; to provide songwriters opportunities to meet other music business professionals by inviting guest speakers to monthly meetings and workshops; and to provide songwriters opportunities to learn more about the craft of songwriting and the business of music by presenting mini-workshops at each monthly meeting. "We offer a chance for the songwriter to learn from peers and industry professionals and an opportunity to belong to a supportive group environment to encourage the individual to continue his/her songwriting endeavors." Offers competitions (including the Annual Song Contest with over $5,000 in prizes, and the Quarterly Lyric Contest), field trips, instruction, lectures, newsletter, performance opportunities, social outings, workshops and seminars. "Our members are eligible for discounts at several local music stores and seminars." Applications accepted year-round. Membership fee: $50. "When inquiring by phone, please leave complete mailing address and phone number or e-mail address where you can be reached day and night."

THE DRAMATISTS
GUILD OF AMERICA, INC.

(formerly The Dramatists Guild, Inc.), 1501 Broadway, Suite 701, New York NY 10036. (212)398-9366. Fax: (212)944-0420. E-mail: rtec@dramatistsguild.com.

Website: www.dramatistsguild.com. **Contact:** Roland Tec, director of membership. "For over three-quarters of a century, The Dramatists Guild has been the professional association of playwrights, composers and lyricists, with more than 6,000 members across the country. All theater writers, whether produced or not, are eligible for Associate membership ($90/year); students enrolled in writing degree programs at colleges or universities are eligible for Student membership ($45/year); writers who have been produced on Broadway, Off-Broadway or on the main stage of a LORT theater are eligible for Active membership ($130/year). The Guild offers its members the following activities and services: use of the Guild's contracts (including the Approved Production Contract for Broadway, the Off-Broadway contract, the LORT contract, the collaboration agreements for both musicals and drama, the 99 Seat Theatre Plan contract, the Small Theatre contract, commissioning agreements, and the Underlying Rights Agreements contract; advice on all theatrical contracts including Broadway, Off-Broadway, regional, showcase, Equity-waiver, dinner theater and collaboration contracts); a nationwide toll-free number for all members with business or contract questions or problems; advice and information on a wide spectrum of issues affecting writers; free and/or discounted ticket service; symposia led by experienced professionals in major cities nationwide; access to health insurance programs; and a spacious meeting room which can accommodate up to 50 people for readings and auditions on a rental basis. The Guild's publications are: *The Dramatist*, a bimonthly journal containing articles on all aspects of the theater (which includes *The Dramatists Guild Newsletter*, with announcements of all Guild activities and current information of interest to dramatists); and an annual resource directory with up-to-date information on agents, publishers, grants, producers, playwriting contests, conferences and workshops, and an interactive website that brings our community of writers together to exchange ideas and share information."

THE FIELD

161 Sixth Ave., 14th Floor, New York NY 10013. (212)691-6969. Fax: (212)255-2053. E-mail: jennifer@ thefield.org. Website: www.thefield.org. Contact: any staff member. Estab. 1986. "Founded by artists for artists, The Field has been dedicated to providing impactful services to thousands of performing artists

in New York City and beyond since 1986. From fostering creative exploration to stewarding innovative fundraising strategies, we are delighted to help artists reach their fullest potential. More than 1,900 performing artists come to The Field annually to build their businesses, 2,000+ new art works are developed under our stewardship each year, and our services are replicated in 11 cities across the US and in Europe. At the same time, we remain true to our grassroots origin and artist-centered mission: to strategically and comprehensively serve the myriad artistic and administrative needs of independent performing artists and companies who work in the fields of dance, theater, music, text, and performance art. Our core values of affordability, accessibility and rigorous delivery infuse all of our interactions. Field services include career-building workshops (grant writing, touring, internet strategies, etc.), fiscal sponsorship, creative residences in New York City and out of town, an 'Artists' Kinkos' Resource Center, and Membership benefits." Offers fiscal sponsorship, arts management & creative workshops, residencies, and performance opportunities. Applications accepted year-round. Membership fee: $100/year.

TIPS "The Field offers the most affordable and accessible fiscal sponsorship program in New York City. The Sponsored Artist Program offered by The Field enables performing artists and groups to accumulate the funds they need to make their artistic and career goals a reality. Fiscal sponsorship provides independent performing artists and groups with: eligibility to apply for most government, foundation, and corporate grants which require a 501(c)(3), not-for-profit status; eligibility to receive tax-deductible donations of both money and goods from individuals; and other services where 501(c)(3) status is necessary."

FORT WORTH SONGWRITERS ASSOCIATION

P.O. Box 162443, Fort Worth TX 76161. (817)654-5400. E-mail: info@fortworthsongwriters.com. Website: www.fwsa.com. President: John Terry. Vice president: Rob Owen. Secretary: Carole Butterfield. Treasurer: Rick Tate. Estab. 1992. Members are ages 18-83, beginners up to and including published writers. Interests cover gospel, country, western swing, rock, pop, bluegrass, and blues. Purpose is to allow songwriters to become more proficient at songwriting; to provide an opportunity for their efforts to be performed before a live audience; to provide songwriters an opportunity to meet cowriters. "We provide our members free critiques of their efforts. We provide a monthly newsletter outlining current happenings in the business of songwriting. We offer competitions and mini workshops with guest speakers from the music industry. We promote a weekly open 'mic' for singers of original material, and hold invitational songwriter showcase events a various times throughout the year. Each year, we hold a Christmas Song Contest, judged by independent music industry professionals. We also offer free web pages for members or links to member Web sites." Applications accepted year-round. Membership fee: $35.

GOSPEL MUSIC ASSOCIATION

1205 Division St., Nashville TN 37203. (615)242-0303. E-mail: info@gospelmusic.org. Website: www.gospelmusic.org. Estab. 1964. Serves songwriters, musicians and anyone directly involved in or who supports gospel music. Professional members include advertising agencies, musicians, songwriters, agents/managers, composers, retailers, music publishers, print and broadcast media, and other members of the recording industry. Associate members include supporters of gospel music and those whose involvement in the industry does not provide them with income. The primary purpose of the GMA is to expose, promote, and celebrate the Gospel through music. A GMA membership offers newsletters, performance experiences and workshops, as well as networking opportunities. Applications accepted year-round. Membership fee: $95/year (professional); $60/year (associate); and $25/year (college student).

◗ THE GUILD OF INTERNATIONAL SONGWRITERS & COMPOSERS

Sovereign House, 12 Trewartha Road, Praa Sands, Penzance, Cornwall TR20 9ST England. (01736)762826. Fax: (01736)763328. email: songmag@aol.com. Website: www.songwriters-guild.co.uk and www.myspace.com/guildofsongwriters. The Guild of International Songwriters & Composers is an international music industry organisation based in England in the United Kingdom. Guild members are songwriters, composers, lyricists, poets, performing songwriters, musicians, music publishers, studio owners, managers, independent record companies, music industry personnel, etc., from many countries throughout the world. The Guild of International Songwriters

& Composers has been publishing *Songwriting and Composing Magazine* since 1986, which is issued free to all Guild members throughout their membership. The Guild of International Songwriters and Composers offers advice, guidance, assistance, copyright protection service, information, encouragement, contact information, Intellectual property/copyright protection of members works through the Guild's Copyright Registration Centre along with other free services and more to Guild members with regard to helping members achieve their aims, ambitions, progression and advancement in respect to the many different aspects of the music industry. Information, advice, and services available to Guild members throughout their membership includes assistance, advice, and help on many matters and issues relating to the music industry in general. Annual membership fees: are £55. For further information please visit the Guild's website or MySpace page.

INTERNATIONAL BLUEGRASS MUSIC ASSOCIATION (IBMA)

2 Music Circle South, Suite 100, Nashville TN 37203. (615)256-3222. Fax: (615)256-0450. E-mail: info@ibma.org. Website: www.ibma.org. Member Services: Jill Crabtree. Estab. 1985. Serves songwriters, musicians, and professionals in bluegrass music. "IBMA is a trade association composed of people and organizations involved professionally and semi-professionally in the bluegrass music industry, including performers, agents, songwriters, music publishers, promoters, print and broadcast media, local associations, recording manufacturers and distributors. Voting members must be currently or formerly involved in the bluegrass industry as full or part-time professionals. A songwriter attempting to become professionally involved in our field would be eligible. Our mission statement reads: 'IBMA: Working together for high standards of professionalism, a greater appreciation for our music, and the success of the worldwide bluegrass music community.' IBMA publishes a bimonthly *International Bluegrass*, holds an annual trade show/convention with a songwriters showcase in the fall, represents our field outside the bluegrass music community, and compiles and disseminates databases of bluegrass related resources and organizations. Market research on the bluegrass consumer is available and we offer Bluegrass in the Schools information and matching grants. The primary value in

this organization for a songwriter is having current information about the bluegrass music field and contacts with other songwriters, publishers, musicians and record companies." Offers workshops, liability insurance, rental car discounts, consultation and databases of record companies, radio stations, press, organizations, and gigs. Applications accepted year-round. Membership fee: for a nonvoting patron $40/year; for an individual voting professional $75/year; for an organizational voting professional $205/year.

◗ INTERNATIONAL SONGWRITERS ASSOCIATION LTD.

P.O. Box 46, Limerick City, Ireland. E-mail: jliddane@songwriter.iol.ie. Website: www.songwriter.co.uk. Contact: Anna M. Sinden, membership department. Serves songwriters and music publishers. "The ISA headquarters is in Limerick City, Ireland, and from there it provides its members with assessment services, copyright services, legal and other advisory services and an investigations service, plus a magazine for one yearly fee. Our members are songwriters in more than 50 countries worldwide, of all ages. There are no qualifications, but applicants under 18 are not accepted. We provide information and assistance to professional or semi-professional songwriters. Our publication, Songwriter, which was founded in 1967, features detailed exclusive interviews with songwriters and music publishers, as well as directory information of value to writers." Offers competitions, instruction, library, newsletter and a weekly e-mail newsletter *Songwriter Newswire*. Applications accepted year-round. Membership fee for European writers is £19.95; for non-European writers, US $30.

JUST PLAIN FOLKS MUSIC ORGANIZATION

5327 Kit Dr., Indianapolis IN 46237. (317)513-6557. E-mail: JPFolksPro@aol.com. Website: www.jpfolks. com. **Contact:** Brian Austin Whitney (brian@jpfolks. com), founder, or Linda Berger (linda@jpfolks.com), projects director. Estab. 1998. "Just Plain Folks is among the world's largest Music Organizations. Our members cover nearly every musical style and professional field, from songwriters, artists, publishers, producers, record labels, entertainment attorneys, publicists and PR experts, performing rights organization staffers, live and recording engineers, educators, music students, musical instrument manufacturers, TV, Radio and Print Media and almost every major Internet Music entity. Representing all 50 US States and over 160 countries worldwide, we have members of all ages, musical styles and levels of success, including winners and nominees of every major music industry award, as well as those just starting out. A complete demographics listing of our group is available on our website. Whether you are a #1 hit songwriter or artist, or the newest kid on the block, you are welcome to join. Membership does require an active e-mail account." The purpose of this organization is "to share wisdom, ideas and experiences with others who have been there, and to help educate those who have yet to make the journey. Just Plain Folks provides its members with a friendly networking and support community that uses the power of the Internet and combines it with good old-fashioned human interaction. We help promote our members ready for success and educate those still learning." Offers special programs to members, including:

○ *Just Plain Notes Newsletter:* Members receive our frequent e-mail newsletters full of expert info on how to succeed in the music business, profiles of members successes and advice, opportunities to develop your career, and tons of first-person networking contacts to help you along the way. (Note: we send this out 2-3 times/month via e-mail only.)

TIPS "Our motto is 'We're All In This Together!'"

KNOXVILLE SONGWRITERS ASSOCIATION

P.O. Box 603, Knoxville TN 37901. (865)573-1025. E-mail: deblair@mindspring.com; JC2NZmusic@hotmail.com. Website: www.knoxvillesongwritersassociation.org. **Contact:** Joyce Brown, membership director. Estab. 1982. Serves songwriters of all ages. "Some have been members since 1982, others are beginners. Members must be interested in learning the craft of songwriting. Not only a learning organization but a support group of songwriters who wants to learn what to do with their song after it has been written. We open doors for aspiring writers. The primary benefit of membership is to supply information to the writer on how to write a song. Many members have received major cuts." Offers showcases, instruction, lectures, library, newsletter, performance opportunities, evaluation services, and workshops. Applications accepted year-round. Membership fee: $40/year.

THE LAS VEGAS SONGWRITERS ASSOCIATION

P.O. Box 42683, Las Vegas NV 89116-0683. (702)223-7255. E-mail: lasvegassongwriters@yahoo.com. **Contact:** Betty Kay Miller, president. Estab. 1980. "We are an educational, nonprofit organization dedicated to improving the art and craft of the songwriter. We want members who are serious about their craft. We want our members to respect their craft and to treat it as a business. Members must be at least 18 years of age. We offer quarterly newsletters, monthly information meetings, workshops three times a month and quarterly seminars with professionals in the music business. We provide support and encouragement to both new and more experienced songwriters. We critique each song or lyric that's presented during workshops, we make suggestions on changes—if needed. We help turn amateur writers into professionals. Several of our songwriters have had their songs recorded on both independent and major labels." Dues: $30/year.

LOS ANGELES MUSIC NETWORK

P.O. Box 2446, Toluca Lake CA 91610-2446. (818)769-6095. E-mail: info@lamn.com. Website: www.lamn.com. **Contact:** Tess Taylor, president. Estab. 1988. "Connections. Performance opportunities. Facts. Career advancement. All that is available with your membership in the Los Angeles Music Network (LAMN). Our emphasis is on sharing knowledge and information, giving you access to top professionals and promoting career development. LAMN is an association of music industry professionals, i.e., artists, singers, songwriters, and people who work in various aspects of the music industry with an emphasis on the creative. Members are ambitious and interested in advancing their careers. LAMN promotes career advancement, communication and education among artists and creatives. LAMN sponsors industry events and educational panels held at venues in the Los Angeles area and now in other major music hubs around the country (New York, Las Vegas, Phoenix, and San Francisco). LAMN Jams are popular among our members. Experience LAMN Jams in L.A. or N.Y. by performing your original music in front of industry experts who can advance your career by getting your music in the hands of hard-to-reach music supervisors. the 'anti-*American Idol*' singer-songwriter contest gives artists an opportunity to perform in front of industry experts and receive instant feedback to their music, lyrics and performance. As a result of the exposure, Tim Fagan won the John Mayer Songwriting Contest and was invited to tour with the Goo Goo Dolls, Lifehouse, and recently, the platinum recording artist Colbie Caillat. This paired him with multi-platinum songwriter and recording artist John Mayer, with whom Fagan co-wrote 'Deeper.' Publisher Robert Walls has pitched music from LAMN Jam performers to hit TV shows like *The OC* and *Grey's Anatomy,* and the flick *The Devil Wears Prada*. Other performers have received offers including publishing and production deals and studio gigs. Offers performance opportunities, instruction, newsletter, lectures, seminars, music industry job listings, career counseling, resume publishing, mentor network, and many professional networking opportunities. See our website for current job listings and a calendar of upcoming events." Applications accepted year-round. Annual membership fee is $15.

LOUISIANA SONGWRITERS ASSOCIATION

P.O. Box 82009, Baton Rouge LA 70884. E-mail: info@louisianamusichalloffame.org. Website: http://louisianamusichalloffame.org. Serves songwriters. Lifetime membership: $40.

☉ MANITOBA MUSIC

1-376 Donald St., Winnipeg MB R3B 2J2 Canada. (204)942-8650. Fax: (204)942-6083. E-mail: info@manitobamusic.com. Website: www.manitobamusic.com. **Contact:** Sara Stasiuk, Executive Director. Estab. 1987. Organization consists of "songwriters, producers, agents, musicians, managers, retailers, publicists, radio, talent buyers, media, record labels, etc. (no age limit, no skill level minimum). Must have interest in the future of Manitoba's music industry." The main purpose of Manitoba Music is to foster growth in all areas of the Manitoba music industry primarily through education, promotion, and lobbying. Offers newsletter, extensive website, directory of Manitoba's music industry, workshops, and performance opportunities. Manitoba Music is also involved with the Western Canadian Music Awards festival, conference, and awards show. Applications accepted year-round. Membership fee: $50 (Canadian funds).

MEET THE COMPOSER

90 John St., Suite 312, New York NY 10038. (212)645-6949. Fax: (212)645-9669. E-mail: mtc@meetthecomposer.org. Website: www.meetthecomposer.org. Estab. 1974. "Meet The Composer serves composers working in all styles of music, at every career stage, through a variety of grant programs and information resources. A nonprofit organization, Meet The Composer raises money from foundations, corporations, individual patrons and government sources and designs programs that support all genres of music—from folk, ethnic, jazz, electronic, symphonic, and chamber to choral, music theater, opera and dance. Meet The Composer awards grants for composer fees to non-profit organizations that perform, present, or commission original works. This is not a membership organization; all composers are eligible for support. Meet The Composer was founded in 1974 to increase artistic and financial opportunities for composers by fostering the creation, performance, dissemination, and appreciation of their music." Offers grant programs and information services. Deadlines vary for each grant program.

MEMPHIS SONGWRITERS' ASSOCIATION

4728 Spottswood, #191, Memphis TN 38117-4815. (901)626-4127 or (901)577-0906. Website: www.memphissongwriters.org. **Contact:** Phillip Beasley, MSA president. Estab. 1973. "MSA is a nonprofit songwriters organization serving songwriters nationally. Our mission is to dedicate our services to promote, advance, and help songwriters in the composition of music, lyrics and songs; to work for better conditions in our profession; and to secure and protect the rights of MSA songwriters. The Memphis Songwriters Association are organizational members of the Folk Alliance (FA.org). We also supply copyright forms. We offer critique sessions for writers at our monthly meetings. We also have monthly open mic songwriters night to encourage creativity, networking and co-writing. We host an annual songwriter's seminar and an annual songwriter's showcase, as well as a bi-monthly guest speaker series, which provide education, competition and entertainment for the songwriter. In addition, our members receive a bimonthly newsletter to keep them informed of MSA activities, demo services and opportunities in the songwriting field." Annual fee: $50; Student/Senior: $35.

MINNESOTA ASSOCIATION OF SONGWRITERS

P.O. Box 4262, Saint Paul MN 55104. E-mail: info@mnsongwriters.org. Website: www.mnsongwriters.

org. "Includes a wide variety of members, ranging in age from 18 to 80; type of music is very diverse, ranging from alternative rock to contemporary Christian; skill levels range from beginning songwriters to writers with recorded and published material. Main requirement is an interest in songwriting. Although most members come from the Minneapolis/St. Paul area, others come in from surrounding cities, nearby Wisconsin, and other parts of the country. Some members are full-time musicians, but most represent a wide variety of occupations. MAS is a nonprofit community of songwriters which informs, educates, inspires and assists its members in the art and business of songwriting." Offers instruction, newsletter, lectures, workshops, performance opportunities and evaluation services. Applications accepted year-round. Membership fee: Individual: $25.

TIPS "Members are kept current on resources and opportunities. Original works are played at meetings and are critiqued by involved members. Through this process, writers hone their skills and gain experience and confidence in submitting their works to others."

○ MUSIC BC INDUSTRY ASSOCIATION

#530-425 Carrall St., Vancouver BC V6B 6E3 Canada. (604)873-1914. 1-888-866-8570 (Toll Free in BC). Fax: (604)873-9686. E-mail: info@musicbc.org; musicb cinfo@gmail.com. Website: www.musicbc.org. Estab. 1990. Music BC (formerly PMIA) is a nonprofit society that supports and promotes the spirit, development, and growth of the BC music community provincially, nationally, and internationally. Music BC provides education, resources, advocacy, opportunities for funding, and a forum for communication. Visit website for membership benefits.

MUSICIANS CONTACT

P.O. Box 788, Woodland Hills CA 91365. (818)888-7879. E-mail: information@musicianscontact.com. Website: www.musicianscontact.com. Estab. 1969. "The primary source of paying jobs for musicians and vocalists nationwide. Job opportunities are posted daily on the Internet. Also offers exposure to the music industry for solo artists and complete acts seeking representation."

NASHVILLE SONGWRITERS ASSOCIATION INTERNATIONAL (NSAI)

1710 Roy Acuff Place, Nashville TN 37203. (615)256-3354 or (800)321-6008. Fax: (615)256-0034. E-mail: nsai@nashvillesongwriters.com. Website: www.nash villesongwriters.com. Executive Director: Bart Herbison. Purpose: a not-for-profit service organization for both aspiring and professional songwriters in all fields of music. Membership: Spans the United States and several foreign countries. Songwriters may apply in one of four annual categories: Active ($150 U.S currency for songwriters are actively working to improve in the craft of writing and/or actively pursuing a career within the songwriting industry); Student ($100 U.S for full-time college, high school, or middle school students); Professional ($100 U.S. currency for songwriters who are staff writers for a publishing company or earn 51 percent of their annual income from songwriting, whether from advances, royalties, or performances, or are generally regarded as a professional songwriter within the music industry); Lifetime (please contact NSAI for details). Membership benefits: music industry information and advice, song evaluations, eNews, access to industry professionals through weekly Nashville workshops and several annual events, regional workshops, use of office facilities, discounts on books and discounts on NSAI's three annual events. There are also "branch" workshops of NSAI. Workshops must meet certain standards and are accountable to NSAI. Interested coordinators may apply to NSAI.

○ Also see the listing for NSAI Songwriters Symposium (formerly NSAI Spring Symposium) in the "Workshops" section of this book.

OPERA AMERICA

330 Seventh Ave., 16th Floor, New York NY 10001. (212)796-8620. Fax: (212)796-8631. E-mail: info@ operaamerica.org. Website: www.operaamerica.org. **Contact:** Paul T. Gosselin, membership and development manager. Estab. 1970. Members are composers, librettists, musicians, singers, and opera/music theater producers. Offers conferences, workshops, and seminars for artists. Publishes online database of opera/music theater companies in the US and Canada, database of opportunities for performing and creative artists, online directory of opera and musical performances worldwide and US, and an online directory of new works created and being developed by current-day composers and librettists, to encourage the performance of new works. Applications accepted year-round. Publishes quarterly magazine and a variety of

electronic newsletters. Membership fee is on a sliding scale by membership level.

OUTMUSIC

Website: http://thelara.org **Contact:** Diedre Meredith, chairwoman/CEO. Estab. 1990. "OUTMUSIC is comprised of gay men, lesbians, bisexuals and transgenders. They represent all different musical styles from rock to classical. Many are writers of original material. We are open to all levels of accomplishment—professional, amateur, and interested industry people. The only requirement for membership is an interest in the growth and visibility of music and lyrics created by the LGBT community. We supply our members with support and networking opportunities. In addition, we help to encourage artists to bring their work 'OUT' into the world." Offers newsletter, lectures, workshops, performance opportunities, networking, industry leads and monthly open mics. Sponsors Outmusic Awards. Applications accepted year-round.

TIPS "OUTMUSIC has spawned *The Gay Music Guide*, The Gay and Lesbian American Music Awards (GLAMA), several compilation albums and many independent recording projects."

PACIFIC NORTHWEST SONGWRITERS ASSOCIATION

P.O. Box 98564, Seattle WA 98198. (206)824-1568. E-mail: pnsapals@hotmail.com. "PNSA is a nonprofit organization, serving the songwriters of the Puget Sound area since 1977. Members have had songs recorded by national artists on singles, albums, videos and network television specials. Several have released their own albums and the group has done an album together. For only $45 per year, PNSA offers monthly workshops, a quarterly newsletter and direct contact with national artists, publishers, producers and record companies. New members are welcome and good times are guaranteed. And remember, the world always needs another great song!"

PORTLAND SONGWRITERS ASSOCIATION

P.O. Box 28355, Portland OR 97228. E-mail: info@portlandongwriters.org; membership@portland songwriters.org. Website: www.portlandsongwriters.org. Estab. 1991. "The PSA is a nonprofit organization providing education and opportunities that will assist writers in creating and marketing their songs. The PSA offers an annual National Songwrit-

ing Contest, monthly workshops, songwriter showcases, special performance venues, quarterly newsletter, mail-in critique service, discounted seminars by music industry pros." Annual dues: $25 (no eligibility requirements).

TIPS "Although most of our members are from the Pacific Northwest, we offer services that can assist songwriters anywhere. Our goal is to provide information and contacts to help songwriters grow artistically and gain access to publishing, recording and related music markets. For more information, please call, write or e-mail."

RHODE ISLAND SONGWRITERS' ASSOCIATION

(RISA) P.O. Box 9246, Warwick RI 02889. E-mail: generalinfo@risongwriters.com; memberships@risongwriters.com. Website: www.risongwriters.com. Estab. 1993. "Membership consists of novice and professional songwriters. RISA provides opportunities to the aspiring writer or performer as well as the established regional artists who have recordings, are published and perform regularly. The only eligibility requirement is an interest in the group and the group's goals. Non-writers are welcome as well." The main purpose is to "encourage, foster and conduct the art and craft of original musical and/or lyrical composition through education, information, collaboration and performance." Offers instruction, newsletter, lectures, workshops, performance opportunities, and evaluation services. Applications accepted year-round. Membership fees: $25/year (individual); $30/year (family/band). "The group holds twice monthly critique sessions; twice monthly performer showcases (one performer featured) at a local coffeehouse; songwriter showcases (usually 6-8 performers); weekly open mikes; and a yearly songwriter festival called 'Hear In Rhode Island,' featuring approximately 50 Rhode Island acts, over two days."

SAN DIEGO SONGWRITERS GUILD

3368 Governor Dr., Suite 326, San Diego CA 92122. E-mail: sdsongwriters@hotmail.com. Website: http://sdsongwriters.org. **Contact:** Annie Rettic, secretary. Estab. 1982. "Members range from their early 20s to senior citizens with a variety of skill levels. Several members perform and work full time in music. Many are published and have songs recorded. Some are getting major artist record cuts. Most members are from San Diego county. New writers are encouraged to participate and meet others. All musical styles are represented." The purpose of this organization is to "serve the needs of songwriters and artists, especially helping them in the business and craft of songwriting through industry guest appearances." Offers competitions, newsletter, workshops, performance opportunities, discounts on services offered by fellow members, in-person song pitches and evaluations by publishers, producers and A&R executives. Applications accepted year-round. Membership dues: $25/year.

TIPS "Members benefit most from participation in meetings and concerts. Generally, one major meeting held monthly. E-mail for meeting details. Can join at meetings."

SESAC INC.

55 Music Square East, Nashville, TN, 37203. (615)320-0055. Fax: (615) 329-9627. Website: www.sesac.com. **New York:** 152 W. 57th St., 57th Floor, New York NY 10019. (212)586-3450. Fax: (212)489-5699. **Los Angeles:** 6100 Wilshire Blvd. Suite 700, Los Angeles CA 90048. (323)937-3722. Fax: (323)937-3733. **Atlanta**: 981 Joseph E. Lowery Blvd NW, Ste 102, Atlanta, GA 30318. (404)897-1330. Fax: (404)897-1306. **Miami:** 420 Lincoln Rd, Suite 502, Miami FL 33139, (305)534-7500. **London:** 67 Upper Berkeley St., London W1H 7QX United Kingdom. (020)76169284. Chief Operating Officer: Pat Collins. "SESAC is a selective organization taking pride in having a repertory based on quality rather than quantity. Serves writers and publishers in all types of music who have their works performed by radio, television, nightclubs, cable TV, etc. Purpose of organization is to collect and distribute performance royalties to all active affiliates. As a SESAC affiliate, the individual may obtain equipment insurance at competitive rates. Music is reviewed upon invitation by the Writer/Publisher Relations dept."

☼ SOCAN

(Society of Composers, Authors and Music Publishers of Canada) Head Office: 41 Valleybrook Dr., Toronto ON M3B 2S6 Canada. English Information Center: (866)(307)6226. French Information Center: (866)(800)55-SOCAN. Fax: (416)445-7108. Website: www.socan.ca. President: Earl Rosen. CEO: Eric Baptiste. "SOCAN is the Canadian copyright collective for the communication and performance of musical works. We administer these rights on behalf of our members (composers, lyricists, songwriters, and their publishers) and those of affiliated international organizations by licensing this use of their music in Canada. The fees collected are distributed as royalties to our members and to affiliated organizations throughout the world. We also distribute royalties received from those organizations to our members for the use of their music worldwide. SOCAN has offices in Toronto, Montreal, Vancouver, Edmonton, and Dartmouth."

SOCIETY OF COMPOSERS & LYRICISTS

8447 Wilshire Blvd., Suite 401, Beverly Hills CA 90211. (310)281-2812. Fax: (310)284-4861. E-mail: execdir@thescl.com. Website: www.thescl.com. The professional nonprofit trade organization for members actively engaged in writing music/lyrics for films, TV, and/or video games, or are students of film composition or songwriting for film. Primary mission is to advance the interests of the film and TV music community. Offers an award-winning quarterly publication, educational seminars, screenings, special member-only events, and other member benefits. Applications accepted year-round. Membership fee: $135 Full Membership (composers, lyricists, songwriters—film/TV music credits must be submitted); $85 Associate/Student Membership for composers, lyricists, songwriters without credits only; $135 Sponsor/Special Friend Membership (music editors, music supervisors, music attorneys, agents, etc.).

☾☉ SODRAC INC.

Tower B, Suite 1010, 1470 Peel Montreal Quebec H3A 1T1 Canada. (514)845-3268. Fax: (514)845-3401. E-mail: sodrac@sodrac.ca; members@sodrac.ca. Website: www.sodrac.ca **Contact:** Alain Lauzon, general manager. Estab. 1985. "SODRAC is a reproduction rights collective society facilitating the clearing of rights on musical and artistic works based on the Copyright Board of Canada tariffs or through collective agreements concluded with any users and is responsible for the distribution of royalties to its national and international members. The Society counts over 6,000 Canadian members and represents musical repertoire originating from nearly 100 foreign countries and manages the right of over 25,000 Canadian and foreign visual artists. SODRAC is the only reproduction rights society in Canada where both songwriters and music publishers are represented, equally and directly." Serves those with an interest in songwriting and music publishing no matter what their age or skill level is. "Members must have written or published at least one musical work that has been reproduced on an audio (CD, cassette, or LP) or audio-visual support (TV, DVD, video), or published five musical works that have been recorded and used for commercial purposes. The new member will benefit from a society working to secure his reproduction rights (mechanicals) and broadcast mechanicals." Applications accepted year-round.

SONGWRITERS ASSOCIATION OF WASHINGTON

PMB 106-137, 4200 Wisconsin Ave. NW, Washington DC 20016. (301)654-8434. E-mail: membership@SAW.org. Website: www.saw.org. Estab. 1979. "SAW is a nonprofit organization operated by a volunteer board of directors. It is committed to providing its members opportunities to learn more about the art of songwriting, learn more about the music business, perform in public, and connect with fellow songwriters. SAW sponsors various events to achieve these goals: workshops, open mics, songwriter exchanges, and showcases. In addition, SAW organizes the Mid-Atlantic Song Contest open to entrants nationwide each year; "the competition in 2011 will be the 27th contest SAW has adjudicated since 1982, making it one of the longest-running song contests in the nation." (Contest information masc@saw.org). As well as maintaining a website, SAW publishes a monthly e-newsletter for members containing information on upcoming local events, member news, contest information, and articles of interest, as well as a member directory, a valuable tool for networking. Joint membership with the Washington Area Music Association as well as a two-year membership are available at a savings. Use the contact information above for membership inquiries.

THE SONGWRITERS GUILD OF AMERICA

5120 Virginia Way, Suite C22, Brentwood TN 37027. (615)742-9945. Fax: (615)630-7501. E-mail: membership@songwritersguild.com. Website: www.songwritersguild.com. Estab. 1931. "The Songwriters Guild of America Foundation offers a series of workshops with discounts for some to SGA members, including online classes and song critique opportunities. There is a charge for some songwriting classes and seminars; however, online classes and some monthly events may be included with an SGA membership. Charges vary depending on the class or event. Current class offerings and workshops vary. Visit website to sign up for the newsletter and e-events, and for more informa-tion on current events and workshops. Some current events in Nashville are the Ask-a-Pro and ProCritique sessions that give SGA members the opportunity to present their songs and receive constructive feedback from industry professionals. Various performance opportunities are also available to members, including an SGA Showcase at the Bluebird. The New York office hosts a weekly Pro-Shop, which is coordinated by producer/musician/award winning singer Ann Johns Ruckert. For each of six sessions an active publisher, producer or A&R person is invited to personally screen material from SGA writers. Participation is limited to 10 writers and an audit of one session. Audition of material is required. Various performance opportunities and critique sessions are also available from time to time. SGAF Week is held periodically and is a week of scheduled events and seminars of interest to songwriters that includes workshops, seminars and showcases."

Also see the Songwriters Guild of America listing in the "Organizations" section.

SONGWRITERS HALL OF FAME (SONGHALL)

E-mail: info@songhall.org. Website: www.songhall.org. **Contact:** Jimmy Webb, chairman. Estab. 1969. "SongHall membership consists of songwriters of all levels, music publishers, producers, record company executives, music attorneys, and lovers of popular music of all ages. There are different levels of membership, all able to vote in the election for inductees, except Associates who pay only $25 in dues, but are unable to vote. SongHall's mission is to honor the popular songwriters who write the soundtrack for the world, as well as providing educational and networking opportunities to our members through our workshop and showcase programs." Offers: newsletter, workshops, performance opportunities, networking meetings with industry pros and scholarships for excellence in songwriting. Applications accepted year-round. Membership fees: $25 and up.

SONGWRITERS OF WISCONSIN INTERNATIONAL

P.O. Box 1027, Neenah WI 54957. E-mail: sowi@new.rr.com. Website: www.SongwritersOfWisconsin.org. **Contact:** Tony Ansems, president. Workshops Coordinator: Mike Heath. Estab. 1983. Serves songwriters. "Membership is open to songwriters writing all styles of music. Residency in Wisconsin is recommended but not required. Members are encouraged to bring tapes and lyric sheets of their songs to the meetings, but it is not required. We are striving to improve the craft of songwriting in Wisconsin. Living in Wisconsin, a songwriter would be close to any of the workshops and showcases offered each month at different towns. The primary value of membership for a songwriter is in sharing ideas with other songwriters, being critiqued and helping other songwriters." Offers competitions (contest entry deadline: June 15), field trips, instruction, lectures, newsletter, performance opportunities, social outings, workshops and critique sessions. Applications accepted year-round. Membership dues: $30/year.

TIPS "Critique meetings every last Thursday of each month, January through October, 7 p.m.-10 p.m. at Sabre Lanes, 1330 Midway Road, Menasha WI. E-mail for more details."

SONGWRITERS RESOURCE NETWORK

E-mail: info@SongwritersResourceNetwork.com. Website: www.SongwritersResourceNetwork.com. **Contact:** Steve Cahill, president. Estab. 1998. "For songwriters and lyricists of every kind, from beginners to advanced." No eligibility requirements. "Purpose is to provide free information to help songwriters develop their craft, market their songs, and learn about songwriting opportunities." Sponsors the annual Great American Song Contest, offers marketing tips and website access to music industry contacts. "We provide leads to publishers, producers and other music industry professionals." Visit website or send SASE for more information.

Also see the listing for Great American Song Contest in the Contests and Awards section of this book.

SOUTHWEST VIRGINIA SONGWRITERS ASSOCIATION

P.O. Box 698, Salem VA 24153. E-mail: svsasongwriters@gmail.com. Website: www.svsasongs.com. **Contact:** Greg Trafidlo, treasurer. Estab. 1981. 80 members of all ages and skill all levels, mainly country, folk, gospel, contemporary and rock but other musical interests too. "The purpose of SVSA is to increase, broaden and expand the knowledge of each member and to support, better and further the progress and success of each member in songwriting and related fields of endeavor." Offers performance opportunities, evaluation services, instruction, newsletter, workshops, monthly meetings, and monthly newsletter. Application accepted year-round. Membership fee: $20/year.

TEXAS ACCOUNTANTS & LAWYERS FOR THE ARTS

1540 Sul Ross, Houston TX 77006. (713)526-4876. Fax: (713)526-1299. E-mail: info@talarts.org. Website: www.talarts.org. **Contact:** Erin Rodgers, staff attorney, or Kristian Salinas, office manager. Estab. 1979. TALA's members include accountants, attorneys, museums, theater groups, dance groups, actors, artists, musicians, and filmmakers. Our members are of all age groups and represent all facets of their respective fields. TALA is a nonprofit organization that provides pro bono legal and accounting services to income-eligible artists from all disciplines and to nonprofit arts organizations. TALA also provides mediation services for resolving disputes as a low cost nonadversarial alternative to litigation. Offers newsletter, lectures, library, and workshops. Applications accepted year-round. Annual membership fee for students: $30; artists: $50; bands: $100; nonprofit organizations: $200.

TIPS TALA's speakers program presents low-cost seminars on topics such as the music business, copyright and trademark, and the business of writing. These seminars are held annually at a location in Houston. TALA's speaker's program also provides speakers for seminars by other organizations.

TEXAS MUSIC OFFICE

P.O. Box 13246, Austin TX 78711. (512)463-6666. Fax: (512)463-4114. E-mail: music@governor.state.tx.us. Website: http://governor.state.tx.us/music. **Contact:** Casey Monahan, director. Estab. 1990. "The Texas Music Office (TMO) is a state-funded business promotion office and information clearinghouse for the Texas music industry. The TMO assists more than 14,000 individual clients each year, ranging from a new band trying to make statewide business contacts to BBC journalists seeking information on Down South Hip hop. The TMO is the sister office to the Texas Film Commission, both of which are within the Office of the Governor. The TMO serves the Texas music industry by using its Business Referral Network: Texas Music Industry (7,880 Texas music businesses in 96 music business categories); Texas Music Events (625 Texas music events); Texas Talent Register (8,036 Texas recording artists); Texas Radio Stations (942 Texas stations); US Music Contacts; Classical Texas (detailed information for all classical music organizations in Texas); and International (1,425 foreign businesses interested in Texas music). Provides referrals to Texas music businesses, talent and events in order to attract new business to Texas and/or to encourage Texas businesses and individuals to keep music business in-state. Serves as a liaison between music businesses and other government offices and agencies. Publicizes significant developments within the Texas music industry."

THE NATIONAL ASSOCIATION OF COMPOSERS/USA (NACUSA)

P.O. Box 49256, Barrington Station, Los Angeles CA 90049. E-mail: nacusa@music-usa.org. Website: www.music-usa.org/nacusa. **Contact:** Daniel Kessner, president. Estab. 1932. Serves songwriters, musicians, and classical composers. "We are of most value to the concert hall composer. Members are serious music composers of all ages and from all parts of the country, who have a real interest in composing, performing, and listening to modern concert hall music. The main purpose of our organization is to perform, publish, broadcast and write news about composers of serious concert hall music—mostly chamber and solo pieces. Composers may achieve national notice of their work through our newsletter and concerts, and the fairly rare feeling of supporting a non-commercial music enterprise dedicated to raising the musical and social position of the serious composer." Offers competitions, lectures, performance opportunities, library, and newsletter. Applications accepted year-round. Membership fee: National (regular): $25; National (students/seniors): $15.

Also see the listing for NACUSA Young Composers' Competition in the Contests section of this book.

TIPS "99% of the money earned in music is earned, or so it seems, by popular songwriters who might feel they owe the art of music something, and this is one way they might help support that art. It's a chance to foster fraternal solidarity with their less prosperous, but wonderfully interesting classical colleagues at a time when the very existence of serious art seems to be questioned by the general populace."

◯ TORONTO MUSICIANS' ASSOCIATION

15 Gervais Dr., Suite 500, Toronto ON M3C 1Y8 Canada. (416)421-1020. Fax: (416)421-7011. E-mail: info@tma149.ca. Website: www.tma149.ca. Executive director: Jim Biros. Estab. 1887. "Local 149 of the American Federation of Musicians of the United States and Canada is the Professional Association for musicians in the greater Toronto Area. A member driven association of 3,500 members, the TMA represents professional musicians in all facets of music in the greater Toronto area. Dedicated to the development of musical talent and skills the Toronto Musicians' Association has for the past 100 years fostered the opportunity through the collective efforts of our members for professional musicians to live and work in dignity while receiving fair compensation." Joining fee: $225. Thereafter, members pay $61.25 per quarter.

VOLUNTEER LAWYERS FOR THE ARTS

1 E. 53rd St., 6th Floor, New York NY 10022. (212)319-ARTS (2787), ext. 1 (Monday-Friday 10am-6pm). Fax: (212)752-6575. E-mail: epaul@vlany.org. Website: www.vlany.org. **Contact:** Elena M. Paul, esq., executive director. Estab. 1969. Serves songwriters, musicians and all performing, visual, literary and fine arts artists and groups. Offers legal assistance and representation to eligible individual artists and arts organizations who cannot afford private counsel and a mediation service. VLA sells publications on arts-related issues and offers educational conferences, lectures, seminars and workshops. In addition, there are affiliates nationwide who assist local arts organizations and artists. Call for information.

WASHINGTON AREA MUSIC ASSOCIATION

6263 Occoquan Forest Dr., Manassas VA 20112. (703)368-3300. Fax: (703)393-1028. E-mail: dcmusic@wamadc.com. Website: www.wamadc.com. Serves songwriters, musicians and performers, managers, club owners, and entertainment lawyers; "all those with an interest in the Washington music scene." The organization is designed to promote the Washington music scene and increase its visibility. Its primary value to members is its seminars and networking opportunities. Offers lectures, newsletter, performance opportunities and workshops. WAMA sponsors the annual Washington Music Awards (the Wammies) and the Crosstown Jam or annual showcase of artists in the DC area. Applications accepted year-round. Annual dues: $35 for one year; $60 for two years.

WEST COAST SONGWRITERS

(formerly Northern California Songwriters Association) 1724 Laurel St., Suite 120, San Carlos CA 94070. (650)654-3966. E-mail: info@westcoastsongwriters. org; ian@westcoastsongwriters.org. Website: www. westcoastsongwriters.org. **Contact:** Ian Crombie, executive director. Serves songwriters and musicians. Estab. 1979. "Our 1,200 members are lyricists and composers from ages 16-80, from beginners to professional songwriters. No eligibility requirements. Our purpose is to provide the education and opportunities that will support our writers in creating and marketing outstanding songs. WCS provides support and direction through local networking and input from Los Angeles and Nashville music industry leaders, as well as valuable marketing opportunities. Most songwriters need some form of collaboration, and by being a member they are exposed to other writers, ideas, critiquing, etc." Offers annual West Coast Songwriters Conference, "the largest event of its kind in Northern California. This 2-day event held the second weekend in September features 16 seminars, 50 screening sessions (over 1,200 songs listened to by industry professionals) and a sunset concert with hit songwriters performing their songs." Also offers monthly visits from major publishers, songwriting classes, competitions, seminars conducted by hit songwriters ("we sell audio tapes of our seminars—list of tapes available on request"), mail-in song-screening service for members who cannot attend due to time or location, a monthly e-newsletter, monthly performance opportunities and workshops. Applications accepted year-round. Dues: $40/year for students; $75/year, regular membership; $99 band membership; $100+ contributing membership.

TIPS "WCS's functions draw local talent and nationally recognized names together. This is of a tremendous value to writers outside a major music center. We are developing a strong songwriting community in Northern and Southern California. We serve the San Jose, Monterey Bay, East Bay, San Francisco, Los Angeles, Sacramento and Portland, WA areas and we have the support of some outstanding writers and publishers from both Los Angeles and Nashville. They provide us with invaluable direction and inspiration."

WORKSHOPS & CONFERENCES

For a songwriter just starting out, conferences and workshops can provide valuable learning opportunities. At conferences, songwriters can have their songs evaluated, hear suggestions for further improvement and receive feedback from music business experts. They are also excellent places to make valuable industry contacts. Workshops can help a songwriter improve his or her craft and learn more about the business of songwriting. They may involve classes on songwriting and the business, as well as lectures and seminars by industry professionals.

Each year, hundreds of workshops and conferences take place all over the country. Songwriters can choose from small regional workshops held in someone's living room to large national conferences such as South by Southwest in Austin, Texas, which hosts more than 6,000 industry people, songwriters, and performers. Many songwriting organizations—national and local—host workshops that offer instruction on just about every songwriting topic imaginable, from lyric writing and marketing strategy to contract negotiation. Conferences provide songwriters the chance to meet one-on-one with publishing and record company professionals and give performers the chance to showcase their work for a live audience (usually consisting of industry people) during the conference. There are conferences and workshops that address almost every type of music, offering programs for songwriters, performers, musical playwrights, and much more.

This section includes national and local workshops and conferences with a brief description of what they offer, when they are held, and how much they cost to attend. Write or call any that interest you for further information.

APPEL FARM ARTS AND MUSIC FESTIVAL

P.O. Box 888, Elmer, NJ 08318. (856)358-2472. Fax: (856)358-6513. E-mail: perform@appelfarm.org. Website: www.appelfarm.org. **Contact:** Sean Timmons, artistic director. Estab Festival: 1989; Series: 1970. "Our annual open air festival is the highlight of our year-round Performing Arts Series which was established to showcase the finest contemporary songwriters. Festival includes a diversity of styles including rock, roots, folk, world music, blues, etc." Past performers have included Gogol Bordello, Josh Ritter & the Royal City Band, Trombone Shorty & Orleans Avenue, Good Old War, the Avett Brothers, Rufus Wainwright, Fountains of Wayne, Indigo Girls, Ani DiFranco, They Might Be Giants, Randy Newman, Jackson Browne, David Gray, and more. Programs for songwriters and musicians include performance opportunities as part of Festival and Performing Arts Series and an emerging artists series, First Fridays @ The Gallery. Programs for musical playwrights also include performance opportunities as part of Performing Arts Series. Festival is a one-day event held in June, and Performing Arts Series is held year-round. Both are held at the Appel Farm Arts and Music Center in southern New Jersey. Up to 20 songwriters/musicians participate in each event. Participants are songwriters, individual vocalists, bands, ensembles, vocal groups, composers, individual instrumentalists, and dance/mime/movement. Participants are selected by online submissions. Applicants should forward links to their websites, MySpace pages etc. Application materials accepted year-round. Faculty opportunities are available as part of residential Summer Arts Program for children, July/August.

ASCAP I CREATE MUSIC EXPO

Estab. 2006. (800)278-1287. Fax: (212)621-6387. E-mail: expo@ascap.com. Website: www.ascap.com. 3-day event held in April.

ASCAP MUSICAL THEATRE WORKSHOP

1 Lincoln Plaza, New York NY 10023. (212)621-6234. E-mail: mkerker@ascap.com. Website: www.ascap.com. **Contact:** Michael A. Kerker, director of musical theatre. Estab. 1981. Workshop is for musical theater composers and lyricists only. Its purpose is to nurture and develop new musicals for the theater. Offers programs for songwriters. Offers programs annually, usually April through May. Event took place in New York City. Four musical works are selected. Others are invited to audit the workshop. Participants are amateur and professional songwriters, composers, and musical playwrights. Participants are selected by demo CD submission. Deadline: see website. Also available: the annual ASCAP/Disney Musical Theatre Workshop in Los Angeles. It takes place in January and February. Deadline is late November. Details similar to New York workshop as above.

ASCAP WEST COAST/LESTER SILL SONGWRITERS WORKSHOP

7920 Sunset Blvd., 3rd Floor, Los Angeles, CA 90046. (323)883-1000. Fax: (323)883-1049. E-mail: info@ascap.com. Website: www.ascap.com. Annual workshop for advanced songwriters sponsored by the ASCAP Foundation. Renamed in 1995 to honor ASCAP's late board member and industry pioneer Lester Sill, the workshop takes place over a four-week period and features prominent guest speakers from various facets of the music business. Workshop dates and deadlines vary from year to year; refer to www.ascap.com for updated info. Applicants must submit two songs on a CD (cassette tapes not accepted), lyric sheets, brief bio and short explanation as to why they would like to participate, e-mail address, and telephone number. Limited number of participants are selected each year.

BMI-LEHMAN ENGEL MUSICAL THEATRE WORKSHOP

7 World Trade Center, 250 Greenwich St., New York, NY 10007. (212)230-3000. E-mail: musicaltheatre@bmi.com. Website: www.bmi.com. **Contact:** Jean Banks, senior director of musical theatre. Estab. 1961. "BMI is a music licensing company which collects royalties for affiliated writers and publishers. We offer programs to musical theatre composers, lyricists and librettists. The BMI-Lehman Engel Musical Theatre Workshops were formed in an effort to refresh and stimulate professional writers, as well as to encourage and develop new creative talent for the musical theatre." Each workshop meets 1 afternoon a week for 2 hours at BMI, New York. Participants are professional songwriters, composers, and playwrights. BMI-Lehman Musical Theatre Workshop Showcase presents the best of the workshop to producers, agents, record and publishing company execs, press, and directors for possible option and production. Go to BMI.com and click on Musical Theatre for application.

Tape and lyrics of 3 compositions required with applications. BMI also sponsors a jazz composers workshop. For more information contact Raette Johnson at rjohnson@bmi.com.

BROADWAY TOMORROW PREVIEWS

c/o Science of Light, Inc., 191 Claremont Ave., Suite 53, New York, NY 10027. E-mail: solministry@earth link.net. Website: www.solministry.com/bway_tom. html. **Contact:** Elyse Curtis, PhD, artistic director. Estab. 1983. Purpose is the enrichment of American theater by nurturing new musicals. Offers series in which composers living in New York city area present self-contained scores of their new musicals in concert. Submission is by CD of music or video, synopsis, cast breakdown, résumé, reviews, if any, acknowledgment postcard, and SASE. Participants selected by screening of submissions. Programs are presented in fall and spring with possibility of full production of works presented in concert.

CMJ MUSIC MARATHON & FILM FESTIVAL

1201 Broadway, Suite 706, New York NY 10001. (212)277-7120. Fax: (212)719-9396. E-mail: market ing@cmj.com. Website: www.cmj.com/marathon/. **Contact:** Operations Manager. Estab. 1981. Premier annual alternative music gathering of more than 9,000 music business and film professionals. Features 5 days and nights of more than 75 panels and workshops focusing on every facet of the industry; exclusive film screenings; keynote speeches by the world's most intriguing and controversial voices; exhibition area featuring live performance stage; over 1,000 of music's brightest and most visionary talents (from the unsigned to the legendary) performing over 5 evenings at more than 80 of NYC's most important music venues. Participants are selected by submitting demonstration tape. Go to website for application (through Sonicbids.com).

CUTTING EDGE MUSIC BUSINESS CONFERENCE

1524 N. Claiborne Ave., New Orleans LA 70116. (504)945-1800. Fax: (504)945-1873. E-mail: cut_edge@bellsouth.net. Website: www.cuttingedgenola.com. Executive producer: Eric L. Cager. Showcase Producer: Nathaniel Franklin. Estab. 1993. "The conference is a five-day international conference which covers the business and educational aspects of the music industry. As part of the conference, the New Works showcase features over 200 bands and artists from around the country and Canada in showcases of original music. All music genres are represented." Offers programs for songwriters and performers. "Bands and artists should submit material for consideration of entry into the New Works showcase." Event takes place during August in New Orleans. 1,000 songwriters/musicians participate in each event. Participants are songwriters, vocalists, and bands. Send for application. Deadline: July 1. "The Music Business Institute offers a month-long series of free educational workshops for those involved in the music industry. The workshops take place each September. Further information is available via our website."

FOLK ALLIANCE ANNUAL CONFERENCE

510 South Main, Memphis, TN 38103. (901) 522-1170. Fax: (901) 522-1172. E-mail: fa@folk.org. Website: www.folk.org. **Contact**: Louis Meyers, Executive Director. Estab. 1989. Conference/workshop topics change each year. Conference takes place late February and lasts 4 days at a different location each year. 2,000-plus attendees include artists, agents, arts administrators, print/broadcast media, folklorists, folk societies, merchandisers, presenters, festivals, recording companies, etc. Artists wishing to showcase should contact the office for a showcase application form. Closing date for official showcase application is in November. 2012 event is February 22-26. Costs vary.

HOLLYWOOD REPORTER/BILLBOARD FILM & TV MUSIC CONFERENCE

Sofitel LA, 8555 Beverly Blvd., Los Angeles, CA 90048. (212)493-4026. E-mail: conferences@billboard.com; Nicole.Carbone@Billboard.com. Website: www.bill boardevents.com. **Contact**: Nicole Carbone. Estab. 1995. Promotes all music for film and television. Offers programs for songwriters and composers. Held at the Directors Guild of America in October. More than 350 songwriters/musicians participate in each event. Participants are professional songwriters, composers, plus producers, directors, etc. Conference panelists are selected by invitation. For registration information, call Nicole Carbone at (212)493-4263. Fee: $349-499/person.

INDEPENDENT MUSIC CONFERENCE

InterMixx.com, Inc., 304 Main Ave., PMB 287, Norwalk, CT 06851. (203)606-4649. E-mail: IMC@inter mixx.com. Website: www.indiemusicon.com. **Executive director:** Noel Ramos. Estab. 1992. "The purpose of the IMC is to bring together rock, hip hop and acoustic music for of panels and showcases. Offers programs for songwriters, composers and performers. 250 showcases at 20 clubs around the city. Also offer a DJ cutting contest." Held annually in the fall. 3,000 amateur and professional songwriters, composers, individual vocalists, bands, individual instrumentalists, attorneys, managers, agents, publishers, A&R, promotions, club owners, etc., participate each year. Send for application.

KERRVILLE FOLK FESTIVAL

Kerrville Festivals, Inc., P.O. Box 291466, Kerrville, TX 78029. (830)257-3600. Fax: (830)257-8680. E-mail: info@kerrville-music.com. Website: www.kerrville folkfestival.com. **Contact:** Dalis Allen, producer. Estab. 1972. Hosts 3-day songwriters' school, a 4-day music business school and New Folk concert competition. Festival produced in late spring and late summer. Spring festival lasts 18 days and is held outdoors at Quiet Valley Ranch. 110 or more songwriters participate. Performers are professional songwriters and bands. Participants selected by submitting demo, by invitation only. Send cassette, or CD, promotional material and list of upcoming appearances. "Songwriter and music schools include lunch, experienced professional instructors, camping on ranch and concerts. Rustic facilities. Food available at reasonable cost. Audition materials accepted at above address. These three-day and four-day seminars include noon meals, handouts and camping on the ranch. Usually held during Kerrville Folk Festival, first and second week in June. Write or check the website for contest rules, schools and seminars information, and festival schedules. Also establishing a Phoenix Fund to provide assistance to ill or injured singer/songwriters who find themselves in distress."

⭕ Also see the listing for New Folk Concerts For Emerging Songwriters in the "Contests & Awards" section of this book.

LAMB'S RETREAT FOR SONGWRITERS

Presented by Springfed Arts, a nonprofit organization, P.O. Box 304, Royal Oak, MI 48068-0304. (248)589-3913. E-mail: johndlamb@ameritech.net. Website: www.springfed.org. **Contact:** John D. Lamb, director. Estab. 1995. Offers programs for songwriters on annual basis. November 3-6, 2011, and November 10-

13, 2011, at the Birchwood Inn, Harbor Springs, MI. 60 songwriters/musicians participate in each event. Participants are amateur and professional songwriters. Anyone can participate. Send for registration or e-mail. Deadline: 2 weeks before event begins. Fee: $289-546, includes all meals. Facilities are single/double occupancy lodging with private baths; 2 conference rooms and hospitality lodge. Offers song assignments, songwriting workshops, song swaps, open mic, and one-on-one mentoring. Faculty are noted songwriters, such as Michael Smith, Jonathan Byrd, Anais Mitchell, Don Henry, Sally Barris, LJ Booth. Partial scholarships may be available by writing: Blissfest Music Organization, Jim Gillespie, P.O. Box 441, Harbor Springs, MI 49740. Deadline: 2 weeks before event.

MANCHESTER MUSIC FESTIVAL

P.O. Box 33, Manchester VT 05254. (802)362-1956 or (800)639-5868. Fax: (802)362-0711. E-mail: info@mmfvt.org. Website: www.manchestermusicfestival.org. Estab. 1974. Offers classical music education and performances. Summer program for young professional musicians offered in tandem with a professional concert series in the mountains of Manchester VT. Up to 23 young professionals, age 19 and up, are selected by audition for the Young Artists Program, which provides instruction, performance, and teaching opportunities, with full scholarship for all participants. Commissioning opportunities for new music, and performance opportunities for professional chamber ensembles and soloists for both summer and fall/winter concert series.

MUSIC BUSINESS SOLUTIONS/CAREER BUILDING WORKSHOPS

P.O. Box 230266, Boston MA 02123-0266. E-mail: success@mbsolutions.com. Website: www.mbsolutions.com. **Contact:** Peter Spellman, director. Estab. 1991. Workshop titles have included "Discovering Your Music Career Niche," "How to Release an Independent Record" and "Promoting and Marketing Music in the 21st Century." Offers programs for music entrepreneurs, songwriters, musical playwrights, composers, and performers. Programs offered year-round, annually, and biannually. Event takes place at various colleges, recording studios, hotels, conferences. 10-100 songwriters/musicians participate in each event. Participants are both amateur and professional songwriters, vocalists, music business professionals, composers, bands, musical playwrights and instrumentalists. Anyone can participate. Fee: varies. "Music Business Solutions offers a number of other services and programs for both songwriters and musicians including: private music career counseling, business plan development and internet marketing; publication of *Music Biz Insight: Power Reading for Busy Music Professionals*, a bimonthly e-zine chock full of music management and marketing tips and resources. Free subscription with e-mail address."

NEWPORT FOLK FESTIVAL

P.O. Box 3865, Newport, RI 02840. (401)848-5055. E-mail: info@newportfolkfest.net. Website: www.new portfolkfest.com. **Contact:** George Wein. Held annually in midsummer at the International Tennis Hall of Fame and Fort Adams State Park.

NEWPORT JAZZ FESTIVAL

Newport, RI. E-mail: jazz@newportjazzfest.net. Website: www.newportjazzfest.com. **Contact:** George Wein. Estab. 1954. "Hailed by the *New York Times* as 'the festival that put jazz festivals on the map,' the Newport Jazz Festival*, now the CareFusion Newport Jazz Festival, was founded by Jazz pianist George Wein in 1954 as the first outdoor music festival of its kind devoted entirely to Jazz, and is now universally acknowledged as the grandfather of all Jazz festivals. During the last half-century, the name Newport has become synonymous with the best in Jazz music. In its long illustrious history, the Newport Jazz Festival has presented a virtual pantheon of Jazz immortals alongside an array of rising young artists: Duke Ellington's 1956 rebirth framing Paul Gonzalves' epic solo; subject of the classic 1958 documentary "Jazz on a Summer's Day; origin of famous recordings by Thelonious Monk, John Coltrane and Miles Davis; showcase for emerging young masters including Wynton Marsalis, Diana Krall, Joshua Redman and Esperanza Spalding. Referred to as a Mecca of Jazz, the event draws thousands of people from all over the world to it's uniquely picturesque outdoor stages at the International Tennis Hall of Fame and Fort Adams State Park."

NORFOLK CHAMBER MUSIC FESTIVAL

September-May address: Woolsey Hall, 500 College St., Suite 301, New Haven, CT 06520. (203)432-1966. Fax: (203)432-2136. E-mail: norfolk@yale.edu. Website: www.yale.edu/norfolk. June-August address: Ellen Battell, Stoeckel Estate, Routes 44 and 272, Nor-

folk, CT 06058. (860)542-3000. Fax: (860)542-3004. **Contact:** Deanne E. Chin, operations manager. Estab. 1941. Festival season of chamber music. Offers programs for composers and performers. Offers programs summer only. Approximately 45 fellows participate. Participants are up-and-coming composers and instrumentalists. Participants are selected by following a screening round. Auditions are held in New Haven, CT. Send for application. Deadline: mid-January. Fee: $50. Held at the Ellen Battell Stoeckel Estate, the Festival offers a magnificent Music Shed with seating for 1,000, practice facilities, music library, dining hall, laundry, and art gallery. Nearby are hiking, bicycling, and swimming.

◐ NORTH BY NORTHEAST MUSIC FESTIVAL AND CONFERENCE

189 Church St., Lower Level, Toronto, ON M5B 1Y7, Canada. (416)863-6963. Fax: (416)863-0828. E-mail: info@nxne.com. Website: www.nxne.com. **Contact:** Andy McClean, managing director. Estab. 1995. "Our festival takes place mid-June at over 30 venues across downtown Toronto, drawing over 2,000 conference delegates, 500 bands and 50,000 music fans. Musical genres include everything from folk to funk, roots to rock, polka to punk and all points in between, bringing exceptional new talent, media front-runners, music business heavies and music fans from all over the world to Toronto." Participants include emerging and established songwriters, vocalists, composers, bands, and instrumentalists. Festival performers are selected by submitting a CD and accompanying press kit or applying through sonicbids.com. Application forms are available by website or by calling the office. Submission period each year is from November 1 to the third weekend in January. Submissions "early bird" fee: $25. Conference registration fee: $149-249. "Our conference is held at the deluxe Holiday Inn on King and the program includes mentor sessions—15-minute one-on-one opportunities for songwriters and composers to ask questions of industry experts, roundtables, panel discussions, keynote speakers, etc."

NSAI SONG CAMPS

1710 Roy Acuff Place, Nashville TN 37023. 1-800-321-6008 or (615)256-3354. Fax: (615)256-0034. E-mail: songcamps@nashvillesongwriters.com. Website: www.nashvillesongwriters.com. **Contact:** Deanie Williams, NSAI events director. Estab. 1992. Offers programs strictly for songwriters. Event held 4 times/

year in Nashville. "We provide most meals and lodging is available. We also present an amazing evening of music presented by the faculty." Camps are 3 days long, with 36-112 participants, depending on the camp. "There are different levels of camps, some having preferred prerequisites. Each camp varies. Please call, e-mail or refer to website. It really isn't about the genre of music, but the quality of the song itself. Song Camp strives to strengthen the writer's vision and skills, therefore producing the better song. Song Camp is known as 'boot camp' for songwriters. It is guaranteed to catapult you forward in your writing! Participants are all aspiring songwriters led by a pro faculty. We do accept lyricists only and composers only with the hopes of expanding their scope." Participants are selected through submission of 2 songs with lyric sheet. Song Camp is open to NSAI members, although anyone can apply and upon acceptance join the organization. There is no formal application form. See website for membership and event information.

○Also see the listing for Nashville Songwriters Association International (NSAI) in the "Organizations" section of this book.

NSAI SONGWRITERS SONGPOSIUM

1710 Roy Acuff Place, Nashville TN, 37203. (615)256-3354 or (800)321-6008. Fax: (615)256-0034. E-mail: songposium@nashvillesongwriters.com. Website: www.nashvillesongwriters.com. Covers "all types of music. Participants take part in publisher evaluations, as well as large group sessions with different guest speakers." Offers annual programs for songwriters. Event takes place annually in downtown Nashville. 300 amateur songwriters/musicians participate in each event. Send for application.

○ ORFORD FESTIVAL

Orford Arts Centre, 3165 Chemim DuParc, Orford QC J1X 7A2 Canada. (819)843-9871 or 1-800-567-6155. Fax: (819)843-7274. E-mail: info@arts-orford.org. Website: www.arts-orford.org. **Contact:** Registrar/information manager. Artistic Coordinator: Nicolas Bélanger. Estab. 1951. "Each year, the Orford Arts Centre produces up to 35 concerts in the context of its Music Festival. It receives artists from all over the world in classical and chamber music." Offers master classes for music students, young professional classical musicians and chamber music ensembles. New offerings include master classes for all instruments, voice, and opera. Master classes last 2 months

and take place at Orford Arts Centre from the end of June to the middle of August. 350 students participate each year. Participants are selected by demo tape submissions. Send for application. Closing date for application is mid to late March. Check website for specific dates and deadlines. Scholarships for qualified students.

● REGGAE SUMFEST

Shops 9 & 10 Parkway Plaza, Rose Hall, Montego Bay, Jamaica. E-mail: office@reggaesumfest.com. Website: reggaesumfest.com. **Contact**: Tina Mae Davis, administration manager and festival manager. "Reggae Sumfest is a musical event to which we welcome 30,000+ patrons each year. The festival showcases the best of Dancehall and Reggae music, as well as top R&B/hip hop performers. The festival also offers delicious Jamaican cuisine as well as arts and crafts from all over the island. The main events of the festival is held at Catherine Hall, Montego Bay, Jamaica over a three-day period which usually falls in the third week of July, from Sunday to Saturday." Reggae Sumfest is presented by Summerfest Productions and accepts press kit submissions for persons wishing to perform at the festival between November and January each year. Send to address above.

SONGWRITERS PLAYGROUND®

75-A Lake Rd., #366, Congers NY 10920. (845)267-5955. E-mail: heavyhitters@earthlink.net. Website: www.songwritersplayground.blogspot.com; book: http://goo.gl/totgq. **Contact:** Barbara Jordan, director. Estab. 1990. "To help songwriters, performers and composers develop creative and business skills through the critically acclaimed programs Songwriters Playground, The 'Reel' Deal on Getting Songs Placed in Film and Television, and the Mind Your Own Business Seminars. We offer programs year-round. Workshops last anywhere from 2-15 hours. Workshops are held at various venues throughout the United States. Prices vary according to the length of the workshop." Participants are amateur and professionals. Anyone can participate. Send or call for application.

SOUTH BY SOUTHWEST MUSIC CONFERENCE

SXSW Headquarters, P.O. Box 685289, Austin, TX 78768. (512)467-7979. Fax: (512)451-0754. E-mail: sxsw@sxsw.com. Website: www.sxsw.com. **Contact:**

Conference Organizer. **UK and Ireland:** Mementomori Ltd, 9 The Coach Yard, Cloughjordan, Co. Tipperary, Ireland. Phone/Fax: (353)505-42570. E-mail: una@sxsw.com. **Contact:** Una Johnston. **Europe:** Einsiedlerweg 6, D-72074 Tuebingen-Pfrondorf 72074, Germany. Phone/Fax: (49)-7071-885-604. E-mail: mirko@sxsw.com. **Contact:** Mirko Whitfield. **Asia:** Meijidori Bldg. #406, 2-3-21 Kabukicho, Shinjuku-ku, Tokyo 160-0021, Japan. Phone: +82 3-5292-5551. Fax: +82 3-5292-5552. E-mail: info@sxsw-asia.com. **Contact:** Hiroshi Asada. **Australia/New Zealand/Hawaii:** 60 Kings St., Coffs Harbour, 2450 NSW, Australia. Phone: 61-2-6652-6675. Fax: 61-2-9557-7788. E-mail: tripp@sxsw.om. **Contact:** Phil Tripp. Estab. 1987. South by Southwest (SXSW) is a private company based in Austin, Texas, with a year-round staff of professionals dedicated to building and delivering conference and festival events for entertainment and related media industry professionals. Since 1987, SXSW has produced the internationally recognized music and media conference and festival (SXSW). As the entertainment business adjusted to issues of future growth and development, in 1994, SXSW added conferences and festivals for the film industry (SXSW Film) as well as for the blossoming interactive media (SXSW Interactive Festival). Now three industry events converge in Austin during a Texas-sized week, mirroring the ever-increasing convergence of entertainment/media outlets. The next SXSW Music Conference and Festival will be held in March. Offers panel discussions, "Crash Course" educational seminars and nighttime showcases. SXSW Music seeks out speakers who have developed unique ways to create and sell music. From Thursday through Saturday, the conference includes over fifty sessions including a panel of label heads discussing strategy, interviews with notable artists, topical discussions, demo listening sessions and the mentor program. And when the sun goes down, a multitude of performances by musicians and songwriters from across the country and around the world populate the SXSW Music Festival, held in venues in central Austin. Write, e-mail, or visit website for dates and registration instructions.
TIPS "Go to the website in August to apply for showcase consideration. SXSW is also involved in North by Northeast (NXNE), held in Toronto, Canada in late Spring."

THE SWANNANOA GATHERING— CONTEMPORARY FOLK WEEK
Warren Wilson College, P.O. Box 9000, Asheville, NC 28815-9000. E-mail: gathering@warren-wilson.edu. Website: www.swangathering.com. Director: Jim Magill. "For anyone who ever wanted to make music for an audience, we offer a comprehensive week in artist development, including classes in Songwriting, Performance, and Vocal Coaching, 2010 staff included Christine Lavin, Peter Mulvey, Catie Curtis, Sara Hickman, Abbie Gardner, Vance Gilbert, Jack Williams, Jon Vezner, David Roth, Siobhan Quinn, and Ray Chesna." For a brochure or other info contact the Swannanoa Gathering at the phone number/address above. Takes place last week in July. 2012 Tuition: See website. Housing (including all meals): $ 350. Annual program of the Swannanoa Gathering Folk Arts Workshops.

THE NEW HARMONY PROJECT
P.O. Box 441062, Indianapolis, IN 46244-1062. (317)464-1103. E-mail: jgrynheim@newharmony project.org. Website: www.newharmonyproject.org. **Contact:** Joel Grynheim, conference director. Estab. 1986. Selected scripts receive various levels of development with rehearsals and readings, both public and private. "Our mission is to nurture writers and their life-affirming scripts. This includes plays, screenplays, musicals and TV scripts." Offers programs for musical playwrights. Event takes place in May/June in southwest Indiana. Participants are amateur and professional writers and media professionals. Send for application.

THE SONGWRITERS GUILD OF AMERICA FOUNDATION
1560 Broadway, Suite #408, New York, NY 10036. (800)524-6742. E-mail: ny@songwritersguild.com. Website: www.songwritersguild.com. Director of Operations: Mark Saxon. The Foundation is in charge of many events, including workshops in the NY, Nashville, and L.A. areas.

UNDERCURRENTS
P.O. Box 94040, Cleveland OH 44101-6040. E-mail: music@undercurrents.com. Website: www.undercurrents.com. **Contact:** John Latimer, executive director. Estab. 1989. A music, event, and art marketing and promotion network with online and offline exposure featuring music showcases, seminars, trade shows,

networking forums. Ongoing programs and performances for songwriters, composers, and performers. Participants are selected by EPK, demo, biography, and photo. Register at www.undercurrents.com.

WEST COAST SONGWRITERS CONFERENCE

(formerly Northern California Songwriters Association Conference) 1724 Laurel St., Suite 120, San Carlos, CA 94070. (650)654-3966. E-mail: info@westcoast-songwriters.org. Website: www.westcoastsongwriters. org. **Contact:** Ian Crombie, executive director. Estab. 1980. "Conference offers opportunity and education. 16 seminars, 50 song screening sessions (1,500 songs reviewed), performance showcases, one on one sessions and concerts." Offers programs for lyricists, songwriters, composers, and performers. "During the year we have competitive live Songwriter competitions. Winners go into the playoffs. Winners of the playoffs perform at the sunset concert at the conference." Event takes place second weekend in September at Foothill College, Los Altos Hills, CA. Over 500 songwriters/musicians participate in this event. Participants are songwriters, composers, musical playwrights, vocalists, bands, instrumentalists, and those interested in a career in the music business. Send for application. Deadline: September 1. Fee: $150-275. "See our listing in the Organizations section."

WESTERN WIND WORKSHOP IN ENSEMBLE SINGING

263 W. 86th St., New York NY 10024. (212)873-2848. Fax: (212)873-2849. E-mail: workshops@western-wind.org. Website: www.westernwind.org. **Contact:** William Zukoff, executive producer. Estab. 1981. Participants learn the art of ensemble singing—no conductor, one on a part. Workshop focuses on blend, diction, phrasing, and production. Offers programs for performers. Limited talent-based scholarship available. Offers programs annually. Takes place June, July, and August in the music department at Smith College, Northampton MA. 70-80 songwriters and/or musicians participate in each event. Participants are amateur and professional vocalists. Anyone can participate. Send for application or register at their website. Arrangers' works are frequently studied and performed. Also offers additional workshops President's Day weekend in Brattleboro VT, and Columbus Day weekend in Woodstock, VT.

WINTER MUSIC CONFERENCE INC.

3450 NE 12th Terrace, Ft. Lauderdale, FL 33334. (954)563-4444. Fax: (954)563-1599. E-mail: info@wintermusicconference.com. Website: www.winter musicconference.com. President: Margo Possenti. Estab. 1985. Features educational seminars and showcases for dance, hip-hop, alternative, and rap. Offers programs for songwriters and performers. Offers programs annually. Event takes place March of each year in Miami FL. 3,000 songwriters/musicians participate in each event. Participants are amateur and professional songwriters, composers, musical playwrights, vocalists, bands and instrumentalists. Participants are selected by submitting demo tape. Send SASE, visit website, or call for application. Deadline: February. Event held at either nightclubs or hotel with complete staging, lights, and sound.

RETREATS & COLONIES

This section provides information on retreats and artists' colonies. These are places for creatives, including songwriters, to find solitude and spend concentrated time focusing on their work. While a residency at a colony may offer participation in seminars, critiques, or performances, the atmosphere of a colony or retreat is much more relaxed than that of a conference or workshop. Also, a songwriter's stay at a colony is typically anywhere from one to twelve weeks (sometimes longer), while time spent at a conference may only run from one to fourteen days.

Like conferences and workshops, however, artists' colonies and retreats span a wide range. Yaddo, perhaps the most well-known colony, limits its residencies to artists "working at a professional level in their field, as determined by a judging panel of professionals in the field." The Brevard Music Center offers residencies only to those involved in classical music. Despite different focuses, all artists' colonies and retreats have one thing in common: they are places where you may work undisturbed, usually in nature-oriented, secluded settings.

SELECTING A COLONY OR RETREAT

When selecting a colony or retreat, the primary consideration for many songwriters is cost, and you'll discover that arrangements vary greatly. Some colonies provide residencies as well as stipends for personal expenses. Some suggest donations of a certain amount. Still others offer residencies for substantial sums but have financial assistance available.

When investigating the various options, consider meal and housing arrangements and your family obligations. Some colonies provide meals for residents, while others require residents to pay for meals. Some colonies house artists in one main building; others provide separate cottages. A few have provisions for spouses and families. Others prohibit families altogether.

Overall, residencies at colonies and retreats are competitive. Since only a handful of spots are available at each place, you often must apply months in advance for the time period you desire. A number of locations are open year-round, and you may find planning to go during the "off-season" lessens your competition. Other colonies, however, are only available during certain months. In any case, be prepared to include a sample of your best work with your application. Also, know what project you'll work on while in residence and have alternative projects in mind in case the first one doesn't work out once you're there.

Each listing in this section details fee requirements, meal and housing arrangements, and space and time availability, as well as the retreat's surroundings, facilities and special activities. Of course, before making a final decision, send a SASE to the colonies or retreats that interest you to receive their most up-to-date details. Costs, application requirements and deadlines are particularly subject to change.

MUSICIAN'S RESOURCE

For other listings of songwriter-friendly colonies, see *Musician's Resource* (available from Watson-Guptill—www.watsonguptill.com), which not only provides information about conferences, workshops, and academic programs but also residencies and retreats. Also check the Publications of Interest section in this book for newsletters and other periodicals providing this information.

BREVARD MUSIC CENTER

P.O. Box 312, 349 Andante Ln., Brevard, NC 28712. (828)862-2100. Fax: (828)884-2036. E-mail: bmc@ brevardmusic.org. Website: www.brevardmusic. org. **Contact:** Dorothy Knowles, admissions coordinator. Estab. 1936. Offers 6-week residencies from June through the first week of August. Open to professional and student composers, pianists, vocalists, collaborative pianists, and instrumentalists of classical music. A 2-week jazz workshop is offered in June. Accommodates 400 at one time. Personal living quarters include cabins. Offers rehearsal, teaching, and practice cabins.

COSTS $4,100 for tuition, room and board. Scholarships are available.

REQUIREMENTS Call for application forms and guidelines. $50 application fee. Participants are selected by audition or demonstration tape and then by invitation. There are 80 different audition sites throughout the US.

ISLE ROYALE NATIONAL PARK ARTIST-IN-RESIDENCE PROGRAM

800 E. Lakeshore Dr., Houghton, MI 49931. (906)482-0984. Fax: (906)482-8753. E-mail: ISRO_Parkinfo@ nps.gov. Website: www.nps.gov/ISRO. **Contact:** Greg Blust, coordinator. Estab. 1991. Offers 2-3 week residencies from mid-June to mid-September. Open to all art forms. Accommodates 1 artist with 1 companion at one time. Personal living quarters include cabin with shared outhouse. A canoe is provided for transportation. Offers a guest house at the site that can be used as a studio. The artist is asked to contribute a piece of work representative of their stay at Isle Royale, to be used by the park in an appropriate manner. During their residency, artists will be asked to share their experience (1 presentation per week of residency, about 1 hour/week) with the public by demonstration, talk, or other means.

REQUIREMENTS Deadline: postmarked February 16, 2012. Send for application forms and guidelines. Accepts inquiries via fax or e-mail. A panel of professionals from various disciplines, and park representatives will choose the finalists. The selection is based on artistic integrity, ability to reside in a wilderness environment, a willingness to donate a finished piece of work inspired on the island, and the artist's ability to relate and interpret the park through their work.

KALANI OCEANSIDE RETREAT

RR2, Box 4500, Pahoa, HI 96778. (808)965-7828 or (800)800-6886. Fax: (808)965-0527. E-mail: kalani@ kalani.com. Website: www.kalani.com. **Contact:** Richard Koob, director. Estab. 1980. Offers 2-week to 2-month residencies. Open to all artists who can verify professional accomplishments. Accommodates 120 at one time. Personal living quarters include private cottage or lodge room with private or shared bath. Full (3 meals/day) dining service. Offers shared studio/library spaces. Activities include opportunity to share works in progress, ongoing yoga, hula and other classes; beach, thermal springs, Volcanoes National Park nearby; olympic pool/spa on 120-acre facility.

COSTS $84-240/night lodging with stipend, including 3 meals/day. Transportation by rental car from $45/day, Kalani service $65/trip, or taxi $90/trip.

REQUIREMENTS Accepts inquiries via fax or e-mail.

THE HAMBIDGE CENTER

Attn: Residency Director, P.O. Box 339, Rabun Gap, GA 30568. (706)746-5718. Fax: (706)746-9933 E-mail: director@hambidge.org. Website: www.hambidge. org. **Contact:** Deb Sanders, residency chair. Estab. 1934 (Center); 1988 (residency). Offers 2-week to 2-month residencies year-round. Open to all artists. Accommodates 8 at one time. Personal living quarters include a private cottage with kitchen, bath, and living/studio space. Offers composer/musical studio equipped with piano. Activities include communal dinners February through December and nightly or periodic sharing of works-in-progress.

COSTS $200/week

REQUIREMENTS Send SASE for application forms and guidelines, or available on website. Accepts inquiries via fax and e-mail. Application fee: $30. Deadlines: January 15, April 15, and September 15.

● THE TYRONE GUTHRIE CENTRE

Annaghmakerrig, Newbliss, County Monaghan, Ireland. (353)(047)54003. Fax: (353)(047)54380. E-mail: info@tyroneguthrie.ie. Website: www.tyroneguthrie.ie. **Contact:** Resident Director. Estab. 1981. Offers year-round residencies. Artists may stay for anything from 1 week to 3 months in the Big House, or for up to 6 months at a time in one of the 5 self-catering houses in the old farmyard. Open to artists of all disciplines.

Accommodates 13 in the big house and up to 7 in the farmyard cottages. Personal living quarters include bedroom with bathroom en suite. Offers a variety of workspaces. There is a music room for composers and musicians with a Yamaha C3M-PE conservative grand piano, a performance studio with a Yamaha upright, a photographic darkroom, and a number of studios for visual artists, one of which is wheelchair accessible. At certain times of the year it is possible, by special arrangement, to accommodate groups of artists, symposiums, master classes, workshops and other collaborations.

COSTS Irish and European artists: €300/week for the big house; €150 for self-catering cottages; others pay €650 per week, all found, for a residency in the Big House and €325 per week (plus gas and electricity costs) for one of the self-catering farmyard houses. To qualify for a residency, it is necessary to show evidence of a significant level of achievement in the relevant field.

REQUIREMENTS Application forms and guidelines are available on the Web. Accepts inquiries via telephone, fax, or e-mail. Submit application form with CV to be reviewed by the selection committee of board members at quarterly meetings.

VIRGINIA CENTER FOR THE CREATIVE ARTS

154 San Angelo Dr., Amherst, VA 24521. (434)946-7236. Fax: (434)946-7239. E-mail: vcca@vcca.com. Website: www.vcca.com. **Contact:** Suny Monk, executive director. Estab. 1971. Offers residencies year-round, typical residency lasts 2 weeks to 2 months. Open to originating artists: composers, writers, and visual artists. Accommodates 25 at one time. Personal living quarters include 22 single rooms, 2 double rooms, bathrooms shared with one other person. All meals are served. Kitchens for fellows' use available at studios and residence. The VCCA van goes into town twice a week. Fellows share their work regularly. Four studios have pianos.

COSTS No transportation costs are covered. "Artists are accepted into the VCCA without regard for their ability to contribute financially to their residency. Daily cost is $180 per Fellow. We ask Fellows to contribute according to their ability."

REQUIREMENTS Send SASE for application form or download from website. Applications are reviewed by panelists. Application fee: $30. Deadline: May 15 for October-January residency; September 15 for February-May residency; January 15 for June-September residency.

VENUES

40 WATT CLUB
285 W. Washington St., Athens GA 30601. (706)549-7871. E-mail: fortywatt@athens.net. Website: www.40watt.com. Music: indie, rock, alternative.

123 PLEASANT STREET
123 Pleasant St., Morgantown WV 26505. (304)292-0800. E-mail: 123pleasantstreet@gmail.com. Website: www.123pleasantstreet.com. "An eclectic crowd can be expected any given night and is as diverse as the bands that grace our stage whether it be rock, bluegrass, punk, jazz, reggae, salsa, country, djs, indie, hardcore, old time, or some mixture of some or all or the above."

11/12 LOUNGE: ENTERTAINMENT & SPORTS BAR
843 Lee Rd., Orlando FL 32810. (407)539-3410. E-mail: the1112lounge@yahoo.com. Website: www.the1112lounge.com. **Contact:** Kathleen W., Marketing & Promotions. Estab. 2008. Music: acoustic, alternative, metal, pop, punk, reggae, rock, and singer/songwriter.

ABG'S BAR
190 W. Center St., Provo UT 84106. (801)373-1200. E-mail: booking@abgsbar.com. Website: http://abgsbar.com. Music: rock, alt-country, alternative, folk, blues, jazz.

ALLEY KATZ
10 Walnut Alley, Richmond VA 23223. (804)643-2816. E-mail: alleykatzva@aol.com. Website: www.alleykatzrva.com. Music: hard rock, punk, metal.

ARMADILLO'S BAR & GRILL
132 Dock St., Annapolis MD 21401. (401)280-0028. E-mail: armadillosannapolis@gmail.com. Website: www.armadillosannapolis.com. "Armadillo's is the top choice for nightlife in downtown Annapolis. We are the only venue in town to provide two levels of live entertainment. Upstairs, Armadillo's brings you the hottest local and national bands, in a casual, intimate setting, while DJ's keep the crowd moving downstairs." Music: rock, acoustic, reggae, soul, pop, indie, alternative.

ART BAR
1211 Park St., Columbia SC 29201. (803)929-0198. E-mail: booking@artbarsc.com. Website: www.artbarsc.com. Music: rock, alternative, indie, punk, hard rock, hip-hop.

ASHLAND COFFEE & TEA
100 N. Railroad Ave., Ashland VA 23005. (804)798-1702. Website: http://ashlandcoffeeandtea.com. "Join us most Thursdays, Fridays and Saturdays in our intimate 'Listening Room' for an evening of Americana, bluegrass, folk, blues, jazz, pop—you never know what

we'll have on tap with our wide range of performers. Don't miss 'Homegrown Wednesday' featuring local Virginia talent, or the 'Songwriter's Showdown', a songwriting and vocal performance competition every Tuesday."

BACKBOOTH

37 W. Pine St., Orlando FL 32801. (407)999-2570. E-mail: bookings@backbooth.com. Website: www.backbooth.com. "BackBooth's reputation as a music venue has grown to being named one of the best live music venues in the city, according to *Orlando Weekly*, and still boasts the most impressive draft selection in downtown. With a capacity of 350, a large stage, a powerful sound/lighting system, balcony, and back bar area; the club still maintains a very comfortable and inviting, almost pub-like atmosphere with an Old English decor including wood work and dark curtains throughout. As a venue, Back Booth continues to play host to many popular national and regional acts, while remaining a favorite among locals. The club is also known for its dance parties; which are among the most popular and recognized in town. Whether it be for an intimate live performance, a rousing rock show, or a night of dancing and drinks, Back Booth is established in the heart of the central Florida community as a favorite destination." Music: reggae, acoustic, alternative, indie, pop, hip-hop, jam, roots, soul, gospel, funk, dubstep, country, rock, metal.

BACK EAST BAR & GRILL

9475 Briar Village Point, Colorado Springs CO 80920. (719)264-6161. Website: www.backeastbarandgrill.com. "We have created the perfect place for you to watch your favorite game and enjoy the incredible food and flavors that we have brought from home. We know you will enjoy every minute that you share with us. So sit back and have a drink, eat some great food, and enjoy your favorite team on one of our many TVs." Music: rock, alternative, R&B, blues, country, pop.

B.B. KING'S MEMPHIS

143 Beale St., Memphis TN 38103. 901-524-5464. E-mail: info@bbkingclubs.com. Website: www.bbking clubs.com. "Come sit with us for a while and enjoy B.B. King's favorite dishes as you listen to the best of Memphis music! Then get ready to get up and dance the night away to the great live music we present to you every night on world-famous Beale Street. B.B. King's features such Memphis music stars as Will Tucker, Preston Shannon, The BB King All-Stars and many more!"

TIPS Send demo CD and photo. No phone or e-mail inquiries will be considered until this information is received.

B.B. KING'S NASHVILLE

152 2nd Ave. N, Nashville TN 37201. 615-256-2727. E-mail: info@bbkingclubs.com. Estab. 2003. "Located in the heart of Downtown Nashville on Historic 2nd Avenue just blocks from Broadway, LP Stadium & The Gaylord Entertainment Center you will find one of Nashville's largest live music venues specializing in speakeasy blues, motown & classic rock. Welcome to Nashville's ultimate entertainment experience!" Also located in Memphis, Las Vegas, Orlando, West Palm Beach.

TIPS Send demo CD and photo. No phone or e-mail inquiries will be considered until this information is received.

BERKELEY CAFE

217 W. Martin St., Raleigh NC 27601. (919)821-0777. E-mail: lakeboonee@bellsouth.net. Website: www.berkeleycafe.net. **Contact:** Jim Shires. Music: rock, bluegrass, alternative, blues, punk, folk.

BILLY'S LOUNGE

1437 Wealthy SE, Grand Rapids MI 49506. (616)459-5757. E-mail: billysbooking@gmail.com. Website: www.billyslounge.com. "In keeping the long standing tradition of service and entertainment, Billy's offers live music. Although deeply rooted in the Blues, acts from all genres, ranging in size from local to international, can be heard blazing from Billy's premier sound system on any given night." Music: blues, country, rock, R&B, Americana, hip-hop, jazz.

BLUE

650A Congress St., Portland ME 04101. (207)774-4111. E-mail: booking@portcityblue.com. Website: http://portcityblue.com. "Located in the heart of Portland's Arts District, Blue is Portland's most intimate live music venue. We present an array of music such as Celtic, Middle Eastern, Blues, Old Time, Jazz, Folk, and more."

BO'S BAR

2310 University Blvd., Tuscaloosa AL 35401. (205)259-1331. E-mail: bosbar2310@gmail.com. Website: www.bos-bar.com. **Contact:** Bo Hines, owner. Music: rock, alternative, country, alt-country, bluesgrass. "The most freedom loving bar in the world!"

BOTTLETREE

3719 Third Ave. S, Birmingham AL 35222. (205)533-6288. E-mail: bottletreevenue@gmail.com. Website: www.thebottletree.com. **Contact:** Kyle; Rebecca. Music: punk, indie, folk, rock, country, soul, alternative.

BOTTOM OF THE HILL

1233 17th St., San Francisco CA 94107. (415)621-4455. E-mail: booking@bottomofthehill.com. **Contact:** Ramona Downey; Ursula Rodriguez, bookers. Music: alternative, rock, rockabilly, punk, hard rock.

BROOKLYN BOWL

61 Wythe Ave., Brooklyn NY 11211. (718)963-3369. E-mail: rock.androll@brooklynbowl.com. E-mail: booking@brooklynbowl.com. Website: www.brooklynbowl.com. "Brooklyn Bowl redefines the entertainment experience for the 21st century. Centered around a 16-lane bowling alley, 600-capacity performance venue with live music 7 nights a week, and food by Blue Ribbon, Brooklyn Bowl stakes out expansive new territory, literally and conceptually, in the 23,000-square foot former Hecla Iron Works (1882), one block from the burgeoning waterfront." Music: rock, indie, hip-hop, R&B, alternative, punk, funk, folk, reggae, soul.

CAFE 939

939 Boylston St., Boston MA 02215. (617)747-6040 or (617)747-6143. E-mail: jindrisano@berklee.edu; swolfgang@berklee.edu. E-mail: 939booking@beklee.edu. **Contact:** Jack Indrisano; Shawn Wolfgang. "Cafe 939 showcases Berklee's emerging student performers and local Boston artists, as well as national acts seeking a more intimate, personal space in which to connect with their fans. The venue is open to the general public and aims to attract musicians and music fans from all walks of life." Music: rock, jazz, folk, Americana, bluegrass, hip-hop, electronica, pop, indie.

CAFE NINE

250 State St., New Haven CT 06511. (203)789-8281. E-mail: bookcafenine@gmail.com. Website: www.cafenine.com. **Contact:** Paul Mayer, booker. "Cafe Nine features live music from national, regional and local acts seven nights a week. Catch some of your favorites getting back to their roots in our intimate setting or see tomorrow's stars on their way to the stadiums." Music: indie, rock, alternative, jazz, punk, garage, alt-country.

CALEDONIA LOUNGE

365 W. Clayton St., Athens GA 30601. (706)549-5577. E-mail: booking@caledonialounge.com. Website: http://caledonialounge.com. Music: indie, rock, alternative, folk.

CAPONES

1201 Third St. SE, Cedar Rapids IA 52401. (319)364-0027. E-mail: caponescr@yahoo.com. Website: www.caponesrestaurantcr.com. **Contact:** Dave Fountain, General Manager. Music: rock, dance, alternative.

CASSELMAN'S BAR & VENUE

2620 Walnut St., Denver CO 80205. (720)242-8923. E-mail: booking@casselmans.com. Website: www.casselmans.com. "Casselman's is a multi-use live music and special events venue located in NoDo (North-Downtown) Denver. Casselman's opened in 2009 and started to brand 'NoDo' as the new entertainment and arts district of Denver. The name Casselman is the maiden name of our great grandmother and was carried as the middle name down to three members of the family business. Casselman's is a proud recipient of the Westword's 2010 Best New Club award!" Music: pop, rock, R&B, hip-hop, alternative.

CHELSEA'S CAFE

2857 Perkins Rd., Baton Rouge LA 70808. (225)387-3679. E-mail: dave@chelseascafe.com. Website: www.chelseascafe.com. **Contact:** Dave, manager. "Chelsea's Cafe is Baton Rouge's favorite place to relax, offering good food, drinks and live music in an intimate, casual atmosphere." Music: rock, indie, alternative, soul.

CHILKOOT CHARLIES

2435 Spenard Rd., Anchorage AK 99503. (907)272-1010. E-mail: promo@koots.com. Website: www.koots.com. "Chilkoot Charlie's features a rustic Alaska atmosphere with sawdust-covered floors, 3 stages, 3 dance floors and 10 bars (11 in the summertime!) with padded tree stumps and beer kegs for seating. Literally filled to the rafters with such things as famous band photos & autographs, huge beer can collections, hilarious gags, and tons of Alaska memorabilia, a person could wander around Chilkoot Charlie's for days and still not see everything." Music: rock, punk, metal.

CHROME HORSE SALOON

1202 Third St. SE, Cedar Rapids IA 52401. (319)365-1234. E-mail: chromehorsesaloon@mchsi.com. Website: www.chromehorsesaloon.net. "In addition to weekly shows inside on Friday and Saturday nights, a series of Friday night outdoor concerts are held in the parking lot during the summer months. The bar also has hosted a variety of national acts, including The Jeff Healey Band, L.A. Guns, Saliva, Hank Williams III, Black Oak Arkansas, The Buckinghams, The Grass Roots, American Idol finalist Amanda Overmyer and Blues Traveler." Music: rock, funk, punk, indie, alternative.

CHURCHILL'S

5501 NE Second Ave., Miami FL 33137. (305)757-1807. E-mail: bookings@churchillspub.com. Website: www.churchillspubs.com. Music: rock, alternative, indie, pop, jazz, hip-hop, electronica, acoustic.

CITY TAVERN

1402 Main St., Dallas TX 75201. (214)745-1402. E-mail: info@citytaverndowntown.com. E-mail: booking@citytaverndowntown.com. Website: www.citytaverndowntown.com. Music: country, rock, jam, pop, alternative.

CLUB 209

209 N. Boulder Ave., Tulsa OK 74103. (918)584-9944. E-mail: thegang@club209tulsa.com. Website: www.club209tulsa.com. Music: indie, Americana, alt-country, folk.

CLUB CONGRESS

311 E. Congress St., Tucson AZ 85701. (520)622-8848. E-mail: clubcongressbooking@gmail.com. Website: www.hotelcongress.com. Contact: David Slutes, entertainment and booking director. Music: rock, alternative, indie, folk, Americana.

CONGRESS THEATER

2135 North Milwaukee Ave., Chicago IL 60647. 773-252-4000. E-mail: alberto@congresschicago.com. Website: www.congresschicago.com. "The Congress Theater is always looking for local/regional talent. Please send us your information through our online form and we'll take a look." Music: alternative, classic rock, electronic/dance/DJ, hip-hop/rap, metal, punk, rock, and urban/R&B.

The theater dates back to the '20s when it was a movie palace in the style of Italian Renaissance and Classical Revival styles.

TIPS "Bands: if you're interested in getting on a current bill, or being considered for a future bill, pursue those opportunities through promoters in the entertainment community. Draw well at smaller venues in the city, and you won't have to call them. They'll call your agent."

CORAZON

401 S. Guadalupe, Santa Fe NM 87505. (505)983-4559. Website: www.corazonsantafe.com. "The Heart of Santa Fe Nightlife; featuring the best Touring & Local Bands, DJs and all around entertainment The City has to offer. We feature Downtown Santa Fe's premier stage (and sound) for live music with plenty of room to dance." Music: rock, indie, techno, reggae, hip-hop, blues, jazz, metal.

CUTTY'S

1140 W. Hwy 22, Jackson WY 83001. (307)732-0001. Website: www.eatatcuttys.com. Music: Americana, indie, rock, country, alt-country, alternative, folk.

D.B.A.

618 Frenchmen St., New Orleans LA 70116. (504)942-3731. E-mail: booking@dbabars.com. Website: http://dbabars.com/dbano. Music: blues, jazz, R&B, Cajun.

DOUG FIR LOUNGE

830 E. Burnside, Portland OR 97214. (503)231-9663. E-mail: booking@dougfirlounge.com. Website: www.dougfirlounge.com. Music: rock, alternative, indie, funk, garage, pop, dance, folk, bluegrass, soul, Americana.

DUFFY'S TAVERN

1412 O St., Lincoln NE 68508. (402)474-3543. E-mail: management@duffyslincoln.com. E-mail: booking@duffyslincoln.com. Website: www.duffyslincoln.com. Contact: Jeremy "Dub" Wardlaw, booking and promotions. "We're known for a lot of things, but if you ask any of us, we will tell you that we're a music venue. Many national acts have graced our stage, including Nirvana, 311, Bright Eyes, the Boss Martians, Slobberbone, Wesley Willis, and many others. A lot of us think some of the local acts are even better, and on any Sunday or Wednesday night, you can be assured Duffy's stage will be jumping with some of the best original music around." Music: rock, folk, Americana, indie, psychedelic, pop, hard rock.

EL BAIT SHOP

200 SW Second St., Des Moines IA 50309. (515)284-1970. E-mail: music@elbaitshop.com. Website: http://elbaitshop.com. Music: rock, alternative, pop, indie, folk, country, Americana, blues, jam, bluegrass, psychedelic.

ELBOW ROOM

1025 Strand Ave., Missoula MT 59801. (406)728-9963. E-mail: paffer17@yahoo.com. Website: www.elbowroombar.com. **Contact:** Josh Paffhausen, owner and general manager. "With entertainment at least five nights a week, ranging from karaoke and red hot DJs to favorite local bands, and major headliners." Music: rock, alternative, country.

EXIT/IN

2208 Elliston Place, Nashville TN 37203. (615)321-3340. Website: www.exitin.com. "The Exit/In began it's role as a Nashville music venue back in 1971. Since then countless shows and great memories have happened within these walls." Music: rock, country, alt-country, folk, punk, pop, psychedelic.

FAT CATZ MUSIC CLUB

440 Bourbon St., New Orleans LA 70130. (504)525-0303. E-mail: info@fatcatzmusicclub.com. Website: www.fatcatzmusicclub.com. "When you are looking for a great place to hang out in New Orleans, look no further! Stop by for a great time any day of the week. We have awesome music all the time, and our staff is second to none. Kick back, relax, and enjoy quality music with us! We have live bands EVERY night of the week that feature a large variety music styles." Music: R&B, rock, alternative, jazz, hip-hop, pop, blues.

FIVE SPOT

1123 Euclid Ave., Atlanta GA 30307. (404)223-1100. E-mail: booking@fivespot-atl.com. **Contact:** Kirk Hollingsworth, General Manager; Dusty Watts, Manager. "On any given night, the Five Spot features live music of all genres, from bluegrass to indie rock, jam bands to acid jazz, and form funk to hip-hop. We also features live art, short films and animations. The Five Spot is Atlanta's most inclusive music and arts venue and features acoustic acts every Monday, a diverse Musician's Jam on Tuesdays, monthly Bluegrass Jams and many touring and national acts Wednesday through Sunday."

FLIPNOTICS

1601 Barton Springs Rd., Austin TX 78704. (512)658-7633. E-mail: flip@flipnotics.com. E-mail: flipsbooking@gmail.com. **Contact:** Blaker Palmer; Chris Copple, general managers. Music: indie, rock, alternative, pop, folk, country, Americana.

FREAKIN' FROG

4700 S. Maryland Pkwy., Las Vegas NV 89119. (702)597-9702. E-mail: tommy@freakinfrog.com. Website: www.freakinfrog.com. **Contact:** Tommy Marth, director of marketing. Music: pop, rock, punk, blues, alternative.

FREIGHT HOUSE DISTRICT

250 Evans Ave., Reno NV 89501. (775)334-7094. E-mail: info@freighthouse.com. Website: www.freighthouse.com. Includes: Duffy's Ale House, 205 Lounge, Bugsy's Sports Bar and Grill, Arroyo Mexican Grill. Music: funk, rock, Latin, pop, dance, alternative, soul, reggae, blues.

GEORGE'S MAJESTIC LOUNGE

519 W. Dickson St., Fayetteville AR 72701. (479)527-6618. E-mail: saxsafe@aol.com. Website: www.georgesmajesticlounge.com. **Contact:** Brian Crowne. "George's is perhaps best known for the incredible musicians that have graced our stages, bringing the best in local, regional, and national acts through our doors. Some artists of note that have performed at Georges through the years include Robert Cray, Leon Russell, Little River Band, Delbert McClinton, Eddie Money, Pat Green, Derek Trucks, Sam Bush, Tower of Power, Leftover Salmon, Bob Margolin, Chubby Carrier, Tommy Castro, Coco Montoya, Anthony Gomes, Bernard Allison, Michael Burks, Charlie Robison, Cross Canadian Ragweed, Jason Boland, Dark Star Orchestra, Steve Kimock, Martin Fierro, North Mississippi Allstars, Robert Randolph, David Lindley, Big Smith, Cate Brothers, Oteil Burbridge, and so many more. Music: rock, folk, alternative, country, bluegrass, punk.

GREAT AMERICAN MUSIC HALL

859 O'Farrell St., San Francisco CA 94109. (415)885-0750. E-mail: booking@gamh.com. Website: www.gamh.com. "The past three decades at the Great American Music Hall have been full of music, with

artists ranging from Duke Ellington, Sarah Vaughan and Count Basie to Van Morrison, the Grateful Dead and Bobby McFerrin." Music: contemporary pop, indie, jazz, folk, rock, alternative, Americana.

GREAT SCOTT

1222 Commonwealth Ave., Allston MA 02134. (617)566-9014. E-mail: submissions@greatscottbos ton.com. Website: www.greatscottboston.com. **Contact:** Carl Lavin. Music: rock, metal, alternative, indie.

GUNPOWDER LODGE

10092 Bel Air Rd., Kingsville MD 21087. (410)256-2626. Website: www.thegunpowderlodge.com. Music: rock, indie, acoustic, classic rock.

HAL & MAL'S

200 S. Commerce St., Jackson MS 39204. (601)948-0888. E-mail: april@halandmals.com. Website: www.halandmals.com. "The most talked about, upscale honky tonk in all of Mississippi. Here, art is made, music is played and locals gather to share community and celebrate the very best of Mississippi's creative spirit." Music: honky-tonk, country, rock, blues, classic rock, alternative.

HANK'S CAFE

1038 Nuuanu Ave., Honolulu HI 96817. (808)526-1410. Website: www.hankscafehonolulu.com. Music: rock, doo-wop, dance, country, pop.

HEADLINERS MUSIC HALL

1386 Lexington Rd., Louisville KY 40206. (502)584-8088. E-mail: booking@headlinerslouisville.com. Website: http://headlinerslouisville.com. "Locally owned and operated, Headliners Music Hall is the premiere live entertainment venue of Louisville, Kentucky. We bring the best local and national acts to our stage, with fantastic sound and a fun atmosphere. We've had the privilege of hosting some amazing rock, metal, acoustic, hip-hop, and alternative bands such as My Morning Jacket, Jimmy Eat World, Neko Case, Clutch, Sharon Jones & The Dap Kings, Umphrey's McGee, Old Crow Medicine Show, Kings of Leon, Talib Kweli, Girl Talk and more." Music: rock, indie, punk, folk, reggae, soul, R&B, psychedelic.

HIGHLANDS TAP ROOM

1279 Bardstown Rd., Louisville KY 40204. (502)459-2337. E-mail: booking@highlandstaproom.com. Website: www.highlandstaproom.com. "Fun, friend-ly neighborhood bar in the heart of the Highlands, Louisville, KY. Live entertainment seven days a week." Music: rock, acoustic, hip-hop, folk, blues, bluegrass, alt-country.

HIGH-NOON SALOON

701A E. Washington Ave., Madison WI 53703. (608)268-1122. E-mail: info@high-noon.com. E-mail: booking@high-noon.com. **Contact:** Cathy Dethmers, owner/manager. "Founded in 2004 in downtown Madison, Wisconsin, High Noon Saloon is a live music venue that features many different styles of music, including rock, alternative, metal, indie, alt-country, pop, punk, bluegrass, folk, jam, world music, and more. We host large national acts, smaller touring bands from around the world, and lots of local music."

HI-TONE CAFE

1913 Poplar Ave., Memphis TN 38104. (901)278-8663. E-mail: thehitonecafe@gmail.com. Website: www.hi-tonememphis.com. **Contact:** Jonathan Kiersky, general manager/talent buyer. Music: rock, alternative, indie, pop, alt-country, Americana.

HOT TUNA

2817 Shore Dr., Virginia Beach VA 23451. (757)481-2888. E-mail: rstreet@hottunavb.com. Website: www.hottunavb.com. Music: rock, acoustic, alternative, dance, pop.

HOWLER'S COYOTE CAFE

4509 Liberty Ave., Pittsburgh PA 15224. (412)682-0320. E-mail: booking@howlerscoyotecafe.com. Website: www.howlerscoyotecafe.com. **Contact:** Stef; Bengt, booking staff. "Howler's Coyote Cafe is an independent mid-level music venue and bar in Pittsburgh's east end hosting local and national acts of all genres 5 days a week." Music: rock, alternative, pop, dance, blues, alt-country, punk, jam, psychedelic, folk, indie.

HUMPY'S

610 W. Sixth Ave., Anchorage AK 99501. (907)276-2337. Website: www.humpys.com. Music: folk, rock, metal, blues, Americana.

JEREMIAH BULLFROGS LIVE

4115 SW Huntoon St., Topeka KS 66604. (785)273-0606. E-mail: bullfrogslive@gmail.com. Website:

www.bullfrogslive.com. **Contact:** Rob Fateley. Music: blues, soul, rock, alternative, dance.

JUANITA'S PARTY ROOM

1300 Main St., Little Rock AR 72202. (501)372-1228. Website: www.juanitas.com. Music: rock, reggae, alternative, country, alt-country, indie.

KILBY COURT

741 S. Kilby Ct., Salt Lake City UT 84101. (801)364-3538. E-mail: will@sartainandsaunders.com. Website: www.kilbycourt.com. **Contact:** Will Sartain. Music: rock, alternative, Americana, indie, pop, ska, punk.

KNICKERBOCKERS

901 O St., Lincoln NE 68508. (402)476-6865. E-mail: mail@knickerbockers.net. Website: www.knickerbockers.net. Music: alternative, rock, metal, punk, indie, folk, electronica, Americana.

LARIMER LOUNGE

2721 Larimer St., Denver CO 80205. (303)296-1003. Website: www.larimerlounge.com; www.booklarimer.com. **Contact:** James Irvine, booking manager. Music: rock, pop, electronica, indie, garage, alternative.

LAUNCHPAD

618 Central Ave. SW, Albuquerque NM 87102. (505)764-8887. Website: www.launchpadrocks.com. Music: rock, punk, reggae, alternative.

LEADBETTERS TAVERN

1639 Thames St., Baltimore MD 21231. (410)675-4794. E-mail: leadbetterstavern@gmail.com. Website: www.leadbetterstavern.com. Music: blues, rock, soul, jazz, punk, alternative, funk, pop, indie.

LIQUID LOUNGE

405 S. 8th St. #110, Boise ID 83702. (208)287-5379. E-mail: liquidbooking@gmail.com. Website: www.liquidboise.com. Music: rock, reggae, funk, ska, bluegrass, dance, soul, folk, punk.

LOW SPIRITS

2823 2nd St., Albuquerque NM 87107. (505)433-9555. Website: www.lowspiritslive.com. Music: rock, indie, blues, alternative, folk.

LUCKEY'S CLUB CIGAR STORE

933 Olive St., Eugene OR 97401. (541)687-4643. Website: www.luckeysclub.com. **Contact:** Sam Hahn. "Today, Luckey's combines art nouveau decor, saloon sensibilities, serious pool players, cutting edge music, and a chair for everyone in the community. It still has echoes of the sounds, smells, pool games, and conversations from the past 100 years. It's like a time capsule with a hip twist." Music: folk, acoustic, blues, indie, Americana, rock.

MAD ANTHONY BREWING COMPANY

2002 Broadway, Ft. Wayne IN 46802. (260)426-2537. E-mail: madbrew@msn.com. Website: www.madbrew.com. "A cool, laid back atmosphere, full food menu and weekly live music." Music: rock, jam, jazz, blues, funk, soul, pop.

MAJESTIC THEATRE

115 King St., Madison WI 53703. (608)255-0901. E-mail: info@majesticmadison.com. Website: www.majesticmadison.com. Estab. 1906. The Majestic Theatre is a world-class venue located in Madison, WI, that hosts major national touring acts. Seeks established local and regional acts to open for high-profile headlining acts. Music: acoustic, alternative, americana, classic rock, country, electronic/dance/DJ, folk, funk, hip-hop/rap, jam band, metal, pop, punk, reggae, rock, singer/songwriter, spoken word, and urban/R&B. **TIPS** Contact/submit online at website.

MARTIN'S DOWNTOWN BAR & GRILL

413 1st St. SW, Roanoke VA 24015. E-mail: jmart1175@aol.com. Website: www.martinsdowntown.com. Estab. 2005. Music: rock, jam band, reggae, grass, funk, ska.

MAXWELL'S

1039 Washington St., Hoboken NJ 07030. (201)653-1703. E-mail: TelstarRec@aol.com. Website: www.maxwellsnj.com. Music: rock, alternative, blues, punk, indie.
TIPS Please mail all booking information via postal mail.

MELODY INN

3826 N. Illinois St., Indianapolis IN 46208. (317)923-4707. E-mail: picwizard@earthlink.net. Website: www.melodyindy.com. Music: punk, rock, metal, indie, pop, rockabilly, bluegrass.

MEMPHIS ON MAIN

55 E. Main St., Champaign IL 61820. (217)398-1097. E-mail: info@memphisonmain.com. Website: http://memphisonmain.com. Music: rock, classic rock, R&B,

blues, soul, funk, folk, country, metal, rockabilly, punk, reggae.

MERCURY LOUNGE

1747 S. Boston Ave., Tulsa OK 74119. (918)382-0012. E-mail: reggiemerc@gmail.com. Website: www.mercurylounge918.com. **Contact:** Reggie Dobson. Music: country, alt-country, Americana, blues, jazz, rock, reggae, rockabilly, pop.

MERCY LOUNGE/CANNERY BALLROOM

One Cannery Row, Nashville TN 37203. (615)251-3020. E-mail: info@mercylounge.com. Website: www.mercylounge.com. **Contact:** John Bruton; Andrew Mischke, managers. "Since the doors to the Mercy Lounge first opened back in January of 2003, the cozy little club on Cannery Row has been both locally-favored and nationally-renowned. Building a reputation for showcasing the best in burgeoning buzz-bands and renowned national talents, the club has maintained its relevance by consistently offering reliable atmosphere and entertainment." Music: pop, country, rock, folk, Americana, indie, funk, soul, psychedelic.

MILLER THEATRE

Columbia University School of the Arts, 2960 Broadway, MC 1801, New York NY 10027. (212)854-6205. Website: www.millertheatre.com. **Contact:** Production Manager. "Miller Theatre's mission is to develop the next generation of cultural consumers, to reinvigorate public enthusiasm in the arts nationwide by pioneering new approaches to programming, to educate the public by presenting specialized, informative programs inviting to a broad audience, to discover new and diverse repertoire and commission new works, and to share Columbia University's intellectual riches with the public." Music: dance, contemporary and early music, jazz, opera, and performance.

MILLY'S TAVERN

500 Commercial St., Manchester NH 03101. (603)625-4444. E-mail: info@millystavern.com. E-mail: petertelge@millystavern.com. Website: www.millys-tavern.com. **Contact:** Peter Telge. "There is always something happening in our lounge. Whether it's from 4-7 pm, or all night, you are bound to have a good time. We offer live music every Tuesday, Thursday, Friday and Saturday." Music: blues, rock, retro, funk, dance.

MISSISSIPPI STUDIOS

3939 N. Mississippi, Portland OR 97227. (503)288-3895. E-mail: info@mississippistudios.com; matt@mississippistudios.com. E-mail: booking@mississippistudios.com. Website: www.mississippistudios.com. **Contact:** Matt King, senior talent buyer. "Portland's premier concert venue, offering guests the best sound and an intimate concert experience." Music: indie, folk, rock, Americana, alternative, pop, blues.

MOJO 13

1706 Philadelphia Ave., Wilmington DE 19809. (302)798-5798. E-mail: mojo13booking@gmail.com. Website: www.mojothirteen.com. "We play host to local and touring music acts as well as a whole host of other forms of entertainment that cater to the rock and roll lifestyle. We're looking to become the home away from home for the alternative minded music community here in Delaware and beyond. . . so if you've got a band, are a musician, entertainer or just a fan. . .please join us." Music: punk, rock, alternative, indie.

MOTR PUB

1345 Main St., Cincinnati OH 45202. (513)381-6687. E-mail: motrpub@gmail.com. Website: www.motrpub.com. Music: rock, alternative, folk, indie, Americana.

MUSE MUSIC CAFE

115 N. University Ave., Provo UT 84106. (801)377-6873. Website: http://musemusiccafe.com. **Contact:** Justin Hyatt; Colin Hatch, general managers. "The hub of Music, Art and Culture in Utah Valley." Music: rock, hard rock, hip-hop, electronica, indie, alternative, pop, Americana.

NATASHA'S BISTRO & BAR

112 Esplanade Alley, Lexington KY 40507. (859)259-2754. Website: www.beetnik.com. **Contact:** Kamilla Olsen. "Natasha's has hosted a wide variety of acts, including jazz, rock, world, comedy, pop, country, Americana, folk, singer/songwriter, indie and blues. Over The Rhine, Punch Brothers, Vienna Teng, Sara Watkins, Michelle Shocked, Richard Shindell, Patty Larkin, and Nellie McKay have all played recently on our stage."

NECTAR'S

188 Main St., Burlington VT 05401. (802)658-4771. E-mail: info@liveatnectars.com. E-mail: alex@liveat

nectars.com. Website: www.liveatnectars.com. **Contact:** Alex Budney, talent buyer. Music: blues, Americana, folk, rock, alternative, punk, indie, jazz, pop, dance, funk, psychedelic.

NEUMOS

925 E. Pike St., Seattle WA 98122. (206)709-9442. E-mail: steven@neumos.com; jason@neumos.com. Website: http://neumos.com. "The Concert Hall side of the business has always been our priority, and the lifeline to all other things that surround it. We pride ourselves on our always relevant and carefully curated music calendar, light production and state of the art sound system. The Concert Hall has 3 full service bars, and a second floor with a nicely seated mezzanine and balcony over looking the showroom. The showroom is fitted with an ample size stage, merch area, and superior unobstructed sight lines. We play host to several musical genres, by national and local artists alike including but not excluded to Indie Rock, Hip Hop, Punk Rock, DJ's , Metal, Singer/Song Writers, Country and much more."

NEUROLUX

111 N. 11th St., Boise ID 83702. (208)343-0886. Website: www.neurolux.com. Music: funk, indie, rock, reggae, folk, country, bluegrass.

NIETZSCHE'S

248 Allen St., Buffalo NY 14201. (716)886-8539. Website: www.nietzsches.com. Music: blues, jazz, rock, alternative, funk, soul.

NORTH STAR BAR & RESTAURANT

2639 Poplar St., Philadelphia PA 19130. (215)787-0488. E-mail: polaris@northstarbar.com. E-mail: booking@sunnydaymusic.com. Website: www.northstarbar.com. Music: rock, indie, psychedelic, pop, funk, jam, ska, punk, alternative.

ONE TRICK PONY GRILL & TAPROOM

136 E. Fulton, Grand Rapids MI 49503. (616)235-7669. E-mail: dvh652@gmail.com. Website: www.onetrick.biz. **Contact:** Dan Verhil, owner. Music: acoustic, rock, country, blues.

ON STAGE DRINKS & GRINDS

802 Kapahulu Ave., Honolulu HI 96816. (808)738-0004. Website: www.onstagedrinksandgrinds.com. "Onstage is our ultimate living room. A cool, 'off the beaten path,' fun & comfortable spot to hang & chill.

Equipped with a stage area complete with sound system, guitars, congas, and drums. We feature live music, and at times, surprise jams by well-known local artists that pop in. A kind of neat, underground music scene." Music: blues, rock, Hawaiian, acoustic.

PARADISE ROCK CLUB

967 Commonwealth Ave., Boston MA 02115. (617)547-0620. E-mail: paradiserockclub@gmail.com. Website: www.thedise.com. **Contact:** Crossroads Presents. Music: pop, reggae, alternative, rock, indie, punk, hip-hop, Americana.

PEARL AT COMMERCE

2038 Commerce St., Dallas TX 75201. (214)655-8824. E-mail: info@pearlatcommerce.com. Website: www.pearlatcommerce.com. Music: jazz, blues, zydeco, reggae, Latin, Americana.

PJ'S LAGER HOUSE

1254 Michigan Ave., Detroit MI 48226. (313)961-4668. E-mail: info@pjslagerhouse.com. E-mail: lagerhousebooking@yahoo.com. Website: www.pjslagerhouse.com. "PJ's features the best of Detroit's original rock'n'roll. Up and coming and established acts along with a variety of touring bands occupy PJ's stage most nights." Music: rock, alternative, hard rock, pop, folk, indie, punk.

PLOUGH AND STARS

912 Massachusetts Ave., Cambridge MA 02139. (617)576-0032. Website: www.ploughandstars.com. "The Plough and Stars Irish pub and restaurant in Cambridge has become a favorite of locals and visitors alike. With it's warm cozy atmosphere and great music scene, The Plough has become a staple of the Cambridge community. There is live music nearly every night." Music: alternative, pop, rock, indie, psychedelic, acoustic, folk.

PLUSH

340 E. Sixth St., Tucson AZ 85705. (502)798-1298. E-mail: plushtucson@gmail.com. Website: www.plushtucson.com. **Contact:** Kris Kerry. "Dynamic and comfy! Plush, yet affordable! Come hither and partake. PLUSH is dedicated to Tucson's live music scene. YES, we book 'em live! Talented local, regional, and national touring acts 5-7 nights a week. AND our rooms and sound system were designed to sound good and look good so you feeeeel good!" Music: rock, indie, garage, electronica, alt-country, rockabilly.

POSITIVE PIE

22 State St., Montpelier VT 05602. (802)229-0453. E-mail: info@positivepie.com. E-mail: music@positivepie.com. Website: www.positivepie.com. Music: hip-hop, pop, R&B.

R BAR & RESTAURANT

1617 Genessee, Kansas City MO 64102. (816)471-1777. E-mail: info@rbarkc.com. Website: www.rbarkc.com. **Contact:** Joy Jacobs, owner. Music: honky tonk, western swing, rockabilly, indie, country, rock, blues, jazz.

RECORD BAR

1020 Westport Rd., Kansas City MO 64111. (816)753-5207. E-mail: booking@therecordbar.com. Website: www.therecordbar.com. "We strive to provide our guests with diverse live entertainment, special events and gourmet food in a comfortable atmosphere. You'll see the best of the Kansas City music scene, as well as nationally known touring artists." Music: rock, punk, indie, jazz, swing, folk, pop, alternative.

RED SQUARE

136 Church St., Burlington VT 05401. (802)859-8909. E-mail: hyle.bradley@gmail.com. Website: www.red-squarevt.com. **Contact:** Bradley Hyle. Music: jazz, blues, rock, reggae.

RHYTHM & BREWS

2308 4th St., Tuscaloosa AL 35401. (205)750-2992. Website: www.rhythmnbrews.com. "Rhythm & Brews first opened in Tuscaloosa, AL. The club has the reputation of being the premiere location for the best live bands in the region. From dance music to performances by Nashville recording artists, the music you find at Rhythm & Brews will please all. We are committed to bringing you a fun and friendly atmosphere by offering a wide variety of drinks, great service, and great entertainment." Music: pop, rock, country, blues.

RICK'S BAR

2721 Main Ave., Fargo ND 58103. (701)232-8356. E-mail: meghanc@ricks-bar.com. Website: www.ricks-bar.com. **Contact:** Meghan Carik. Music: rock, metal, alternative.

ROCK ISLAND LIVE

101 N. Rock Island, Wichita KS 67202. (316)303-9800. Website: www.rockislandlive.com. Music: rock, alternative, pop, indie, dance.

SAM BONDS GARAGE

407 Blair, Eugene OR 97405. (541)431-6603. E-mail: info@sambonds.com. E-mail: bondsbooking@hotmail.com. Website: www.sambonds.com. "Opened in 1995, we've strived to represent the uniqueness of the neighborhood with a warm, laid back atmosphere, always changing local and regional microbrew selection, a full bar, quality vittles and of course, one of the west coast's best places to see diverse local, regional and worldly entertainment on a nightly basis." Music: bluegrass, rock, Irish jam, funk, alternative, folk, Americana.

SANTA FE SOL

37 Fire Place, Santa Fe NM 87508. (505)474-7322. Website: www.solsantafelive.com. Music: rock, Mexicana, Latin, alternative.

SCHUBAS TAVERN

3159 N. Southport, Chicago IL 60657. (773)525-2508. E-mail: rucins@schubas.com. Website: www.schubas.com. Paul Massaro, production manager. **Contact:** Matt Rucins, talent buyer. Schubas presents a diverse line-up of live music seven nights a week. From honky-tonk to indie rock, from Americana to jazz, from pop to country.

Building is a brick and masonry neo-Gothic neighborhood landmark built in 1903.

TIPS "Have a confirmed show? Use the Media and Retail link on the website to help better promote your show. Advance your show with our Production Manager, Paul Massaro. Send any promotional materials (posters, cds, bios, photos) to Rob Jensen."

SHANK HALL

1434 N. Farewell Ave., Milwaukee WI 53202. (414)276-7288. E-mail: shank@wi.rr.com. Website: www.shankhall.com. Music: indie, rock, alternative, Americana, pop, folk, bluegrass.

SILVER DOLLAR

478 King St., Charleston SC 29403. (843)722-7223. E-mail: daveb@Charlestoncocktail.com. Website: www.charlestoncocktail.com/silverdollar.html. **Contact:** David Beiderman. Music: rock, pop, dance, hip-hop, R&B, funk.

SMITH'S OLD BAR

1578 Piedmont Ave., Atlanta GA 30307. (404)876-8436. E-mail: nolenreevesbooking@gmail.com. Website: www.smithsoldebar.com. **Contact:** Dan Nolen,

Talent Buyer. "Smith's Olde Bar is an Atlanta institution, offering some of the best music to be found anywhere in the city. Our atmosphere is very relaxed, and you can find something good to eat and something fun to do almost every night." Music: rock, indie, punk, hip-hop, alternative, garage, bluegrass, reggae, jazz, funk.

SOUTHGATE HOUSE

24 E. Third St., Newport KY 41071. (859)431-2201. E-mail: sghrock@gmail.com. E-mail: sghbooking@gmail.com. Website: www.southgatehouse.com. **Contact:** Rick McCarty, general manager. "Presently the Southgate House is nationally recognized as a premier music venue, and it has also been incredibly supportive of the local music scene, heralded for its intimate setting and friendly atmosphere. The first floor, Juney's Lounge, offers pool tables, comfortable seating, and one of the most incredible jukeboxes in the area, filled with obscure and classic country and rock 'n' roll. Our downstairs Ballroom features multiple bars, a state-of-the-art stage and sound system, room for 600 music fans and a balcony to accomodate larger performances. A second-floor Parlour offers a more intimate and personal environment for relaxed performances." Music: rock, alternative, indie, pop, R&B, Americana, folk, bluegrass.

STATION 4

201 E. Fourth St., St. Paul MN 55101. (651)224-6372. E-mail: info@station-4.com. E-mail: dawn@station-4.com. Website: www.station-4.com. "Station 4 is a fully independent live music venue seven nights a week in St. Paul, MN. We support all genres of local and national talent." Music: rock, alternative, punk, metal, indie.

STRANGE BREW TAVERN

88 Market St., Manchester NH 03101. (603)666-4292. E-mail: info@strangebrewtavern.net. Website: www.strangebrewtavern.net. Music: blues, acoustic, rock, alternative.

SULLY'S PUB

2701 Park St., Hartford CT 06106. (860)231-8881. E-mail: sully@sullyspub.com. Website: www.sullyspub.com. **Contact:** Darrell "Sully" Sullivan, owner; Rob Salter, manager. "This mantra though is an important one in any community. Original Music must be supported on every level of society. Sully's is proud to stand on the front lines of musical evolution. Blazing a trail with the very musicians composing and performing." Music: pop, rock, alternative, indie.

THE 4TH AVENUE TAVERN

210 E. Fourth Ave., Olympia WA 98501. (360)951-7887. E-mail: the4thave@gmail.com. Website: www.the4thave.co. Music: indie, alternative, funk, rock, punk.

THE BARLEY STREET TAVERN

2735 N. 62nd St., Omaha NE 68104. (402)408-0028. E-mail: bookings@barleystreet.com. Website: www.barleystreet.com. "We have live music performances on scheduled nights, featuring some great local and regional performers, as well as, national touring acts. This is the music venue to find the best in all music styles." Music: rock, alternative, folk, indie, country, pop, Americana.

THE BLUE DOOR

2805 N. McKinley Ave., Oklahoma City OK 73106. (405)524-0738. E-mail: bluedoormusic@yahoo.com. Website: www.bluedoorokc.com. **Contact:** Greg Johnson. "We have grown to become Oklahoma's premiere venue for performing songwriters, hosting such legends as Jimmy Webb, Joe Ely, Ramblin' Jack Elliott, David Lindley and Tom Rush. We love working with new songwriters who are developing their audience and always welcome the best in bluegrass, folk, rock, country and blues."

THE BOTTLENECK

737 New Hampshire, Lawrence KS 66044. (785)841-5483. E-mail: booking@pipelineproductions.com. Website: www.thebottlenecklive.com. "The Bottleneck is considered by many to be a Rock & Roll historical landmark. The Bottleneck cemented its status as a scheduled stop on many major-city, national tours, giving nearby University of Kansas students access to some of the best names in modern music." Music: indie, rock, alternative, folk, jazz, blues, funk, dance, ska, psychedelic.

THE BRASS RAIL

1121 Broadway, Ft. Wayne IN 46802. (260)422-0881. E-mail: corey@brassrailfw.com. Website: www.brassrailfw.com. **Contact:** Corey Rader. Music: rock, punk, metal, alternative.

THE BREWERY

3009 Hillsborough St., Raleigh NC 27607. (919)838-6789. E-mail: tom@brewerync.com. Website: www.brewerync.com. **Contact:** Tom, general manager. "The Brewery has been a staple of the NC music scene since 1983. Having hosted some of the biggest names in the music industry, The Brewery is the perfect spot to see the best local musicians as well as the stars of tomorrow." Music: rock, pop, alternative, hip-hop.

THE BRICKYARD

129 N. Rock Island, Wichita KS 67202. (316)263-4044. E-mail: booking@brickyardoldtown.com. Website: www.brickyardoldtown.com. Music: rock, indie, alternative, punk, classic rock, country.

THE BROTHERHOOD LOUNGE

119 Capital Way N, Olympia WA 98501. (360)352-4153. Website: www.thebrotherhoodlounge.com. Music: soul, funk, rock, pop, hip-hop, R&B.

THE BUNKHOUSE SALOON

124 S. 11th St., Las Vegas NV 89101. (702)384-4536. E-mail: booking@bunkhouselv.com. Website: ww.bunkhouselv.com. **Contact:** Keith Fox, general manager. Music: indie, rock, punk, alternative, pop.

THE CACTUS CLUB

2496 S. Wentworth Ave., Milwaukee WI 53207. (414)897-0663. E-mail: cactuscl@execpc.xom. Website: www.cactusclubmilwaukee.com. Music: punk, rock, alternative, indie, funk, psychedelic.

THE CANOPY CLUB

708 S. Goodwin Ave., Champaign-Urbana IL 61801. (217)344-2263. E-mail: seth@jaytv.com; mikea@jaytv.com. Website: www.canopyclub.com. **Contact:** Seth Fein; Mike Armintrout. "In striving to achieve the highest level of entertainment, the Canopy Club prides itself on being able to offer entertainment for all walks of life. Whether you like rock, country, hip hop, jazz, funk, indie or anything in between, the Canopy Club has something to offer you. If you're a fan of live music and entertainment, the Canopy Club is your home in central Illinois!"

THE CAVE

452 1/2 W. Franklin St., Chapel Hill NC 27516. (919)968-9308. E-mail: info@caverntavern.com. Website: http://caverntavern.com. Music: pop, rock, country, twang, folk, acoustic, funk, indie, punk, blues, bluegrass.

TIPS Use online booking form.

THE CLUBHOUSE

1320 E. Broadway Rd., Tempe AZ 85282. (460)968-3238. E-mail: clubhousegigs@hotmail.com. Website: www.theclubhousemusicvenue.com. **Contact:** Eugenia. "A club that features the best in Local, Touring, and Regional acts. Voted Best Local Music Venue by The New Times Magazine, We have been in the valley of the sun for 6 years hosting shows for all age groups on a nightly basis." Music: rock, punk, metal, alternative.

THE DOGFISH BAR & GRILLE

128 Free St., Portland ME 04101. (207)772-5483. E-mail: michele@thedogfishcompany.com. Website: www.thedogfishbarandgrille.com. Music: jazz, be-bop, blues, soul, jam, acoustic.

THE DOUBLE DOOR INN

1218 Charlottetowne Ave., Charlotte NC 28204. (704)376-1446. E-mail: info@doubledoorinn.com. E-mail: info@doubledoorinn.com; jeff.dillon72@gmail.com. Website: www.doubledoorinn.co. **Contact:** Micah Davidson, talent buyer/promotions; Jeff Dillon, assistant talent buyer/assistant promotions. "Established in 1973 and recognized as the 'Oldest Live Music Venue East of the Mississippi,' the Double Door Inn oozes musical tradition. Looking at our walls, packed with 35 years of autographed photos, has been described as being like 'viewing a timeline for live music in the Queen City.' Also holding the title 'Oldest Blues Club In The U.S. Under Original Ownership,' the Double Door Inn strives to bring the best in local, regional, and national touring and recording artists to the discriminating music lover. Legendary performers like Eric Clapton, Stevie Ray Vaughn, Dave Alvin, Leon Russell, Buddy Guy, Junior Brown, Bob Margolin, and others, have graced the stage of our historic and intimate venue." Music: blues, rock, soul, pop, funk, jazz, bluegrass, acoustic, folk, alt-country, R&B, Americana, reggae.

THE ECHO

1822 Sunset Blvd., Los Angeles CA 90026. (213)413-8200. Website: www.attheecho.com. Music: funk, punk, rock, indie, folk, hip-hop, electronica, Mexicana, pop.

THE EMPTY BOTTLE

1035 N. Western Ave., Chicago IL 60622. (773)276-3600. E-mail: pete@emptybottle.com. Website: www.emptybottle.com. **Contact:** Peter Toalson, Booking Agent/Talent Buyer. Music: rock, indie, psychedelic, anti-pop, garage, metal, country, dance, electronica, soul, blues, folk.

THE EMPTY GLASS

410 Elizabeth St., Charleston WV 25311. (304)345-3914. E-mail: booking@emptyglass.com. Website: www.emptyglass.com. Music: blues, jazz, rock, folk, bluegrass, indie.

THE FINELINE MUSIC CAFE

318 First Ave., Minneapolis MN 55401. (612)338-8100. E-mail: finelinemusiccafe@gmail.com. E-mail: davidjoe.flbooking@gmail.com; brad.flbooking@gmail.com; finelinebooking@gmail.com. Website: www.finelinemusic.com. **Contact:** David-Joe Holiday; Brad Danielson; Kim King. Music: rock, acoustic, indie, folk, alternative.

THE FREQUENCY

121 W. Main St., Madison WI 53703. (608)819-8777. E-mail: contact@madisonfrequency.com. E-mail: booking@madisonfrequency.com. Website: www.madisonfrequency.com. **Contact:** Darwin. "The Frequency is serving up a wide variety of live music in downtown Madison seven nights a week featuring a smattering of local, regional, national and international acts playing bluegrass, punk, metal, jazz, electronic, indie, hip hop."

THE GOLDEN FLEECE TAVERN

132 W. Loockerman St., Dover DE 19904. (302)674-1776. E-mail: goldenfleecetavern@gmail.com. Website: www.thegoldenfleecetavern.com. Music: rock, indie, classic rock, pop, alternative.

THE GRAMOPHONE

4243 Manchester Ave., St. Louis MO 63110. (314)531-5700. E-mail: info@thegramophonelive.com. Website: http://thegramophonelive.com. "The Gramophone features an eclectic schedule of live music and DJs in an intimate concert setting." Music: hip-hop, funk, soul, indie, rock, Americana.

THE GREAT NORTHERN BAR & GRILL

27 Central Ave., Whitefish MT 59937. (406)862-2816. E-mail: info@greatnorthernbar.com. Website: www.greatnorthernbar.com. "The Great Northern Bar & Grill is the premiere destination in the Flathead Valley for good food, good music, and good times." Music: rock, alternative.

THE GREEN LANTERN

497 W. Third St., Lexington KY 40508. (859)252-9539. Website: www.myspace.com/greenlanternbar. "Making the best neighborhood bar in Lex a reality." Music: rock, alternative, indie, folk, punk, metal.

THE HAVEN

6700 Aloma Ave., Winter Park FL 32792. (407)673-2712. E-mail: thehavenproductions@gmail.com. Website: www.thehavenrocks.com. The Haven is a 350-plus capacity venue with a full-liquor bar located in the Aloma Square Shopping Center in Winter Park, FL. Music: alternative, classic rock, cover band, funk, jam band, metal, punk, reggae, rock, and singer/songwriter—all types of live music with local, regional, and national bands, and most shows are age 18 and up.

TIPS See House P.A., stage and lighting specs, mains, monitors, microphones, and stage dimensions at: www.thehavenrocks.com/specs/.

THE HIDEOUT

1354 W. Wabansia, Chicago IL 60642. (773)227-4433. Website: www.thehideout.com. "The Hideout is music, art, performance, plays, poetry, rock and rebellion." Music: indie, folk, rock, alternative, country.

THE JEWISH MOTHER

600 Nevan Rd., Virginia Beach VA 23451. (757)428-1515. E-mail: jmomsmusic@aol.com. Website: www.jewishmother.com. Music: rock, Americana, indie, alternative, funk, soul.

THE LOFT

2502 W. Colorado Ave., #301, Colorado Springs CO 80904. (719)445-9278. Website: www.theloftmusic.wordpress.com. "We are here to bring you the best musical experience in Colorado Springs with an intimate atmosphere, amazing sound and GREAT music. We hope you come often and tell your friends about our place." Music: rock, pop, country, acoustic, indie, blues, jazz, bluegrass, folk.

THE LOST LEAF BAR & GALLERY

914 N. Fifth St., Phoenix AZ 85004. (602)481-4004. E-mail: solnotes@hotmail.com. Website: www.the

lostleaf.org. **Contact:** Tato Caraveo. Music: Latin, blues, salsa, hip-hop, R&B, funk, outlaw country, Americana.

THE LOUNGE AT HOTEL DONALDSON

101 Broadway, Fargo ND 58102. (701)478-1000 or (888)478-8768. E-mail: info@hoteldonaldson.com. Website: www.hoteldonaldson.com. **Contact:** Karen Stoker, founder/owner. Music: Americana, folk, indie, country, bluegrass.

THE MAJESTIC/MAGIC STICK

4140 Woodward Ave., Detroit MI 48201. (313)833-9700. E-mail: dave@majesticdetroit.com; traci@majesticdetroit.com. E-mail: booking@majesticdetroit.com. **Contact:** Dave Zainea, owner/general manager; Traci Zainea, talent buyer. Music: funk, Americana, rock, indie, alternative, hip-hop, punk, hard rock, soul, electronica.

THE MANGY MOOSE RESTAURANT & SALOON,

3285 McCollister Dr., Teton Village WY 83025. (307)733-4913. E-mail: info@mangymoose.net. E-mail: booking@mangymoose.net. Website: www.mangymoose.net. Music: funk, punk, electronica, indie, folk, rock, bluegrass.

THE MET

1005 Main Sr., Pawtucket RI 02860. (401)729-1005. E-mail: info@themetri.com. Website: www.themetri.com. Music: rock, funk, folk, blues, soul, punk, alternative.

THE MIDDLE EAST NIGHTCLUB

472 Massachusetts Ave., Cambridge MA 02139. (617)864-3278. E-mail: booking@mideastclub.com. Downstairs room capacity is 575. Upstairs is 195. Parking garage is attached to the Meridian Hotel. Music: funk, rock, alternative, dance, pop, hip-hop, punk, Americana.

THE MOHAWK PLACE

47 E. Mohawk Place, Buffalo NY 14203. (716)465-2368. E-mail: buffalomohawk@gmail.com. E-mail: erikspicoli@gmail.com. Website: www.themohawkplace.com. **Contact:** Erik Spicoli. Music: indie, rock, alternative, punk.

THE MONKEY HOUSE

30 Main St., Winooski VT 05404. (802)655-4563. E-mail: info@monkeyhousevt.com. Website: http:// monkeyhousemusic.com. Music: folk, indie, hard rock, punk, rock, alternative, Americana, funk, blues.

THE M ROOM

15 W. Girard Ave., Philadelphia PA 19123. (215)739-5577. E-mail: info@mroomphilly.com. E-mail: booking@mroomphilly.com. Website: http://mroomphilly.com. Music: blues, folk, soul, bluegrass, classic rock, rock, alt-country, pop, jazz, electronica, dance.

THE MUSIC HALL AT CAPITAL ALE HOUSE

619 E. Main St., Richmond VA 23219. (804)780-2537. E-mail: booking@capitalalehouse.com. Website: www.capitalalehouse.com. **Contact:** Kyle Johnson, booking. Music: indie, rock, jazz, blues, pop.

THE NATIONAL UNDERGROUND

159 E. Houston Street, New York NY 10002. (212)475-0611. E-mail: joey@thenationalunderground.com. E-mail: booking@thenationalunderground.com. Website: www.thenationalunderground.com. **Contact:** Joey DeGraw. "Musican brothers Joey & Gavin DeGraw opened The National Underground to provide a home for New York City and the nation's best independent musicians to showcase their talents to an appreciative audience. Featuring live music seven days and nights a week on two floors, The National Underground has more live bands performing per week than any club in New York City. We are a throwback NYC Rock/Americana/Country venue. Celebrity appearances have included Joss Stone, Norah Jones, Moby, John Popper of Blues Traveler, Robert Randolph, Billy Joe Armstrong of Green Day, Ryan Reynolds, Scarlett Johannson and NASCAR driver Jimmie Johnson."

THE NICK ROCKS

2514 10th Ave. S, Birmingham AL 35205. (205)252-3831. E-mail: nolenreevesmusic@mindspring.com. Website: www.thenickrocks.com. **Contact:** Dan Nolen, talent buyer. "The music heard almost every night of the week include local, regional and national acts. The diverse range of acts add to the appeal of an evening at the Nick. One can hear blues, rock, punk, emo, pop, country, metal, bluegrass, rock-a-billy, roots rock or whatever your genre of choice. The Nick has had it all. It is an upclose and personal room voted three times in a row as Birmingham's best live music venue by *Birmingham Weekly*."

THE OLD ROCK HOUSE

1200 S. Seventh St., St. Louis MO 63104. (314)588-0505. E-mail: tweber@oldrockhouse.com. Website: http://oldrockhouse.com. **Contact:** Tim Weber, co-owner. Music: rock, indie, alternative, punk, folk, pop.

THE POUR HOUSE

1977 Maybank Hwy., Charleston SC 29412. (843)571-4343. E-mail: alex@charlestonpourhouse.com. Website: www.charlestonpourhouse.com. **Contact:** Alex Harris, owner/booking. Music: bluegrass, classic rock, indie, rock, funk, folk, country.

THE QUARTER

2504 13th St., Gulfport MS 39501. (228)863-2650. E-mail: info@thequarterbar.com. E-mail: manager@thequarterbar.com. Website: www.thequarterbar.com. "Our goal is to provide the coast with live music up to 5 nights a week or more in a relaxing French Quarter-like atmosphere." Music: metal, pop, rock, country, blues, classic rock.

THE RAVE/EAGLES CLUB

2401 W. Wisconsin Ave., Milwaukee WI 53233. (414)342-7283. E-mail: info@therave.com. Website: www.theravelive.com. "The Rave/Eagles Club is a multi-room entertainment complex. Bands like Pearl Jam, Dave Matthews Band, and Creed all played their first gig at The Rave on The Rave Bar stage." Music: rock, alternative, pop, indie, hip-hop, funk, metal.

THE SHED

15094 Mills Rd., Gulfport MS 39503. (228)832-7240. E-mail: contact@theshedbbq.com. E-mail: booking@theshedbbq.com. Website: http://theshedbbq.com. **Contact:** Brett Orrison. Music: blues, folk, country, bluegrass, rock, alternative.

THE SLOWDOWN

729 N. 14th St., Omaha NE 68102. (402)345-7569. E-mail: info@theslowdown.com. Website: www.theslowdown.com. Music: rock, indie, alternative, psychedelic, punk, folk, pop.

THE SMILING MOOSE

1306 E. Carson St., Pittsburgh PA 15203. (412)431-4668. Website: www.smiling-moose.com. Music: rock, alt-country, indie, country, acoustic, pop, garbage, funk, hip-hop, metal.

THE SOUND FACTORY

812 Kanawha Blvd. E, Charleston WV 25301. (304)342-8001. E-mail: soundfactorybooking@yahoo.com. Website: www.soundfactorywv.com. **Contact:** John Sanese, agent/owner. Music: dance, rock, pop, reggae, country, Americana, psychedelic, funk, punk.

THE SPACE

295 Treadwell St., New Haven CT 06514. (203)288-6400. E-mail: spacebooking@gmail.com. Website: www.thespace.tk. **Contact:** Steve Rodgers; Erick Alfisi. "The Space (since 2003) exists to build a safe, positive community for people of all ages through music and the arts. Physically, we are a listening room venue located in an unlikely industrial park in a sleepy suburb of New Haven." Music: alternative, rock, blues, Latin, folk, pop, indie, dance, hip-hop, Americana.

THE SPANISH MOON

1109 Highland Rd., Baton Rouge LA 70802. (225)383-6666. E-mail: moonbooking@hotmail.com. Website: www.thespanishmoon.com. **Contact:** Aaron Scruggs. Music: rock, pop, dubstep, indie, alternative, Americana.

THE SPOT UNDERGROUND

15 Elbow St., Providence RI 02903. (401)383-7133. E-mail: 725@TheSpotOnThayer.com. E-mail: 725@TheSpotProvidence.com. Website: www.thespotprovidence.com. **Contact:** Kevin Blanchette, director of operations. Music: rock, indie, world, hip-hop, R&B, funk, dance, jam, pop.

THE TREEHOUSE

887 Chambers Rd., Columbus OH 43212. (614)294-2264. E-mail: booking@treehousecolumbus.com. Website: http://treehousecolumbus.com. Music: rock, classic rock, alternative, indie, Americana, folk, pop.

THE TRIPLE ROCK SOCIAL CLUB

629 Cedar Ave., Minneapolis MN 55454. (612)333-7399. E-mail: booking@triplerocksocialclub.com. Website: www.triplerocksocialclub.com. Music: pop, hip-hop, rock, metal, punk, electronica.

THE UNDERGROUND

555 E. Fourth St., Reno NV 89512. (775)786-2582. E-mail: contact@renounderground.com. Website: http://renounderground.com. "The Underground is one of Reno's largest music venues and cannot be classified easily. Shows here range from all-ages top 40

parties, national, regional and local artist concerts. The music style varies wildly depending on the night, with shows ranging from hardcore to world beat, just about any other genre you can think of." Music: rock, alternative, pop, funk, hip-hop, Latin, World, acoustic, jazz, electronica, reggae, dubstep.

THE VAGABOND

30 NE 14th St., Miami FL 33132. (305)379-0508. E-mail: bookings@thevagabondmiami.com. Website: http://thevagabondmiami.com. Music: rock, punk, soul, jam, dance.

THE VISULITE THEATRE

1615 Elizabeth Ave., Charlotte NC 28204. (704)358-9200. E-mail: info@visulite.com. E-mail: booking@visulite.com. Website: www.visulite.com. Music: rock, pop, funk, Americana, indie, blues, folk.

THE VOLLRATH TAVERN

118 E. Palmer, Indianapolis IN 46225. (317)632-5199. E-mail: thevollrath@gmail.com. Website: www.vollrathindy.com. "Now host to Indianapolis' finest local and nationally-touring artists , the Vollrath Tavern has become one of Indy's most respected underground live music venues, proud to feature original music several nights a week." Music: indie, rock, alternative, pop, soul, funk, metal, acoustic.

THE WEBSTER UNDERGROUND

21 Webster St., Hartford CT 06114. (860)246-8001. E-mail: booking@webstertheater.com. Website: www.webstertheater.com. "The Main Theater is a great room for sizeable events or concerts. Book now and share the same stage that launched careers such as Staind, Marilyn Manson, Sevendust, Incubus, 311, Jay Z, Method Man, Godsmack, Fall Out Boy, and many more. The Underground is our intimate room equipped for shows and more. It is perfect for national, regional, locals that are looking to create their own show in a historic room." Music: rock, reggae, punk, alternative, pop, soul, indie, funk, hard rock.

THE WHITE MULE

1530 Main St., Columbia SC 29201. (803)661-8199. E-mail: management@thewhitemule.com. E-mail: tmayn.ent@hotmail.com; davebritt@sc.rr.com. Website: www.thewhitemule.com. Contact: Travis Maynard; Dave Britt, booking. "The White Mule, simply put, is an establishment with great food and great music brought to you by people who love great food and

great music. We want you to have a memorable experience from the minute you walk in the door." Music: rock, alternative, pop.

THE WINCHESTER

12112 Madison Ave., Cleveland OH 44107. (216)226-5681. E-mail: jams@thewinchester.net. Website: http://thewinchester.net. Estab. 2002. Music: blues, jazz, prog, fusion, rock, classic rock, alternative, rockabilly, alt-country, bluegrass and swing/big band. The Winchester Music Hall is well known for featuring the best musicians both nationally and locally.

TOAD

1912 Massachusetts Ave., Cambridge MA 02140. (617)499-6992. E-mail: bookagig@toadcambridge.com. Website: www.toadcambridge.com. Contact: Billy Beard. "Toad is a small neighborhood bar and music club featuring live music seven nights a week." Music: folk, alternative, rock, acoustic, Americana, indie.

TRACTOR TAVERN

5213 Ballard Ave. NW, Seattle WA 98107. (206)789-3599. E-mail: schedule@tractortavern.com. E-mail: booking@tractortavern.com. Website: www.tractortavern.com. "The Tractor hosts live shows 5-7 nights a week featuring a wide range of local and national acts. Check out all of your favorite Rock, Alternative Country, Rockabilly, Groove & Psychedelia, Celtic, Cajun & Zydeco, Folk, Blues, Jazz, and Bluegrass acts to name a few."

TRIPLE CROWN

206 N. Edward Gary St., San Marcos TX 78666. (512)396-2236. E-mail: booking@triplecrownlive.com. Website: www.triplecrownlive.com. Contact: Eric Shaw. Music: rock, country, Americana, jazz, blues, bluegrass, punk, hip-hop, folk.

TRIPLE ROCK SOCIAL CLUB

629 Cedar Ave., Minneapolis MN 55454. (612)333-7399. E-mail: info@triplerocksocialclub.com. E-mail: booking@triplerocksocialclub.com. Website: www.triplerocksocialclub.com. Estab. 2003. The Triple Rock has become one of the big destination punk, indie rock, and underground hip-hop clubs in the Twin Cities—a good-sized music venue with a capacity of 400. The Triple Rock is owned and operated by the members of punk rock band Dillinger Four. Music: acoustic, alternative, blues, classic rock, country, cov-

er band, electronic/dance/DJ, folk, funk, goth, hip-hop/rap, jam band, metal, pop, punk, reggae, rock, singer/songwriter, soul, and urban/R&B.

TIPS To advance shows that have been confirmed, please contact Zartan via e-mail at: zartan@triple rocksocialclub.com

TROCADERO

1003 Arch St., Philadelphia PA 19107. (215)922-6888. E-mail: trocadero@thetroc.com. Website: www.thetroc.com. Music: pop, indie, Americana, alternative, rock, hip-hop, rap, folk, bluegrass.

TROUBADOUR

9081 Santa Monica Blvd., West Hollywood CA 90069. (310)276-1158. Website: www.troubadour.com. Estab. 1958. "The Troubadour is rich with musical history. Elton John, Billy Joel, James Taylor and Joni Mitchell have all made debuts at the Troubadour. The legendary musical line-ups at the Troubadour continue til today. The Troubadour schedule features a wide arrangement of musical performances. Nada Surf, Bob Schneider, The Morning Benders and Manchester Orchestra were some of the performances featured on the Troubadour schedule for 2010." Music: pop, indie, alternative, rock, hip-hop, Americana, jazz, blues.

   ○ To contact use form online at http://www.troubadour.com/contact-booking/. See also lighting plot, stage layout, technical rider links at same site.

TURF CLUB

1601 University Ave. W, St. Paul MN 55104. (651)647-0486. E-mail: booking@turfclub.net. Website: www.turfclub.net. "Turf Club is a perfect setting for rock. The long, prominent bar scales one side of the narrow interior; the stage is at the back and the entire space is enveloped in dark woods. The music is loud, the crowd is devoted." Music: rock, indie, alternative, punk, classic rock.

UNDERGROUND 119

119 S. President St., Jackson MS 39201. (601)352-2322. E-mail: booking@underground119.com. Website: www.underground119.com. **Contact:** Bill Ellison, Entertainment Director. Music: blues, jazz, bluegrass, country, funk, rock, alternative.

UNION POOL

484 Union Ave., Brooklyn NY 11211. (718)609-0484. E-mail: unionpoolbooking@gmail.com. Website:

www.unionpool.blogspot.com. Music: rock, indie, alternative, Americana.

URBAN LOUNGE

241 S. 500 E, Salt Lake City UT 84102. (801)824-1000. E-mail: will@sartainandsaunders.com. Website: www.theurbanloungeslc.com. **Contact:** Will Sartain. "The Urban Lounge has been a staple in the Salt Lake City, Utah music community for more than a decade. What started off as a local live music bar has flourished into a regular stop for headlining national acts-hosting a variety of music from independent artists of all genres including rock, hip hop, folk, electronic, reggae, experimental. Nearly every night of the week you can find a fresh take on a familiar scene."

VAUDEVILLE MEWS

212 Fourth St., Des Moines IA 50309. (515)243-3270. E-mail: booking@vaudevillemews.com. Website: www.vaudevillemews.com. Music: folk, pop, blues, rock, alternative, Americana, hip-hop, soul, rap, country, hard rock, electronica.

WHISKEY BAR

125 Washington St. #G, Hoboken NJ 07030. (201)963-3400. E-mail: whiskeybar.nj@gmail.com. E-mail: whiskeybands@yahoo.com. Website: www.whiskey-bar.com. Music: rock, alternative, punk, pop.

WHISKY A GO-GO

8901 W. Sunset Blvd., West Hollywood CA 90069. (310)360-1110. E-mail: celina@whiskyagogo.com. Website: www.whiskyagogo.com. **Contact:** A. Celina Denkins, talent buyer/booking agent. "As long as there has been a Los Angeles rock scene, there has been the Whisky A Go-Go. An anchor on the Sunset Strip since its opening in 1964, the Whisky A Go-Go has played host to rock 'n' roll's most important bands, from the Doors, Janis Joplin, and Led Zeppelin to today's up and coming new artists." Music: hip-hop, rock, punk, metal, alternative, reggae, pop, classic rock, indie, Americana.

WHITE ROOM MIAMI

(786)444-8647. E-mail: heynastie@gmail.com. Website: www.whiteroomshows.com. "White Room is a cutting edge nightclub and premier live music venue located in downtown Miami's entertainment district. We offer 3 distinct areas of sound from up and coming local bands to national acts to Djs and producers. White Room hosts live performances of different genres such as rock, alternative, electronica, funk, fusion, D&B, and more. Artists may be compensated by merchandise sales and ticket sales depending on the draw. The age restriction is 18 and over." Capacity is 500-1,000. Music: alternative, house, pop / top 40, techno.

WHITE WATER TAVERN

2500 W. Seventh St., Little Rock AR 72205. (501)375-8400. E-mail: whitewaterbooking@gmail.com. Website: www.whitewatertavern.com. Music: rock, country, alternative, Americana, punk.

WILD WILLY'S ROCK HOUSE & SPORTS SALOON

2072 Somerville Rd., Annapolis MD 21401. (410)841-5599. E-mail: wild@wildwillyssaloon.com. Website: www.wildwillyssaloon.com. "Wild Willy's Rock House & Sports Saloon features live entertainment with a rock and roll edge. The venue features weekly live music, ongoing special events, optimum sports viewing, classic food & signature drinks." Music: rock, pop, alternative.

WOODLANDS TAVERN

1200 W. Third Ave., Columbus OH 43212. (614)299-4987 or (614)406-4799. E-mail: woodlandja@gmail.com. Website: www.woodlandstavern.com. **Contact:** Jimmy. Music: bluegrass, acoustic, psychedelic, reggae, jam, funk, rock, classic rock, jazz, blues.

WORMY DOG SALOON

311 E. Sheridan Ave., Oklahoma City OK 73104. (405)601-6276. E-mail: booking@wormydog.com. Website: www.wormydog.com. Music: country, bluegrass, rock, Americana, rockabilly, folk.

YOUNG AVENUE DELI

2119 Young Ave., Memphis TN 38104. (901)278-0034. E-mail: phillip@youngavenuedeli.com. Website: www.youngavenuedeli.com. **Contact:** Phillip Stroud. Music: rock, country, pop, folk.

STATE & PROVINCIAL GRANTS

//

Arts councils in the United States and Canada provide assistance to artists (including poets) in the form of fellowships or grants. These grants can be substantial and confer prestige upon recipients; however, **ONLY STATE OR PROVINCE RESIDENTS ARE ELIGIBLE**. Because deadlines and available support vary annually, query first (with a SASE) or check websites for guidelines.

UNITED STATES ARTS AGENCIES

ALABAMA STATE COUNCIL ON THE ARTS, 201 Monroe St., Montgomery AL 36130-1800. (334)242-4076. E-mail: staff@arts.alabama.gov. Website: www.arts.state.al.us.

ALASKA STATE COUNCIL ON THE ARTS, 411 W. Fourth Ave., Suite 1-E, Anchorage AK 99501-2343. (907)269-6610 or (888)278-7424. E-mail: aksca_info@eed.state.ak.us. Website: www. eed. state.ak.us/aksca.

ARIZONA COMMISSION ON THE ARTS, 417 W. Roosevelt St., Phoenix AZ 85003-1326. (602)771-6501. E-mail: info@azarts.gov. Website: www.azarts.gov.

ARKANSAS ARTS COUNCIL, 1500 Tower Bldg., 323 Center St., Little Rock AR 72201. (501)324-9766. E-mail: info@arkansasarts.com. Website: www.arkansasarts.com.

CALIFORNIA ARTS COUNCIL, 1300 I St., Suite 930, Sacramento CA 95814. (916)322-6555. E-mail: info@caartscouncil.com. Website: www.cac.ca.gov.

COLORADO COUNCIL ON THE ARTS, 1625 Broadway, Suite 2700, Denver CO 80202. (303)892-3802. E-mail: online form. Website: www.coloarts.state.co.us.

CONNECTICUT COMMISSION ON CULTURE & TOURISM, Arts Division, One Financial Plaza, 755 Main St., Hartford CT 06103. (860)256-2800. Website: www.cultureandtourism.org.

DELAWARE DIVISION OF THE ARTS, Carvel State Office Bldg., 4th Floor, 820 N. French St., Wilmington DE 19801. (302)577-8278 (New Castle Co.) or (302)739-5304 (Kent or Sussex Counties). E-mail: delarts@state.de.us. Website: www.artsdel.org.

DISTRICT OF COLUMBIA COMMISSION ON THE ARTS & HUMANITIES, 410 Eighth St. NW, 5th Floor, Washington DC 20004. (202)724-5613. E-mail: cah@dc.gov. Website: http://dcarts.dc.gov.

FLORIDA ARTS COUNCIL, Division of Cultural Affairs, R.A. Gray Building, Third Floor, 500 S. Bronough St., Tallahassee FL 32399-0250. (850)245-6470. E-mail: info@florida-arts.org. Website: http://dcarts.dc.gov.

GEORGIA COUNCIL FOR THE ARTS, 260 14th St., Suite 401, Atlanta GA 30318. (404)685-2787. E-mail: gaarts@gaarts.org. Website: www.gaarts.org.

GUAM COUNCIL ON THE ARTS & HUMANITIES AGENCY, P.O. Box 2950, Hagatna GU 96932. (671)646-2781. Website: www.guam.net.

HAWAII STATE FOUNDATION ON CULTURE & THE ARTS, 2500 S. Hotel St., 2nd Floor, Honolulu HI 96813. (808)586-0300. E-mail: ken.hamilton@hawaii.gov. Website: http.state.hi.us/sfca.

IDAHO COMMISSION ON THE ARTS, 2410 N. Old Penitentiary Rd., Boise ID 83712. (208)334-2119 or (800)278-3863. E-mail: info@arts.idaho.gov. Website: www.arts.idaho.gov.

ILLINOIS ARTS COUNCIL, James R. Thompson Center, 100 W. Randolph, Suite 10-500, Chicago IL 60601. (312)814-6750. E-mail: iac.info@illinois.gov. Website: www.state.il.us/agency/iac.

INDIANA ARTS COMMISSION, 150 W. Market St., Suite 618, Indianapolis IN 46204. (317)232-1268. E-mail: IndianaArtsCommission@iac.in.gov. Website: www.in.gov/arts.

IOWA ARTS COUNCIL, 600 E. Locust, Des Moines IA 50319-0290. (515)281-6412. Website: www.iowaartscouncil.org.

KANSAS ARTS COMMISSION, 700 SW Jackson, Suite 1004, Topeka KS 66603-3761. (785)296-3335. E-mail: KAC@arts.state.ks.us. Website: http://arts.state.ks.us.

KENTUCKY ARTS COUNCIL, 21st Floor, Capital Plaza Tower, 500 Mero St., Frankfort KY 40601-1987. (502)564-3757 or (888)833-2787. E-mail: kyarts@ky.gov. Website: http://artscouncil.ky.gov.

LOUISIANA DIVISION OF THE ARTS, Capitol Annex Bldg., 1051 N. 3rd St., 4th Floor, Room #420, Baton Rouge LA 70804. (225)342-8180. Website: www.crt.state.la.us/arts.

MAINE ARTS COMMISSION, 193 State St., 25 State House Station, Augusta ME 04333-0025. (207)287-2724. E-mail: MaineArts.info@maine.gov. Website: www.mainearts.com.

MARYLAND STATE ARTS COUNCIL, 175 W. Ostend St., Suite E, Baltimore MD 21230. (410)767-6555. E-mail: msac@msac.org. Website: www.msac.org.

MASSACHUSETTS CULTURAL COUNCIL, 10 St. James Ave., 3rd Floor, Boston MA 02116-3803. (617)727-3668. E-mail: mcc@art.state.ma.us. Website: www.massculturalcouncil.org.

MICHIGAN COUNCIL OF HISTORY, ARTS AND LIBRARIES, 702 W. Kalamazoo St., P.O. Box 30705, Lansing MI 48909-8205. (517)241-4011. E-mail: artsinfo@michigan.gov. Website: www.michigan.gov.

MINNESOTA STATE ARTS BOARD, Park Square Court, 400 Sibley St., Suite 200, St. Paul MN 55101-1928. (651)215-1600 or (800)866-2787. E-mail: msab@arts.state.mn.us. Website: www.arts.state.mn.us.

MISSISSIPPI ARTS COMMISSION, 501 N. West St., Suite 701B, Woolfolk Bldg., Jackson MS 39201. (601)359-6030. Website: www.arts.state.ms.us.

MISSOURI ARTS COUNCIL, 815 Olive St., Suite 16, St. Louis MO 63101-1503. (314)340-6845 or (866)407-4752. E-mail: moarts@ded.mo.gov. Website: www.missouriartscouncil.org.

MONTANA ARTS COUNCIL, 316 N. Park Ave., Suite 252, Helena MT 59620-2201. (406)444-6430. E-mail: mac@mt.gov. Website: www.art.state.mt.us.

NATIONAL ASSEMBLY OF STATE ARTS AGENCIES, 1029 Vermont Ave. NW, 2nd Floor, Washington DC 20005. (202)347-6352. E-mail: nasaa@nasaa-arts.org. Website: www.nasaa-arts.org.

NEBRASKA ARTS COUNCIL, 1004 Farnam St., Plaza Level, Omaha NE 68102. (402)595-2122 or (800)341-4067. Website: www.nebraskaartscouncil.org.

NEVADA ARTS COUNCIL, 716 N. Carson St., Suite A, Carson City NV 89701. (775)687-6680. E-mail: online form. Website: http://dmla.clan.lib.nv.us/docs/arts.

NEW HAMPSHIRE STATE COUNCIL ON THE ARTS, 2 1/2 Beacon St., 2nd Floor, Concord NH 03301-4974. (603)271-2789. Website: www.nh.gov/nharts.

NEW JERSEY STATE COUNCIL ON THE ARTS, 225 W. State St., P.O. Box 306, Trenton NJ 08625. (609)292-6130. Website: www.njartscouncil.org.

NEW MEXICO ARTS, Dept. of Cultural Affairs, P.O. Box 1450, Santa Fe NM 87504-1450. (505)827-6490 or (800)879-4278. Website: www.nmarts.org.

NEW YORK STATE COUNCIL ON THE ARTS, 175 Varick St., New York NY 10014. (212)627-4455. Website: www.nysca.org.

NORTH CAROLINA ARTS COUNCIL, 109 East Jones St., Cultural Resources Building, Raleigh NC 27601. (919)807-6500. E-mail: ncarts@ncmail.net. Website: www.ncarts.org.

NORTH DAKOTA COUNCIL ON THE ARTS, 1600 E. Century Ave., Suite 6, Bismarck ND 58503. (701)328-7590. E-mail: comserv@state.nd.us. Website: www.state.nd.us/arts.

COMMONWEALTH COUNCIL FOR ARTS AND CULTURE (NORTHERN MARIANA ISLANDS), P.O. Box 5553, CHRB, Saipan MP 96950. (670)322-9982 or (670)322-9983. E-mail: galaidi@vzpacifica.net. Website: www.geocities.com/ccacarts/ccacwebsite.html.

OHIO ARTS COUNCIL, 727 E. Main St., Columbus OH 43205-1796. (614)466-2613. Website: www.oac.state.oh.us.

OKLAHOMA ARTS COUNCIL, Jim Thorpe Building, 2101 N. Lincoln Blvd., Suite 640, Oklahoma City OK 73105. (405)521-2931. E-mail: okarts@arts.ok.gov. Website: www.arts.state.ok.us.

OREGON ARTS COMMISSION, 775 Summer St. NE, Suite 200, Salem OR 97301-1280. (503)986-0082. E-mail: oregon.artscomm@state.or.us. Website: www.oregonartscommission.org.

PENNSYLVANIA COUNCIL ON THE ARTS, 216 Finance Bldg., Harrisburg PA 17120. (717)787-6883. Website: www.pacouncilonthearts.org.

INSTITUTE OF PUERTO RICAN CULTURE, P.O. Box 9024184, San Juan PR 00902-4184. (787)724-0700. E-mail: www@icp.gobierno.pr. Website: www.icp.gobierno.pr.

RHODE ISLAND STATE COUNCIL ON THE ARTS, One Capitol Hill, Third Floor, Providence RI 02908. (401)222-3880. E-mail: info@arts.ri.gov. Website: www.arts.ri.gov.

SOUTH CAROLINA ARTS COMMISSION, 1800 Gervais St., Columbia SC 29201. (803)734-8696. E-mail: info@arts.state.sc.us. Website: www.southcarolinaarts.com.

SOUTH DAKOTA ARTS COUNCIL, 711 E. Wells Ave., Pierre SD 57501-3369. (605)773-3301. E-mail: sdac@state.sd.us. Website: www.artscouncil.sd.gov.

TENNESSEE ARTS COMMISSION, 401 Charlotte Ave., Nashville TN 37243-0780. (615)741-1701. Website: www.arts.state.tn.us.

TEXAS COMMISSION ON THE ARTS, E.O. Thompson Office Building, 920 Colorado, Suite 501, Austin TX 78701. (512)463-5535. E-mail: front.desk@arts.state.tx.us. Website: www.arts.state.tx.us.

UTAH ARTS COUNCIL, 617 E. South Temple, Salt Lake City UT 84102-1177. (801)236-7555. Website: http://arts.utah.gov.

VERMONT ARTS COUNCIL, 136 State St., Drawer 33, Montpelier VT 05633-6001. (802)828-3291. E-mail: online form. Website: www.vermontartscouncil.org.

VIRGIN ISLANDS COUNCIL ON THE ARTS, 5070 Norre Gade, St. Thomas VI 00802-6872. (340)774-5984. Website: http://vicouncilonarts.org.

VIRGINIA COMMISSION FOR THE ARTS, Lewis House, 223 Governor St., 2nd Floor, Richmond VA 23219. (804)225-3132. E-mail: arts@arts.virginia.gov. Website: www.arts.state.va.us.

WASHINGTON STATE ARTS COMMISSION, 711 Capitol Way S., Suite 600, P.O. Box 42675, Olympia WA 98504-2675. (360)753-3860. E-mail: info@arts.wa.gov. Website: www.arts.wa.gov.

WEST VIRGINIA COMMISSION ON THE ARTS, The Cultural Center, Capitol Complex, 1900 Kanawha Blvd. E., Charleston WV 25305-0300. (304)558-0220. Website: www.wvculture.org/arts.

WISCONSIN ARTS BOARD, 101 E. Wilson St., 1st Floor, Madison WI 53702. (608)266-0190. E-mail: artsboard@arts.state.wi.us. Website: www.arts.state.wi.us.

WYOMING ARTS COUNCIL, 2320 Capitol Ave., Cheyenne WY 82002. (307)777-7742. E-mail: ebratt@state.wy.us. Website: http://wyoarts.state.wy.us.

CANADIAN PROVINCES ARTS AGENCIES

ALBERTA FOUNDATION FOR THE ARTS, 10708-105 Ave., Edmonton AB T5H 0A1. (780)427-9968. Website: www.affta.ab.ca/index.shtml.

BRITISH COLUMBIA ARTS COUNCIL, P.O. Box 9819, Stn. Prov. Govt., Victoria BC V8W 9W3. (250)356-1718. E-mail: BCArtsCouncil@gov.bc.ca. Website: www.bcartscouncil.ca.

THE CANADA COUNCIL FOR THE ARTS, 350 Albert St., P.O. Box 1047, Ottawa ON K1P 5V8. (613)566-4414 or (800)263-5588 (within Canada). Website: www.canadacouncil.ca.

MANITOBA ARTS COUNCIL, 525-93 Lombard Ave., Winnipeg MB R3B 3B1. (204)945-2237 or (866)994-2787 (in Manitoba). E-mail: info@artscouncil.mb.ca. Website: www.artscouncil.mb.ca.

NEW BRUNSWICK ARTS BOARD (NBAB), 634 Queen St., Suite 300, Fredericton NB E3B 1C2. (506)444-4444 or (866)460-2787. Website: www.artsnb.ca.

NEWFOUNDLAND & LABRADOR ARTS COUNCIL, P.O. Box 98, St. John's NL A1C 5H5. (709)726-2212 or (866)726-2212. E-mail: nlacmail@nfld.net. Website: www.nlac.nf.ca.

NOVA SCOTIA DEPARTMENT OF TOURISM, CULTURE, AND HERITAGE, Culture Division, 1800 Argyle St., Suite 601, P.O. Box 456, Halifax NS B3J 2R5. (902)424-4510. E-mail: cultaffs@ gov.ns.ca. Website: www.gov.ns.ca/dtc/culture.

ONTARIO ARTS COUNCIL, 151 Bloor St. W., 5th Floor, Toronto ON M5S 1T6. (416)961-1660 or (800)387-0058 (in Ontario). E-mail: info@arts.on.ca. Website: www.arts.on.ca.

PRINCE EDWARD ISLAND COUNCIL OF THE ARTS, 115 Richmond St., Charlottetown PE C1A 1H7. (902)368-4410 or (888)734-2784. E-mail: info@peiartscouncil.com. Website: www. peiartscouncil.com.

QUÉBEC COUNCIL FOR ARTS & LITERATURE, 79 boul. René-Lévesque Est, 3e étage, Québec QC G1R 5N5. (418)643-1707 or (800)897-1707. E-mail: info@calq.gouv.qc.ca. Website: www. calq. gouv.qc.ca.

THE SASKATCHEWAN ARTS BOARD, 2135 Broad St., Regina SK S4P 1Y6. (306)787-4056 or (800)667-7526 (Saskatchewan only). E-mail: sab@artsboard.sk.ca. Website: www.artsboard. sk.ca.

YUKON ARTS FUNDING PROGRAM, Cultural Services Branch, Dept. of Tourism & Culture, Government of Yukon, Box 2703 (L-3), Whitehorse YT Y1A 2C6. (867)667-8589 or (800)661-0408 (in Yukon). E-mail: arts@gov.yk.ca. Website: www.tc.gov.yk.ca/216.html.

PUBLICATIONS OF INTEREST

Knowledge about the music industry is essential for both creative and business success. Staying informed requires keeping up with constantly changing information. Updates on the evolving trends in the music business are available to you in the form of music magazines, music trade papers, and books. There is a publication aimed at almost every type of musician, songwriter, and music fan, from the most technical knowledge of amplification systems to gossip about your favorite singer. These publications can enlighten and inspire you and provide information vital in helping you become a more well-rounded, educated, and, ultimately, successful musical artist.

This section lists all types of magazines and books you may find interesting. From songwriters' newsletters and glossy music magazines to tip sheets and how-to books, there should be something listed here that you'll enjoy and benefit from.

PERIODICALS

ALLEGHENY MUSIC WORKS, 1611 Menoher Blvd., Johnstown PA 15905. (814)255-4007. Website: www.alleghenymusicworks.com. *Monthly tip sheet.*

ALTERNATIVE PRESS, 1305 West 80th Street, Suite 2F, Cleveland OH 44102-1996. (216)631-1510. Email: subscriptions@altpress.com. Website: http://altpress.com. *Reviews, news, and features for alternative and indie music fans.*

AMERICAN SONGWRITER MAGAZINE, 50 Music Square W., Suite 604, Nashville TN 37203-3227. (615)321-6096. E-mail: info@americansongwriter.com. Website: www.americansongwriter.com. *Bimonthly publication for and about songwriters.*

BACK STAGE EAST, 770 Broadway, 4th Floor, New York NY 10003. (646)654-5700.

BACK STAGE WEST, 5055 Wilshire Blvd., Los Angeles CA 90036. (323)525-2358 or (800)745-8922. Website: www.backstage.com. *Weekly East and West Coast performing artist trade papers.*

BASS PLAYER, P.O. Box 57324, Boulder CO 80323-7324. (800)234-1831. E-mail: bassplayer@ neodata.com. Website: www.bassplayer.com. *Monthly magazine for bass players with lessons, interviews, articles, and transcriptions.*

BILLBOARD, 1515 Broadway, New York NY 10036. (800)745-8922. E-mail: bbstore@billboard. com. Website: www.billboard.com. *Weekly industry trade magazine.*

CANADIAN MUSICIAN, 23 Hannover Dr., Suite 7, St. Catharines ON L2W 1A3 Canada. (877)746-4692. Website: www.canadianmusician.com. *Bimonthly publication for amateur and professional Canadian musicians.*

CHART, 200-41 Britain St., Toronto ON M5A 1R7 Canada. (416)363-3101. E-mail: chart@ chartnet.com. Website: www.chartattack.com. *Monthly magazine covering the Canadian and international music scenes.*

CMJ NEW MUSIC REPORT/CMJ NEW MUSIC MONTHLY, 151 W. 25th St., 12 Floor, New York NY 10001. (917)606-1908. Website: www.cmj.com. *Weekly college radio and alternative music tip sheet.*

COUNTRY LINE MAGAZINE, 16150 S. IH-35, Buda TX 78610. (512)295-8400. E-mail: editor@ countrylinemagazine.com. Website: www.countrylinemagazine.com. *Monthly Texas-only country music cowboy and lifestyle magazine.*

DAILY VARIETY, 5700 Wilshire Blvd., Suite 120, Los Angeles CA 90036. (323)857-6600. Website: www.variety.com. *Daily entertainment trade newspaper.*

ENTERTAINMENT LAW & FINANCE, New York Law Publishing Co., 345 Park Ave. S., 8th Floor, New York NY 10010. (212)545-6174. *Monthly newsletter covering music industry contracts, lawsuit filings, court rulings, and legislation.*

EXCLAIM!, 7-B Pleasant Blvd., Suite 966, Toronto ON M4T 1K2 Canada. (416)535-9735. E-mail: exclaim@exclaim.ca. Website: http://exclaim.ca. *Canadian music monthly covering all genres of non-mainstream music.*

FAST FORWARD, Disc Makers, 7905 N. Rt. 130, Pennsauken NJ 08110-1402. (800)468-9353. Website: www.discmakers.com/music/ffwd. *Quarterly newsletter featuring companies and products for performing and recording artists in the independent music industry.*

GUITAR PLAYER, 1601 W. 23rd St., Suite 200, Lawrence KS 60046-0127. (800)289-9839. Website: www.guitarplayer.com. *Monthly guitar magazine with transcriptions, columns, and interviews, including occasional articles on songwriting.*

JAZZTIMES, 8737 Colesville Rd., 9th Floor, Silver Spring MD 20910-3921. (301)588-4114. Website: www.jazztimes.com. *10 issues/year magazine covering the American jazz scene.*

MUSIC BUSINESS INTERNATIONAL MAGAZINE, 460 Park Ave., S. of 9th, New York NY 10116. (212)378-0406. *Bimonthly magazine for senior executives in the music industry.*

MUSIC CONNECTION MAGAZINE, 16130 Ventura Blvd., Suite 540, Encino CA 91436. (818)795-0101. E-mail: contactMC@musicconnection.com. Website: www.musicconnection.com. *Biweekly music industry trade publication.*

MUSIC MORSELS, P.O. Box 2760, Acworth GA 30102. (678)445-0006. Fax: (678)494-9269. E-mail: SergeEnt@aol.com. Website: www.serge.org/musicmorsels.htm. *Monthly songwriting publication.*

MUSIC ROW MAGAZINE, 1231 17th Ave. S, Nashville TN 37212. (615)321-3617. E-mail: info@ musicrow.com. Website: www.musicrow.com. *Biweekly Nashville industry publication.*

OFFBEAT MAGAZINE, OffBeat Publications, 421 Frenchman St., Suite 200, New Orleans LA 70116. (504)944-4300. E-mail: offbeat@offbeat.com. Website: www.offbeat.com. *Monthly magazine covering Louisiana music and artists.*

THE PERFORMING SONGWRITER, P.O. Box 40931, Nashville TN 37204. (800)883-7664. E-mail: order@performingsongwriter.com. Website: www.performingsongwriter.com. *Bimonthly songwriters' magazine.*

RADIO AND RECORDS, 2049 Century Park East, 41st Floor, Los Angeles CA 90067. (310)553-4330. Fax: (310)203-9763. E-mail: subscribe@radioandrecords.com. Website: www.radio andrecords.com. *Weekly newspaper covering the radio and record industries.*

RADIR, Radio Mall, 2412 Unity Ave. N., Dept. WEB, Minneapolis MN 55422. (800)759-4561. E-mail: info@bbhsoftware.com. Website: www.bbhsoftware.com. *Quarterly radio station database on disk.*

SING OUT!, P.O. Box 5460, Bethlehem PA 18015. (888)SING-OUT. Fax: (610)865-5129. E-mail: info@singout.org. Website: www.singout.org. *Quarterly folk music magazine.*

SONGCASTING, 15445 Ventura Blvd. #260, Sherman Oaks CA 91403. (818)377-4084. *Monthly tip sheet.*

SONGLINK INTERNATIONAL, 23 Belsize Crescent, London NW3 5QY England. Website: www. songlink.com. *10 issues/year newsletter including details of recording artists looking for songs; contact details for industry sources; also news and features on the music business.*

VARIETY, 5700 Wilshire Blvd., Suite 120, Los Angeles CA 90036. (323)857-6600. Fax: (323)857-0494. Website: www.variety.com. *Weekly entertainment trade newspaper.*

WORDS AND MUSIC, 41 Valleybrook Dr., Don Mills ON M3B 2S6 Canada. (416)445-8700. Website: www.socan.ca. *Monthly songwriters' magazine.*

BOOKS & DIRECTORIES

101 SONGWRITING WRONGS & HOW TO RIGHT THEM, by Pat & Pete Luboff, Writer's Digest Books, 4700 E. Galbraith Rd., Cincinnati OH 45236. (800)448-0915. Website: www.writ ersdigest.com.

THE A&R REGISTRY, by Ritch Esra, SRS Publishing, 7510 Sunset Blvd. #1041, Los Angeles CA 90046-3418. (800)377-7411 or (800)552-7411. E-mail: musicregistry@compuserve.com.

THE BILLBOARD GUIDE TO MUSIC PUBLICITY, rev. ed., by Jim Pettigrew, Jr., Billboard Books, 1695 Oak St., Lakewood NJ 08701. (800)344-7119.

BREAKIN' INTO NASHVILLE, by Jennifer Ember Pierce, Madison Books, University Press of America, 4501 Forbes Rd., Suite 200, Lanham MD 20706. (800)462-6420.

CMJ DIRECTORY, 151 W. 25th St., 12th Floor, New York NY 10001. (917)606-1908. Website: www.cmj.com.

THE CRAFT AND BUSINESS OF SONGWRITING, by John Braheny, Writer's Digest Books, 4700 E. Galbraith Rd., Cincinnati OH 45236. (800)448-0915. Website: www.writersdigest.com.

THE CRAFT OF LYRIC WRITING, by Sheila Davis, Writer's Digest Books, 4700 E. Galbraith Rd., Cincinnati OH 45236. (800)448-0915. Website: www.writersdigest.com.

DISC MAKERS, by Jason Ojalvo, Disc Makers, 7905 N. Rt. 130, Pennsauken NJ 08110. (800)468-9353. E-mail: discman@discmakers.com. Website: www.discmakers.com.

HOLLYWOOD CREATIVE DIRECTORY, 3000 W. Olympic Blvd. #2525, Santa Monica CA 90404. (800)815-0503. Website: www.hcdonline.com. *Lists producers in film and TV.*

THE HOLLYWOOD REPORTER, 5055 Wilshire Blvd., Los Angeles CA 90036. (323)525-2150. Website: www.hollywoodreporter.com.

HOW TO GET SOMEWHERE IN THE MUSIC BUSINESS FROM NOWHERE WITH NOTHING, by Mary Dawson, CQK Books, CQK Music Group, 2221 Justin Rd., Suite 119-142, Flower Mound TX 75028. (972)317-2720. Fax: (972)317-4737. Website: www.FromNowhereWithNothing.com.

HOW TO PROMOTE YOUR MUSIC SUCCESSFULLY ON THE INTERNET, by David Nevue, Midnight Rain Productions, P.O. Box 21831, Eugene OR 97402. Website: www.rainmusic.com.

HOW TO MAKE IT IN THE NEW MUSIC BUSINESS: LESSONS, TIPS, AND INSPIRATIONS FROM MUSIC'S BIGGEST AND BEST, by Robert Wolff, Billboard Books. Website: www.billboard.com.

HOW YOU CAN BREAK INTO THE MUSIC BUSINESS, by Marty Garrett, Lonesome Wind Corporation, P.O. Box 2143, Broken Arrow OK 74013-2143. (800)210-4416.

LOUISIANA MUSIC DIRECTORY, OffBeat, Inc., 421 Frenchmen St., Suite 200, New Orleans LA 70116. (504)944-4300. Website: www.offbeat.com.

LYDIAN CHROMATIC CONCEPT OF TONAL ORGANIZATION, VOLUME ONE: THE ART AND SCIENCE OF TONAL GRAVITY, by George Russell, Concept Publishing Company, 258 Harvard St., #296, Brookline MA 02446-2904. E-mail: lydconcept@aol.com. Website: www.lydian chromaticconcept.com.

MELODY IN SONGWRITING, by Jack Perricone, Berklee Press, 1140 Boylston St., Boston MA 02215. (617)747-2146. E-mail: info@berkleepress.com. Website: www.berkleepress.com.

MUSIC ATTORNEY LEGAL & BUSINESS AFFAIRS REGISTRY, by Ritch Esra and Steve Trumbull, SRS Publishing, 7510 Sunset Blvd. #1041, Los Angeles CA 90046-3418. (800)552-7411. E-mail: musicregistry@compuserve.com or srspubl@aol.com.

THE MUSIC BUSINESS REGISTRY, by Ritch Esra, SRS Publishing, 7510 Sunset Blvd. #1041, Los Angeles CA 90046-3418. (800)552-7411. E-mail: musicregistry@compuserve.com or srspu bl@aol.com. Website: www.musicregistry.com.

MUSIC DIRECTORY CANADA, 7th ed., Norris-Whitney Communications Inc., 23 Hannover Dr., Suite 7, St. Catherines ON L2W 1A3 Canada. (877)RING-NWC. E-mail: mail@nor. com. Website: http://nor.com.

MUSIC LAW: HOW TO RUN YOUR BAND'S BUSINESS, by Richard Stin, Nolo Press, 950 Parker St., Berkeley CA 94710-9867. (510)549-1976. Website: www.nolo.com.

MUSIC, MONEY AND SUCCESS: THE INSIDER'S GUIDE TO THE MUSIC INDUSTRY, by Jeffrey Brabec and Todd Brabec, Schirmer Books, 1633 Broadway, New York NY 10019.

THE MUSIC PUBLISHER REGISTRY, by Ritch Esra, SRS Publishing, 7510 Sunset Blvd. #1041, Los Angeles CA 90046-3418. (800)552-7411. E-mail: musicregistry@compuserve.com or srspubl@aol.com.

MUSIC PUBLISHING: A SONGWRITER'S GUIDE, rev. ed., by Randy Poe, Writer's Digest Books, 4700 E. Galbraith Rd., Cincinnati OH 45236. (800)448-0915. Website: www.writersdigest.com.

THE MUSICIAN'S GUIDE TO MAKING & SELLING YOUR OWN CDS & CASSETTES, by Jana Stanfield, Writer's Digest Books, 4700 E. Galbraith Rd., Cincinnati OH 45236. (800)448-0915. Website: www.writersdigest.com.

MUSICIANS' PHONE BOOK, THE LOS ANGELES MUSIC INDUSTRY DIRECTORY, Get Yourself Some Publishing, 28336 Simsalido Ave., Canyon Country CA 91351. (805)299-2405. E-mail: mpb@earthlink.net. Website: www.musiciansphonebook.com.

NASHVILLE MUSIC BUSINESS DIRECTORY, by Mark Dreyer, NMBD Publishing, 9 Music Square S., Suite 210, Nashville TN 37203. (615)826-4141. E-mail: nmbd@nashvilleconnection.com. Website: www.nashvilleconnection.com.

NASHVILLE'S UNWRITTEN RULES: INSIDE THE BUSINESS OF THE COUNTRY MUSIC MACHINE, by Dan Daley, Overlook Press, One Overlook Dr., Woodstock NY 12498. (845)679-6838. E-mail: overlook@netstep.net.

NATIONAL DIRECTORY OF INDEPENDENT RECORD DISTRIBUTORS, P.O. Box 452063, Lake Mary FL 32795-2063. (407)834-8555. E-mail: info@songwriterproducts.com. Website: www.songwriterproducts.com.

THE OFFICIAL COUNTRY MUSIC DIRECTORY, ICMA Music Directory, P.O. Box 271238, Nashville TN 37227.

PERFORMANCE MAGAZINE GUIDES, 1203 Lake St., Suite 200, Fort Worth TX 76102-4504. (817)338-9444. E-mail: sales@performancemagazine.com. Website: www.performancemagazine.com.

RADIO STATIONS OF AMERICA: A NATIONAL DIRECTORY, P.O. Box 452063, Lake Mary FL 32795-2063. (407)834-8555. E-mail: info@songwriterproducts.com. Website: www.songwriterproducts.com.

THE REAL DEAL—HOW TO GET SIGNED TO A RECORD LABEL FROM A TO Z, by Daylle Deanna Schwartz, Billboard Books, 1695 Oak St., Lakewood NJ 08701. (800)344-7119.

RECORDING INDUSTRY SOURCEBOOK, Music Books Plus, P.O. Box 670, 240 Portage Rd., Lewiston NY 14092. (800)265-8481. Website: www.musicbooksplus.com.

REHARMONIZATION TECHNIQUES, by Randy Felts, Berklee Press, 1140 Boylston St., Boston MA 02215. (617)747-2146. E-mail: info@berkleepress.com. Website: www.berkleepress.com.

THE SONGWRITERS IDEA BOOK, by Sheila Davis, Writer's Digest Books, 4700 E. Galbraith Rd., Cincinnati OH 45236. (800)448-0915. Website: www.writersdigest.com.

SONGWRITER'S MARKET GUIDE TO SONG & DEMO SUBMISSION FORMATS, Writer's Digest Books, 4700 E. Galbraith Rd., Cincinnati OH 45236. (800)448-0915. Website: www.writersdigest.com.

SONGWRITER'S PLAYGROUND—INNOVATIVE EXERCISES IN CREATIVE SONGWRITING, by Barbara L. Jordan, Creative Music Marketing, 1085 Commonwealth Ave., Suite 323, Boston MA 02215. (617)926-8766.

THE SONGWRITER'S WORKSHOP: HARMONY, by Jimmy Kachulis, Berklee Press, 1140 Boylston St., Boston MA 02215. (617)747-2146. E-mail: info@berkleepress.com. Website: www.berkleepress.com.

THE SONGWRITER'S WORKSHOP: MELODY, by Jimmy Kachulis, Berklee Press, 1140 Boylston St., Boston MA 02215. (617)747-2146. E-mail: info@berkleepress.com. Website: www.berkleepress.com.

SONGWRITING AND THE CREATIVE PROCESS, by Steve Gillette, Sing Out! Publications, P.O. Box 5640, Bethlehem PA 18015-0253. (888)SING-OUT. E-mail: singout@libertynet.org. Website: www.singout.org/sopubs.html.

SONGWRITING: ESSENTIAL GUIDE TO LYRIC FORM AND STRUCTURE, by Pat Pattison, Berklee Press, 1140 Boylston St., Boston MA 02215. (617)747-2146. E-mail: info@berkleepress.com. Website: www.www.berkleepress.com.

SONGWRITING: ESSENTIAL GUIDE TO RHYMING, by Pat Pattison, Berklee Press, 1140 Boylston St., Boston MA 02215. (617)747-2146. E-mail: info@berkleepress.com. Website: www.berkleepress.com.

THE SONGWRITING SOURCEBOOK: HOW TO TURN CHORDS INTO GREAT SONGS, by Rikky Rooksby, Backbeat Books, 600 Harrison St., San Francisco CA 94107. (415)947-6615. E-mail: books@musicplayer.com. Website: www.backbeatbooks.com.

THE SOUL OF THE WRITER, by Susan Tucker with Linda Lee Strother, Journey Publishing, P.O. Box 92411, Nashville TN 37209. (615)952-4894. Website: www.journeypublishing.com.

SUCCESSFUL LYRIC WRITING, by Sheila Davis, Writer's Digest Books, 4700 E. Galbraith Rd., Cincinnati OH 45236. (800)448-0915. Website: www.writersdigest.com.

THIS BUSINESS OF MUSIC MARKETING AND PROMOTION, by Tad Lathrop and Jim Pettigrew, Jr., Billboard Books, Watson-Guptill Publications, 770 Broadway, New York NY 10003. E-mail: info@watsonguptill.com.

TIM SWEENEY'S GUIDE TO RELEASING INDEPENDENT RECORDS, by Tim Sweeney, TSA Books, 31805 Highway 79 S., Temecula CA 92592. (909)303-9506. E-mail: info@tsamusic.com. Website: www.tsamusic.com.

TIM SWEENEY'S GUIDE TO SUCCEEDING AT MUSIC CONVENTIONS, by Tim Sweeney, TSA Books, 31805 Highway 79 S., Temecula CA 92592. (909)303-9506. Website: www.tsamusic.com.

TEXAS MUSIC INDUSTRY DIRECTORY, Texas Music Office, Office of the Governor, P.O. Box 13246, Austin TX 78711. (512)463-6666. E-mail: music@governor.state.tx.us. Website: www.governor.state.tx.us/music.

TUNESMITH: INSIDE THE ART OF SONGWRITING, by Jimmy Webb, Hyperion, 77 W. 66th St., 11th Floor, New York NY 10023. (800)759-0190.

VOLUNTEER LAWYERS FOR THE ARTS GUIDE TO COPYRIGHT FOR MUSICIANS AND COMPOSERS, One E. 53rd St., 6th Floor, New York NY 10022. (212)319-2787.

WRITING BETTER LYRICS, by Pat Pattison, Writer's Digest Books, 4700 E. Galbraith Rd., Cincinnati OH 45236. (800)448-0915. Website: www.writersdigest.com.

WRITING MUSIC FOR HIT SONGS, by Jai Josefs, Schirmer Trade Books, 257 Park Ave. S., New York NY 10010. (212)254-2100.

THE YELLOW PAGES OF ROCK, The Album Network, 120 N. Victory Blvd., Burbank CA 91502. (800)222-4382. Fax: (818)955-9048. E-mail: ypinfo@yprock.com.

WEBSITES OF INTEREST

The Internet provides a wealth of information for songwriters and performers, and the number of sites devoted to music grows each day. Below is a list of websites that can offer you information, links to other music sites, contact with other songwriters, and places to showcase your songs. Due to the dynamic nature of the online world, this is certainly not a comprehensive list, but it gives you a place to start on your Internet journey to search for opportunities to get your music heard.

ABOUT.COM MUSICIANS' EXCHANGE http://musicians.about.com/
Site features headlines and articles of interest to independent musicians and songwriters, as well as links and label profiles.

ABSOLUTE PUNK www.absolutepunk.net
Searchable online community focusing on punk and rock music, including news, reviews, articles, and interviews; forums to discuss music and pop culture.

AMERICAN MUSIC CENTER www.amc.net
Classical and jazz archives. Includes a list of organizations and contacts for composers.

AMERICAN SOCIETY OF COMPOSERS, AUTHORS AND PUBLISHERS (ASCAP) www.ascap.com
Database of works in ASCAP's repertoire. Includes performer, songwriter, and publisher information as well as membership information and industry news.

***AMERICAN SONGWRITER MAGAZINE* HOMEPAGE** www.americansongwriter.com
This is the official homepage for *American Songwriter* Magazine. Features an online article archive, e-mail newsletter, and links.

BACKSTAGE COMMERCE www.backstagecommerce.com

Provides secure online support for the sale of music goods for independent artists.

BATHTUB MUSIC www.bathtubmusic.com

Online distributor of independent music; receives commission on any sales made.

BEAIRD MUSIC GROUP DEMOS www.beairdmusicgroup.com

Nashville demo service which offers a variety of demo packages.

BILLBOARD.COM www.billboard.com

Industry news and searchable online database of music companies by subscription.

THE BLUES FOUNDATION www.blues.org

Nonprofit organization located in Memphis, TN; website contains information on the foundation, membership, and events.

BROADCAST MUSIC, INC. (BMI) www.bmi.com

Offers lists of song titles, writers, and publishers of the BMI repertoire. Includes membership information and general information on songwriting and licensing.

THE BUZZ FACTOR www.thebuzzfactor.com

Website offers free tips on the music marketing and self-promotion ideas.

BUZZNET www.buzznet.com

Searchable networking and news site featuring music and pop culture; photos, videos, concert reviews, more.

CDBABY www.cdbaby.com

An online CD store dedicated to the sales of independent music.

CDFREEDOM www.cdfreedom.com

An online CD store for independent musicians.

CADENZA www.cadenza.org

Online resource for contemporary and classical music and musicians, including methods of contacting other musicians.

CENTER FOR THE PROMOTION OF CONTEMPORARY COMPOSERS (CPCC) www.under.org/cpcc

Website for CPCC, an Internet-based service organization for composers.

CHORUS AMERICA www.chorusamerica.org

The website for Chorus America, a national organization for professional and volunteer choruses. Includes job listings and professional development information.

FINETUNE www.finetune.com

Internet radio/streaming audio. User can create personalized channels and playlists online.

FILM MUSIC NETWORK www.filmmusicworld.com or www.filmmusic.net
Network of links, news, and job listings within the film music world.

FOURFRONT MEDIA AND MUSIC www.knab.com
Site offers information on product development, promotion, publicity, and performance.

GARAGEBAND www.garageband.com
Online music hosting site where independent musicians can post music and profiles that can be critiqued by listeners.

GET SIGNED www.getsigned.com
Interviews with musicians, songwriters, and industry veterans, how-to business information, and more.

GOVERNMENT LIAISON SERVICES www.trademarkinfo.com
An intellectual property research firm. Offers a variety of trademark searches.

GUITAR NINE RECORDS www.guitar9.com
Offers articles on songwriting, music theory, guitar techniques, etc.

GOOGLE www.google.com
Online search engine can be used to look up music, information, lyrics.

HARMONY CENTRAL www.harmony-central.com
Online community for musicians with in-depth reviews and discussions.

HARRY FOX AGENCY www.harryfox.com
Offers a comprehensive FAQ about licensing songs for use in recording, performance, and film.

ILIKE www.ilike.com
Music networking site. Signed and unsigned artists can sign up for free artists' page and upload songs and events. Works with other social networks such as www.face book.com.

INDEPENDENT DISTRIBUTION NETWORK www.idnmusic.com
Website of independent bands distributing their music with advice on everything from starting a band to finding labels.

INDEPENDENT SONGWRITER WEB MAGAZINE www.independentsongwriter.com/
Independent music reviews, classifieds, message board, and chat sessions.

INDIE-MUSIC.COM http://indie-music.com/

Website of how-to articles, record label directory, links to musicians and venue listings.

JAZZ CORNER www.jazzcorner.com

Portal for the websites of jazz musicians and organizations. Includes the jazz video share, jukebox, and the "Speakeasy" bulletin board.

JUST PLAIN FOLKS www.jpfolks.com or www.justplainfolks.org

Website for songwriting organization featuring message boards, lyric feedback forums, member profiles and music, contact listings, chapter homepages, and more.

LAST.FM www.last.fm/

Music tracking and social networking site.

LI'L HANK'S GUIDE FOR SONGWRITERS IN L.A. www.halsguide.com

Website for songwriters with information on clubs, publishers, books, etc. Links to other songwriting sites.

LIVE365 www.live365.com/index.live

Internet radio/audio stream search engine.

LIVEJOURNAL www.livejournal.com

Social networking community using open source technology; music communities provide news, interviews, and reviews.

LOS ANGELES GOES UNDERGROUND http://lagu.somaweb.org/

Website dedicated to underground rock bands from Los Angeles and Hollywood.

LYRICAL LINE www.lyricalline.com

Offers places to upload original songs for critique or exposure, industry news, and more.

LYRIC IDEAS www.lyricideas.com

Offers songwriting prompts, themes, and creative techniques for songwriting.

LYRICIST www.lyricist.com/

Site offers advice, tips, and events in the music industry.

MI2N (THE MUSIC INDUSTRY NEWS NETWORK) www.mi2n.com

Offers news on happenings in the music industry and career postings.

THE MUSE'S MUSE www.musesmuse.com/

Classifieds, catalog of music samples, songwriting articles, newsletter, and chat room.

MOG http://mog.com/

Internet radio/streaming audio. Contains music news and concert reviews, personalized recommendations.

MUSIC BOOKS PLUS www.musicbooksplus.com
Online bookstore dedicated to music books on every music-related topic, plus a free newsletter.

MUSIC PUBLISHERS ASSOCIATION www.mpa.org/
Ofers directories for music publishers and imprints, copyright resource center, and information on the organization.

MUSIC YELLOW PAGES www.musicyellowpages.com/
Listings of music-related businesses.

MYSPACE www.myspace.com
Social networking site featuring music Web pages for musicians and songwriters.

NASHVILLE SONGWRITERS ASSOCIATION INTERNATIONAL (NSAI) www.nashvillesongwriters.com
Official NSAI homepage. Offers news, links, online registration, and message board for members.

NATIONAL ASSOCIATION OF COMPOSERS USA (NACUSA) www.music-usa.org/nacusa
A nonprofit organization devoted to the promotion and performance of American concert hall music.

NATIONAL MUSIC PUBLISHERS ASSOCIATION www.nmpa.org
Organization's online site filled with information about copyright, legislation, and other concerns of the music publishing world.

ONLINE ROCK www.onlinerock.com/
Range of membership options including a free option, offers webpage services, articles, chat rooms, links, and more.

OPERA AMERICA www.operaamerica.org/
Website of Opera America features information on advocacy and awareness programs, publications, conference schedules, and more.

OUTERSOUND www.outersound.com
Information on educating yourself in the music industry and a list of music magazines to advertise in or get reviewed by.

PANDORA www.pandora.com
A site created by the founders of the Music Genome Project; a searchable music radio/streaming audio site.

PERFORMER MAG www.performermag.com
Offers articles, music industry news, classifieds and reviews.

PERFORMING SONGWRITER MAGAZINE HOMEPAGE www.performingsongwriter.com
Official homepage for the magazine features articles and links.

PITCHFORK www.pitchforkmedia.com
Offers Indie news, reviews, media, and features.

PUBLIC DOMAIN MUSIC www.pdinfo.com/
Articles on public domain works and copyright including public domain song lists, research sources, tips and FAQs.

PUMP AUDIO www.pumpaudio.com/
License music for film and television on a non-exclusive basis. No submission fees, rights retained by songwriter.

PUREVOLUME www.purevolume.com
Music hosting site with searchable database of songs by signed and unsigned artists. Musicians and songwriters can upload songs and events.

THE RECORDING PROJECT www.recordingproject.com/
Online community for musicians and recording artists, every level welcome.

RECORD PRODUCER.COM www.record-producer.com
Extensive site dedicated to audio engineering and record production. Offers a free newsletter, online instruction, and e-books on various aspects of record production and audio engineering.

RHYTHM NET www.rhythmnet.com
Online CD store for independent musicians.

ROCK AND ROLL HALL OF FAME + MUSEUM www.rockhall.com/
Website for the Rock and Roll Hall of Fame and Museum, including events listings, visitor info, and more.

SESAC INC. www.sesac.com
Website for performing rights organization with songwriter profiles, industry news updates, licensing information, and links to other sites.

SINGERSONGWRITER www.singersongwriter.ws
Resources for singer-songwriters, including an extensive list, featured resources, and lists of radio stations organized geographically.

SLACKER www.slacker.com

Internet radio/streaming audio. User can create personalized channels and playlists online.

SOMA FM www.somafm.com

Internet underground/alternative radio with commercial-free broadcasting from San Francisco.

SONG CATALOG www.songcatalog.com

Online song catalog database for licensing.

SONGLINK www.songlink.com

Offers opportunities to pitch songs to music publishers for specific recording projects and industry news.

SONGRAMP www.songramp.com

Online songwriting organization with message boards, blogs, news, and streaming music channels. Offers variety of membership packages.

SONGSALIVE! www.songsalive.org

Online songwriters organization and community.

SONGWRITER 101 www.songwriter101.com

Offers articles, industry news, and message boards.

SONGWRITER'S GUILD OF AMERICA (SGA) www.songwritersguild.com

Industry news, member services information, newsletters, contract reviews, and more.

SONGWRITER'S RESOURCE NETWORK www.songwritersresourcenetwork.com

News and education resource for songwriters, lyricists, and composers.

SONGWRITERUNIVERSE www.songwriteruniverse.com

In-depth articles, business information, education, and recommended reading.

THE SONGWRITING EDUCATION RESOURCE www.craftofsongwriting.com

An educational website for songwriters. Offers discussion boards, articles, and links.

SONIC BIDS www.sonicbids.com

Features an online press kit with photos, bio, music samples, date calendar. Free trial period first month for artists/bands to sign up, newsletter.

SOUNDPEDIA http://soundpedia.com

Internet Radio/streaming audio. User can create personalized channels and playlists online.

STARPOLISH www.starpolish.com

Features articles and interviews on the music industry.

SUMMERSONGS SONGWRITING CAMPS www.summersongs.com

Information about songwriting camps, staff, and online registration.

TAXI www.taxi.com

Independent A&R vehicle that shops demos to A&R professionals.

UNITED STATES COPYRIGHT OFFICE www.copyright.gov

Homepage for the US Copyright office. Offers information on registering songs.

THE VELVET ROPE www.velvetrope.com

Famous/infamous online music industry message board.

WEIRDO MUSIC www.weirdomusic.com

Online music magazine with articles, reviews, downloads, and links to Internet radio shows.

YAHOO! http://new.music.yahoo.com/

Search engine with radio station guide, music industry news, and listings.

YOUTUBE www.youtube.com

Social networking site which hosts audiovisual content. Searchable database provides links to music videos, interviews, and more.

GLOSSARY

A CAPPELLA. Choral singing without accompaniment.

AAA FORM. A song form in which every verse has the same melody; often used for songs that tell a story.

AABA, ABAB. A commonly used song pattern consisting of two verses, a bridge, and a verse, or a repeated pattern of verse and bridge, where the verses are musically the same.

A&R DIRECTOR. Record company executive in charge of the Artists and Repertoire Department who is responsible for finding and developing new artists and matching songs with artists.

A/C. Adult contemporary music.

ADVANCE. Money paid to the songwriter or recording artist, which is then recouped before regular royalty payment begins. Sometimes called "up front" money, advances are deducted from royalties.

AFIM. Association for Independent Music (formerly NAIRD). Organization for independent record companies, distributors, retailers, manufacturers, etc.

AFM. American Federation of Musicians. A union for musicians and arrangers.

AFTRA. American Federation of Television and Radio Artists. A union for performers.

AIMP. Association of Independent Music Publishers.

AIRPLAY. The radio broadcast of a recording.

AOR. Album-Oriented Rock. A radio format that primarily plays selections from rock albums as opposed to hit singles.

ARRANGEMENT. An adaptation of a composition for a recording or performance, with consideration for the melody, harmony, instrumentation, tempo, style, etc.

ASCAP. American Society of Composers, Authors and Publishers. A performing rights society. (See the "Organizations" section.)

ASSIGNMENT. Transfer of rights of a song from writer to publisher.

AUDIO VISUAL INDEX (AVI). A database containing title and production information for cue sheets which are available from a performing rights organization. Currently, BMI, ASCAP, SOCAN, PRS, APRA and SACEM contribute their cue sheet listings to the AVI.

AUDIOVISUAL. Refers to presentations that use audio backup for visual material.

BACKGROUND MUSIC. Music used that creates mood and supports the spoken dialogue of a radio program or visual action of an audiovisual work. Not feature or theme music.

B&W. Black-and-white.

BED. Prerecorded music used as background material in commercials. In rap music, often refers to the sampled and looped drums and music over which the rapper performs.

BLACK BOX. Theater without fixed stage or seating arrangements, capable of a variety of formations. Usually a small space, often attached to a major theater complex, used for workshops or experimental works calling for small casts and limited sets.

BMI. Broadcast Music, Inc. A performing rights society. (See the "Organizations" section.)

BOOKING AGENT. Person who schedules performances for entertainers.

BOOTLEGGING. Unauthorized recording and selling of a song.

BUSINESS MANAGER. Person who handles the financial aspects of artistic careers.

BUZZ. Attention an act generates through the media and word of mouth.

B/W. Backed with. Usually refers to the B-side of a single.

C&W. Country and western.

CATALOG. The collected songs of one writer, or all songs handled by one publisher.

CD. Compact-disc (*see* below).

CD-R. A recordable CD.

CD-ROM. Compact Disc-Read Only Memory. A computer information storage medium capable of holding enormous amounts of data. Information on a CD-ROM cannot be deleted. A computer user must have a CD-ROM drive to access a CD-ROM.

CHAMBER MUSIC. Any music suitable for performance in a small audience area or chamber.

CHAMBER ORCHESTRA. A miniature orchestra usually containing one instrument per part.

CHART. The written arrangement of a song.

CHARTS. The trade magazines' lists of the best-selling records.

CHR. Comtemporary Hit Radio. Top 40 pop music.

COLLABORATION. Two or more artists, writers, etc., working together on a single project; for instance, a playwright and a songwriter creating a musical together.

COMPACT DISC. A small disc (about 4.7 inches in diameter) holding digitally encoded music that is read by a laser beam in a CD player.

COMPOSERS. The men and women who create musical compositions for motion pictures and other audio visual works, or the creators of classical music composition.

COPUBLISH. Two or more parties own publishing rights to the same song.

COPYRIGHT. The exclusive legal right giving the creator of a work the power to control the publishing, reproduction, and selling of the work. Although a song is technically copyrighted at the time it is written, the best legal protection of that copyright comes through registering the copyright with the Library of Congress.

COPYRIGHT INFRINGEMENT. Unauthorized use of a copyrighted song or portions thereof.

COVER RECORDING. A new version of a previously recorded song.

CROSSOVER. A song that becomes popular in two or more musical categories (e.g., country and pop).

CUT. Any finished recording; a selection from a LP. Also to record.

DAT. Digital Audio Tape. A professional and consumer audiocassette format for recording and playing back digitally encoded material. DAT cassettes are approximately one-third smaller than conventional audiocassettes.

DCC. Digital Compact Cassette. A consumer audio cassette format for recording and playing back digitally encoded tape. DCC tapes are the same size as analog cassettes.

DEMO. A recording of a song submitted as a demonstration of a writer's or artist's skills.

DERIVATIVE WORK. A work derived from another work, such as a translation, musical arrangement, sound recording, or motion picture version.

DISTRIBUTOR. Wholesale marketing agent responsible for getting records from manufacturers to retailers.

DONUT. A jingle with singing at the beginning and end and instrumental background in the middle. Ad copy is recorded over the middle section.

E-MAIL. Electronic mail. Computer address where a company or individual can be reached via modem.

ENGINEER. A specially trained individual who operates recording studio equipment.

ENHANCED CD. General term for an audio CD that also contains multimedia computer information. It is playable in both standard CD players and CD-ROM drives.

EP. Extended play record or cassette containing more selections than a standard single, but fewer than a standard album.

EPK. Electronic press kit. Usually contains photos, sound files, bio information, reviews, tour dates, etc., posted online. Sonicbids.com is a popular EPK hosting website.

FINAL MIX. The art of combining all the various sounds that take place during the recording session into a two-track stereo or mono tape. Reflects the total product and all of the energies and talents the artist, producer, and engineer have put into the project.

FLY SPACE. The area above a stage from which set pieces are lowered and raised during a performance.

FOLIO. A softcover collection of printed music prepared for sale.

FOLLOWING. A fan base committed to going to gigs and buying albums.

FOREIGN RIGHTS SOCIETIES. Performing rights societies other than domestic which have reciprocal agreements with ASCAP and BMI for the collection of royalties accrued by foreign radio and television airplay and other public performance of the writer members of the above groups.

HARRY FOX AGENCY. Organization that collects mechanical royalties.

GRAMMY. Music industry awards presented by the National Academy of Recording Arts and Sciences.

HIP-HOP. A dance-oriented musical style derived from a combination of disco, rap, and R&B.

HIT. A song or record that achieves top 40 status.

HOOK. A memorable "catch" phrase or melody line that is repeated in a song.

HOUSE. Dance music created by remixing samples from other songs.

HYPERTEXT. Words or groups of words in an electronic document that are linked to other text, such as a definition or a related document. Hypertext can also be linked to illustrations.

INDIE. An independent record label, music publisher, or producer.

INFRINGEMENT. A violation of the exclusive rights granted by the copyright law to a copyright owner.

INTERNET. A worldwide network of computers that offers access to a wide variety of electronic resources.

IPS. Inches per second; a speed designation for tape recording.

IRC. International reply coupon, necessary for the return of materials sent out of the country. Available at most post offices.

JINGLE. Usually a short verse set to music designed as a commercial message.

LEAD SHEET. Written version (melody, chord symbols, and lyric) of a song.

LEADER. Plastic (non-recordable) tape at the beginning and between songs for ease in selection.

LIBRETTO. The text of an opera or any long choral work. The booklet containing such text.

LISTING. Block of information in this book about a specific company.

LP. Designation for long-playing record played at 33 1/3 rpm.

LYRIC SHEET. A typed or written copy of a song's lyrics.

MARKET. A potential song or music buyer; also a demographic division of the record-buying public.

MASTER. Edited and mixed tape used in the production of records; the best or original copy of a recording from which copies are made.

MD. MiniDisc. A 2.5-inch disk for recording and playing back digitally encoded music.

MECHANICAL RIGHT. The right to profit from the physical reproduction of a song.

MECHANICAL ROYALTY. Money earned from record, tape and CD sales.

MIDI. Musical instrument digital interface. Universal standard interface that allows musical instruments to communicate with each other and computers.

MINI DISC. (See MD above.)

MIX. To blend a multi-track recording into the desired balance of sound, usually to a 2-track stereo master.

MODEM. MOdulator/DEModulator. A computer device used to send data from one computer to another via telephone line.

MOR. Middle of the road. Easy-listening popular music.

MP3. File format of a relatively small size that stores audio files on a computer. Music saved in a MP3 format can be played only with a MP3 player (which can be downloaded onto a computer).

MS. Manuscript.

MULTIMEDIA. Computers and software capable of integrating text, sound, photographic-quality images, animation, and video.

MUSIC BED. (*see* Bed above.)

MUSIC JOBBER. A wholesale distributor of printed music.

MUSIC LIBRARY. A business that purchases canned music, which can then be bought by producers of radio and TV commercials, films, videos, and audiovisual productions to use however they wish.

MUSIC PUBLISHER. A company that evaluates songs for commercial potential, finds artists to record them, finds other uses (such as TV or film) for the songs, collects income generated by the songs, and protects copyrights from infringement.

MUSIC ROW. An area of Nashville, TN, encompassing Sixteenth, Seventeeth and Eighteenth avenues where most of the major publishing houses, recording studios, mastering labs, songwriters, singers, promoters, etc., practice their trade.

NARAS. National Academy of Recording Arts and Sciences.

THE NATIONAL ACADEMY OF SONGWRITERS (NAS). The largest U.S. songwriters' association. (See the "Organizations" section.)

NEEDLE-DROP. Refers to a type of music library. A needle-drop music library is a licensed library that allows producers to borrow music on a rate schedule. The price depends on how the music will be used.

NETWORK. A group of computers electronically linked to share information and resources.

NMPA. National Music Publishers Association.

ONE-OFF. A deal between songwriter and publisher that includes only one song or project at a time. No future involvement is implicated. Many times a single song contract accompanies a one-off deal.

ONE-STOP. A wholesale distributor of who sells small quantities of records to "mom and pop" record stores, retailers and jukebox operators.

OPERETTA. Light, humorous, satiric plot or poem, set to cheerful, light music with occasional spoken dialogue.

OVERDUB. To record an additional part (vocal or instrumental) onto a basic multi-track recording.

PARODY. A satirical imitation of a literary or musical work. Permission from the owner of the copyright is generally required before commercial exploitation of a parody.

PAYOLA. Dishonest payment to broadcasters in exchange for airplay.

PERFORMING RIGHTS. A specific right granted by U.S. copyright law protecting a composition from being publicly performed without the owner's permission.

PERFORMING RIGHTS ORGANIZATION. An organization that collects income from the public performance of songs written by its members and then proportionally distributes this income to the individual copyright holder based on the number of performances of each song.

PERSONAL MANAGER. A person who represents artists to develop and enhance their careers. Personal managers may negotiate contracts, hire and dismiss other agencies and personnel relating to the artist's career, review material, help with artist promotions, and perform many services.

PIRACY. The unauthorized reproduction and selling of printed or recorded music.

PITCH. To attempt to solicit interest for a song by audition.

PLAYLIST. List of songs a radio station will play.

POINTS. A negotiable percentage paid to producers and artists for records sold.

PRODUCER. Person who supervises every aspect of a recording project.

PRODUCTION COMPANY. Company specializing in producing jingle packages for advertising agencies. May also refer to companies specializing in audiovisual programs.

PROFESSIONAL MANAGER. Member of a music publisher's staff who screens submitted material and tries to get the company's catalog of songs recorded.

PROSCENIUM. Permanent architectural arch in a theater that separates the stage from the audience.

PUBLIC DOMAIN. Any composition with an expired, lapsed, or invalid copyright, and therefore belonging to everyone.

PURCHASE LICENSE. Fee paid for music used from a stock music library.

QUERY. A letter of inquiry to an industry professional soliciting his interest.

R&B. Rhythm and blues.

RACK JOBBER. Distributors who lease floor space from department stores and put in racks of albums.

RATE. The percentage of royalty as specified by contract.

RELEASE. Any record issued by a record company.

RESIDUALS. In advertising or television, payments to singers and musicians for use of a performance.

RIAA. Recording Industry Association of America.

ROYALTY. Percentage of money earned from the sale of records or use of a song.

RPM. Revolutions per minute. Refers to phonograph turntable speed.

SAE. Self-addressed envelope (with no postage attached).

SASE. Self-addressed stamped envelope.

SATB. The abbreviation for parts in choral music, meaning Soprano, Alto, Tenor, and Bass.

SCORE. A complete arrangement of all the notes and parts of a composition (vocal or instrumental) written out on staves. A full score, or orchestral score, depicts every orchestral part on a separate staff and is used by a conductor.

SELF-CONTAINED. A band or recording act that writes all their own material.

SESAC. A performing rights organization, originally the Society of European Stage Authors and Composers. (See the "Organizations" section.)

SFX. Sound effects.

SHOP. To pitch songs to a number of companies or publishers.

SINGLE. 45 rpm record with only one song per side. A 12£ single refers to a long version of one song on a 12£ disc, usually used for dance music.

SKA. Fast-tempo dance music influenced primarily by reggae and punk, usually featuring horns, saxophone, and bass.

SOCAN. Society of Composers, Authors and Music Publishers of Canada. A Canadian performing rights organization. (*see* the "Organizations" section.)

SOLICITED. Songs or materials that have been requested.

SONG PLUGGER. A songwriter representative whose main responsibility is promoting uncut songs to music publishers, record companies, artists, and producers.

SONG SHARK. Person who deals with songwriters deceptively for his own profit.

SOUNDSCAN. A company that collates the register tapes of reporting stores to track the actual number of albums sold at the retail level.

SOUNDTRACK. The audio, including music and narration, of a film, videotape, or audiovisual program.

SPACE STAGE. Open stage that features lighting and, perhaps, projected scenery.

SPLIT PUBLISHING. To divide publishing rights between two or more publishers.

STAFF SONGWRITER. A songwriter who has an exclusive agreement with a publisher.

STATUTORY ROYALTY RATE. The maximum payment for mechanical rights guaranteed by law that a record company may pay the songwriter and his publisher for each record or tape sold.

SUBPUBLISHING. Certain rights granted by a U.S. publisher to a foreign publisher in exchange for promoting the U.S. catalog in his territory.

SYNCHRONIZATION. Technique of timing a musical soundtrack to action on film or video.

TAKE. Either an attempt to record a vocal or instrument part, or an acceptable recording of a performance.

TEJANO. A musical form begun in the late 1970s by regional bands in south Texas, its style reflects a blended Mexican-American culture. Incorporates elements of rock, country, R&B, and jazz, and often features accordion and 12-string guitar.

THRUST STAGE. Stage with audience on three sides and a stagehouse or wall on the fourth side.

TOP 40. The first 40 songs on the pop music charts at any given time. Also refers to a style of music which emulates that heard on the current top 40.

TRACK. Divisions of a recording tape (e.g., 24-track tape) that can be individually recorded in the studio, then mixed into a finished master.

TRADES. Publications covering the music industry.

12-SINGLE. A 12-inch record containing one or more remixes of a song, originally intended for dance club play.

UNSOLICITED. Songs or materials that were not requested and are not expected.

VOCAL SCORE. An arrangement of vocal music detailing all vocal parts, and condensing all accompanying instrumental music into one piano part.

WEBSITE. An address on the World Wide Web that can be accessed by computer modem. It may contain text, graphics, and sound.

WING SPACE. The offstage area surrounding the playing stage in a theater, unseen by the audience, where sets and props are hidden, actors wait for cues, and stagehands prepare to chance sets.

WORLD MUSIC. A general music category that includes most musical forms originating outside the U.S. and Europe, including reggae and calypso. World music finds its roots primarily in the Caribbean, Latin America, Africa, and the South Pacific.

WORLD WIDE WEB (WWW). An Internet resource that utilizes hypertext to access information. It also supports formatted text, illustrations, and sounds, depending on the user's computer capabilities.

GENERAL INDEX

11/12 Lounge: Entertainment & Sports Bar 287

123 Pleasant Street 287

40 Watt Club 287

4AD 161

4th Avenue Tavern, The 297

A

A Major Sound Corporation 187

Abear Publishing 122

ABG's Bar 287

Academy of Country Music 258

Acadiana Symphony Orchestra 230

Ackerman, William 187

Ad Agency, The 219

ADR Studios 187

Advertel, Inc. 219

AGO Award in Organ Composition 247

AGO/ECS Publishing Award in Choral
    Composition 247

Air Tight Management 202

ALEA III International Composition Prize 247

Alert Music, Inc. 202

All Rock Music 122

Allegro Music 219

Allen Entertainment Development,
    Michael 202

Alley Katz 287

ALLRS Music Publishing Co. 187

Alpha Music Inc. 122

Alternative Tentacles 161

American Bands Management 202

American Boychoir, The 230

American Music Center, Inc. 258

American Opera Musical Theatre Co. 230

American Recordings 161

American Society of Composers, Authors and
    Publishers (ASCAP) 258

American Songwriter Lyric Contest 247

Andersen, Tim 188

Anderson Symphony Orchestra 230

Angel Records 161

Angelini Enterprises, Bill/BookYourEvent.com
    202

Annual NSAI Song Contest 248

Antelope Publishing Inc. 123

Apodaca Promotions Inc. 203

Appel Farm Arts and Music Festival 276

Appel Farm Arts and Music Festival 276

Ariana Records 161

Arizona Songwriters Association 259

Arkadia Entertainment Corp. 162

Arkansas Repertory Theatre 223

Armadillo's Bar & Grill 287

Art Bar 287

Art of Music Annual Writing Contest, The 253

Artist Representation and Management 203

ASCAP Deems Taylor Awards, The 253

ASCAP I Create Music Expo 276

ASCAP Musical Theatre Workshop 276

ASCAP West Coast/Lester Sill Songwriters Workshop 276

Ashland Coffee & Tea 287

Association des Professionel.le.s de la chanson et de la musique 259

Association of Independent Music Publishers 259

Astralwerks 162

Atlan-Dec/Grooveline Records 162

Atlanta Young Singers of Callanwolde, The 230

Atlantic Records 162

Audio 911 188

Augsburg Choir 231

Austin Songwriters Group 259

Avita Records 162

AWAL UK Limited 163

Aware Records 163

B

Back East Bar & Grill 288

BackBooth 288

Backstreet Booking 203

Baitstring Music 123

Baker's Plays 227

Baltimore Songwriters Association 259

Barkin' Foe the Master's Bone 123

Barley Street Tavern, The 297

Basse, Willie 188

Bearsongs 123

Beigel, Evan 188

Berkeley Cafe 288

Big Bear 188

Big Bear Records 163

Big Fish Music Publishing Group 124

Billings Symphony 231

Billy's Lounge 288

Birmingham-Bloomfield Symphony Orchestra 231

Bixio Music Group & Associates/IDM Music 125

Black Rock Coalition, The 260

Blackheart Records 163

Blank & Blank 204

Blank Theatre Company Young Playwrights Festival, The 254

Blowin' Smoke Productions/Records 204

Blue 288

Blue Cat Agency, The 204

Blue Door, The 297

Blues Alley Records 188

BMI-Lehman Engel Musical Theatre Workshop 276

Bo's Bar 288

Boston Philharmonic, The 231

Bottleneck, The 297

Bottletree 289

Bottom of the Hill 289

Bouquet-Orchid Publishing 125

Bourne Co. Music Publishers 125

Brandon Hills Music, LLC 125

Brass Rail, The 297

BRAVO! L.A. 232

Bread & Butter Productions 204

Brevard Music Center 285

Brewery, The 298

Brickyard, The 298

Broadcast Music, Inc. (BMI) 260

Broadway Tomorrow Previews 277

Brodsky, Cliff 189

Brooklyn Bowl 289

Brotherhood Lounge, The 298

Brothers Management Associates 204

Bug Music, Inc. 126

Bunkhouse Saloon, The 298

C

Cabin-on-the-Lake Music 189

Cactus Club, The 298

Cafe 939 289

Cafe Nine 289

Caledonia Lounge 289

Calgary Boys Choir 232

California Country Music 126

California Lawyers for the Arts 260

Cambria Records & Publishing 163

Canada Council for the Arts/
    Conseil des Arts du Canada 261

Canadian Academy of Recording Arts &
    Sciences (CARAS) 261

Canadian Country Music Association 261

Canadian Musical Reproduction Rights
    Agency Ltd. 261

Canadian Opera Company 232

Canopy Club, The 298

Cantata Academy 232

Cantilena Records 164

Capitol Records 164

Capones 289

CAPP Records 164

Carey University Dinner Theatre,
    William 223

Carmel Symphony Orchestra 233

Casselman's Bar & Venue 289

Cave, The 298

Cedar Crest Studio 219

Celt Musical Services, Jan 192

Central Carolina Songwriters Association
    (CCSA) 262

Central Oregon Songwriters Association 262

Chattanooga Girls Choir 233

Chelsea's Cafe 289

Cherry Street Records 164

Cheyenne Symphony Orchestra 233

Chilkoot Charlies 289

Christmas & Holiday Music 126

Chrome Horse Saloon 290

Chrysalis Music Group 126

Churchill's 290

Cimarron Circuit Opera Company 233

Circa '21 Dinner Playhouse 223

City Tavern 290

Class Act Productions/Management/Peter
    Kimmel's Music Catalog 205

Clousher Productions 205

Club 209 290

Club Congress 290

Clubhouse, The 298

CMJ Music Marathon & Film Festival 277

Coachouse Music 189

Collector Records 164

College Music Society, The 262

Columbia Records 165

Come Alive Communications, Inc. 127

Communications for Learning 219

Concept 2000 Inc. 206

Congress Theater 290

Connecticut Choral Artists/Concora 234

Connecticut Songwriters Association 262

Copperfield Music Group 127

Corazon 290

Corelli Music Group 127

Corne, Eric 189

Cornelius Companies/Gateway
    Entertainment, Inc., The 127

Cosmotone Records 165

Creative Improvised Music Projects
    (CIMP) Records 165

Creative Soul 189

Cringe Music (PRS, MCPS) 128

Crosswind Corporation, The 128

CRS National Composers Competition 248

Curb Music 128

Curb Records 166

Cutting Edge Music Business Conference 277

Cutty's 290

D

Dallas Songwriters Association 263

DAS Communications, Ltd. 206

Dave Music, Jof 128

D.B.A. 290

dbf A Media Company 220

DCA Productions 206

De Miles Music Company, The Edward 129

De Miles Music Company, The Edward 190

De Miles Music Company, The Edward 206

Deep South Entertainment 166

Define Something in Nothing Music 128

Delev Music Company 128

DeLory and Music Makers, Al 187

Dental Records 166

Desisto, Marc 190

Deva, Jeannie 190

Diamond Entertainment, Joel 190

Disk Productions 220

Disney Music Publishing 129

Divine Industries 207

Dogfish Bar & Grille, The 298

Double Door Inn, The 298

Doug Fir Lounge 290

Dramatists Guild of America, Inc., The 263

Drumbeat Indian Arts, Inc. 166

Duane Music, Inc. 129

Dudek, Les 190

Duffy's Tavern 290

Dunsdon Music Publishing 129

Duo Clasico 234

E

Earache Records 166

Earthscream Music Publishing Co. 129

Echo, The 298

Eckert Entertainment Consultants, John 207

El Bait Shop 291

Elbow Room 291

Electric Mule Publishing Company 130

Elektra Records 167

EMF Productions 130

EMI Christian Music Publishing 130

EMI Music Publishing 130

Empty Bottle, The 299

Empty Glass, The 299

Emstone Music Publishing 130

Epic Records 167

Epitaph Records 167

European International Competition for
    Composers/IBLA Music Foundation 248

European Union Chamber Orchestra 234

Evans Productions, Scott 213

Exit/In 291

Eyeball Records 167

F

Fat Catz Music Club 291

Fat Wreck Chords 167

Fatt Chantz Music 131

Fearless Records 167

Feldman & Associates & Macklam Feldman
    Management, S.L. 207

Fiedler Management, B.C. 203

Field, The 263

Final Mix Inc. 190

Fine Art Productions/Richie Suraci Pictures,
    Multimedia, Interactive 220

Fineline Music Cafe, The 299

Fink IV, Richard 191

Fireant 167

First Time Management 207

First Time Music (Publishing) U.K. 131

Five Spot 291

Flipnotics 291

Flying Heart Records 168

Folk Alliance Annual Conference 277

Fontana Concert Society 234

Fools Company, Inc. 224

Fort Worth Children's Opera 235

Fort Worth Songwriters Association 264

Freakin' Frog 291

Freight House District 291

Frequency, The 299

Fricon Music Company 132

Fueled By Ramen 168

G

Gainen, Maurice 191

Garcia, Brian 191

Garner, McKay 191

Garrett Entertainment, Marty 171

Gaul Composition Contest, Harvey 249

George's Majestic Lounge 291

Glad Music Co. 132

G Major Publishing 132

Golden Fleece Tavern, The 299

Good Publishing, L.J. 133

Goodnight Kiss Music 132

Gospel Music Association 264

Gotham Records 168

Gramophone, The 299

Grassy Hill Kerrville New Folk
    Competition 249

Great American Music Hall 291

Great American Song Contest 249

Great Northern Bar & Grill, The 299

Great Scott 292

Greater Grand Forks Symphony
    Orchestra 235

Green Lantern, The 299

Grillo, Carmen 191

Guild of International Songwriters &
    Composers, The 264

Gunpowder Lodge 292

Guthrie Centre, The Tyrone 285

H

Hacienda Records & Recording Studio 168

Hailing Frequency Music Productions 191

Hal & Mal's 292

Hambidge Center, The 285

Hammel Associates, Inc., R L 133

Hank's Cafe 292

Hardison International
    Entertainment Corporation 208

Haven, The 299

Headliners Music Hall 292

Heads Up Int., Ltd. 169

Heart Consort Music 191

Heart Music, Inc. 169

Heartland Men's Chorus 235

Helena Symphony 236

Hendersonville Symphony Orchestra 236

Hermann Sons German Band 236

Hershey Symphony Orchestra 237

Heuer Publishing Co. 227

Heupferd Musikverlag GmbH 133

Hickory Lane Publishing and Recording 133

Hideout, The 299

Highlands Tap Room 292

High-Noon Saloon 292

Hi-Tone Cafe 292

Hitsburgh Music Co. 134

Holley, Heather 192

Hollywood Reporter/Billboard Film & TV
  Music Conference 277

Holographic Recording Company 169

Home Town Hero's Publishing 134

Home, Inc. 220

Hot Tuna 292

Hottrax Records 169

Howler's Coyote Cafe 292

Hudson Valley Philharmonic 237

Humpy's 292

Hunter, Jimmy 192

I

IAMA (International Acoustic Music
  Awards) 134, 249

Idol Publishing 134

Idol Records 170

Illa, Simon 192

Independent Music Conference 277

Indiana University New Music Ensemble 237

Inside Records/OK Songs 134

Integrated Entertainment 192

International Bluegrass Music Association
  (IBMA) 265

International Entertainment Bureau 208

International Songwriters Association
  Ltd. 265

Interscope/Geffen/A&M Records 170

Intoxygene Sarl 135

Island Culture Music Publishers 135

Island/Def Jam Music Group 170

Isle Royale National Park Artist-in-Residence
  Program 285

Ivory Pen Entertainment 135

J

Jae Enterprises, Jana 208

Jae Music, Jana 135

Ja/Nein Musikverlag GmbH 135

Jeremiah Bullfrogs Live 292

Jerjoy Music 136

Jerome Productions 170

Jewish Mother, The 299

Jones Music, Quincy 136

Jost, Michael 192

J Records 170

Juanita's Party Room 293

Julian, Chris 192

Just Plain Folks 265

K

K&R All Media Productions LLC 221

Kalani Oceanside Retreat 285

Kane Producer/Engineer, Karen 193

Kaupps & Robert Publishing Co. 136

Kaysarah Music 137

Kelly, Tim David 193

Ken-Del Productions Inc. 221

Kentucky Opera 238

Kerrville Folk Festival 278

Kilby Court 293

Kill Rock Stars 170

King's Memphis, B.B. 288

King's Nashville, B.B. 288

Kinley Memorial Fellowship, Kate Neal 250

Knickerbockers 293

Knoxville Songwriters Association 266

Kuper Personal Management/Recovery
  Recordings 209

L

L.A. Designers' Theatre Music Awards 250

L.A. Entertainment, Inc. 193

La Jolla Playhouse 224

Lake Transfer Productions & Music 137

Lamarca American Variety Singers 238

Lamb's Retreat for Songwriters 278

Landmark Communications Group 171

Landmark Communications Group 193

Larimer Lounge 293

Lark Record Productions, Inc. 171

Lark Talent & Advertising 193

Las Vegas Songwriters Association, The 266

Launchpad 293

Leadbetters Tavern 293

Lennon Songwriting Contest, The John 254

Levy Management, Rick 211

Lexington Philharmonic Society 238

Lima Symphony Orchestra 238

Liquid Lounge 293

Lita Music 138

Loft, The 299

Loggins Promotion 209

Los Angeles Designers' Theatre 224

Los Angeles Music Network 266

Lost Leaf Bar & Gallery, The 299

Louisiana Songwriters Association 267

Lounge at Hotel Donaldson, The 300

Low Spirits 293

Luckey's Club Cigar Store 293

Luna, Bob 194

Lyric Opera of Chicago 239

M

M & T Waldoch Publishing, Inc. 138

Mac-Attack Productions 194

Mad Anthony Brewing Company 293

Magna Carta Records 171

Majestic Theatre 293

Majestic/Magic Stick, The 300

Makers Mark Gold 138

Malick, Peter 194

Management by Jaffe 209

Management Trust Ltd., The 214

Manchester Music Festival 278

Manitoba Music 267

Many Lives Music Publishers 139

Marshall, Guy 194

Martin Productions, Rick 209

Martin, Pete/Vaam Music Productions 195

Martin's Downtown Bar & Grill 293

Marvin Publishing, John Weller 139

Matador Records 172

Material Worth Publishing 139

Mathews, d/b/a Hit or Myth Productions Inc., Scott 196

Maui Arts & Music Association/Survivor Records/Ten of Diamonds Music 139

Maxwell's 293

Mazumdar New Play Competition, Maxim 250

MCA Nashville 172

McClure & Trowbridge Publishing, Ltd. 139

McCoy Music, Jim 140

McJames Music Inc. 140

Meet the Composer 267

Mega Truth Records 194

Megaforce Records 172

Melody Inn 293

Memphis On Main 293

Memphis Songwriters' Association 267

Mercury Lounge 294

Mercy Loung/Cannery Ballroom 294

Met, The 300

Metal Blade Records 172

Metoyer, Bill 194

Mid-Atlantic Song Contest 251

Midcoast, Inc. 210

Middle East Nightclub, The 300

MIDI Track Publishing 140

Miller Theatre 294

Milly's Tavern 294

Milwaukee Youth Symphony Orchestra 239

Minnesota Association of Songwriters 267

Mississippi Studios 294

Mitchell, Billy 194

Modal Music, Inc. 172

Mohawk Place, The 300

Mojo 13 294

Monk International Jazz Composers
    Competition, Thelonious 251

Monkey House, The 300

Moores Opera Center 239

Moseley, Adam 194

MOTR Pub 294

M Room, The 300

Muse Music Cafe 294

Music BC Industry Association 268

Music Business Solutions/Career Building
    Workshops 278

Music Hall at Capital Ale House, The 300

Music Room Publishing Group, The 141

Musicians Contact 268

MusicJones Records 195

Must Have Music 141

N

NACUSA Young Composers'
    Competition 251

Nashville Songwriters Association
    International 268

Natasha's Bistro & Bar 294

Nathan, Xavier 195

National Association of Composers/USA
    (NACUSA), The 273

National Underground, The 300

Nectar's 294

Nervous Publishing 141

Nervous Records 173

Nestico Award, Sammy/USAF Band Airmen
    of Note 252

Neu Electro Productions 195

Neumos 295

Neurodisc Records, Inc. 173

Neurolux 295

New Harmony Project, The 281

New Rap Jam Publishing, A 122

Newbraugh Brothers Music 142

Newcreature Music 142

Newport Folk Festival 279

Newport Jazz Festival 279

Nick Rocks, The 300

Nietzsche's 295

Norfolk Chamber Music Festival 279

North by Northeast Music Festival and
    Conference 279

North Shore Music Theatre 225

North Star Bar & Restaurant 295

North Star Music 173

Noteworthy Productions 210

Novus Communications 221

NSAI Song Camps 279

NSAI Songwriters SongPosium 280

O

Oglio Records 173

Old Rock House, The 301

Old Slowpoke Music 142

Olson, Carla 195

Omni Communications 221

On Stage Drinks & Grinds 295

One Trick Pony Grill & Taproom 295

Open Eye Theater, The 225

Opera America 268

Opera Memphis 239

Orchestra Seattle/Seattle Chamber
Singers 240

Orford Festival 280

Outmusic 269

Outstanding Records 173

P

Pacific Northwest Songwriters
Association 269

Palmetto Mastersingers 240

Panama Music Group of Companies, The 174

Paper + Plastick 174

Paradigm Talent Agency 210

Paradise Rock Club 295

Parliament Records 175

Peacock Productions, Deborah 206

Pearl at Commerce 295

PeerMusic 142

Pegasus Music 143

Perla Music 143

Peters Music, Justin 143

Phoebob Music 143

Piano Press 143

Piccolo Opera Company Inc. 240

PJ's Lager House 295

Platinum Planet Music, Inc. 144

Platinum Studios 195

Plough and Stars 295

Plush 295

Portage Music 144

Portland Songwriters Association 269

Positive Pie 296

Pour House, The 301

Primary Stages 225

Prime Time Entertainment 210

Prince Music Theater 225

Princeton Symphony Orchestra 240

Prism Saxophone Quartet 240

Pulitzer Prize in Music 252

Q

Qually & Company Inc. 221

QUARK, Inc. 144

Quarter, The 301

R

R Bar & Restaurant 296

Radical Records 175

Rainbow Music Corp. 144

Rainbow Talent Agency LLC 210

Ranco Music Publishing 145

Raspberry Jam Music 211

RAVE Records, Inc. 175

Rave/Eagles Club, The 301

Ray, Will 196

Razor & Tie Entertainment 145

RCA Records 175

Record Bar 296

Red Admiral Records, LLP 176

Red Onion Records 176

Red Square 296

Red Sundown Records 145

Reggae Sumfest 280

Reign Music and Media, LLC 211

Repertory Theatre of St. Louis, The 226

Reprise Records 176

Rhode Island Songwriters' Association 269

Rhythm & Brews 296

Rick's Bar 296

Riohcat Music 212

Rise Records 176

RN'D Distribution, LLC 196

Roadrunner Records 176

Robbins Entertainment LLC 176

Robert Entertainment 212

Rock Island Live 296

Rocky Mountain Folks Festival Songwriter Showcase 252

Rodgers Awards, Richard 252

Roll On Records 177

Rome Prize Competition Fellowship 252

Rondor Music International/Almo/Irving Music 145

Rosenberg, Todd 196

Rotten Records 177

Rough Trade Records 177

R.T.L. Music 145

Rustic Records 177

Rustic Records, Inc Publishing 145

Rustron Music Publishers/Whimsong Music 146

S

Sabteca Music Co. 146

Sacramento Master Singers 241

Sahara Records and Filmworks Entertainment 178

Salt Works Music 147

Sa'Mall Management 212

Sam Bonds Garage 296

San Diego Songwriters Guild 269

San Francisco Girls Chorus 241

Sandalphon Management 212

Sandalphon Music Publishing 147

Sandalphon Records 178

Santa Fe Sol 296

Satkowski Recordings, Steve 197

Saunders, Mark 196

Schubas Tavern 296

Serge Entertainment Group 213

SESAC Inc. 270

Shakespeare Santa Cruz 226

Shank Hall 296

Shawnee Press, Inc. 147

Shed, The 301

Siegel Entertainment Ltd. 213

Silicon Music Publishing Co. 147

Silver Blue Music/Oceans Blue Music 148

Silver Dollar 296

Silver Wave Records 178

Simply Grand Music Inc 178

Singing Boys of Pennsylvania 242

Sinus Musik Produktion, Ulli Weigel 148

Sizemore Music 148

Skeleton Crew 178

Skorman Productions, Inc., T. 213

Slowdown, The 301

Small Stone Records 179

SME Publishing Group 149

Smeltzer Productions, Gary 208

Smiling Moose, The 301

Smith's Old Bar 296

S.M.C.L. Productions, Inc. 148

Smog Veil Records 179

SOCAN (Society of Composers, Authors, and Music Publishers of Canada) 270

Society of Composers & Lyricists 270

SODRAC Inc. 270

Soli Deo Gloria Cantorum 242

Songwriters Association of Washington 271

Songwriters Guild of America Foundation, The 281

Songwriters Guild of America, The 271

Songwriters Hall of Fame (SongHall) 271

Songwriters of Wisconsin International 271

Songwriters Playground 280

Songwriters Resource Network 272

Sonic Unyon Records Canada 179

Sony BMG 179

Sony Music Nashville 179

Sony/ATV Music Publishing 149

Sound Arts Recording Studio 197

Sound Cellar Music 149

Sound Factory, The 301

South by Southwest Music Conference 280

Southeastern Attractions 214

Southgate House 297

Southwest Virginia Songwriters
 Association 272

Space, The 301

Spanish Moon, The 301

Spot Underground, The 301

St. John Artists 214

St. Louis Chamber Chorus 242

Stamey, Chris 197

Starkravin' Management 214

Station 4 297

Still Working Music Group 149

Strange Brew Tavern 297

Studio Seven 197

Succes 150

Sugar Hill Records 180

Sully's Pub 297

Supreme Enterprises Int'l Corp. 150

Susquehanna Symphony Orchestra 243

Swannanoa Gathering--Contemporary Folk
 Week, The 281

T

Tas Music Co./Dave Tasse Entertainment 214

T.C. Productions/Etude Publishing Co. 150

Telluride Troubadour Contest 253

Texas Accountants & Lawyers
 for the Arts 272

Texas Music Cafe 180

Texas Music Office 272

Texas Rose Records 180

Thistle Hill 150

Thunder Bay Theatre 226

Tiki Studios-O'Neal Productions 151

T.L.C. Booking Agency 214

Toad 302

Tobin, Randall Michael 198

Tommy Boy Entertainment LLC 180

Ton Records 180

Topcat Records 180

Toronto Mendelssohn Choir 243

Toronto Musicians' Association 273

Touch and Go/Quarterstick Records 181

Tough, Dave 198

Tourmaline Music, Inc. 151

Tower Music Group 151

Tractor Tavern 302

Transamerika Musikverlag KG 151

Transdreamer Records 181

Transition Music Corporation 152

Treehouse, The 301

Trio Productions, Inc./Songscape Music,
 LLC 152

Triple Crown 302

Triple Rock Social Club 302

Triple Rock Social Club, The 301

Trocadero 303

Troubadour 303

Turf Club 303

U

UAR Records 181

Undercurrents 281

Underground 119 303

Underground, The 301

Union Pool 303

Universal Motown Records 182

Universal Music Marketing 215

Universal Music Publishing 152

Unknown Source Music 152

Urban Lounge 303

U.S.A. Songwriting Competition 254

U.S.-Japan Creative Artists Exchange Fellowship Program 254

Utopian Empire Creativeworks 221

V

Vaam Music Group 152

Vagabond, The 302

Vagrant Recprds 182

Vancouver Chamber Choir 243

Vancouver Youth Symphony Orchestra Society 243

Vaudeville Mews 303

Verve Music Group, The 182

Victory Records 182

Video I-D, Teleproductions 222

Vine Creek Music 153

Virgin Music Group 182

Virginia Center for the Creative Arts 286

Virginia Opera 244

Visulite Theatre, The 302

Vollrath Tavern, The 302

Volunteer Lawyers for the Arts 273

Vorndick, Bil 198

W

Wagner, Dick 198

Walkerbout Music Group 153

Warehouse Creek Recording Corp. 182

Warner Bros. Records 183

Warner Productions, Cheryl K. 205

Warner/Chappell Music, Inc. 153

Washington Area Music Association 273

Waterbury, Dave 198

Waterdog Music 183

Weaver of Words Music 153

Webster Underground, The 302

Wengert, Berthold (Musikverlag) 153

West Coast Songwriters 274

West Coast Songwriters Conference 282

West End Artists 226

Western Wind Workshop in Ensemble Singing 282

Westwires Recording USA 198

Wheaton Symphony Orchestra 244

Whiskey Bar 303

Whisky A Go-Go 303

White Mule, The 302

White Room Miami 303

White Water Tavern 304

Wilcom Publishing 153

Wild Willy's Rock House & Sports Saloon 304

Winchester Records 183

Winchester, The 302

Wind-Up Entertainment 183

Winter Music Conference Inc. 282

WLM Music/Recording 198

Woodlands Tavern 304

Woodrum, Michael 198

World Beatnik Records 184

World Records 199

WorldSound, LLC 215

Wormy Dog Saloon 304

X

Xemu Records 184

XL Recordings 184

Y

Y.E.S. Festival of New Plays 255

Young Avenue Deli 304

Z

Zane Management, Inc. 215

Zig Productions 199

Zomba Music Publishing 154

Zonana, Saul 199

NAMES INDEX

A

Ackerman, William 187

Abrahamsen, Daniel (DCA Productions) 206

Abrahamsen, Geraldine (DCA Productions) 206

Adams, Sheelah (RustRon Music Publishers/ Whimsong Music) 146

Allen, Dalis (Grassy Hill Kerriville New Folk Competition) 249

Allen, Dalis (Kerrville Folk Festival) 278

Allen, Michael (Michael Allen Entertainment Development) 202

Allyn, Stuart J. (ADR Studios) 187

Almodovar, Diane J. (Broadcast Music, Inc. (BMI)) 260

Ambach, Dahlia (The Verve Music Group) 182

Andersen, Tim 188

Anderson Jr., Bill (NewCreature Music) 142

Anderson Jr., Bill (Landmark Communications Group) 171, 193

Anderson, Roger (Artist Representation and Management) 203

Angelini, Bill (Bill Angelini Enterprises/ BookYourEvent.com) 202

Ansems, Tony (Songwriters of Wisconsin International) 271

Anthony, Debra (Hendersonville Symphony) 236

Antoine, Tina (Lake Transfer Productions & Music) 137

Arble, Stephanie (John Weller Marvin Publishing) 139

Armintrout, Mike (The Canopy Club) 298

Asada, Hiroshi (South by Southwest Music Conference) 281

Ashley, Christopher (La Jolla Playhouse) 224

Ashman, Christopher (Cringe Music) 128

Ashman, Chris (Red Admiral Records LLP) 176

Austin, Darlene (Vine Creek Music) 153

Axford, Elizabeth C. (Piano Press) 143

Axford, Elizabeth C. (The Art of Music Annual Writing Contest) 253

B

Bair, Sheldon (Susquehanna Symphony Orchestra) 243

Baker, Brian (EarthScream Music Publishing Co.) 129

Bakshi, Brandon (Broadcast Music, Inc. (BMI)) 260

Banks, Jean (BMI-Lehman Engel Musical Theatre Workshop) 276

Baptiste, Eric (SOCAN) 270

Bare, Jon (Mega Truth Records) 194

Barkan, Jonathan L. (Communications For Learning) 219

Barnes, Philip (St. Louis Chamber Chorus) 242

Barrera, Domingo A. (Apodaca Promotions Inc.) 203

Barricelli, Marco (Shakespeare Santa Cruz) 226

Barr, Shonda (Barkin' Foe the Master's Bone) 123

Bartling, Tab (Heart Music, Inc.) 169

Baxendale, Nancy (Texas Rose Records) 180

Baylock, Alan (Sammy Nestico Award/USAF Band Airmen of Note) 252

Beard, Billy (Toad) 302

Beasley, Phillip (Memphis Songwriters' Association) 267

Beck, Crafton (Lima Symphony Orchestra) 238

Becker, Wayne (Westwires Recording USA) 198

Beecher, Earl (Outstanding Records) 173

Beiderman, David (Silver Dollar) 296

Beigel, Evan 188

Bell, Claudia (Connecticut Choral Artists/ Concora) 234

Benson, Madge (Fricon Music Company) 132

Beran, Paul (Advertel, Inc.) 219

Berger, Linda (Just Plain Folks Music Organization) 265

Berkey, Almeda (Soli Deo Gloria Cantorum) 242

Berry, Clyde (Fort Worth Children's Opera) 235

Berry, Melanie (Canadian Academy of Recording Arts & Sciences (CARAS)) 261

Berry, W. Tom (Alert Music Inc.) 202

Biafra, Jello (Alternative Tentacles) 161

Biddy, Ken (Copperfield Music Group/

Penny Annie Music/Top Brass Music/ Biddy Baby Music) 127

Bilhartz, Herbery (Hermann Sons German Band) 236

Binkley, Phoebe (Phoebob Music) 143

Biros, Jim (Toronto Musicians' Association) 273

Bishop, Eddie (Tower Music Group) 151

Black, Gary (Big Fish Music Publishing Group) 124

Black, Zell (Big Fish Music Publishing Group) 124

Blakeman, Jennifer (Zomba Music Publishing) 154

Blanchette, Kevin (The Spot Underground) 301

Bland, Antony (American Recordings) 161

Blank, E. Robert (Blank & Blank) 204

Blomstrom, John (American Bands Management) 202

Blust, Greg (Isle Royale National Park Artist-in-Residence Program) 285

Bohannon, Bill (Bouquet-Orchid Publishing) 125

Bolin, Bruce (Kaupps & Robert Publishing Co.) 137

Bolster, Jane (Richard Rodgers Awards) 252

Bossert, Bruce Andrew (Midcoast, Inc.) 210

Bossy, Michelle (Primary Stages) 225

Bowling, Lance (Cambria Records & Publishing) 163

Brabec, Jeffery (Music, Money and Success: The Insider's Guide to the Music Industry) 315

Brabec, Todd (American Society of Composers, Authors and Publishers (ASCAP)) 258

Brabec, Todd (Music, Money and Success: The Insider's Guide to the Music Industry) 315

Braheny, John (The Craft and Business of Songwriting) 314

Brandon, Jessica (IAMA) 249

Brauer, Tina (Augsburg Choir) 231

Brewton, Catherine (Broadcast Music, Inc. (BMI)) 260

Brincat, Edgar J. (California Country Music) 126

Brincat, Edgar J. (Roll On Records) 177

Britt, Dave (The White Mule) 302

Brockway, Amie (The Open Eye Theater) 225

Brodsky, Cliff 189

Brown, Joyce (Knoxville Songwriters Association) 266

Brown, Leonard (Thelonious Monk International Jazz Composers Competition) 251

Brown, Marsha (Brandon Hills Music, LLC.) 125

Brown, Tanya (Zomba Music Publishing) 154

Bruton, John (Mercy Lounge/Cannery Ballroom) 294

Bryant, Del R. (Broadcast Music, Inc. (BMI)) 260

Buchart, Manus (Capp Records) 164

Buckley, Suzanne (Raspberry Jam Music) 211

Budney, Alex (Nectar's) 295

Burdell, George (HotTrax Records) 169

Busby, Rick (Austin Songwriters Group) 259

Butterfield, Carole (Fort Worth Songwriters Association) 264

Byrd, Cheryl (American Bands Management) 202

C

Cager, Eric L. (Cutting Edge Music Business Conference) 277

Cahill, Steve (Songwriters Resource Network) 272

Calhoun, Harold (AGO Award in Organ Composition) 247

Calhour Harold, (AGO/ECS Publishing Award in Choral Composition) 247

Callazzo, Missi (Megaforce Records) 172

Camillo, Tony (T.C. Productions/Etude Publishing Co.) 150

Cane, Barbara (Broadcast Music, Inc. (BMI) 260

Caputo, Greg (Transdreamer Records) 181

Caraveo, Tato (The Lost Leaf Bar & Gallery) 300

Carbone, Bruce (Universal Motown Records) 182

Carbone, Nicole (Hollywood Reporter/ Billboard Film & TV Music Conference) 277

Carik, Meghan (Rick's Bar) 296

Carotenuto, Henry (ALLRS Music Publishing Co.) 187

Caruso, Ron (RustRon Music Publishers/ Whimsong Music) 146

Catanese, Susan (Cantata Academy) 232

Celt, Jan (Flying Heart Records) 168

Celt, Jan (Jan Celt Musical Services) 192

Chalk, Richard (TopCat Records) 181

Chin, Deanne E. (Norfolk Chamber Music Festival) 279

Choate, Terry (The Crosswind Corporation) 128

Chugg, Andrew (Virginia Opera) 244

Clark, Rich (John Eckert Entertainment Consultants) 207

Clark, William (Wilcom Publishing) 153

Clousher, Fred (Clousher Productions) 205

Coffey, Richard (Connecticut Choral Artists/ Concora) 234

Cohen, Steve Barri (Lake Transfer Productions & Music) 137

Cole, Roger (Vancouver Youth Symphony Orchestra Society) 243

Collins, Pat (SESAC, Inc.) 270

Colon, Wandaliz (Ivory Pen Entertainment) 135

Conners, Jack (World Records) 199

Cook, H.R. (Weaver of Words Music) 153

Cooper, Nick (EarthScream Music Publishing Co.) 129

Copeland, Eric (Creative Soul) 189

Copenhaver, Dave (Studio Seven) 197

Copple, Chris (Flipnotics) 291

Coquoz, Gary (St. John Artists) 214

Corbin, Paul (Broadcast Music, Inc. (BMI)) 260

Corelli, Jerry (Corelli Music Group) 127

Corne, Eric 189

Cornelius, Ron (The Cornelius Companies/ Gateway Entertainment, Inc.) 127

Cox, Amy (Deep South Entertainment) 166

Crabtree, Jill (International Bluegrass Music Association (IBMA)) 265

Crombie, Ian (West Coast Songwriters) 274

Crombie, Ian (West Coast Songwriters Conference) 282

Crowne, Brian (George's Majestic Lounge) 291

Culhane, Sandra (Billings Symphony) 231

Curtis, Elyse (Broadway Tomorrow Previews) 277

Curtis, Kevin (Barkin' Foe the Master's Bone) 123

Cuttino, Walter (Palmetto Mastersingers) 240

D

Dackow, Dr. Sandra (Hershey Symphony Orchestra) 237

Daily, Wes (Glad Music Co.) 132

Daley, Dan (Nashville's Unwritten Rules: Inside the Business of the Country Music Machine) 316

Danielson, Brad (The FineLine Music Café)

D'Arduini, Matt (Robbins Entertainment LLC) 176

Davidson, Micah (The Double Door Inn) 298

Davis, Allen (Carmel Symphony Orchestra) 233

Davis, LaRonda (The Black Rock Coalition) 260

Davis, Sheila (The Craft of Lyric Writing) 317

Davis, Sheila (The Songwriters Idea Book) 317

Davis, Sheila (Successful Lyric Writing) 314

Davis, Tina Mae (Reggae Sumfest) 280

Dawson, Jeremy (McJames Music Inc.) 140

Dawson, Mary (How to Get Somewhere in the Music Business From Nowhere with Nothing) 315

Decker, Joey (Disk Productions) 220

DeLory, Al (Al DeLory and Music Makers) 187

De Miles, Edward (Sahara Records and Filmworks Entertainment) 178

De Miles, Edward (The Edward De Miles Music Company) 190, 206

Denkins, A. Celina (Whisky A Go-Go) 303

Desisto, Marc 190

Dethmers, Cathy (High-Noon Saloon) 292

Deva, Jeannie 190

Devlin, Shannon (The College Music Society) 262

Diamond, Joel (Joel Diamond Entertainment) 190

Diamond, Joel (Silver Blue Music/Oceans Blue Music) 148

Dickens, Tony (Central Carolina Songwriters Association (CCSA)) 262

Dickson, Ron (R.T.L. Music) 145

Dillon, Jeff (The Double Door Inn) 298

DiMatteo, Panfilo (Ranco Music Publishing) 145

Dobson, Reggie (Mercury Lounge) 294

Doehrer, Terran (Modal Music, Inc.) 172

Dostal, Mary (Ja/Nein Musikverlag GMBH) 135

Douglas, Jim (Prime Time Entertainment) 210

Dowdall, James (Warner Bros. Records) 183

Downey, Ramona (Bottom of the Hill) 289

Draghi, Robert (Bixio Music Group & Associates/IDM Music) 125

Drakoulias, George (American Recordings)

161

Dreyer, Mark (Nashville Music Business
Directory) 316

Dudek, Les 190

Duffy, Lee (Austin Songwriters Group) 259

Dunsdon, Ian (Dunsdon Music Publishing)
129

Dzubay, David (Indiana University New
Music Ensemble) 237

E

Ealy, Jonathan (Opera Memphis) 239

Eckert, John (John Eckert Entertainment
Consultants) 207

Edwards, Roy (BaitString Music) 123

Elliott, Jeff (Salt Works Music) 147

Ellison, Bill (Underground 119) 303

Ervin, Jim (L.A. Entertainment, Inc.) 193

Esra, Ritch (The A&R Registry) 314

Esra, Ritch (Music Attorney Legal & Business
Affairs Registry) 315

Esra, Ritch (The Music Business Registry) 315

Esra, Ritch (The Music Publisher Registry) 316

Evans, Karlene (Bixio Music Group &
Associates/IDM Music) 125

Ezzell, Mary (Scott Mathews, D/B/A Hit or
Myth Productions Inc.) 196

F

Fateley, Rob (Jeremiah Bullfrogs Live) 293

Faucera, Allen A. (Brothers Management
Associates) 204

Faye, Lisa (Big Fish Music Publishing
Group) 124

Fehribach, Barbara (Hudson Valley
Philharmonic) 237

Feigelson, Danzyl (Awal UK Limited) 163

Fein, Seth (The Canopy Club) 298

Feldman, Charlie (Broadcast Music, Inc.
(BMI)) 260

Felts, Randy (Reharmonization Techniques) 317

Fielder, B.C. (B.C. Fielder Management) 203

Fink IV, Richard 191

Fisher, Janet (Goodnight Kiss Music) 132

Fishman, Shirley (La Jolla Playhouse) 224

Fletcher, Russell (BearSongs) 123

Forchette, Jack (Air Tight Management) 202

Forman, Sandra (Y.E.S. Festival of New
Plays) 255

Fountain, Dave (Capones) 289

Fox, Keith (The Bunkhouse Saloon) 298

Foy, Janice (Bravo! L.A.) 232

Franklin, Nathaniel (Cutting Edge Music
Business Conference) 277

Frank, Theresa (Final Mix Inc.) 190

Freeman, Michael (Coachouse Music) 189

Fruge, Ed (EMF Productions) 130

G

Gainen, Maurice 191

Garcia, Brian 191

Garcia, Rick (Hacienda Records & Recording
Studio) 168

Garcia, Roland (Hacienda Records &
Recording Studio) 168

Garner, McKay 191

Garrett, Marty R. (How You Can Break Into
the Music Business) 315

Garrett, Marty R. (Marty Garrett
Entertainment) 171

Gates, Byron (RN'D Distribution, LLC) 196

Gilbert, Harold (Hitsburg Music Co.) 134

Gillette, Steve (Songwriting and the Creative
Process) 317

Gilpin, Greg (Shawnee Press, Inc.) 147

Gladson, Steve (Bread & Butter
Productions) 204

Glaza, Ken (K&R All Media Productions
LLC) 221

Glenn, Melissa (Kaupps & Robert Publishing
Co.) 136

Glover, McShane (Noteworthy Productions) 210

Gold, Jake (The Management Trust, Ltd.) 214

Gomez, Eddie (Bug Music, Inc.) 126

Good, Lonnie (L.J. Good Publishing) 133

Gordon, Marjorie (Piccolo Opera Company Inc.) 240

Gordon, Rusty (RustRon Music Publishers/ Whimsong Music) 146

Gosselin, Paul T. (Opera America) 268

Graham, Phillip (Broadcast Music, Inc. (BMI)) 260

Greenwell, Charles (Birmingham-Bloomfield Symphony Orchestra) 231

Grillo, Carmen 191

Grindlay, Paul (Calgary Boys Choir) 232

Grynheim, Joel (The New Harmony Project) 281

Guha, R.J. (The Management Trust, Ltd.) 214

Gurewitz, Brett (Epitaph Records) 167

Gutberlet, Ken (Baltimore Songwriters Association) 259

Guthrie, Mary (Dallas Songwriters Association) 263

H

Hagelstein, Aubin (Texas Music Café) 180

Hahn, Sam (Luckey's Club Cigar Store) 293

Hamilton, Ken (Hawai'i State Foundation on Culture & the Arts) 306

Hamilton, Scott (Small Stone Records) 179

Hammel, Randal L. (RL Hammel Associates, Inc.) 133

Hammett, Ollie (Mark Saunders) 196

Hanlon, Jerry (Jerjoy Music) 136

Hanlon, Jerry (UAR Records) 181

Hanlon, Jerry (KaySarah Music) 137

Hanney, Bill (North Shore Music Theatre) 225

Hardison, Dennis K. (Hardison International Entertainment Corporation) 208

Hardison, Travis J. (Hardison International Entertainment Corporation) 208

Harner, Bud (The Verve Music Group) 182

Harrelson, Darryl (Big Fish Music Publishing Group) 124

Harris, Alex (The Pour House) 301

Hartwell, M'Lynn (Utopian Empire Creativeworks) 222

Hatch, Colin (Muse Music Café) 294

Hawkins, Cynthia (Toronto Mendelssohn Choir) 243

Heath, Mike (Songwriters of Wisconsin International) 271

Hebert, Ron (A Bear Publishing/SongTown Publishing) 122

Hendrickson, Peter A. (Augsburg Choir) 231

Herman, Lew (Fireant) 168

Herring, Duane (Sabteca Music Co.) 146

Herring, Romare (Sabteca Music Co.) 146

Herzig, Bill (Zig Productions) 199

Hilton, Paul (Platinum Studios) 195

Hines, Bo (Bo's Bar) 288

Holiday, David-Joe (The FineLine Music Café) 299

Holley, Heather 192

Hollingsworth, Kirk (Five Spot) 291

Holvay, Jim (Lake Transfer Productions & Music) 137

Hooker, Joseph L. (Come Alive Communications, Inc.) 127

Hoover, Alex (G Major Publishing) 132

Hopkins, Paul (Makers Mark Gold) 138

Horse, Dylan (Landmark Communications Group) 171

Hughes, Ralph (Sacramento Master Singers) 241

Hunter, Jimmy 192

Hupp, Robert (Arkansas Repertory Theatre) 223

Hyatt, Justin (Muse Music Café) 294

Hylak, Bridget G. (Come Alive Communications, Inc.) 127

Hyle, Bradley (Red Square) 296

I

Indrisano, Jack (Café 939) 289

Iger, Jon (Arizona Songwriters Association) 259

Illa, Simon 192

Irvine, James (Larimer Lounge) 293

Iva, Michael (Qually & Company, Inc.) 221

J

Jacobs, Joy (R Bar & Restaurant) 296

Jae, Jana (Lark Talent & Advertising) 193

Jaffe, Jerry (Management by Jaffe) 209

James, Tim (McJames Music Inc.) 140

Jammes, Patrick (Intoxygene Sarl) 135

Jerome, Bill (Fatt Chantz Music) 131

Jerome, Bill (Jerome Productions) 170

John, Robert (Megaforce Records) 172

John, Robert (Transdreamer Records) 181

Johnson, David (Jof Dave Music) 128

Johnson, Greg (The Blue Door) 297

Johnson, James (Unknown Source Music) 152

Johnson, Kyle (The Music Hall at Capital Ale House) 300

Johnson, Raette (BMI-Lehman Engel Musical Theatre Workshop) 277

Johnston, Una (South by Southwest Music Conference) 281

Jones, Andi (Rotten Records) 177

Jones, Michael E. (Music Jones Records) 195

Jones, Paul (Rough Trade Records) 177

Jones, Quincy (Quincy Jones Music) 136

Jones, Roderick G. (First Time Management) 207

Jones, Roderick G. (First Time Music Publishing UK) 131

Jones, Roderick G. (The Panama Music Group of Companies) 174

Jones, Ted (Scott Evans Productions) 213

Joos, Todd (Sound Cellar Music) 149

Jordan, Barbara (Songwriters Playground) 280

Jordan, Barbara (Songwriter's Playground— Innovative Exercises in Creative Songwriting) 317

Josefs, Jai (Writing Music For Hit Songs) 318

Jost, Michael 192

Julian, Chris 192

K

Kachulis, Jimmy (The Songwriter's Workshop: Harmony) 317

Kachulis, Jimmy (The Songwritr's Workshop: Melody) 317

Kaminsky, Pia (Transamerika Musikverlag KG) 151

Kane, Karen (Karen Kane Producer/ Engineer) 193

Karwelis, Erv (Idol Publishing) 134

Kayne, Robert (Avita Records) 162

Kayne, Robert (Riohcat Music) 212

Kelly, Tim David 193

Kennedy, Edwin (Ken-Del Productions Inc.) 221

Kerker, Michael A. (ASCAP Music Theatre Workshop) 276

Kerry, Kris (Plush) 295

Kessner, Daniel (NACUSA Young Composers' Competition) 250

Kessner, Daniel (The National Association of Composers/USA (NACUSA)) 273

Ketchum, Bob (Cedar Crest Studio) 219

Kickham, Maureen (Birmingham-Bloomfield Symphony Orchestra) 231

Kiersky, Jonathan (Hi-Tone Café) 292

Kimmel, Peter (Class Act Productions/ Management/Peter Kimmel's Music Catalog) 205

Kinard, Sharon (SME Publishing Group) 149

Kindig, Karen (The Blue Cat Agency) 204

King, Kim (The FineLine Music Café) 299

King, Matt (Mississippi Studios) 294

Kinley, Kate Neal (Kate Neal Kinley Memorial Fellowship) 250

Klar, Kenneth R. (Must Have Music) 141

Klop, Cees (All Rock Music) 122

Klop, Cees (Collector Records) 165

Knauss, Nicole (Chattanooga Girls Choir) 233

Knight, Larry (Blowin' Smoke Productions/ Records) 204

Knight, Larry (Hailing Frequency Music Productions) 191

Knought, Brenna (Canadian Academy of Recording Arts & Sciences (CARAS)) 261

Knowles, Dorothy (Brevard Music Center) 285

Koob, Richard (Kalani Oceanside Retreat) 285

Krebs, Margitta (Vancouver Youth Symphony Orchestra Society) 243

Krueger, Jenny (Acadiana Symphony Orchestra) 230

Kuper, Koop (Kuper Personal Management/ Recovery Recordings) 209

L

Labate, Carl (Rainbow Talent Agency LLC) 211

LaMarca-Kandell, Priscilla (LaMarca American Variety Singers) 238

Lamb, John D. (Lamb's Retreat for Songwriters) 278

LaPole, Larry (Portage Music) 144

Lapsansky, Carrie (T.L.C. Booking Agency) 214

Lapsansky, Tom (T.L.C. Booking Agency) 214

Lathrop, Tad (The Business of Music Marketing and Promotion) 318

Latimer, John (Undercurrents) 281

Latterman, Gregg (Aware Records) 163

Lauzon, Alain (SODRAC Inc.) 270

Lavin, Carl (Great Scott) 292

LaVorgna, Tony (Antelope Publishing Inc.) 123

Lawhon, Ryan (McJames Music Inc.) 140

Lawson, Catherine (Heart Consort Music) 191

Lee, Tanya (R.T.L. Music) 145

Lee, Xavier (R.T.L. Music) 145

LeFort, Christian (S.M.C.L. Productions, Inc.) 148

LeMatt, Katrine (R.T.L. Music) 145

Levy, Matthew (Prism Saxophone Quartet) 240

Levy, Rick (Rick Levy Managament) 211

Lewis, Sonya (Ivory Pen Entertainment) 135

Lewis, Steven (Ivory Pen Entertainment) 135

Lewis, Tiana (The John Lennon Songwriting Contest) 254

Lily, Leatrice (Helena Symphony) 236

LoFrumento, John (American Society of Composers, Authors and Publishers (ASCAP)) 258

Loggins, Paul (Loggins Promotion) 209

Long, S.M. (Omni Communications) 221

Long, W.H. (Omni Communications) 221

Love, Dave (Head Up Int., Ltd.) 169

Love, Pasha (Neurodisc Records, Inc.) 173

Lovett, Kim E. (Cheyenne Symphony Orchestra) 233

Luboff, Pat (101 Songwriting Wrongs & How to Right Them) 314

Luboff, Pete (101 Songwriting Wrongs & How to Right Them) 314

Lucas, Darryl (Delev Music Company) 128

Lucas, William L. (Delev Music Company) 128

Lucchesi, Linda (Simply Grand Music Inc.) 178

Luekens, Tom (Scott Mathews, D/B/A Hit or Myth Productions, Inc.) 196

Luna, Bob 194

M

Mackie, Michael (Canadian Musical Reproduction Rights Agency Ltd.) 261

Madden, Brenda (Vine Creek Music) 153

Magill, Jim (The Swannanoa Gathering-

Contemporary Folk Week) 281

Magnum, Watts Lee (WLM Music/ Recording) 198

Malick, Peter 194

Malvar-Ruiz, Fernando (The American Boychoir) 230

Marienthal, James (Silver Wave Records) 178

Marshall, Guy 194

Marth, Tommy (Freakin' Frog) 291

Martin, Joseph M. (Shawnee Press, Inc.) 147

Martin, Pete (Vaam Music Group) 152, 195

Martin, Rick (Rick Martin Productions) 209

Massaro, Paul (Schubas Tavern) 296

Mathews, Scott (Scott Mathews, D/B/A Hit or Myth Productions Inc.) 196

Mathis, Paige F. (The Atlanta Young Signers of Callanwolde) 230

Mattison, Don (Wheaton Symphony Orchestra) 244

Mauceri, Frank (Smog Veil Records) 179

Mayer, Paul (Café Nine) 289

Maynard, Travis (The White Mule) 302

Mazur, Wendy (Zig Productions) 199

McCabe, Meghan (Canadian Academy of Recording Arts & Sciences (CARAS)) 261

McCarty, Rick (Southgate House) 297

McClean, Andy (North by Northeast Music Festival and Conference) 279

McClintock, Cathy-Anne (McJames Music Inc.) 140

McClintock, Steven (McJames Music Inc.) 140

McClure, George (McClure & Trowbridge Publishing, Ltd.) 140

McCoy, Bertha (Jim McCoy Music) 140

McCoy, Bertha (Winchester Records) 183

McCoy, Jim (Jim McCoy Music) 140

McCoy, Jim (Winchester Records) 183

McDonald, Bob (ALLRS Music Publishing Co.) 187

McLane, B.C. (Starkravin' Management) 214

McMane, Susan (San Francisco Girls Chorus) 241

McNamee, Michael (Mac-Attack Productions) 194

Mechutan, Bryan (Radical Records) 175

Medill, Laurie (Orchestra Seattle/Seattle Chamber Singers) 240

Meeusen, Jean (Inside Records/OK Songs) 134

Meredith, Diedre (OUTMUSIC) 269

Merrihew, Nancy L. (Kaupps & Robert Publishing Co.) 136

Metoyer, Bill 194

Meyers, Louis (Folk Alliance Annual Conference) 277

Michel, Alan (Home, Inc.) 220

Migliorelli, Leslie (ALLRS Music Publishing Co.) 187

Migliorelli, Leslie (Midi Track Publishing) 140

Mihori, Margaret (U.S.-Japan Creative Artists Exchange Fellowship Program) 254

Miksche, James (Cabin-on-the-Lake Music) 189

Milanov, Rossen (Princeton Symphony Orchestra) 240

Miller, Ambrose (Eurpoean Union Chamber Orchestra) 234

Miller, Arden (Thistle Hill) 150

Miller, Betty Kay (The Las Vegas Songwriters Association) 266

Miller, James (Sound Cellar Music) 149

Milligan, James (A New Rap Jam Publishing) 122

Mills, Brandi (Canadian Country Music Association) 261

Milne, Mark (Sonic Unyon Records Canada) 179

Milner, Paul C. (Many Lives Music Publishers) 139

Milner, Paul C. (A Major Sound Corporation) 187

Minardi, Johnny (Fueled by Ramen) 168

Mischke, Andrew (Mercy Lounge/
Cannery Ballroom) 294

Mitchell, Billy 194

Moltisanti, Dr. Salvatore (European
International Competition for Composers/
IBLA Foundation) 248

Monahan, Casey (Texas Music Office) 272

Mondor, Christian (Canada Council for the
Arts) 261

Monk, Suny (Virginia Center for the Creative
Arts) 286

Monsanto Jr., Liston (Island Culture Music
Publishers) 135

Morgan, Buck (Dallas Songwriters
Association) 263

Morgan, Mike (Salt Works Music) 147

Morticelli, Pete (Magna Carta Records) 171

Moseley, Adam 194

Moseley, Jeff (Electric Mule Publishing
Company/Neon Mule Music) 130

Moy, Allen (Divine Industries) 207

Mullet, Jim (Omni Communications) 221

N

Nadeau, Joseph (Heartland Men's Chorus) 235

Nathan, Xavier 195

Neef, Alexander (Canadian Opera Company)
232

Negri, Jayne (Vine Creek Music) 153

Neumann, Bob (Neu Electro Productions) 195

Nevue, David (How to Promote Your Music
Successfully on the Internet) 315

Newbraugh, John S. (Newbraugh Brothers
Music) 142

Newtown, Ashley (RCA Records) 175

Neysmith, Claudene (Bixio Music Group &
Associates/IDM Music) 125

Niederberg, Richard (L.A. Designers' Theatre
Music Awards) 250

Niederberg, Richard (Los Angeles Designers'
Theatre) 224

Nolen, Dan (Smith's Olde Bar) 296

Nolen, Dan (The Nick Rocks) 300

Noone, Rose (Epic Records) 167

Nurko, Michael (Alpha Music Inc.) 122

Nuss, Bob (Drumbeat Indian Arts, Inc.) 166

Nytch, Jeffrey (Harvey Gaul Composition
Contest) 249

O

O'Brien, Daniel (Allegro Music) 219

O'Hara, Billy (Big Fish Music Publishing
Group) 124

Ojalvo, Jason (Disc Makers) 314

O'Keefe, Tom (Neurodisc Records, Inc.) 173

Oland, Pamela Phillips (McJames Music Inc.)
140

Oliva, Michael (Capp Records) 164

Oliver, Alise (Kentucky Opera) 238

Olsen, Kamilla (Natasha's Bistro & Bar) 294

Olson, Carla 195

O'Neal, Gradie (Tiki Studios-O'Neal
Productions) 151

O'Neal, Jeannine (Tiki Studios-O'Neal
Productions) 151

Orbison, Barbara (Still Working Music
Group) 149

Orrison, Brett (The Shed) 301

Otey, Ruth (Sandalphon Management) 212

Otey, Ruth (Sandalphon Music Publishing) 147

Otey, Ruth (Sandalphon Records) 178

Owen, Rob (Fort Worth Songwriters
Association) 264

Ozier, John (Curb Records) 166

P

Paffhausen, Josh (Elbow Room) 291

Palmer, Blake (Flipnotics) 291

Paredes, Dino (American Recordings) 161

Pattison, Pat (Songwriting: Essential Guide to

Lyric Form and Structure) 317

Pattison, Pat (Songwriting: Essential Guide to Rhyming) 317

Pattison, Pat (Writing Better Lyrics) 318

Paul, Elena M. (Volunteer Lawyers for the Arts) 273

Peacock, Deborah (Deborah Peacock Productions) 206

Pere, Bill (Connecticut Songwriters Association) 262

Perla, Gene (Perla Music) 143

Perricone, Jack (Melody in Songwriting) 315

Perrota, Suzanne (DCA Productions) 206

Perry, Ruby (Red Sundown Records) 145

Peters, Erol (Pegasus Music) 143

Peters, Ginny (Pegasus Music) 143

Peters, Justin (Lita Music) 138

Peters, Justin (Justin Peters Music) 143

Peters, Justin (Platinum Planet Music, Inc.) 144

Peters, Justin (Tournaline Music, Inc.) 151

Peterson, Ron (Rotten Records) 177

Petree, Chad (McJames Music Inc.) 140

Petree, Stephen (McJames Music Inc.) 140

Petrelli, David (Annual NSAI Song Contest) 248

Pettigrew, Jr., Jim (The Billboard Guide to Music Publicity) 314

Pettigrew, Jr., Jim (The Business of Music Marketing and Promotion) 318

Pickens, Tyler (Bug Music, Inc.) 126

Pierce, Jennifer Ember (Breakin' into Nashville) 314

Pixley, Kathleen (Jana Jae Enterprises) 208

Pixley, Kathleen (Jana Jae Music) 135

Pixley, Kathleen (Lark Talent & Advertising) 193

Pixley, Kathleen (Lark Record Productions, Inc.) 171

Platt, Alexander (Greater Grand Forks Symphony Orchestra) 235

Poe, Randy (Music Publishing: A Songwriter's Guide) 316

Porter, Fred (Raspberry Jam Music) 211

Possenti, Margo (Winter Music Conference Inc.) 282

Potocic, Tim (Sonic Unyon Records Canada) 179

Prescott, Ashley M. (Cantata Academy) 232

Q

Quave, O.L. (William Carney University Dinner Theatre) 223

R

Rader, Corey (The Brass Rail) 297

Ramos, Noel (Independent Music Conference) 278

Ray, Will 196

Reed, John (The Music Room Publishing Group) 141

Remick, Lloyd Z. (Zane Management, Inc.) 215

Resnick, Felix (Birmingham-Bloomfield Symphony Orchestra) 231

Rettic, Annie (San Diego Songwriters Guild) 269

Reynolds, Jaime (Define Something in Nothing Music) 128

Rhine, Gail (Sizemore Music) 148

Richman, Fran (Milwaukee Youth Symphony Orchestra) 239

Roach, William (A New Rap Jam Publishing) 122

Robertson, Eddie (Robertson Entertainment) 212

Robinson, Alma (California Lawyers for the Arts) 260

Rodgers, Erin (Texas Accountants & Lawyers for the Arts) 272

Rodgers, Steve (The Space) 301

Rodriguez, J.R. (Thunder Bay Theatre) 226

Rodriguez, Ursula (Bottom of the Hill) 289

Romeo, Bob (Academy of Country Music) 258

Rooksby, Rikky (The Songwriting Sourcebook: How to Turn Chords into Great Songs) 317

Rosenberg, Todd 196

Rosen, Earl (SOCAN) 270

Ross, Buck (Moores Opera Center) 239

Ross, Doreen Ringer (Broadcast Music, Inc. (BMI)) 260

Roundtree, Cornelius (Ivory Pen Entertainment) 135

Rucins, Matt (Schubas Tavern) 296

Rull, Joe (Big Fish Music Publishing Group) 124

Runyon, Randy (DBF A Media Company) 220

Rusch, Bob (Creative Improvised Music Projects Records) 165

Russell, Ed (Tower Music Group) 151

Russell, George (Lydian Chromatic Concept of Total Organization, Volume One: The Art and Science of Tonal Gravity) 315

Rybacki, Karl (Warner Bros. Records) 183

S

Salinas, Kristian (Texas Accountants & Lawyers for the Arts) 272

Sanders, Deb (The Hambidge Center) 285

Sanese, John (The Sound Factory) 301

Sanford, Rick (Dental Records) 166

SanSaurus, Esther (The ASCAP Deems Taylor Awards) 253

Sardella, Frank (Material Worth Publishing) 139

Sartain, Will (Kilby Court) 293

Sartain, Will (Urban Lounge) 303

Satkowski, Steve (Steve Satkowski Recordings) 197

Saxon, Mark (The Songwriters Guild of America Foundation) 281

Schade, K Bernard (Singing Boys of Pennsylvania) 242

Schneider, Jack (Rustic Records, Inc. Publishing) 145

Schneider, Jack (Rustic Records) 177

Schneider, Nell (Rustic Records) 177

Schwartz, Daylle Deanna (The Real Deal—How to Get Signed to a Record Label From A to Z) 316

Schwartz, Mara (Bug Music, Inc.) 126

Score, G.L. (NewCreature Music) 142

Scott, Allan R. (Helena Symphony) 236

Scott, Laura (Bug Music, Inc.) 126

Scruggs, Aaron (The Spanish Moon) 301

Sengupta, Ab (Fontana Concert Society) 234

Serge, Sandy (Serge Entertainment Group) 213

Sfarnas, James (Backstreet Booking) 203

Sfarnas, James (Holographic Recording Company) 169

Shaw, Eric (Triple Crown) 302

Shelder, Cliff (SME Publishing Group) 149

Shires, Jim (Berkeley Café) 288

Siegel, Robert (Siegel Entertainment Ltd.) 213

Silvestri-Bushey, Renee (ALLRS Music Publishing Co.) 187

Silvestri-Bushey, Renee (Midi Track Publishing) 140

Silvestri, F. John (ALLRS Music Publishing Co.) 187

Silvestri, F. John (Midi Track Publishing) 140

Simpson, Jim (BearSongs) 123

Simpson, Jim (Big Bear Records) 163

Sinden, Anna M. (International Songwriters Association Ltd.) 265

Skelton, David (Central Orgeon Songwriters Association) 262

Skorman, Ted (T. Skorman Productions, Inc.) 213

Slutes, David (Club Congress) 290

Smeltzer, Gary (Gary Smeltzer Productions) 208

Smith, Alison (Broadcast Music, Inc. (BMI)) 260

Smith, Kevin W. (Cimarron Circuit Opera Company) 233

Smith, Ramon (RN'D Distribution, LLC) 196

Smith, Steve (Aware Records) 163

Smolij, Mariusz (Acadiana Symphony Orchestra) 230

Southall, Claude (Rustic Records, Inc. Publishing) 145

Sowers, Dr. Richard (Anderson Symphony Orchestra) 230

Spellman, Peter (Music Business Solutions/ Career Building Workshops) 278

Spicoli, Erik (The Mohawk Place) 300

Sprague, Lora (Big Fish Music Publishing Group) 124

Stack-Slutsky, Courtney (Bixio Music Group & Associates/IDM Music) 125

Stamey, Chris 197

Stamm, David (Chrysalis Music Group) 126

Stanfield, Jana (The Musician's Guide to Making & Selling Your Own CDs & Cassettes) 316

Starrett, Carla (Great American Song Contest) 249

Starrett-Guillermo, Christie (The American Boychoir) 230

Stasiuk, Sara (Manitoba Music) 267

Steele, Ted (Sa'mall Management) 212

Stember, Rudolf (Capp Records) 164

Stertz. Shelley (The Management Trust, Ltd.) 214

Stin, Richard (Music Law: How to Run Your Band's Business) 315

St. John, Jon (St. John Artists) 214

Stoker, Karen (The Lounge at Hotel Donaldson) 300

Stone, Madeline (Emstone Music Publishing) 130

Stone, Mitchell (Emstone Music Publishing) 130

Stoner, Brian (McJames Music Inc.) 140

Strother, Linda Lee (The Soul of the Writer) 317

Stroud, Phillip (Young Avenue Deli) 304

Stuart, Fred (Rainbow Music Corp.) 144

Sturgis, Billy (Warehouse Creek Recording Corp.) 182

Sullivan, Darrell (Sully's Pub) 297

Sullivan, Dave (Tower Music Group) 151

Summers, Deanna L. (Silicon Music Publishing Co.) 147

Summers, Gene (Silicon Music Publishing Co.) 147

Summers, Steve (Silicon Music Publishing Co.) 147

Suraci, Richard (Fine Art Productions/Richie Suraci Pictures, Multimedia, Interactive) 220

Sweeney, Tim (Tim Sweeney's Guide to Releasing Independent Records) 318

Sweeney, Tim (Tim Sweeney's Guide to Succeeding at Music Conventions) 318

Swiger, Joshua (Blues Alley Records) 188

Syzmanski, Steve (Rocky Mountain Folks Festival Songwriter Showcase) 252

Syzmanski, Steve (Telluride Troubadour Contest) 253

T

Tachoir, Jerry (Avita Records) 162

Tamimi, Radi (Capp Records) 164

Tasse, David (Tas Music Co./Dave Tasse Entertainment) 214

Tate, Rick (Fort Worth Songwriters Association) 264

Taylor-Drake, Robyn (Trio Productions, Inc./ Songscape Music, LLC.) 152

Taylor, Tess (Los Angeles Music Network) 266

Tec, Roland (The Dramatists Guild of America, Inc.) 263

Telge, Peter (Milly's Tavern) 294

Templeman, Tom (McJames Music Inc.) 140

Tennin, Chuck (Big Fish Music Publishing Group) 124

Terrell, Scott (Lexington Philharmonic Society) 238

Terry, John (Fort Worth Songwriters Association) 264

Thompson, Garrie (Duane Music, Inc.) 129

Thompson, Mike (Sound Cellar Music) 149

Timmons, Sean (Appel Farm Arts and Music Festival) 276

Toalson, Peter (The Empty Bottle) 299

Tobin, Randall Michael 198

Tolson, Nell (Rustic Records, Inc. Publishing) 145

Torchia, Andrea (Zomba Music Publishing) 154

Tough, Dave 198

Toulon, Dominique (Capp Records) 164

Towry, Arik (World Beatnik Records) 184

Trafidlo, Greg (Southwest Virginia Songwriters Association) 272

Tripp, Phil (South by Southwest Music Conference) 281

Trumbull, Steve (Music Attorney Legal &Business Affairs Registry) 315

Tucker, Susan (The Soul of the Writer) 317

U

Urbanski, Chris (Hickory Lane Publishing and Recording) 133

Urbina, Curtis (Quark, Inc.) 144

V

Vasquez, Jay (Ton Records) 180

Verhil, Dan (One Trick Pony Grill & Taproom) 295

Verkerk, Peter (Red Onion Records) 176

Visvardis, Peter (Zomba Music Publishing) 154

Vorndick, Bil 198

W

Wagner, Dick 198

Waldoch, Mark T. (M&T Waldoch Publishing, Inc.) 138

Waldoch, Timothy J. (M&T Waldoch Publishing, Inc.) 138

Walker, Jack (ADR Studios) 187

Wallace, Brian (Concept 2000 Inc.) 206

Wardlaw, Jeremy (Duffy's Tavern) 290

Warner, Cheryl K. (Cheryl K. Warner Productions) 205

Washburn, Jon (Vancouver Chamber Choir) 243

Waterbury. Dave 198

Waterman, Richard (North Star Music) 173

Watkins, Matt (Walkerbout Music Group) 153

Watts, Dusty (Five Spot) 291

Weber, Tim (The Old Rock House) 301

Webb, Jimmy (Songwriters Hall of Fame (SongHall)) 271

Webb, Jimmy (Tunesmith: Inside the Art of Songwriting) 318

Webb, Rick (Kaupps & Robert Publishing Co.) 137

Weigel, Ulli (Sinus Musik Produktion) 148

Wein, George (Newport Folk Festival) 279

Wein, George (Newport Jazz Festival) 279

Weisberg, Lawrence (Hailing Frequency Music Productions) 191

Weisman, Ben (Parliament Records) 175

Wells, Jeff (EarthScream Music Publishing Co.) 129

Wells, Jeff (Red Onion Records) 176

Wells, Jeff (Sound Arts Recording Studio) 197

Wengert, Berthold (Berthold Wengert Musikverlag) 153

Westercappel, Miriam (Bixio Music Group & Associates/IDM Music) 125

Whims, Davilyn (RustRon Music Publishers/ Whimsong Music) 146

Whitfield, Mirko (South by Southwest Music Conference) 281

Whitney, Brian Austin (Just Plain Folks Music Organization) 265

Wilde, Justin (Christmas & Holiday Music) 126

Williams, Deanie (NSAI Song Camps) 279

Williams, Ed (Bug Music, Inc.) 126

Williams, Paul (American Society of Composers, Authors and Publishers (ASCAP)) 258

Williams, Roy (Nervous Publishing) 141

Willson, Frank (Universal Music Marketing) 215

Witten, David (Duo Classico) 234

Wolff, Robert (How to Make It in the New Music Business: Lessons, Tips, and Inspirations From Music's Biggest and Best) 315

Wolff, Zander (Blackheart Records) 163

Wolfgang, Shawn (Café 939) 289

Woodrum, Michael 198

Wood, Tammy (Hometown Hero's Publishing) 134

Woof, Tanya (R.T.L. Music) 145

Woolf, Steven (The Repertory Theatre of St. Louis) 226

Wright, James (Willie Basse) 188

Wyatt, Warren (Worldsound, LLC) 215

Wytas, Steven J. (Audio 911) 188

Y

Yasenak, Michael (European International Competition for Composers/IBLA Foundation) 248

Young, Rodney (Cherry Street Records) 164

Young, Thomas (Lyric Opera of Chicago) 239

Z

Zainea, Dave (The Majestic/Magic Stick) 300

Zainea, Traci (The Majestic/Magic Stick) 300

Zander, Benjamin (The Boston Philharmonic) 231

Zhang, Jin (Vancouver Youth Symphony Orchestra Society) 243

Zonana, Saul 199

Zucker, Laurel (Cantilena Records) 164

Zukoff, William (Western Wind Workshop in Ensemble Singing) 282